Application Developer's Handbook for the AS/400

By Michael Otey

A Division of
DUKE COMMUNICATIONS
INTERNATIONAL
Loveland, Colorado

Library of Congress Cataloging-in-Publication Data

Application developer's handbook for the AS/400 : practical, ready-to-use AS/400 programming tools, techniques, and advice / edited by Michael Otey. — 1st ed.

p. cm.

Includes index.

ISBN 0-9628743-3-7

1. IBM AS/400 (Computer)—Programming 2. Application software..

I. Otey, Michael, 1958-

QA76.8.I25919A66 1992

005. 2'45—dc20 92-33175

CIP

DUKE COMMUNICATIONS INTERNATIONAL
Loveland, Colorado

This book was printed and bound in the United States of America.
First Edition: January 1993

ISBN 0-9628743-3-7

2 3 4 5 6 BP 9 8 7 6 5

To my family for their love, support, and extra proofreading.
Without their help this book would not have been possible.

Acknowledgments

Although this book is the result of the fine work of many authors and editors, I would particularly like to acknowledge the accomplishments of Paul Conte. As his many contributions to this book attest, Paul's exceptional, quality work over the past decade have served as a guide to the midrange community. In addition to his many articles, Paul also contributed his expertise to assist me with various questions that arose during the editing process and I am extremely grateful for his help. Without Paul's endeavors this book would not exist.

I would also like to acknowledge the significant efforts of several other key individuals whose work made this book a reality:

Dave Bernard for helping to get this project under way and for providing insightful guidance and feedback that significantly improved and shaped this work.

Sharon Hamm for her countless hours of editing and numerous questions that helped to fill in many details and to provide this book with clarity and consistency. Her creative suggestions, endurance, and occasional reminders helped to keep this book moving ahead.

Jan Caufman for turning the many pages of editorial into production-quality manuscript.

Jan Hazen for taking care of the administrative support and thousands of other details.

Trish Frease for her help in collecting and sometimes rekeying the original source material.

Sharon Vaughn for compiling the Table of Contents and List of Figures.

Steve Adams for the cover concept and design.

Steve Rath for providing the index.

The authors of the chapters of this book, in alphabetical order, are: Marshall Akins, J.H. Botterill, Paul Conte, Carol-Ann Doucher, Brian Gordon, Ron Harvey, Gerry Kaplan, Ken Kelley, Nicholas Knowles, Wayne Madden, Bryan Meyers, Frieda Parker, Douglas T. Parrish, Jeffery Pisarczyk, John Rittenhouse, Richard M. Rubin, Carson Soule, and Jon Vote.

Contents

List of Figures

Code on Diskette

While not all of the code examples contained in the *Application Developer's Handbook for the AS/400* are on diskette, all of the complete programs and large code examples are included on the accompanying diskette. This code has been taken directly from the original material submitted by the authors. All of the textual headings and comments that were not a part of the original code have been removed to facilitate copying and compiling the source on your AS/400.

The diskette subdirectory and file structure have been arranged to correspond to the chapters and figures presented in this book. The diskette contains a directory for each chapter that contains a code example that is included on the diskette. For instance, the first code example is found in Chapter 6, Figure 2. On the diskette, there is a subdirectory called CHAPTER.06. Within subdirectory CHAPTER.06 there is a file called FIG_06.02 that contains the code from Figure 2. A directory of the code on diskette follows:

Subdirectory/File

/CHAPTER.06
- /FIG_06.02

/CHAPTER.08
- /FIG_08.13
- /FIG_08.15
- /FIG_08.16

/CHAPTER.14
- /FIG_14.01
- /FIG_14.02

/CHAPTER.16
- /FIG_16.01
- /FIG_16.02
- /FIG_16.03
- /FIG_16.04
- /FIG_16.09

/CHAPTER.18
- /FIG_18.02
- /FIG_18.03

/CHAPTER.24
- /FIG_24.07

/CHAPTER.26
- /FIG_26.05
- /FIG_26.06
- /FIG_26.07

/CHAPTER.29
- /FIG_29.01
- /FIG_29.02
- /FIG_29.03
- /FIG_29.04
- /FIG_29.05
- /FIG_29.06

/CHAPTER.30
/FIG_30.01
/FIG_30.02

/CHAPTER.33
/FIG_33.05
/FIG_33.06
/FIG_33.07

/CHAPTER.36
/FIG_36.01
/FIG_36.02
/FIG_36.03
/FIG_36.04
/FIG_36.05
/FIG_36.06
/FIG_36.07

/CHAPTER.37
/FIG_37.01
/FIG_37.02
/FIG_37.04
/FIG_37.05

/CHAPTER.39
/FIG_39.01

/CHAPTER.41
/FIG_41.01
/FIG_41.03
/FIG_41.05
/FIG_41.06
/FIG_41.09
/FIG_41.10
/FIG_41.13
/FIG_41.15

/CHAPTER.42
/FIG_42.06
/FIG_42.07
/FIG_42.08
/FIG_42.09
/FIG_42.10
/FIG_42.11
/FIG_42.12

/CHAPTER.43
/FIG_43.02
/FIG_43.03
/FIG_43.04

/CHAPTER.44
/FIG_44.03

/CHAPTER.45
/FIG_45.04
/FIG_45.05

/CHAPTER.46
/FIG_46.05
/FIG_46.07
/FIG_46.08

/CHAPTER.47
/FIG_47.01
/FIG_47.02
/FIG_47.04

/CHAPTER.48
/FIG_48.08
/FIG_48.09
/FIG_48.10
/FIG_48.12
/FIG_48.13
/FIG_48.14

/APPENDIX
/FIG_A.04
/FIG_A.05
/FIG_C.01
/FIG_C.02
/FIG_C.03
/FIG_D.ALL

Foreword

The AS/400 provides an advanced platform for business applications, offering application developers a relational database management system, integrated security and transaction recovery facilities, object-based system management features, and numerous other resources to create robust and flexible applications. As part of the AS/400's well-structured architecture, these facilities can be smoothly incorporated into all of a company's applications.

The AS/400's wealth of integrated facilities presents the application developer with a dilemma, however — there's an overwhelming amount to learn before you can effectively use the AS/400's capabilities in your applications. For example, a sophisticated facility, such as AS/400 security, presents hundreds of alternatives, some good, some bad, and some that can be safely ignored. Although with a little guidance it's not too difficult to use even the most advanced AS/400 security features, figuring out the right approach by yourself can take a lot of time digesting manuals and trial-and-error programming.

In many companies, there's just not enough time to explore all of the AS/400 on your own. In my experience, the fastest and most effective way to discover how to use an AS/400 facility is to find someone who's already spent a lot of time working with it, and who's using the facility successfully in production applications. By learning from people who've already mastered various areas of the AS/400, you can get a rapid start applying what they've learned to your own application development.

This book is an attempt to get you in touch with just such people — the ones who've done the legwork and can suggest the smoothest paths to working with the AS/400. Mike Otey, who is a knowledgeable AS/400 developer in his own right, has worked with a large group of AS/400 developers and consultants to cover many of the most challenging and rewarding AS/400 application facilities. This collaboration has produced a reference book that can help you the moment you start learning about an AS/400 facility, and that will remain helpful as you continue to delve into more advanced features.

Each chapter combines technical explanations and practical suggestions for AS/400 application development. You'll find two things that don't appear in the standard manuals: clear and simple explanations of each topic, and "rules of thumb" for using various AS/400 features. Reference manuals are there to document every detail of a facility; this book tells you what you really need to know to use a facility effectively.

In addition to the specific advice you'll find in each chapter, this book, taken as a whole, offers you an opportunity to see how a diverse group of experienced AS/400 developers views the system. By reflecting on their techniques and recommendations, you'll strengthen your own approach to AS/400 development. Reading through this collection is the next best thing to having the authors working as part of your development team.

Paul Conte
President, Picante Software, and *NEWS 3X/400* Senior Technical Editor

AS/400 CONCEPTS AND DESIGN

Chapter 1

Historical Perspective

by Michael Otey and Paul Conte

> **Today's AS/400 could well be tomorrow's primary mainframe computer system**

Since its introduction in 1988, the AS/400 has been one of the most successful business computers ever made. To date, more than 100,000 AS/400s have been sold. The AS/400 originated as the successor to the S/38 and the S/36. While it consistently received the highest ratings for user satisfaction, the S/38 was not extremely popular. Nor was the S/38 considered as easy to use as its smaller and more popular cousin, the S/36. By 1988, each of these systems had been in use for a number of years and both had become dated. Many users of both systems had reached their systems' capacity limits and were desperately looking for an upward migration path. Recognizing this situation, IBM introduced the AS/400 as the solution to both groups. Not only did the AS/400 provide a growth path for both S/36 and S/38 users, but it also allowed IBM to consolidate its own support and development onto a single platform. Instead of being forced to split its internal resources between multiple systems, IBM could accelerate its progress by having a single focus in the midrange market.

Built on the advanced S/38 architecture, the AS/400 provided the growth path that S/38 and S/36 users were looking for. It also combined the best features of both systems. From the S/36, the AS/400 got its menu-driven approach and its context-sensitive help facilities. From the S/38, it got its built-in relational database and its underlaying operating system. The AS/400 is so closely related to the S/38 that objects can be saved on the S/38 and restored directly onto the AS/400. This is not the case with the S/36. To support the upward path for S/36 users, the AS/400 introduced the S/36 Environment (S/36E). The S/36E is a clever program that emulates most of the S/36 features by converting S/36 job control into native AS/400-equivalent instructions. While this approach didn't give S/36 users the immediate advantages of the AS/400 advancements, it did

Figure 1.1

The Capability

Access rights	Address

provide a convenient method to move existing software applications quickly to the new platform to gain relief from current capacity constraints.

To quell immediate concerns from new users about once again reaching their system's capacity limits, IBM promised to double the AS/400's size every two years. IBM has kept this promise in spades. At its introduction, the top-of-the-line AS/400 model was a B60 with 96 MB of main storage. IBM quickly followed this with the release of the bigger, faster model 70 and then the new D series of processors. Today, the top-of-the-line AS/400 is a multiple processor E90 that sports 512 MB of main storage. The new E90 offers six times the performance of the original B60. The AS/400 line now extends from the small two- and three-user model E02 upward into the mainframe-size E90 model. If this growth rate continues, today's AS/400 could well be tomorrow's primary mainframe computer system, supplanting the aging S/370 models. IBM certainly has recognized this potential and already has coined the term "midframe" when referring to the upper AS/400 models. The AS/400 has bridged the traditional gap separating midrange minicomputers and mainframe systems.

While the roots of AS/400 technology spring from the S/38, both the S/38 and the AS/400 share an architectural base that is unlike the more traditional computer systems. The AS/400 and the S/38 both use a "capability-based" address scheme rather than the more traditional "process-oriented" address scheme found in most computer systems such as the S/36, the S/370, and the DEC VAX. Essentially, a capability is a pointer to an object in the computer system. The capability associates the object's access rights with that object's physical location. Figure 1.1 shows the basic construction of a capability.

Capability-based systems possess several characteristics that differentiate them from the more traditional systems. First, capability-based systems support a single-level storage implementation. Single-level storage means that objects in main storage and objects in auxiliary storage are both addressed using the same mechanism. Essentially, the operating system does not need to know in advance if the object will be located in main storage or if it is on disk. Next, as each capability is associated with a set of access rights, capability-based systems can have a deeply integrated security implementation. This allows every object in the system to have its own set of access rights. Perhaps most importantly, capability-based systems provide the foundation for an object-based system. To access a given object on a capability-based computer system, you do not need to know that object's physical location. Instead, the named capability provides the access

Figure 1.2

Major Developments in Capability-Based Systems

1967 — Dennis and Van Horn define the first capability-based system supervisor.

1967 — A group from the University of Chicago attempts to build the first integrated hardware and software capability-based system.

1968 — The CAL-TSS project at the University of California attempts to build a capability-based operating system for the CDC 6400.

1969 — The Plessey 250 becomes the first commercially available capability-based system.

1971 — The Hydra, the first object-based system, is developed at Carnegie-Mellon University. This marks the first time that capability-based addressing is used to provide data abstraction in the design of a complex system.

1978 — IBM announces the S/38, in which capability-based addressing is used to support a complete object-based architecture.

1988 — IBM announces the AS/400.

to the physical entity. This object-oriented approach raises the level of abstraction, thus simplifying the methods needed to build complex systems.

The IBM S/38 was the first commercially successful capability-based computer system. Figure 1.2 presents a brief synopsis of the historical development of capability-based computer systems.

The S/38 was the result of IBM's Future Systems project during the late 1960s and early 1970s. The Future Systems project actually was an aborted attempt to plan the successor to the S/360. IBM eventually terminated this plan because of the difficulty of moving to a more advanced computing platform and maintaining the existing S/360 machine instruction set. While the S/36 designers in Rochester incorporated many of the ideas that came from that project, the Future Systems project itself did not result in the S/38. The S/38 housed a complete object-oriented architecture. Its designers implemented the system using a layered structure with a high-level interface. This approach gave them the flexibility to be able to change the underlaying hardware layer without requiring the higher layers to be rewritten. Using the capability-based addressing scheme, they also implemented single-level storage and an object-level security system. The next chapter of this book covers the implementation of the AS/400's unique architecture in detail. Figure 1.3 presents a simplified look at the layered architecture implemented in the S/38.

Using this layered approach insulates the OS/400 operating system from the underlaying hardware. When IBM implemented the AS/400, it took advantage of this foundation by retaining and extending the basic OS/400 operating system.

Figure 1.3

S/38 Layered Architecture

User Applications Layer
CPF Operating System Layer
MI Microcode Layer
Hardware Layer

Figure 1.4

A Little 3X/400 History

The AS/400 has deep "roots" and even a few skeletons in the closet. Here are some of the events that brought the midrange to where it is today.

1959 — Design begins on RPG as a replacement for EAM wired boards.

June 1961 — ACM symposium paper describes ATLAS computer with a "one-level storage system."

April 1964 — IBM announces the S/360.

June 1969 — IBM announces the S/3.

Late 1960s and early 1970s — IBM's secret Future Systems project team meets regularly to design the S/360's successor. The project eventually disbands because no one can figure out how to build an advanced machine that is instruction-compatible with the S/360. Some members of the Future Systems project join the S/38 development team.

January 1970 — Frank Soltis and Dean Zimmerman, two IBM engineers, sketch the beginnings of a machine architecture based on single-level addressability. Eventually this design will be expanded to the S/38.

June 1970 — Edgar Codd introduces the relational database model.

Summer 1971 — Frank Soltis, Dick Bains, and Roy Hoffman complete initial S/38 architecture concepts.

September 1973 — IBM officially designates Pacific (S/38) a development project. G. Glenn Henry becomes programming manager of the team that eventually develops MI into an object-oriented, high-level "machine" interface.

1973 through 1978 — S/38 development proceeds in the lingerie and toy departments of a retrofitted Wells Discount store in Rochester, Minnesota.

January 1975 — IBM announces the S/32.

April 1977 — IBM announces the S/34.

October 1978 — IBM announces the S/38; performance problems delay first shipments.

Figure 1.4 Continued

Figure 1.4

A Little 3X/400 History *Continued*

July 1980	—	The first S/38 ships.
May 1983	—	IBM announces the S/36.
1984 and 1985	—	Rochester puzzles over a way to converge the S/36 and S/38 and considers a multiprocessor solution.
December 1985	—	Seven Rochester engineers demonstrate S/36 application software running on a S/38 equipped with software support for OCL, RPG II, and other S/36 facilities. The decision is made to build Olympic using S/38 architecture with software for S/36 and S/38 environments.
January 1986	—	IBM announces the RT PC; IBMer G. Glenn Henry is the proud parent of another high-level machine architecture.
1986 through June 1988	—	Rumors of Olympic and Silverlake keep business booming for industry consultants and trade press.
June 21, 1988	—	IBM announces the AS/400. Industry watchers begin predictions of a system to converge the AS/400 and S/370. Life goes on in Rochester, Minnesota.

The major changes took place in the hardware and microcode layers. This approach allowed IBM to leverage its investment in the operating system and still take full advantage of the latest hardware improvements. IBM did the same thing when it introduced the "D" series of processors. In an era of rapid hardware advancements, this high-level machine implementation could pay substantial dividends many times over. IBM spent a good deal of time evolving this approach. Figure 1.4 presents a brief development history of IBM's 3X/400 line.

Rumors of the AS/400 persisted for almost two years prior to its actual announcement. When IBM actually introduced the AS/400, the system did fulfill most expectations that awaited it. It perpetuated the S/38 architecture, it preserved the customer's investment in existing software, it vastly increased the capacity limits of the S/36 and S/38, and it did this using modern hardware and a rack-mounted design. In terms of growth potential, only the DEC VAX line rivals the AS/400. Figure 1.5 presents the broad range of the current AS/400 models.

With its integrated architecture, the AS/400 has already gained a reputation as a highly productive platform. IBM has provided new languages and has made enhancements to the existing languages since the AS/400's introduction. IBM's announcements concerning the software development lifecycle promise continued improvement in the future. Given the foundation of the AS/400 with its layered implementation and the continued IBM improvements, we can conclude that the AS/400 will be a major factor in the computing world for years to come.

Figure 1.5

Relative Performance of AS/400 Models

Model	RAMP-C	Memory (MB)	DASD (GB)
9402 E02	1.5	24	1.976
9402 E04	1.9	24	3.952
9404 E06	2.6	40	3.952
9404 E10	2.6	40	11.856
9404 E20	3.5	72	11.856
9406 E25	4.2	80	15.808
9406 E35	3.4	72	28.680
9406 E45	4.8	80	28.680
9406 E50	6.4	128	49.180
9406 E60	10.2	192	76.680
9406 E70	14.2	256	76.680
9406 E80	25.2	384	124.680
9406 E90	34.4	512	124.680

Chapter 2

AS/400 Architecture

by Paul Conte

Sophisticated design and ease-of-use come together in the AS/400

The AS/400 attacks both traditional and emerging business applications with an innovative architecture originally established on the S/38. IBM set out with the S/38 — and has continued on the AS/400 — to provide an easy-to-use architecture that offers a complete set of application services and lets users take advantage of rapid improvements in hardware without modifications to application or system service software. The AS/400 builds on three key design elements: a software "machine" definition, an advanced system supervisor, and an integrated user interface.

IBM hopes the AS/400's architectural principles will support improved programmer productivity for conventional record-keeping applications *and* foster new end-user-driven applications such as Office functions. IBM has good reason to believe the AS/400 will meet these objectives: The S/38 already has established the highest user-approval ratings of any commercial computer and has earned a reputation as one of the most productive development systems available. IBM has made significant strides in the ongoing development of the AS/400. In 1991, IBM's Rochester, Minnesota plant, home of the AS/400, received the Malcolm-Baldrige award for quality production standards.

Because it offers a wider range of price/performance than the S/38, the AS/400 expands the community of programmers and end users who can enjoy the benefits of the well-received S/38 architecture. An operational AS/400 model E02 is available for as low as about $12,000, and a fully loaded AS/400 model E90 provides performance that many companies previously could get only with a S/370.

As S/34/36/38 programmers and those from other systems move onto the AS/400, they will discover elements unlike those on their previous systems. S/38 programmers will find the AS/400 architecture itself familiar because the AS/400 incorporates no major changes at the *architectural* level. S/38 programmers, however, will notice many differences between the S/38 and AS/400 *implementations* of the two systems' common architecture, especially in the underlying hardware and external interfaces. Programmers familiar with the S/36 or other conventional systems, such as the S/370 and DEC VAX, will find the AS/400 architecture dramatically different — and more advanced — than their accustomed systems. Regardless which systems you've programmed on, this chapter guides you through the AS/400 architecture and some of its implementation and interface details.

Layered Architecture

The AS/400's most significant architectural characteristic is that the "machine" is defined as a *software interface*, not as a hardware instruction set. To support this high-level machine interface, IBM incorporated several unique features into AS/400 hardware and developed an advanced, *object-oriented* operating system supervisor. IBM built tightly integrated system-command and service interfaces for application development on top of the AS/400's high-level machine interface. The AS/400 also includes two alternative "environments" that mimic existing S/36 and S/38 interfaces.

The AS/400 is designed with five major layers (Figure 2.1). Three of these layers — hardware, microcode, and supervisor routines — implement the machine interface (MI) that defines the AS/400. Above MI, two layers — integrated system services and high-level language (HLL) compilers — provide the application programming interface (API) for developing application software. Each layer of the AS/400 provides a consistent interface to the next higher layer so that higher layers do not need to know the implementation details of lower layers.

The AS/400 design not only encourages application development using higher-level layers; it also enforces this practice. For example, it is impossible for an application programmer to use microcode or hardware-level instructions directly. Most sites cannot even use MI instructions directly, because IBM restricts the license of the MI assembler. A typical AS/400 data processing organization develops all its applications in an HLL such as RPG III, COBOL, or PL/I using the integrated system services for database and device access.

Because AS/400 applications cannot use any interface lower than MI — and rarely can they use MI — IBM can substantially change the AS/400 hardware and supervisor without disrupting either the system services or the application software of existing sites. MI has enabled the AS/400's hardware predecessor — the S/38 — to incorporate five hardware technology changes without changes to application software. And as dramatic evidence of its effectiveness, MI lets S/38 applications be ported to the AS/400 without recompilation, even though the S/38 uses 16-bit register instructions and the AS/400 uses 32-bit register instructions. In the future, with MI, the AS/400 will be able to take advantage of new hardware developments quickly because there will be little inertial drag from either the customer base or IBM's own operating system programmers.

The AS/400 high-level machine definition differs from conventional system architectures such as the S/36 and S/370 or DEC's VAX. Figure 2.1 shows the

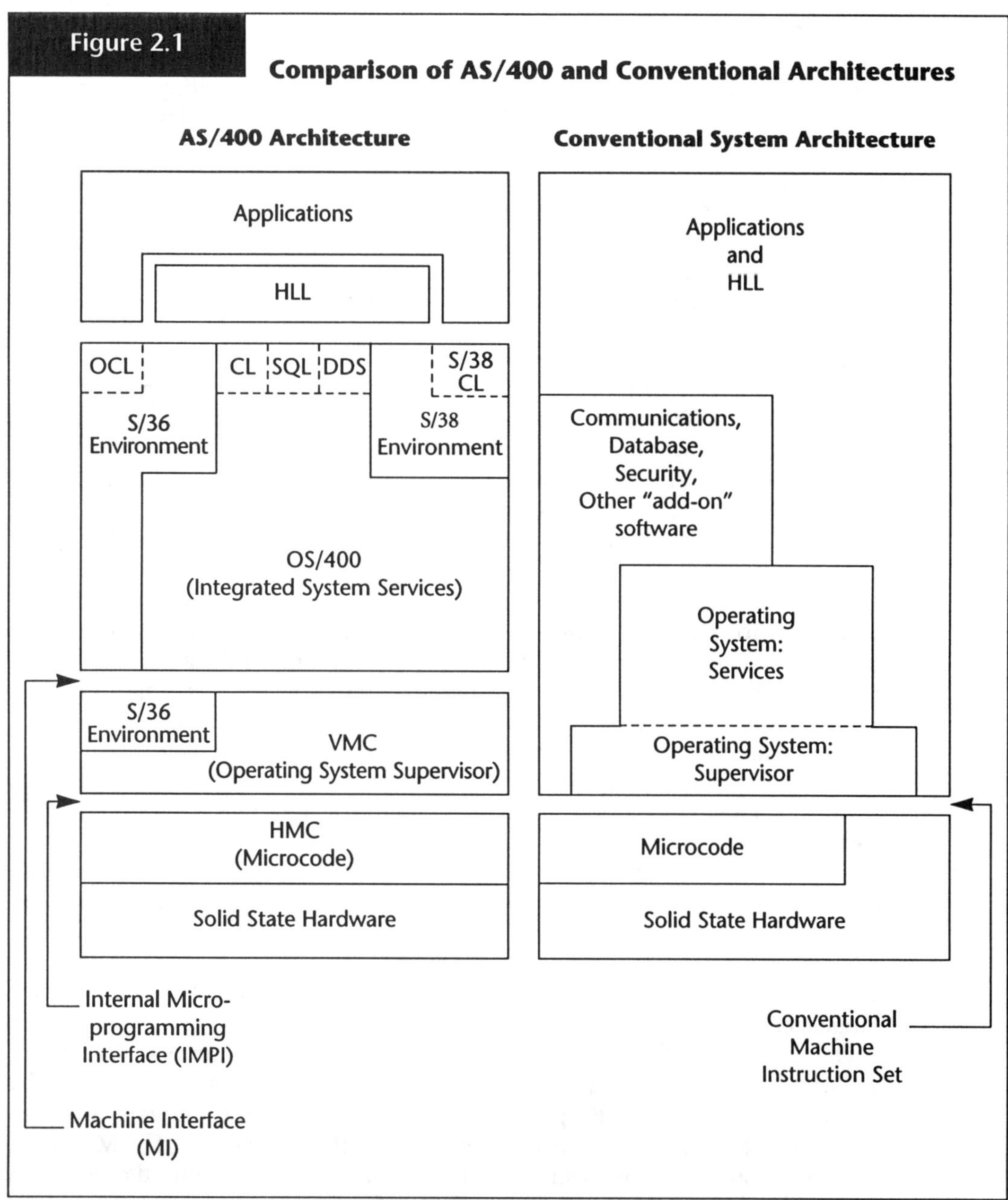

correspondence between a conventional architecture and the AS/400 architecture. Conventional architectures are defined by a microcode or hardware interface, and programmers are free to use machine-level instructions. As a consequence, local system programmers often use this capability to modify the operating system supervisor and services. By defining their architectures at the hardware level, conventional systems create application dependency on the hardware structure. This dependency means that changes to the hardware can require modifications to application and system-service software — modifications that can be costly. In addition, by allowing local changes to the operating system code, conventional systems make installation of new operating system releases or vendor modifications more difficult and error-prone. Both of these problems reduce the pace and increase the cost of incorporating new hardware technology into a system. The limited development of the S/360, S/370, and S/370-XA since it was first shipped in 1965 — and the difficulties that have accompanied the two major changes in its lifetime — are evidence of the problems that arise from a hardware-level system definition.

Machine Interface

As the comparison with other architectures suggests, MI is the key to understanding the AS/400. Although MI is the abbreviation for machine interface, it is really a software layer interface masquerading as a machine with a very powerful instruction set. MI consists of more than 260 instructions, such as Add Numeric, Branch, Compute Math Function, Create Cursor, Initiate Process, and Resolve System Pointer. The MI instruction set includes all of the arithmetic, logic, and control instruction types that a hardware processor typically provides. MI also includes high-level instructions, such as ones to create database objects and control processes, that implement functions typically provided by procedure interfaces to subsystems of an operating system. Both traditional and high-level types of MI instructions have formats that look like conventional machine instructions, including specific hexadecimal operation codes and a fixed layout for the bytes that contain operands. An MI "assembler" even converts instruction mnemonics and symbolic operand references into a binary MI program template similar to, but not the same as, the binary program an assembler on a conventional system would create.

Unlike a conventional system's machine instructions, however, MI defines a *logical*, rather than a *physical* machine — currently no AS/400 hardware can directly execute an MI program. Instead, all MI programs are translated into a form that the AS/400 hardware can execute directly. In other words, MI is a hybrid between an HLL and a true machine language. It looks like a machine language, but it requires translation just like an HLL.

On the AS/400, the translation process for an MI program is called *encapsulation*. As Figure 2.2 illustrates, you invoke MI program translation by executing an MI Create Program instruction; a part of the software provided with the operating system supervisor carries out the translation. (The MI Create Program instruction you execute is contained in a system program that has been encapsulated previously, normally by IBM before it ships the operating system.) The input for the translation process is an MI program *template*, a string of bytes that contain MI instructions and operands. The output is a set of instructions and operands in a lower-level, true machine instruction set. These true machine instructions are known as *Internal Microprogramming Interface (IMPI)* instructions and are defined by the microcoded central processor.

Figure 2.2

AS/400 Program Encapsulation

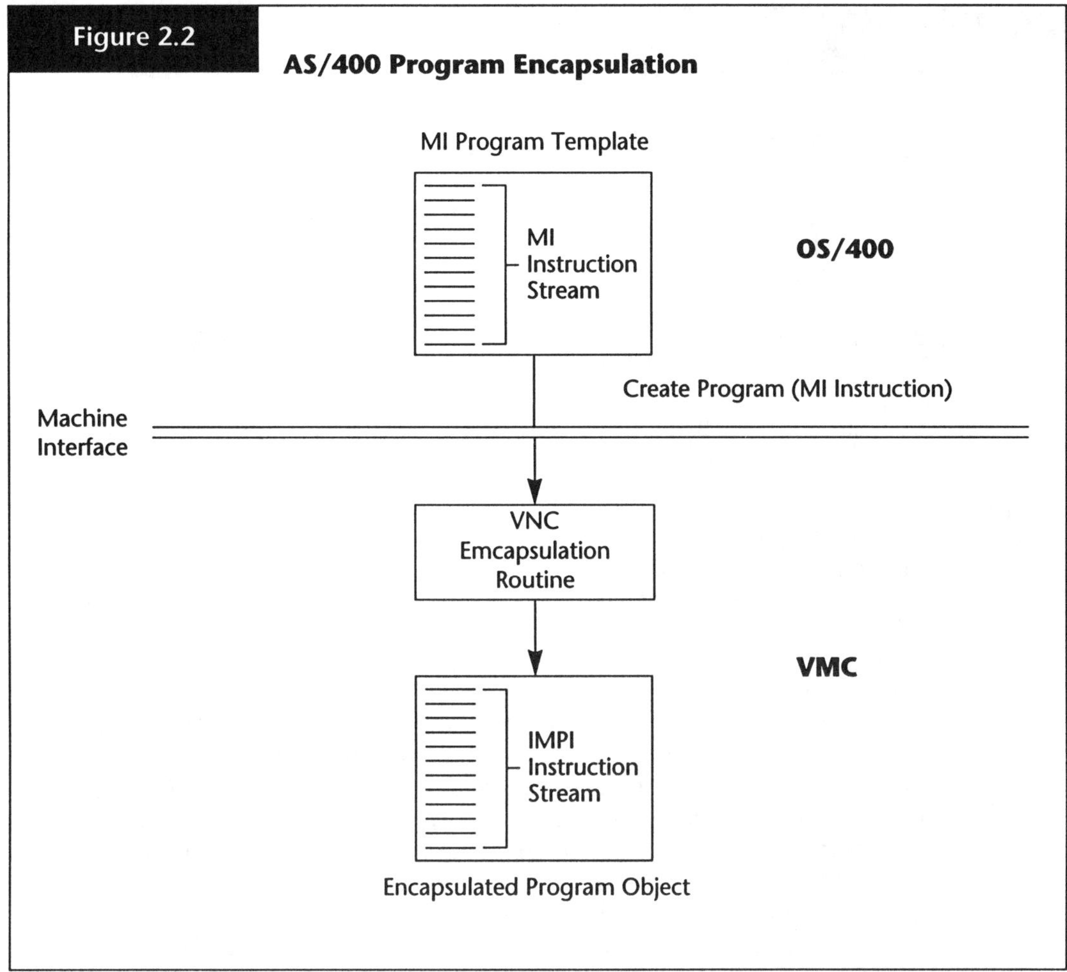

Just as HLL compilers in conventional systems generate object program calls to runtime libraries (e.g., for I/O services), the encapsulation process for an MI program also generates IMPI calls to routines that IBM supplies with the supervisor. For example, the IMPI code generated for an MI Activate Cursor instruction includes calls to object management routines that IBM supplies. IBM uses the term *Vertical Microcode (VMC)* to identify the supervisor code and the runtime routines that support MI. The VMC supervisor code, the MI program translator (encapsulator), and the VMC runtime routines that encapsulated MI programs use all consist of IMPI instructions, which are the only directly executable instructions on the AS/400.

Vertical Microcode

The term Vertical Microcode can be confusing because the code it refers to is not actually microcode. The code in the VMC layer is IMPI, or machine code. IMPI instructions have formats similar to S/370 machine instructions, including

Figure 2.3

Examples of S/370 and AS/400 Instruction Formats

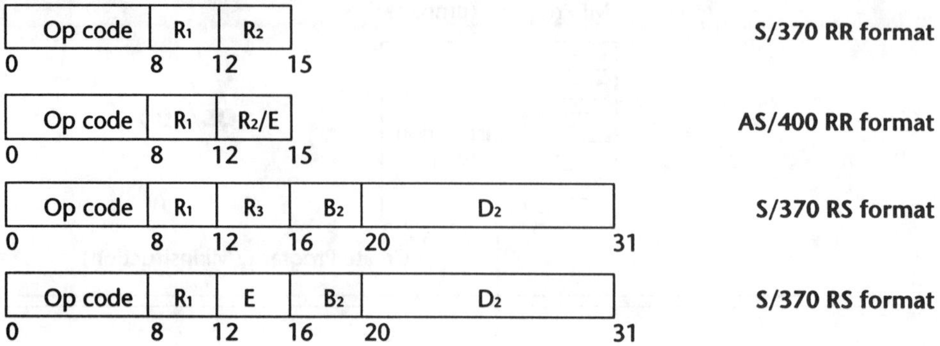

Op code	R_1	R_2			S/370 RR format
0	8	12	15		

Op code	R_1	R_2/E			AS/400 RR format
0	8	12	15		

Op code	R_1	R_3	B_2	D_2		S/370 RS format
0	8	12	16	20	31	

Op code	R_1	E	B_2	D_2		S/370 RS format
0	8	12	16	20	31	

Key

R_n = Register for operand n
B_n = Base address register for operand n
Dn = address displacement for operand n
E = AS/400 op code extension

register-to-register (RR), register-immediate (RI), register-and-storage (RS), storage-to-storage (SS), storage-immediate (SI), and branch instructions. IMPI instructions also use base-register addressing similar to the S/370 (see Figure 2.3 for examples). The closest analogue to VMC in a conventional architecture is the operating system supervisor and resource manager. VMC includes routines to support process management, virtual memory, device management, security, and other facilities available on the MI-defined "machine." As I mentioned earlier, VMC also includes the translator and runtime routines for encapsulating MI programs.

The support for MI — a single, uniform interface to the supervisor and underlying hardware — is unique to the AS/400. Other systems provide at least two distinct interfaces: the hardware instruction set and a collection of procedure interfaces to the operating system supervisor. The interfaces to the supervisor often are inconsistent among various subsystems such as process management, memory management, security, device management, and communications. Through MI, the AS/400 provides a high-level "virtual" machine that makes it easier for IBM and third-party developers to implement system services and compilers in the layers that sit above MI. MI also keeps clever assembler programmers from tying a site's applications or operations too closely to low-level hardware interfaces. And IBM can change the underlying IMPI instruction set without disrupting AS/400 customers. In theory, IBM could choose between hardware alternatives as radically different as a direct hardware implementation of MI or a RISC IMPI instruction set. In either case, the VMC layer would insulate the higher layers from the change.

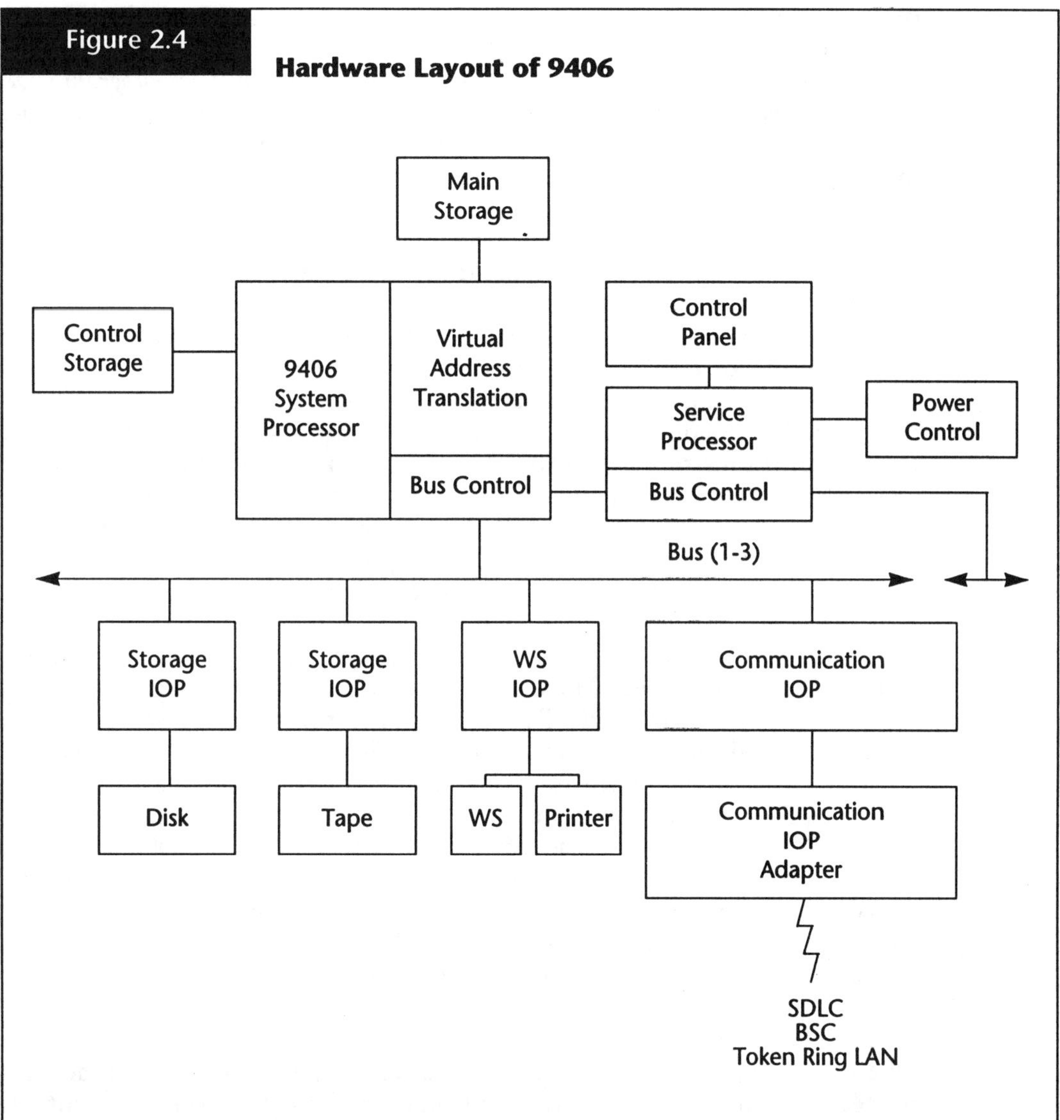

Figure 2.4
Hardware Layout of 9406

Horizontal Microcode and Hardware

A microcoded processor implements the IMPI instruction set that the VMC layer currently uses. This instruction set resembles the S/370 instruction set. (Figure 2.4 shows a simplified layout of the AS/400 9406 models' — E35 through E90 — hardware.) The microcode used to implement IMPI is called *Horizontal Microcode (HMC)*. HMC is true microcode with 42-bit micro-instructions (also called control words) that directly control the solid-state circuits at a low level by having particular bits on or off in the micro-instruction. Simple IMPI instructions, such as arithmetic operations, require only a single HMC micro-instruction and execute in a single processor cycle. More complex IMPI instructions may execute several micro-instructions, including HMC "subroutines."

When an AS/400 is powered up, a process known as *Initial Microprogram Load (IMPL)* loads HMC micro-instructions from DASD into fast-control storage, and subsequent IMPI instructions are carried out by the processor that executes these HMC micro-instructions. Different models of the AS/400 have different control storage sizes (either 4 K or 8 K 42-bit words) and processor cycle speeds (from 60 to 120 nanoseconds), which yield a range of processor power across the models. Because microcode and solid-state logic are so closely related and because their specific boundary is not of primary importance to the AS/400 architecture, the inclusive term "hardware" is used to mean HMC, control storage, and solid-state logic in the discussion that follows.

IMPI instructions provide a fairly standard register-oriented hardware interface. The current IMPI instruction set supports an array of 16 48-bit registers. IMPI instructions include 8-, 16-, and 32-bit arithmetic and logical register operations. Special addressing instructions allow 48-bit operands to be added to a pointer offset in a single instruction. In addition, AS/400 hardware implements several types of instructions to support performance-critical aspects of the high-level MI interface. For example, interprocess communication and memory allocation is handled mostly in hardware rather than VMC.

Data moves through the AS/400 on internal data paths that are 32 data bits wide and on one to three I/O buses, also 32 data bits wide. Processor-to-memory data paths are 64 data bits wide. The largest current model of the AS/400, the E90, supports 512 MB of main storage built from 16-megabit chips. The models E50 through E90 also feature laser-driven fiber optics to increase the data access speed.

The AS/400 uses I/O processors (IOPs) to offload much of the device-control and data-stream assembly processing. IBM uses Motorola 68000 chips, Intel 80286 chips, and on-board memory for the IOPs. The IOPs are hefty little computers in their own right and accelerate the net throughput of an AS/400. As an example, the workstation IOP with 1 MB to 2 MB of memory provides most of the function and speed of IBM's 3705 communications controller.

Tagged Memory

One of the most important AS/400 hardware functions is a special address protection scheme known as tagged memory. On the AS/400, 64-bit MI addresses are stored in 128-bit pointers. Special "tag" bits protect these pointers from inadvertent or intentional corruption. The protection of pointers is supported by a memory bus that is 80 bits wide. Of the 80 bits, 64 bits (eight bytes) are for data, 14 bits are for data error detection and correction, one bit is for address parity checking, and one bit is a pointer tag bit. If an 8-byte memory transfer contains scalar data or instructions, the memory bus tag bit is off. But if a special IMPI pointer instruction is used to store an AS/400 128-bit pointer (in two memory references), the hardware sets the memory bus tag bit on during the transfer. The tag bits are then stored in memory with the pointer value. Similarly, when memory contents are transferred to the processor, the bus tag bit is set on or off depending upon whether or not the fetched contents are tagged as a pointer. During instruction execution, AS/400 hardware checks every attempt to use a pointer to make sure the tag bits are on; if they are not on, an addressing error occurs. Only special IMPI pointer instructions (e.g., Add Fullword Space Pointer Offset) can be used to modify a pointer value and leave the tag bits on. If a pointer value is modified by a nonpointer instruction, the hardware turns off the tag bits in memory, thus invalidating the pointer. This hardware mechanism to protect addresses stored in pointers provides the foundation for the AS/400 object-oriented architecture.

Virtual Address Space

AS/400 hardware also supports a large, uniformly addressable, virtual address space. MI instructions have 64-bit addresses stored as part of a 128-bit pointer, providing an address space of approximately 18 quintillion (10^8) bytes. However, current AS/400 hardware supports only 48-bit virtual address calculations, providing 281 trillion bytes of addressability. The current AS/400 processors can use any of the 16 48-bit registers for calculating a virtual address. IBM has designed the AS/400 so that in the future it can modify the hardware to use 64-bit registers for address operations, thus increasing the hardware address size to the full 64-bit MI address size.

The full 64-bit MI addresses are always stored as part of the header of any AS/400 object. When MI instructions use a 64-bit address, VMC routines map the address to a 48-bit hardware address and then check the header of the referenced object to make sure all 64 bits match. This partial, but effective, implementation of 64-bit MI addresses is another example of how the VMC implementation of MI allows the AS/400 to balance hardware price and performance but still have the potential for smooth incorporation of more powerful hardware as costs drop.

The AS/400's very large address space allows all AS/400 objects (e.g., programs, database files, queues) to have a permanent virtual address. When any new object is created, the object is assigned a unique virtual address that will be used as its identifier in all future references to the object. This means, for example, that all processes' programs execute within a single, system-wide virtual address space. The AS/400 approach to addressing is different from conventional virtual memory systems, such as the S/370, that distinguish between an object's permanent identifier — usually a qualified disk file name — and an object's virtual address while in use within a specific process. (Figures 2.5 through 2.8 compare the AS/400 and S/370 virtual address space definitions and translations.) Most conventional systems don't allow any objects other than programs to be referenced by a virtual memory address (although the S/370-XA has recently added "memory mapped files" to provide this facility for data files).

The AS/400's uniform address space provides *single-level addressability* to storage. This facility sometimes is referred to by the misnomer "single-level storage"; however, like other virtual memory systems, the AS/400 uses a multilevel memory hierarchy of solid-state chips and DASD to provide a flexible and fast, but cost-effective, virtual memory system. The AS/400 is different from other systems, though, in that all references to objects, whether they contain data

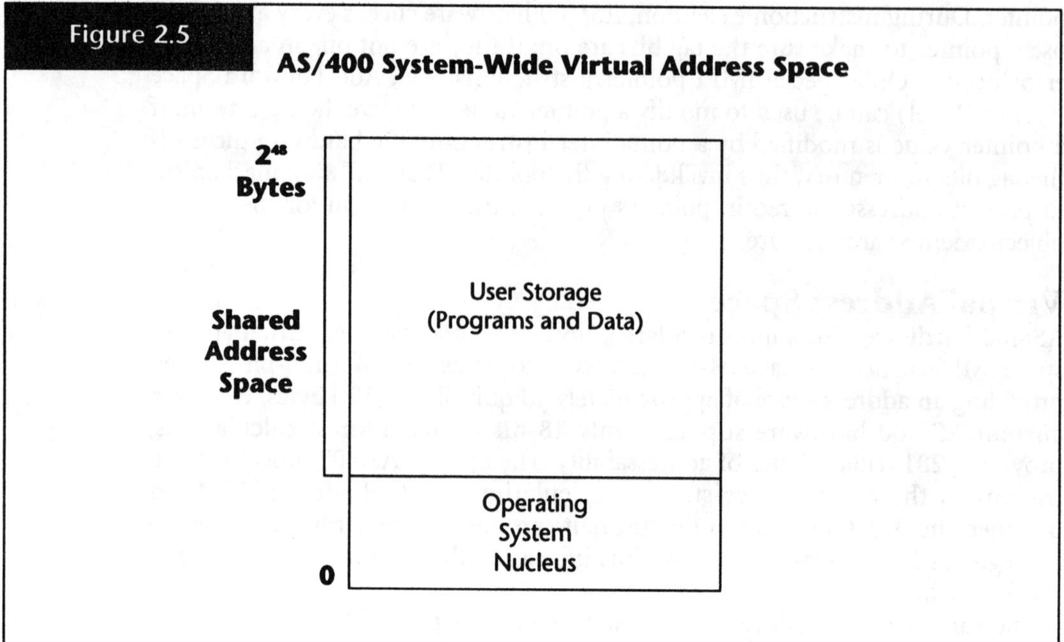

or instructions, use the same pointer addressing mechanism. Only a very small portion of VMC and HMC code handles the virtual address translation to real memory or DASD locations.

This uniform addressing mechanism greatly simplifies the operating system design of the AS/400 and makes multiprocess sharing of objects straightforward. For example, on the AS/400 all programs are created as re-entrant and do not need to be put in special libraries or directories for different processes to share a single copy of the program's instruction portion. In fact, the AS/400 has no link editor because all programs are dynamically accessible by their permanent virtual address. To the application developer, the ease with which objects can be shared on the AS/400 means both higher productivity and better performance. In particular, modular application designs are well-suited to the AS/400.

Object-Oriented Design and Capability-Based Addressing

The AS/400's sophisticated hardware design and VMC supports an interface that not only is a high-level "machine" relative to the actual hardware interfaces of other systems, but also is an advanced interface relative to other operating systems. MI is defined as an *object-oriented* interface and uses an object referencing mechanism known as *capability-based* addressing. Both of these design characteristics add to the flexibility and security of the AS/400.

Most permanent or complex (i.e., not a simple program data type) operands for MI instructions are known as *objects.* There are more than a dozen different MI objects, including programs, data spaces, indexes, queues, process control spaces, logical unit descriptions, contexts, and user profiles. All MI objects have several attributes in common: a name, an object type and subtype, an owner (which is a user profile object), a context (a one-level directory), and a text description.

Each object is uniquely identified by its name, type-subtype, and context. A symbolic reference to an object requires a name, type-subtype, and a context (either explicit or implicit). A symbolic object name is resolved by VMC routines that search for a matching name and type-subtype entry in a context. If a matching entry is found, a system pointer stored in the context entry provides the permanent virtual address of the object. The virtual address is used to locate the referenced object through either the Associative Translation Buffer (ATB) or the Page Directory Table (PDT) if it is in memory (see Figure 2.6), or through a

Figure 2.6

AS/400 Virtual Address Translation

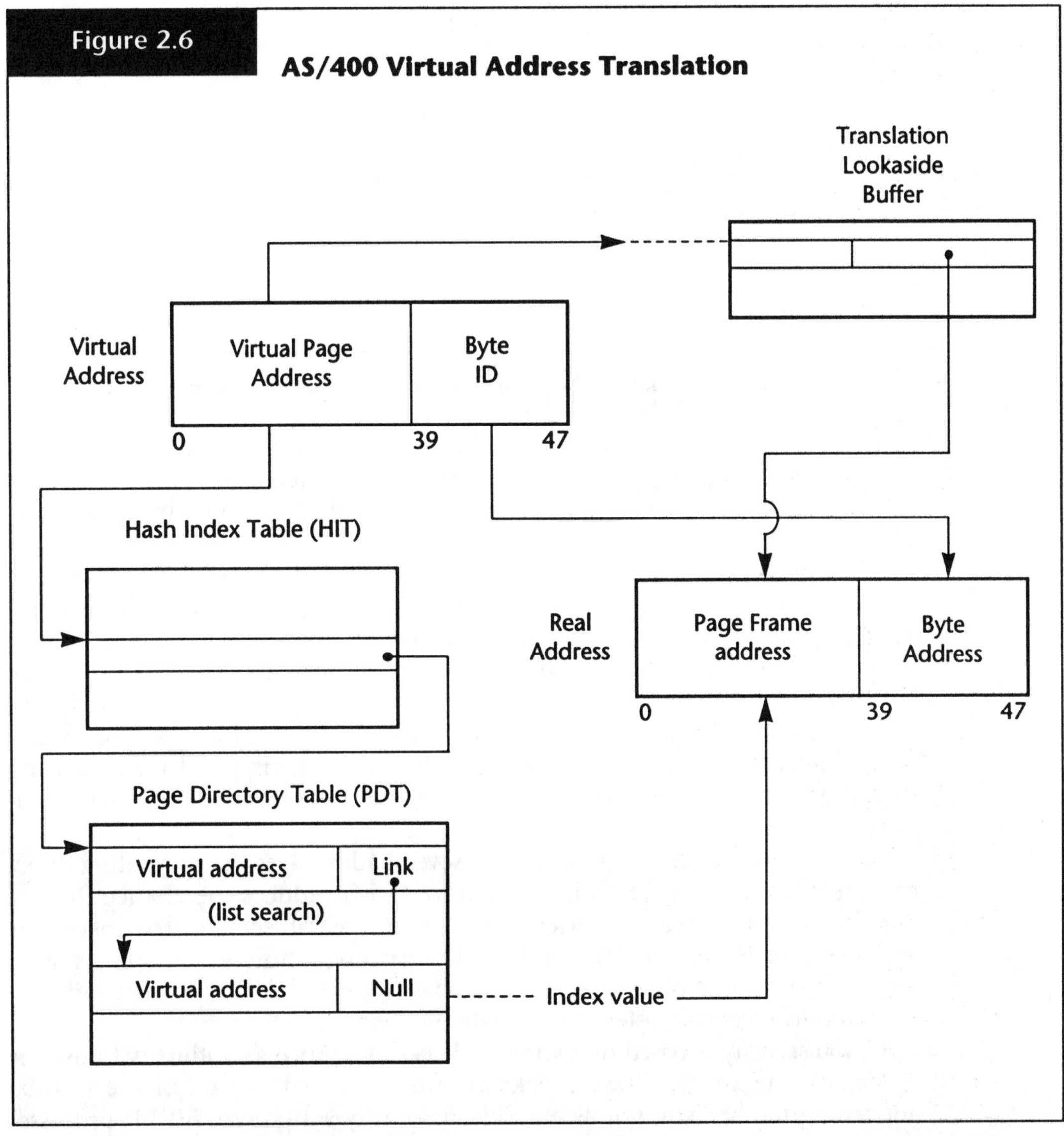

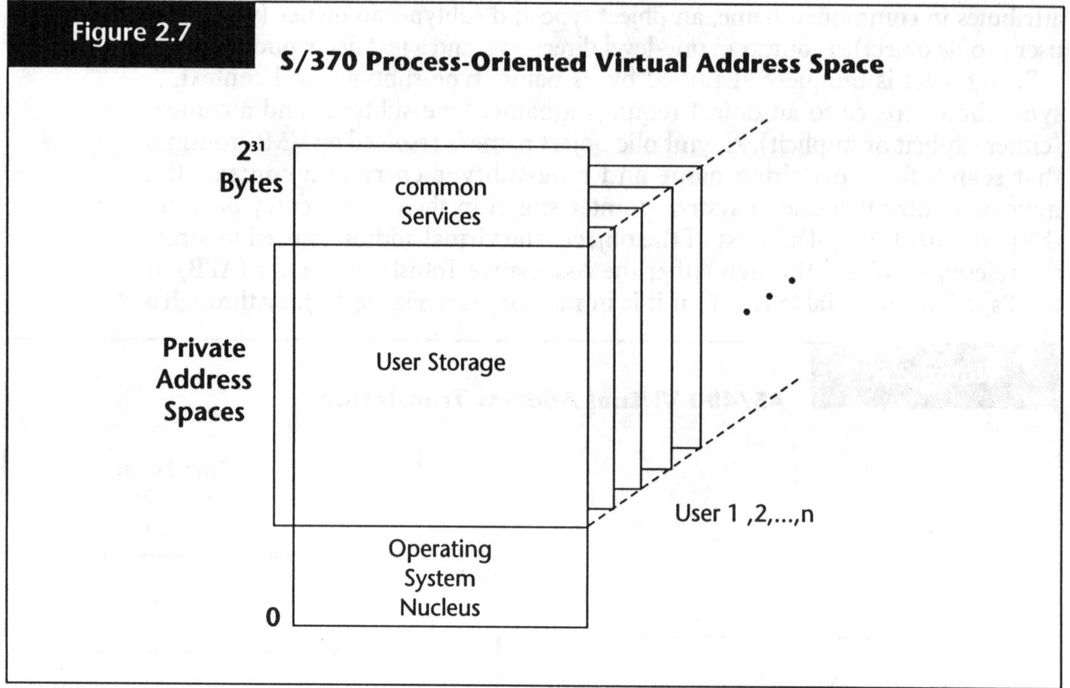

Permanent Directory that contains one entry for each object's permanent virtual address and its current location on DASD.

The AS/400's consistent mechanism for identifying and referencing all objects aids object management and security. All AS/400 operations to move objects between contexts, change object owners, back up and recover objects, dynamically allocate objects, and control object access are the same for all object types.

In addition, only certain types of operations are valid for each object type. For example, a program object can be created, executed, or destroyed, but cannot have its internal contents directly altered with byte-oriented operations. A queue object can have entries added or removed at either end, but also cannot be altered by byte-oriented instructions. Data space objects hold the description and contents of database files and allow record-oriented operations. Space objects provide an unrestricted array of bytes for storing and manipulating pointer and scalar values. The contents of an object are effectively "hidden" from direct manipulation.

The object-oriented design of MI has several advantages. By preventing direct manipulation of an object's internal storage, MI reduces the chance that an object will be damaged inadvertently. The high-level, object-oriented operations available with MI also aid IBM and third-party programmers developing system service software and compilers. And the object-oriented design is the foundation for a uniform security system that is tight but flexible.

AS/400 security is based on dynamic checks of a process's authority to use the objects it references. These checks are implemented as part of the AS/400 addressing mechanism, not as an add-on security subsystem. All MI processes

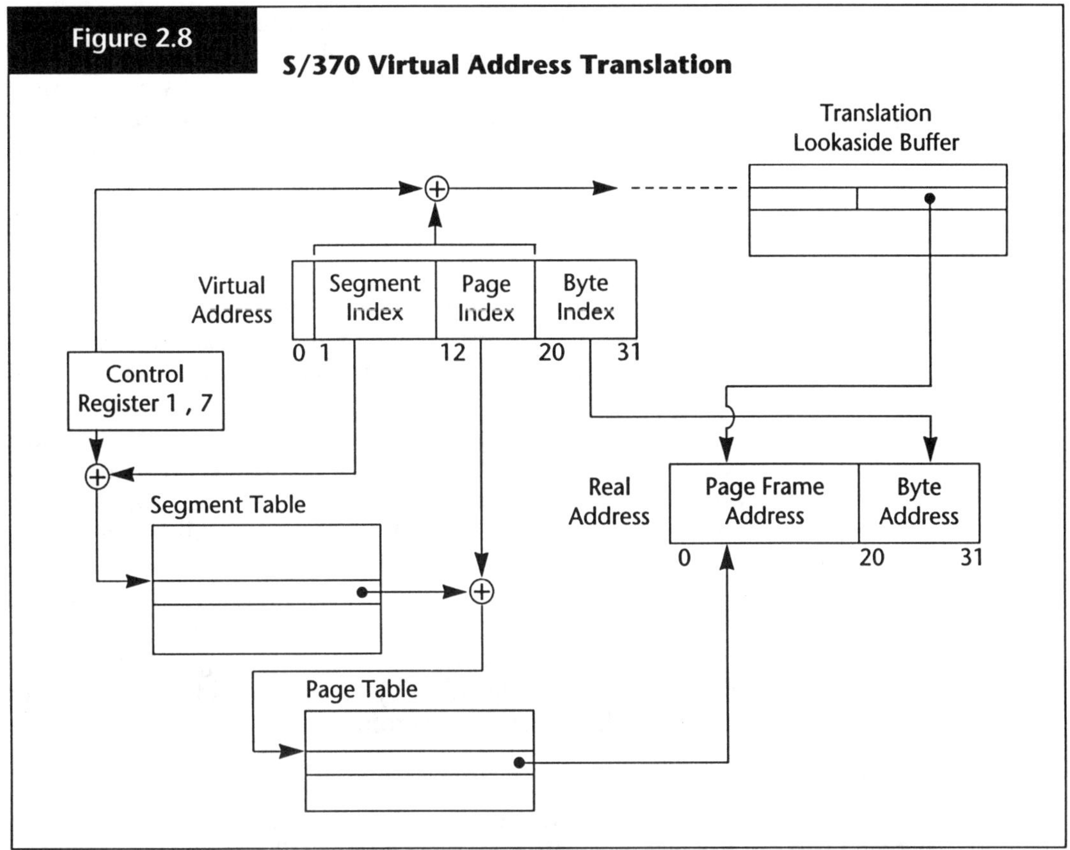

Figure 2.8 **S/370 Virtual Address Translation**

are temporarily associated with a user profile during the life of the process. When a process references an object, it uses a pointer that contains the object's permanent virtual address. (A reference also may use the object's name, type-subtype, and context; and VMC routines will resolve the symbolic reference into a pointer that contains the object's permanent virtual address.)

In addition to the object's virtual address, a resolved pointer also may contain a set of predefined rights to manipulate the object. These rights may include read access, update access, object management rights, or other rights. A pointer that contains predefined rights is known as an *authorized* pointer on the AS/400. In more widely used system architecture terminology, an AS/400 MI authorized pointer represents a *capability* — a symbolic address and a set of rights to an object. If a pointer does not contain adequate rights to an object for the requested operation, the AS/400 searches either the current user profile or an *authorization list* (a special object that contains explicit user-object authorizations) to see whether the user has been explicitly granted (or excluded from) access to the object. If the combination of rights included in the pointer and those included in the user profile or authorization list are adequate for the intended operation, the operation is permitted; otherwise, a security exception occurs and the operation is blocked.

The MI approach to object security allows an optimal combination of the flexibility and ease of interprocess sharing of capabilities and the tighter security management of authorization lists. Generally, only system software uses capabilities, while user applications use authorization lists. Tagged memory is an important element in MI security, because it provides hardware protection against counterfeit pointers that contain improper object rights.

MI also has features to make object security management even more flexible. A program object can be created with a special attribute that allows any process that executes the program to have temporarily all the rights of the program owner as long as the program is invoked. This *adopted authority* can be limited to instructions in the specific program or can be passed on to programs called by the program that adopts authority. By temporarily granting object rights, special programs can provide specific functions to otherwise unauthorized users.

Three other AS/400 options simplify object authorization. Objects can allow *public authority* to the object. The use of a public authorization entry avoids having to list every user profile that should be granted access. Coupled with public authority, a specific user can be *excluded* from access available to the rest of the users. And an individual user profile can be designated as a member of a *group*, in which case the individual user profile automatically inherits all the rights granted to the group user profile. This one-level hierarchy of user profiles simplifies the assignment of authority to user roles (e.g., a "Personnel Department Employee" group profile) filled by several individual user profiles (e.g., "Mary Smith" and "John Walters" user profiles).

Operating System/400

The object-oriented design of MI provides a secure, high-level interface upon which IBM has implemented other parts of the AS/400 operating system — integrated system services and a user interface. The original S/38 designers intended MI to be a base for a variety of operating systems; however, only *Operating System/400 (OS/400)* (and of course, its S/38 predecessor *Control Program Facility*) has been implemented so far. On the AS/400, the term "operating system" really applies to both VMC and OS/400. VMC includes supervisory and resource management portions, which control the execution of other programs in processes, manage memory, and handle security and access rights to programs and data. OS/400 includes system services such as file-management and work-management facilities. OS/400 also includes two languages — *Control Language* and *Data Description Specifications* — that provide the primary user interfaces to the operating system.

The programs that make up OS/400 are implemented as MI templates encapsulated by VMC before being shipped to customers. Thus, OS/400 is dependent only on MI, not on any specific hardware. OS/400 programs use MI objects such as cursors, data spaces, and data-space indices to implement an application-oriented set of higher-level objects, such as database files, available to AS/400 programmers and users. By building more complex system components out of MI objects, OS/400 retains the object-oriented nature of MI but presents a less operating-system-oriented user interface. OS/400 provides more than 40

Figure 2.9 **OS/400 Objects**

Authorization List	Folder	Message Queue
Chart Format	Forms Control Table	Mode Description
Class	Graphics Symbol Set	Output Queue
Class of Service Description	Ideographic Character Table	Panel Group Definition
Command	Ideographic Dictionary	Product Definition
Configuration List	Ideographic Sort Table	Program
Controller Description	Information Search Index	Query Definition
Data Dictionary	Job Description	Reference Code Translate Table
Device Description	Job Queue	S/36 Machine Description
Document	Journal	Session Description
Document List	Journal Receiver	Spelling Aid Dictionary
Data Area	Library	Subsystem Description
Data Queue	Line Description	Table
Edit Description	Menu Definition	User Profile
File	Message File	

objects (Figure 2.9) that encompass all application and system resources including programs, data, and hardware. The same advantages that accrue for MI objects also are realized with OS/400 objects — a consistent approach to object management and security, protection against inadvertent misuse of an object, and high-level, object-specific operations.

Control Language and REXX

The Control Language (CL) is a set of OS/400 commands that control system configuration, system operation, programming, object management, process management, and security. CL is the single command-level interface to the AS/400. (The S/36 and S/38 environments provide alternative S/36 OCL and S/38 CL interfaces for S/36/38 compatibility.) OS/400 CL provides a uniform interface to all system functions; and because it is extensible, CL also can be used for application interfaces. CL even controls installation and configuration of VMC and OS/400 — there is no "system generation" process on the AS/400, nor are there any directly accessible operating system tables.

CL is one of the most exceptional aspects of the OS/400 interface, and its design conveys the AS/400's highly integrated nature. Every command has a verb-object form; for example, the Create COBOL Program (CRTCBLPGM) and Delete Message Queue (DLTMSGQ) commands follow this form. The set of CL verbs is small (a dozen verbs cover almost all of the commands) and consistent. When a new object is required, it is always created with a Create (CRTxxx) command for the object type. A display/update of an object is always obtained with a Work (WRKxxx) command. Most commands have keyworded parameters with accompanying descriptive text. You can supply command

Figure 2.10

OS/400 CL Prompting — Partial Copy File Command

```
                         Copy File (CPYF)

Type choices, press Enter.

From File . . . . . . . .   __________     Name
 library name . . . . . .    *LIBL         Name, *LIBL, *CURLIB
To file name. . . . . . .   __________     Name, *PRINT
 library name . . . . . .    *LIBL         Name, *LIBL, *CURLIB
From member . . . . . . .   *FIRST         Name, generic*, *FIRST, *ALL
To member or label. . . .   *FIRST         Name, *FIRST, *FROMMBR
Replace or add records. .   *NONE          *NONE, *ADD, *REPLACE
Create File . . . . . . .   *NO            *NO, *YES
Print format. . . . . . .   *CHAR          *CHAR, *HEX

                                                              Bottom
F3=Exit F4=Prompt F5=Refresh F10=Additional parameters F12=Cancel
F13=How to use this display F24=More keys
```

parameter values using the keywords or by entering them positionally. OS/400 also supplies command and object menus and prompting aids (Figure 2.10).

You can use CL in any AS/400 context. Both batch and interactive jobs use the same version of CL, and you can use CL interpretively or in compiled programs. CL is accessible from HLL programs and CL programs can call HLL programs. The prompting facility is available when you use the standard command line on a display, when you use the source editor, or when you execute CL from an HLL program.

CL also includes commands to define new commands. The command-definition commands provide table-driven and procedural checking of parameter values, as well as a parameter value translation capability. User-defined command objects are handled exactly the same way as the command objects shipped with OS/400 — full prompting is supported and locally written commands can be used in all contexts, including CL programs.

CL, more than any other OS/400 facility, makes the AS/400, although very sophisticated, one of the easiest systems to use.

In conforming to SAA guidelines, OS/400 also supports REXX as the *control* portion of command procedures. REXX provides interpreted instructions for structured programming and string manipulation. These commands let you build CL command strings and control which CL commands in a procedure are executed.

Data Description Specifications and SQL

Data Description Specifications (DDS) are a set of statements used to define OS/400 database and device file objects. Database files are either physical files that contain actual data or logical files that are views of the data. Device files are mappings from devices such as displays, printers, and communications controllers to program storage areas (buffers). DDS provides a *field-level* description of the contents of a physical file or of the mapping for a logical or device file. In addition, DDS has specific statements that apply only to certain file types; for example, display file DDS includes keywords to control display attributes such as high-intensity or reverse image.

DDS statements are entered into source files and are compiled by one of several OS/400 Create commands (e.g., Create Physical File). The result is an OS/400 object that contains an encapsulated description of the file. For example, a physical file contains not only data but also a field-level description of the data. All AS/400 HLL compilers and utilities use the encapsulated file descriptions when the object is accessed. By using DDS-defined files, a programmer can isolate many device dependencies from the logical structure of a program. During compilation, the HLL compilers also store a hashed identifier for each version of a file object used in the program; then, when the program executes, the program checks its object version identifier against the version identifier stored in the accessed object to make sure the object description has not changed since the program was compiled.

MI support for DDS-defined database files in conjunction with other OS/400 facilities available through CL provide many of the capabilities of a database management system (DBMS). Primary and alternate indices, record selection by field values, and file joins are some of the options OS/400 database files offer. Although the AS/400 does not include a standalone application generator, database files significantly increase the productivity of HLL applications development.

OS/400 also supports SQL as a data-definition language (DDL) alternative to DDS for database files for use in SQL procedures. SQL/400 provides a subset of the ANSI standard data manipulation language (DML) as well. IBM has implemented SQL/400 as a front-end to the MI database functions rather than as a separate subsystem such as DB2 on the S/370. By implementing AS/400 database facilities in a single place (MI), IBM maintains complete consistency between the S/38 DDS derivative interface and the new Systems Application Architecture (SAA) SQL interface. This consistency will be a tremendous aid to migrating applications from the S/38 DDS to the SQL/400 database interface. In early releases of OS/400, however, this coupling of SQL to MI means SQL can provide only a subset of the SAA defined capabilities.

Besides CL, DDS, and SQL, OS/400 includes a number of other productivity aids, including a unique interprogram message mechanism that aids signaling, detecting, and handling runtime errors, and a multijob-per-workstation capability that allows a user to access several applications simultaneously. In addition, OS/400 has comprehensive backup and recovery features, including transaction commit/rollback and journaling. Applications implemented in HLLs can use all of these facilities through a common set of OS/400 CL interfaces.

High-Level Languages

The final layer of the AS/400 is a set of HLL compilers. The languages of primary interest to S/36 and S/38 sites are RPG II, RPG III and RPG/400. COBOL (both 1974 and 1985 standards), PL/I, Pascal, BASIC and C/400 are also available. RPG/400, COBOL-85, and PL/I fully support all OS/400 facilities, and all have language extensions to support DDS-defined files and SQL. Neither Pascal nor BASIC is as comprehensive; for example, Pascal does not support the full range of database access included in the other languages. C/400 does have full database facilities, but its poor execution-time performance limits its applicability for general business applications.

As I've already mentioned, the HLL compilers retrieve database and device file descriptions during compilation. These descriptions are used to create program data structures that correspond to the layout of file buffers. You can manipulate these generated data structures with normal program computation and assignment statements and read them from or write them to a file using extended HLL I/O statements. This integration between the HLLs and OS/400 adds capabilities to the HLLs provided on conventional systems by calls to such utilities as a DBMS or a screen I/O package. IBM has extended this same mechanism for retrieving file definitions during compilation to support SQL "cursor" declarations in HLL programs.

The AS/400 source editor (SEU) is also integrated with the HLL compiler front-ends and provides syntax checking and prompting during editing sessions.

You can better understand the integration of HLL programs with the AS/400 architecture by examining the steps an HLL source program goes through as it is compiled into an executable program object (Figure 2.11). First, the HLL compiler reads the HLL source and the descriptions stored with any file object the program references. From this input, the compiler generates a temporary form known as *Intermediate Representation of a Program (IRP)*. IRP is essentially the same format as MI and is the target language for all HLL compilers. Next, the *Program Resolution Monitor (PRM)*, a part of OS/400, makes a few minor transformations to create an MI program template from the IRP. And finally, an MI Create Program instruction is executed to translate the MI program template into an executable, encapsulated program object. This multistep compilation process — called *cascading* — simplifies the design of the HLL compiler code-generation routines. It also enables all HLL programs to take advantage of the "peep-hole" optimizer that is part of the VMC encapsulation routine.

User Interface Manager

Although OS/400 CL provides a consistent, easy-to-use interface for the experienced programmer and can be used effectively by advanced end users, all OS/400 facilities are also available through a set of menus and fill-in-the-blank displays. IBM designed all OS/400 displays to SAA Common User Access standards, giving them a high degree of consistency across all functions.

Figure 2.11

AS/400 HLL Program Compilation

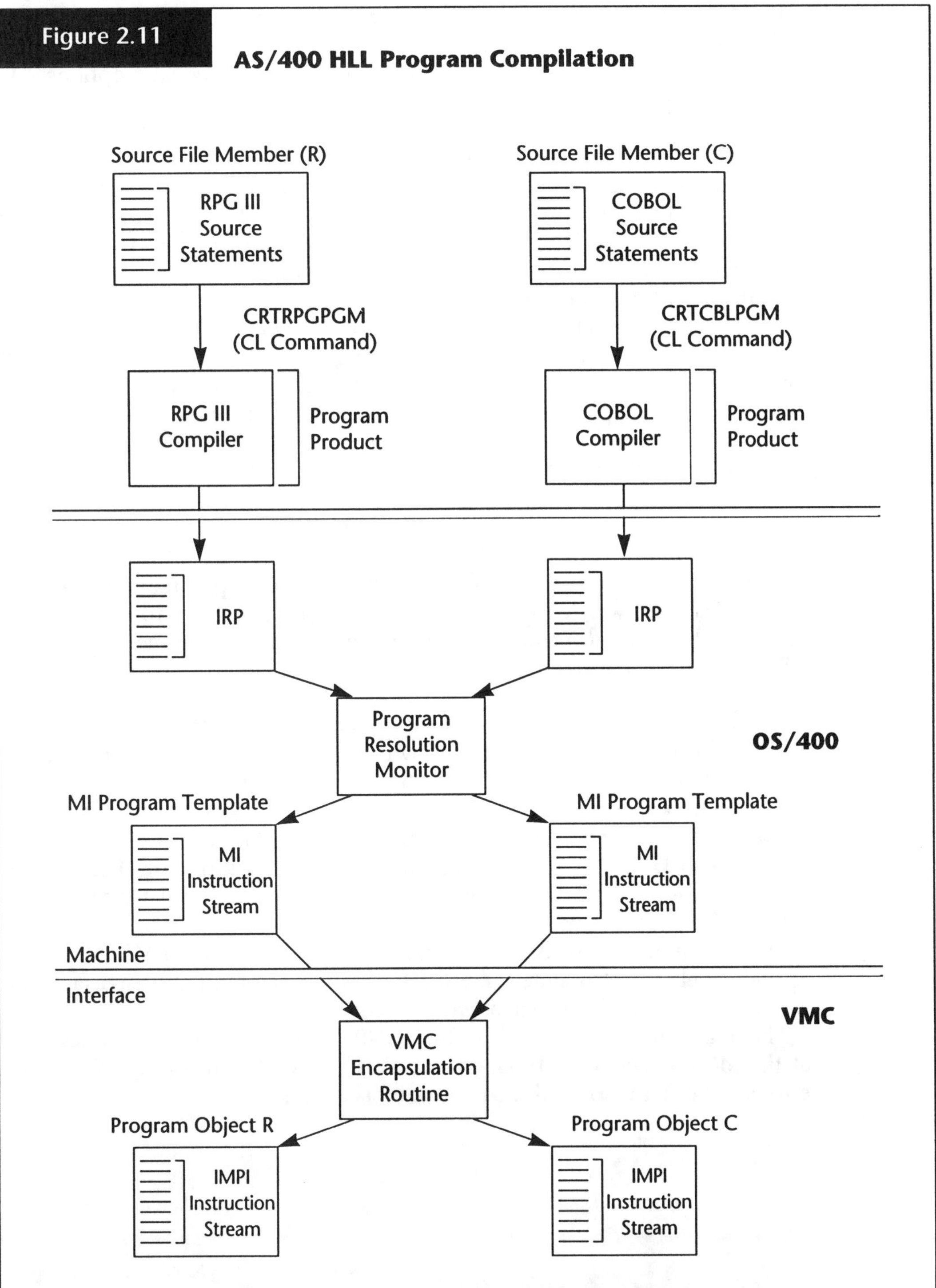

Source File Member (R)
RPG III Source Statements
CRTRPGPGM (CL Command)
RPG III Compiler
Program Product
Source File Member (C)
COBOL Source Statements
CRTCBLPGM (CL Command)
COBOL Compiler
Program Product
IRP
IRP
Program Resolution Monitor
OS/400
MI Program Template
MI Instruction Stream
MI Program Template
MI Instruction Stream
Machine
Interface
VMC
VMC Encapsulation Routine
Program Object R
IMPI Instruction Stream
Program Object C
IMPI Instruction Stream

The OS/400 interface displays are controlled by the *User Interface Manager (UIM)*, which is a "smart" display manager that knows about functional dependencies between parameter values and which presents only valid options. The UIM also supports context-sensitive, field-level help.

S/36 and S/38 Environments

To support smooth migration paths for S/36 and S/38 applications, the AS/400 includes two environments that coexist with OS/400. OS/400 is so close to S/38 CPF that the S/38 environment consists mainly of an alternative set of displays and some minor differences in CL syntax (e.g., many DSPxxx commands on the S/38 are named WRKxxx on the AS/400.)

The S/36 environment is more complex than the S/38 environment. Some S/36 facilities, such as S/36 assembly language, are not supported at all on the AS/400. The S/36 facilities supported on the AS/400 are implemented in two ways: either as a complete re-implementation of the facility (e.g., the RPG II compiler) or as a mapping to an existing OS/400 facility (e.g., the S/36 Status Print command is mapped to the AS/400 Work with Spooled Files command.)

In either case, the S/36 function is carried out using AS/400 MI objects and encapsulated programs. There is no emulation of S/36 machine code, nor is there a separate path to AS/400 IMPI that circumvents MI. By using the same MI facilities as OS/400 and many of the OS/400 functions, programs ported from the S/36 coexist well with OS/400 and S/38 environment applications. In addition, the S/36 environment programmer can take advantage of additional OS/400 features on a gradual basis.

The Significance of the AS/400 Architecture

The layered design of the AS/400 provides a well-structured set of interfaces appropriate for the layers built upon them. IMPI is effective for implementing the operating system supervisor and resource managers; MI is effective for implementing integrated system services, compilers, and database facilities; and OS/400 and HLLs are effective for application development. This layered approach not only provides functional interfaces, it also insulates each layer's software from lower-level changes.

In addition to layering AS/400 interfaces, IBM designed both MI and OS/400 as high-level, object-oriented interfaces. This object-oriented design facilitates resource use and management as well as security.

The final major characteristic of the AS/400 — the high degree of integration at the MI and OS/400 interfaces — makes the AS/400 relatively easy to use, especially given the sophisticated nature of its design.

Section II

SYSTEM MANAGEMENT

Chapter 3

Security: Concepts

by Douglas T. Parrish

Implement and maintain appropriate AS/400 security from the beginning

Your new AS/400 arrives, and the challenge begins to get the system in operation as soon as possible. Everyone pitches in and works overtime, and in the rush to get the system set up, security is thrown out the window. New applications can be developed and installed much faster if programmers have access to the security officer's password. And when the time comes to install sensitive applications such as payroll, everyone's password can be changed, right?

If this scenario sounds familiar, you may find that you've opened wide the proverbial barn door and let out far more than just the horse. If your AS/400 security is lax in the beginning, it probably will continue to be compromised — no matter how many times you change passwords.

In this chapter we look at how AS/400 security works, so you can implement the appropriate security levels for your particular situation from the start — or find ways to plug security loopholes if your system lacks the security it needs.

Object Authority

AS/400 security is controlled by the Operating System/400 (OS/400), and it centers on users, objects, and users' authority to use those objects. There are no object orphans on the AS/400: When an object is created, it must be owned by someone. An owner with object authority can use the object, delete it, give it to another user, or let other users use it. When a user tries to access an object, OS/400 determines whether or not the user has authority to use it. If proper authority exists, the object can be used; if not, an escape message notifies the user of the problem. This process applies to system routines as well as to user programs and files.

Object authority, or the right to use or control an object, comes in two categories: object rights and data rights. Object rights are concerned with the object itself; data rights apply to the data contained within the object. Object rights assign a user the following authority:

Operational Rights (*OPER): the authority to use an object, look at its description, and restore it. A user must have operational rights to a program to execute it.

Object Management Rights (*OBJMGT): the authority to grant and revoke user rights, move and rename objects, and add members to database files.

Object Existence Rights (*OBJEXT): the authority to delete, free storage, save, restore, or transfer ownership of an object.

Four types of data rights exist:

Read (*READ): the authority to retrieve the contents of an object entry.

Add (*ADD): the authority to add entries to an object. For example, adding records to a database file requires ADD rights for the file. Adding objects to a library requires ADD rights for the library.

Update (*UPD): the authority to change the entries in an object. For example, changing records in a database file requires UPD rights for the file.

Delete (*DLT): the authority to remove objects in an object. For example, deleting a program from a library requires DLT rights for the library. Deleting records from a database file requires DLT rights for the database file.

The seven rights can be mixed and matched depending on the requirements of your system. Their interrelated use can use make security quite powerful — and complex. IBM's *Security Concepts and Planning* manual (SC41-8083) contains a detailed explanation of the object authorities required to use OS/400 commands. Figure 3.1 presents an overview of the OS/400 authority rights.

Figure 3.1

OS/400 Authority Rights

	*OBJOPR	*OBJMGT	*OBJEXIST	*READ	*ADD	*UPD	*DLT
*ALL	X	X	X	X	X	X	X
*CHANGE	X		X	X	X	X	X
*USE	X			X			
*EXCLUDE				none			

Public Authority

Most create commands include a parameter for Authority (AUT). This parameter always defaults to *LIBCRTAUT, which assigns the default public authority based on the CRTAUT keyword that is associated with each library. By default, this value will be the system value QCRTAUT, which in turn defaults to *CHANGE. Authority also can be specified as *ALL, which adds object-existence and object-management rights. Entering *EXCLUDE revokes public authority; objects created this way are known as private objects.

Public authority is stored with the object and object rights are stored with each user profile. When you want to use an object, OS/400 will perform a sequence of three main authority checks. First, it will check the individual user profile and adopted authorities. OS/400 will check for *ALLOBJ authority, then for specific authority to the object, and next for specific authority from an authorization list. Second, if a Group Profile exists, OS/400 will check it exactly as it does the individual profile. The system will check the group profile for *ALLOBJ authority, then it will look at any specific authorities of the group profile, and finally it will check for specific authorities of the group profile from an authorization list. The third and last set of authorities that OS/400 checks are the Public Authorities. It examines the public authority of the object and, finally, the public authority for the object from an authority list. Figure 3.2 presents the OS/400's authority-checking sequence.

Since the system first checks the authorities from the individual profile, a user's authority to use an object can be more restrictive than the public authority for that object. The public authority cannot be more restrictive than the individual authorities. For example, if public authority on a data file is *ALL, any specific rights can be revoked from a specific user. Any of the seven previously mentioned object rights, as well as public authorities, can be revoked at any time. The Revoke Object Authority (RVKOBJAUT) command is used to revoke public authority.

Figure 3.2

Authority Checking Sequence

1. Individual User Profile
   *ALLOBJ
   Specific Authorities
   Specific Authority from AUTL

2. Group Profile
   *ALLOBJ
   Specific Authorities
   Specific Authority from AUTL

3. Public

   Public Authority from Object
   Public Authority from AUTL

Special Authority

Special authority is required to perform certain system functions. Special rights are All Object (*ALLOBJ), Save System (*SAVSYS), Job Control (*JOBCTL), Security Administrator (*SECADM), Spool Control (*SPLCTL) and Service (*SERVICE). These rights are assigned with the Special Authority (SPCAUT) parameter in the Create User Profile (CRTUSRPRF) and Change User Profile (CHGUSRPRF) commands.

**ALLOBJ* special authority permits full access to all system resources. A user with All Object rights has the rights to use, change, or delete any object on the system. This special authority is usually granted if more than one person has security-officer functions.

**SAVSYS* grants authority to save, restore, and free storage for all objects on the system regardless of whether or not the user has object existence rights for the objects. This special authority eliminates the need to grant object-existence rights to the user who performs save/restore.

**JOBCTL* grants authority to change, display, hold, release, and cancel all jobs that are executing, that are in a job queue, or that are in an output queue that has OPRCTL(*YES) specified. Special authority usually is granted only to the system operator and those users who must have authority to perform special functions.

**SECADM* authority allows the user to create, change, and delete user profiles. It also provides the ability to add users to the distribution directory. This authority is usually given to the person responsible for office enrollment. It is also used when someone besides the security officer performs the user profile administration.

**SPLCTL* authority allows the user to control spooled files. This allows the user to hold, release, cancel, delete, and display the spooled files of other users. Spool Control authority is usually given to system operators and other personnel who handle printed output.

**SERVICE* allows the user to use the system service functions such as display, alter, and dump. This authority can provide access to secure data, so it is usually given only to the QSRV and QSECOFR profiles.

Authority Adoption

At the root of many AS/400 security problems is a feature known as authority adoption. This feature allows a program to adopt its owner's authority when executed. Although in many instances authority adoption can be used effectively, it *can* create security problems.

To illustrate authority adoption, let's examine a payroll application. Assume that the payroll manager owns an employee master file containing salary information. The payroll manager has exclusive authority to the object, which allows him to run payroll without authorization problems. Authority has not been granted to other users.

But suppose department heads need access to a listing of employee names and telephone numbers. Without file authority to use the employee master file, the department heads cannot execute the list. If read authority is granted to the department heads, then those who have access to DFU, QUERY, or Copy File (CPYF) can list the file and extract salary information.

Therein lies the dilemma. Without authority, the list cannot be executed. If authority is granted, file security is compromised. One solution is to create a logical view of the file that excludes sensitive salary information. Another solution is to use authority adoption to give department heads authority to access the file. To use authority adoption, a programmer would compile the listing program as USRPRF(*OWNER). Then the security officer would change the object's owner to the payroll manager. Then, whenever the authorized users execute the list program, authority for the master file will be adopted, but only during program execution. Because the listing program does not print or display salaries, the file remains secure. In this case, using authority adoption is one way to allow user access to a file without compromising security.

Adoption Problems

You should use the adoption feature with great care, however — particularly when the security officer's authority is adopted. As mentioned earlier, programmers frequently receive the security officer's password when the system is first installed. But after the password is changed, programmers still may be able to perform security officer tasks. Understanding how this happens is key to reclaiming AS/400 security.

Programmers who can perform security officer tasks may have coded a program similar to the one below, compiled it with USRPRF(*OWNER) while they were acting as the security officer, and filed it away for future use:

```
PGM
CALL PGM(QCMD)
ENDPGM
```

It doesn't take a genius to figure out that if a user has operational rights to this program, the command entry screen will be displayed. When the command entry screen is displayed, the user has the same authority as the security officer and can enter any command, including Display Authorized Users (DSPAUTUSR). Ask yourself how many of these programs exist on *your* system.

In this case, the person who distributed the security officer's password is the culprit. Obviously, if the password is kept secret, a program cannot be created to adopt the security officer's authorities.

You also must be careful when using programs restored from another AS/400. OS/400 revokes all authority to restored programs that adopt authorities if someone other than the program owner or the security officer restores the program. After restoration, a user must inform the security officer that a program was restored and that operational authority needs to be granted. If the security officer fails to inquire about the program's purpose and blindly grants authority, security will be compromised if the restored program adopts the security officer's authorities. As you can see, strict company policies are as important as machine security.

Library Lists and Adoption

When used with library lists, authority adoption can further compromise security. Suppose program PGMA performs a function for the security officer but a programmer executes it. Assume the program uses the Display Object Description (DSPOBJD) command to list all objects on the system and then calls PGMB to list them on the printer. The code for PGMA might look like this:

```
PGM
DSPOBJD OBJ(*ALL/*ALL) OBJTYP(*ALL) OUTFILE(QGPL/OBJECTS)
CALL   PGM(PGMB)
ENDPGM
```

To ensure that all objects are listed, the security officer compiles the program with USRPRF(*OWNER). PGMB is an RPG program that reads the file QGPL/OBJECTS and lists the objects. PGMA and PGMB reside in library QGPL.

Suppose that an enterprising programmer creates a program called PGMB and places it in his library PGMRLIB. The program could be coded as follows:

```
PGM
CALL PGM(QCMD)
ENDPGM
```

This is the same program shown earlier, except that the programmer owns it, and the program does not adopt authority. It is perfectly normal for a programmer to create a program in this fashion.

But by adding library PGMRLIB to the front of his library list and calling program PGMA, the programmer can cause the following steps to occur. First, the DSPOBJD command will execute as normal, and the outfile will be created. When PGMB is called, however, the called program will be PGMRLIB/PGMB and not the intended program QGPL/PGMB. Because PGMRLIB/PGMB calls QCMD and because PGMA adopts the security officer's authority, the programmer is presented with the command entry screen with full security-officer authority.

Reclaiming Control

While your goal is to establish solid security practices from the beginning, you may find yourself in a situation where authority adoption has been used with less-than-ideal discrimination. Reclaiming total security once the security officer's password has been placed in the hands of unauthorized users is difficult — but it can be done. Here are my recommendations for reclaiming security:

- Change the security officer's password immediately. Execute Display Object Description (DSPOBJD) to list all programs in all libraries. This step is best done overnight because it is quite lengthy.

- Use the Display Program Adopt (DSPPGMADP) command to display programs that adopt security-officer authority.
- Examine the source for all programs that adopt authority. Check the date and time the source was last modified. You can do this with the Display File Description (DSPFD) command by specifying the member list option. The date and time of modification should match the compile date and time stored with the program and the date and time shown on the DSPPGM display. If not, the source being examined may not be the source from which the program was created. This discrepancy is suspect!
- Recompile all programs with USRPRF(*USER) that adopt authority but don't need adoption capability. This step will help eliminate unnecessary authority adoption.
- Extend restrictions on commands and programs that need to adopt authority. For instance, specify QSYS for all system commands — QSYS/DSPOBJD, for example. This step prevents user commands with the same name from being executed.
- Monitor the history log for job-initiation messages that belong to the security officer. The log records each time the security officer signs on.
- Revoke public authority to the diskette and tape drive device descriptions in extreme cases. Revoking public authority to these devices will prevent unauthorized program restoration. Assign device description authority to one person — the system operator, for example.

After you reclaim control, the most important recommendation is that you use the security officer's user profile to perform only security-related functions. Do not program or operate the machine as the security officer; otherwise, you'll continue to court disaster. Remember: Think AS/400 security at all times. Tight security will reduce your vulnerability.

Chapter 4

Security: Object Authorization

by Paul Conte

Object-oriented security provides a powerful base for foolproof security

The AS/400 uses the same general mechanisms for object authority — capabilities and access lists — as the S/38. But the AS/400 makes several significant changes in how you use object authorization to implement your organization's security, and not all of the changes are for the better.

Capabilities, or *authorized pointers* as they're called on the AS/400 and S/38, contain both an object's virtual address and access rights to the object. Capabilities are ideal for internal use by system software because they are fast (no authorization lookup is necessary) and simple (they can be passed between programs and processes). Capabilities are not good for general authorization management, however, because once a capability is passed out, there's no simple way to get it back. Both OS/400 and the S/38 CPF use authorized pointers only for internal functions, and authorized pointers are not directly available to the end user.

Access lists, on the other hand, are used by OS/400 and CPF to provide end-user facilities for authority management. Access lists are slower than capabilities but allow more control over granting and revoking authority. An access list logically contains a set of user-object pairs, with each user-object pair specifying the access rights a user has to an object. The system looks up rights in the access list when a user tries to access an object. You manage authority by creating or deleting user-object pairs or changing the specific rights associated with a user-object pair.

The S/38 implements an access list as a list of authorized objects in a user profile object. Each entry in a user profile's authorized object list includes the object's virtual address (rather than its name, type, and library) and a set of one to seven access rights. On the S/38, these seven rights are categorized as *specific authority* to distinguish them from other rights (e.g., job control), known as

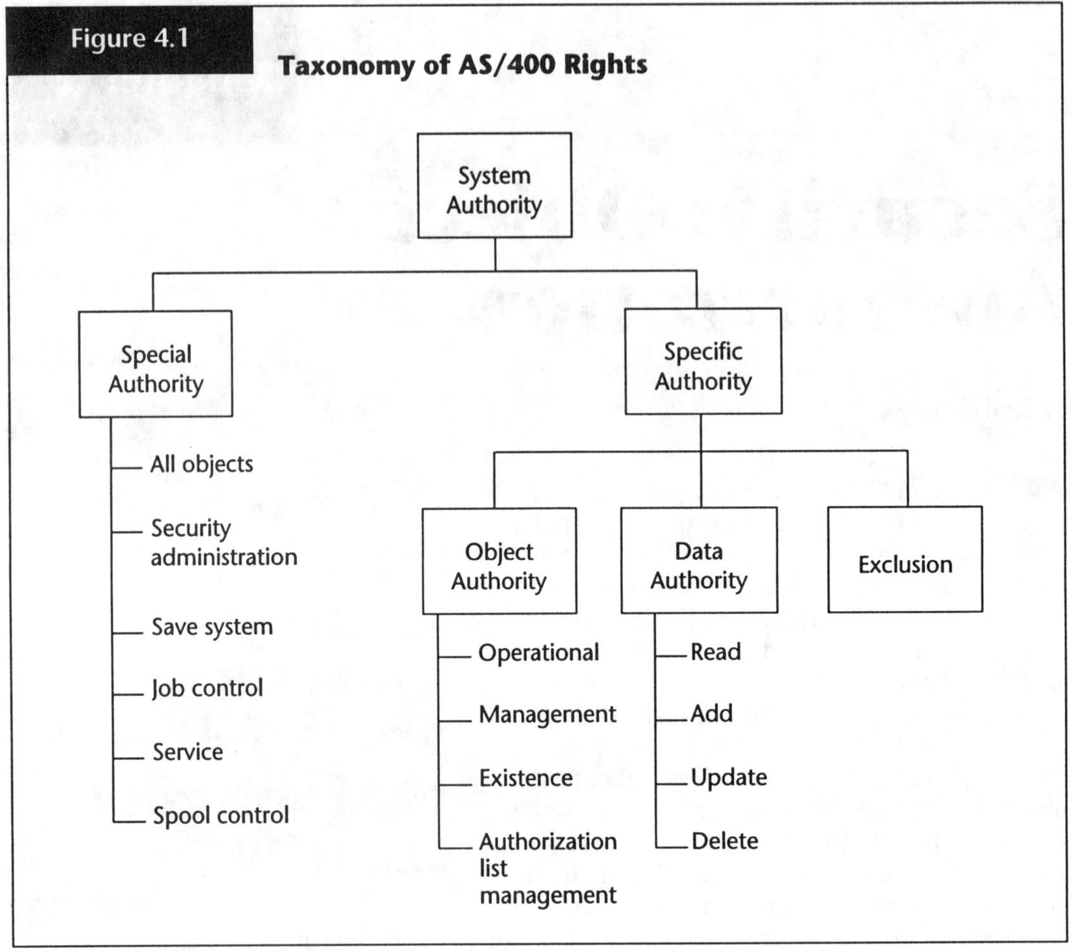

special authority, that do not apply to specific objects. The rights included in S/38 specific authority are further divided into two categories: three *object authority* rights — existence, management, and use; and four *data authority* rights — read, add, update, and delete.

Like the S/38, the AS/400 supports user-profile-authorized object lists. To the seven rights included in S/38 specific authority, the AS/400 adds two new ones: authorization list management, which falls in the object-authority category; and exclusion, which is a new category of authority that specifies no rights at all. Figure 4.1 provides a taxonomy of rights on the AS/400.

The authorization list management right applies only to an *authorization list* object type (discussed below). The exclusion right is not really a right; it is a placeholder that means the user profile has no rights to the object. If exclusion is specified, it must be the only right specified for that object.

Both the AS/400 and S/38 support *group profiles*, which provide one level of nesting for user-profile object authority. Group profiles let you manage the authority of a set of user profiles through a single group profile. On the S/38, if user profile USR has GRP as its group profile, USR adds all of GRP's authority to its own. Group profiles work differently on the AS/400. USR adds GRP's authority only for objects not on USR's own list. For example, suppose USR has only read rights to file FIL, and GRP has read and update rights to file FIL. On the S/38 USR can read and update FIL, but on the AS/400 USR can only read FIL. Neither the AS/400 nor the S/38 lets a group profile itself have a group profile (thus, the one-level limit to the profile nesting). Nor does either system let a user profile belong to more than one group. Both of these missing facilities are essential to model real-world business environments, which are not hierarchies with only one level of nesting. For example, an employee may work part of his or her time in two different divisions. We can hope that a future version of OS/400 will complete the group profile concept.

In addition to letting you manage a set of user profiles, the AS/400 now lets you use a new object, the authorization list, to manage authority for a set of objects. An authorization list contains a list of user profiles and a list of objects. Each user profile entry contains a set of rights to all objects in the authorization list. If a new object is added to the object list, any user in the user profile list immediately has rights to the object. As with group profiles, the authorization list provides only one level of nesting. In addition, an object can be in only one authorization list; however, a user profile can be in more than one authorization list.

The AS/400 checks for a user profile entry in an authorization list only after it has checked the specific user profile's authorized objects list. If the object is in the user profile's list, the rights in that entry are the only rights the user has to the object.

Like the S/38, the AS/400 also allows an object to have public authority. On the S/38, an object's public authority allows access by any user. On the AS/400, only user profiles not otherwise authorized to the object can access the object using the object's public authority.

The AS/400 continues the S/38 adopted authority feature whereby a program can add the authorities of its owner to those of the user executing the program for the duration of the program.

The AS/400 adds several miscellaneous security features. You now can include a new special authority, *ALLOBJ, for a user or group profile, allowing the profile unrestricted access to all objects.

The AS/400 also lets you specify a *user class* for a user profile. Each of the five user classes (security officer, security administrator, programmer, system operator, and user) is just a short-form equivalent to a different set of special authorities. For example, specifying the system operator class is the same as specifying "save system" and "job control" special authorities.

For S/36 compatibility, you can create an authority holder, which is a "shadow" program-described database file object. You can grant and revoke authority to the authority holder as if to a file of the same name. Rights to the authority holder are transferred to a file by the same name if one is created, and those rights persist even if the file is deleted. Because an authority holder can be used only for program-described database files, it won't be generally useful. And

Figure 4.2

AS/400 Search Sequence for Object Authority

1. User profile *ALLOBJ special authority
2. User profile explicit object authority
3. User profile entry in authorization list containing object
4. Group profile *ALLOBJ special authority
5. Group profile explicit object authority
6. Group profile entry in authorization list containing object
7. Public authority specified for object not in authorization list
8. Public authority entry in authorization list containing object

finally, as another S/36 migration aid, or for those who like to live dangerously, on the AS/400, you can turn off security altogether.

Overall, the biggest change to security in moving from the S/38 to the AS/400 is that S/38 individual, group, and public rights are additive, whereas the AS/400 uses only the first set of object rights found following a strictly ordered search for an authorization to the object. Figure 4.2 shows the order of the search.

One result of this search order is that if an AS/400 user profile has explicit, individual rights to an object, these rights are the only rights the user has. They cannot be augmented by group profile, authorization list, or object public rights. Another implication is that if the first authorization found during a search specifies *EXCLUDE, the user has no rights to the object regardless of rights specified elsewhere.

IBM intends the ordered search list and the *EXCLUDE pseudo-right to provide convenient "authorization by exception." Some smaller organizations may, in fact, find it easy to assign all users to one of several groups and then limit or exclude access by specific profiles.

But at its foundation, the ordered search approach is a kludge that may cause more problems than it solves. The "real world" doesn't think about authority as if people were members of a single group and had individual restrictions. Instead, a typical organization thinks about people as belonging to one or more groups and having the combined authority of all the groups to which they belong.

Given the poor match between "real-world" and AS/400 models of security, the person responsible for a typical large organization's security will have to hand map the organization's authorization model into the AS/400's model, being careful to keep consistent all the places where a person's authority can be specified. Here is a simple example of the problems that may be encountered:

1. Suppose group profile GRP has READ and UPDATE authority to file FIL.
2. And suppose user profile USR is a member of group profile GRP.

3. But suppose USR is the profile of a person who should not be allowed to update a FIL record, so USR has been granted explicit READ (only) authority to FIL.
4. Then suppose that at some point, a policy change occurs that allows everyone in the work group represented by GRP to add new entries to FIL, so GRP is granted ADD authority to FIL.
5. Surprise! Although USR also should now be allowed to add entries to FIL, it can't because of the explicit authority.

The implication of this example is significant: To revise authority of members of a work group (or of an entry in an authorization list), you must check all places in the ordered search list where an authorization entry could "short-circuit" your change. And you must check all these locations for all members of the group.

A preferable authorization scheme is conceptually simple — allow a user profile to be a member of more than one group and have the combined authority of all groups. This alternate approach would not only simplify the initial implementation of an organization's view of security, but it also would make authorization changes simpler and less error-prone.

With S/38 object-oriented security, IBM established an elegant, powerful base for convenient, foolproof security. Apparently, IBM also heard from customers that additional authorization aids were needed to make object-oriented security easier to use on the AS/400. Unfortunately, IBM didn't "fix" anything with the ordered search approach; it simply muddied an otherwise clean system. We can hope that IBM will recognize this mistake quickly and that we'll see a more viable solution before too many more releases of OS/400.

Chapter 5

Security: OS/400 Exposures

by Paul Conte

Existing gaps in OS/400 security can be closed with level 40

The AS/400, like the S/38, has a reputation for carefully architected security. Both systems provide an object-oriented machine interface (MI) that requires a process (i.e., a job) to have appropriate authority to an object before the process can access the object. MI's architecture provides a tight but flexible foundation for security. To support MI's security architecture, the hardware also includes logic to block counterfeiting of object pointer values, thus assuring the integrity of storage locations that contain MI-level authorities.

Unfortunately, gaps in Release 2.0 (and previous releases) of OS/400 (and all releases of CPF) compromise the well-architected security facilities in the hardware and MI. For the numerous installations that take only a casual approach to security, these gaps do not substantially increase security risks. However, installations that require maximum security should be aware of the exposure they face due to these gaps. In this chapter, I explain the OS/400 gaps and show how you can reduce your potential exposure to security breeches (The issues I discuss about OS/400 apply to CPF as well). I also outline the changes IBM has made to OS/400 to correct the problems.

Although the OS/400 security gaps are potentially serious, you should be aware that many commonly used security practices can increase your security risks more than the problems I describe. In particular, if you set your system value QSECURITY to operate your AS/400 with security level 10 (no security) or 20 (password security), you already allow more access than the gaps in OS/400 do. You also are more exposed to security breeches if you let programmers sign on as the QSECOFR user profile or give them *ALLOBJ or *SERVICE special authority. Essentially, in all these cases, you give anyone who signs on complete access to your system, and OS/400's gaps don't really matter.

The problems with OS/400 apply to your installation only if you are concerned enough with maintaining strict security to use security level 30 (resource security) and to tightly control use of the QSECOFR user profile and special authorities. Even in these cases, additional exposure from OS/400's gaps may be limited because a potential security violator must use an MI-level technique to take advantage of the gaps. Relatively few people have the technical skill to use the necessary MI-level techniques. In general, with the OS/400 gaps, nontechnical individuals do not pose a risk unless they have a technical accomplice. But, unfortunately, it is difficult — if not impossible —to completely block a knowledgeable programmer who has access to an MI assembler or the AS/400 service facility from exploiting the gaps.

Note, however, that a person need not have an MI assembler to use MI-level techniques. Several published articles have described how to patch S/38 programs to get at MI-level capabilities without an assembler. Although IBM has removed the S/38 PCHPGM (Patch Program) command from the AS/400, the AS/400 service facility allows MI program patches. (Access to the AS/400 service facility is limited to users with *SERVICE special authority.)

AS/400 Security

MI is the foundation of AS/400 security. In simplest terms, MI requires a process to have specific authorities (e.g., existence, read, update) to any MI object (e.g., space, cursor, program) that the process accesses. MI provides several mechanisms for a process to obtain authority to an object: by getting authority from the user and group profile objects associated with the process, by executing programs that *adopt* authority temporarily, or by using special object pointers with predefined authorities.

As a starting point, every process has associated user and group profile objects that contain lists of object authorities. These authorities are available for the process's duration.

For specific functions that require authority not contained in a process's associated profiles, the process can execute a program (to which the process has authority) that has the *adopt* attribute and that is owned by a user profile with the authority required for the function. When a program is created with the adopt attribute, a process executing the program adds the program owner's authority to those of the process's associated profiles while the program is invoked.

As another way to get authority, a process can use an *authorized* MI object pointer (to which the process has authority) to access an object. A process that has authority to an object creates an authorized object pointer. The pointer contains not only the virtual address of the object but also a list of specific authorities to the object. Once a process creates an authorized pointer, the process can store the pointer and make it available to other processes, thus giving the other processes the object authorities stored in the pointer.

OS/400 uses these and other MI objects and MI security mechanisms to implement another level of objects and object authority. For example, an OS/400 data-area object is implemented as an MI space object. Some OS/400 objects are composites of several MI objects: An OS/400 physical file, for instance, consists of MI data spaces, spaces, cursors, and data-space indexes. OS/400 also uses MI

Figure 5.1

AS/400 Security Level 30

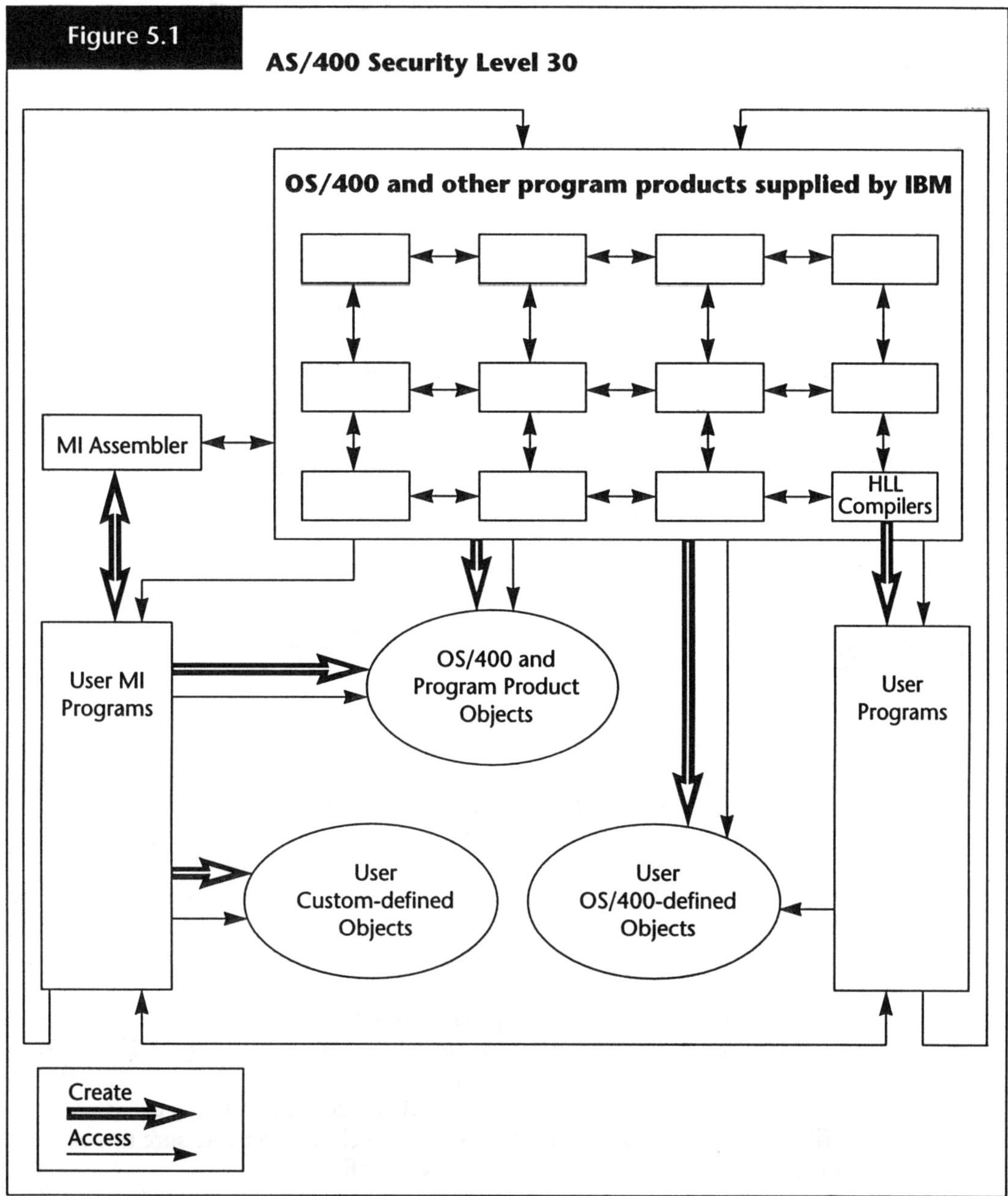

objects for internal operations. For example, one MI space that OS/400 uses contains information about processes.

OS/400 uses both profile object authorities and other MI security facilities, such as programs that adopt authority and authorized pointers. In some cases, OS/400 uses MI's facilities for performance reasons — authorized pointers are the fastest way to reference a frequently used object. In other cases, OS/400 uses

Figure 5.2

HLL Programmer's View with Level 10-30

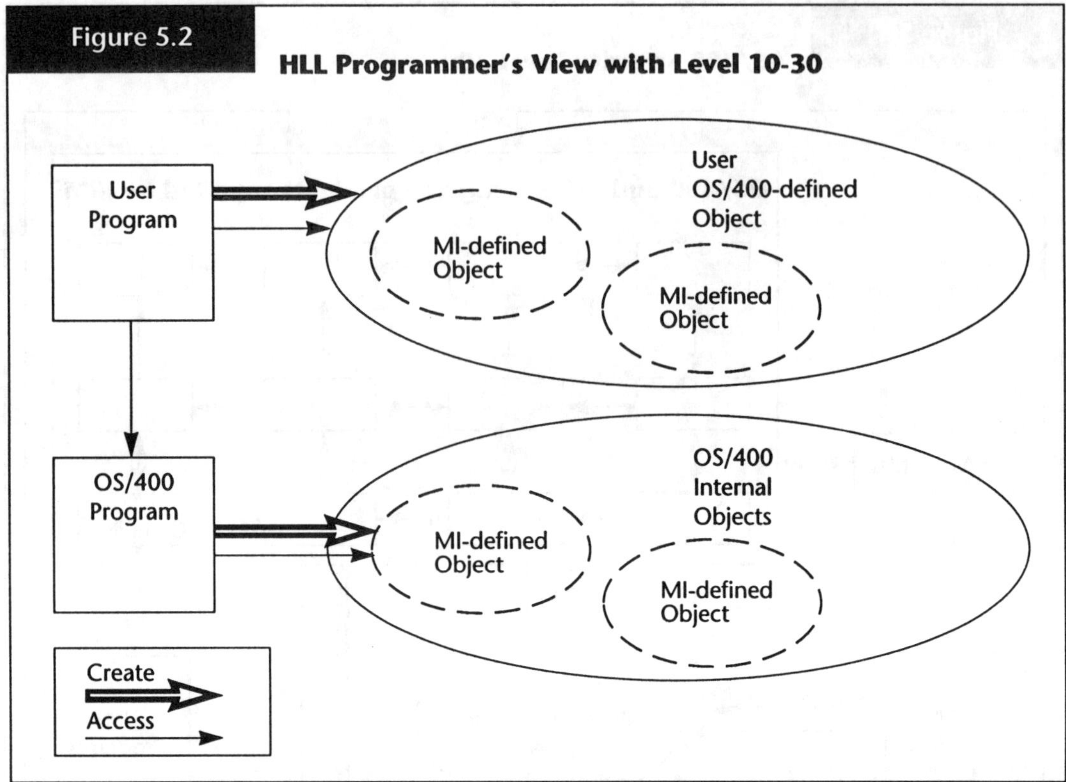

MI's facilities to simplify the implementation of certain operations. For example, using a program that adopts authority is a way to implement a restricted function, such as logging information to the system history log even when a process is not otherwise authorized to modify the history log object.

Figure 5.1 shows a simplified view of OS/400's approach to security with level 30. For the most part, AS/400 installations create and access MI objects only through OS/400 or other IBM program products, or through code an IBM-supplied high-level-language (HLL) compiler (e.g., RPG/400 or COBOL/400) generates. Because IBM-supplied programs control access to MI objects, if IBM has done its job well, a user working just with IBM products and HLL programs can't circumvent OS/400's security design. For example, if an OS/400 routine uses an authorized pointer to access an MI object, thereby bypassing MI user-profile-authority checking, the OS/400 routine checks to make sure this action is appropriate for the process's associated user profile.

Figure 5.2 shows an HLL programmer's conceptual view of OS/400 objects. A user-written HLL program appears to access OS/400 objects (e.g., a database file) directly. This access can be through built-in HLL operations (e.g., an RPG/400 CHAIN) or through CL commands. Of course, under the covers, OS/400 programs actually manipulate MI objects. The important point is that IBM-supplied programs control the manipulation of MI objects. An HLL program also indirectly manipulates OS/400 internal objects by executing CL commands

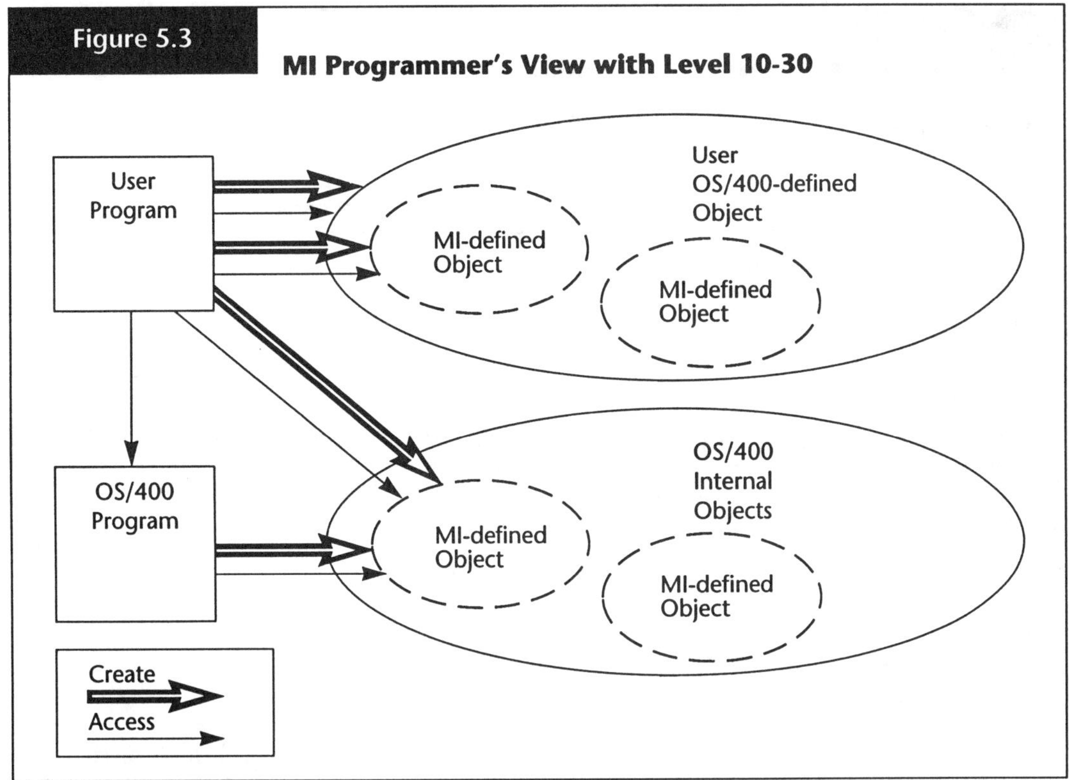

that control job execution, authority, and so forth. For example, an HLL program can indirectly manipulate the OS/400 Process Control Block (an MI space object) by submitting a job. Generally, HLL programmers don't even concern themselves with details of OS/400 internal objects.

OS/400 security level 30 depends on the insulation of MI objects from direct user-program manipulation. Yet, as Figure 5.1 shows, a user MI program can directly access any MI object to which a process is authorized. Although IBM doesn't offer an MI assembler on the AS/400, one is available from a third-party vendor, and you can find several techniques for making a homegrown MI assembler. IBM does *not* control the code an MI assembler generates — in contrast to that of available HLL compilers. Figure 5.3 shows a conceptual view of OS/400 objects with security level 30. All the object manipulation paths available from an HLL program are also available from an MI program. In addition, an MI program can *directly* manipulate both the MI objects that make up an OS/400 object and the MI objects OS/400 uses internally.

Level 30 Gaps

By itself, an MI program's ability to manipulate MI objects directly does not circumvent MI-level security. A process executing an MI program still must have or get authority to any objects it accesses. However, OS/400 security level 30 has gaps that let an MI program improperly obtain object authorities by accessing

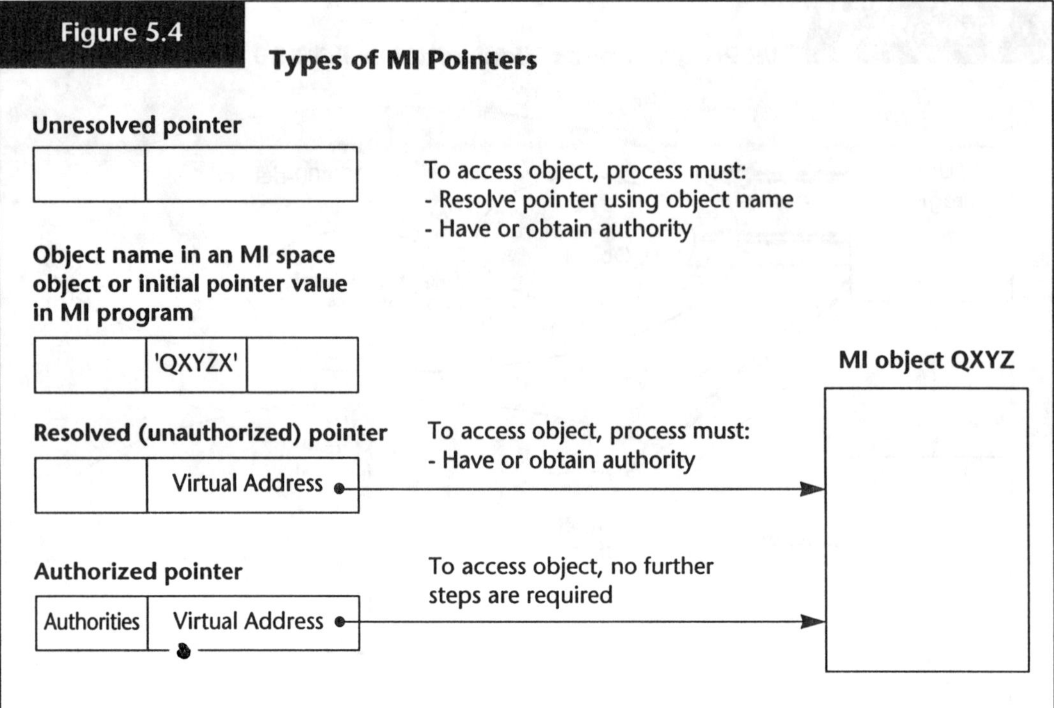
Unresolved pointer
To access object, process must:
- Resolve pointer using object name
- Have or obtain authority
Object name in an MI space object or initial pointer value in MI program
'QXYZX'
MI object QXYZ
Resolved (unauthorized) pointer
To access object, process must:
- Have or obtain authority
Virtual Address
Authorized pointer
To access object, no further steps are required
Authorities
Virtual Address
Figure 5.4
Types of MI Pointers

internal OS/400 objects that have public authority. Although I don't disclose the specifics of these gaps, you can understand the nature of the exposure by seeing how OS/400 uses symbolic object names and pointers at the MI level.

Figure 5.4 shows three types of MI object pointers. The first type is an *unresolved* pointer. To use this pointer, the symbolic object name (i.e., a character string) must be resolved to the virtual address that is the object's system identifier. You achieve this resolution by specifying an object name and context (i.e., library) as the initial value for a pointer when you declare it in an MI program or by specifying the object name and context as operands for the RSLVSP (Resolve System Pointer) MI instruction. In either case, to use the object, either the process's associated user or group profile must have authority to the object, or the process must get the required authority.

The security exposure with unresolved pointers is that some OS/400 programs create an *authorized* pointer from an unresolved pointer by retrieving an object's name from an unprotected space object. The process that creates the authorized pointer from the object name either has an associated user profile with adequate authorities or executes a program that adopts adequate authorities to access the target object. The gap here is that an MI program can use character operations to alter the original object name stored in an unprotected-space object and thus fool OS/400 into creating an authorized pointer to an object that the process should not be able to access.

The second type of MI object pointer is a *resolved* pointer, which contains an object's virtual address but no authorities. An MI program can get a resolved (but not authorized) pointer, even if the process has no authority to the object, as long as the process has authority to the context used to locate the object. Essentially, this approach results in the same type of exposure as with unprotected object names, but exploits different OS/400 internal interfaces. Although OS/400 checks against adding improper authorities in pointers that it creates, an MI program can fool OS/400 into setting authority in a pointer that a user program, not an OS/400 program, creates.

The final type of MI object pointer is an *authorized* pointer, which contains an object's virtual address and one or more authorities to the object. When a process uses an authorized pointer, the process has all the authorities in the pointer in addition to those of the process's associated user and group profiles. You can think of authorized pointers as master keys to objects — any process that gets the key can access the object. Unfortunately, OS/400 has stashed various authorized pointers (i.e., the keys) in space objects that are accessible to processes with no specific authority. An MI program can retrieve these authorized pointers and use them improperly.

These examples show that exploiting OS/400 security gaps requires MI operations. But keep in mind that an MI assembler is not the only way to execute an MI instruction. In addition, once encapsulated (i.e., compiled into an executable form), an MI program can masquerade as an RPG/400 or COBOL/400 program. In other words, you cannot eliminate from your attention those program objects that don't have "MI" as their program type.

Closing the Gaps: Level 40

To close the OS/400 security gaps, IBM added security level 40 to Version 1 Release 3 of OS/400. Level 40 provides several new facilities that block exploitation of level 30 security gaps.

When using level 40, levels 10, 20, and 30 will continue to work as they currently do; however, an AS/400 running at level 10, 20, or 30 will log operations that are potential MI security breeches. This log will let an AS/400 installation assess what changes are required in application or utility programs before an installation moves to level 40 security, which blocks these operations. When ready, an installation will be able to change the QSECURITY system value to level 40 and gain the increased protection.

Level 40 will introduce three new concepts to MI security: object *domains*, program invocation *states*, and MI *privileged instructions*. OS/400 will use these concepts to close the gaps that exist with level 30 security. Figures 5.5, 5.6, and 5.7 show how these concepts interrelate.

All MI objects will have a new *domain* attribute that specifies the program invocation state required to access the object. Looking at Figure 5.5, you can see the two possible domains: *system* and *user*.

To control object access, program invocations will have an execution-time attribute: *state*. It will be possible for a program invocation to be in either the *system* or *user* state. As Figures 5.5 and 5.6 show, a program invocation in the system state will be able to access both system and user domain objects. One implication of this rule is that a program invocation in the system state will be

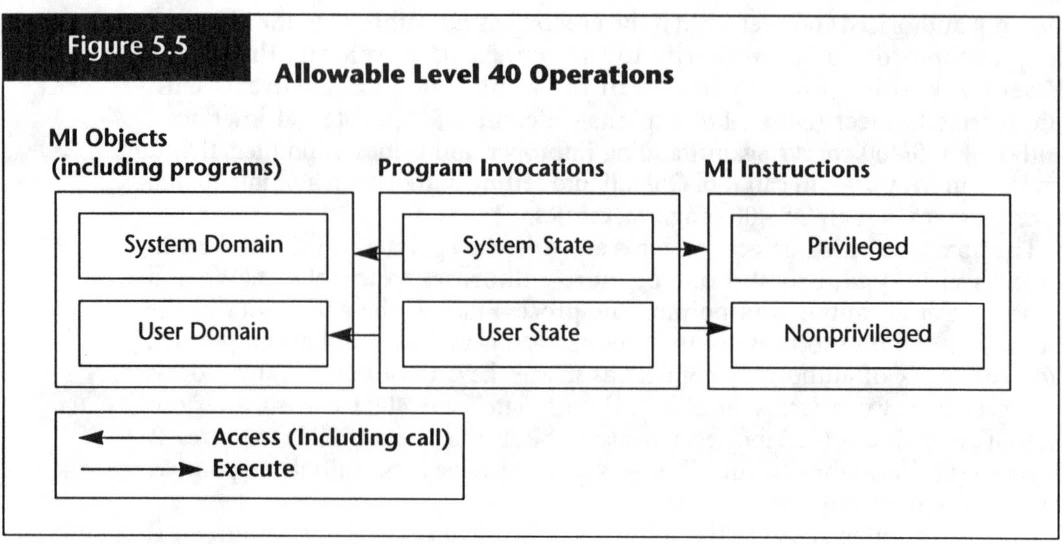

Figure 5.5
Allowable Level 40 Operations

Figure 5.6
Table of Allowable Level 40 Operations

Security Level	Program Invocation	MI Instructions		Access Object/Call Program	
		Not Privileged	Privileged	User Domain	System Domain
10, 20, 30	User State	Allowed	Logged	Allowed	Logged
	System State	Allowed	Allowed	Allowed	Allowed
40	User State	Allowed	Not Allowed	Allowed	Not Allowed
	System State	Allowed	Allowed	Allowed	Allowed

able to call both system and user domain programs. A program invocation in the user state will be able to directly access only user domain objects. Consequently, a program invocation in the user state will be able to call only user domain programs. (Unlike object authorities — which include various specific types of access, such as existence, read, and update — the state-domain access control will be all or none.)

A program invocation's state will be set in several ways. Every program object will have a default state that is one of three values: *system*, *user*, or *inherit*. When a program is invoked, it will assume its default state if the default is either system or user. If the default is inherit, the invocation will assume the current state of its caller. Invocations in the system state will be able to execute an instruction to change their current state to user. (For obvious reasons, a program invocation in the user state will not be able to change its state to system.) Only IBM-supplied

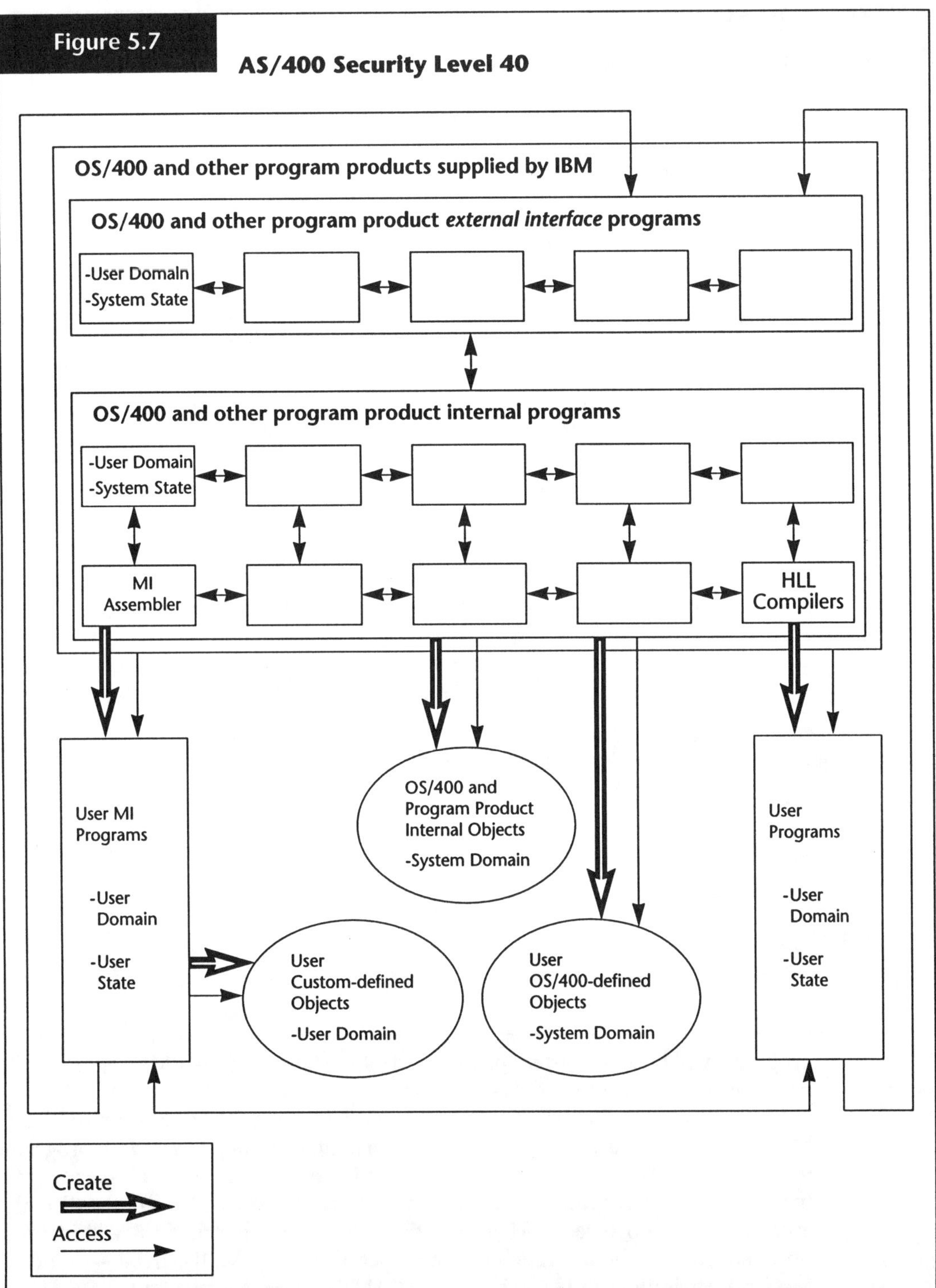
Figure 5.7
AS/400 Security Level 40
OS/400 and other program products supplied by IBM
OS/400 and other program product external interface programs
-User Domain
-System State
OS/400 and other program product internal programs
-User Domain
-System State
MI
Assembler
HLL
Compilers
User MI
Programs
-User
Domain
-User
State
OS/400 and
Program Product
Internal Objects
-System Domain
User
Custom-defined
Objects
-User Domain
User
OS/400-defined
Objects
-System Domain
User
Programs
-User
Domain
-User
State
Create
Access

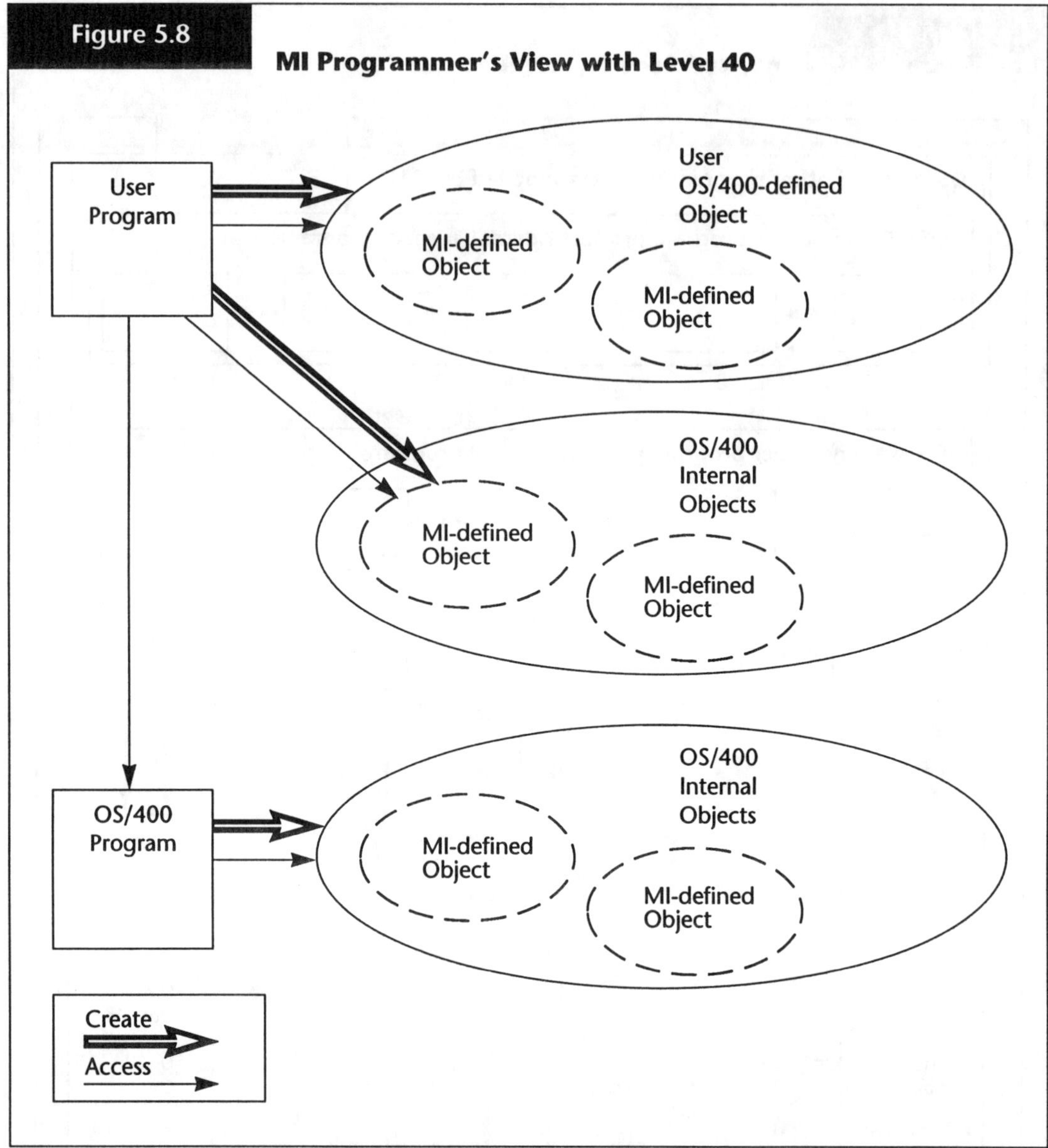

programs will have the system or inherit default state, so non-IBM programs will never be able to execute in the system state.

The program invocation state will also control execution of MI instructions. MI instructions will be in two classes: *privileged* and *nonprivileged.* A program invocation in the system state will be able to execute both classes of MI instructions. A program invocation in the user state will be able to directly execute only nonprivileged MI instructions. Privileged instructions will include ones that control the machine's internal operation (e.g., MODMATR — Modify Machine Attributes) and security (e.g., GRANT — Grant Authority).

Nonprivileged instructions will include problem-oriented ones such as ADDN (Add Numeric) and SETSPP (Set Space Pointer). With level 40, the use of privileged MI instructions will be controlled at execution time. This approach means that you will not be able to circumvent the restrictions by patching an encapsulated MI program.

With levels 10, 20, and 30, a program invocation in the user state will still be able to execute privileged MI instructions; however, the system will log these instructions. With all security levels, the IBM-supplied Licensed Internal Code (i.e., Vertical Microcode — VMC) encapsulation routine will no longer allow an MI program template that contains a privileged instruction. In other words, you will not be able to create new programs that contain privileged instructions.

Figure 5.7 shows how these changes affect OS/400 security. With level 40, non-IBM MI programs will be able to manipulate their own objects (or any user domain object) directly. But permanent MI objects for OS/400-defined user objects and for OS/400 internal operations will all have the system domain attribute and be directly accessible only by program invocations in the system state (and only if the process has authority to the object). The AS/400 will not let a user create a program that executes in the system state; only IBM-supplied programs will do so.

Essentially, level 40 will make OS/400 an opaque interface in the same way that MI has been since its inception. Although IBM's VMC developers could always work below MI and directly manipulate the internal structures of MI objects, other programmers (even with MI) have no way to bootstrap their programs to directly translate them into IMPI (Internal Microprogram Interface — the AS/400's true machine language) and access internal structures of MI objects. Level 40 will impose the same barrier on programs that work with OS/400 objects; the MI objects that are internal to OS/400 objects will not be directly accessible by user-state program invocations (i.e., all non-IBM-supplied and IBM-supplied programs that execute in the user state).

Figure 5.8 shows an MI programmer's conceptual view of OS/400 objects with level 40 security. User-written MI programs will still be possible, and they will still be able to directly manipulate MI objects. But user-written MI programs will be able to access only user domain MI objects. These objects will usually be ones a user-written MI program creates. In addition, user-written MI programs will be blocked from executing MI instructions that could disrupt the machine's operation or breech security.

Many OS/400 programs, especially those that control machine operations and security, will have the system-domain attribute and thus, with level 40, will not be directly callable by program invocations in the user state. Selected OS/400 programs (e.g., supported external interface programs, including QCMD, QPGMMENU, and QSNDDTAQ) will have the user-domain attribute and provide the only external entry points to OS/400. Most IBM-supplied OS/400 programs, whether system- or user-domain, will have a default state of either system or inherit and will be able to execute in the system state. When in the system state, these programs will be able to access system-domain MI objects internal to OS/400 and call other OS/400 programs. Thus, a program invocation in the user state will be able to indirectly execute any OS/400 program, as long as the indirect execution is done via a call to one of the OS/400 user-domain programs that executes in the system state. Level 40 will not only seal off direct manipulation of MI objects managed by OS/400, but will also govern calls to internal OS/400 programs that have greater authority than should be directly available to user programs.

The use of object domains, program invocation states, and MI privileged instructions closes three gaps in level 30 security: OS/400's MI objects will no longer be directly accessible, OS/400 programs will no longer be improperly callable, and security-related MI instructions will no longer be directly executable. In addition, the new version of OS/400 will log all access of system-domain objects by program invocations in the user state. This logging capability will be available with any security level (10 through 40), and you will be able to use logging with levels 30 and lower to find and modify programs that will not run with level 40.

As a further barrier to security violations, save operations (e.g., SAVOBJ — Save Object) will store a checksum of each saved program object. When a program object is restored, the checksum will be recomputed and must match the saved checksum, or the program object will not be restored. This technique increases the difficulty of modifying a saved version of a program and then restoring it.

Closing these gaps will not prevent you from using MI for non-OS/400-related purposes. Level 40 will, however, block one of the most typical uses of MI — direct access of OS/400 objects to build tools for business or utility software. For example, with level 30, an MI program can directly access the MI space that contains an OS/400 database file's field descriptions. This method of retrieval is not available in any HLL, and the CL DSPFFD (Display File Field Description) command, which uses an output file, is too slow for many applications. Under level 40, such direct access of a file's space object by a user-domain MI program will not be possible.

To address the need for fast interfaces to OS/400 information and functions not already available through CL, IBM is developing a library of Application Programming Interfaces (APIs), or callable programs, that go with level 40 security. This library includes functions for retrieving information, such as a file's field description, by using program parameters rather than database files. This strategy places a burden on IBM to deliver a comprehensive set of functions to replace the tools implemented in MI with callable programs that run efficiently with level 40. A benefit of this program library will be that HLL programs, as well as MI programs, will be able to use fast, IBM-supported interfaces.

Protecting Your Installation

To protect your installation from level 30 security gaps, you should move to level 40 as soon as it is available. Until then, you should carefully separate program-development objects and production-application objects. For locally written programs, you should inspect the source code and recompile programs when you move them from development to production. You should acquire object-only programs only from reliable vendors and ask them what controls they use to prevent Trojan horses in the software they ship. Software vendors should have a well-thought-out approach to their software quality control, including controlling security-related defects. You should not install freeware or shareware object-only programs — use such programs only if you can recompile the source.

Of course, you should follow other good security practices, including physical security, limiting use of service interfaces, and restricting the restore of program objects.

For S/38 installations, the same gaps exist in CPF as in OS/400. IBM does not intend to change CPF to close these gaps. If you are considering moving to an AS/400, you should consider this fact in your planning. In addition to the precautions suggested for AS/400 installations, you should also allow only the security officer authority to the PCHPGM command and limit access to the system console to control use of the service aids.

As you consider the OS/400 level 30 security gaps, keep in mind no method can guarantee to protect any system perfectly. Your actions concerning the exposures this article describes should be consistent with your current approach to security, including careful selection and evaluation of your technical staff. With appropriate care and with improvements in OS/400, you can maintain effective security on your AS/400.

Chapter 6

Security: User Profiles

by Paul Conte

The standards you set for user profiles are key to AS/400 security

The AS/400 has a very sophisticated approach to security, and a key component of the security facilities is the user profile object. User profiles are AS/400 objects that have two security-related purposes: They establish an object that owns other objects, and they establish the object that will be checked for access rights during execution of a job. User profiles also contain information about users — for example, their default message and output queues. Like many aspects of AS/400 architecture, user profiles do little good unless they are used properly. On the one hand, if everyone in an organization shares a single user profile, neither access security nor an audit trail is possible. On the other hand, if all authorizations are "hand-tailored," the application developers face a burdensome addition to their maintenance responsibilities — that of maintaining a spider's web of individual authorizations. By carefully laying out your organization's security requirements, however, you can establish your user profiles, object ownership, and authorization in a manner that will avoid both extremes.

In this chapter I prescribe some ways to establish and maintain user profiles. The user profiles I describe are grouped into logically related sets, based on the role of the person who will be signed on as the user profile. Because some employees of an organization may function in different roles at different times, an individual employee may have the password for more than one user profile. In such cases, the person signs on under the user profile appropriate to the tasks he or she wants to perform. The related sets of user profiles include:

- *Security function* user profiles to own objects restricted to security officer access and to establish special-purpose functional access to objects using adopted authority.

- *System* user profiles to own objects supplied by IBM for OS/400 and other systems software.
- *Ersatz IBM-supplied* user profiles for IBM-supplied passwords.
- *IBM service* user profiles for IBM personnel to use.
- *Local configuration-related* user profiles to own device descriptions, job queues, output queues, and other, locally defined systemwide objects. This set also includes a user profile for operation of the system.
- *Application system* user profiles to own the organization's database files, programs that use the database, and other related objects. This set also includes "group" user profiles to establish authorization to application objects.
- *Public access* user profiles to allow otherwise unauthorized personnel access to training programs and other unrestricted facilities.
- *Individual* user profiles for each person with access to the system.

Figure 6.1 provides a summary of the user profiles, their uses, and the libraries that contain objects they own. The "Libraries for Owned Objects" column refers to either IBM-supplied libraries (those that have the form Qxxx) or user-created libraries. In some cases, a user profile may own objects in a library other than one listed beside the user profile in Figure 6.1. For simplicity, I have not listed these special cases but instead have shown the libraries generally associated with the user profile.

Security-Function User Profiles

The AS/400 has a predefined user profile (QSECOFR) with unique built-in authority for creating user profiles and for other restricted functions, such as displaying passwords for user profiles. Anyone signed on as QSECOFR has unrestricted authority to the entire system; thus, QSECOFR is a user profile that must be available only to personnel who should have such extensive authority.

In organizations especially sensitive to security violations, the security officer may not be a member of the technical staff, and no one on the technical staff may know the QSECOFR password. Operating with this level of security is somewhat difficult because the security officer must control many configuration details to preserve the desired security. If the security officer is not a technical person, support mechanisms (e.g., CL programs) must be created to handle these tasks, and the support mechanisms themselves must be secure. Setting up this type of security system is beyond the scope of this chapter, and I assume in the recommendations that follow that the security officer is a member of the technical staff or shares the password with a member of the staff, so the required functions can be handled with the IBM-supplied OS/400 facilities.

The objects QSECOFR owns include all user-profile objects locally created with the CRTUSRPRF (Create User Profile) command. (IBM-supplied system user profiles, such as QSPL, are owned by QSYS.) IBM also ships many of its software packages with objects owned by QSYS. Some of these packages and their

Figure 6.1

User Profiles

User Profile Set	User Profile	Libraries For Owned Objects	Usage
Security Functions	QSECOFR	SCRxxx	Security officer
	AUTxxxxxx	PRDEXC QGPL SCREXC	Specific authority combination to be adopted by program
System	QRJE	QRJE	For Remote Job Entry Facility
	QSPL QSPLJOB	QSPL	For spooling
	QDBSHR QSYS	QGDDM QRCL QRECOVERY QSYS QCBL QIDU QRPG etc.	For machine and CPF operation
Ersatz IBM-supplied Profiles	IBMQCE	None	Password "CE"
	IBMQPGMR	None	Password "PGMR"
	IBMQSECOFR	None	Password "SECOFR"
	IBMQSYSOPR	None	Password "SYSOPR"
IBM Service	QSRV	QSRV	Customer Engineer
Local Configuration related Profiles	QPGMR	ALTQSYS ALTQSYSSRC GPLSRC QGPL QSYS	System Configuration
	QSYSOPR	None	Operator
Application System	APPADM	PRDxxx EXPxxx	Application System Administrator
	APPPGMR	None	Application Programmer group profile
	group_name	None	General access level; e.g. by division and position
	proto_name	None	"Prototype" profile with authorizations to be granted to a profile using GRTUSRAUT
Public Access	QUSER	None	For signon without password, and password "USER"
	TRAINING	TSTxxxTRN	Training use with password "TRAINING"
Individual Employees	unique_name	TSTxxxiii	Technical and non-technical staff

corresponding libraries are Interactive Data Utilities (QIDU), RPG/400 (QRPG), COBOL (QCBL), and PC Support (QIWS). While QPGMR more logically might own these software packages' objects, most shops find it simpler to leave them under the ownership of QSYS.

You should define device descriptions for workstations at which the security officer may work as owned by or explicitly authorized to QSECOFR. Other objects may be created in the SCRxxx libraries (library containing security-related objects) to facilitate security functions. QSECOFR should own these objects.

One security-related object should be a file in which to keep information about previous and current user profiles beyond that provided in the user profile object. Figure 6.2 shows the DDS (Data Description Specifications) for the file USRINF. USRINF has one or more records for each user profile ever created on the system. The USRPRF and AUTENDDAT (Authorization Ending Date) fields serve as the unique key. The date the user profile was created and the date it was deleted are kept for all user profiles. The file provides a permanent record of who has been authorized to the system and the periods during which they were authorized — important information for audits occurring years after a user profile has been deleted. This approach requires that user profile names be unique throughout the life of the system, although the same person may have more than one period of authorization. This requirement is considered in the discussion of individual user profiles later in this section.

Using a database file such as USRINF to extend the user profile not only provides historical information but also lets you customize security and other aspects of application programs. A high-level language (HLL) program (e.g., a COBOL program GETUSRINF) can return information from USRINF by a file-read operation and from the user profile object by a RTVUSRPRF (Retrieve User Profile) command. This HLL program, which is owned by the security officer, adopts the owner's profile when called. By revoking public authority to the USRINF file and to the RTVUSRPRF command, you can make GETUSRINF the only access to the USRINF file and to user profiles. This technique lets you restrict access to private information that may be kept in the USRINF file yet make the information for a job's current user profile easily accessible to application programs.

The GETUSRINF program can return information such as the organizational division in which a job's user profile works. An application program can use this information to tailor display files or menus. For example, GETUSRINF can be used to control the *effective* initial program when a user signs on to a workstation. In this case, all employees' user profiles would have the same INLPGM (Initial Program) specified on the CRTUSRPRF command. If INLPGM(SYSINLPGM) were specified, the locally created SYSINLPGM program would call GETUSRINF, determine the user's division, and execute a TFRCTL (Transfer Control) command to the appropriate division-oriented menu program.

Maintenance of user profiles is simpler when a single program is specified for the initial program in all user profiles. For instance, if users change divisions, you need not modify their user profiles; you need modify only the division information in USRINF.

Figure 6.2

Data Description Specifications (DDS) for File USRINF

```
      *... ... 1 ... ... 2 ... ... 3 ... ... 4 ... ... 5 ... ... 6

 *  USRINF

 *  Authorized user information

 *  A currently authorized user can be accessed by using the key:
 *    USRPRF    - User profile name
 *    AUTENDDAT - 99991231

                                        UNIQUE

          R USRINF

 *  Fields in alphabetical order:

            AUTBGNDAT      8P00         COLHDG('Authorization ' +
                                               'Beginning'      +
                                               'Date'           )
                                        RANGE(00000101 99991231)
 *                                      Format is YYYYMMDD.

            AUTENDDAT      8P00         COLHDG('Authorization'  +
                                               'Ending'         +
                                               'Date'           )
                                        RANGE(00000101 99991231)
 *                                      Format is YYYYMMDD.
 *                                      Set to 99991231 while user
 *                                      is still authorized.

            DVNABR         3A           COLHDG('Division'       +
                                               'Abbreviation'   )
 *                                      Division in which user is
 *                                      currently employed.
 *                                      e.g., 'PRS' for Personnel

            DVNDIR         1A           COLHDG('Division'       +
                                               'Director'       )
                                        VALUES('Y' 'N')
 *                                      'Y' means person is
 *                                      current division director.

            USRABR         3A           COLHDG('User'           +
                                               'Abbreviation'   )
 *                                      Unique 3-letter identifier
 *                                      used in library names, etc.
```

Figure 6.2 Continued

Figure 6.2 Data Description Specifications (DDS) for File USRINF *Continued*

```
     *                                                e.g., MRS for Mary R. Smith;
     *                                                with libraries TSTxxxMRS.
     *                                                A logical file with key
     *                                                fields USRABR and AUTENDDAT
     *                                                can be used to assure
     *                                                uniqueness.

                 USRFNM         15A                   COLHDG('User'            +
                                                             'First'           +
                                                             'Name'            )
     *                                                Use CHECK(LC) in display
     *                                                file for upper/lower case.

                 USRINLPGM       1A                   COLHDG('User-written'    +
                                                             'Initial Pgm.'    +
                                                             'Allowed'         )
                                                      VALUES('Y' 'N')
     *                                                'Y' means person can have
     *                                                their own initial program.

                 USRLNM         30A                   COLHDG('User'            +
                                                             'Last'            +
                                                             'Name'            )
     *                                                Use CHECK(LC) in display
     *                                                file for upper/lower case.

                 USRMNM         15A                   COLHDG('User'            +
                                                             'Middle'          +
                                                             'Name'            )
     *                                                Use CHECK(LC) in display
     *                                                file for upper/lower case.

                 USRPRF         10A                   COLHDG('User'            +
                                                             'Profile'         +
                                                             'Name'            )
                                                      CHECK(VN)
     *                                                AS/400 user profile.
     *                                                Must be valid CPF name.

     *
               K USRPRF
               K AUTENDDAT
```

Also, controlling the effective initial program through the file USRINF provides a high degree of flexibility. This approach can be extended to permit user-written initial programs, a useful facility for programmers. One way to implement this extension is to adopt a convention for naming a user-written initial program (e.g., USRINLPGM). Users with a "Y" in the USRINLPGM field of USRINF can have a user-written initial program. A user must create these programs in the library that holds his or her programs (i.e., TSTEXCiii, where iii is a user's unique, three-letter identifier — stored in the USRABR field of USRINF). Program SYSINLPGM first attempts a

```
TFRCTL PGM(TSTEXCiii/USRINLPGM)
```

and monitors for CPF messages. If the transfer to the user-written initial program fails, a transfer is made instead either to a default initial program or to QCMD (for COMMAND ENTRY).

Another useful object QSECOFR might own is a CL program that uses a DSPOBJD (Display Object Description) command to create a file of object descriptions. Only the user profile QSECOFR can be certain that all objects will be included in output from the DSPOBJD command, because the user must have read rights for the library and must have one of the object rights (i.e., existence, management, or operational rights) for an object, or it will not be included. For purposes such as generating reports on auxiliary storage used by large objects, a complete list of objects is necessary. This special-purpose program should adopt the owner's profile, and the user profiles QPGMR and APPADM (Application Administrator) should have operational (*OPER) rights to it.

Special-purpose programs for other functions also can be useful. QSECOFR should own such programs only if the authority required cannot be provided by a program owned by QPGMR, APPADM, or one of the access-defining user profiles discussed below. The general ownership rule should be to have the owner of a program that adopts authority be the user profile with the *lowest level of authority* that meets the required level.

When the authority needed for a specific function is greater than that provided by any single user profile, but you do not want to use a program that adopts all the authority of QSECOFR, you can create a user profile for the sole purpose of establishing this specific authorization set. You should create these user profiles by using PASSWORD(*NONE) so that no one can sign on under these profiles. The required function is built into a program owned by this access-defining user profile, and you specify USRPRF(*OWNER) when you create the program.

This approach also can be used to establish adopted authority that is a subset of a single user profile's object authority. (Note that a program cannot adopt a user's special authority, such as job control rights.) For example, instead of QSECOFR owning program GETUSRINF, a new user profile AUTUSRINF (Authority to User Information) could own the program. AUTUSRINF would be the only user profile on the system, besides QSECOFR, with authority to use the USRINF file and the RTVUSRPRF command. The AUTUSRINF profile would have no authority other than that needed to execute the GETUSRINF program successfully. This provides less chance for security violations through program-adopted authority because the authority adopted while the program is invoked is very limited. Programs that adopt the authority of an access-defining profile belong in the library with other programs that have a similar function (QGPL for configuration-related, PRDEXC for application-related, and SCREXC for security-related programs. (See Chapter 7 for guidelines on setting up user libraries.)

System User Profiles

IBM supplies several user profiles to own objects for the machine definition, OS/400, and other system software. These user profiles also may be used for jobs initiated by the system. QSYS owns commands, programs, and other machine and OS/400-related objects in libraries QSYS, QGDDM, QRCL, and QRECOVERY. The QDBSHR profile is used for system functions. QSPL owns the database files in library QSPL where spooled files are stored. Spool jobs run under the QSPLJOB user profile. The Remote Job Entry Facility (RJEF) is supplied with the QRJE user profile, which owns objects in the QRJE library and which is used for QRJE subsystem jobs.

Ersatz IBM-Supplied User Profiles

When IBM ships OS/400, it includes user profiles with standard passwords. These passwords are published in the *Security Concepts and Planning* manual (SC41-8083) and other places. Obviously, one of the first things your security officer must do is change all these passwords (except for QUSER). Otherwise, you run the risk of having anyone who has read the manual sign on as your IBM Customer Engineer (CE), posing a major threat to your system. After you have changed these passwords, you should verbally provide the new passwords to the appropriate IBM service manager, who is then responsible for their secure storage. The password for the security officer should be written down and stored with other similarly sensitive material under care of an officer of the organization. Other than these actions, no written record of passwords should exist.

After locking these doors to your system, you may find it will help IBM personnel and new technical staff if you create new, "ersatz" user profiles with the published passwords. These profiles have no authority other than that granted the public. They all should have the same initial program that executes a SNDRCVF (Send/Receive File) command for a display file that states that the passwords have been changed and explains who in the organization should be contacted for more information. After the SNDRCVF completes, the program should execute a SIGNOFF. This simple setup will win you the friendship of your IBM CE, who is probably used to entering the password "CE" at most customer sites, and who will appreciate more than "Invalid password" as an indication that "CE" is no longer the customer engineer password on your system.

IBM Service User Profiles

The IBM-supplied user profiles QSRV and QSRVBAS are for use by IBM service personnel. These profiles have extensive authority and must be as secure as the QSECOFR profile. Besides changing the passwords, you should limit QSRV and QSRVBAS to certain workstations. Neither profile is included when you grant public authorization to a workstation device description, so you can limit QSRV and QSRVBAS to workstation devices that you explicitly authorize those profiles to use. You may even want to make the system console, which should be in a secure location, their only means of access.

You should change the passwords for QSRV and QSRVBAS regularly. Although you may hear some grumbling from the CE or PSR, this step is as important as regularly changing the password for QSECOFR. Of course, you should inform the appropriate IBM service manager as soon as you make a change. You also need to be sure that no one is writing down the password somewhere in your machine room, for instance in the CE's service log.

Local Configuration-Related User Profiles

One user profile should be the "configurator" — the person who is responsible for creating line, control unit, and device descriptions; subsystems; classes; job queues; and other systemwide objects for system operation. The IBM-supplied user profile QPGMR can serve this purpose (or you may want to create a new profile, SYSPGMR). This profile is for use with general system configuration and operation, not with application-oriented tasks handled by the APPADM profile or the individual user profiles. For example, QPGMR should own an output queue created for a workstation printer, but an individual programmer's user profile should own his or her private output queue for compiler output.

Objects owned by QPGMR belong in QSYS, ALTQSYS (the library for objects that replace IBM-supplied objects), and QGPL. The source for these objects should be in ALTQSYSSRC and GPLSRC. To restrict the creation of an object type such as a device description, only QPGMR should be authorized to the CRTDEVD (Create Device Description) command. Most OS/400 "create" (CRTxxx) commands have no public authorization, but QPGMR is authorized to them. You may want to review all OS/400 and software package "create" commands to modify their authorizations. Any GRTOBJAUT (Grant Object Authority) and RVKOBJAUT (Revoke Object Authority) commands you use to change command authorization should be saved in a CL program or database file for use if authorizations must be modified again.

The person responsible for operations such as periodic backup and changing print writers for special forms can use the IBM-supplied profile QSYSOPR. If you have several employees who act as operators, you may prefer to have QSYSOPR as the group profile for these employees' user profiles and to have each operator sign on as his or her own user profile. This approach facilitates an audit trail that is tied to individual profiles, rather than to a shared profile.

Generally the QSYSOPR profile owns no objects. QPGMR should own any objects, such as CL programs, needed for system operation; or, when adopted authority is needed, QSECOFR or an access-defining user profile should own the objects.

Application System User Profiles

For integrated application systems that share files, programs, and other objects among several divisions, one user profile — APPADM — should own all application-related objects. The password for this profile should be used only by the person responsible for creating new application objects or for replacing existing objects in a production library with new versions from one of the programmer's test libraries. If these responsibilities are distributed among technical staff members, it will be necessary to use programs with adopted authority to perform some functions. No programmer should have APPADM as his group profile unless he is, in fact, the application administrator. One of the purposes of the user profile structure laid out here is to separate system administration, which embodies a high level of organizational responsibility, from program development, which is primarily a technical responsibility.

There is no absolute rule about the types of objects that the APPADM profile, rather than either QSECOFR or QPGMR, should own. A personal message queue is a good example of an object that any one of these profiles might own. Such message queues are assigned to a specific user profile, and the message queue name may be included in the MSGQ parameter of the CRTUSRPRF command. Alternatively, the name may be stored in a field in the USRINF file or in a separate file, USRMSGQ. QSECOFR, QPGMR, or APPADM could own the USRMSGQ file. Which solution is best? Any of them will work fine, as long as you document who owns such objects and in which library they are kept.

In this example, you would want to consider who should create the message queues and maintain message queue attributes such as sender information and maximum size. Another consideration is that, while a personal message queue is not really a security-related object, the message queue is most naturally created and deleted at the same time as the user profile. The solution here is to document procedures for authorizing and deauthorizing a user and include in the procedures who is to own the message queue object and how its name is to be associated with the user profile name. The procedures may be carried out using programs that adopt authority if someone other than the security officer has this responsibility.

To use application objects owned by APPADM, other user profiles must have authority to them. An effective and reasonably simple approach to most authorization is to create all programs, except those that adopt authority, with AUT(*CHANGE), and to create physical and logical files with AUT(*EXCLUDE). Authority to physical and logical files then is granted to division group profiles, as discussed below. This protects the data and requires authorization maintenance on only the file objects. You generally have many fewer files than programs, and files are not re-created as frequently; thus, the maintenance is simpler. In addition, controlling access via program authorization restricts only individual means of access; it does not protect the data itself. Most programs that adopt authority also should have AUT(*EXCLUDE) and explicit authorization to group profiles.

Application objects other than programs and files will also require authorization. Locally created commands can have AUT(*CHANGE) as long as the objects upon which the command processing program operates are properly protected. Data areas should be authorized like physical files because they are directly accessible from HLL programs (e.g., by RPG III IN and OUT operations). Other objects that are not files, but contain data-like information (e.g., message queues and journal receivers) are not accessible except by OS/400 commands or programs that execute these commands. This inaccessibility lets you protect the contents of these nonfile objects by controlling authorization either to the related OS/400 commands or to the objects themselves. If you have many such objects, and they are frequently re-created, you may find that controlling authority to the OS/400 commands requires less work. Again, it is important that you document the approach you take, so it will be followed consistently throughout your system.

Group Profiles

For production objects, authority generally is not granted to individual users, but rather is granted to *group* profiles. A group profile is a user profile that is named in the GRPPRF (Group Profile) parameter of the CRTUSRPRF (Create User Profile) command. A user profile with a group profile will adopt all authority (both object and special authority) of the group profile at the time the user profile starts a job. Authority can be granted to group profiles as a means of indirectly granting authority to all users with that group profile. You can use PASSWORD(*NONE) when you create group profiles so that no one can sign on under a group profile.

Using group profiles reduces authorization maintenance because fewer authorizations must be specified. Each group profile represents a class of authorization based on factors the organization establishes. An individual employee has a group profile that represents the authorization class in which the employee belongs. When employees are hired, transferred, or leave, no object authorization changes are necessary. Instead, you can create the user profile with the appropriate group profile, which then can be changed if necessary when the employee assumes a new position. When an employee leaves, the only action necessary is to delete the user profile.

Unfortunately, the AS/400 permits a user profile to have only a single group profile, and a profile used as a group profile must itself have GRPPRF(*NONE) specified. These restrictions limit the flexibility of group profiles and necessitate careful planning before you establish the group profile structure. The goal is to minimize the number of specific authorizations of user profiles to objects while preserving the desired object security.

A user profile must never have a group profile with more authority than appropriate for the user because there is no way to negate an authority adopted from the group profile. Thus, if you have too few group profiles, most of your user profiles will have a low-authority group profile and still require specific authorizations to objects the user profiles use. If you have too many group profiles, you simply exchange the problem of maintaining authorizations for many user profiles with the only slightly easier problem of maintaining authorizations for many group profiles.

One approach that has been found effective is to create a "management" level and a "staff" level group profile for each operating division. This approach provides a group profile scheme that incorporates the cross-product of an employee's level of responsibility (and presumably corresponding authority) in the organization and his or her operational area within the organization (e.g., personnel or sales). The group profile names are a concatenation of the division's abbreviation (stored for each user in the DVNABR field of USRINF) and "MGT" for management or "STF" for staff.

A group profile such as PRSMGT (Personnel/Management) would be granted all data rights to all personnel physical files and operational rights to all personnel physical and logical files. Thus, any user with PRSMGT as a group profile can update any part of the personnel database. The PRSSTF (Personnel/Staff) profile might have all data rights to the personnel physical files, but operational rights only to logical files that exclude salary. Because operational rights are required to open a physical file, users with the PRSSTF group profile would have more restricted access than those users with the PRSMGT group profile. The public might have authority to read data in the physical files, but again have only operational rights to logical files that, through field selection, provide a limited view of the data.

A consideration in establishing group profiles is that database jobs must have a //JOB command that references a job description with a *specific user profile*; the SBMDBJOB (Submit Data Base Job) command does not have the provision the SBMJOB (Submit Job) command has for specifying the current job's user as the user for the submitted job. Thus, because database jobs are an important tool for users to build and submit their own jobs, at least one job description must be created for each group profile for use with database jobs submitted by users. Each respective job description (e.g., PRSMGTJOBD) has the corresponding user specified (e.g., USER(PRSMGT)), is owned by APPADM, has no public authorization, and is authorized for use by the corresponding group profile (e.g., PRSMGT).

In addition, at least one job description is needed for use with the SBMJOB command when USER(*CURRENT) is specified. This job description should have USER(*RQD), so that the submitted job's user profile comes from the job that executed the SBMJOB command. This job description can be used by any user profile regardless of the group profile because the batch job will use the submitting job's user profile. A natural choice for this job description is the IBM-supplied job description QBATCH. However, QBATCH is shipped with USER(QPGMR), which must be changed to USER(*RQD).

The careful structuring of group profiles is perhaps the most difficult and important task you face in establishing standards for user profiles. Variations on the structure suggested here may suit your needs better. For example, you may want to add an "ADM" (administrator) level above the "MGT" and "STF" levels or use functional areas rather than organizational areas to divide the groups. Some completely different scheme may work better. Whatever approach you take, it should be worked out as a joint effort of the data processing and user divisions. After being established, it should be committed to writing along with the rest of the user profile standards.

Application programmers should have APPPGMR as their group profile. When programmers sign on or submit batch jobs, they will have the specific authorizations of their own user profiles as well as those of the group profile APPPGMR. APPPGMR, not the specific user profiles, should be granted authority to the create commands such as CRTPF (Create Physical File) and

CRTCLPGM (Create CL Program). Similarly, special authorities, such as job control rights, should be granted to APPPGMR only. Using APPPGMR as a group profile makes specific authorizations for each programmer unnecessary, thus simplifying authorization maintenance.

Programmers will need a job description, APPPGMRJOBD, for database jobs as previously described for the other group profiles. Individual programmers also will probably want to create their own job descriptions for use with the SBMJOB command and the Create Object option on the Programmer's Menu. These personalized job descriptions should have the programmer's test libraries included in the library list and should name a private default output queue for compiler spooled file output.

No matter what group profile structure you use, some specific authorizations may still be necessary. A frequent example is an employee who performs a single function that requires management-level authorization in the employee's division. Rather than give full management-level authorization by using the xxxMGT group profile, you can grant explicit authority to the user profile. The division director usually determines cases such as these, and you can distribute some of the responsibility if you grant object management rights to the management-level group profile. With object management rights, the division director can use GRTOBJAUT (Grant Object Authority) to extend the access rights the director has to another user. Before you use this approach, it is best to have users familiar with concepts such as "objects," "user profiles," and "authority." This can be achieved with a training program targeted at supporting user-driven computing.

With trained users in the operating divisions, a variation on the ownership of production objects is possible. The division management group profile rather than APPADM can own the objects. Division profile object ownership fits into a more sophisticated approach to security, with authorization control by non-technical staff.

Another problem you may encounter is an employee who should be a member of two groups. No matter how carefully you structure group profiles, some cases of dual membership will arise. In such circumstances you can use the GRTUSRAUT (Grant User Authority) command to do a one-time copying of authority from a group profile to a specific user profile. For instance, if SMITH_J holds two positions, one in the Personnel Division and one in the Sales Division, the SMITH_J user profile can be created with GRPPRF(PRSSTF). This command provides personnel staff authority through the group profile. Then

```
GRTUSRAUT USER(SMITH_J) REFUSER(SLSSTF)
```

can be executed. This command provides SMITH_J with sales staff authority by explicit authorization of the user profile. If the authority of SLSSTF subsequently changes, you must also change SMITH_J. Keeping a file of GRTUSRAUT commands that have been used will prove helpful in tracking this type of authorization.

In some cases, a set of authorities will be granted regularly using GRTUSRAUT with a REFUSER profile that is never used as a group profile. This occurs, for example, if you grant authority to some OS/400 and IDU commands only to users who have completed a training program. The intent of restricting authority to these commands is not so much to protect data security as it is to avoid inadvertent misuse of sophisticated AS/400 capabilities. You can create a "prototype" user profile with the desired set of authorizations and use that profile as the REFUSER. An employee's user profile may be granted authority from one or more of the prototype profiles. The prototype profiles should own no objects and should never be used directly (i.e., by signing on with the password).

Public Access

The QINTER job description is shipped with USER(*RQD), which requires that all users must enter a valid user profile name in order to sign on. To permit convenient access of training or other public information, you could create another user profile, TRAINING, with the password TRAINING, as the group profile for QUSER. TRAINING could be granted the necessary authority to the publicly accessible objects. The TRAINING user profile could also own small test files or other objects in TSTxxxTRN libraries.

When a user signs on to either QUSER or TRAINING, the initial program would be a menu that lists training or other public options. When the menu and other display files include support for the Help key, a new employee can begin learning how to use the system from the day the employee is hired. You also could modify the CPF message for invalid password with

```
CHGMSGD MSGID(CPF1107) MSG('Invalid password. Enter          +
        "TRAINING" for training menu.')
```

The revised message helps novices along if they attempt to sign on with an invalid password.

Individual User Profiles

Last, but not least, among user profiles are the individual user profiles you create for employees and other system users. Each person should have a unique user profile. No two people should share the same user profile because their actions on the system become indistinguishable. With unique user profiles, DFU and application programs can record the user profile adding a database record; HLL programs can record the user profile last changing a record; and journals and job accounting information can be used to determine when users were signed on and what resources they used.

For audit purposes, all user profile names must be unique for the life of the system. That is, if Mike J. Smith is authorized from January 1, 1982, through July 23, 1983, and Mary R. Smith is authorized from January 1, 1984, through August 1, 1985, user profiles for these two people must be different. Mike Smith might have been assigned SMITH_M and Mary Smith assigned SMITH_MR. Unique user profile names are necessary so the record of the user profile clearly points to the correct person. Unique names also enable Mike Smith to assume his original user profile name if he returns to work while Mary Smith is still employed.

The USRINF file described earlier provides the mechanism for tracking user profile names and the person to whom each is assigned. The user profile name should be formulated in a standard way, the simplest being the LASTNAME_I format derived from the last name and first initial. Obviously, some people could have the same user profile name, and in these cases, a reasonable alteration to achieve uniqueness is required. Similarly, last names longer than 10 characters must be truncated. To avoid complications that can arise when people change names, you may want to use a meaningless series of values for user profile names.

Documenting User Profiles and Object Authorizations

Several tools are available to help you keep track of user profiles and object authorizations. The OS/400 command WRKUSRPRF (Work with User Profile) will show all current user profiles. WRKUSRPRF can only be executed if the user profile has the authority of *SECADM. An alternative way to get a file of user profiles on the system is to execute DSPAUTUSR (Display Authorized Users). To get a list of all of the user profiles in a database file you can use the DSPOBJD (Display Object Description) command:

```
DSPOBJD OBJ(QSYS/*ALL) OBJTYPE(*USRPRF) OUTFILE(USRPRFOBJD)
```

under the authority of QSECOFR. This output file can be joined with USRINF for a file of user information.

To determine the owner of an object, use the DSPOBJD (Display Object Description) command with DETAIL(*ALL). To determine the objects owned by a user profile, use the WRKUSRPRF (Work with User Profile) command with TYPE(*OBJOWN).

To get a file of object authorizations, you need a CL program using the DSPOBJD and DSPOBJAUT (Display Object Authority) commands and an HLL program to process the resulting records.

In conclusion, all objects on the AS/400 must be owned by another object (the user profile). This object ownership is part of the *existence matrix* for objects on your system. An existence matrix, which provides the foundation for organized application development and maintenance, includes standards for object names, libraries to contain the objects, and user profiles to own the objects.

There are many ways you can structure user profiles on your AS/400. The well-planned use of group and individual user profiles can gain for your organization the full capabilities of OS/400 security without entangling your programmers and users in a web of authorizations. As with any plan, your approach to user profiles should be in writing and closely followed as objects are created. The standards for user profiles should be developed in coordination with the standards for libraries and object names. Because security is fundamentally an organizational policy issue and not a data processing issue, the entire approach to security, including user profile standards, is best developed as a coordinated effort of the data processing and operational divisions. With a comprehensive plan, you and your users will feel more secure.

Chapter 7

Library Standards

by Paul Conte

A well structured library supports application development, simplifies backup, and improves security

What would it be like if your data processing staff had no filing cabinets in which to keep hard-copy documents, but instead tossed everybody's work into one big cardboard box? Or what if you had no copying machine and the only place revisions could be made was on the original document? Do such work conditions sound impossible?

Then consider what chaos there would be if the AS/400 had *no libraries* — if everybody's programs, files, and other objects were lumped together and if required revisions had to be made to the original objects rather than to copies. Fortunately, the AS/400 does have libraries, and by using them effectively to organize objects, you can keep chaos at bay, ease application development, simplify backup procedures, and improve security.

Because all AS/400 objects must exist in a library, libraries are the *de facto* way in which AS/400 objects are organized. Although an AS/400 library is an object, it functions primarily as a "directory" of the objects it contains. Libraries always are stored in QSYS, the "machine context" or highest level directory. For consistency, QSYS also is treated as a library by the Operating System/400 (OS/400), although QSYS has unique properties that no other library has (such as being able to contain library objects).

You can use various approaches to grouping objects into libraries to accomplish different purposes. For instance, you can group objects into libraries to separate production and test versions of programs or files; to separate objects that require special security from more generally available objects; to give individual programmers or users their own private sets of objects; or to separate vendor-supplied software from other applications. You might also want to group objects with similar properties into a library to facilitate backup operations. Finally, even if there are no production/test, security, or backup reasons for libraries, you might want to group logically related objects, just as people use file cabinets to organize documents.

No matter what approach to library organization your shop takes, library standards should be clearly documented in writing along with standards for naming objects and object ownership. Standards for libraries, object names, and object ownership define for your system an "existence matrix," which structures how objects will be owned and where they will be stored. An existence matrix provides the foundation for organized application development and maintenance.

As a step toward a good existence matrix, I recommend organizing libraries into sets according to their uses. Library sets should include libraries provided by IBM (libraries with names beginning with "Q") as well as libraries created locally using the CRTLIB (Create Library) command. My recommended library sets include:

- *System* libraries for operating system (including spooling and recovery) objects
- The *temporary* library created for every job
- *Local configuration-related* libraries for job queues, output queues, personal message queues, and other systemwide objects that are locally defined
- *Vendor-supplied software* libraries
- *Local production* libraries for the integrated database, programs that use the database, and other related objects
- *Local "experimental"* libraries for pre-production objects that are application-related and are in general use
- *Test libraries* (multiple sets) for programmers to use during development and for user-driven computing
- *Security function* libraries for highly restricted security officer functions

Figure 7.1 provides a summary of the libraries and their contents. Now let's consider what objects you should put into the specific library sets.

System Libraries

The most important system library is QSYS, the IBM-supplied library that contains all OS/400 commands and programs. In addition, QSYS contains all control unit descriptions, device descriptions, edit descriptions, libraries, line descriptions, workstation message queues, and user profiles. These are the only locally created objects that should be put into QSYS, and QSYS is the only library in which objects of these types can be created.

Many shops also find it useful to have an alternate QSYS (ALTQSYS) library, which contains locally created objects that supercede IBM-supplied objects in QSYS. For instance, in ALTQSYS you can create a new CRTDSPF (Create Display File) command definition that has RSTDSP(*YES) (restore display, yes) as the default rather than RSTDSP(*NO), which is the default for the IBM-supplied

Figure 7.1

Library Sets with Library Names, Types, Contents

Library Set	Libraries	Type	Contents
System	QSYS	*TEST	IBM-supplied commands, programs, etc. for CPF. Libraries; line, control unit, and device descriptions; edit descriptions; user profiles; and workstation message queues.
	ALTQSYS	*TEST	Local commands and other objects used in place of IBM supplied objects in QSYS.
	ALTQSYSSRC	*TEST	Source files for objects in ALTQSYS.
	QGDDM	*TEST	Graphics support.
	QRECOVERY	*TEST	For system recovery.
	QRCL	*TEST	Reclaimed objects.
	QSPL	*TEST	Spooled files.
	QSRV	*TEST	For IBM service.
Temporary	QTEMP	*TEST	Created and deleted for each job.
Local Configuration	QGPL	*TEST	IBM-supplied work management objects, device files, etc. Local configuration-related objects.
	GPLSRC	*TEST	Source files for objects in QGPL.
Vendor-supplied Software	QCBL	*PROD	COBOL/400.
	QIDU	*PROD	DFU, Query, SEU, SDA.
	QRPG	*PROD	RPG/400.
	QRJE	*PROD	RJE Facility.
	QOFC	*PROD	OfficeVision/400.
	etc.		
Local Production Applications	PRDDTA	*PROD	Physical and logical files, journals, and journal receivers.
	PRDDEV	*PROD	Device files.
	PRDEXC	*PROD	Commands, programs, DFU and Query applications.
	PRDDOC	*PROD	Source files for documentation.
	PRDSRC	*PROD	Source files for programs, files, etc.
	PRDMSC	*PROD	Data areas, message files, other object types not in one of the other five libraries.
Local Experimental Applications	EXPDTA	*PROD	Same organization as the production library set.
	EXPDEV	*PROD	
	EXPEXC	*PROD	
	EXPDOC	*PROD	
	EXPSRC	*PROD	
	EXPMSC	*PROD	

Figure 7.1 Continued

Figure 7.1 **Library Sets with Library Names, Types, Contents** *Continued*

Library Set	Libraries	Type	Contents
Test	TSTDTAxxx TSTDEVxxx TSTEXCxxx TSTDOCxxx TSTSRCxxx TSTMSCxxx	*TEST *TEST *TEST *TEST *TEST *TEST	Same organization as the production library set, one set for each programmer. Additional sets for user-driven computing.
	(xxx should be a unique identifier of the user of the library. Programmer initials or a division abbreviation can be used.)		
Security Functions	SCRDTA SCRDEV SCREXC SCRDOC SCRSRC SCRMSC	*TEST *TEST *TEST *TEST *TEST *TEST	Same organization as the production library set.

CRTDSPF command in QSYS. If ALTQSYS is placed before QSYS in the system portion of the library list, then whenever the CRTDSPF command is given without a library specified, the local version is used. If ALTQSYS is used, the related library ALTQSYSSRC also should be created. ALTQSYSSRC should contain source files for objects created in ALTQSYS (e.g., the source file ALTQSYSSRC/CMDSRC will be used for commands created in ALTQSYS).

There are other IBM-supplied libraries related to OS/400 and its operation. For example, AS/400 recovery tasks use library QRECOVERY. Library QRCL contains objects with no known library which the RCLSTG (Reclaim Storage) command reclaims. Such objects should be moved to their proper library or deleted, not left in QRCL. Library QSPL contains the physical files used for storing spooled output files and other spooling related objects. QSRV is the IBM-supplied service library for use primarily by the IBM program service representative (PSR). If you have graphic devices, library QGDDM contains objects needed for Presentation Graphics Routines (PGR) and Graphical Data Display Manager (GDDM). None of these system libraries should have any locally created objects in them.

Temporary System Library

One additional system library that should not be overlooked is the temporary library the system creates when a job starts. This library, QTEMP, can be referenced only by the job for which it was created. At the end of a job, the job's QTEMP library is deleted. QTEMP is used for temporary files or other objects that are created for use by the job but that will not be needed when the job ends. Vendor-supplied software packages often use QTEMP.

Local Configuration-Related Libraries

Local configuration-related libraries should contain all the local configuration objects (including both IBM-supplied objects and locally created objects) except those required to be in QSYS. The primary (and often only) library for these objects is the IBM-supplied QGPL library. The IBM-supplied objects in QGPL include classes, job descriptions, job queues, and subsystem descriptions for QBATCH, QINTER, QPGMR, and QSPL. These objects are the standard work management objects. In addition, QGPL contains device files for card, diskette, printer, punch, and tape; the print image and table for QSYSIMAGE; and the output queues for diskette, printer, and punch. Finally, IBM supplies several empty source files (such as QCLSRC and QCMDSRC) for local use.

Because library QGPL already contains IBM-supplied configuration objects, it provides a natural place for locally created configuration objects. These objects should be ones generally available systemwide. For example, an output queue for a workstation printer belongs in QGPL, but a programmer's private output queue for compiler output does not. The locally created objects in library QGPL should include object types like those IBM supplies in QGPL (classes, job descriptions, job queues, output queues, subsystem descriptions, device files, print images, and tables), but they also may include commands, programs, files, and other locally created objects used to configure and operate the system. For example, if you have customized IBM-supplied messages using CHGMSGD (Change Message Description) commands, these commands should be in a CL program or database job for use after installing the next release of OS/400. Such objects should be in QGPL. Also, any general-purpose (not application-specific) commands you have created to help the operator run the AS/400 should be in QGPL. The source files for objects in QGPL should be in the library GPLSRC.

Some shops use QGPL solely for configuration-related objects and use separate libraries, OPRMSC (Operations Miscellaneous), and OPRSRC (Operations Source) for operations-related objects. Still others put the operations-related objects, both general-purpose and application-specific, into the set of production libraries.

Any of these approaches will work if you clearly document what goes into each library. One thing that any shop other than the smallest should avoid, though, is putting application-related objects in QGPL. At least one library (QGPL) should be reserved for systemwide configuration-related objects. This practice makes it much easier for the person charged with configuration responsibilities to control the necessary objects. The practice also simplifies a more comprehensive "system" backup because SAVSYS can be followed by SAVLIB LIB(ALTQSYS QGPL), thus capturing the local system configuration completely.

Vendor-Supplied Libraries

When IBM or another vendor distributes a software package, it typically comes as one or two libraries. For example, the IBM utilities DFU, Query, SEU, and SDA come in library QIDU. Other libraries supplied with IBM software packages include QRPG for RPG/400, QCBL for COBOL/400, QOFC for OfficeVision/400, and QRJE for the RJE (Remote Job Entry) Facility. The only objects that should be locally created directly in these libraries (e.g., using the CRTPF (Create Physical File) or CRTDSPF (Create Display File) commands) are ones necessary for installation of the software package. For example, the RJE Facility requires a session description, a forms control table, and other objects. These objects can be created in QRJE. An alternate approach is to create objects required for a software package in library QGPL or in production libraries.

Local Production Libraries

All application-related objects that meet production-level standards should be put into a set of production libraries. Such objects will generally include locally defined database files; display, printer, and other device files; programs; commands; source code; documentation; and other object types used to implement application systems. Having a set of production libraries lets you separate production versions of objects from "experimental" or test versions and application-related objects from configuration-related objects.

Some objects will not fall clearly into either the configuration category or the application category, reinforcing the recommendation that each shop have consistent, written standards of what goes in each set of libraries. Similarly, the question of whether an object adequately meets production-level standards or whether it is still an experimental or prototype version that has been put into general use (and hence belongs in the experimental library set discussed next) is not always simple to answer. Again, clear standards are the solution.

Once you have decided to put production application objects into their own set of libraries, the question of how to structure the set arises. For shops with simple applications and small physical files, it may be adequate to have only a single library (PRDLIB) in the set; production application objects of all types can go into this library.

More complex organizations will require more than a single library. The current limit of 40 libraries in a job's library list sets the upper boundary for how many libraries can be in this set. However, a maximum of six libraries in this set will make it easier to construct a library list that contains all the libraries required by a job. Many shops have chosen an approach that uses one library for each application system — accounts receivable, inventory, payroll, etcetera. This approach works well if *all* the following are true: The different application systems number no more than six; the application systems are totally independent — they do not share data, subroutines, or anything else; and the database files are small or medium size (of a size that allows a fairly simple backup strategy).

Grouping production objects by application systems can work even if all the conditions listed above are not met, but a variety of *ad hoc* procedures for backup will be required. If you decide to use this approach, pay special attention to your save/restore planning for physical files, logical files, and journals. Any time a logical file or a journal is not in the same library as the related physical file, the restore operation follows some rules that can cause problems.

A strategy better suited to shops that have integrated applications that share data, programs, and other objects is the one I will detail below. The set of production libraries is comprised of libraries that contain items with related *functional* properties. The following six libraries are used:

- PRDDTA (Production Data) — Physical and logical files, journals, and journal receivers
- PRDEXC (Production Executable objects) — Commands; programs; and, for applications generated by DFU, the related display file
- PRDDEV (Production Device files) — All device files for displays, printers, and communications
- PRDSRC (Production Source) — All source code for high-level languages, data description specifications (DDS), and utility definition specifications (UDS) for DFU and Query applications
- PRDDOC (Production Documentation) — Source physical files that contain system documentation, including on-line help text, if such a facility is provided and uses source file members
- PRDMSC (Production Miscellaneous objects) — Objects including message queues, data areas, and others not in the other five production libraries

Whether you break the production library set into six specific libraries, as I suggest here, or whether you choose an alternate approach, you should follow several guidelines when deciding what specific libraries to use.

First, with an eye toward the recovery process, at least keep all physical files, logical files, and journals in the same library. In a save/restore procedure, all physical files must exist on the system before any logical files based on them are restored. If the physical and logical files are in the same library, OS/400 provides the proper sequencing; otherwise, you must sequence the restores correctly. In addition, if you restore a logical file whose access path has been saved, and the logical file is not in the same library as the physical file upon which it is based, the AS/400 will re-create the logical file access path, which can significantly lengthen your recovery time. However, if the physical file and the logical file are in the same library, they can easily be saved and restored in the same command, eliminating any potential problem.

Second, for journaled physical files, if the journal is not in existence when the physical file is restored, journaling of the physical file ends. If the journal being restored is in a different library from the physical file, it must be restored first for the file to remain journaled. A simpler and more reliable practice is to put the journal into the same library as the physical file. Journal receivers can be kept in a different library from the physical file, but doing so offers no particular advantage, and your save/restore is easier to manage if the journal receiver is found in the same library as the journal and physical file.

Third, *within a library set* all objects should have unique names and types even if they are in different libraries. While the AS/400 will let you create a display file in PRDDEV called ACTRCV and a database file in PRDDTA also called ACTRCV, the referencing of objects via the library list will not work properly because all the libraries in a set are normally in the library list at the same time. You could encounter the problem of having a program search the libraries in the library list for the display file ACTRCV and come upon the database file ACTRCV first. The wrong file then would be accessed by the program. Unique object names and types within a library set avert this problem.

Fourth, whatever method you use to structure the production library set also should be used to structure the experimental version library set, all the test library sets for programmers and users, and the security functions library set. A consistent structure makes finding and moving objects straightforward. This principle should be followed even though some libraries contain few objects.

Production Library Source Files

Source for all objects created in the production libraries also should be in a production library. I recommend library PRDSRC for this. Source files should be created to organize source code in the same way that libraries are set up to organize objects. Figure 7.2 provides one approach to establishing source files.

Note that the IBM-supplied source files, such as QCLSRC and QCMDSRC, are *not* used. I ignore the IBM-supplied set of source files because they do not provide an adequate breakdown of DDS source (it should be split into different file types), nor do they break down COBOL source into the desired program source and copy library source files. You may want to set up additional types of source files that are not provided by IBM; for example, if you use RJE to submit jobs to a System/370 host, you may want a Job Control Language Source file (JCLSRC). To add new types of source files, you must either follow the IBM naming standard (beginning each file name with "Q") or make up your own names for the added files. Naming your files beginning with "Q" can present a problem because you no longer can be sure that all objects on your system that have names beginning with "Q" are IBM-supplied. Making up names that do not begin with "Q" for any source files you add while still using the IBM-supplied files creates its own dilemma because then you have a confusing inconsistency in source file names.

A simpler, more consistent approach is to use all locally defined names and ignore the IBM-supplied source files. The particular names you choose are not critical, but you should document what goes into each source file and what library contains objects created from the source file. Source files required in other library sets (e.g., security functions or test libraries) should use the same file names used in PRDSRC.

Experimental Version Libraries

Not all objects will meet full production standards before users begin using them. While this approach may not be the ideal theoretical approach to application development, it is the reality in almost all shops. As long as such experimental versions of objects (often referred to as "beta," "preproduction," or "prototype" versions) are adequately controlled, you can take advantage of them by familiarizing users with them and getting user reactions to them before they become production versions.

Figure 7.2

Source File Contents and Related Libraries

Source File	Library for Objects Created From Source	Contents
CBLCPY	xxxEXC	COBOL statements copied into programs using the COPY verb.
CBLSRC	xxxEXC	COBOL statements for programs.
CLPSRC	xxxEXC	CL statements for programs.
CMDSRC	xxxEXC	Command definitions.
CMNSRC	xxxDEV	DDS for BSC and SNA communication files.
DFUSRC	xxxEXC	UDS for DFU applications.
DSPSRC	xxxDEV	DDS for display files.
JCLSRC		Job Control Language submitted to System/370 via RJE Facility.
JOBSRC		CL statements for database jobs.
LFSRC	xxxDTA	DDS for logical files.
MSCSRC	xxxMSC	Print images, tables, other miscellaneous source.
PRTSRC	xxxDEV	DDS for printer files.
PFSRC	xxxDTA	DDS for physical files.
QRYSRC	xxxEXC	UDS for Query applications.
RPGCPY	xxxEXE	RPG statements copied into programs using /COPY.
RPGSRC	xxxEXE	RPG source for programs.

You can implement this practice quite naturally with a set of experimental libraries that corresponds in structure to the production set. The guidelines for inclusion in a particular experimental library are the same as those for the corresponding production library, except that the object is a prototype. The library names (shown in Figure 7.1) all begin with EXP (experimental). (PRO, for "prototype," is not used as a prefix because of the visual similarity to PRD, which could lead to confusion. You can pick any three-letter prefix you like.)

Be aware that one area of conflict can arise when you use both a production library set and an experimental library set. If a logical file created in EXPDTA is based on a physical file in PRDDTA, the logical file restore problems discussed earlier can occur. Such an occurrence is the penalty you pay when logical files do not meet production standards. Never should a logical file in PRDDTA be based on a physical file in EXPDTA because the logical file obviously cannot satisfy production level standards if the physical file does not meet them. Similarly, physical files in EXPDTA should have a journal in EXPDTA. Generally, most of the objects in the experimental libraries will be for totally independent (i.e., not integrated), small applications, or they will be programs and related objects for use against data that is in PRDDTA. Thus, the potential conflicts described do not pose a large problem in actual practice.

Test Libraries

Every programmer should have a set of libraries corresponding to the production set. These libraries should contain private objects, such as customized job descriptions or output queues for the programmer's compiler output. The libraries also should contain copies of production and experimental objects, such as programs, which the programmer is modifying. All development work should occur on the *copies* of the production and experimental objects, never on the original objects themselves. Because two objects with the same name and object type can exist in different libraries, the original objects can remain in production use while a copy having the same name can be under development.

To use programmers' test library sets, a defined set of procedures for copying production objects to a test library is required. The procedures should establish methods for object check-out and check-in so a programmer can systematically copy the objects he needs to a test library and systematically return the objects to the production library when finished with them. It is essential that an object and its source be checked out to only one person at a time; otherwise, more than one person at a time may be modifying different copies of the same object.

Test library sets are also useful for user-driven computing. Some organizations give specific users their own library sets; others find it adequate to provide a single set of libraries for each operating division. These libraries can contain the applications from Query, Applications Made Easy (AME), spreadsheets, and other general-purpose software. Small database files and source files with Text Management documents and database jobs can also be kept in these libraries.

Security Function Libraries

The final set of libraries to consider is a set created for and owned by the security officer. The public should have, at most, read authorization to these libraries, and many of the objects in the libraries should have no public rights. These libraries should contain objects used for security functions. Programs to facilitate authorizing/deauthorizing users and a database file to maintain information about all user profiles created on the system are two examples of objects that should be kept in this set of libraries. In addition, special-function programs that adopt the security officer's user profile during execution should be kept here. The specific libraries in the set should be identical in structure to those established for the production libraries. Thus, the set of security libraries would be SCRDEV (security device files), SCRDOC (documentation), SCRDTA (data), SCREXC (executable objects), SCRMSC (miscellaneous), and SCRSRC (source).

Library Types

When a library is created, you must specify its type as *PROD or *TEST on the CRTLIB (Create Library) command. If you specify TYPE(*PROD), then no database files in the library can be opened for update if a job is in debug mode and UPDPROD(*NO) has been specified on the STRDBG (Start Debug) command. This affords some protection of production database files. If you specify the library type as *TEST, no such protection exists. Figure 7.1 shows the library type IBM has established for its libraries and the library type I recommend for the libraries discussed in the article. Note that making a library *PROD type does not prevent a database file from being deleted nor does it prevent other objects, such as data areas, from being modified. Proper object authorization is still essential for all production objects.

The library type I recommend for security-function libraries requires further explanation. I designated all security-function libraries *TEST type. The use of *TEST provides less protection than *PROD if testing is done on the actual data in these libraries, but it reduces the likelihood that sensitive data will need to be copied into a programmer's test library. This tradeoff is one of many that arise between tight security and ease of application modification. Each data processing shop should carefully consider the relative weight of tight security versus convenience before deciding how to set the library types and how to handle application development for the security officer, who may not be a programmer.

Library Lists

Once you have established what the libraries will be on your system — following the scheme I have outlined or one of your own — you must establish how these libraries will be used in library lists. On the AS/400, if an object is referred to by its *qualified* name (e.g., PRDDTA/MYFILE), the system looks for the object in the specified library. However, when an object is referred to by name only, with no specific library qualifier (e.g., *LIBL/MYFILE), the job's library list is used to find the object. The library list is an ordered list of library names that are searched one by one until an object is found with the specified name and the proper object type.

A library list has two parts: system and user. The system part of a library list can contain up to 15 libraries and these are searched before the libraries in the user part of the library list. The system part should be established by using the CHGSYSVAL (Change System Value) command to set the value of QSYSLIBL to "ALTQSYS QSYS QGPL" (Figure 7.3). This library list puts configuration-related libraries (QGPL) into the system part of the library list. After setting QSYSLIBL, the system part should be left alone (i.e., it should *not* be changed by the CHGSYSLIBL — Change System Library List — command).

The user part of a library list can contain up to 25 libraries. While user libraries or vendor-supplied software package libraries can be put in the system part of the library list, they are more logically put in the user part.

The user part of a library list is initially taken from the system value QUSRLIBL. At the time a job is submitted, this value may be overridden entirely

Figure 7.3

Recommended Values for QSYSLIBL and QUSRLIBL

QSYSLIBL (maximum of 15 libraries)	ALTQSYS QSYS QGPL
QUSRLIBL (maximum of 25 libraries)	PRDDTA PRDDEV PRDEXC PRDMSC PRDDOC PRDSRC EXPDTA EXPDEV EXPEXC EXPMSC EXPDOC EXPSRC QIDU QADM QADMFLS QTEMP

by a user library list specified in a job description or by a list specified in the //JOB command or SBMJOB (Submit Job) command. Once a job has started, the entire user part of the library list can be replaced with the RPLLIBL (Replace Library List) command, or the list can be incrementally modified with the ADDLIBLE (Add Library List Entry) and RMVLIBLE (Remove Library List Entry) commands. The EDTLIBL command can also be used to selectively modify the current library list.

Figure 7.3 shows the recommended values for QUSRLIBL. This library list provides the necessary libraries for normal production work, including use of Query, Administrative Management, and Text Management. If you use other software packages, they should be added to the ones shown. The local production libraries head the list because their lead position will provide a slight performance advantage when a search for an object is made.

Because the user part of the library list is limited to 25 libraries, I recommended earlier that the production library set be broken into six libraries. This approach allows enough slots to include production, experimental, and one test set of libraries, as well as six vendor-supplied libraries in a library list. If more than the recommended six libraries are defined for the production set, then

Figure 7.4 Using the RPLLIBL Command to Set Up a Programmer's Library List

```
RPLLIBL LIBL(TSTDTAPTC     TSTDEVPTC     TSTEXCPTC     +
             TSTMSCPTC     TSTDOCPTC     TSTSRCPTC     +
             PRDDTA        PRDDEV        PRDEXC        +
             PRDMSC        PRDDOC        PRDSRC        +
             EXPDTA        EXPDEV        EXPEXC        +
             EXPMSC        EXPDOC        EXPSRC        +
             QCBL          QRPG          QIDU          +
             QRJE          QTEMP)
```

some adjustment to the library lists will be required. All libraries included in either QSYSLIBL or QUSRLIBL should have at least public operational rights, so that any user profile can access them.

Programmers and users involved in user-driven computing will need the appropriate set of test libraries added to their library lists. A convenient way to handle this addition is by using a RPLLIBL command in an initial program that is executed at sign-on to establish an extended library list. This same extended library list should also be included in a job description that each programmer has for submitting compiles and other batch jobs. Figure 7.4 shows a sample RPLLIBL (Replace Library List) command to establish a new user part of the job's library list for an application programmer.

In a programmer's library list, the test libraries must precede the production and experimental libraries so that the objects with the same name and type will be found in the programmer's test library. Each programmer's library list should include his own set of test libraries. The new library list for a programmer responsible for configuration might also include ALTQSYSSRC or GPLSRC instead of the TSTSRCxxx library.

There are many ways in which libraries can be set up on your AS/400. This section has suggested an approach that will allow several levels of application development (test, experimental, and production) across an integrated database. Your organization may find a different approach works better for you; but because libraries are the major object organization facility on the AS/400, it is important to have a clearly defined library structure as soon as you begin installing OS/400. A very small AS/400 shop with a single programmer/operator may choose simply to use the system library, QSYS, and the general-purpose library QGPL, as supplied by IBM. However, even a small AS/400 shop, and especially larger organizations with more complex application systems, should follow a more structured approach toward organizing objects to smooth subsequent application development.

Chapter 8

Work Management

by Wayne Madden

Good work management skills facilitate problem solving and operations

Work management on the AS/400 refers to the set of objects that define jobs and how the system processes those jobs. With a good understanding of work management concepts, you can easily perform such tasks as finding a job on the system, solving problems, improving performance, or controlling job priorities. I can't imagine anyone operating an AS/400 in a production environment without having basic work management skills to facilitate problem solving and operations. Let me illustrate two situations in which work management could enhance system operations.

Perhaps you are plagued with end users who complain that the system takes too long to complete short jobs. You investigate and discover that, indeed, the system is processing short jobs slowly because they spend too much time in the job queue behind long-running end-user batch jobs, operator-submitted batch jobs, and even program compiles. You could tell your operators not to submit jobs, or you could have your programmers compile interactively, but those approaches would be impractical and unnecessary. The answer lies in understanding the work management concepts of multiple subsystems and multiple job queues.

Perhaps when your "power users" and programmers share a subsystem, excessive peaks and valleys in performance occur due to the heavy interaction of these users. Perhaps you want to use separate storage pools (i.e., memory pools) based on user profiles so that you can place your power users in one pool, your programmers in another, and everyone else in a third pool, thereby creating consistent performance for each user group. You could do this if you knew the work management concepts of memory management.

Figure 8-1

Work Management Objects

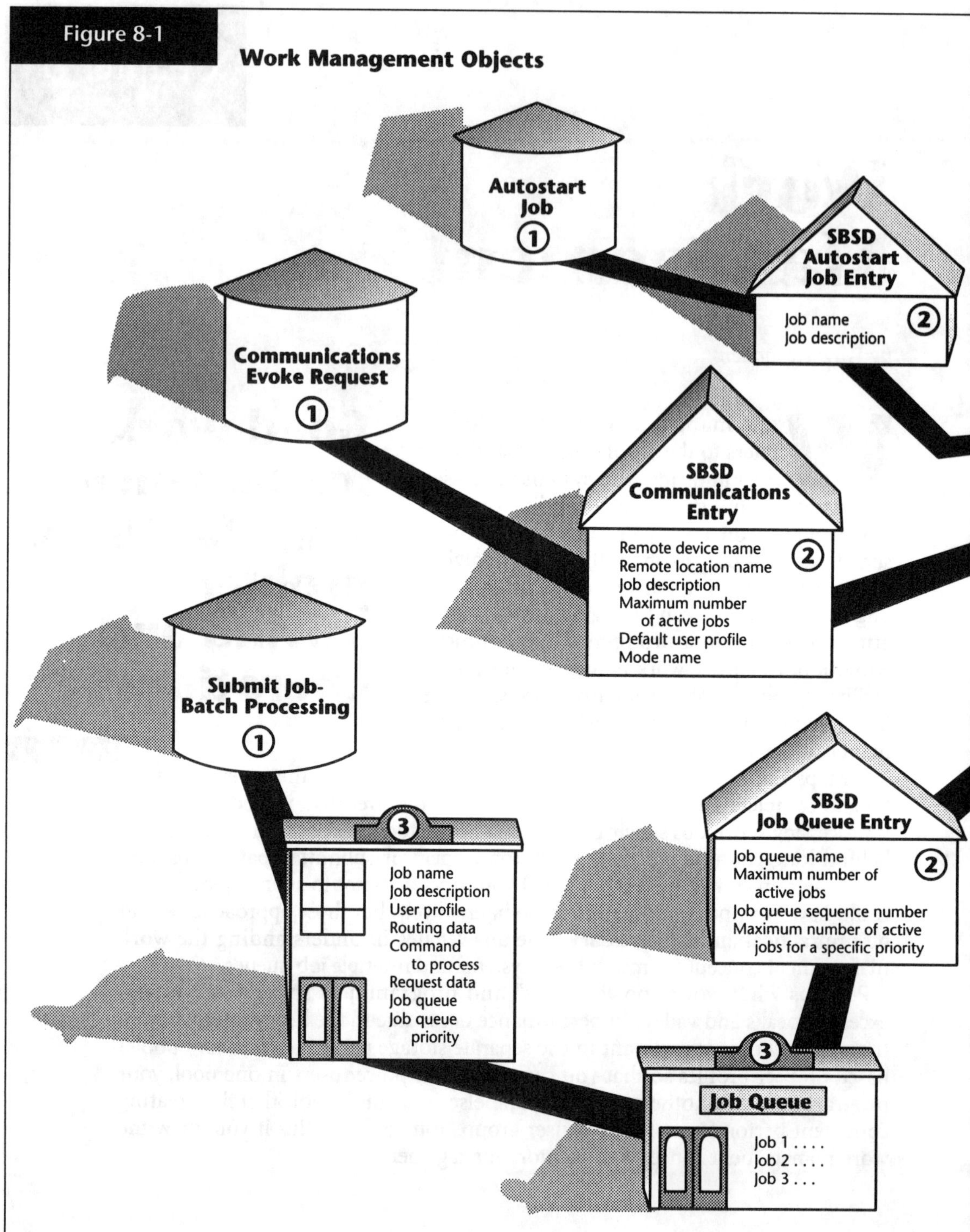
Autostart
Job
1
SBSD
Autostart
Job Entry
Job name
Job description
2
Communications
Evoke Request
1
SBSD
Communications
Entry
Remote device name
Remote location name
Job description
Maximum number
of active jobs
Default user profile
Mode name
2
Submit Job-
Batch Processing
1
SBSD
Job Queue Entry
Job queue name
Maximum number of
active jobs
Job queue sequence number
Maximum number of active
jobs for a specific priority
2
3
Job name
Job description
User profile
Routing data
Command
to process
Request data
Job queue
Job queue
priority
3
Job Queue
Job 1 . . . .
Job 2 . . . .
Job 3 . . .

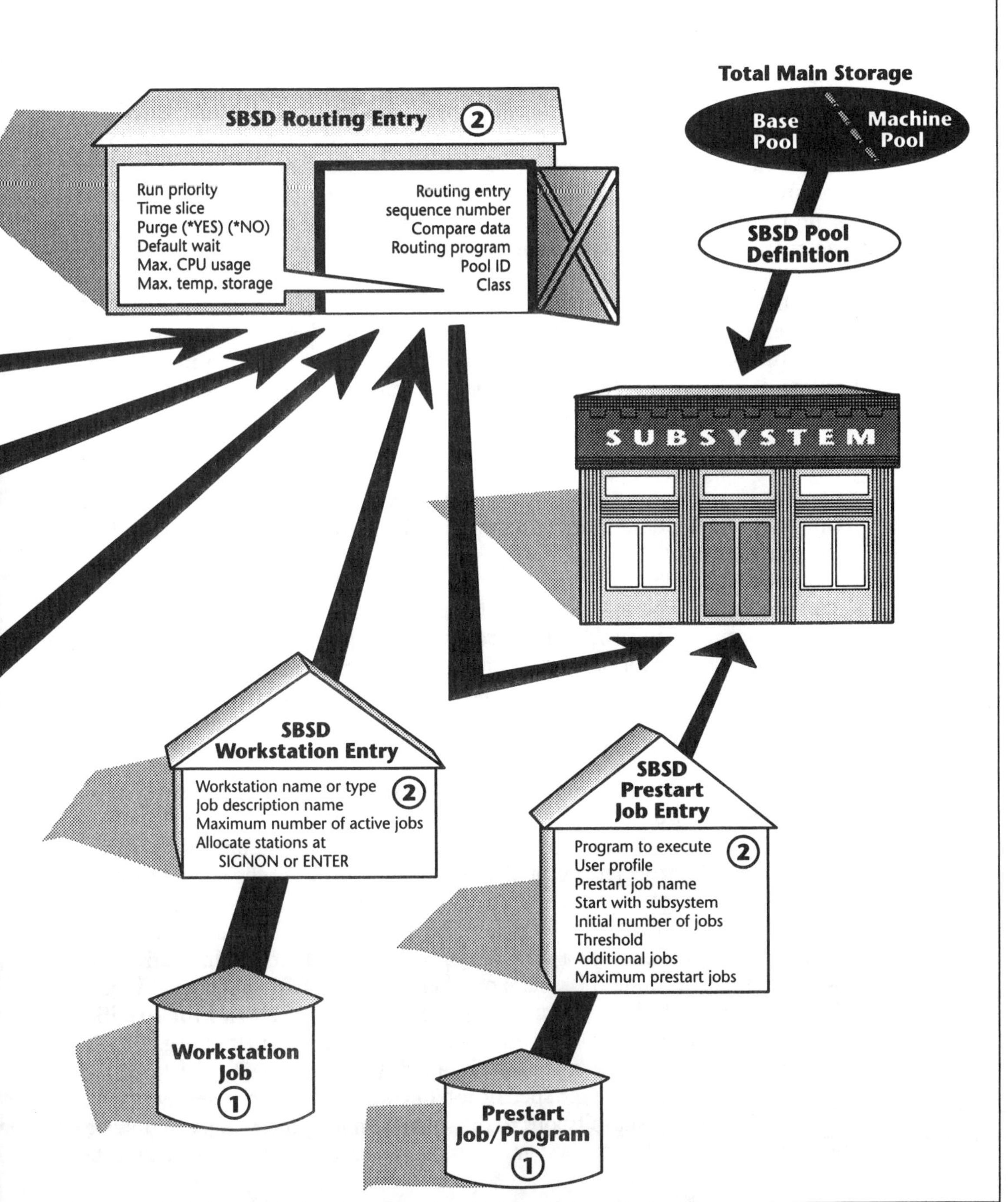
Total Main Storage
Base Pool
Machine Pool
SBSD Pool Definition
SBSD Routing Entry ②
Run priority
Time slice
Purge (*YES) (*NO)
Default wait
Max. CPU usage
Max. temp. storage
Routing entry sequence number
Compare data
Routing program
Pool ID
Class
SUBSYSTEM
SBSD Workstation Entry
Workstation name or type ②
Job description name
Maximum number of active jobs
Allocate stations at SIGNON or ENTER
SBSD Prestart Job Entry
Program to execute ②
User profile
Prestart job name
Start with subsystem
Initial number of jobs
Threshold
Additional jobs
Maximum prestart jobs
Workstation Job ①
Prestart Job/Program ①

Getting Oriented

Just as a road map gives you the information you need to find your way in an unfamiliar city, Figure 8.1 serves as a guide to understanding work management. It shows the basic work management objects and how they relate to one another. The objects designated by a 1 represent jobs that enter the system, the objects designated by a 2 represent parts of the subsystem description, and the objects designated by a 3 represent additional job environment attributes (e.g., class, job description, and user profile) that affect the way a job interacts with the system.

You will notice that all the paths in Figure 8.1 lead to one destination — the subsystem. In the Roman Empire all roads led to Rome. On the AS/400, all jobs must process in a subsystem. So what better place to start our study of work management than with the subsystem?

Defining a Subsystem

A subsystem, defined by a subsystem description, is where the system brings together the resources needed to process work. As shown in Figure 8.2, the subsystem description contains seven parts that fall into three categories. Let me briefly introduce you to these components of the subsystem description.

- *Subsystem attributes* provide the general definition of the subsystem and control its main storage allocations. The general definition includes the subsystem name, description, and the maximum number of jobs allowed in the subsystem.

  Storage pool definitions are the most significant subsystem attributes. A subsystem's storage pool definition determines how the subsystem uses main storage for processing work. The storage pool definition lets a subsystem either share an existing pool of main storage (e.g., *BASE and *INTERACT) with other subsystems, establish a private pool of main storage, or both. The storage pool definition also lets you establish the activity level — the maximum number of jobs allowed in the subsystem — for a particular storage pool.

- *Work entries* define how jobs enter the subsystem and how the subsystem processes that work. They consist of autostart job entries, workstation entries, job queue entries, communications entries, and prestart job entries.

  Autostart job entries let you predefine any jobs you want the system to start automatically when it starts the subsystem.

  Workstation entries define which workstations the subsystem will use to receive work. You can use a workstation entry to initiate an interactive job when a user signs on to the system or when a user transfers an interactive job from another subsystem. You can create workstation entries for specific workstation names (e.g., DSP10 and OH0123), for generic names (e.g., DSP*, DP*, and OH*), or by the type of workstations (e.g., 5251, 3476, and 3477).

  Job queue entries define the specific job queues from which to receive work. A job queue, which submits jobs to the subsystem for processing, can only be allocated by one active subsystem. A single subsystem, however, can allocate

Figure 8.2

Subsystem Description Components

Subsystem Attributes
- Storage pool definitions

Work Entries
- Autostart job entries
- Workstation entries
- Job queue entries
- Communications entries
- Prestart job entries

Routing Entries

multiple job queues, prioritize them, and specify for each a maximum number of active jobs.

Communications entries define the communications device associated with a remote location name from which you can receive a communications evoke request.

Prestart job entries define jobs that start on a local system before a remote system sends a communications request. When a communications evoke request requires the program running in the prestart job, the request attaches to that prestart job, thereby eliminating all overhead associated with initiating a job and program.

- *Routing entries* identify which programs to call to control routing steps that will execute in the subsystem for a given job. Routing entries also define in which storage pool the job will be processed and which basic execution attributes (defined in a job class object associated with a routing entry) the job will use for processing.

All these components of the subsystem description determine how the system uses resources to process jobs within a subsystem. Now that we've covered some basic terms, let's take a closer look at subsystem attributes and how subsystems can use main storage for processing work.

Main Storage and Subsystem Pool Definitions

When the AS/400 is shipped, all of main storage resides in two system pools: the machine pool (*MACHINE) and the base pool (*BASE). You must define the machine pool to support your system hardware; the amount of main storage you allocate to the machine pool is hardware-dependent and varies with each AS/400.

The base pool is the main storage that remains after you reserve the machine pool. You can designate *BASE as a shared pool for all subsystems to use to process work, or you can divide it into smaller pools of shared and private main storage. A shared pool is an allocation of main storage where multiple subsystems can process work. *MACHINE and *BASE are both examples of shared pools. Other shared storage pools that you can define include *INTERACT (for

Figure 8.3

Work with Shared Pools Panel

```
                         Work with Shared Pools
                                                  System:   MYSYSTEM
 Main storage size (K)   :      20480

 Type pool size, activity level, and description changes, press enter.

              Defined     Max    Allocated    Pool
 Pool         Size (K)   Active   Size (K)     ID
 *MACHINE       3500      +++       3500        1
 *BASE          4820       15       4820        2
 *INTERACT      8000       16       8000        4
 *SPOOL          160        3        160        3
 *SHRPOOL1         0        0
 *SHRPOOL2         0        0
 *SHRPOOL3         0        0
 *SHRPOOL4         0        0
 *SHRPOOL5         0        0
 *SHRPOOL6         0        0
                                                          More ...
 Command
 ===>
 F3=Exit   F4=Prompt   F5=Refresh   F11=Description   F12=Cancel
```

interactive jobs), *SPOOL (for printers), and *SHRPOOL1 to *SHRPOOL10 (for pools that you can define for your own purposes).

You can control shared pool sizes by using the CHGSHRPOOL (Change Shared Storage Pool) or WRKSHRPOOL (Work with Shared Storage Pools) commands. Figure 8.3 shows a WRKSHRPOOL screen, on which you can modify the pool size or activity level simply by changing the entries.

The AS/400's default controlling subsystem (QBASE) and the default spooling subsystem (QSPL) are configured to take advantage of shared pools. QBASE uses the *BASE pool and the *INTERACT pool, while QSPL uses *BASE and *SPOOL.

To see what pools a subsystem is using, you use the DSPSBSD (Display Subsystem Description) command. For instance, when you execute the command

```
DSPSBSD QBASE OUTPUT(*PRINT)
```

you will find the following pool definitions for QBASE listed (if the defaults have not been changed):

```
QBASE   ((1 *BASE) (2 *INTERACT))
```

Parentheses group together two definitions, each of which can contain two distinct parts (the subsystem pool number and size). In this example of the QBASE pool definitions, the (1 *BASE) represents the subsystem pool number 1 and a size of *BASE, meaning that the system will use all of *BASE as a shared pool. A third part of the pool definition, the activity level, doesn't appear for *BASE because system value QBASACTLVL maintains the activity level. The second pool definition for QBASE is (2 *INTERACT). Because you can use the CHGSHRPOOL or WRKSHRPOOL commands to modify the activity level for shared pool *INTERACT, the activity level is not listed as part of the subsystem description, nor is it specified when you use the CRTSBSD or CHGSBSD commands.

Be careful not to confuse *subsystem* pool numbering with *system* pool numbering. The AS/400's two predefined system pools, *MACHINE and *BASE, are defined as system pool number 1, and system pool number 2, respectively. Pool numbering within a subsystem is unique to that subsystem, and only the routing entries in that subsystem use it to determine which pool jobs will use, based on the routing data associated with each job. As subsystems define new storage pools (shared or private) in addition to the two predefined system pools, the system simply assigns the next available system pool number to use as a reference on the WRKSYSSTS display. For example, with the above pools for QBASE and the following pools for QSPL,

```
QSPL   ((1 *BASE) (2 *SPOOL))
```

the system pool numbering might correspond to the subsystem pool numbering as shown in Figure 8.4.

A private pool is a specific allocation of main storage reserved for one subsystem. It's common to use a private pool when the system uses the controlling subsystem QCTL instead of QBASE. If you change your controlling subsystem to QCTL, the system startup program starts several subsystems (i.e., QINTER, QBATCH, QCMN, and QSPL) at IPL that are designed to support specific types of work. Although using QBASE as the controlling subsystem lets you divide main storage into separate pools, using QCTL is inherently easier to manage and administer in terms of controlling the number of jobs and performance tuning.

IBM ships the following pool definitions for the multiple subsystem approach:

```
QCTL   ((1 *BASE))
QINTER ((1 *BASE) (2 *INTERACT))
QBATCH ((1 *BASE))
QCMN   ((1 *BASE))
QSPL   ((1 *BASE) (2 *SPOOL))
```

As you can see, the initial configuration of these subsystems is like the initial configuration of subsystem QBASE, in that shared pools reserve areas of main storage for specific types of jobs. However, pool sharing does not provide optimum performance in a diverse operations environment where various types of work process simultaneously. In such cases, subsystems with private pools may be necessary to improve performance.

Look at the pool definitions in Figure 8.5, in which two interactive subsystems (QINTER and QPGMR) provide private pools for both end users and programmers. Both QINTER and QPGMR define specific amounts of main storage to be allocated to the subsystem instead of sharing the *INTERACT pool. Also, both storage definitions require a specific activity level, whereas shared

Figure 8.4

System and Subsystem Pool Numbering

System Pool Number	Subsystem Pool Number QBASE	QSPL
1 Machine Pool		
2 *BASE Pool	1	1
3 *INTERACT Shared Pool	2	
4 *SPOOL Shared Pool		2

Figure 8.5

Sample Subsystem Pool Definitions

Controlling subsystem
```
QCTL        ((1 *BASE))
```
Interactive subsystems
```
QINTER      ((1 *BASE) (2 20000 50))
QPGMR       ((1 *BASE) (2 2000 5))
```
Batch subsystems
```
QBATCH      ((1 *BASE))
DAYQ        ((1 *BASE) (2 1000 2))
QPGMRB      ((1 *BASE) (2 500 1))
```
Communications subsystem
```
QCMN        ((1 *BASE))
```
Spooling subsystem
```
QSPL        ((1 *BASE) (2 *SPOOL))
```

pool activity levels are maintained as part of the shared pool definitions (using the CHGSHRPOOL or WRKSHRPOOL commands). The private pool configuration in this example, with private main storage and private activity levels, prevents unwanted contention for resources between end users and programmers.

Figure 8.5 also demonstrates how you can use multiple batch subsystems. Three batch subsystems (QBATCH, DAYQ, and QPGMRB, respectively) provide for daytime and nighttime processing of operator-submitted batch jobs, daytime end-user processing of short jobs, and program compiles. A separate communications subsystem, QCMN, is configured to handle any communications requests, and QSPL handles spooling.

The decision about whether to use shared pools or private pools should depend on the storage capacity of your system. On one hand, because shared pools ensure efficient use of main storage by letting more than one subsystem share a storage pool, it's wise to use shared pools if you have a system with limited main storage. On the other hand, private pools provide a reserved pool of main storage and activity levels that are constantly available to a subsystem without contention from any other subsystem. They are easy to manage when dealing with multiple subsystems. Therefore, private pools are a wise choice for a system with ample main storage.

Starting a Subsystem

A subsystem definition is only that — a definition. To start a subsystem, you use the STRSBS (Start Subsystem) command. Figure 8.6 outlines the steps your system takes to activate a subsystem after you execute a STRSBS command.

First, it uses the storage pool definition to allocate main storage for job processing. Next, it uses the workstation entries to allocate workstation devices and present the workstation sign-on displays. If the system finds communications entries, it uses them to allocate the named devices. The system then allocates job queues so that when the subsystem completes the start-up process, the subsystem can receive jobs from the job queues. Next, it starts any defined prestart or autostart jobs. When the system has completed all these steps, the subsystem is finally ready to begin processing work.

Running Jobs

One of OS/400's most elegant features is the concept of a "job," a unit of work with a tidy package of attributes that lets you easily identify and track a job throughout your system. The AS/400 defines this unit of work with a job name, a user profile associated with the job, and a computer-assigned job number; it is these three attributes that make a job unique. For example, when a user signs on to a workstation, the resulting job might be known to the system as

Job name . . . : DSP10 (Workstation ID)
User profile . : WMADDEN
Job number . : 003459

Any transaction OS/400 completes is associated with an active job executing on the system. But where do these jobs come from? A job can be initiated when you sign on to the system from a workstation, when you submit a batch job, when your system receives a communications evoke request from another system, when you submit a prestart job, or when you create autostart job entries that the system automatically executes when it starts the associated subsystem.

Understanding how jobs get started on the system is crucial to grasping AS/400 work management concepts. So let's continue by focusing on *work entries*, the part of the description that defines how jobs gain access to the subsystem for processing.

Types of Work Entries

There are five types of work entries: workstation, job queue, communications, prestart job, and autostart job. The easiest to understand is the *workstation entry*, which describes how a user gains access to a particular subsystem (for interactive

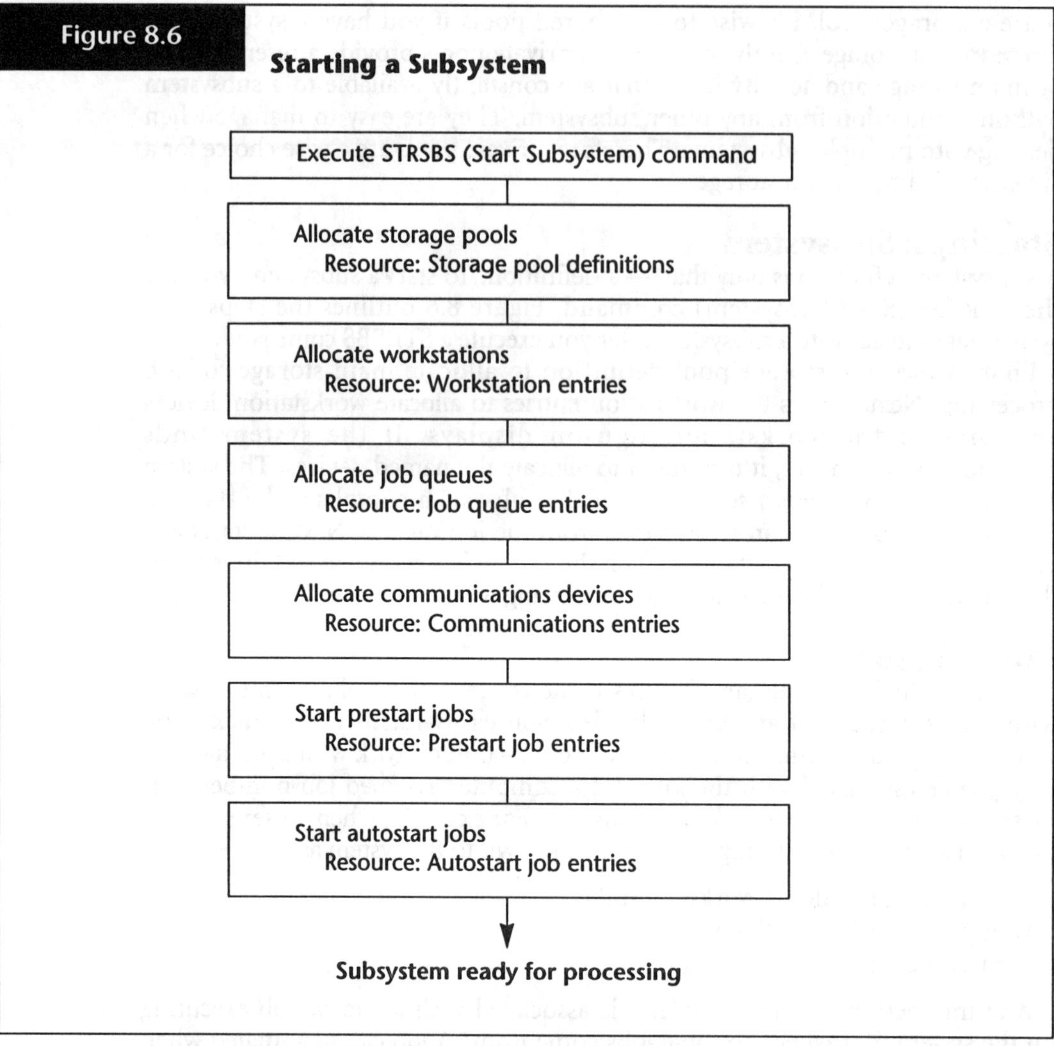

Figure 8.6
Starting a Subsystem

jobs) using a workstation. To define a workstation entry, you use the ADDWSE (Add Work Station Entry) command. A subsystem can have as many workstation entries as you need, all of which have the following attributes:

- WRKSTNTYPE (workstation type) or WRKSTN (workstation name)
- JOBD (job description name)
- MAXACT (maximum number of active workstations)
- AT (when to allocate workstation)

When defining a workstation entry, you can use either the WRKSTNTYPE or WRKSTN attribute to specify which workstations the system should allocate. For instance, if you want to allocate all workstations, you specify WRKSTN TYPE(*ALL) in the workstation entry. This entry tells the system to allocate all workstations, regardless of the type (e.g., 5250, 5291, 3476, or 3477). Or you can use the WRKSTNTYPE attribute in one or more workstation entries to tell the system to allocate a specific type of workstation (e.g., WRKSTNTYPE(3477)).

You can also define workstation entries using the WRKSTN attribute to specify that the system allocate workstations by name. You can enter either a specific name or a generic name. For example, an entry defining WRKSTN(DSP01) tells the subsystem to allocate device DSP01. The generic entry, WRKSTNN(OHIO*), tells the subsystem to let any workstation whose name begins with "OHIO" establish an interactive job.

You must specify a value for either the WRKSTNTYPE parameter or the WRKSTN parameter. In addition, you cannot mix WRKSTNTYPE and WRKSTN entries in the same subsystem. If you do, the subsystem recognizes only the entries that define workstations by the WRKSTN attribute and ignores any entries using the WRKSTNTYPE attribute.

The JOBD workstation entry attribute specifies the job description for the workstation entry. You can give this attribute a value of *USRPRF (the default) to tell the system to use the job description named in the user profile of the person who signs on to the workstation. Or you can specify a value of *SBSD to tell the system to use the job description of the subsystem. You can also use a qualified name of an existing job description. For security reasons, it's wise to use the default value *USRPRF for the JOBD attribute so that a user profile is required to sign on to the workstation. If you use the value *SBSD or a job description name and there is a valid user profile associated with the job description via the USER attribute, any user can simply press Enter and sign on to the subsystem. In such a situation, the user then assumes the user ID associated with the default job description named on the workstation entry.

There may be times when you want to define a workstation entry so that one user profile is always used when someone accesses the system via a particular workstation (e.g., if you wanted to disseminate public information at a courthouse, mall, or school). In such cases, be sure to construct such configurations so that only certain workstation entries have a job description that provides this type of access.

The workstation entry's MAXACT attribute determines the maximum number of workstations allowed in the subsystem at one time. When this limit is reached, the subsystem must de-allocate one workstation before it can allocate another. The value that you should normally use for this attribute is the default, *NOMAX, because you typically control (i.e., you physically limit) the number of devices. In fact, supplying a number for this attribute could cause confusion if one day the limit is reached and some poor soul has to figure out why certain workstations aren't functioning. It could take days to find this seldom-used attribute and change the value.

The AT attribute tells the system when to allocate the workstation. The default value, AT(*SIGNON), tells the system to allocate the workstation (i.e., initiate a sign-on screen at the workstation) when the subsystem is started. AT(*ENTER) tells the system to let jobs enter the subsystem only via the TFRJOB (Transfer

Job) command. (To transfer a job into an interactive subsystem, a job queue and a subsystem description job queue entry must exist.)

Now you're acquainted with the workstation entry attributes, but how can you use workstation entries? Let's say you want to process all your interactive jobs in subsystem QINTER. When you look at the default workstation entries for QINTER, you see the following:

```
WRKSTNTYPE   JOBD       MAXACT    AT
*ALL         *USRPRF    *NOMAX    *SIGNON
*CONS        *USRPRF    *NOMAX    *ENTER
```

The first set of values tells the system to allocate all workstations to subsystem QINTER when the subsystem is started. The second set of values tells the system to let the console transfer into the subsystem, but not to allocate the device.

What about a multiple subsystem environment for interactive jobs? Let's say you want to configure three subsystems: one for programmers (PGMRS), one for local end-user workstations (LOCAL), and one for remote end-user workstations (REMOTE). How can you make sure the system allocates the workstations to the correct subsystem?

Perhaps you're thinking you can create individual workstation entries for each device. You can, but such a method would be a nightmare to maintain, and it would require you to end the subsystem each time you added a new device. Likewise, it would be impractical to use the WRKSTNTYPE attribute, because defining types does not necessarily define specific locations for certain workstations.

So you have only two good options for ensuring that the correct subsystem allocates the devices. One is to name your various workstations so you can use generic WRKSTN values in the workstation entry. For example, you can allocate programmers' workstations to the proper subsystem by first giving them names like PGMR01 or PGMR02 and then creating a workstation entry that specifies WRKSTN(PGMR*). You might preface all local end-user workstation names with ADMN and LOC and then create workstation entries in the local subsystem using WRKSTN(ADMN*) and WRKSTN(LOC*). For the remote subsystem, you could continue to create workstation entries using generic names like the ones described above, or simply specify WRKSTNTYPE(*ALL), which would cause the subsystem to allocate the remaining workstations. However, you will need to read on to learn how subsystems allocate workstations to ensure that those workstations in the programmer and local subsystems are allocated properly.

Your second option for ensuring that the correct subsystem allocates the devices is to use routing entries to reroute workstation jobs to the correct subsystem (I explain how to do this later).

Conflicting Workstation Entries

Can workstation entries in different subsystems conflict with each other? You bet they can! Consider what happens when two different subsystems have workstation entries that allocate the same device. If AT(*SIGNON) is specified in the workstation entry, the first subsystem will allocate the device, and the device will show a sign-on display. When the system starts another subsystem with a workstation entry that applies to that same device (with AT(*SIGNON) specified), the subsystem will try to allocate it. If no user is signed on to the workstation, the second subsystem will allocate the device.

This arrangement isn't all bad. In fact, you can make it work for you. Imagine that you want to establish an interactive environment for two subsystems: QINTER (for all end-user workstations) and QPGMR (for all programmer workstations). You supply WRKSTNTYPE(*ALL) for subsystem QINTER and WRKSTN(PGMR*) for subsystem QPGMR.

To ensure that each workstation is allocated to the proper subsystem, you should start QINTER first. Consequently, the system will allocate all workstations to QINTER. After a brief delay, start QPGMR, which will then allocate (from QINTER) only the workstations whose names begin with "PGMR". Every workstation has its rightful place by simply using the system to do the work.

What about you? Can you see how your configuration is set up to let interactive jobs process? Take a few minutes to examine the workstation entries in your system's subsystems. You can use the DSPSBSD (Display Subsystem Description) command to display the work entries that are part of the subsystem description.

Job Queue Entries

Job queue entries control job initiation on your system and define how batch jobs enter the subsystem for processing. To submit jobs for processing, you must assign one or more job queues to a subsystem. A job queue entry associates a job queue with a subsystem. The attributes of a job queue entry are as follows:

- JOBQ (job queue name)
- MAXACT (maximum number of active jobs from this job queue)
- SEQNBR (sequence number used to determine order of selection among all job queues)
- MAXPTYn (maximum number of active jobs with this priority)

The JOBQ attribute, which is required, defines the name of the job queue you are attaching to the subsystem. The subsystem will search this job queue to receive jobs for processing. You can name only one job queue for a job queue entry, but you can define multiple job queue entries for a subsystem.

The MAXACT attribute defines the maximum number of jobs that can be active in the subsystem from the job queue named in this entry. This attribute controls only the maximum number of jobs allowed into the subsystem from the job queue. The default for MAXACT is 1, which lets only one job at a time from this job queue process in the subsystem.

The MAXACT (yes, same name) attribute of the subsystem description controls the maximum number of jobs in the subsystem from all entries (e.g., job queue and communications entries).

You can use the SEQNBR attribute to sequence multiple job queue entries associated with the subsystem. The subsystem searches each job queue in the order specified by the SEQNBR attribute of each job queue entry. The default for this attribute is 10, which you can use to define only one subsystem job queue entry; however, when defining multiple job queue entries, you should determine the appropriate sequence numbers desired to prioritize the job queues.

The MAXPTYn attribute is similar to the MAXACT attribute except that MAXPTYn controls the number of active jobs from a job queue that have the same priority (e.g., MAXPTY1 defines the maximum for jobs with priority 1, MAXPTY2 defines the maximum number for jobs with priority 2). The default for MAXPTY1 through MAXPTY9 is *NOMAX.

To illustrate how job queue entries work together to create a proper batch environment, Figure 8.7 shows a scheme that includes three subsystems: DAYSBS, NIGHTSBS, and BATCHSBS. DAYSBS processes daytime, short-running end-user batch jobs. NIGHTSBS processes nighttime, long-running end-user batch jobs. BATCHSBS processes operator-submitted requests and program compiles. To create the batch work environment in Figure 8.7, you first create the subsystems using the following CRTSBSD (Create Subsystem) commands:

```
CRTSBSD SBSD(QGPL/DAYSBS) POOL((1 *BASE) (2 400 1)) MAXACT(1)
CRTSBSD SBSD(QGPL/NIGHTSBS) POOL((1 *BASE) (2 2000 2)) MAXACT(2)
CRTSBSD SBSD(QGPL/BATCHSBS) POOL((1 *BASE) (2 1500 3) MAXACT(3)
```

Notice that each subsystem has an established maximum number of active jobs (MAXACT(n)). The maximum limit matches the activity level specified in the subsystem pool definition so that each active job is assigned an activity level without having to wait for one.

The next step is to create the appropriate job queues with the following CRTJOBQ (Create Job Queue) commands:

```
CRTJOBQ JOBQ(QGPL/DAYQ)
CRTJOBQ JOBQ(QGPL/NIGHTQ)
CRTJOBQ JOBQ(QGPL/PGMQ)
CRTJOBQ JOBQ(QGPL/BATCHQ)
```

Then, add the job queue entries to associate the job queues with the subsystems:

```
ADDJOBQE SBSD(DAYSBS) JOBQ(DAYQ) MAXACT(*NOMAX) SEQNBR(10)
ADDJOBQE SBSD(NIGHTSBS) JOBQ(NIGHTQ) MAXACT(*NOMAX) SEQNBR(10)
ADDJOBQE SBSD(BATCHSBS) JOBQ(PGMQ) MAXACT(1) SEQNBR(10)
ADDJOBQE SBSD(BATCHSBS) JOBQ(BATCHQ) MAXACT(2) SEQNBR(20)
```

Now let's walk through this batch work environment. Subsystem DAYSBS is a simple configuration that lets one job queue feed jobs into the subsystem. Because the MAXACT attribute value of DAYSBS is 1, only one job filters into the subsystem at a time, despite the fact that you specified the attribute MAXACT(*NOMAX) for the DAYQ job queue entry. Later, you can change the subsystem pool size and activity level, along with the MAXACT subsystem attribute, to let more jobs from the job queue process without having to re-create the job queue entry to modify MAXACT.

Figure 8.7

Sample Batch Work Environment

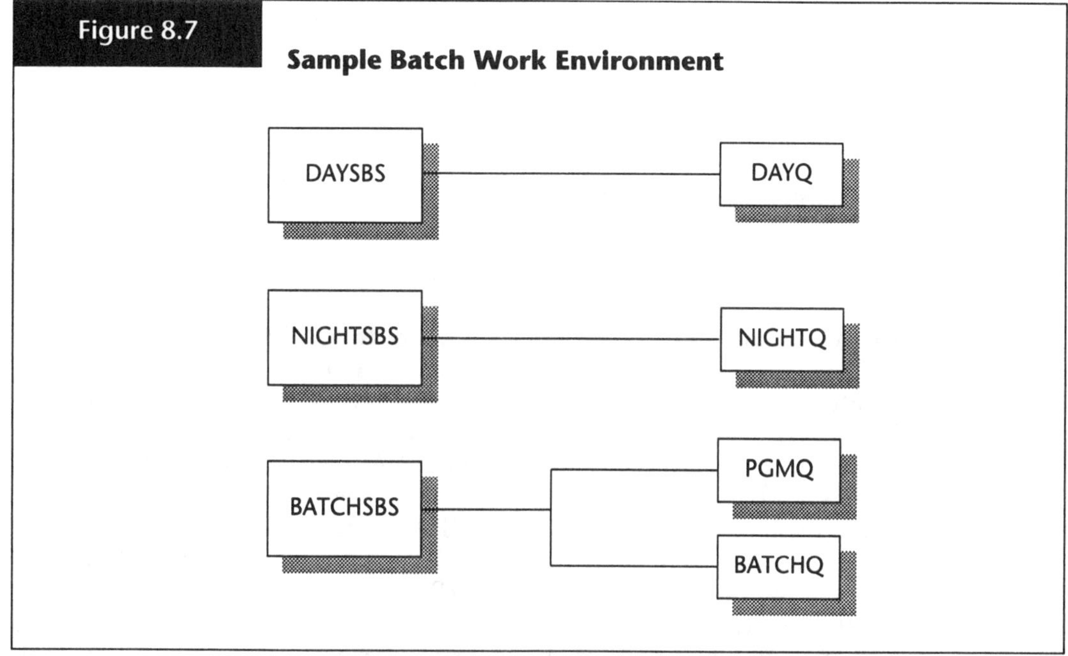

The configuration of NIGHTSBS is similar to the configuration of DAYSBS, except that it lets two jobs process at the same time. This subsystem is inactive during the day and starts at night via the STRSBS (Start Subsystem) command. When a subsystem is inactive, no job queues are allocated and no jobs are processed. Therefore, application programs can send batch jobs to the NIGHTQ job queue, where they wait to process at night. When NIGHTSBS starts, the system allocates job queue NIGHTQ and jobs can be processed.

To show you how job queues can work together to feed into one subsystem, I configured the BATCHSBS subsystem with two job queue entries. Notice that BATCHSBS supports a maximum of three jobs (MAXACT(3)). Job queue entry PGMQ lets one job from that queue be active (MAXACT(1)), while job queue entry BATCHQ lets two jobs be active (MAXACT(2)).

As with workstation entries, job queue entries can conflict if you define the same job queue as an entry for more than one subsystem. When a subsystem starts, the job queues defined in the job queue entries are allocated. And when a job queue is allocated to an active subsystem, that job queue cannot be allocated to another subsystem until the first subsystem ends. In other words, first come, first served...or first come, first queued!

Communications Entries

After you establish a workstation and a physical connection between remote sites, you need a *communications entry*, which enables the subsystem to process the program start request. If there are no communications entries, the system rejects any program start request. There's no real pizazz to this entry; you simply need it to link the remote system with your subsystem.

A communications entry has the following attributes:

- DEV (name or type of communications device)
- RMTLOCNAME (remote location name)
- JOBD (job description name)
- DFTUSR (default user profile name)
- MODE (mode description name)
- MAXACT (maximum number of jobs active with this entry)

The DEV attribute specifies the particular device (e.g., COMMDEV or REMSYS) or device type (e.g., *APPC) needed for communications. The RMTLOCNAME attribute specifies the remote location name you define when you use the CRTDEVxxxx command to create the communications device. There is no default for the DEV or the RMTLOCNAME attribute. As with the WRKSTNTYPE and WRKSTN attributes, you must specify one or the other, but not both.

The next two attributes, JOBD and DFTUSR, are crucial. JOBD specifies the job description to associate with this entry. As you do with the workstation entry, you should use the default value *USRPRF to ensure that a user profile is used and that the system uses the job description associated with the user making the program start request. As with workstation entries, using a specific job description can cause a security problem if that job description names a default user. DFTUSR defines the default user for the communications entry. You should specify *NONE for this attribute to ensure that any program start request supplies a valid user profile and password.

The MODE attribute defines specific communications boundaries and variables. For more information about the MODE attribute, see the CRTMODD (Create Mode Description) command description in IBM's *Control Language Reference (SC41-0030)*.

The MAXACT attribute defines the maximum number of program start requests that can be active at any time in the subsystem for this communications entry.

You can add a communications entry by using the ADDCMNE (Add Communications Entry) command, as in the following example:

```
ADDCMNE SBSD(COMMSBS) RMTLOCNAME(NEWYORK) JOBD(*USRPRF)       +
        DFTUSR(*NONE) MODE(*ANY) MAXACT(*NOMAX)
```

If you are communicating already and you want to know what entries are configured, use the DSPSBSD (Display Subsystem Description) command to find out.

Prestart Job Entries

The *prestart job entry* goes hand-in-hand with the communications entry, telling the subsystem which program to start when the subsystem itself is started. The program does not execute — the system simply performs all the opens and initializes the job named in the prestart job entry and then waits for a program start request for that particular program. When the system receives a program start request, it starts a job by using the prestart program that is ready and waiting, thus saving valuable time in program initialization.

The prestart job entry is the only work entry that defines an actual program and job class to be used. (Other jobs get their initial routing program from the routing data entries that are part of the subsystem description.) The two key attributes of the prestart job entry are PGM and JOBD. The PGM attribute specifies the program to use and the JOBD attribute specifies the job description to be used.

To add a prestart job entry, use an ADDPJE (Add Prestart Job Entry) command similar to the following:

```
ADDPJE SBSD(COMMSBS) PGM(OEPGM) JOBD(OEJOBD)
```

Then, when the communications entry receives a program start request (an EVOKE) and processes the request, it will compare the program evoke to the prestart job program defined. In this case, if the program evoke is also OEPGM, the system has no need to start a job because the prestart job is already started.

Autostart Job Entry

An *autostart job entry* specifies the job to be executed when the subsystem starts. For instance, if you want to print a particular history report each time the system is IPLed, you can add the following autostart job entry to the controlling subsystem description:

```
ADDAJE SBSD(sbs_name) JOB(HISTORY) JOBD(MYLIB/HISTJOBD)
```

The JOB and JOBD attributes are the only ones the autostart job entry defines, which means that the job description must use the request data or routing data to execute a command or a program. In the example above, HISTJOBD would have the correct RQSDTA (Request Data) attribute to call the program that generates the history report (e.g., RQSDTA('call histpgm')). The job HISTORY, defined in the autostart job entry, starts each time the associated subsystem starts, ensuring that the job runs whether or not anyone remembers to submit it.

OS/400 uses an autostart job entry to assist the IPL process. When you examine either the QBASE or QCTL subsystem description (using the DSPSBSD command), you will find that an autostart job entry exists to submit the QSTRUPJD job using the job description QSYS/QSTRUPJD. This job description uses the request data to call a program used in the IPL process.

One reminder. If you decide to create or modify the system-supplied work management objects such as subsystem descriptions and job queues, you should place the new objects in a user-defined library. When you are ready to start using your new objects, you can change the system startup program QSYS/QSTRUP to use your new objects for establishing your work environment (to change the system startup program, you modify the CL source and recompile the program). By having your new objects in your own library, you can easily document any changes.

Routing Entries

So far, I have explained how jobs are defined and started on the AS/400. We've seen that jobs are processed in a subsystem, which is where the system combines all the resources needed to process work. And we've seen how work entries control how jobs gain access to the subsystem. Now we need to talk about routing, which determines how jobs are processed after they reach the subsystem. I am constantly surprised by the number of AS/400 programmers who have never fully examined routing. In fact, it's almost as though routing is some secret whose meaning is known by only a few. Here, I will prove to you, once and for all, that you have nothing to fear!

The AS/400 uses routing to determine where jobs go. To understand routing, it might help to think of street signs, which control the flow of traffic from one place to another. The AS/400 uses the following routing concepts to process each and every job:

- *Routing data* — A character string, up to 80 characters long, that determines the routing entry the subsystem will use to establish the routing step.
- *Routing entry* — A subsystem description entry, which you create, that determines the program and job class the subsystem will use to establish a routing step.
- *Routing step* — The processing that starts when the routing program executes.

To execute in a subsystem, AS/400 jobs must have routing data. Routing data determines which routing entry the subsystem will use. For most jobs, routing data is defined by either the RTGDTA (Routing Data) parameter of the job description associated with the job or by the RTGDTA parameter of the SBMJOB (Submit Job) command. Now let's look at each of these job types to see how routing data is defined for each.

Routing Data for Interactive Jobs

Users gain access to a given subsystem for interactive jobs via workstations, defined by workstation entries. The key to determining routing data for an interactive job is the JOBD (Job Description) parameter of the workstation entry that the subsystem uses to allocate the workstation being used. If the value for the JOBD parameter is *USRPRF, the routing data defined on the job description associated with the user profile is used as the routing data for the interactive job. If the value of the JOBD parameter of the workstation entry is *SBSD (which instructs the system to use the job description that has the same name as the subsystem description) or an actual job description name, the routing data of the specified job description will be used as the routing data for the interactive job. Let me give you a couple examples.

Let's say you create a user profile using the CRTUSRPRF (Create User Profile) command and do not enter a specific job description. The system uses QDFTJOBD (the default job description) for that user profile. Executing DSPJOBD QDFTJOBD reveals that the RTGDTA attribute has a value of

'QCMDI'. When a user signs on to a workstation that uses a subsystem workstation entry where *USRPRF is defined as the JOBD attribute, the routing data for that interactive job would be the routing data defined on the job description associated with the user profile; in this case, the JOBD would be QDFTJOBD, and the routing data would be 'QCMDI'.

Now look at Figure 8.8, in which the workstation entry defines SPJOBD as the job description. Instead of using the job description associated with the user profile, the subsystem uses the SPJOBD job description to establish job attributes, including the RTGDTA value of 'SPECIAL'.

Routing Data for Batch Jobs

Establishing routing data for a batch job is simple; you use the RTGDTA parameter of the SBMJOB (Submit Job) command. The RTGDTA parameter on this command has four possible values:

- JOBD — the routing data of the job description.
- RQSDTA — the value specified in the RQSDTA (Request Data) parameter on the SBMJOB command. (Because the request data represents the actual command or program to process, specifying *RQSDTA is practical only if specific routing entries have been established in a subsystem to start specific routing steps based on the command or program being executed by a job.)

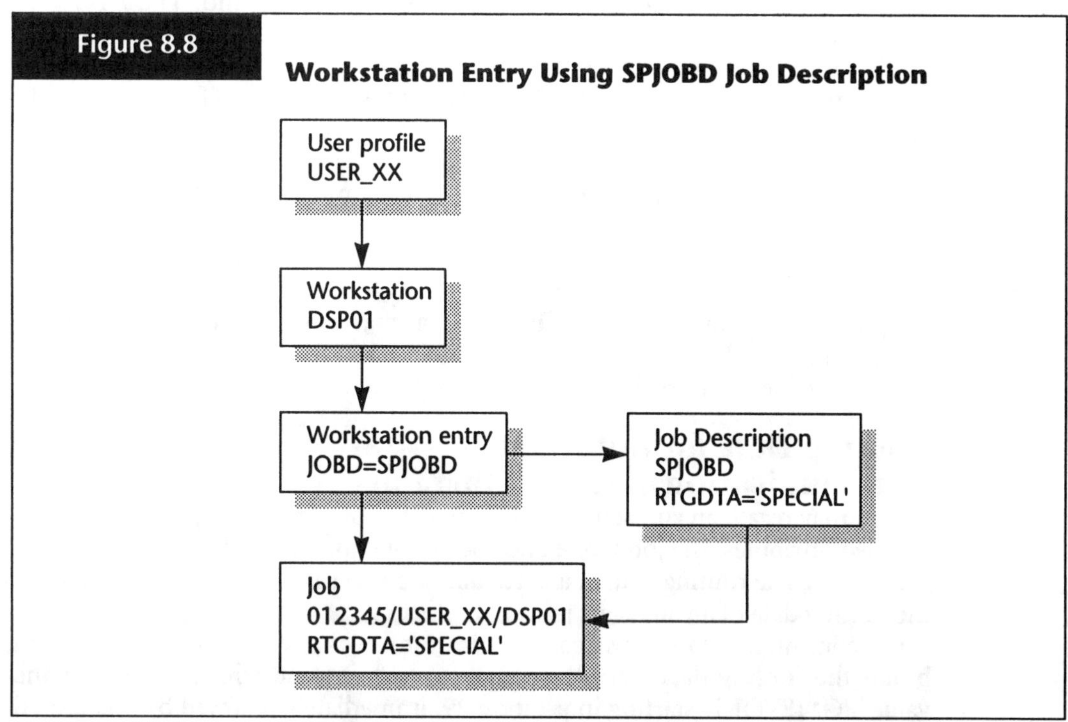

Figure 8.8 Workstation Entry Using SPJOBD Job Description

- QCMDB — the default routing data used by the IBM-supplied subsystems QBASE or QBATCH to route batch jobs to the CL processor QCMD (more on this later).
- 'routing-data' — up to 80 characters of user-defined routing data.

Keeping these values in mind, let's look at a SBMJOB command. To submit a batch job that sends the operator the message "hi," you would enter the command

```
SBMJOB JOB(MESSAGE) CMD('SNDMSG"hi" TOMSGQ(QSYSOPR)')
```

This batch job would use the routing data of 'QCMDB'. How do I know that? Because, as I stated above, the value 'QCMDB' is the default. If you submit a job using the SBMJOB command without modifying the default value for the RTGDTA parameter, the routing data is always 'QCMDB' — as long as this default has not been changed via the CHGCMDDFT (Change Command Default) command.

Now examine the following SBMJOB command:

```
SBMJOB JOB(PRIORITY) CMD('call user-pgm')                          +
       RTGDTA('high-priority')
```

In this example, a routing data character string ('high-priority') is defined. By now you are probably wondering just how modifying the routing data might change the way a job is processed. We'll get to that in a minute.

Figure 8.9 provides an overview of how the routing data for a batch job is established. A user submits a job via the SBMJOB command. The RTGDTA parameter of the SBMJOB command determines the routing data, and the resulting job (012345/USER_XX/job_name) is submitted to process in a subsystem. We can pick any of the four possible values for the RTGDTA attribute on the SBMJOB command and follow the path to see how that value eventually determines the routing data for the submitted batch job.

If you specify RTGDTA(*JOBD), the system examines the JOBD parameter of the SBMJOB command and then uses either the user profile's job description or the actual job description named in the parameter. If you define the RTGDTA parameter as *RQSDTA, the job uses the value specified in the RQSDTA (Request Data) parameter of the SBMJOB command as the routing data. Finally, if you define the RTGDTA parameter as 'QCMDB' or any user-defined routing data, that value becomes the routing data for the job.

Routing Data for Autostart, Communications, and Prestart Jobs

As you may recall, an autostart job entry in the subsystem description consists of just two attributes: the job name and the specific job description to be used for processing. The routing data of a particular job description is the only source for the routing data of an autostart job.

For communications jobs (communications evoke requests), the subsystem builds the routing data from the program start request, which always has the value 'PGMEVOKE' starting in position 29, immediately followed by the desired program name. The routing data is not taken from a permanent object on the AS/400, but is instead derived from the program start request that the communications entry in the subsystem receives and processes.

Prestart jobs use no routing data. The prestart job entry attribute, PGM, specifies the program to start in the subsystem. The processing of this program *is* the routing step for that job.

The Importance of Routing Data

When a job enters a subsystem, the subsystem looks for routing data that matches the compare value in one or more routing entries of the subsystem description — similar to the way you would check your written directions to see which highway exit to take. The subsystem seeks a match to determine which program to use to establish the routing step for that job. Routing entries, typically defined when you create a subsystem, are defined as part of the subsystem description via the ADDRTGE (Add Routing Entry) command. Before we take a closer look at the various attributes of a routing entry, let me explain how routing entries relate to routing data.

Figure 8.9

Method for Determining Batch Job Routing Data

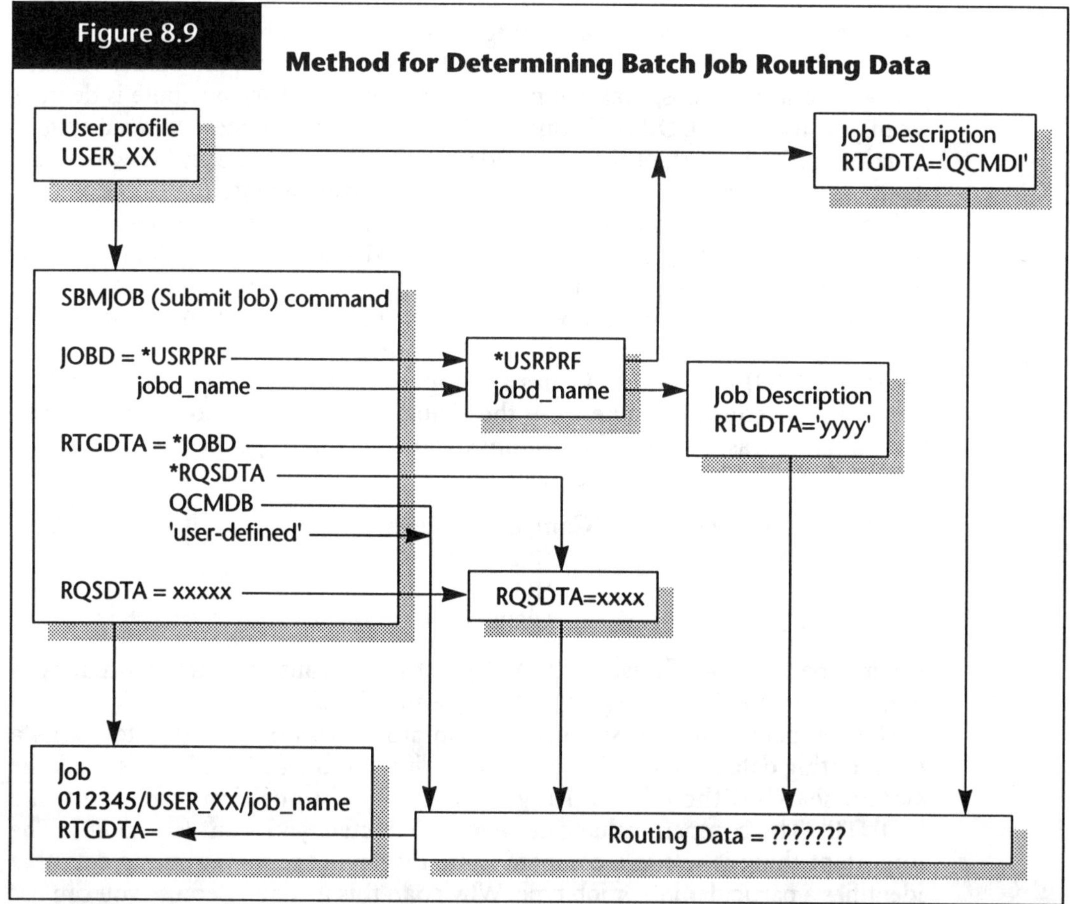

Figure 8.10 shows how the subsystem uses routing data for an interactive job. When USER_XX signs on to workstation DSP01, the interactive job is started, and the routing data ('QCMDI') is established. When the job enters the subsystem, the system compares the routing data in the job to the routing data of each routing entry until it finds a match. (The search is based on the starting position specified in the routing entry and the literal specified as the compare value.)

In Figure 8.10, the compare value for the first routing entry (SEQNBR(10)) and the routing data for job 012345/USER_XX/DSP01 are the same. Because the system has found a match, it executes the program defined in the routing entry (QCMD in library QSYS) to establish the routing step for the job in the subsystem. In addition to establishing the routing step, the routing entry also provides the job with specific runtime attributes based on the job class specified. In this case, the specified class is QINTER.

Jobs that require routing data (all but prestart jobs) follow this same procedure when being started in the subsystem. Now that you have the feel of how this process works, let's talk about routing entries and associated job classes.

Previously I said that routing entries identify which programs to call, define which storage pool the job will be processed in, and specify the execution attributes the job will use for processing. As shown in Figure 8.10, a routing entry consists of a number of attributes: sequence number, compare value, starting position, program, class, maximum active, and pool ID. Each attribute is defined when you use the ADDRTGE command to add a routing entry to a subsystem description. It's important that you understand these attributes and how you can use them to create the routing entries you need for your subsystems.

The sequence number is simply a basic numbering device that determines the order in which routing entries will be compared against routing data to find a match. When assigning a sequence number, you need to remember two rules. First, always use the compare value *ANY with SEQNBR(9999) so it will be used only when no other match can be found. (Notice that routing entry SEQNBR(9999) in Figure 8.10 has a compare value of *ANY.) Second, when using similar compare values, use the sequence numbers to order the values from most to least specific. For example, you would arrange the values 'PGMR', 'PGMRS', AND 'PGMRS1' this way:

Sequence Number	Compare Value
10	'PGMRS1'
20	'PGMRS'
30	'PGMR'

Placing the least specific value ('PGMR') first would cause a match to occur even when the intended value (e.g., 'PGMRS1') is more specific.

The compare value and starting position attributes work together to search a job's routing data for a match. For example, if the value ('ROUTE' 5) is used, the system searches the job's routing data starting in position 5 for the value 'ROUTE'. The compare value can be any characters you want (up to 80). The important thing is to use a compare value that matches some routing data that identifies a particular job or job type. Why go to this trouble? Because you can use

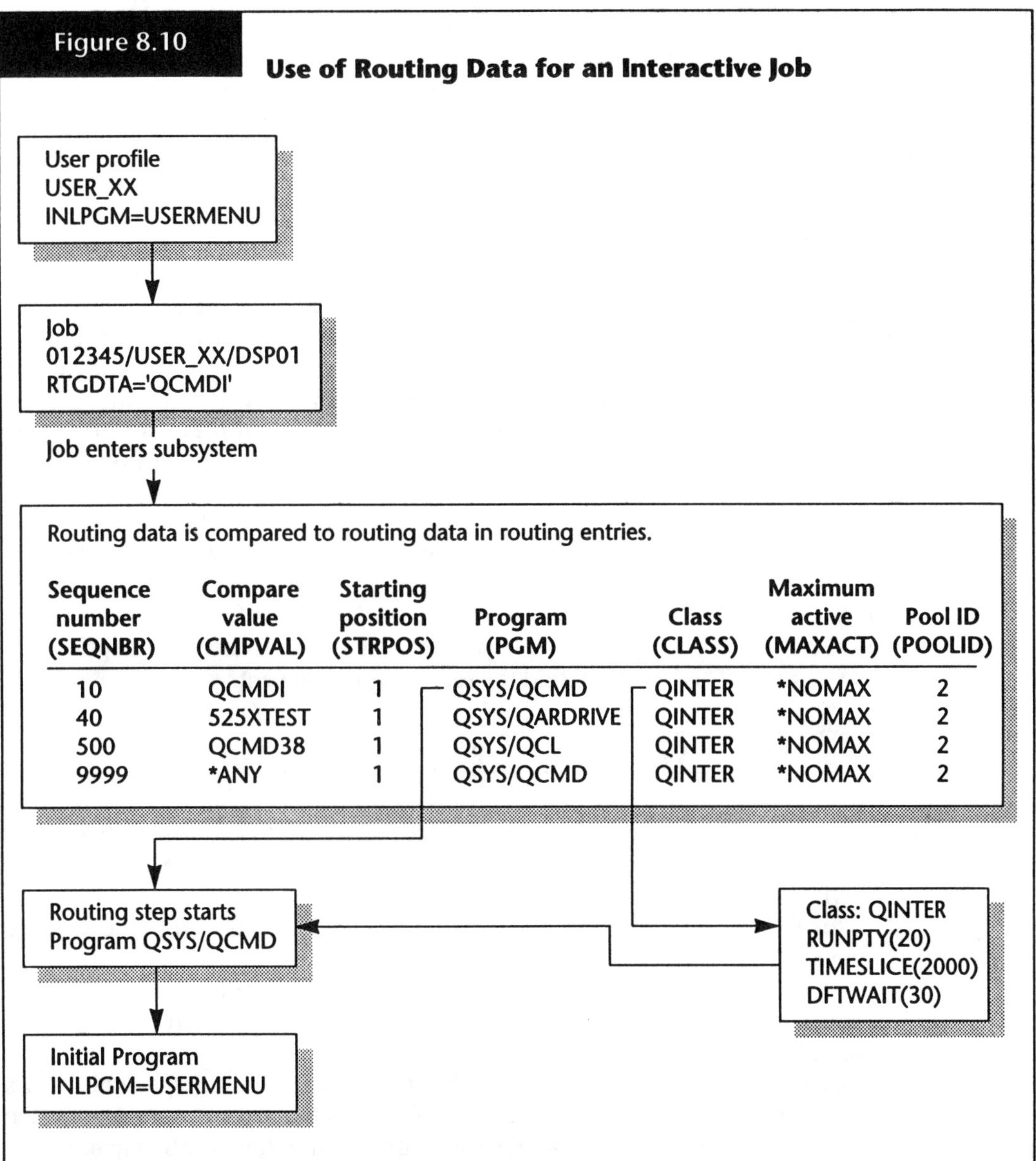

this matching routing entry to determine a lot about the way a job is processed on the system (e.g., subsystem storage pool, run priority, and time slice).

The PGM attribute determines what program is called to establish the routing step for the job being processed. Remember, a routing step simply starts the program named in the routing entry. Normally, this program is QCMD (the IBM CL processor), but it can be any program. When QCMD is the routing program, it waits for a request message to process. For an interactive job, the request message would be the initial program or menu request; for a batch job, it would be the request data (i.e., the command or program to execute). If the routing program is a user-defined program, the program simply executes. The routing entry program is the first program executed in the routing step. The routing entry can be used to make sure that a specific program is executed when certain routing data is found, regardless of the initial program or specific request data for a job. Later in this chapter, I explain how this might be beneficial to you.

Runtime Attributes

The CLASS (job class) is an important performance-related object that defines the run priority of the job, as well as the time slice for a job. (The time slice is the length of time, in CPU milliseconds, a job will process before being bumped from the activity level to wait while another job executes a time slice.) A routing entry establishes a job's run priority and time slice much the way speed limit or yield signs control the flow of traffic. For more information on these performance-related attributes of the CLASS object, see IBM's *Work Management Guide (SC41-8078).*

In Figure 8.10, all the routing entries use class QINTER, which is defined to represent the run priority and time slice typical for an interactive job. Because you would not want to process a batch job using these same values, the system also has an IBM-supplied class, called QBATCH, that defines attributes more typical for batch job processing. If you look at the subsystem description for QBASE or QBATCH, you will find the following routing entry:

Sequence Number	Compare Value	Program	Class
1Ø	'QCMDB'	QSYS/QCMD	QBATCH

This entry uses program QCMD and directs the system to use class QBATCH to define the runtime attributes for jobs having routing data 'QCMDB'. To route jobs with the correct routing program and job class, the system-supplied routing data for the default batch job description QBATCH is 'QCMDB'. You can use different classes to create the right performance mix.

MAXACT determines the maximum number of active jobs that can use a particular routing entry. You will rarely need to change this attribute's default (*NOMAX).

The last routing entry attribute is the POOLID (subsystem storage pool ID). As I explained earlier, the subsystem definition includes the specific storage pools the subsystem will use. These storage pools are numbered in the subsystem, and these numbers are used only within that particular subsystem description; they do not match the numbering scheme of the system pools. The routing entry attribute POOLID tells the system which subsystem storage pool to use for processing this job. Look at the following pool definition and abbreviated routing entry:

Pool Definition:

```
((1 *BASE) (2 1ØØØØ 2Ø))
```

Sequence Number	Compare Value	Pool ID
1Ø	'QCMDI'	1

This routing entry tells the system to use subsystem pool number 1 (*BASE). Considering that 10,000 K of storage is set aside in pool number 2, this routing entry is probably incorrectly specifying pool number 1. Beginners commonly make the mistake of leaving the default value in the routing entry definition when creating their own subsystems and defining their own routing entries. Just remember to compare the pool definition with the routing entry definition to ensure that the correct subsystem pool is being used.

Is There More Than One Way to Get There?

So far, we've discussed how routing data is created, how routing entries are established to search for that routing data, and how routing entries establish a routing step for a job and control specific runtime attributes of a job.

Now for one more hurdle... A job can have more than one routing step. But why would you want it to? One reason might be to use a new class to change the runtime attributes of the job.

After a job is started, you can reroute it using the RRTJOB (Reroute Job) command or transfer it to another subsystem using the TFRJOB (Transfer Job) command. Both commands have the RTGDTA parameter, which lets you modify the job's current routing data to establish a new routing step. Suppose you issue the following command during the execution of a job:

```
RRTJOB RTGDTA('FASTER') RQSDTA(*NONE)
```

Your job would be rerouted in the same subsystem but use the value 'FASTER' as the value to be compared in the routing entries.

Do-It-Yourself Routing

To reinforce your understanding of routing and tie together some of the facts you've learned about work management, consider the following example.

Let's say you want to place programmers, OfficeVision/400 (OV/400) users, and general end users in certain subsystems based on their locations or functions. You need to do more than just separate the workstations; you need to separate the users, no matter what workstation they are using at the time. Figures 8.11 through 8.16 describe the objects and attributes needed to define such an environment.

Figure 8.11 lists three job descriptions that have distinct routing data. User-defined INTERJOBD has 'QINTER' as the routing data. OFFICEJOBD and PGMRJOBD have 'QOFFICE' and 'QPGMR' specified, respectively, as their routing data. (Note that the routing data need not match the job description name.) To enable users to work in separate subsystems, you first need to create or modify their user profiles and supply the appropriate job description based on the subsystem in which each user should work. In our example, general end users would have INTERJOBD, OV/400 users would have OFFICEJOBD, and programmers would have the job description PGMRJOBD.

Next, you must build subsystem descriptions that use the routing entries associated with the job descriptions. Figure 8.12 shows some sample subsystem definitions. All three subsystems use the WRKSTNTYPE (workstation type) entry with the value *ALL. However, only the workstation entry in QINTER uses

Figure 8.11

Sample Job Descriptions

Job Descriptions

```
INTERJOBD...RTGDTA('QINTER')
OFFICEJOBD...RTGDTA('QOFFICE')
PGMRJOBD...RTGDTA('QPGMR')
```

Note: Only the RTGDTA parameter of the job descriptions is addressed for the purpose of this example. You will need to supply the desired values for the remaining parameters on the CRTJOBD (Create Job Description) command. One easy way to establish these job descriptions is to use the CRTDUPOBJ (Create Duplicate Object) command to duplicate the QDFTJOBD job description and then simply change the routing entry.

the AT(*SIGNON) entry to tell the subsystem to allocate the workstations. This means that subsystem QINTER allocates *all* workstations, and QOFFICE and QPGMR (both with AT(*ENTER)) only allocate workstations as jobs are transferred *into* those subsystems. Also, notice that each workstation entry defines JOBD(*USRPRF) so that the routing data from the job descriptions of the user profiles will be the routing data for the job.

After a user signs on to a workstation in subsystem QINTER, the routing entries do all the work. The first routing entry looks for the compare value 'QOFFICE'. When it finds 'QOFFICE', program QOFFICE in library SYSLIB is called to establish the routing step. In Figure 8.13, program QOFFICE simply executes the TFRJOB command to transfer this particular job into subsystem QOFFICE. However, if you look carefully at Figure 8.13, you will see that the TFRJOB command also modifies the routing data to become 'QCMDI', so that when the job enters subsystem QOFFICE, routing data 'QCMDI' matches the corresponding routing entry and uses program QCMD and class QOFFICE. If an error occurs on the TFRJOB command, the MONMSG CPF0000 EXEC(RRTJOB RTGDTA('QCMDI')) command reroutes the job in the current subsystem. Figure 8.14 shows how class QOFFICE might be created to provide the performance differences needed for OV/400 users.

Look again at Figure 8.12. The next routing entry in the QINTER subsystem looks for compare value 'QPGMR'. When it finds 'QPGMR', it calls program QPGMR (Figure 8.15) to transfer the job into subsystem QPGMR. Routing data 'QCMDI' calls program QCMD and then processes the initial program or menu of the user profile. The same is true for routing data *ANY.

In our example, subsystems QOFFICE and QPGMR use similar routing entries to make sure each job enters the correct subsystem. Notice that each subsystem has a routing entry that searches for 'QINTER'. If this compare value is found, program QINTER (Figure 8.16) is called to transfer the job into subsystem QINTER.

As intimidating as they may at first appear, routing entries are really plain and simple. Basically, you can use them to intercept jobs as they enter the subsystem and then control the jobs using various run-time variables. I strongly recommend that you take the time to learn how your system uses routing entries.

Figure 8.12

Sample Subsystem Descriptions

QINTER - General end user subsystem

Workstation entries

```
WRKSTNTYPE(*ALL)  JOBD(*USRPRF) AT(*SIGNON) MAXACT(*NOMAX)
```

Job queue entries

```
JOBQ(QINTER) SEQNBR(10) MAXACT(*NOMAX)
```

Routing entries

```
SEQNBR(10)     CMPVAL('QOFFICE') PGM(SYSLIB/QOFFICE) CLASS(QINTER)
SEQNBR(20)     CMPVAL('QPGMR')   PGM(SYSLIB/QPGMR)   CLASS(QINTER)
SEQNBR(30)     CMPVAL('QCMDI')   PGM(QSYS/QCMD)      CLASS(QINTER)
SEQNBR(9999)   CMPVAL(*ANY)      PGM(QSYS/QCMD)      CLASS(QINTER)
```

QOFFICE - OV/400 end-user subsystem

Workstation entries

```
WRKSTNTYPE(*ALL)  JOBD(*USRPRF) AT(*ENTER)  MAXACT(*NOMAX)
```

Job queue entries

```
JOBQ(QOFFICE) SEQNBR(10) MAXACT(*NOMAX)
```

Routing entries

```
SEQNBR(10)     CMPVAL('QINTER') PGM(SYSLIB/QINTER) CLASS(QOFFICE)
SEQNBR(20)     CMPVAL('QPGMR')  PGM(SYSLIB/QPGMR)  CLASS(QOFFICE)
SEQNBR(30)     CMPVAL('QCMDI')  PGM(QSYS/QCMD)     CLASS(QOFFICE)
SEQNBR(9999)   CMPVAL(*ANY)     PGM(QSYS/QCMD)     CLASS(QOFFICE)
```

QPGMR - Programmer subsystem

Workstation entries

```
WRKSTNTYPE(*ALL)  JOBD(*USRPRF) AT(*ENTER)  MAXACT(*NOMAX)
```

Job queue entries

```
JOBQ(QPGMR) SEQNBR(10) MAXACT(*NOMAX)
```

Routing entries

```
SEQNBR(10)     CMPVAL('QINTER')  PGM(SYSLIB/QINTER)  CLASS(QPGMR)
SEQNBR(20)     CMPVAL('QOFFICE') PGM(SYSLIB/QOFFICE) CLASS(QPGMR)
SEQNBR(30)     CMPVAL('QCMDI')   PGM(QSYS/QCMD)      CLASS(QPGMR)
SEQNBR(9999)   CMPVAL(*ANY)      PGM(QSYS/QCMD)      CLASS(QPGMR)
```

Start by studying subsystem descriptions to learn what each routing entry controls. Once you understand them, you will find that you can use routing entries as solutions to numerous work management problems.

Figure 8.13

Source for Program QOFFICE

```
/*--------------------------------------------------------------------*/
/* Program: QOFFICE                                                   */
/* Purpose: To transfer general users into QOFFICE subsystem with    */
/*          QCMDI routing data.                                       */
/*--------------------------------------------------------------------*/

 PGM

/* Transfer any job using this program to QOFFICE subsystem */
 TFRJOB JOBQ(QOFFICE) RTGDTA('QCMDI')

/* If error occurs, simply reroute job in current subsystem */
 MONMSG CPF0000 EXEC(RRTJOB RTGDTA('QCMDI'))

 ENDPGM
```

Figure 8.14

Sample CLASS Object Definitions

```
QINTER      RUNPTY(20)
            TIMESLICE(2000)
            DFTWAIT(30)
            TEXT('general interactive user job class')

QOFFICE     RUNPTY(21)
            TIMESLICE(3000)
            DFTWAIT(30)
            TEXT('OV/400 user job class')

QPGMR       RUNPTY(20)
            TIMESLICE(2500)
            DFTWAIT(30)
            TEXT('programmer job class')
```

Note: These are only sample values for RUNPTY, TIMESLICE, and DFTWAIT. When configuring for your system, you should research these parameters to determine the values that best suit your environment.

Figure 8.15

Source for Program QPGMR

```
/*==================================================================*/
/* Program: QPGMR                                                   */
/* Purpose: To transfer general users into QPGMR subsystem with     */
/*          QCMDI routing data.                                     */
/*==================================================================*/

 PGM

/* Transfer any job using this program to QPGMR subsystem */
 TFRJOB JOBQ(QPGMR) RTGDTA('QCMDI')

/* If error occurs, simply reroute job in current subsystem */
 MONMSG CPF0000 EXEC(RRTJOB RTGDTA('QCMDI'))

 ENDPGM
```

Figure 8.16

Source for Program QINTER

```
/*==================================================================*/
/* Program: QINTER                                                  */
/* Purpose: To transfer general users into QINTER subsystem with    */
/*          QCMDI routing data.                                     */
/*==================================================================*/

 PGM

/* Transfer any job using this program to QINTER subsystem */
 TFRJOB JOBQ(QINTER) RTGDTA('QCMDI')

/* If error occurs, simply reroute job in current subsystem */
 MONMSG CPF0000 EXEC(RRTJOB RTGDTA('QCMDI'))

 ENDPGM
```

Chapter 9

Controlling Output

by Wayne Madden

> **With output queues, you can master AS/400 print operations**

Printing. It's one of the most common things any computer does, and it's relatively easy with the AS/400. What complicates this basic task is that the AS/400 provides many functions you can tailor for your printing needs. For example, you can use multiple printers to handle various types of forms. You can use printers that exist anywhere in your configuration — whether the printers are attached to local or remote machines or even to PCs on a LAN. You can let users view, hold, release, or cancel their own output; or you can design your system so their output simply prints on a printer in their area without any operator intervention except to change and align the forms.

The cornerstone for all this capability is the AS/400 output queue. Understanding how to create and use output queues can help you master AS/400 print operations.

What Is an Output Queue?

An output queue is an object containing a list of spooled files that you can display on a workstation or write to a printer device. (You can also use output queues to write spooled output to a diskette device, but this chapter does not cover that function.) The AS/400 object type identifier for the output queue is *OUTQ.

Figure 9.1 shows the AS/400 display you get on a workstation when you enter the WRKOUTQ (Work with Output Queue) command for the output queue QPRINT. As the figure shows, the Work with Output Queue display lists each spooled file that exists on the queue you specify. For each spooled file, the display also shows the spooled file name, the user of the job that created the spooled file, the user data identifier, the status of that spooled file on the queue, the number of pages in the spooled file, the number of copies requested, the form type, and that spooled file's output priority (which is defined in the job that generates the spooled file). You can use function key F11=View 2 to view additional information (e.g., job name and number) about each spooled file entry.

Figure 9.1

Work with Output Queue Panel

```
                         Work with Output Queue

Queue:   QPRINT          Library:   QUSRSYS          Status:   RLS/WTR

Type options, press Enter.
  1=Send   2=Change   3=Hold   4=Delete   5=Display   6=Release   7=Messages
  8=Attributes        9=Work with printing status

Opt  File        User        User Data    Sts    Pages   Copies   Form Type    Pty
 _   QSYSPRT     QSYSOPR                  WTR        1        1   *STD          5
 _   PRINTKEY    QSYSOPR                  HLD        1        1   *STD          5
 _   QQRYPRT     DPJLASK                  HLD       23        2   *STD          5
 _   QPDSPLIB    QSECOFR                  SAV       73        1   *STD          5
 _   ARLIST      ACKWISP                  HLD       25        3   F8X11         5

                                                                            Bottom
Parameters for options 1, 2, 3, or command
===> ____________________________________________________________________________
F3=Exit   F11=View 2   F12=Cancel    F22=Printers    F24=More keys
```

The status of a spooled file can be any of the following:

- `OPN` The spooled file is being written and cannot be printed at this time (i.e., the SCHEDULE parameter of the print file is *FILEEND or *JOBEND.
- `CLO` The file is spooled but unavailable for printing (i.e., the SCHEDULE parameter's value for the print file is *JOBEND).
- `HLD` The file is spooled and on hold in the output queue. You can use option 6 to release the spooled file for printing.
- `RDY` The file is spooled and waiting to be printed when the writer is available. You can use option 3 to hold the spooled file.
- `SAV` The spooled file has been printed and is now saved in the output queue. (The spooled file attribute SAVE has a value of *YES. In contrast, a spooled file with SAVE(*NO) will be removed from the queue after printing.)
- `WTR` The spooled file is being printed. You can still use option 3 to hold the spooled file and stop the printing, and the spooled file will appear on the display as HLD.

I have mentioned two options for spooled files — option 3, which holds spooled files, and option 6, which releases them. The panel in Figure 9.2 lists and explains each option.

Figure 9.2

Output Queue Options

You Select	
`1=Send`	to send a copy of a specified spooled file to someone in your network (local or remote).
`2=Change`	to change some or all the attributes of a spooled file (e.g., changing the OUTQ parameter to a different output queue name by moving the spooled file to a particular queue).
`3=Hold`	to hold a spooled file (if it has a status of RDY or WTR, the spooled file will be held and returned to a HLD status).
`4=Delete`	to delete spooled files you have authority to delete.
`5=Display`	to view spooled data. (When you view spooled files on your workstation, you should keep in mind that the system does not display blank lines. The spacing does not look exactly as it will when printed.)
`6=Release`	to release a spooled file for printing.
`7=Messages`	to work with any messages pending for a spooled file.
`8=Attributes`	to display spooled file attributes.
`9=Work with printing status`	to work with the current printing status of a spooled file.

How to Create Output Queues

Now that we've seen that output queues contain spooled files and let you perform actions on them, we can focus on creating output queues. The most common way output queues are created is through a printer device description. Yes, you read correctly! When you create a printer device description using the CRTDEVPTR (Create Device Description (Printer)) command or through autoconfiguration, the system automatically creates an output queue in library QUSRSYS by the same name as that assigned to that printer. This output queue is the default for that printer. In fact, the system places "Default output queue for PRINTER_NAME" in the output queue's TEXT attribute.

An alternative method is to use the CRTOUTQ (Create Output Queue) command. The parameter values for this command determine attributes for the output queue. When you use the CRTOUTQ command, after entering the name of the output queue and of the library in which you want that queue to exist, you are presented with two categories of parameters — the procedural ones (i.e., SEQ, JOBSEP, and TEXT) and those with security implications (i.e., DSPDTA, OPRCTL, AUTCHK, and AUT). For a look at some of the parameters you can use, see the CRTOUTQ panel in Figure 9.3.

The first of the procedural parameters, SEQ, controls the order of the spooled files on the output queue. You can choose values of either *FIFO (first in, first out) or *JOBNBR. If you select *FIFO, the system places new spooled files on the

Figure 9.3

Create Output Queue Panel

```
                    Create Output Queue (CRTOUTQ)

Type choice, press Enter.

Output queue . . . . . . . . . . OUTQ       __________
  Library  . . . . . . . . . . .              *CURLIB
Order of files on queue  . . . SEQ          *FIFO
Text 'description' . . . . . . TEXT         *BLANK

__________________

                     Additional Parameters

Display any file . . . . . . . . DSPDTA     *NO
Job separators . . . . . . . . . JOBSEP     0
Operator controlled  . . . . . . OPRCTL     *YES
Authority to check . . . . . . . AUTCHK     *OWNER
Authority  . . . . . . . . . . . AUT        *USE

                                                                  Bottom
F3=Exit   F4=Prompt   F5=Refresh   F12=Cancel   F13=How to use this display
F24=More keys
```

queue following all other entries already on the queue that have the same output priority as the new spooled files (the job description you use during job execution determines the output priority).

Using *FIFO can be tricky because the following changes to an output queue entry cause the system to reshuffle the queue's contents and place the spooled file behind all others of equal priority:

- A change of output priority when you use the CHGJOB (Change Job) or CHGSPLFA (Change Spooled File Attributes) command;
- A change in status from HLD, CLO, or OPN to RDY;
- A change in status from RDY back to HLD, CLO, or OPN.

The other possible value for the SEQ parameter, *JOBNBR, specifies that the system sort queue entries according to their priorities, using the date and time the job that created the spooled file entered the system. I recommend using *JOBNBR instead of *FIFO, because with *JOBNBR you don't have to worry about changes to an output queue entry affecting the order of the queue's contents.

The next procedural parameter is JOBSEP (job separator). You can specify a value from 0 through 9 to indicate the number of job separators (i.e., pages) the system should place at the beginning of each job's output. The job separator contains the job name, the job user's name, the job number, and the date and time the job is run. This information can help in identifying jobs. If you'd rather not use a lot of paper, you can lose the job separator by selecting a value of 0. Or you can enter *MSG for this value, and each time the end of a print job is reached, the system will send a message to the message queue for the writer.

Don't confuse the JOBSEP parameter with the FILESEP (file separator) parameter, which is an attribute of print files. When creating or changing print files, you can specify a value for the FILESEP parameter to control the number of file separators at the beginning of each spooled file. The information on the file separators is similar to that printed on the job separator but includes information about the particular spooled file.

When do you need the file separator, the job separator, or both? You need file separators to help operators separate the various printed reports within a single job. You need job separators to help separate the printed output of various jobs and to quickly identify the end of one report and the beginning of the next. However, if you program a header page for all your reports, job separators are probably wasteful. Another concern is that for output queues that handle only a specific type of form, such as invoices, a separator wastes an expensive form.

In reality, a person looking for a printed report usually pays no attention to separator pages but looks at the first page of the report to identify the contents and destination of the report. And as you can imagine, a combination of file separators and job separators could quickly launch a major paper recycling campaign. If you use both, you'll need to stock up on containers to hold the paper. Understand, I am *not* saying these separators have no function. I *am* saying you should think about how helpful the separators are and explicitly choose the number you need.

The security-related CRTOUTQ command parameters help control user access to particular output queues and particular spooled data. To appreciate the importance of controlling access, remember that you can use output queues not only for printing spooled files but also for displaying them. What good is it to prevent people from watching as payroll checks are printed, if they can simply display the spooled file in the output queue?

The DSPDTA (display data) parameter specifies what kind of access to the output queue is allowed for users who have *READ authority. A value of *YES says that any user with *READ access to the output queue can display, copy, or send the data of any file on the queue. A value of *NO specifies that users with *READ authority to the output queue can display, copy, or send the output data only of their *own* spooled files unless they have some other special authority. (Special authorities that provide additional function are *SPLCTL and *JOBCTL.)

The OPRCTL (operator control) parameter specifies whether or not a user who has *JOBCTL special authority can manage or control the files on an output queue. The values are *YES, which allows control of the queue and provides the ability to change queue entries, or *NO, which blocks this control for users with the *JOBCTL special authority.

It is important to note that Release 3.0 corrects a problem with controlling output queue security. In past releases, when you wanted to let a user start, change, and end writers, the user needed *JOBCTL special authority on his or her user profile. This special authority gave the user spool-control abilities that could bypass some spool file security.

With Release 3.0, a program can adopt a user profile's special authorities. Now, when a user who does not have *JOBCTL special authority needs to start, change, and end writers to the queue, you can write a program to perform such writer functions. The program adopts the authority of a user who has *JOBCTL authority. When the program ends, the user has not adopted *JOBCTL authority and thus cannot take advantage of a security hole.

The AUTCHK (authority check) parameter specifies whether the commands that check the requester's authority to the output queue should check for ownership authority (*OWNER) or for just data authority (*DTAAUT). When the value is *OWNER, the requester must have ownership authority to the output queue to pass the output queue authorization test. When the value is *DTAAUT, the requester must have *READ, *ADD, and *DELETE authority to the output queue.

Finally, the AUT parameter specifies the initial level of authority allowed for *PUBLIC users. You can modify this level of authority by using the EDTOBJAUT (Edit Object Authority), GRTOBJAUT (Grant Object Authority), or RVKOBJAUT (Revoke Object Authority) command.

As you can see, creating output queues requires more than just selecting a name and pressing Enter. Given some appropriate attention, output queues can provide a proper level of procedural (e.g., finding print files and establishing the order of print files) and security (e.g., who can see what data) support.

Who Should Create Output Queues?

Who should create output queues? Although this seems like a simple question, it is important for two reasons: First, the owner can modify the output queue attributes as well as grant/revoke authorities to the output queue, which means the owner controls who can view or work with spooled files on that queue. Second, the AUTCHK parameter checks the ownership of the output queue as part of the authorization test when the output queue is accessed. So ownership is a key to your ability to secure output queues.

Here are a few suggestions. The system operator should be responsible for creating and controlling output queues that hold data considered public or nonsecure. With this ownership and the various authority parameters on the CRTOUTQ command, you can create an environment that lets users control their own print files and print on various printers in their area of work.

For secure data (e.g., payroll, human resources, financial statements), the department supervisor profile (or a similar one) should own the output queue. The person who owns the output queue is responsible for maintaining the security of the output queue and can even explicitly deny access to DP personnel.

How Spooled Files Get on the Queue

It is very important to understand that *all spooled output generated on the AS/400* uses a print file. Whether you enter the DSPLIB (Display Library) command using the OUTPUT(*PRINT) parameter to direct your output to a report, create and execute an AS/400 query, or write a report-generating program, you are going to use a print file to generate that output. A print file is the means to spool output to a file that can be stored on a queue and printed as needed. Also, a print file determines the attributes printed output will have. This means you can create a variety of print files on the system to accommodate various form requirements.

Another essential fact to understand about spooling on the AS/400 is that *all printed output must be placed on an output queue to be printed.* When a job generates a spooled file, that file is placed on an output queue. The output queue is determined by one of two methods — if the print file has a specifically defined output queue or is overridden to a specific output queue, the output from that print file is placed on that specific queue; if the print file does not specifically direct the spool file, it is placed on the output queue currently defined as the output queue for that particular job.

Figure 9.4 illustrates how one job can place spooled files on different output queues. The job first spools the nightly corporate A/R report to an output queue

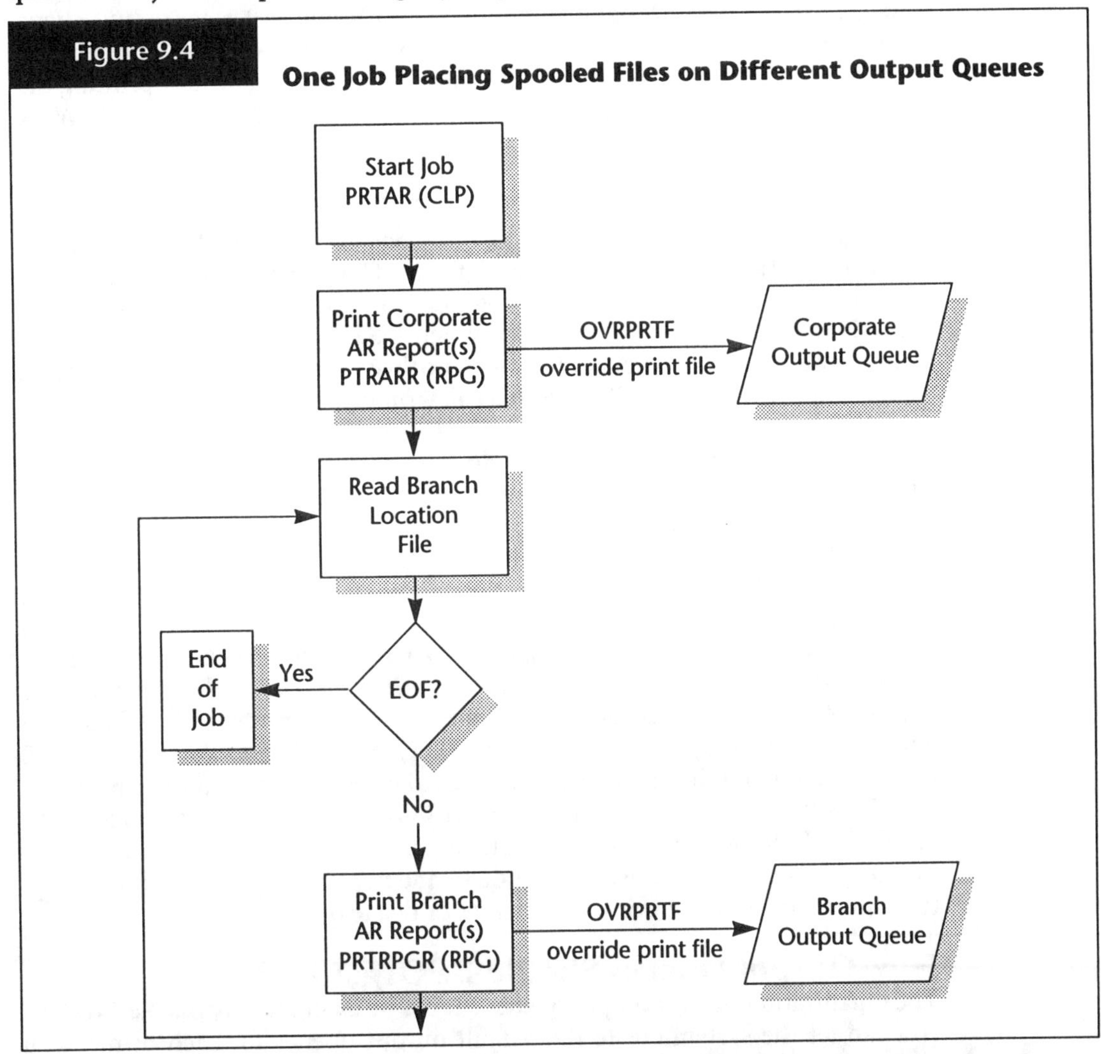

Figure 9.4

One Job Placing Spooled Files on Different Output Queues

at the corporate office. Then the program creates a separate A/R report for each branch office and places the report on the appropriate output queue.

How Spooled Files are Printed from the Queue

So how do the spooled files get printed from the queue? The answer is no secret. You must start (assign) a writer to an output queue. You make spooled files available to the writer by releasing the spooled file, using option 6. You then use the STRPRTWTR (Start Printer Writer) command. The OUTQ parameter on that command determines the output queue to be read by that printer.

When the writer is started to a specific output queue and you use the WRKOUTQ command for that specific output queue, the letters WTR appear in the Status field at the top of the Work with Output Queue display to indicate that a writer is assigned to print available entries in that queue.

You can start a writer for any output queue (only one writer per output queue and only one output queue per writer). You don't have to worry about the name of the writer matching the name of the queue. For instance, to start printing the spooled files in output queue QPRINT, you can execute the STRPRTWTR command

```
STRPRTWTR WRITER(writer_name) OUTQ(QPRINT)
```

(Messages for file control are sent to the message queue defined in the printer's device description unless you also specify the MSGQ parameter.)

When you IPL your system, the program QSTRUP controls whether or not the writers on the system are started. When QSTRUP starts the writers, each printer's device description determines both its output queue and message queue. You can modify QSTRUP to start all writers, to start specific writers, or to control the output queues by using the STRPRTWTR command. After a writer is started, you can redirect the writer to another output queue by using the CHGWTR (Change Writer) command or by ending the writer and restarting it for a different output queue.

To list the writers on your system and the output queues they are started to, type the WRKOUTQ command and press Enter. You will see a display similar to the one in Figure 9.5. You can also use the WRKWTR (Work with Writer) command by typing WRKWTR and pressing Enter to get a display like the one in Figure 9.6.

It is important to understand that *the output queue and the printer are independent objects*, so output queues can exist with no printer assigned and can have entries. The Operational Assistant (OA) product in OS/400 Release 3.0 illustrates some implications of this fact. OA lets you create two output queues (i.e., QUSRSYS/QEZJOBLOG and QUSRSYS/QEZDEBUG) to store job logs and problem-related output, respectively. These output queues are not default queues for any printers. Entries are stored in these queues, and the people who manage the system can decide to print, view, move, or delete them.

How Output Queues Should Be Organized

The organization of your output queues should be as simple as possible. To start, you can let the system create the default output queues for each printer you

Figure 9.5

Work with All Output Queues Panel

```
                    Work with All Output Queues

 Type options, press Enter.
   2=Change   3=Hold   5=Work with   6=Release   8=Description

 Opt    Queue         Library        Files    Writer        Status
  _     PGMROUTQ      QUSRSYS            6    PGMRWTR        RLS
  _     PRT01         QUSRSYS           10    PRT01          RLS
  _     QPRINT        QUSRSYS            0                   RLS
  _     QPJOBLOG      QUSRSYS           75                   HLD
  _     TAAOUTQ       QUSRSYS            2                   RLS

                                                                  Bottom
 Command
 ===> ____________________________________________________________________
 F3=Exit   F4=Prompt   F5=Refresh   F12=Cancel   F24=More keys
```

Figure 9.6

Work with All Printers Panel

```
                       Work with All Printers

 Type options, press Enter.
   1=Start   2=Change   4=End   5=Work with   6=Release
   7=Display messages   8=Work with output queue

 Opt  Device     Sts   Sep    Form Type   File       User       User Data
  _   ACCTWTR    END
  _   PGMRWTR    STR   *FILE  *ALL
  _   PRT01      STR   *FILE  *ALL        ARCP010    AC01RLM

                                                                  Bottom
 Command
 ===> ____________________________________________________________________
 F3=Exit   F11=View 2   F12=Cancel   F17=Top   F18=Bottom   F24=More keys
```

create. Of course, you may want to modify ownership and some output queue attributes. At this point, you can send output to an output queue and there will be a printer assigned to print from that queue.

How can you use output queues effectively? Each installation must discover its own answer, but I can give you a few ideas. If your installation generates relatively few reports, having one output queue per available printer is the most efficient way to use output queues.

Installations that generate large volumes of printed output need to control when and where these reports might be printed. For example, a staff of programmers might share a single printer. If you spool all compiled programs to the same queue and make them available to the writer, things could jam up fast; and important reports might get delayed behind compile listings being printed just because they were spooled to a queue with a writer. A better solution is to create an output queue for each programmer. Each programmer can then use a job description to route printed output to his or her own queue. When a programmer decides to print a spooled file, he or she moves that file to the output queue with the shared writer active. This means that the only reports printed are those specifically wanted. Also, you can better schedule printing of a large number of reports.

What about the operations department? Is it wise to have one output queue (e.g., QPRINT or PRT01) to hold all the spooled files that nightly, daily, and monthly jobs generate? You should probably spend a few minutes planning for a better implementation.

I recommend you do not assign any specific output to PRT01. You should create specific output queues to hold specific types of spooled files. For instance, if you have a nightly job that generates sales, billing, and posting reports, you might consider having either one or three output queues to hold those specific files. When the operations staff is ready to print the spooled files in an output queue, they can use the CHGWTR command to make the writer available to that output queue. Another method is to move the spooled files into an output queue with a printer already available. This method lets you browse the queue to determine whether or not the reports were generated and lets you print these files at your convenience.

For some end users, you may want to make the output queue invisible. You can direct requested printed output to an output queue with an available writer in the work area of the end user who made the request. Long reports should be generated and printed only at night. The only things the user should have to do are change or add paper and answer a few messages.

What a mountain of information! And I've only discussed a few concepts for managing output queues. But this information should be enough to get you started and on your way to mastering output queues.

Chapter 10

Journal Management

by Paul Conte

Use journal management to recover critical data in AS/400 files

If a hardware or software malfunction damages an AS/400 physical file that an on-line application uses, you must be able to restore the file to the last valid state before the failure occurred. You can use the save commands — SAVCHGOBJ (Save Changed Object), SAVLIB (Save Library), or SAVOBJ (Save Object) — to make a tape or diskette copy of a physical file, and you can use this copy to restore members of the physical file should they become damaged. But a save command provides only a partial backup because it creates a static "snapshot" of the file's data; that is, it captures the state of the file at one point in time. As soon as subsequent updates are made to the file's data (records are added, deleted, or changed), the "snapshot" is out of date. Another data protection method is disk mirroring. While disk mirroring can provide you with added protection from hardware failure, not everyone can afford its double-disk requirements; and mirroring can not do anything to protect you from malfunctioning software.

If you wanted to use a save command to provide *up-to-the-minute* recovery capability, you would need to do a save after every update to the file, which is obviously impractical. Even frequent saves (hourly or twice a day) usually are not practical. During a save, a file member may be unavailable for updating. In addition, a significant amount of time is required to complete a save for a large file.

When you cannot afford to lose or re-enter transactions, another alternative is to include in critical applications custom-written routines to create a copy of changes made to files. This copy can be a separate disk or tape file that another custom-written program can use to re-apply changes should the file become damaged. But such custom-written routines require considerable programmer effort.

However, you need not wrestle with frequent saves or custom-written programs if you use AS/400 *journal management*. Journal management automatically creates a separate copy of file changes and, if necessary, uses the copy to recover data in a file. Because of journal management's facilities for backing up and recovering changes made to the data in physical files, using journal management with save/restore functions gives you the capability of restoring database files up to the very minute an unexpected failure damaged the physical file. You also can reduce the time needed to create backups for physical files.

The Basics of Journaling

Before discussing how to use journal management for enhanced database file recovery, let's review how a journal works. A journal is an AS/400 object used primarily to record changes to data in a physical file member and, optionally, changes to a logical file's access path. (In case you are wondering, a journal cannot be used to record changes to the contents of other objects such as data areas or message queues.) To help a user during recovery, a journal also records file opens, file closes, system IPLs, user-generated entries, and other types of activity related to physical files.

A journal does not discriminate when it records changes made to data in a physical file member; it doesn't matter whether the data is changed by a DFU application accessing the physical file member, or by an RPG/400 program accessing a logical file over the physical file member, or by a CPYF (Copy File) command accessing the member. In all cases, if the data in the physical file member is changed, the journal records the changes in the exact sequence they occur to the member. That is, if two programs are simultaneously updating the same physical file member, the journal records any changes these two programs cause in the same order in which the AS/400 data-management facility processes the changes to the physical file member. Because a journal records all changes to a physical file member in precise time sequence, these changes can be used later to recover the physical file member to an exact point in time.

In addition, a single journal can be used for a group of files, in which case the journal will record in proper time sequence the changes to all members of all files in the group. This sequencing allows synchronization of a group of files during recovery, either under explicit user control or automatically if commitment control (an additional recovery mechanism beyond journal management) is in use.

I said the journal "records" changes to a physical file member's data, but what is recorded and where? A journal records a change to the data by placing a "journal entry" into an object known as a journal receiver. Although access to a journal receiver is not the same as access to a database file, you can think of the journal receiver as the "container" for journal entries in the same sense that a file member is a "container" for file records.

The distinction between the journal and the journal receiver is important. The *journal* is the control mechanism — it maintains information about which physical files it is journaling and about which journal receiver is being used. It also maintains a directory of journal receivers it has used. The *journal receiver* is the actual repository of the entries that record the changes to the data in a physical file member.

Each entry a journal places into a journal receiver contains system-generated information, including a journal code and entry-type code that identifies the type of entry, a sequence number, and a date-time stamp. For changes to a file's data, the system-generated portion of an entry includes job name, job user, job number, program name, file name, library name, member name, and relative record number. Journal entries for changes to data also contain a complete copy of the physical file member's affected record. This copy is bit-for-bit the same as the record, either before it was changed (known as a "before image") or after it was changed (known as an "after image").

When data is changed, a journal always puts after-image journal entries into a journal receiver. Optionally, you can specify that the journal should put both before images and after images into the journal receiver. A journal entry's after image for an add operation to a physical file member contains the new record's data. A journal entry's after image for a change to an existing record contains the revised version of the data. When an existing record is deleted, an after image is a meaningless concept; the journal entry-type code indicating a delete operation and the relative record number provide adequate record-specific information.

Because the journal receiver contains properly sequenced after images for every change made to the data, it is straightforward for journal management to recover a file member to a point in time just before a failure occurred. First, the file member is restored from a previous save tape or diskette. Then journal management steps through the after images beginning with the first one after the time of the file save. Each after image has the relative record number of the affected record as well as every bit of the record after a change, so journal management simply replaces, adds, or marks as deleted the record to which the relative record number points. As the affected record is updated, any access path over the physical file member also is updated.

So that the journal will reflect all changes made to the data, journal entries are forced to auxiliary storage (disk) before the change is made to the database record. Thus, if a system failure occurs during a database operation, the journal receiver may contain the change, but the database file may not. At IPL the AS/400 always attempts to synchronize the file member and journal by applying any changes recorded in the journal receiver but not recorded in the file. This approach provides almost foolproof recovery... unless the disk on which your journal receiver resides suffers a head crash and is damaged irretrievably. Later in the chapter I discuss ways to survive a head crash.

Setting Up Journaling

Now that I have covered the basics of how a journal works, let's look at some guidelines for setting up journaling to provide enhanced database file recovery. First, you must decide which files to journal and how to group them. Some of your files may be small, inactive, or easily recoverable without journaling. If these files are not involved in transactions that use the files you decide to journal and if they are not related to journaled files by logical files, they need not be journaled. Periodic saves of these files will provide adequate recovery. However, you should journal files that are large, active, have critical transactions applied, or that are related to files with these characteristics.

Once you have identified files to be journaled, you need to decide how to group them. A single journal can be used for a single physical file, or one journal can be used for a group of physical files. You can create as many journals on your system as you need, using the CRTJRN (Create Journal) command. Each journal will cover one or more physical files. However, a physical file can use only one journal at a time.

If a journal is used for a group of files, the journal covers all members of those physical files using the journal. You should group files so that a single journal is used by all physical files that are related closely in an application system, or have members included in the same logical file, or may be open at the same time by a job using commitment control. In general, although on some occasions performance can be improved in concurrent jobs by using multiple journals, the simplest approach is to use a single journal for all physical files within an application system.

Second, establish for each file to be journaled whether to keep after images or both before and after images. Only after images are required for journal management recovery operations. However, if you want to be able to back out changes or to analyze specific changes to records using journal management, you need both before and after images. In addition, when a file is in use under commitment control, the system always keeps both before and after images, regardless of how you have set up the physical file to be journaled, so you do not need to specify that both images be kept just to use commitment control.

Also consider that keeping both before and after images increases the disk-space requirement, but does not necessarily double it. Add and delete operations always generate a single journal entry; the add always contains an after image, and the delete contains a before image (if they are being kept). Only a change operation generates two journal entries, one for the before image and one for the after image, if both types of images are being kept. Keeping both images has a negligible impact on runtime performance.

Third, decide whether you need a single journal receiver or dual journal receivers. A journal can be set up so that instead of just one receiver for journal entries, there are two. Every entry is duplicated and placed in both receivers. Dual receivers provide extra protection against damaged receivers because if one receiver is damaged, the other one still can be used for recovery. The disk space required for dual receivers is twice that for a single receiver; however, the runtime performance with dual receivers is only slightly slower than with a single receiver and should not be an impediment to using dual receivers. If disk space isn't a constraint, I recommend starting with dual receivers; you always can revert to a single receiver if disk space becomes more limited.

Finally, you should decide on which user ASP unit you want to place each journal receiver. The AS/400's default value of *LIBASP will allocate storage for the journal receiver in the same auxiliary storage pool as the library that contains the journal receiver. If you use dual receivers and are using multiple-user ASPs, you will probably want to assign each journal receiver to a different ASP, as this will reduce the chance of a disk malfunction damaging both journal receivers.

The Journaling Process

Having made these decisions, you are ready to go into action. The following steps describe (in the order you will need to carry out the commands) how to create the objects you need for journaling, how to start journaling your files, and how to save journal management objects to tape periodically for off-line backup.

Your first steps are to create the journal receivers and then the journals. When you do so, you should create both receivers and journals in the same library as the physical files that use them. This practice simplifies backup/restore operations. If a journaled physical file is in a different library from its journal and the journal is not in existence when the physical file is restored, journaling of the physical file ends. Putting the journal and the journal receivers into the same library as the physical file is simpler and more reliable.

With that in mind, first create one or both receivers needed for each journal. Journal receivers should be given "generic" receiver names with one to six characters and then a four-digit number (e.g., RCVA0001). A generic receiver name enables the system to build new receiver names automatically when you want to detach one receiver and attach a new one. I will cover detaching and attaching receivers later in this section. With generic receiver names, the system will increment the numeric portion of the currently attached receiver to form the name of the next receiver in the chain. Generic names also make it easier for you to see the order in which receivers have been used. To create a single receiver:

```
CRTJRNRCV JRNRCV(PRDDTA/RCVA0001)                              +
          ASP(2) TEXT('Primary receiver')
```

To create a second receiver for dual receivers:

```
CRTJRNRCV JRNRCV(PRDDTA/RCVB0001)                              +
          ASP(3) TEXT('Secondary receiver')
```

After you have created the journal receivers, you create the journal. If you use a single journal receiver:

```
CRTJRN JRN(PRDDTA/PRDJRN) JRNRCV(PRDDTA/RCVA0001)              +
       TEXT('Production File Journal: single receiver')
```

If you use dual receivers:

```
CRTJRN JRN(PRDDTA/PRDJRN) JRNRCV(PRDDTA/RCVA0001               +
       PRDDTA/RCVB0001) TEXT('Production File                  +
       Journal: dual receivers')
```

When you create the journal, the first receiver or pair of dual receivers are attached to the journal and ready for use.

With the journal receivers and journals created, you can begin journaling physical files by using one or more STRJRNPF (Start Journal Physical File) commands. Each STRJRNPF command includes one to 50 physical files and specifies for them the type of images to keep.

To keep only after images:

```
STRJRNPF FILE(PRDDTA/PEOPLE) JRN(PRDDTA/PRDJRN) IMAGES(*AFTER)
```

To keep both before and after images for several files:

```
STRJRNPF FILE(PRDDTA/LONAPP PRDDTA/LONTRN PRDDTA/DFTCLM)       +
      JRN(PRDDTA/PRDJRN) IMAGES(*BOTH)
```

You can keep only after images for some of the files using a journal and keep both before and after images for other files using the same journal. For example, both preceding STRJRNPF commands could be used for the journal PRDJRN.

To provide recovery capability for a physical file, you must save a file immediately after you begin journaling it. During recovery, journal entries can be applied only to a version of the physical file that was being journaled. In addition, you must save a physical file immediately after adding a member to it, so the new member also can be recovered. You can use any of the save commands. Recovery of logical files over the physical file will be faster if you save their access paths at the same time you save the physical file; however, saving logical file access paths is not required for recovery.

After you begin journaling a physical file, the journal records any changes made to the data in the file's members. The file itself has the name of the journal stored in its description. You can find out which journal, if any, a physical file is using with the DSPFD (Display File Description) command.

Finally, you need to establish the frequency for saving the physical files, journal, and journal receivers. Many approaches to making periodic saves offer you adequate recovery capability. One commonly used guideline is to follow procedures that produce one disk copy for recovering up-to-the-minute, one disk and one tape copy for recovering to the beginning of the current day, one disk and two tape copies for recovering to the beginning of the prior day, and three tape copies for recovering to the beginning of two days prior. If you follow this guideline, you have redundant coverage with more copies available for older versions of the data. Maintaining on-line (disk) copies makes recovery more convenient, while additional tape copies provide coverage in case of disk damage.

The following procedures provide this graduated level of backup:

- At the end of each workday, before the daily save of the journal and journal receivers, detach the current receiver and attach a new receiver. (Instead of changing receivers at the end of the day, you may choose to do it before the beginning of the next workday. You also would want to do the daily save then.) With generic receiver names, you can do this with a single CHGJRN (Change Journal) command. For journals with a single receiver:

  ```
  CHGJRN JRN(PRDDTA/PRDJRN) JRNRCV(*GEN)
  ```

  For journals with dual receivers:

  ```
  CHGJRN JRN(PRDDTA/PRDJRN) JRNRCV(*GEN *GEN)
  ```

If you use dual receivers, be sure to include two *GEN values for the JRNRCV parameter, as shown in the preceding command. If you use only one *GEN, the command succeeds, but the journal is switched to using a single receiver.

- At the end of each workday, after you have changed receivers, save the journal and the journal receivers for the current day and past two days. Do not omit the daily save on the last day of the workweek, even though you also will do a weekly save on that day. This last day's save tape is a necessary element in the redundant backup coverage. Do not free storage with the save command.

  To save the journals and journal receivers, you can use any of the save commands; a SAVCHGOBJ command like the following one does not require that you identify the journal receiver names. Instead, the command saves the journal (that was changed by the CHGJRN command) and the journal receivers used during the current and previous two days. Cycle 10 to 14 sets of tapes (two times the number of workdays in a week).

```
SAVCHGOBJ OBJ(*ALL) LIB(PRDDTA) OBJTYPE(*JRN *JRNRCV)        +
          REFDATE(mm/dd/yy)
```

  (The REFDATE, mm/dd/yy, is the current date minus two days.)

- At the end of the workweek, after the last workday's daily save, save all files, journals, and journal receivers (as well as other objects you may want to save weekly). Do not free storage. Again, you can use any of the save commands. Cycle three or more sets of tapes.

- After the weekly save, save a second copy of all journals and journal receivers. Free the storage of the journal receivers. Use a SAVOBJ command similar to the following one. Cycle two or more sets of tapes.

```
SAVOBJ OBJ(*ALL) LIB(PRDDTA) OBJTYPE(*JRN *JRNRCV)           +
       STG(*FREE)
```

  Although you specify that storage is freed, the save will not free storage for the journal or for any attached receiver. This is precisely what you want because the journal and the attached receiver remain usable, while the disk space used by detached journal receivers is made available.

- After making this second copy, delete detached, saved journal receivers more than two weeks old. You can determine which journal receivers these are by using the WRKJRNA (Work with Journal Attributes) command to display the journal receiver directory. The date on which each journal receiver was attached will guide you in selecting the journal receivers to delete. Use DLTJRNRCV (Delete Journal Receiver) commands similar to this one:

```
DLTJRNRCV JRNRCV(PRDDTA/RCVA0015)
```

  If you used dual receivers, you must delete both sets; for example, you would use

```
DLTJRNRCV JRNRCV(PRDDTA/RCVB0015)
```

in addition to the previous DLTJRNRCV command. You can use a generic form of the receiver name in the DLTJRNRCV command; for example,

```
DLTJRNRCV JRNRCV(RCVA001*)
```

will delete all journal receivers with names that begin with "RCVA001." You should exercise care when you use a generic receiver name to make sure you do not inadvertently delete the wrong receivers.

You will not reduce your coverage if you delete all detached, saved journal receivers at this time, rather than just the ones that are more than two weeks old. However, when you delete a receiver, it is removed from the journal's receiver directory. By leaving receivers on the system for up to three weeks, you can take advantage of journal management's use of the receiver directory to control recovery. Little extra disk space is used because the storage is freed for the detached, saved receivers.

Many variations on this approach are workable. The key aspects are that the procedures should be clearly documented and carefully followed; the entire file should be saved periodically (weekly, biweekly, or monthly); the journal and journal receivers should be saved daily; the journal receivers should be changed daily; and saves should be done in a way to produce multiple copies for recovery.

If your disk constraints are severe, a similar level of backup can be obtained by making multiple copies of the journal and journal receivers daily. After these daily saves, delete detached, saved journal receivers to free disk space.

Handling Critical Recovery Requirements

When you complete all the preceding steps, you will have the additional recovery protection of journal management. All of the journal entries except those for the current workday will be on tape. Thus, if a disk malfunction damages both the file and the journal receiver, you can use an off-line copy to restore a damaged receiver before using journal management recovery. If the currently attached receiver is damaged, though, journal management cannot recover beyond the last saved journal receiver's entries. Transactions entered during the current workday would be lost. Installations that cannot afford to lose part of a day's transactions must take additional measures to protect against this type of damage.

One alternative is to detach and save the current receiver more frequently than once a day. Because the CHGJRN command can be executed while journaled files are being updated, changing journal receivers has no impact, other than performance, on application systems that update the files. As soon as a receiver is detached, it should be saved. Appropriate procedures for freeing storage of detached, saved receivers or for deleting them should be followed. This strategy will cover most critical recovery situations.

For the most comprehensive recovery requirements, you can create a tape (or diskette or communication) file with one record added to the file each time a journal entry is put into the journal receiver. This approach requires that a tape device be dedicated to the job that is writing the tape records. It provides a means of writing an off-line copy of a journal entry immediately after it is put into the receiver. This off-line copy can be used for recovery if the currently attached receiver is damaged. However, you need a user-written program to apply the changes reflected in the tape records. Because these records are not in the same format as journal entries, journal management cannot use them for recovery.

To produce an off-line copy of journal entries, you can use the RCVJRNE (Receive Journal Entry) command to invoke a user-written program to process a journal entry as it is put into a journal receiver. Besides specifying the types of journal entries that should be passed to the user-written program, RCVJRNE must include the EXITPGM (Exit Program) parameter to specify the program to be invoked. When the RCVJRNE command is executed, the IBM-supplied command processing program (CPP) repeats a loop in which it receives a journal entry if one has been generated by journal management, converts the entry to a fixed-field format, and calls the user-written program with the converted journal entry (if any) as the first program parameter. A control code is passed as a second program parameter to indicate whether a journal entry is being passed (code equals "1") or no journal entries are currently available (code equals "0"). This loop continues until the user-written program puts a "9" in the control code parameter and returns to the CPP.

Each time the user-written program is called, it can check the control code to see whether the CPP has passed it a journal entry. If an entry has been passed, the user-written program can move the entry to a tape record and write it. The user-written program also controls when the RCVJRNE command should end by setting the control-code parameter before it returns to the CPP.

As long as the RCVJRNE command continues to execute, it receives, converts, and passes as a program parameter each journal entry as it is put into the receiver. RCVJRNE does not operate like the DSPJRN (Display Journal) and RTVJRNE (Retrieve Journal Entry) commands that get a set of old journal entries all at one time. The RCVJRNE command requires its own job, so it can continue looping while other jobs are generating journal entries. Journal management provides the synchronization between jobs generating journal entries and the job executing the RCVJRNE command.

Because the RCVJRNE command converts the variable-length internal format of the journal entry to a fixed-field format that is passed to the user-written program, journal management cannot use a tape copy of a journal entry for recovery. Further details about the RCVJRNE command and a sample program for using copies of journal entries for recovery is included in IBM's *Backup and Recovery Guide* (SC41-8079).

Journaling Considerations

One of the main reasons separate objects (journals and journal receivers) are used in journal management is to facilitate disk-space management. As journal entries are put into a journal receiver, it consumes increasing amounts of disk space. At some point, you need to make a tape or diskette copy of the accumulated journal entries and free the disk space for new ones. Journal management provides this capability by using a "chain" of journal receivers. A journal receiver into which a journal is currently putting entries is considered an "attached" receiver. Using the CHGJRN (Change Journal) command, you can change the receiver the journal is using. The current receiver is "detached," and the journal no longer uses it to store journal entries. A new receiver is attached in its place. Journal management synchronizes this change, so no journal entries are lost, even if you change receivers while journaled files are being updated. A sequence of journal entries will span the two receivers without interruption.

Once a receiver is detached, it can be saved with its storage freed, thus releasing the disk space it was using. The journal maintains a journal receiver directory that includes all receivers a journal used and that still exist on the system, even if their storage has been freed. This directory includes when journal receivers were saved. Journal management uses this directory during recovery operations to restore journal receivers containing the journal entries necessary for the recovery. Because journal management tracks the order in which the journal receivers were used (i.e., the names of "prior" and "next" receivers) you can perform recovery operations based on date/time periods or events (file opens and closes); journal management will find the necessary journal entries in the chain of journal receivers, which greatly simplifies recovery.

Journal management also provides several commands to obtain information about a journal. The DSPJRN (Display Journal) command is used to display the journal entries in on-line journal receivers used by the journal. The receivers can be either attached or detached, as long as they exist on the system and their storage has not been freed. If you want to find out what files are covered by a journal or what receivers have been used by a journal, use the WRKJRNA (Work with Journal Attributes) command. To see how many entries are in a journal receiver, what the prior and next receivers are in the current receiver chain, or other related information, use the DSPJRNRCVA (Display Journal Receiver Attributes) command. These and other journal management commands are included on the Journal Menu and Journal Receiver Menu, which you can get with the commands GO CMDJRN and GO CMDJRNRCV, respectively.

Using Journal Management for Recovery

Hopefully, after you have taken the time to set up journaling, you never will need to use it for recovery. If you are not that fortunate, however, journal management provides a menu-driven recovery facility. Figures 10.1 and 10.2 show the journal management menus.

This facility is entered by the GO CMDJRN (Journal Commands Menu) command and selection of option 15 (Work with Journal). This will call the WRKJRN command, as shown in Figure 10.3, where you select option 2 for the journal you want to forward recovery. The options on the Work with Journal command will step you through any RSTOBJ (Restore Object) and APYJRNCHG (Apply Journaled Changes) commands necessary to recover the desired file members. Using the menu-driven facility is simpler than entering individual commands, especially because you probably will not have to enter them often. The menu-driven recovery also makes certain that important recovery functions such as recovering all damaged physical file members used by a logical file are done. If you follow the guidelines laid out in this chapter for

Figure 10.1

Journal Commands Panel

```
CMDJRN                     Journal Commands
Select one of the following:

  Commands
     1. Apply Journaled Changes                          APYJRNCHG
     2. Change Journal                                   CHGJRN
     3. Compare Journal Images                           CMPJRNIMG
     4. Create Journal                                   CRTJRN
     5. Delete Journal                                   DLTJRN
     6. Display Journal                                  DSPJRN
     7. End Journal Access Path                          ENDJRNAP
     8. End Journaling PF Changes                        ENDJRNPF
     9. Receive Journal Entry                            RCVJRNE
    10. Remove Journaled Changes                         RMVJRNCHG
    11. Retrieve Journal Entry                           RTVJRNE
    12. Send Journal Entry                               SNDJRNE
    13. Start Journal Access Path                        STRJRNAP

More...
 Selection or command
 ===>

 F3=Exit   F4=Prompt   F9=Retrieve   F12=Cancel   F16=Major menu
```

Figure 10.2

Journal Commands Panel

```
 CMDJRN                              Journal Commands
Select one of the following:

    14. Start Journal Physical File                      STRJRNPF
    15. Work with Journal                                WRKJRN
    16. Work with Journal Attributes                     WRKJRNA

  Related Command Menus
    17. Accounting Commands                              CMDACG
    18. Commit Commands                                  CMDCMT
    19. File Commands                                    CMDFILE
    20. Journal Receiver Commands                        CMDJRNRCV
    21. Receive Commands                                 CMDRCV

                                                            Bottom
Selection or command
 ===>

F3=Exit   F4=Prompt   F9=Retrieve   F12=Cancel   F16=Major menu
```

Figure 10.3

Work with Journals Panel

```
                      Work with Journals

 Type options, press Enter.
   2=Forward recovery          3=Backout recovery   5=Display
journal status
   6=Recover damaged journal   7=Recover damaged journal
receivers

 Opt  Journal     Library     Text
      QACGJRN     QSYS
      QSXJRN      QUSRSYS     JOURNAL FOR PROBLEM DATABASE
      PRDJRN      PRDDTA

                                                          Bottom
 Command
 ===>
 F3=Exit   F4=Prompt   F9=Retrieve   F12=Cancel
```

setting up journaling, most recoveries should be straightforward using just the WRKJRN command.

Recovery of an individual file normally involves restoring the most recently saved version of the file and then using the APYJRNCHG command to bring it up to the most recent change. If you choose to use individual commands (rather than the menu-driven facility) to do this, you first must use one of the restore commands to restore the file. Then you use a command similar to the following:

```
APYJRNCHG JRN(PRDDTA/PRDJRN) FILE(PRDDTA/MYFILE *ALL)
```

This example uses default values for most APYJRNCHG command parameters. Among the parameters for which default values are used, the RCVRNG(*LASTSAVE) default specifies that the system should determine what journal receivers to use by using system-stored information about when the file was saved. The FROMENT(*LASTSAVE) default specifies that the first journal entry to be applied to the file is the first one after the file was last saved. The TOENT(*LASTRST) default specifies that the last journal entry to be applied is the last one occurring before the date and time the file was last restored. These defaults result in the file being fully recovered.

If you want to recover the file up to a specific file update, you can use an explicit journal entry sequence number for the TOENT (To Entry) parameter rather than taking the default. The journal entry sequence numbers are displayed by the DSPJRN (Display Journal) command. If you want to recover the file up to some particular time, you can specify the date and time in the TOTIME parameter rather than using a TOENT parameter. In addition to these options, the APYJRNCHG command also provides other alternatives for specifying the first and last journal entries to be applied.

If the journal or a journal receiver is damaged or if the last saved version of the file is unusable, other steps (such as restoring the journal or receivers) will be necessary. Most of these are incorporated in the menu-driven recovery facility mentioned earlier.

In conclusion, journal management used with save/restore functions can significantly increase your recovery capabilities with a minimum of programmer effort. Journal management also reduces the time you must dedicate to saving physical files. The key to successful use of journal management is careful planning of the journals and receivers that you will use and developing written procedures for saving files, journals, and journal receivers. With these in place, your data will have up-to-the-minute protection.

Chapter 11

Commitment Control

by Paul Conte

Automate user- and source-file disaster recovery

In this chapter, I'm going to show you how performing a little black magic on the AS/400 can double your money, make your last parking ticket disappear, and make an RPG program add 2 + 2 and get 5 as an answer. You'll also learn how to *prevent* similar magic from unexpectedly spellbinding your AS/400 applications. The sources of database "black magic" are transactions that update multiple records and concurrent updating of database files by multiple jobs. The "white magic" that protects your applications from these data-corrupting forces is commitment control, an AS/400 facility that protects the integrity of your database and helps you recover from abnormal system terminations.

Before I explain how the white magic of commitment control counters the black magic of non-commitment control, you'd probably like to learn how to double your money, make a parking ticket disappear, and get 5 when you add 2 + 2. Figure 11.1 shows a typical funds-transfer transaction.

If you're really set on doubling your money, just pull the CPU power plug between time **t5** and time **t6**. Or you can use a more sophisticated technique like building a logical file with a unique access path over file CHKACT, using the balance field as a key field. If you have previously added another CHKACT record with a value of .01 for the balance field, the update at **t6** will fail. Whether caused by a power outage or a program error, a failure to complete the transaction results in an inconsistent database.

Rollback Procedure Issues

What's needed to prevent this error is a facility that guarantees "all-or-none" execution of a multiple-record update transaction. Another way to phrase this is that the system must consider a multiple-record transaction as an "atomic" (i.e., indivisible) unit of work. Commitment control provides just such a mechanism.

Figure 11.1

Typical Funds Transfer Transaction

Time	Action	File CHKACT	File SAVACT
t0	"Transfer 500 from checking to savings"	500.01	0
t1	Read SAVACT for update	500.01	0
t2	Read CHKACT for update	500.01	0
t3	Add 500 to SAVACT	500.01	0
t4	Subtract 500 from CHKACT	500.01	0
t5	Update SAVACT	500.01	500.00
t6	Update CHKACT	.01	500.00

Figure 11.2

Interrupted Transaction with Commitment Control

Time	Action	File CHKACT	File SAVACT
t0	Commitment boundary established	500.01	0
t1	"Transfer 500 from checking to savings"	500.01	0
t2	Read SAVACT for update	500.01	0
t3	Read CHKACT for update	500.01	0
t4	Add 500 to SAVACT	500.01	0
t5	Subtract 500 from CHKACT	500.01	0
t6	Update SAVACT	.01	500.00
t7	"Pull power plug"	500.01	500.00
t8	IPL — Automatic system "rollback" of uncommitted transactions	500.01	0

Figure 11.2 shows what happens when commitment control is used and a transaction is interrupted.

The AS/400 automatically will "roll back" (i.e., back out) the file updates that had been performed as part of the incomplete transaction. If an abnormal system termination (such as a power failure) occurs, the rollback is performed at the next

Figure 11.3

Losing an Update by Backing Out a Partial Transaction

Time	Job A Action	Job B Action	File PRKACT
t0	"Apply 5.00 payment"	—	8.00
t1	Read PRKACT for update	"Charge 2.00 for ticket"	8.00
t2	Subtract 5.00 from PRKACT	Read PRKACT for update	8.00
t3	Update PRKACT	Wait for record lock	3.00
t4	Failed Write 5.00 entry to CHKRCV (file full)	Add 2.00 to PRKACT	3.00
t5	Update PRKACT	5.00	
t6	Update PRKACT with old copy of record	—	8.00
t7	Send error message	—	8.00
t8	—	—	8.00
t9	Redo "Apply 5.00 payment" successfully	—	3.00

IPL and is completed before the affected records can be accessed. If an abnormal *routing step* termination (such as an immediate job cancellation) occurs, the AS/400 performs the rollback during routing-step termination processing.

Figure 11.3 shows a sequence of events in *two* jobs that concurrently update file PRKACT, a file of parking fine accounts receivable. Job A posts a payment, a two-file transaction that reduces the account balance in PRKACT and then writes a new entry to CHKRCV, the file of checks received. At the same time, Job B posts a ticket for the same person, which increases the account balance in PRKACT. To make the parking ticket disappear, limit the size of file CHKRCV so that Job A's attempt to add a new record at time t4 fails. Assume that, in this non-commitment control environment, a conscientious programmer built into the payment-posting program a "backout" procedure that is executed if part of the transaction fails. This backout procedure uses a copy of the original PRKACT record (saved after the read at time t1) to "correct" the file at time t6. This custom-coded version of a backout operation wipes out the Job B ticket-posting update that occurred at time t5.

With commitment control, though, you can simplify programs and prevent updates from being "wiped out" when a backout occurs. Figure 11.4 shows the same updates to file PRKACT, but this time both jobs use commitment control. With commitment control, Job A locks the PRKACT record from the time it is read for update (t2) until the rollback operation (t6) ends the transaction. This record lock prevents Job B from completing a read-for-update operation (started

Figure 11.4

Preventing Lost Updates by Using Commitment Control

Time	Job A Action	Job B Action	File PRKACT
t0	Commitment boundary established	—	8.00
t1	"Apply 5.00 Payment" established	Commitment boundary	8.00
t2	Read PRKACT for update	"Charge 2.00 for ticket"	8.00
t3	Subtract 5.00 from PRKACT (Begin wait for record lock)	Read PRKACT for update	8.00
t4	Update PRKACT	Wait for record lock	3.00
t5	Failed write 5.00 entry to CHKRCV (file full)	Wait for record lock	3.00
t6	Rollback transaction	Wait for record lock	8.00
t7	Send error message	Add 2.00 to PRKACT	8.00
t8	—	Update PRKACT	10.00
t9	—	Commit transaction	10.00
t10	Redo "Apply 5.00 Payment" successfully	—	5.00
t11	Commit transaction	—	5.00

at time **t3**) until the rollback is completed (after **t6**) and the PRKACT record is restored to its original value. With commitment control, no update can be wiped out by another job's rollback operation because the second update is blocked until the first job releases its record locks at the end of the transaction.

When 2 + 2 = 5

Doubling your money and making parking tickets disappear are fit challenges for a sorcerer's apprentice, but to convince people that your magic is potent enough to make two plus two equal anything but four, you'll need to outwit RPG. Figure 11.5 shows two jobs concurrently accessing file INV, a parts inventory by warehouse and part number. Job A updates the quantity on hand for a part in two warehouses and Job B sums the total quantity on hand for the part, using an RPG program. The file ends up at time **t10** with "2" as the quantity on hand for part XYZ at each warehouse. But the RPG program reports a total of "5." This occurs because the RPG program adds the quantity on hand for warehouse 678 *after* it has been updated, but adds the quantity on hand for warehouse 123 *before* it is updated.

You chuckling COBOL and PL/I programmers shouldn't be so smug, because the same problem can arise in *any* language. Furthermore, even the normal lock level (*CHG) of AS/400 commitment control lets this error slip by because the

Figure 11.5

Invalid Totaling Caused by Concurrent Updating

Time	Job A	Job B	File INV Whse 123	File INV Whse 678
t0	"Transfer 1 part XYZ from Whse '123' to Whse '678'	—	3	1
t1	Read Whse '678' for update	—	3	1
t2	Read Whse '123' for update	—	3	1
t3	Add 1 to Whse '678'	—	3	1
t4	Subtract 1 from Whse '123'	—	3	1
t5	Update Whse '678'	"Total part XYZ"	3	2
t6	—	Read Whse '678' for input	3	2
t7	—	Add to total (2)	3	2
t8	—	Read Whse '123' for input	3	2
t9	Update Whse '123'	Add to total (5)	2	2
t10	—	Print total: '5'	2	2

record locks obtained at time **t1** and **t2** do not normally prevent a read-for-input such as the ones by Job B at time **t6** and time **t8**. "Industrial strength" commitment control, using lock level *ALL, however, will clean up the tarnished total. Figure 11.6 shows the Figure 11.5 operations with Job A using the low lock level (*CHG) of commitment control and Job B using the high lock level (*ALL) of commitment control. Under the high lock level of commitment control, Job B acquires a record lock even when it reads a record for input. Thus, Job B begins waiting for the record lock at time **t7** and completes the read only after Job A has completed its transaction and released its record locks (after time **t10**).

Having shown you that white magic will beat black magic every time, I can now give you the key that unleashes the power of AS/400 commitment control. With commitment control, your programs will become very obedient if you follow these six simple steps:

- Identify which files will be placed under commitment control
- Specify in your CL and high-level language (HLL) programs those files that will be opened under commitment control
- Add commit and rollback statements to your application programs to define commitment control boundaries for both successful and unsuccessful transactions

Figure 11.6

Correct Totaling with Commitment Control Level *ALL

Time	Job A Lock level *CHG	Job B Lock level *ALL	File INV Whse 123	 Whse 678
t0	Commitment boundary established	—	3	1
t1	"Transfer 1 part XYZ from Whse '123' to Whse '678'	—	3	1
t2	Read Whse '678' for update	—	3	1
t3	Read Whse '123' for update	—	3	1
t4	Add 1 to Whse '678'	—	3	1
t5	Subtract 1 from Whse '123'	Commitment boundary established	3	1
t6	Update Whse '678'"	Total part XYZ"	3	2
t7	—	Read Whse '678' for input (Begin wait for record lock)	3	2
t8	—	Wait for record lock	3	2
t9	Update Whse '123'	Wait for record lock	2	2
t10	Commit transaction	Wait for record lock	2	2
t11	—	Add to total (2)	2	2
t12	— input	Read Whse '123' for	2	2
t13	—	Add to total (4)	2	2
t14	—	Commit transaction	2	2
t15	—	Print total: '4'	2	2

- Journal physical files that are accessed under commitment control
- Start a commitment control environment in a job before opening any files under commitment control
- End the commitment control environment when it is no longer needed in a job

Identifying Which Files to Place Under Commitment Control

Identifying which physical and non-join logical files to access under commitment control requires looking at each application program's use of database files. If a commitment control. This guarantees that no partial update will be left in the database because of an abnormal termination and assures that recovery can begin with the first transaction that was not completed. (As an alternative for stand-alone batch jobs that use small files, you might get better performance than with commitment control by creating a backup copy of all files updated in a multiple-record transaction and by allocating the file members exclusive-allow-read (*EXCLRD), using the ALCOBJ (Allocate Object) command, before executing the program. Recovery is then possible by re-creating the files from the backup copy and restarting the program with the first transaction.)

A file should also be opened under commitment control when you do not want to allow records from the file to be read if the records are involved in an incompleted transaction in a different job (as in the totaling program in Figure 11.6). (Another way to prevent a job from reading records from a partially complete transaction is to allocate the file member (*EXCLRD) or share-no-update (*SHRNUP). Either of these object locks will prevent other jobs from updating the files; thus, no transactions can occur in other jobs. Allocating a file member to prevent updates is feasible only when there is no requirement for multiple jobs updating the member concurrently.) Finally, a file must be opened under commitment control if it is opened as a shared file and the other shared open places the file under commitment control.

It is possible to have some files in a single program that are opened under commitment control and other files that are not. Such a mixture of *update* files is indivisible, however, because if a file is not placed under commitment control when it is opened for update, the commitment control environment does not encompass updates to the file (i.e., updates are permanent; they cannot be rolled back). Similarly, record locks are not held for the duration of a transaction; they are released by the next read-for-update or update operation to the file. Commitment control doesn't affect input-only files unless the high lock level (*ALL) is in effect, so in most cases input-only files can be left outside the commitment control environment, except when they are opened as a shared file and the other open is for update under commitment control.

Specifying Files Under Commitment Control in HLL and CL Programs

The second step in using commitment control is to specify in HLL and CL programs those files that will be opened under commitment control. A key point to remember is that in all HLL programs (except Pascal) you must decide how the file will be opened *before* you compile the program; an execution-time option to open a file under commitment control is available only in Pascal and CL. To specify that a file will be opened under commitment control in RPG, you code a K in position 53 and COMIT in positions 54 through 59 of a file continuation specification (Figure 11.7). In COBOL you must include the internal (COBOL) file name in the COMMITMENT CONTROL clause of an I-0-CONTROL paragraph entry (Figure 11.8). In PL/I you must include the COMMITABLE option in the ENVIRONMENT attribute of the file declaration (Figure 11.9). In Pascal you must specify COMMIT(*YES) in the file open options string (Figure 11.10). In CL you must specify COMMIT(*YES) on the OPNDBF (Open Data Base File) command (Figure 11.11). BASIC does not support commitment control.

Figure 11.7

Specifying a File Under Commitment Control in RPG III

```
*... ... 1 ... ... 2 ... ... 3 ... ... 4 ... ... 5 ... ... 6 ... ... 7
     FPRKACT  UF  E              K         DISK          KCOMIT
```

Figure 11.8

Specifying a File Under Commitment Control in COBOL

```
INPUT-OUTPUT SECTION.
FILE-CONTROL.

          SELECT     PRKACT-FILE
                     ASSIGN              TO    DATABASE-PRKACT
                     ORGANIZATION        IS    INDEXED
                     ACCESS              IS    DYNAMIC
                     RECORD KEY          IS    EXTERNALLY-DESCRIBED-KEY
                     FILE STATUS         IS    PRKACT-STATUS.


I-O-CONTROL.  COMMITMENT CONTROL FOR PRKACT-FILE.
```

Figure 11.9

Specifying a File Under Commitment Control in PL/I

```
DECLARE      PRKACT-FILE    FILE          RECORD
                            INTERNAL      DIRECT        UPDATE
                        ENV(INDEXED       COMMITABLE    DESCRIBED);
```

Figure 11.10

Specifying a File Under Commitment Control in Pascal

```
UPDATE(PRKACT,'COMMIT(*YES)')
```

Figure 11.11

Specifying a File Under Commitment Control in CL

```
      OPNDBF    FILE(PRKACT)   OPTION(*ALL)    COMMIT(*YES)
```

Placing Commit and Rollback Statements in HLL and CL Programs

The third step is to place commit and rollback statements in your programs to define commitment boundaries. Before I describe the statement syntax, let's briefly look at the concept of a "transaction" and a "commitment boundary." Figure 11.12 shows a sequence of events in a job using commitment control.

Before time **t1**, the job doesn't use commitment control. At **t1** the job establishes a commitment control environment, but no transaction has begun. When the first database file is opened under commitment control (**t2**), the beginning commitment boundary of the first transaction is established. This first transaction includes all activity on files opened under commitment control (**t3**) that occurs before the next commitment boundary. Any database file updates are temporary until the next commitment boundary is reached. A new commitment boundary is established when either a commit (**t4**) or rollback (**t6**, **t8**) operation occurs. The rollback may be explicit (**t6**), or it may occur because the commitment control environment ends (**t8**) or because the routing step abnormally terminates.

When a commit or rollback operation establishes a new commitment boundary, the current transaction ends and a new transaction begins. Execution of the commit operation causes all database file updates executed during the transaction to be made permanent, whereas a rollback — whatever its cause — removes all database file updates performed since the previous commitment boundary. In addition, a rollback resets all file pointers (i.e., the "current" record pointer for sequential access) to their values at the last successful commitment boundary. Both the commit and rollback operations cause all record locks in the job to be released.

The commit statements should be placed in your programs before you worry about rollbacks. Place RPG COMIT, COBOL COMMIT, PL/I CALL PLICOMMIT, Pascal SYSTEM('COMMIT',RTNCDE), or CL COMMIT statements at those points in your program logic where a transaction is successfully completed (e.g., in the funds transfer example in Figure 11.2, after both the checking and savings account files have been updated). There may be more than one place where you should place a commit statement, and there is no significant disadvantage to having multiple commit statements in a program. Also, there is no harm in executing a commit (or a rollback) when there are no uncommitted file updates; the only action that occurs is placement of a commit entry in the journal and establishment of a new commitment boundary. On the other hand, if you execute a COMMIT (or ROLLBACK) command in a CL or Pascal program and the commitment control environment has not been established, escape message CPF8350 will be sent. Similarly, executing an RPG COMIT (or ROLBK) in a noncommitment control environment causes escape message RPG0802 to be sent. In COBOL and PL/I programs, the runtime systems ignore COMMIT (or ROLLBACK) and CALL PLICOMMIT (or CALL PLIROLLBACK) statements if they are executed in a noncommitment control environment, and no error occurs.

Keep two points in mind when you add the commit statements. First, neither closing a file nor ending a program establishes a new commitment boundary. Thus, you must make certain that the last successfully completed transaction in

Figure 11.12

Transactions and Commitment Boundaries

Time	Action	
t0	—	
t1	Start commitment control (STRCMTCTL)	
	—	
	—	
----------	----------	Commitment boundary
t2	Open first file under commitment control	
	—	
	—	
t3	Other opens, closes, reads, updates	Transaction 1
	—	
	—	
t4	Commit	
----------	----------	Commitment boundary
	—	
	—	
t5	Other opens, closes, reads, updates	Transaction 2
	—	
	—	
t6	Rollback	
----------	----------	Commitment boundary
	—	
	—	
t7	Other opens, closes, reads, updates	Transaction 3
	—	
	—	
t8	End commitment control (ENDCMTCTL); implicit rollback	
----------	----------	Commitment boundary
	—	
	—	

an update program is followed by a commit operation. Second, a transaction encompasses *all* activity on files opened under commitment control within a job; if separate programs and separate Open Data Paths (ODPs) are used to update files, the updates still are included in the same transaction. (In a single job you cannot have more than one transaction in progress at a time.) Therefore, you must be sure that a commit statement is not executed too soon (i.e., before all files involved in the transaction have been updated) or too late (i.e., after file updates occur that are not involved in a completed transaction).

After adding the commit statements, you must add the rollback statements. Within an HLL program, you need to code an RPG ROLBK, a COBOL ROLLBACK, a PL/I CALL PLIROLLBACK, or a Pascal SYSTEM('ROLLBACK', RTNCDE) statement only if the program logic determines that the transaction cannot be completed successfully. Occasions for using rollback include handling database file I/O errors and applications where multiple records in the same file must be updated before the validity of the transaction can be determined.

A good practice to follow in CL "shell" programs that call HLL programs is to place a ROLLBACK operation within a MONMSG (Monitor Message) command after the CL CALL command that invokes an HLL program. Figure 11.13 shows a "generic" MONMSG that will trap RPG, COBOL, and PL/I program abnormal terminations. The ROLLBACK prevents a "dangling" transaction, which might accidentally be committed if a commit operation were subsequently executed in the same job.

In addition, if commitment control is ended or the routing step is terminated and partial, uncommitted updates exist, an error condition occurs, and escape message CPF8356 is sent. Executing a rollback after abnormal program termination helps prevent this error. IBM's *Backup and Recovery Guide* (SC41-8079), and the HLL programmer's guides provide detailed examples of programs using the commit and rollback statements.

Journaling Physical Files

The fourth step in implementing commitment control is journaling the physical files that will be opened under commitment control or that are within the scope of a logical file that will be opened under commitment control. You must journal to the same journal all physical files accessed under commitment control in the same commitment control environment (i.e., within a job, after a STRCMTCTL command and before an ENDCMTCTL command or the end of the routing step). The easiest approach is to journal all physical files to the same journal; for performance improvement, however, you may want to use multiple journals and journal all physical files within each self-contained application system to the same journal. If you use multiple journals, you must use them in *separate* commitment environments. Thus, multiple journals can be used only in separate jobs or within a single job by executing an ENDCMTCTL to end one commitment environment and then by executing a STRCMTCTL to establish a new commitment environment. Keep in mind that there are save/restore, as well as commitment control, considerations in setting up your journals; a complete discussion of journal management is provided in Chapter 10, "Journal Management."

To perform rollback operations, commitment control requires that both the before and the after record images be placed in the journal. You can still specify IMAGES(*AFTER) on the AS/400 STRJRNPF (Start Journal Physical File) command, however, because the AS/400 automatically switches to journaling

Figure 11.13

Monitoring for Errors After CALL Command

```
CALL        PGM(HLL_PGM)
MONMSG      MSGID(RPG9001  CBE9000   PLI9000)  +
            EXEC(ROLLBACK)
```

both images while a file is open under commitment control. Besides journaling before and after record images, commitment control also places an entry in the journal for each commit and rollback operation. Chapters 3 and 4 of the *Backup and Recovery Guide* provide a detailed description of the entries commitment control places in a journal.

Establishing a Commitment Control Environment in a Job

The fifth step is to establish, by executing the AS/400 STRCMTCTL command, a commitment control environment in a job *before* you open database files under commitment control. The STRCMTCTL parameter LCKLVL (Lock Level) specifies the type of record locking that occurs when files under commitment control are accessed. The low lock level specified by parameter value *CHG causes locks to be placed on records read for update and records that are updated, added, or deleted. The high lock level specified by *ALL causes locks to be placed on all records accessed, even those read for input. The lock level applies only within the job executing the STRCMTCTL command; record locking in a different job is determined by whether the job has established a commitment control environment and, if it has, which lock level is in effect. Also keep in mind that the lock level doesn't affect files that are not opened under commitment control. One further consideration is that the lock level applies to all files under commitment control; you cannot lock input-only records in some files and not in others. To change the lock level, you must end commitment control and start it again with a different lock level.

The other STRCMTCTL parameter, NFYOBJ (Notify Object), optionally specifies a message queue, character data area, or physical file in which an entry is placed if a routing step or system termination occurs and uncommitted updates exist. The entry, known as the "commit ID," identifies the last successfully completed transaction and can be used to restart processing with the first transaction *after* the one the commit ID identifies. The commit ID is a user-defined character string up to 9,999 bytes long that is specified in the commit statement. In RPG you can specify a field or data structure name up to 9,999 bytes long in Factor 1 of the COMIT operation. In PL/I you can specify a character expression of up to 2,000 bytes as the argument of the PLICOMMIT built-in subroutine. In Pascal and CL you can specify a character expression of up to 2,000 bytes in the CMTID parameter of the COMMIT command. COBOL does not directly support commit IDs; to use them, you can execute the commit operation by calling a CL, RPG, or PL/I subroutine.

Chapter 4 of the *Backup and Recovery Guide* provides numerous examples of using a notify object to support application restart. I include the following recommendations to help you use these examples more effectively.

If you use a manual approach to restarts, the simplest method is to use a single message queue, for example CMTNFY (Commit Notify), as the notify object for all jobs. Create this message queue with SENDER(*JOB *DTS) to capture the ID of the job that sent the message and the date and time the message was sent. The commit ID should include an application name, the name of the application program executing the commit operation, and an identifier (such as order number or customer number) that unambiguously identifies the transaction. If a failure occurs, the message queue can be displayed to determine where processing was interrupted. Only those jobs that were using commitment control and that had uncommitted updates will have sent a message to the message queue. If the information in the message is not sufficient to determine a restart point (e.g., if there were two or three transactions for the same customer in a short time interval), the DSPJRN (Display Journal) command will provide record-specific details about successful and interrupted transactions. Together, the message containing the commit ID and the journal entries provide adequate information to determine a restart point.

To implement a programmed restart facility, you should use a *single* physical file for the notify object. The record format in this file should include fields for job name, user profile name, job number, application name, and program name. (The examples in the AS/400 *Backup and Recovery Guide* mention only the user profile name portion of the job ID, but this will not guarantee a unique key for the records in the file because a user may be signed on to more than one interactive job or own multiple batch jobs when an abnormal system termination occurs.) Optional fields for date and time provide helpful information, especially in the case of batch jobs that may have failed at night or over the weekend. There should be a "generic" restart field large enough to contain the largest commit ID that any application generates. Each application must place sufficient information into the commit ID to enable it to restart at the proper processing point. The restart information will vary from application to application and may include record keys, program processing cycle count, and program totals.

While commit IDs provide the foundation for a flexible and reliable general purpose restart capability, there are significant performance considerations when using commit IDs. The commit ID is included in the commit journal entry and if it is large, considerable auxiliary storage is used during normal transaction processing. In addition, the throughput of the journal will be degraded, and thus transaction rates may be reduced. You can minimize storage requirements by using short commit IDs and the informal approach, based on a message queue notify object, for restarting interactive jobs. For batch jobs, you can use other restart techniques, such as updating a status field in successfully completed transaction records and writing "checkpoint" records with intermediate totals. In batch jobs, the commit ID can be omitted entirely from commit operations except for the commit operation immediately after the "checkpoint." In both interactive and batch jobs, the full integrity protection of commitment control can still be used, even with a more limited approach to automatic recovery.

Ending Commitment Control in a Job

The final step in implementing commitment control is to end commitment control. Because commitment control protects you from partially completed transactions, it requires an orderly end to processing. First, you must complete the last transaction with a commit or rollback operation. Next, you must close all files that were opened under commitment control (this may be done automatically by ending an HLL program or run unit). Finally, you must end the commitment control environment. The ENDCMTCTL (End Commitment Control) command can be used explicitly or you can end commitment control by terminating the routing step (e.g., with a SIGNOFF, or the ENDGRPJOB (End Group Job) command).

If any uncommitted updates remain when you end commitment control, escape message CPF8356 is sent and the updates are rolled back. Also, if you execute the ENDCMTCTL command when no commitment control environment exists, escape message CPF8350 is sent.

Record Locking

The preceding six steps put commitment control to work for you; but to use commitment control effectively, you must consider how record locking operates under commitment control. Otherwise, you may experience problems with conflicting record locks arising from concurrent access of the database by multiple jobs. Commitment control introduces additional locking rules. Most importantly, while record locks for files not under commitment control are always held by individual Open Data Paths (ODPs), record locks under commitment control are held by ODPs when the records are first read and then transferred to the job's commitment control environment control block when the records are updated.

Though subtle, this difference is important. It means that without commitment control, when a record is locked by an ODP and a *different* ODP in the same job attempts to lock the same record before the first ODP's lock is released, the second lock will not be granted and the read will fail. To better understand this concept, consider two logical files, FILEX and FILEY, that are defined over the same physical file (FILEP) and that are both opened for update without commitment control in the same program. The following sequence of operations results in a failed read operation:

READ record 123 from FILEX
— lock is obtained by ODP for FILEX
READ record 123 from FILEY
— lock request by ODP for FILEY fails

Under the same conditions, an update operation between the two reads releases the first lock and lets the second read obtain the required lock:

READ record 123 from FILEX
— lock is obtained by ODP for FILEX
UPDATE record 123 in FILEX
— lock held by ODP for FILEX is released
READ record 123 from FILEY
— lock is obtained by ODP for FILEY

With commitment control, the handling of locks is different. Within a transaction, when a record is read for update (or for input with lock level *ALL), its lock is held by the ODP. Until the lock is released or transferred to the commitment control environment control block, the same record cannot be read with a lock through a different ODP in the same job. Using FILEX and FILEY again, but with commitment control (either lock level), the following sequence of operations results in a failed read operation:

READ record 123 from FILEX
— lock is obtained by ODP for FILEX
READ record 123 from FILEY
— lock request by ODP for FILEY fails

Under lock level *CHG, if the first lock is released by a read to FILEX for a different record, the FILEY read succeeds. As the following sequence demonstrates, locks are not retained by commitment control lock level *CHG unless an update (or add or delete occurs):

READ record 123 from FILEX
— lock on 123 is obtained by ODP for FILEX
READ record 987 from FILEX
— lock on 123 is released
— lock on 987 is obtained by ODP for FILEX
READ record 123 from FILEY
— lock on 123 is obtained by ODP for FILEY

When a record is updated, its record lock is transferred from the ODP to the commitment control environment control block. As long as a record lock is held by the control block — but not by any ODP, the same record can be reread in the same job:

READ record 123 from FILEX
— lock on 123 is obtained by ODP for FILEX
UPDATE record 123 in FILEX
— lock on 123 is transferred to job's commitment control environment control block
READ record 123 from FILEY
— lock on 123 is held by job's commitment control environment control block but not by any ODP, so read succeeds
— lock on 123 is obtained by ODP for FILEY

Note that at the end of this sequence of operations, the ODP for FILEY holds a lock on record 123, and this lock prevents any other ODP in the same job (including the ODP for FILEX) from reading record 123 with a lock until the FILEY ODP lock is released or transferred.

The commitment control handling of locks is necessary because locks on updated records are held until the next commit or rollback operation, rather than released when the update occurs, as happens without commitment control. To be able to re-access records that were previously updated in the same transaction (and therefore still locked), it must be possible to satisfy a second lock request within the same job.

Another important aspect of record locking under commitment control is the duration of the record locks. Figure 11.14 shows, for each I/O operation, when a record is locked and when the lock is released. As the last three rows of the figure show, both lock levels of commitment control hold record locks on updated, added, and deleted records until the next commitment boundary. In a noncommitment control environment, the record lock is released after the update, add, or delete occurs. The first two rows illustrate the differences between the two lock levels. Records read for input are locked only when the high lock level (*ALL) is used. Similarly, records read for update — but released without being updated — are normally unlocked when the release occurs; with the high lock level, however, the lock is retained until the next commitment boundary. A record that has been read for update can be "released" in an HLL program by performing, before any update of the record, another read-for-update via the same ODP.

Figure 11.15 shows the allowable access of a record by a second job (Job B) when another job (Job A) has already read the record, but has not yet released or updated it. As you may have determined from the lock duration rules of Figure 11.14, the rules for a second job's access are the same for a non-commitment control environment and for the low lock level (*CHG) of commitment control. The high lock level (*ALL), on the other hand, requires a

Figure 11.14

Record Lock Duration

I/O Operation	Commitment Control Environment	This I/O ▼	Release ▼	Update ▼	Commit or Rollback ▼
Read-for-input	None or *CHG	*			
	*ALL	*————	————	————	————*
Read-for-update, then release	None or *CHG	*————	————*		
	*ALL	*————	————	————	————*
Read-for-update, then update	None	*————	————	————*	
	*CHG or *ALL	*————	————	————	————*
Add	None	*			
	*CHG or *ALL	*————	————	————	————*
Delete	None	*			
	*CHG or *ALL	*————	————	————	————*

(Time ———→)

Figure 11.15

Allowable Record Access

Job A		Allowable Type of Read by Job B		
Commitment Environment	Record Read for	Non-Commitment Environment	Lock Level *CHG	Lock Level *ALL
None	Input	Update	Update	Update
	Update	Input	Input	None
Lock Level *CHG	Input	Update	Update	Update
	Update	Input	Input	None
Lock Level *ALL	Input	Input	Input	None
	Update	Input	Input	None

record lock to perform a read-for-input *and* holds a record lock on input-only records until the next commitment boundary.

Because the use of commitment control is likely to increase both the number and duration of record locks, you must design your applications, particularly interactive applications, to avoid holding record locks for long periods of time. The best design for concurrent interactive database updating avoids long-duration record locks by *not* locking records when they are first read. Instead, records are read without a lock (i.e., for input); a *copy* of each record is made in program variables; and the records are displayed for update. If the workstation user changes the records, the update proceeds by re-retrieving the records with a lock (i.e., for update), validating the records by comparing the re-retrieved records with their respective original copies, and, if the re-retrieved records are the same as the originals, performing the update operations. If any record was changed during the interval between the original retrieval and the re-retrieval, the update is rejected and the workstation user notified.

To extend this algorithm to a commitment control environment, you must declare a program variable for each file involved in a multiple-file transaction. If a transaction can involve more than one record from a single file, the program variable for that file's record copies must be an array. In addition, with multiple records from the same file, you cannot simply re-retrieve and validate all records from the file before beginning the update phase. Unless you are using the high lock level, a sequence of read-for-update operations to the same file will release the lock on the previously read record. The proper way to handle this condition is to re-retrieve, validate, and update each record in turn. If a record is re-retrieved that does not match its original copy, a rollback must be executed and the update rejected.

Other techniques, such as maintaining an "in use" flag in a field of a retrieved record or using the WAITRCD (Wait for Record) parameter on display files, may offer a partial solution to the problem of record lock conflicts. But these methods do not work well in all environments, particularly with large numbers of interactive users and when group jobs are used. The read-copy-validate-update technique, on the other hand, always minimizes lock contention.

One variant of the recommended read-copy-validate-update technique reduces the memory required to maintain copies of original records. A field, for example UPDCNT (Update Count), is included in every physical file. *Every* update program adds one to this field just before an update operation. This enables any program using the read-copy-validate-update algorithm to make a copy of the update count field rather than of the entire record. The validation step can compare the update count in the re-retrieved record to the original update count; if these values are the same, the record has not been changed. Although this method saves memory, it requires extreme care to be certain that *all* update programs observe the convention of incrementing the update count. Of course, DFU is unable to automatically increment a field when a record is updated, so this technique effectively rules out DFU use.

Handling record locks with a high lock level is a further challenge. The first thing to determine is when to use the high lock level. If you require a summary report on a file and want to be certain no record updates occur that will make the report inconsistent, consider using object allocation, instead of a high lock level, to prevent all updates while the report executes. If object allocation cannot be used for a *read-only* (i.e., report) application, make certain that the locks on input records are held only while the analysis phase executes. Once that phase ends, execute a commit operation to release record locks, and then display or print the results. Keep in mind that a job can hold a maximum of 9,999 record locks on the AS/400 at one time. When you attempt an input-output operation that would exceed this limit, you receive escape message CPF5079 (RPG file status code 1299, COBOL file status '90') and the operation fails. The current transaction is not rolled back or committed, and all updates and record locks remain pending. You should monitor for this error and execute a rollback or commit operation to free the locks and restart or continue the transaction. If you have transactions that approach the record lock limit, use object allocation instead of record locking.

Finally, you may encounter cases where an input-only record is involved in an update transaction and you want to guarantee that the record is not changed by another job until the transaction is complete. In batch jobs, you can use the high lock level and open the input files, as well as update files, under commitment control. You should not use this method in interactive jobs because the high lock level causes record locking to occur during the original "read-copy" phase of the read-copy-validate-update process. (The read-copy-validate-update algorithm is normally implemented with shared opens for the input-only and update access to a file; thus, *both* program files must be placed under commitment control.) In interactive jobs, the simplest alternative to locking a record used only for input is to handle it the same way that update records are handled — make a copy and validate it before committing the transaction. By reading the "input only" record for update during the validation step, the necessary record lock is obtained. Thus, the read-copy-validate-update technique can use the low lock level to handle most of the circumstances when the high lock level seems necessary.

As anyone who has seen *The Wizard of Oz* knows, there are good witches and there are bad witches. With AS/400 commitment control, you can pick which you want to be — ignore it and continue to practice the "black magic" of lost and inconsistent updates, or implement it and practice the "white magic" of automatic database recovery and consistent concurrent file updating.

Chapter 12

Job Accounting

by John Rittenhouse

Track jobs and system resource use with job accounting

Deep down in their heart of hearts accountants are all alike. They want to see everything counted, indexed, and cross-referenced to everything else. For the accountant in you or in your enterprise, IBM provides job accounting on the AS/400.

Job accounting could well be your best friend. With it, you can monitor CPU use, charge back system overhead to other organizational units inside or outside your company, and even find out who is using so much paper. If your system is overloaded, job accounting can help you justify new hardware expenditures and determine who should pay for them. If talk like this awakens in you the accountant's zeal for tracking and shifting costs, follow along and see how easy it is to implement job accounting on your system. I'll describe how to set up a job accounting system using the job accounting journal and how to retrieve information from the journal.

Setting Up the System

Job accounting on the AS/400 is based on the use of the job accounting journal. Once the journal is up and running, the system automatically generates an entry for every job, recording information like job name and number, total transaction time, completion code, and number of database and communications operations. Figure 12.1 shows the field layout for the job accounting journal entries, which are the same as IBM-supplied *TYPE1 outfiles on the AS/400.

Because job accounting is optional, you need to do some chores to set it up. First, you need to identify job users to the system, and then you need to create journal receivers to hold the accounting information generated by the system.

To identify users for accounting purposes, you must assign an accounting code to each system user. Of course, you should first determine how job accounting can serve your organization and then assign accounting codes accordingly. For

Figure 12.1

Job Accounting File Field Layout

Generic fields common to all (JB, SP, and DP) entries

FIELD NAME	DESCRIPTION	ATTRIBUTES
JAENTL	Entry length	*DEC(5,0) Zoned
JASEQN	Sequence Number	*DEC(10,0) Zoned
JACODE	Journal Code	*CHAR(1)
JAENTT	Entry Type	*CHAR(2)
JADATE	Entry Date	*CHAR(6)
JATIME	Entry Time	*DEC(6,0) Zoned
JARES	Reserved Area	*CHAR(95)
JAJOB	Job name	*CHAR(10)
JAUSER	User profile	*CHAR(10)
JANBR	Job number	*DEC(6,0) Zoned
JACDE	Accounting code	*CHAR(15)

Additional job accounting (JB) fields generated to output file
*LIBL/QAJBACG for entry type of JB only

FIELD NAME	DESCRIPTION	ATTRIBUTES
JACPU	CPU time used (milliseconds)	*DEC(11,0) Packed
JARTGS	Number of routing steps	*DEC(5,0) Packed
JAEDTE	Date job entered system (mmddyy)	*CHAR(6)
JAETIM	Time job entered system (hhmmss)	*CHAR(6)
JASDTE	Date job started (mmddyy)	*CHAR(6)
JASTIM	Time Job started (hhmmss)	*CHAR(6)
JATRNT	Total transaction time (seconds)	*DEC(11,0) Packed
JATRNS	Number of transactions	*DEC(11,0) Packed
JAAUX	Auxiliary I/O and DB operations (including Page faults)	*DEC(11,0) Packed
JATYPE	Job type A = Autostart B = Batch I = Interactive M = Subsystem Monitor R = Spooling Reader W = Spooling Writer	*CHAR(1)
JCCDE	Completion code 000 = Normal completion 010 = Normal completion during controlled cancel 020 = Job exceeded cancel severity 030 = Job terminated abnormally 040 = Job cancelled before active 050 = Job cancelled while active 060 = Subsystem terminated abnormally while job was active 070 = System terminated abnormally while job was active 080 = Job completed within the time limit 090 = Job forced to complete after time limit expired 099 = Accounting entry caused by CHGACGCOD command	*DEC(3,0) Packed
JALINE	Number of print lines	*DEC(11,0) Packed
JAPAGE	Number of printed pages	*DEC(11,0) Packed
JAPRTF	Number of print files	*DEC(11,0) Packed
JADBPT	Number of DB put operations	*DEC(11,0) Packed
JADBGT	Number of DB get operations	*DEC(11,0) Packed
JADBUP	Number of DB update, delete, FEOD, release, commit, and rollback operations	*DEC(11,0) Packed

Figure 12.1 Continued

Figure 12.1

Job Accounting File Field Layout *Continued*

FIELD NAME	DESCRIPTION	ATTRIBUTES
JACMPT	Number of communications puts	*DEC(11,0) Packed
JACMGT	Number of communications gets	*DEC(11,0) Packed
JAACT	Time job was active (milliseconds)	*DEC(11,0) Packed
JASPN	Time job suspended (milliseconds)	*DEC(11,0) Packed
	Additional fields generated to output file *LIBL/QAPTACG for Entry Type of DP or SP Only	
JADFN	Device file name	*CHAR(10)
JADFNL	Device file library	*CHAR(10)
JADEVN	Device name	*CHAR(10)
JADEVT	Device type	*CHAR(4)
JADEVM	Device model	*CHAR(4)
JATPAG	Number of printed pages produced	*DEC(11,0) Packed
JATLIN	Number of printed lines produced	*DEC(11,0) Packed
JASPFN	Spool file name (SP)	*CHAR(10)
JASPNB	Spool file number (SP)	*CHAR(4)
JAOPTY	Output priority (SP)	*CHAR(1)
JAFMTP	Form type (SP)	*CHAR(10)
JABYTE	Total bytes sent to printer (SP)	*DEC(11,0) Packed
JAUSRD	User Data (AS/400 only)	*CHAR(10)

instance, to charge CPU use to other departments, you can assign the same accounting code to each user profile in a department. Or perhaps you want to isolate users or programmers you suspect of burdening the system with CPU-intensive interactive functions while nobody is looking — copying half a million records, for instance. Assigning one accounting code to this group of user profiles would produce documentation of such abuse.

Once you decide how you want to organize and use job accounting, you can assign codes to existing user profiles with the CHGUSRPRF (Change User Profile) command. The Job accounting commands are listed in Figure 12.2.

For example, to journal Smith's activity so it can be charged to the finance division, you would execute the following command:

```
CHGUSRPRF USRPRF(SMITH1) ACGCDE(FINANCE)
```

If you want to change more than one user profile at the same time, you can use the WRKUSRPRF (Work with User Profiles) command. You can assign accounting codes to new users with the CRTUSRPRF (Create User Profile) command.

Once you group users and assign accounting codes to them, you need to create a receiver using the CRTJRNRCV (Create Journal Receiver) command as follows:

```
CRTJRNRCV JRNRCV(receiver_name)
```

You should treat this receiver, and the journal itself, like all other journals on the system: Attach a new receiver to the journal periodically, and archive the old receiver for backup purposes. (For more information about journaling, see "Journal Management," Chapter 10.)

Figure 12.2

Job Accounting Commands

CHGUSRPRF ACGCOD(code_name)	Assign code to current user
CRTUSRPRF ACGCOD(code_name)	Assign code to new user
CRTJRNRCV JRNRCV(receiver_name)	Create journal receiver to hold job accounting journal entries.
CRTJRN JRN(QSYS/QACGJRN) + JRNRCV(receiver_name)	Create AS/400 accounting journal
CHGSYSVAL SYSVAL(QACGLVL) + VALUE(*JOB)	Establish accounting level
RTVJOBA ACGCOD(&ACGCOD)	Retrieve accounting code within a job stream
CHGACGCOD ACGCOD(code_name)	Change accounting code within a job stream

It's a good idea to give journal receivers a generic name indicating what they are used for. For instance, you might name the receiver JOBACC. Then when you detach one receiver and attach another by specifying CHGJRN JRNRCV(*GEN), the system automatically names the next receiver by appending a sequential number starting with 0001. You should also consider giving journal receivers their own auxiliary storage pool to isolate journal operations from other disk operations and enhance recovery capability.

Now that you have the receiver, you must attach it to a journal. Use the CRTJRN (Create Journal) command to create the journal with the name QACGJRN in library QSYS and attach the receiver. For example, the AS/400 command would be

```
CRTJRN JRN(QSYS/QACGJRN) JRNRCV(JOBACC)
```

You must be authorized to add objects to QSYS to create the accounting journal.

After you create the journal, you can change the accounting level system value (QACGLVL) to tell the system what types of journal entries it should generate. You can do this with the CHGSYSVAL (Change System Value) command:

```
CHGSYSVAL SYSVAL(QACGLVL) VALUE(*JOB)
```

VALUE(*JOB) produces job-resource accounting journal entries (designated JB) containing summaries of resources a job uses (e.g., processing unit time, number of routing steps, total transaction time). VALUE(*PRINT) produces direct-print (DP) output accounting and spooled-print (SP) output accounting entries. The system produces a DP entry whenever a SPOOL(*NO) output file is printed. However, when you specify SPOOL(*YES) on the print file definition, no printed output is created until the file is released to the printer; job accounting then generates an SP entry when the job is printed. The SP entry shows how many printed lines and pages were actually produced. (DP and SP entries record actual printer output: A 50-page report with ten copies generates one SP entry of 500 pages. A 75-page report printed five times (not five copies) generates five SP entries of 75 pages.) VALUE(*JOB *PRINT) for QACGLVL directs the system to generate all three types of entries (i.e., JB, DP, and SP). (IBM's *AS/400 Work Management Guide* (SC41-8078) provides more information about job accounting entries.)

That's all there is to it. Jobs that enter the system after you execute the CHGSYSVAL command run under job accounting. The system records information for each interactive and batch job executed.

In some cases, you may want to charge a job to a different accounting code than the one assigned to the user running the job — if the system operator (with an information services department accounting code) submits a job for a user department, for example. You can use the CHGACGCOD (Change Accounting Code) command as many times as you wish to segment a procedure, charging different parts of a program to different accounting units.

Figure 12.3 shows a CL program that executes jobs for the finance, marketing, and internal auditing departments. Before each job is run, the CHGACGCOD command causes the system to write a job completion entry to the appropriate accounting code. Be aware that a user authorized to execute the CHGACGCOD command can also change the ACGCOD parameter in the job description for the user's current job (if the user has authority to create or change job descriptions).

Retrieving Information

Even though the system is now making journal entries to receivers, you will need to retrieve the information so you can analyze it. To do this, you must first convert the accounting data into physical files. The system provides two field reference files as source statements for the physical files: QAJBACG for JB entries, and QAPTACG for DP and SP entries. You can combine these two files into a multiple-format logical file if you want to retrieve all three types of entries with one file-read operation.

Figure 12.3

Sample Program for Segmenting Jobs

```
PGM
CHGACGCOD  ACGCOD(FINANCE)
CALL PGM(JOB#1)
CHGACGCOD ACGCOD(MARKETING)
CALL PGM(JOB#2)
CHGACGCOD  ACGCOD(AUDITING)
CALL PGM(JOB#3)
ENDPGM
```

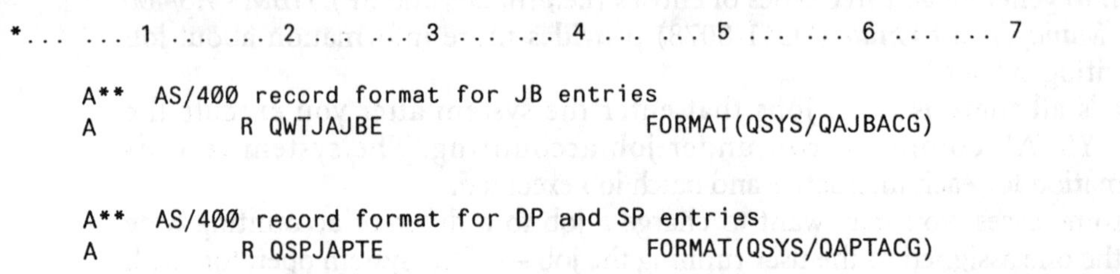

Figure 12.4

DDS for AS/400 Physical Files

```
*... ... 1 ... ... 2 ... ... 3 ... ... 4 ... ... 5 ... ... 6 ... ... 7

A**  AS/400 record format for JB entries
A          R QWTJAJBE                   FORMAT(QSYS/QAJBACG)


A**  AS/400 record format for DP and SP entries
A          R QSPJAPTE                   FORMAT(QSYS/QAPTACG)
```

Before you can create the physical files, you need to tell the system where to find their field layouts. Figure 12.4 shows DDS source for the system-supplied layouts. Once you define the DDS, use the CRTPF (Create Physical File) command to create data files with those layouts (see Figure 12.5). Then simply use the DSPJRN (Display Journal) command (Figure 12.6) to convert the journal entries into data records. As you set up this procedure, remember that whoever executes the DSPJRN command must have existence rights to the journal.

File field formats for the physical file correspond to the format of the journal receiver entry. The formats are straightforward except for some quirks in the way job accounting collects database information. For QAJBACG and QAPTACG, database I/O counts (fields JADBPT, JADBGT, and JADBUP — see Figure 12.1) do not include I/O to readers and writers or I/O generated from the CPYSPLF (Copy Spooled File) and DSPSPLF (Display Spooled File) commands. Also, if SEQONLY(*YES) is in effect (i.e., sequential-only processing is to be used on the file), the total will show blocks of records read, not the number of individual records. Sequential-only processing can occur in the following cases:

- when you request SEQONLY(*YES) in the OVRDBF (Override with Database File) command;
- when the system reads a file in arrival sequence;
- when the system writes a file in blocks; or
- when you use the SEQONLY parameter in the OPNQRYF (Open Query File) command.

Using The Job Accounting System

Now that you have all this data at your disposal, it's up to you to make good use of it. The uses you can find for this information are virtually limitless.

For instance, by selecting JATYPE = 'I', you can look at interactive jobs. Or take JATRNT (total transaction time) and divide it by JATRNS (total transactions) to get the average response time for a single interactive job, an accounting code, or a particular user, depending on how you sort and summarize the transactions. Query is a fine reporting tool for this purpose; for response time analysis, you can get a minimum, maximum, and average for any group you select. You can

Figure 12.5

CRTPF Commands for the AS/400

```
CRTPF FILE(*LIBL/QAJBACG) SRCFILE(*LIBL/QDDSSRC) +
      SRCMBR(QAJBACG)       /*   —AS/400 (JB)    */

CRTPF FILE(*LIBL/QAPTACG) SRCFILE(*LIBL/QDDSSRC) +
      SRCMBR(QAPTACG)          /*    —AS/400 (DP,SP)*/
```

Figure 12.6

DSPJRN Commands for the AS/400

```
DSPJRN JRN(QSYS/QACGJRN) ENTTYP(JB) +
       OUTPUT(*OUTFILE) OUTFILE(*LIBL/QAJBACG)     /*  AS/400 (JB) */

DSPJRN JRN(QSYS/QACGJRN) ENTTYP(DP SP) +
       OUTPUT(*OUTFILE) OUTFILE(*LIBL/QAPTACG)     /*  AS/400 (DP & SP)*/
```

also use a high-level language program to track system performance over time using whatever measures of performance or degradation you find appropriate. The only limit is your imagination.

System Performance

Your system should suffer no significant performance degradation using job accounting. Much of the data, in slightly different form, is written to the QHST log anyway, and the only overhead to journal job accounting is writing the journal entry itself. If you notice a response-time degradation, you can change the QACGLVL system value to *NONE to stop job accounting. Note that CPU usage figures in the job accounting journal will differ slightly from those in the QHST log. The journal includes the time required to write the job log, which the QHST log entry does not. (For more information about QHST, see the *Work Management Guide.*)

That's it. As you can see, job accounting lets you control your system, rather than your system controlling you. Never forget the old saw, though, about the three types of lies being lies, damn lies, and statistics. All good accountants know that statistics can be used to prove almost anything. Did the user running the on-line inventory program eat up so much CPU time because the user is a trainee, or was the inventory program written so poorly that hundreds of lines of code were executed when 10 or 20 would do? Is the average response time for a user so high because the applications being run are CPU-intensive, or is your system overloaded? When you analyze job-accounting data, be prudent about the conclusions you reach, as some measurements can be easily misinterpreted. With this caveat, go forth and let job accounting help you to conquer!

Chapter 13

Message Handling

by Douglas T. Parrish

Enhance your AS/400 communications with its message handling capabilities

When the AS/400's operating system, OS/400, was originally being developed by IBM, a design objective was to find a way to control communication between objects in the system. On most computer systems, messages are used primarily to send status information from program to user, or from user to user. But there is a need for a facility to communicate information among programs, users, history logs, job logs, the system operator, and even among machine components.

Designing separate routines to handle communications among all possible object types (is there an object type called *HUMAN?) is cumbersome and places too much of a burden on programmers. Thus, IBM incorporated a generalized message handler into OS/400 which uses message facilities to control object communication.

Messages provide information that is unique in content and meaning; they can be either impromptu or predefined. Impromptu messages are created by the sender when needed; a good example is "System Will Be Powered Down at 6 p.m." Predefined messages are stored within the system so they can be used repeatedly; they reside in an object called a Message File (MSGF). For instance, OS/400 messages reside within the system message file QCPFMSG in library QSYS. There also are message files for RPG, COBOL, and the system utilities. To store your own predefined messages, you must create a message file. This is done using the Create Message File (CRTMSGF) command. For example,

```
CRTMSGF MSGF(MYLIB/MYMSGF) TEXT('Example message file')
```

creates a message file called MYMSGF in library MYLIB. The message file can be given any name except when the RPG operation code DSPLY is used. In this case, the name of the message file must be QUSERMSG.

Predefined messages are identified by a seven-character ID code and are described by a message description. They are added to the message file using the Add Message Description (ADDMSGD) command, changed using the Change Message Description (CHGMSGD) or the Work with Message Descriptions (WRKMSGD) command, and removed using the Remove Message Description (RMVMSGD) command.

The first character of every message code must be alphabetic, the next two can be alphanumeric, and the last four must be numeric. IBM recommends that all user messages begin with the letter U to distinguish them from IBM-supplied messages. The last four digits are not significant except during message monitoring.

You can specify two levels of message text. First-level text normally is displayed when the message is sent. It can be up to 132 characters in length. Second-level text, up to 3,000 characters in length, can be displayed upon request. Second-level text normally is used for additional explanation such as problem determination.

Handling Human and Program Needs

Potential conflict exists between humans and programs using messages because of differences in their message data needs. Humans understand messages that are in a readable text format; programs, on the other hand, more easily process messages containing fields of data with predefined attributes. The message handler must be able to meet the data needs of both types of users — often with the same message.

The solution is to allow message fields to be specified with predefined attributes and length. A collective name for these fields is Message Data (MSGDTA). When a predefined message is sent using the Send Program Message (SNDPGMMSG) command, message data can be sent with the message. If a program is the recipient of a message, it can examine the message data and easily process the information since it is in field format. If the message recipient is a user, text can be combined with the message data in the form of substitution parameters, giving more meaning to the message. For example,

```
ADDMSGD MSGID(USR0001) MSGF(MYLIB/MYMSGF)                        +
  MSG('Program &1 terminated successfully')                      +
  FMT((CHAR 10))
```

adds a message USR0001 to the message file MYMSGF in library MYLIB. The &1 specified in the MSG parameter refers to the FMT parameter where the message data fields are defined. If message data fields are used in the message text, they are called message substitution parameters, and are specified within the first- or second-level text (MSG or SECLVL). They are preceded by the ampersand character (&) and followed by a number from one to 99. In the example, the first substitution parameter is in character format with a length of 10.

If a message is sent from a CL program, the SNDPGMMSG command looks something like this:

```
SNDPGMMSG MSGID(USR0001) MSGF(MYLIB/MYMSGF)                      +
  MSGDTA(&PGM) TOMSGQ(QSYSOPR)
```

Either constants or variables or a concatenation of both can be specified for the MSGDTA parameter. Notice that the message queue to which the message is sent is QSYSOPR, the system operator message queue. The example uses the variable &PGM. Let's assume &PGM has been previously defined as a character with length of 10 and a value of "PGMA". The message, when received by the system operator, will look like this:

```
Program PGMA terminated successfully
```

Notice that the message handler has truncated trailing blanks from the 10-character substitution parameter. In the same way, leading zeros of numeric substitution parameters are dropped when the message is displayed.

Up to nine types of substitution values (i.e., *QTDCHAR, character string with apostrophes; *CHAR, character string; *HEX, hexadecimal; *SPP, space pointer; *DEC, packed decimal; *BIN, binary; *DTS, date time stamp; *SYP, system pointer; or *ITV, time interval) are allowed in a message, and up to 99 message data fields can be specified in the message FMT parameter.

Let's look at an example. Assume a message is sent to an operator, notifying him of the rebuilding of a logical file access path. The message requires two message data fields, a file name, and a library name. First,

```
ADDMSGD MSGID(USR0002) MSGF(MYLIB/MYMSGF)                            +
   MSG('Access path for file &1/&2 rebuilt.')                       +
   FMT((*CHAR 10) (*CHAR 10))
```

adds message USR0002 to message file MYMSGF in library MYLIB.
A message can be sent from a CL program:

```
SNDPGMMSG MSGID(USR0002) MSGF(MYLIB/MYMSGF)                          +
  MSGDTA(('PRDDTA    ' *CAT 'FILE01    ')) TOMSGQ(QSYSOPR)
```

And it would appear at the system operator's message queue like this:

```
Access path for file PRDDTA/FILE01 rebuilt
```

Notice the use of concatenated constants instead of a variable in the message data parameter.

So far we have discussed only informational messages (*INFO), which convey information about certain conditions. There are several other types of messages, including inquiry messages (*INQ), completion messages (*COMP), diagnostic messages (*DIAG), notification messages (*NOTIFY), escape messages (*ESCAPE), request messages (*RQS), and status messages (*STATUS).

Inquiry Messages

Inquiry messages describe a condition and wait for a reply. A response is entered by the system operator, a user, or another program. Validity checking, if specified in the Add Message Description (ADDMSGD) command, can be performed on the returned response. Response type (character or decimal) and length can be specified. Valid values, range, or relationship also can be specified.

Send User Message (SNDUSRMSG), an OS/400 command, can send an inquiry message then wait for a response from the user. SNDUSRMSG is easier to use but eliminates some of the SNDPGMMSG command parameters. One of these parameters is the WAIT value, which will be demonstrated later.

An example of inquiry message processing shows some interesting message-processing functions. For instance, assume a program is being used to perform payroll file backup. The system operator is prompted to mount the payroll backup tape. Response codes C and G are tested for in the program and appropriate action taken. First,

```
ADDMSGD MSGID(USR0003) MSGF(MYLIB/MYMSGF)                    +
  MSG('Mount payroll backup tape (C G)')                     +
  TYPE(CHAR) LEN(1) VALUES('C' 'G')                          +
  SPCVAL(('c' 'C') ('g' 'G')) DFT('C')
```

adds the predefined message to the message file. TYPE specifies that the valid reply is character in format, with a length of one. Valid values are capitalized letters C and G. The SPCVAL parameter translates lowercase responses to uppercase.

In the CL program, two variables are needed: &MSGKEY and &RPY. &MSGKEY contains a value assigned by the system when the message is sent. It identifies the message so that when a response is sent, the system can determine to which message the response belongs. &RPY is the variable into which the response is placed. The variables are coded like this:

```
DCL VAR(&MSGKEY) TYPE(*CHAR) LEN(4)
DCL VAR(&RPY) TYPE(*CHAR) LEN(1)
```

The message processing follows:

```
SNDPGMMSG MSGID(USR0003) MSGF(MYLIB/MYMSGF)                  +
  TOMSGQ(QSYSOPR) MSGTYPE(*INQ)                              +
  KEYVAR(&MSGKEY)
RCVMSG MSGTYPE(*RPY)                                         +
  MSGKEY(&MSGKEY) WAIT(MAX) MSG(&RPY)
```

First, the inquiry message is sent to the system operator's message queue with the SNDPGMMSG command. The system places the unique message key into the variable &MSGKEY. The Receive Message (RCVMSG) command is then executed. It will wait for an indefinite period of time (WAIT(*MAX)) to receive the response to the message. The message key value set in the Send Program Message command is used to identify the message for which a reply is requested. When the system operator responds with a correct character, it will be placed into the variable &RPY and control will be passed to the next statement in the program. Response validation and translation is controlled by the message handler. Valid responses to the message are c, g, C, or G; but since the lowercase responses are translated to uppercase, the only values returned in the &RPY variable are C or G.

Since WAIT(*MAX) is used, the program will wait forever until the operator enters a valid response. A numeric value indicating the number of seconds to wait also can be used to continue to another function if a response is not received after a specified period of time. If the wait time is exceeded, the reply variable, &RPY, will have a blank value. Other data that can be received using the RCVMSG command include message identification, text (first and second level), message data, and severity. IBM's *CL Programmer's Guide* (SC41-8077) can give you more information.

Completion and Diagnostic Messages

Completion and diagnostic messages are treated much the same as informational messages. For example, you can send a completion message to signal successful completion of a program, or a diagnostic message to report processing errors to a calling program. Diagnostic messages usually are followed by an escape message that informs the caller that diagnostic messages were sent.

Status Messages

Status messages have several different purposes, and are quite useful when used with interactive jobs. A status message, sent to the job message queue of an interactive job, is displayed on the active message line of a workstation. If you have used the Copy File (CPYF) command, you may have noticed that during execution the operator is informed that the copy is in progress and is given the number of records successfully copied. OS/400 uses status messages to perform this function, and you can do the same thing.

Status messages must be predefined. They can be described with substitutional parameters and appropriate message data. They are sent to the job message queue using TOPGMQ(*EXT). For example,

```
SNDPGMMSG MSGID(USR0002) MSGF(MYLIB/MYMSGF)                        +
MSGDTA(('PRDDTA    ' *CAT 'FILE01    ')) TOPGMQ(*EXT)              +
  TYPE(STATUS)
```

displays the following message on the bottom line of the workstation:

```
Access path for file PRDDTA/FILE01 rebuilt
```

The line for status message display is the active message line. If your display files use a line other than line 24 for messages, the messages are displayed there. CPF normally defaults the message line to line 24. If you change the active message line using the DDS keyword MSGLOC, status messages sent from interactive jobs will be displayed on the line specified.

Escape Messages

Escape messages are sent by commands to inform the sender that a problem was encountered and that the called program was terminated. Escape messages can be monitored, allowing appropriate corrective action to be taken. In CL, this is accomplished using the Monitor Message (MONMSG) command.

When using MONMSG, the first MONMSG parameter, MSGID, is required. A list of up to 50 message IDs can be specified, and either the message ID or a group of messages can be specified. For example, MONMSG MSGID(CPF1234) monitors for message CPF1234, MONMSG MSGID(CPF1200) monitors for messages CPF1200 through CPF1299, and MONMSG MSGID(CPF0000) monitors for messages CPF0000 through CPF9999.

The MONMSG command also has an EXEC parameter associated with it. The EXEC parameter contains a command that is executed if the specified message is intercepted. For example, MONMSG MSGID(CPF1234) EXEC(GOTO END) will cause program control to go to the label END: if message CPF1234 is received. The parameter is optional; if not specified, no action occurs.

In addition to the monitor, message data accompanying the message can be compared to a string specified in the MONMSG command parameter CMPDTA. The string can be up to 28 bytes long. If the specified message is received and its associated message data matches the compare value, the command specified in EXEC is executed.

Messages can be monitored at the program level or at the command level. At the program level, if an escape message is sent to the program, it will be intercepted. Up to 100 MONMSG commands for program-level monitoring can be specified immediately after the last declare command (DCL, DCLDTAARA, or DCLF). The EXEC parameter, which is optional, can specify any command except PGM, ENDPGM, IF, ELSE, DCL, DCLF, ENDDO, and MONMSG. If no command is specified, the escape message is ignored and the program continues with the command immediately after the command from which the escape message was sent.

Messages also can be monitored at a command level. This is done by coding the MONMSG command immediately after a command. Up to 100 MONMSG commands can be placed after a command. Again, the EXEC parameter is optional and can use any command except PGM, ENDPGM, IF, ELSE, DCL, DCLDTAARA, DCLF, ENDDO, and MONMSG. Although both types of monitoring can be used in a program, command level monitoring overrides program level monitoring. No more than 1,000 MONMSG commands can exist in a program.

Message Queues

All messages on the AS/400 are sent to message queues. The following message queues are supplied as part of OS/400:

- The system operator message queue, QSYSOPR.
- A message queue for each workstation.
- A job message queue for each job in the system.
- A program message queue for each program started within a job.
- The system history log message queue, QHST.

The system operator message queue QSYSOPR is the target for messages to the system operator. Workstation message queues are used for communication among workstation users. They have the same name as their workstations and are created when devices are described to the system using the Create Device Description (CRTDEVD) command.

Job message queues are used to receive messages that are sent during the course of a job. A job message queue is created for each job and exists until the job terminates. If you want to send a message to the job message queue, the TOMSGQ parameter should be specified as *EXT, which is the job message queue. When a job terminates, the job log, if specified, is generated from the messages which are in the job message queue.

Program message queues exist for each program started within a job and are used to receive messages from called programs. They are created automatically when a program is invoked and are deleted when the program terminates.

The system log message queue QHST provides a path to the system history log. Messages to be placed in any of these logs are sent to the corresponding message queue. For example,

```
SNDPGMMSG MSGID(USR0001) MSGF(MYLIB/MYMSGF)                    +
  TOMSGQ(QSYS/QHST) MSGDTA('ARP010')
```

sends the following message to the system history log QHST:

```
Program ARP010 terminated successfully
```

This technique can be used by a program to send a user message to the system history log when a sensitive function is performed, such as payroll master file maintenance. By monitoring the history log, you can determine how often the function was requested.

Chapter 14

Disk Space Management

by Carson Soule

Use these strategies to make the most of your AS/400's disk space

The AS/400 loves disk. And as it gets older, it loves disk even more. Each subsequent release is up to 10 percent bigger than the previous release. And as the AS/400 is used more, it wants even more disk. Left on its own, the AS/400 will consume all the disk it has, even if your program and data libraries don't grow a byte.

So what do you do with this disk space glutton? There are only two choices: Regularly buy more disk (Volume Procurement Agreements (VPAs) are available from IBM), or manage the disk you have. This chapter is about the second choice. Granted, disk management takes time; but like many AS/400 tasks, knowing what to do and having a few key programs can keep this time to a minimum.

After plowing through many manuals, finagling internal-use-only SE newsletters, going to COMMON, pestering Rochester developers, and monitoring the space on our company's own systems, we have arrived at a list of management tasks. The tasks help you identify many of the space-consuming objects and the operations you must perform to recover the extra space they use. The list contains two kinds of actions: things to do once and things you must do regularly. Some of the latter you can program and execute as part of a normal IPL or nightly/weekly process. Note that many of these actions require security-administrator or spool-control authority.

First Things First

To see how much disk space you have and what portion of it objects occupy, run the WRKSYSSTS (Work with System Status) command. In the upper right part of the screen, this command displays the total disk space on your system in megabytes and, as a percentage of the total disk space, the disk space objects use.

Armed with information about how much disk space your objects use, let's look at exactly what is on your disk and which objects you can remove. IBM shipped many systems with the operating system and utilities already loaded. IBM SEs or Business Partners loaded many others. In either case, extra utilities or options were probably loaded onto your disk. To review the IBM program products on your disk, key

```
GO LICPGM
```

and run Option 12 = Delete licensed programs. This option displays all installed licensed programs and options.

Items to consider for deletion include any utility that is not at the current release level, unused languages, the migration utility, PC Support options for OS/2 and the double-byte character set (DBCS), language dictionaries other than ones you actually use, Advanced Function Printing and fonts, previous release support (*PRV) for the compilers, S/36 and S/38 environment support, S/36 and S/38 RPG compiler support, on-line education, and QUSRTOOL — the example tools library. In Appendix C of the AS/400 manual, *Licensed Programs and New Releases Installation Guide* (SC41-9878), you'll find a list of the licensed programs and options. This list shows the space each program/option requires on disk and the time required to install it. The time required to delete the product is close to the time required to install it.

Before deleting any licensed program, make sure you have a backup copy. (You can save licensed programs from the GO LICPGM menu with Option 13 = Save licensed programs.) Your distribution tapes may be a sufficient backup, but remember that you will have to apply PTFs to a licensed program if you restore it from the distribution tapes. You can use GO LICPGM's Option 11 = Install licensed programs to reinstall a licensed program that has been deleted.

By removing unused licensed programs, we have reduced the amount of IBM overhead on an AS/400 by more than 70 MB. That was more than 10 percent of the disk on our model 20.

If you migrated your software to the AS/400 using the IBM Migration Aid, you may find that it left a number of unused objects on your system. Use the WRKLIB (Work with Libraries) command

```
WRKLIB QMGU*
```

to display all migration libraries. Library QMGU itself contains the migration utility programs and should only be deleted using Option 12 = Delete licensed programs from the GO LICPGM menu. However, any other library name that starts with QMGU and is followed by six digits is a migration work library. You should delete these libraries as soon as the migration is complete and verified. To delete them, use Option 4 on the WRKLIB command, or use the DLTLIB (Delete Library) command. You don't need to back up these work libraries before deleting them.

Another set of objects left over from migration is found in your application program libraries. Source files QS36LOD and QS36DDSSRC contain work members created during migration and compilation. All members should be removed from these files with the RMVM (Remove Member) command. (You don't need to back up these files before removing the members.) In addition, you can remove DFU source members from the QS36SRC files as the members serve no purpose on the AS/400.

The next step is to use the command

```
WRKLIB *ALL
```

to review all the libraries on your system. You can save and then delete unused or infrequently used user libraries. When looking at infrequently used libraries, consider your source code. It often takes as much space as the object programs. Note that you cannot remove your S/36 environment procedures or the source for sorts, but you can save all other source offline or even online in a compressed save file. I recommend that at least two backups of the source code exist before you delete it from disk. Starting with OS/400 Version 2.1 you also have the option to compress your library objects, including source code; but you must remember that the system decompresses these objects when they are used. If an object is used frequently and you want it to be stored compressed, you will need to set up a regular method to recompress it.

A more controversial option is to remove the observable information from your object programs. Some vendors do this as a matter of course, but many do not. When you remove observable information from a program, you remove the program template, which reduces the size of the program by 40 to 50 percent. However, the debug facility (STRDBG — Start Debug, ADDBKP — Add Breakpoint) cannot be used against a program without its template. Also, you may not be able to restore the program on a previous release. While this option has these serious drawbacks, it saves a significant amount of disk space and reduces backup time and tape. You should seriously consider it for all your stable production systems. To remove observable information from all programs in a library, use the following CHGPGM (Change Program) command:

```
CHGPGM PGM(library/*ALL) RMVOBS(*ALL)
```

Be sure to back up the library before running this command.

Spring Cleaning

Now that the one-time steps are complete, you can consider the steps that you must take periodically. First on the list is to IPL. On systems that have been IPLed infrequently, we have retrieved as much as 30 percent of the disk space. This space was tied up in system control areas, other temporary spaces, and unused spool file members that are not freed until the next IPL. On our company's moderately busy system (model B40 with 40 users), a weekly IPL returns between 3 and 5 percent of our 3.2 GB of disk space.

Periodically (about every six months for us), you should run a RCLSTG (Reclaim Storage) and RCLDLO (Reclaim Document Library Object) command. Both commands require a dedicated system, and both can take quite a while to run (RCLSTG took more than eight hours the last time we ran it). RCLSTG puts lost objects into library QRCL where you can review and recover or delete them.

Note that if you have a critical storage condition while running RCLSTG, the system will halt and issue the critical storage message. The low-level text for this message says to run RCLSTG! To avoid this problem, use the following command to change the job to ignore break messages just before you run the RCLSTG command:

```
CHGJOB BRKMSG(*NOTIFY)
```

If you have Office on your system, or if you use PC Support's shared folders, review the contents of library QDOC using the WRKFLR (Work with Folders) command. Save unused or infrequently used folders with the SAVDLO (Save Document Library Object) command, and then delete them from the system. Do not remove any IBM folders whose names start with the letter Q.

System Upkeep

More frequently, there are a number of areas of disk usage to review. Use the WRKJOBQ (Work with Job Queues) command to review all job queues on your system. Look at each job queue with jobs in it using Option 5 = Work with. End old jobs that were held (if they will never be released) using Option 4 = End. You may find jobs submitted to job queues that are not attached to an active subsystem. These jobs should be transferred to an active job queue or ended with Option 4. (Another interesting way to see all the jobs on the system is with the WRKUSRJOB *ALL command. You can use the second parameter (STATUS) to limit the jobs displayed to those in a JOBQ, ACTIVE, or OUTQ status.)

You should also review output queues frequently. Use the WRKOUTQ (Work with Output Queues) command to review all output queues on your system. Look at each output queue with files in it using Option 5 = Work with. Pressing F11 = View 2 will show you the date, time, and user when the file was created. Delete old spool files that are no longer required using Option 4 = Delete. Deleting old spool files not only frees the space used by the spool file but it also allows the job that created the spool file to be removed from the system.

Use Operational Assistant

You can simplify the process of performing your system upkeep chores by taking advantage of OS/400's Operational Assistant. Operational Assistant makes it easy to manage those system objects on disk that seem to grow and grow. Operational Assistant submits the cleanup job to a job queue of your choice, where it waits until the specified time to run. For each category of objects, you can set the number of days (1 to 366) you want to keep the objects. The default time for the daily cleanup is 10 p.m., but you can designate any time for the routine to run. Each time it does, it:

- Deletes user messages older than the number of days specified. The default is seven days, but I recommend four days, which keeps user messages to a minimum but lets a user see messages received over the weekend.
- Deletes system messages (QSYSOPR and workstation message queues) older than the number of days specified. The default is one day, but I recommend

seven days, which affords a margin of safety (once messages are deleted, you can't go back and see what happened on the system).

- Deletes job logs, program dumps, and service dumps older than the number of days specified. The IBM-supplied default is seven days. If your programmer is on site, you may want to delete job logs, program dumps, and service dumps every two or three days. If, however, your programmer is off site, you may want to keep these objects longer so that, if a problem emerges, the programmer can still refer to the job log. When Operational Assistant is set up, this output is routed to a specific output queue (job log output to QEZJOBLOG and dumps to QEZDEBUG).
- Deletes system journals and system logs older than the number of days specified. The default is 30, but again, I recommend every seven days or less if you do regular saves. Operational Assistant deletes the journal receivers for Office, Distributed System Network Executive, System Network Architecture Distribution Services (SNADS), problems, and security changes.

As Operational Assistant deletes old records, it also reorganizes files to free the space used by the deleted entries.

There's More...

In addition to the various objects mentioned above, OS/400 leaves a number of other objects on your system, and programmers may create even more. If you download PTFs using ECS, the PTFs are placed in QGPL as save files with a name that begins with P and is followed by the PTF number. You can delete these save files after the PTFs are loaded and applied. To delete all PTF save files, first use the WRKOBJ (Work with Objects) command to be sure there are no user files in QGPL that start with the letter P. If there are other files, use WRKOBJ's Option 4 = Delete to delete just the PTF save files. If there are only PTF files, execute the command

```
DLTF QGPL/P*
```

While you are working in QGPL, look for user-created objects that ended up in QGPL by accident. Because it is the default library, simple mistakes by programmers can result in programs or files in QGPL that are not needed. Use

```
WRKOBJ QGPL/*ALL
```

to review the contents of QGPL and Option 4 = Delete to delete unnecessary objects. It's a good idea to back up library QGPL before deleting objects — in case you make a mistake and need to recover an object.

When IBM ships its compilers, it includes a verification program in a source file (QxxxSRC) in QGPL. If you are not using these source files and you have verified the installation of the compilers on your system, you can remove all members from these files with the command

```
RMVM FILE(QGPL/QXXXSRC) MBR(*ALL)
```

Replace the xxx with BAS, CBL, CL, DDS, LBL, PAS, PLI, RJX, or RPG — depending on the compilers installed on your system. Note that QDDSSRC contains the source code for the sign-on screen, which you may want to save.

When you use the performance measurement tools, performance data is collected in library QPFRDATA (or another, user-specified, library). The data in this library should be deleted when the performance analysis is complete. You may want to save this data before deleting it. You can delete performance data with the STRPFRT (Start Performance Tools) command or by clearing library QPFRDATA with the CLRLIB (Clear Library) command.

Gone, But Not Forgotten

Office users can use space in a number of ways. Just like old libraries can take up space, old folders and documents can take up precious disk. Periodically review folders and documents to see whether they should be archived. Individual documents may be marked for off-line storage with an option to delete the document, delete its content (equivalent to the free option with other objects), or keep the document. You can find the total space required to hold documents by running the DSPLIB (Display Library) command against library QDOC.

In addition to documents and folders, Office users have mail and calendar entries. Make sure that users receive their mail and then file it or delete it. Note that if the QSNADS subsystem is not started, mail for indirect users will not print and thus will consume space on the system. Calendar entries must be deleted through the office administration option to work with Office files. Run the delete option against each calendar on the system specifying a date in the past before which calendar entries may be deleted. You can save the entries before deleting them, if necessary. Note that deleting the calendar entries just marks the calendar records as deleted but does not actually free any space. (In a minute, I'll explain how to reorganize files in library QUSRSYS to retrieve the space deleted records use.) Office data, including calendar entries, is stored in the QAO* files in QUSRSYS.

Problem records created by the system or by users running problem analysis can also build up on your system. Because problem records form a history of system problems, you may not want to delete them too quickly. However, in a communications environment, the system may log dozens of problems every day that you will never process. The DLTPRB (Delete Problem) command deletes problems older than a specified number of days. But, as with calendar entries, the space is not actually freed. Problem data, including PTF data, is stored in the QASX* files in QUSRSYS.

Students enrolled in System Delivered Education also use up space, particularly if they use bookmarks (up to 1 MB per bookmark!). Be sure to remove students from the system after they have completed their education using the STREDU (Start Education) command to work with student information. Again, records are deleted but space is not freed. Education data is stored in the QAE* files in QUSRSYS.

If you are in a communications network and your system receives alerts indicating network problems, be sure to use the WRKALR (Work with Alerts) command to delete alerts once they have been handled. Again, records are deleted but space is not freed. Alternately, all the alerts can be deleted and the space freed with the command:

```
CLRPFM FILE(QUSRSYS/QAALRT) MBR(QAALRT)
```

I have noted in a number of steps above that records are deleted but the space they occupy is not freed. On the AS/400, a deleted record keeps its space until the file it is in is reorganized with the RGZPFM (Reorganize Physical File Member) command. This command reorganizes a file, removing the deleted records and returning the space they occupy to the system as available space. Most application systems perform this function on application files periodically. IBM does not. You must run the command on each file to be reorganized. The system files containing deleted records are all in library QUSRSYS and their names are noted above. To see how many deleted records are in your files and how much space they occupy, run the command:

```
DSPFD FILE(QUSRSYS/*ALL) TYPE(*MBR) FILEATR(*PF)
```

An easier way to see this information is to use the above command to an outfile and then build a Query over the outfile.

Rather than having to reorganize each file separately, I have created command RGZPF (Figure 14.1 contains the command; Figure 14.2 contains the CPP), which reorganizes all the files in QUSRSYS. RGZPF lets you name the library and files(s) (including *ALL) to be reorganized. The KEYVAL parameter indicates whether the records should be left in the order they are currently in or reorganized in the order of the file key (if any). This matches the parameter of IBM's RGZPFM command. The DLTPCT parameter sets the threshold value to trigger the reorganize. Files with fewer deleted records, as a percent of all records in the file, are not reorganized. The default is 10 percent, but when using this command against QUSRSYS, I use 0 percent. The DLTMIN sets an absolute minimum number of deleted records required to trigger the reorganize. The default is 1. The DLTMAX sets an absolute maximum number of deleted records over which a reorganize is forced. The default is 999999999.

The steps outlined above, followed by a reorganize of all files in QUSRSYS, will retrieve most of the excess space AS/400 objects consume.

Figure 14.1

Command RGZPF

```
/*****************************************************************************/
/*                                                                           */
/*  Description:  RGZPF - Reorganize Physical Files                          */
/*                                                                           */
/*  Parameters:  File, Member, Library, Keyfile, Delete options              */
/*                                                                           */
/*  Written for CAS By:  CS / May, 1990                                      */
/*                                                                           */
/*****************************************************************************/

          CMD        PROMPT('Reorganize Physical Files')

          PARM       KWD(FILE) TYPE(*GENERIC) LEN(10) +
                       SPCVAL((*ALL)) MIN(1) FILE(*UPD) +
                       CHOICE('Name, generic*, *all') +
                       PROMPT('Data base file')

          PARM       KWD(LIB) TYPE(*NAME) LEN(10) DFT(*CURLIB) +
                       SPCVAL((*CURLIB) (*LIBL)) MIN(0) +
                       CHOICE('Name, *CURLIB, +
                       *LIBL') PROMPT('Library')

          PARM       KWD(KEYFILE) TYPE(*NAME) LEN(10) DFT(*NONE) +
                       SPCVAL((*NONE) (*FILE)) MIN(0) FILE(*IN) +
                       CHOICE('Name, *NONE, *FILE') +
                       PROMPT('Key file')

          PARM       KWD(DLTPCT) TYPE(*DEC) LEN(2) DFT(10) MIN(0) +
                       CHOICE('00 - 99') +
                       PROMPT('Delete percent')

          PARM       KWD(DLTMIN) TYPE(*DEC) LEN(10) DFT(1) MIN(0) +
                       CHOICE('1 - +
                       9999999999') PROMPT('Minimum records to +
                       delete')

          PARM       KWD(DLTMAX) TYPE(*DEC) LEN(10) +
                       DFT(9999999999) MIN(0) +
                       CHOICE('0 - 9999999999') +
                       PROMPT('Maximum deleted records')
```

Figure 14.2

CPP for Command RGZPF

```
/***************************************************************************/
/*                                                                         */
/*  Description:                                                           */
/*    RGZPFC - Reorganize Physical Files                                   */
/*                                                                         */
/*  Parameters:                                                            */
/*    &FILE    - File name, generic name or *ALL                           */
/*    &LIB     - Library name                                              */
/*    &KEYFILE - Key file name, *NONE, *FILE                               */
/*    &DLTPCT  - Delete percent (percent of deleted records to trigger reorg) */
/*    &DLTMIN  - Minimum deleted records (do no reorg is less than minimum)   */
/*    &DLTMAX  - Maximum deleted records (reorg if over maximum)           */
/*                                                                         */
/*  Written for CAS By:  cs, May 1990                                      */
/*                                                                         */
/***************************************************************************/
 RGZPF:      PGM        PARM(&FILE  &LIB &KEYFILE &DLTPCT &DLTMIN +
                          &DLTMAX)

/* Declare parameters */
             DCL        VAR(&FILE   )  TYPE(*CHAR) LEN(10)
             DCL        VAR(&LIB    )  TYPE(*CHAR) LEN(10)
             DCL        VAR(&KEYFILE)  TYPE(*CHAR) LEN(10)
             DCL        VAR(&DLTPCT )  TYPE(*DEC )  LEN( 2 0)
             DCL        VAR(&DLTMIN )  TYPE(*DEC )  LEN(10 0)
             DCL        VAR(&DLTMAX )  TYPE(*DEC )  LEN(10 0)

/* Declare program variables */
             DCL        VAR(&ACTDLTPCT) TYPE(*DEC) LEN(3 0) /* actual +
                        delete record percent of file */

/* Declare error handling variables */
             DCL        VAR(&ERRFLG) TYPE(*LGL) /* error flag */

/* Declare data file for DSPFD */
             DCLF       FILE(QAFDMBR) /* DSPFD member list outfile */

/* Global monitor */
             MONMSG     MSGID(MCH0000 CPF0000 CPF9999) EXEC(GOTO +
                          CMDLBL(ENDERR)) /* exception handler */

/* Display physical file members */
             DSPFD      FILE(&LIB/&FILE) TYPE(*MBR) OUTPUT(*OUTFILE) +
                          FILEATR(*PF) OUTFILE(QTEMP/QAFDMBR) /* +
                          display member information for selected +
                          files */
             MONMSG     MSGID(CPF3020 CPF3012) EXEC(GOTO +
                          CMDLBL(ENDPGM)) /* no physical files found */

/* Read list of physical file members and reorganize as requested */
```

Figure 14.2 Continued

Figure 14.2

CPP for Command RGZPF *Continued*

```
            OVRDBF      FILE(QAFDMBR) TOFILE(QTEMP/QAFDMBR)
 RCVFIL:    RCVF        /* do while member records found */
            MONMSG      MSGID(CPF0864) EXEC(GOTO CMDLBL(ENDPGM)) /* +
                          end of file reached */

            IF          COND(&MBNDTR >= &DLTMIN) THEN(CHGVAR +
                          VAR(&ACTDLTPCT) VALUE((&MBNDTR * 100) / +
                          (&MBNDTR + &MBNRCD))) /* if the file +
                          contains deleted records over the minimum +
                          allowed, calculate actual deleted record +
                          percentage */

            IF          COND((&MBNDTR >= &DLTMIN) *AND (&ACTDLTPCT >= +
                          &DLTPCT) *OR (&MBNDTR > &DLTMAX)) THEN(DO) +
                          /* if this member matches the +
                          reorganization requirements */

            IF          COND((&KEYFILE *EQ '*FILE') *AND (&MBACCP *NE +
                          'A')) THEN(DO) /* if reorganize by key +
                          requested and file is keyed */
            RGZPFM      FILE(&MBLIB/&MBFILE) MBR(&MBNAME) +
                          KEYFILE(*FILE) /* reorganize file by key */
            MONMSG      MSGID(CPF2981 CPF2986) /* cannot allocate +
                          file */
            ENDDO       /* if reorganize by key */

            ELSE        CMD(DO)
            RGZPFM      FILE(&MBLIB/&MBFILE) MBR(&MBNAME) +
                          KEYFILE(*NONE) /* reorganize file */
            MONMSG      MSGID(CPF2981 CPF2986) /* cannot allocate +
                          file */
            ENDDO       /* if reorganize not by key */

            ENDDO       /* if reorganize requirements met */

            GOTO        CMDLBL(RCVFIL) /* end do next member record */

/* End program */
ENDPGM:     RETURN

/* Standard error handler */
 ENDERR:    IF          COND(*NOT &ERRFLG) THEN(DO)
            SNDPGMMSG   MSGID(CPF9898) MSGF(QCPFMSG) +
                          MSGDTA('RGZPF failed.  See job log for +
                          errors causing the failure') MSGTYPE(*ESCAPE) +
                          /* function check */
            MONMSG      MSGID(CPF0000) /* avoid error loop */
            CHGVAR      VAR(&ERRFLG) VALUE('1')
            ENDDO       /* if error condition */
            ENDPGM
```

DATA MANAGEMENT

Chapter 15

Physical File Structures

by Wayne Madden

Effective application development depends on understanding AS/400 file structures

If you count the various types of files the AS/400 supports, how many do you get? The answer is five. And 10. The AS/400 supports five *types* of files — database files, source files, device files, DDM files, and save files. So if you count types, you get five. However, if you count the file *subtypes* — all the objects designated as OBJTYPE(*FILE) — you get 10. Still puzzled? Figure 15.1 lists the five file types that exist on the AS/400, as well as the 10 subtypes and the specific CRTxxxF (Create xxx File) commands used to create them. Each file type (and subtype) contains unique characteristics that provide unique functions on the AS/400. In this chapter, I look at the various types of files and describe the way each file type functions.

Structure Fundamentals

If there is any one AS/400 concept that is the key to unlocking a basic understanding of application development, it is the concept of AS/400 file structure. It's not that the concept is difficult to grasp; it's just that there are quite a few facts to digest. So let's start by looking at how files are described.

On the AS/400, all files are described at four levels (Figure 15.2). First is the *object-level description*. A file is an AS/400 object whose object type is *FILE. The AS/400 maintains the same object description information for a file (e.g., its library and size) as it does for any other object on the system. You can look at the object-level information with the DSPOBJD (Display Object Description) command.

The second level of description the system maintains for *FILE objects is a *file-level description*. The file description is created along with the file when you execute a CRTxxxF command. It describes the attributes or characteristics of a

Figure 15.1

AS/400 File Types and Subtypes

File Type	Subtype	File Description	Create Command
Database File	PF	Physical File	CRTPF
	LF	Logical File	CRTLF
Source File	PF	Physical Source File	CRTSRCPF
Device File	DSPF	Workstation Display File	CRTDSPF
	PRTF	Printer File	CRTPRTF
	TAPF	Tape File	CRTTAPF
	DKTF	Diskette File	CRTDKTF
	ICFF	Intersystem Communications Function File	CRTICFF
DDM File	DDMF	Distributed Data Management File	CRTDDMF
Save File	SAVF	Save File	CRTSAVF

particular file and is embedded within the file itself. You can display or print a file description with the DSPFD (Display File Description) command.

The file subtype is one of the attributes maintained as part of the file description. This allows OS/400 to present the correct format for the description when using the DSPFD command. This also provides OS/400 with the ability to determine which commands can operate on which types of files. For instance, the DLTF (Delete File) command works for any type of file on the system, but the ADDPFM (Add Physical File Member) command only works for physical files. OS/400 uses the description of the file to maintain and enforce each file's object identity.

The third level of descriptive information the system maintains for files is the *record-level description.* This level describes the various, if more than one, record formats that exist in the file. A record format describes a set of fields that make a record. If the fourth level of description — field descriptions — is not used when creating the file, the record format is described by a specific record length.

All files have at least one record format, and logical files can have multiple record formats (we'll cover this topic in a future chapter). Applications perform I/O by using specific record formats. An application can further break the record format into fields by either explicitly defining those fields within the application or by working with the external field definitions if they are defined for a record format. While there is the DSPOBJD command and the DSPFD command, there is no Display Record Description command. You use the DSPF command and the DSPFFD (Display File Field Description) command to display or print the record-level information.

Figure 15.2

File Description Levels

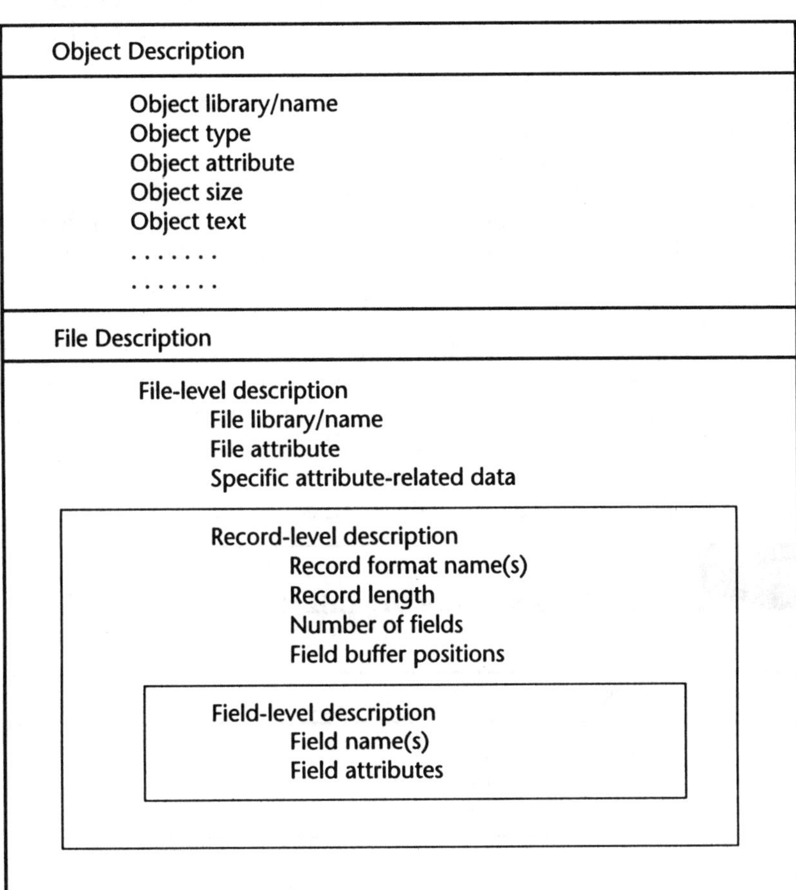

Object Description
Object library/name
Object type
Object attribute
Object size
Object text
....
....
File Description
File-level description
File library/name
File attribute
Specific attribute-related data
Record-level description
Record format name(s)
Record length
Number of fields
Field buffer positions
Field-level description
Field name(s)
Field attributes

The final level of descriptive information the system maintains for files is the *field-level description*. Field descriptions do not exist for all types of files; tape files, diskette files, DDM files, and save files have no field descriptions because they have no fields. (In the case of DDM files, the field descriptions of the target system file are used.) For the remaining files — physical, logical, source, display, printer, and ICF — a description of each field and field attribute is maintained. You can use the DSPFFD command to display or print the field-level descriptions for a file.

Data Members: A Challenge

Now that you know how files are described, you need a challenge! We now need to consider a particular organizational element that applies only to database and source files, the two types of files that actually contain records of data. You may be saying, "Wait, you don't have to tell us that. Each file is described (as discussed), and each file has records, right?"

I wish it were that simple, but on the AS/400 there is an additional element of file organization, the *data member*, that has caused even the best application programmers to cry in anguish. Examine Figure 15.3, which introduces you to the concept of the file data member. You traditionally think of a file containing a set of records, and usually an AS/400 database file has a description and a data member that contains all the records that exist in that database file. If you create a physical file using the CRTPF (Create Physical File) command and take the defaults for member name and maximum number of members, which are MBR(*FILE) and MAXMBRS(1), respectively, you will create a file that contains only one data member, and the name of that member will be the same name as the file itself.

So far, so good. Now comes the tricky part. Believe it or not, AS/400 database and source files can have *no* data members. If you create a physical file and specify MBR(*NONE), the file will be created without any data member for records. If you try to add records to that file, the system will issue an error stating that no data member exists. You would have to use the ADDPFM command to create a data member in the file before you could add records to the file.

Figure 15.3

Usual Database File Organization

File Name: TEST

File-level description
Record-level description
Field-level description

Data Member   Member name: TEST

Record 1 ....
Record 2 ....
Record 3 ....
Record 4 ....
Record 5 ....
Record 6 ....
Record 7 ....
Record 8 ....
Record 9 ....
Record 10..............................

At the other end of the scale is the fact that you can have *multiple* data members in a file. A source file offers a good example. Figure 15.4 represents the way a source file is organized. Each source member is a different data member in the file. When you create a new source member, you are actually creating another data member in this physical source file. Whether you are using PDM (Programming Development Manager) or SEU (Source Entry Utility), by specifying the name of the source member you want to work with, you are instructing the software to override the file to use that particular member for record retrieval.

Consider another example — a user application that views both current and historical data by year. Each year represents a unique set of records. This type of

Figure 15.4

Source File Organization

Source File: QRPGSRC

File-level description
Record-level description
Field-level description

Data Member Member name: INLT01

Source data record 1 ....
Source data record 2 ....
Source data record 3 ....
Source data record 4 ....
Source data record 5 ....

Data Member Member name: INLT02

Source data record 1 ....
Source data record 2 ....
Source data record 3 ....
Source data record 4 ....
Source data record 5 ....

Data Member Member name: INLT03

Source data record 1 ....
Source data record 2 ....
Source data record 3 ....
Source data record 4 ....
Source data record 5 ....

application might use a database file to store each year's records in separate data members, using the year itself to construct the name of the data member. Figure 15.5 represents how this application might use a single physical file to store these records. As you can see, each year has a unique data member, and each member has a various number of records. All members have the same description in terms of record format and fields, but each member contains unique data. The applications that access this data must use the OVRDBF (Override with Database File) command to open the correct data member for record retrieval (Chapter 17 will discuss file overrides in detail).

Wow! No database members...one database member... multiple database members... Why? That's a fair question. Using multiple data members provides a unique manner to handle data that uses the same record format and same field descriptions and yet must be maintained separately for business reasons. One set of software can be written to support the effort, but the data can be maintained, even saved, separately.

Having sorted through the structure of AS/400 files and dealt with data members, let's look specifically at the types of files and how they are used.

Figure 15.5

Physical File with Multiple Data Members

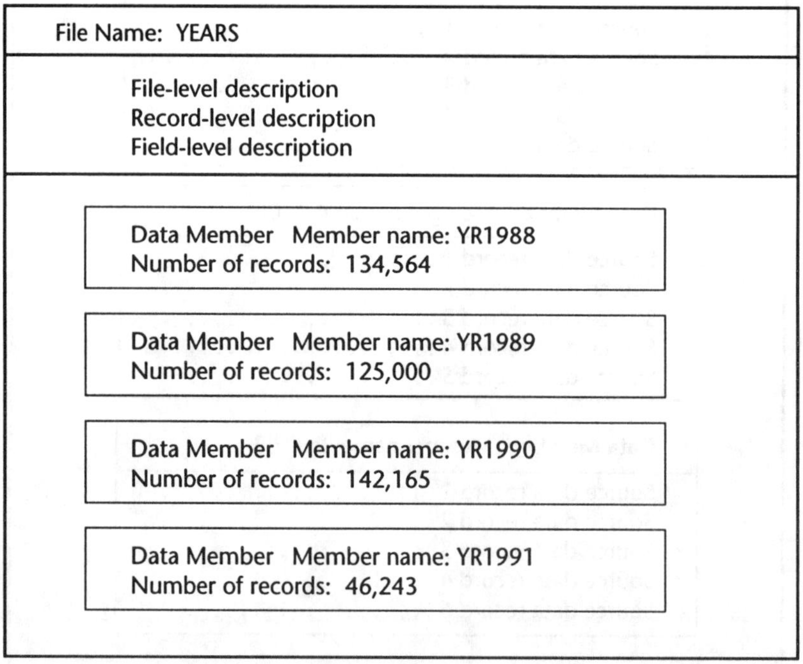

File Name: YEARS

File-level description
Record-level description
Field-level description

Data Member Member name: YR1988
Number of records: 134,564

Data Member Member name: YR1989
Number of records: 125,000

Data Member Member name: YR1990
Number of records: 142,165

Data Member Member name: YR1991
Number of records: 46,243

Database Files

Database files are AS/400 objects that actually contain data or provide access to data. Two types of files are considered database files — physical files and logical files. A *physical file*, denoted as TYPE(*FILE) and ATTR(PF), has file-, record-, and field-level descriptions and can be created with or without using externally described source specifications. Physical files — so called because they contain your actual data (e.g., customer records) — can have only one record format. The data entered into the physical file is assigned a relative record number based on arrival sequence. As I indicated earlier, database files can have multiple data members, and special program considerations must be implemented to ensure that applications work with the correct data members. You can view the data that exists in a specific data member of a file using the DSPPFM (Display Physical File Member) command.

A *logical file*, denoted as TYPE(*FILE) and ATTR(LF), is created in conjunction with physical files to determine how data will be presented to the requestor. For those of you coming from a S/36, the nearest kin to a logical file is an index or alternate index. Logical files contain no data but instead are used to specify key fields, select/omit logic, field selection, or field manipulation. The key fields serve to specify the access paths to use for accessing the actual data records that reside in physical files. Logical files must be externally described using DDS and can be used only in conjunction with externally described physical files.

Source Files

A source file, like QRPGSRC where RPG source members are maintained, is simply a customized form of a physical file; and as such, source files are denoted as TYPE(*FILE) and ATTR(PF). (Note: If you work with objects using PDM, physical data files and physical source files are distinguished by using two specific attributes — PF-DTA and PF-SRC.) All source files created using the CRTSRCPF (Create Source Physical File) command have the same record format and thus the same fields. When you use the CRTSRCPF command, the system creates a physical file that allows multiple data members. Each program source is one physical file member. When you edit a particular source member, you are simply editing a specific data member in the file.

Device Files

Device files contain no actual data. They are files whose descriptions provide information about how an application is to use particular devices. The device file must contain information valid for the device type the application is accessing. The types of device files are display, printer, tape, diskette, and ICF.

Display files, denoted by the system as TYPE(*FILE) and ATTR(DSPF), provide specific information relating to how an application can interact with a workstation. While a display file contains no data, the display file does contain various record formats that represent the screens the application will present to the workstation. Each specific record format can be viewed and maintained using IBM's Screen Design Aid (SDA), which is part of the Application Development Tools licensed program product.

Interactive high-level language (HLL) programs include the workstation display file as one of the files to be used in the application. The HLL program writes a display file record format to the screen to present the end user with formatted data and then reads that format from the screen when the end user presses Enter or another appropriate function key. Whereas I/O to a database file accesses disk storage, I/O to a display file accesses a workstation.

Printer files, denoted by the system as TYPE(*FILE) and ATTR(PRTF), provide specific information relating to how an application can spool data for output to a writer. The print file can be created with a maximum record length specified and one format to be used with a HLL program and program-described printing, or the print file can be created from external source statements that define the formats to be used for printing. Like display files, the print files themselves contain no data and therefore have no data member associated with them. When an application program performs output operations to a print file, the output becomes spooled data that can be printed on a writer device.

Tape files, denoted by the system as TYPE(*FILE) and ATTR(TAPF), provide specific information relating to how an application can read or write data using tape media. The description of the tape file contains information such as the device name for tape read/write operations, the specific tape volume requested (if a specific volume is desired), the density of the tape to be processed, the record and block length to be used, and other essential information relating to tape processing. Without the use of a tape file, HLL programs cannot access the tape media devices.

Diskette files, denoted by the system as TYPE(*FILE) and ATTR(DKTF), are identical to tape files except that these files support diskette devices. Diskette files have attributes that describe the volume to be used and the record and block length.

ICF (Intersystem Communications Function) files, denoted by the system as TYPE(*FILE) and ATTR(ICFF), provide specific attributes to describe the physical communications device used for application peer-to-peer communications programming. When a local application wants to communicate with an application on a remote system, the local application turns to the ICF file for information regarding the physical device to use for those communications. The ICF file also contains record formats used to read and write data from and to the device and the peer program.

DDM Files

DDM (Distributed Data Management) files, denoted by the system as TYPE(*FILE) and ATTR(DDMF), are objects that represent files that exist on a remote system. For instance, if your customer file exists on a remote system, you can create a DDM file on the local system that specifically points to that customer file on the remote system. DDM files provide you with an interface that lets you access the remote file just as you would if it were on your local system. You can compile programs using the file, read records, write records, and update records while the system handles the communications. Figure 15.6 represents a typical DDM file implementation.

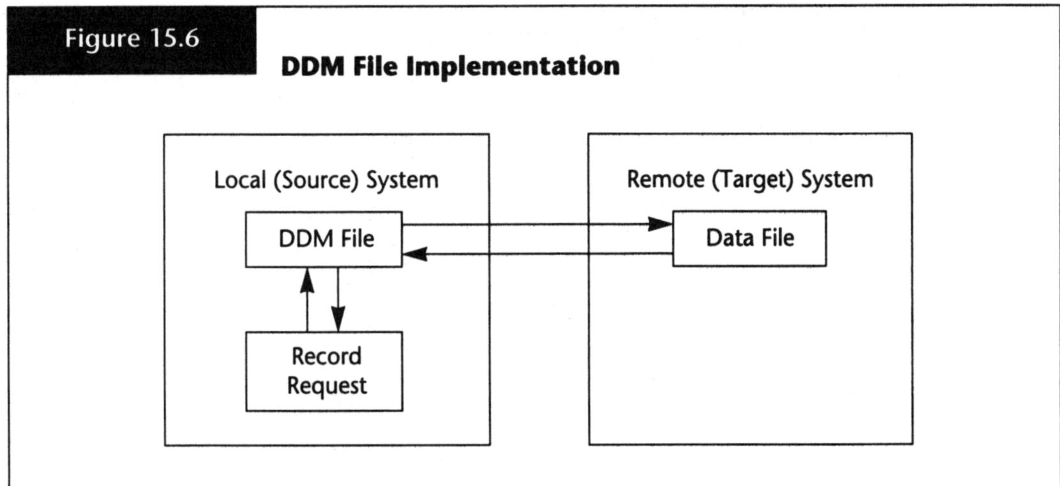

Figure 15.6
DDM File Implementation

Save Files

Save files, denoted by the system TYPE(*FILE) and ATTR(SAVF), are a special form of file designed specifically to handle save/restore data. You cannot determine the file-, record-, and field-level descriptions for a save file. The system creates a specific description used for all save files to make them compatible with save/restore operations.

Save files can be used to receive the output from a save operation and then be used as input for a restore operation. This works just as performing save/restore operations with tape or diskette, except that the saved data is maintained on disk, which enhances the save/restore process because I/O to the disk file is faster than I/O to a tape or diskette device. Save file data also can be transmitted electronically or transported via a sneaker network or overnight courier network to another system and then restored.

We have briefly looked at the various types of files that exist on the AS/400. Understanding these objects is critical to effective application development and maintenance on the AS/400. One excellent source for further reading is IBM's *Data Management Guide* (SC41-9658).

Chapter 16

Logical Files

by Wayne Madden

For many years, IBM sold the S/38 on the premise that it was the "logical choice." Yes, that play on words was corny, but true. One of the S/38's strongest selling points was the relational database implementation provided by logical files, and now the AS/400 has inherited that feature.

Logical files are the backbone of the AS/400's relational database implementation

So what's so special about logical files? They are the backbone of the AS/400's relational database implementation. (For an introduction to database design, see Chapter 19 — "Relational Database Principles.") Logical files provide the flexibility needed to build a database for an interactive multiuser environment.

There are two kinds of database files: physical files and logical files. Physical files contain data; logical files do not. Logical files control how data in physical files is presented, most commonly using key fields (whose counterpart on the S/36 is the alternate index) so that data can be retrieved in key-field sequence. However, the use of key fields is not the only function logical files provide. Let me introduce you to the following basic concepts about logical files:

- record format definition/physical file selection
- key fields
- select/omit logic
- multiple logical file members

Record Format Definition/Physical File Selection

To define a logical file, you must select the record formats to be used and the physical files to be referenced. You can use the record format found in the physical file, or you can define a new record format. If you use the physical file record format, every field in that record format is accessible through the logical file. If you create a new record format, you must specify which fields will exist in

Figure 16.1

DDS for Physical File HREMFP

```
*... ... 1 ... ... 2 ... ... 3 ... ... 4 ... ... 5 ... ... 6 ... ... 7

     *--------------------------------------------------------------*
     * Human Resources Applications                                 *
     * Employee Master File - Physical File                         *
     *--------------------------------------------------------------*
     *
     A                                      REF(DBDICT)
     A          R HREMFR                    TEXT('Employee Master')
     *
     A            EMEMP#    R
     A            EMFNAM    R
     A            EMMINT    R
     A            EMLNAM    R
     A            EMSTRT    R
     A            EMCITY    R
     A            EMST      R
     A            EMZIP     R
     A            EMPHON    R
     A            EMDEPT    R
     A            EMSTRD    R
     A            EMTRMD    R
     A            EMSSN#    R
     A            EMTYPE    R
     A            EMPAYR    R
```

the logical file. A logical file field must either reference a field in the physical file record format or be derived by using concatenation or substring functions.

Because the logical file does not contain any data, it must know which physical file to access for the requested data. You use the DDS PFILE keyword to select the physical file referenced by the logical file record format. You specify the physical file in the PFILE keyword as a qualified name (i.e., library_name\file_name) or as the file name alone.

Figure 16.1 lists the DDS for physical file HREMFP, and Figure 16.2 shows the DDS for logical file HREMFL1. Notice that the logical file references the physical file's record format (HREMFR). Consequently, every field in the physical file will be presented in logical file HREMFL1. Also notice that the PFILE keyword in Figure 16.2 references physical file HREMFP.

In Figure 16.3, logical file HREMFL2 defines a record format not found in PFILE-referenced HREMFP. Therefore, this logical file must define each physical file field it will use. A logical file can thus be a *projection* of the physical file — that is, contain only selected physical file fields. Notice that fields EMEMP#, EMSSN#, and EMPAYR all appear in the physical file but are not included in file HREMFL2.

Key Fields

Let's look at Figures 16.2 and 16.3 again to see how key fields are used. File HREMFL1 identifies field EMEMP# as a key field (in DDS, key fields are identified by a K in position 17 and the name of the field in positions 19 through

Figure 16.2

DDS for Logical File HREMFL1

```
*... ... 1 ... ... 2 ... ... 3 ... ... 4 ... ... 5 ... ... 6 ... ... 7

      *==============================================================*
      * Human Resources Applications                                 *
      * Employee Master File - Logical File 1                        *
      *                                                              *
      * Key Fields:     EMEMP# - Employee Number  (Unique)           *
      *==============================================================*
      *
     A                                      UNIQUE
     A          R HREMFR                    PFILE(HREMFP)
      *
     A          K EMEMP#
```

Figure 16-3

DDS for Logical File HREMFL2

```
*... ... 1 ... ... 2 ... ... 3 ... ... 4 ... ... 5 ... ... 6 ... ... 7

      *==============================================================*
      * Human Resources Applications                                 *
      * Employee Master File - Logical File 2                        *
      *                                                              *
      * Key Fields:     EMLNAM - Last name                           *
      *                 EMFNAM - First name                          *
      *                 EMMINT - Middle initial                      *
      *==============================================================*
      *
     A                                      REF(DBDICT)
     A          R HREMFR2                   PFILE(HREMFP)
      *
     A            EMFNAM    R
     A            EMMINT    R
     A            EMLNAM    R
     A            EMSTRT    R
     A            EMCITY    R
     A            EMST      R
     A            EMZIP     R
     A            EMDEPT    R
     A            EMSTRD    R
     A            EMTRMD    R
     A            EMTYPE    R
      *
     A          K EMLNAM
     A          K EMFNAM
     A          K EMMINT
```

28). When you access this logical file by key, the records will be presented in employee number sequence. The logical file simply defines an *access path* for the access sequence — it does not physically sort the records.

The UNIQUE keyword in this source member tells the system to require a unique value for EMEMP# for each record in the file, thus establishing EMEMP# as the primary key to physical file HREMFP. Should the logical file be deleted, records could be added to the physical file with a non-unique key, giving rise to a question that has been debated over the years: Is it better to use a keyed physical file or a keyed logical file to establish a file's primary key?

You could specify EMEMP# as the key in the DDS for physical file HREMPF and enforce it as the primary key using the UNIQUE keyword. Making the primary key a part of the physical file has a distinct advantage: The primary key is always enforced because the physical file cannot be deleted without deleting the data. Even if all dependent logical files were deleted, the primary key would be enforced. However, placing the key in the physical file also has a disadvantage. Should the access path for a physical file data member be damaged (a rare, but possible, occurrence), the damaged access path prevents access to the data. Your only recourse in that case would be to delete the member and restore it from a backup. Another minor inconvenience is that any time you want to process the file in arrival sequence, you must use the OVRDBF (Override with Database File) command or specify arrival sequence in your high-level language program.

Placing the primary key in a logical file, as I did in Figure 16.2, ensures that access-path damage results only in the need to recompile the logical file — the physical file remains intact. This method also means that you can access the physical file in arrival sequence. As I mentioned earlier, the negative effect is that deleting the logical file results in leaving the physical file without a primary key.

Let me make a few comments concerning the issue of where to place the primary key. Access path maintenance is costly; when records are updated, the system must determine whether any key fields have been modified, requiring the access path to be updated. The overhead for this operation is relatively small in an interactive environment where changes are made randomly based on business demands. However, for files where batch purges or updates result in many access-path updates, the overhead can be quite detrimental to performance. With that in mind, here are some suggestions.

- For work files, which are frequently cleared and reloaded, create the physical file with no keys, and place the primary and alternate keys in logical files. Then delete the logical files (access paths) before you clear and reload the file. The update will be much faster with no access-path maintenance to perform. After the update, rebuild or restore the logical files.
- The same method works best for very large files. When you need to update the entire file, you can delete the logical files, perform the update, and then rebuild or restore the logical files.
- For files updated primarily through interactive maintenance programs, putting the key in the physical file poses no performance problems. The only problem is that of data integrity in the event of a damaged physical file access path.

The UNIQUE keyword is also expensive in terms of system overhead, so you should use it only to maintain the primary key. Logical file HREMFL2 specifies three key fields — EMLNAM (employee last name), EMFNAM (employee first

Figure 16.4

DDS for Logical File HREMFL3

```
*... ... 1 ... ... 2 ... ... 3 ... ... 4 ... ... 5 ... ... 6 ... ... 7
     *---------------------------------------------------------------*
     * Human Resources Applications                                  *
     * Employee Master File - Logical File 3                         *
     *                                                               *
     * Key Fields:     EMEMP# - Employee Number  (Unique)            *
     * SELECT          EMTRMD EQ 0                                   *
     *---------------------------------------------------------------*
     *
    A          R HREMFR                    PFILE(HREMFP)
     *
    A          K EMEMP#
    A          S EMTRMD                    COMP(EQ 0)
```

name), and EMMINT (employee middle initial). The UNIQUE keyword is not used here because the primary key is the employee number and there is no advantage in requiring unique names (even if you could ensure that no two employees had the same name). A primary key protects the integrity of the file, while alternative keys provide additional views of the same data.

Select/Omit Logic

Another feature that logical files offer is the ability to select or omit records from the referenced physical file. You can use the keywords COMP, VALUES, and RANGE to provide select or omit statements when you build logical files.

Figure 16.4 shows logical file HREMFL3. Field EMTRMD (employee termination date) is used with keyword COMP to compare values, forming a SELECT statement (notice the S in position 17). This DDS line tells the system to select records from the physical file in which field EMTRMD is equal to 0 (i.e., no termination date has been entered for that employee). Therefore, when you create logical file HREMFL3, OS/400 builds indexed entries in the logical file only for records in which employee termination date is equal to zero, thus omitting terminated employees (EMTRMD NE 0). When a program accesses the logical file, it reads only the selected records.

Before looking at some examples, I want to go over some of the basic rules for using select/omit statements.

1. You can use select/omit statements only if the logical file specifies key fields (the value *NONE in positions 19 through 23 satisfies the requirement for a key field) or if the logical file uses the DYNSLT keyword. (I'll go into more detail about this keyword later.)
2. To locate the field definitions for fields named on a select/omit statement, OS/400 first checks the field name specified in positions 19 through 28 in the record format definition and then checks fields specified as parameters on CONCAT (concatenate) or RENAME keywords. If the field name is found in more than one place, OS/400 uses the first occurrence of the field name.

3. Select/omit statements are specified by an S or an O in position 17. Multiple statements coded with an S or an O form an OR connective relationship. The first true statement is used for select/omit purposes.
4. You can follow a select/omit statement with other statements containing a blank in position 17. Such additional statements form an AND connective relationship with the initial select or omit statement. All related statements must be true before the record is selected or omitted.
5. You can specify both select and omit statements in the same file, but the following rules apply:
   a. If you specify both select and omit for a record format, OS/400 processes the statements only until one of the conditions is met. Thus, if a record satisfies the first statement or group of related statements, the record is processed without being tested against the subsequent select/omit statements.
   b. If you specify both select and omit, you can use the ALL keyword to specify whether records that do not meet any of the specified conditions should be selected or omitted.
   c. If you do not use the ALL keyword, the action taken for records not satisfying any of the conditions is the converse of the last statement specified. For example, if the last statement was an omit, the record is selected.

Now let's work through a few select/omit examples to see how some of these rules apply. Consider the statements in Figure 16.5. Based on rule 3, OS/400 selects any record in which employee termination date equals 0 or employee type equals H (i.e., hourly). Both statements have an S coded in position 17, representing an OR connective relationship.

Contrast the statements in Figure 16.5 with the statements in Figure 16.6. Notice that the second statement in Figure 16.6 does not have an S or an O in position 17. According to rule 4, the second statement is related to the previous statement by an AND connective relationship. Therefore, *both* comparisons must be true for a record to be selected, so all current hourly employees will be selected.

To keep it interesting, let's change the statements to appear as they do in Figure 16.7. At first glance, you might think this combination of select and omit would provide the same result as the statements in Figure 16.6. However, it doesn't — for two reasons. As rule 5a explains, the order of the statements is significant. In Figure 16.7, the first statement determines whether employee type equals H. If it does, the record is selected and the second test is not performed, thus allowing records for terminated hourly employees to be selected.

The second reason the statement in Figures 16.6 and 16.7 produce different results is because of the absence of the ALL keyword, which specifies how to handle records that do not meet either condition. According to rule 5c, records that do not meet either comparison are selected because the system performs the converse of the last statement listed (e.g., the omit statement).

Figure 16.8 shows the correct way to select records for current hourly employees using both select and omit statements. The ALL keyword in the last statement tells the system to omit records that don't meet the conditions

Figure 16.5

Statements Forming an OR Relationship

```
*... ... 1 ... ... 2 ... ... 3 ... ... 4 ... ... 5 ... ... 6 ... ... 7

                S EMTRMD                     COMP(EQ Ø)
                S EMTYPE                     COMP(EQ 'H')
```

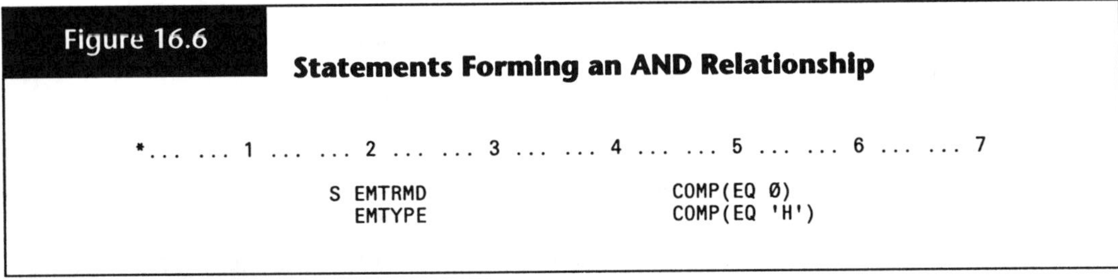

Figure 16.6

Statements Forming an AND Relationship

```
*... ... 1 ... ... 2 ... ... 3 ... ... 4 ... ... 5 ... ... 6 ... ... 7

                S EMTRMD                     COMP(EQ Ø)
                  EMTYPE                     COMP(EQ 'H')
```

Figure 16.7

An Incorrect Variation of Figure 16.6

```
*... ... 1 ... ... 2 ... ... 3 ... ... 4 ... ... 5 ... ... 6 ... ... 7

                S EMTYPE                     COMP(EQ 'H')
                O EMTRMD                     COMP(NE Ø)
```

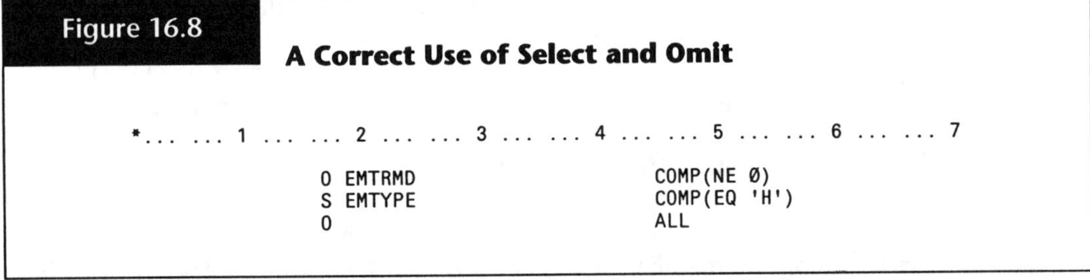

Figure 16.8

A Correct Use of Select and Omit

```
*... ... 1 ... ... 2 ... ... 3 ... ... 4 ... ... 5 ... ... 6 ... ... 7

                O EMTRMD                     COMP(NE Ø)
                S EMTYPE                     COMP(EQ 'H')
                O                            ALL
```

specified by the first two statements. In general, however, it is best to use only one type of statement (either select or omit) when you define a logical file. By limiting your definitions this way, you will avoid introducing errors that result when the rules governing the use of select and omit are violated.

Select/omit statements give you dynamic selection capabilities via the DDS DYNSLT keyword. DYNSLT lets you defer the select/omit process until a program requests input from the logical file. When the program reads the file, OS/400 presents only the records that meet the select/omit criteria. Figure 16.9 shows how to code the DYNSLT keyword.

So now I guess you are wondering just how this differs from an example *without* the DYNSLT keyword. It differs in one significant way: performance.

Figure 16.9

Coding the DYNSLT Keyword

```
*... ... 1 ... ... 2 ... ... 3 ... ... 4 ... ... 5 ... ... 6 ... ... 7
     *-----------------------------------------------------------------*
     * Human Resources Applications                                    *
     * Employee Master File - Logical File                             *
     *-----------------------------------------------------------------*
     *
     A                                      DYNSLT
     A          R HREMFR                    PFILE(HREMFP)
     *
     A          K EMEMP#
     A          S EMTRMD                    COMP(EQ Ø)
```

In the absence of the DYNSLT keyword, OS/400 builds indexed entries only for those records that meet the stated select/omit criteria. Access to the correct records is faster, but the overhead of maintaining the logical file is increased. When you use DYNSLT, *all* records in the physical file are indexed, and the select/omit logic is not performed *until the file is accessed.* You only retrieve records that meet the select/omit criteria, but the process is dynamic. Because DYNSLT decreases the overhead associated with access path maintenance, it can improve performance in cases where that overhead is considerable. As a guideline, if you have a select/omit logical file that uses more than 75 percent of the records in the physical file member, the DYNSLT keyword can reduce the overhead required to maintain that logical file without significantly affecting the retrieval performance of the file, because most records will be selected anyway. If the logical file uses less than 75 percent of the records in the physical file member, you can usually maximize performance by omitting the DYNSLT keyword and letting the select/omit process occur when the file is created.

Multiple Logical File Members

The last basic concept you should understand is the way logical file members work. The CRTLF (Create Logical File) command has several parameters related to establishing the member or members that will exist in the logical file. These parameters are MBR (the logical file member name), DTAMBRS (the physical file data members upon which the logical file member is based), and MAXMBRS (the maximum number of data members the logical file can contain). The default values for these parameters are *FILE, *ALL, and 1, respectively.

Typically, a physical file has one data member. When you create a logical file to reference such a physical file, these default values instruct the system to create a logical file member with the same name as the logical file itself, base this logical file member on the single physical file data member, and specify that a maximum of one logical file member can exist in this file.

When creating applications with multiple-data-member physical files, you often don't know precisely what physical and logical members you will eventually need. For example, for each user you might add members to a temporary work file for each session when the user signs on. Obviously, you (or, more accurately, your program) don't know in advance what members to create. In such a case, you would normally

- Create the physical file with no members:

```
CRTPF FILE(TESTPF) MBR(*NONE)
```

- Create the logical file with no members:

```
CRTLF FILE(TESTLF) MBR(*NONE)
```

- For every user that signs on, add a physical file member to the physical file:

```
ADDPFM FILE(TESTPF) MBR(TESTMBR) TEXT('Test PF Data Member')
```

- For every physical file member, add a member to the logical file and specify the physical file member on which to base the logical member:

```
ADDLFM FILE(TESTLF) MBR(TESTMBR) DTAMBRS((TESTPF TESTMBR))     +
       TEXT('Test LF Data Member')
```

When a logical file member references more than one physical file member, and your application finds duplicate records in the multiple members, the application processes those records in the order in which the members are specified on the DTAMBRS parameter. For instance, if the CRTLF command specifies

```
CRTLF FILE(TESTLIB/TESTLF) MBR(ALLYEARS)                        +
      DTAMBRS((YRPF DT1988) (YRPF DT1989) (YRPF DT1990))
```

a program that processes logical file member ALLYEARS first reads the records in member DT1988, then in member DT1989, and finally in member DT1990.

Keys to the AS/400 Database

Understanding logical files will take you a long way toward creating effective database implementations on the AS/400. Since I have introduced the basic concepts only, I strongly recommend that you spend some time in the manuals to increase your knowledge about logical files. Start with the description of the CRTLF command in IBM's *Control Language Reference* (SC41-0030). As you master the methods presented, you will discover many ways in which logical files can enhance your applications.

Chapter 17

File Overrides

by Wayne Madden

You can change file attributes at run time with high-performance override commands

In Chapters 15 and 16, I looked closely at the various kinds of files that exist on the AS/400, each of which has unique characteristics or *attributes*. These attributes not only provide the file definition, but determine how the system controls the file. In this chapter, I introduce file overrides, which you can use to temporarily modify the attributes (i.e., definition) of a file during program execution.

The basic purpose of overrides is to temporarily change the attributes of a file so you don't have to create permanent files for every combination of attributes your application might need. The reasons for performing an override vary according to the type of file being accessed. Overrides give you the flexibility to use existing model files and dynamically change their attributes, but not without a few requirements that you must be aware of.

To perform an override, you use a specific override command designed to override the particular type of file you want to access. Figure 17.1 lists the override commands and some of the reasons for performing each one. (This chapter does not address the OVRMSGF (Override with Message File) command, although the command exists in OS/400. I focus here on OBJTYPE(*FILE) objects; message files are OBJTYPE(*MSGF) objects.) As Figure 17.1 shows, override commands exist for most *FILE objects on the AS/400. Each override command has specific parameters that correspond to the file attributes of the file type the command was designed to operate on. For instance, you cannot use the OVRTAPF (Override with Tape File) command to specify a data member, because there aren't any data members in a tape file. Likewise, the OVRDBF (Override with Database File) command cannot specify a tape volume number, because a database file does not require a tape when you

Figure 17.1

Override Commands and their Functions

Override Command	Type of File	Possible Reasons for Using
OVRDBF (Override with Database File)	Database (and source)	To select data member to process To change SHARE attribute (sharing an Open Data Path) To select a starting position for record retrieval
OVRDKTF (Override with Diskette File)	Device	To select the physical device name to associate with file To establish record and block length
OVRDSPF (Override with Display File)	Device	To select defer write option To select restore display option
OVRICFDEVE (Override with Intersystem Communications Function Program Device Entry)	Device	To select physical device name to associate with file
OVRPRTF (Override with Printer File)	Device	To select a specific output queue To select font, characters per inch, lines per inch, page rotation, and form type
OVRSAVF (Override with Save File)	Save	To specify whether to delete previous records or resume output by adding records to the existing data
OVRTAPF (Override with Tape File)	Device	To select physical device name to associate with file To establish record and block length To select volume label ID

Note: Because the chapter does not discuss message files, this list does not include the OVRMSGF command.

access it directly. You get the idea — a command for each type of file and appropriate override parameters for each command.

Suppose you want to override a tape file so you can write records from a disk file to tape using a high-level language (HLL) program. You can specify this override in a CL program before calling the HLL program, or you can execute the override command interactively before calling the program. The override and call would appear as follows:

```
OVRTAPF FILE(QSYSTAP) DEV(TAP01) RCDLEN(256) BLKLEN(5120)    +
        ENDOPT(*UNLOAD)
CALL HLLPROGRAM
```

The override provides the attributes for device, record length, block length, and end-of-job tape options. The HLL program opens file QSYSTAP using the new attributes, calculates the records, and writes them to tape.

Consider another example. Suppose you need an override to a print file to correctly set the number of copies you want to print. Because the number of copies will vary depending on each particular job, you can specify the desired number of copies as a parameter to a CL program that calls the HLL print program. The code in the CL program would look something like this:

```
OVRPRTF FILE(REPORT) TOFILE(QPRINT) COPIES(&COPIES)
CALL HLLPRINT
```

The HLL print program tries to open file REPORT, but due to the override, the program opens print file QPRINT instead and generates the specified number of reports.

As you see, performing an override is easy. You simply execute the appropriate override command, modifying the particular attributes you need. For a detailed look at the various override commands and the parameters associated with them, refer to IBM's *Control Language Reference* (SC41-0030).

Override Rules

Although overrides are not complicated, the rules governing their use require some consideration. The rules focus on two areas of concern: the order in which overrides are processed within a job's program call levels and overrides to the same file. Call levels identify the relationship between active programs. When one program calls another, the calling program and the called program exist at different call levels. Look at the example in Figure 17.2. Notice that when PGMA (call level 1) calls PGMB, a new call level is established (call level 2). But when PGMB uses the TFRCTL (Transfer Control) command to transfer control to PGMC, the call level remains the same because TFRCTL causes the program named in the command to replace the program that executed the TFRCTL command in the program stack. (A program stack is a list of a job's active programs, in call-level order.)

Figure 17.2 also shows the misuse of override statements within the programs. PGMA tries to execute two override commands for a single file (QPRINT), violating the first law of overrides: You can apply only one override per file in a single call level. You can see that the two overrides are at the same call level, because both are within the same program. A program uses the last override it encounters at any given call level. When PGMA calls PGMB, the printer file has the attribute COPIES(5). The first override, with the attribute FORMTYPE (LETTER), is ignored.

The second rule governing the use of overrides is that the system applies overrides in inverse call-level order. In Figure 17.2, PGMB overrides QPRINT with OVRPRTF QPRINT COPIES(3) FORMTYPE(LTR_3HOLE) before transferring control to PGMC. Does this mean that when PGMB executes TFRCTL PGMC, QPRINT has the attribute COPIES(3)? No. Because the system applies overrides in inverse calling order, it first applies the override for QPRINT

Figure 17.2

Overrides within Program Call Levels

Level 1

```
PGMA
  .
  .
  .
OVRPRTF QPRINT FORMTYPE(LTR_3HOLE)
OVRPRTF QPRINT COPIES(5)
  .
  .
  .
CALL PGMB
```

Level 2

```
PGMB
  .
  .
  .
OVRDBF   MYFILE MBR(MBR1988)
OVRPRTF QPRINT COPIES(3) FORMTYPE(LETTER)
  .
  .
  .
TFRCTL PGMC

PGMC
  .
  .
  .
OVRDBF   MYFILE MBR(MBR1991)
  .
  .
  .
CALL PGMD
```

Level 3

```
PGMD
  .
  .
  .
DLTOVR QPRINT
  .
  .
  .
OVRPRTF QPRINT FORMTYPE(LEGAL)
CALL PGMDX
RETURN
```

Level 2

```
PGMC
  .
  .
  .
DLTOVR *ALL
CALL PGME
RETURN
```

Level 1

```
PGMA
  .
  .
  .
RETURN
```

at call level 2, making COPIES(3) FORMTYPE(LETTER); then it applies the override at call level 1 (PGMA), changing COPIES(3) to COPIES(5). When PGMC begins, the values are COPIES(5) and FORMTYPE(LETTER).

Are you still with me? Great! Let's step through the rest of Figure 17.2.

As I've explained, TFRCTL causes the program receiving control to replace the program that executed the TFRCTL command in the program stack, thus retaining the same call level. Therefore, the OVRDBF MYFILE MBR(MBR1991) command that PGMC executes before calling PGMD exists at the same call level as the OVRDBF performed in PGMB. PGMC ignores the first override to the same file at the same call level and uses MBR(MBR1991) when it calls PGMD.

Now — final test time. What are the values for COPIES and FORMTYPE when PGMD calls PGMDX and PGMDX opens file QPRINT? The answer: COPIES(5) and FORMTYPE(LETTER). You probably noticed the Delete Override command, DLTOVR QPRINT, that precedes the override and program call in PGMD. That DLTOVR doesn't work because there are no overrides for file QPRINT at call level 3. Thus, we encounter another rule: A DLTOVR statement only deletes overrides that are invoked at the same call level. The system automatically deletes overrides when a call level is terminated.

What about the DLTOVR *ALL command that PGMC executes before calling PGME? The command deletes the two existing overrides at that call level — OVRPRTF COPIES(3) FORMTYPE(LETTER) and OVRDBF MBR(MBR1991). When PGMC calls PGME, the only override in effect is COPIES(5).

Again, these are the rules to keep in mind when you use overrides:

- You can apply only one override per file at any single call level (subsequent overrides to the same file render earlier overrides obsolete).
- The system applies overrides in inverse call-level order (remember that TFRCTL does not change the current call level).
- You can use the DLTOVR command only to delete overrides that exist in the same call level as the DLTOVR command.
- When a call level ends in the program stack (i.e., a program ends execution and is freed from the stack), any overrides existing at that call level are deleted.
- If you issue an invalid override, the system gives you no indication (you will not get an error message).

For more information about the use of file overrides, see IBM's *Data Management Guide* (SC41-9658).

Why Use Overrides?

If asked "What functions require file overrides?" my honest reply would have to be "None." However, if you try to create operation automation applications, system applications, or even user business applications on the AS/400 without using overrides, you may create an unmanageable nightmare. As an experienced AS/400 applications developer, my opinion is that there are certain applications for which overrides provide needed flexibility. Let's look at some applications

Figure 17.3

Data Flow in Sample Order-Entry Application

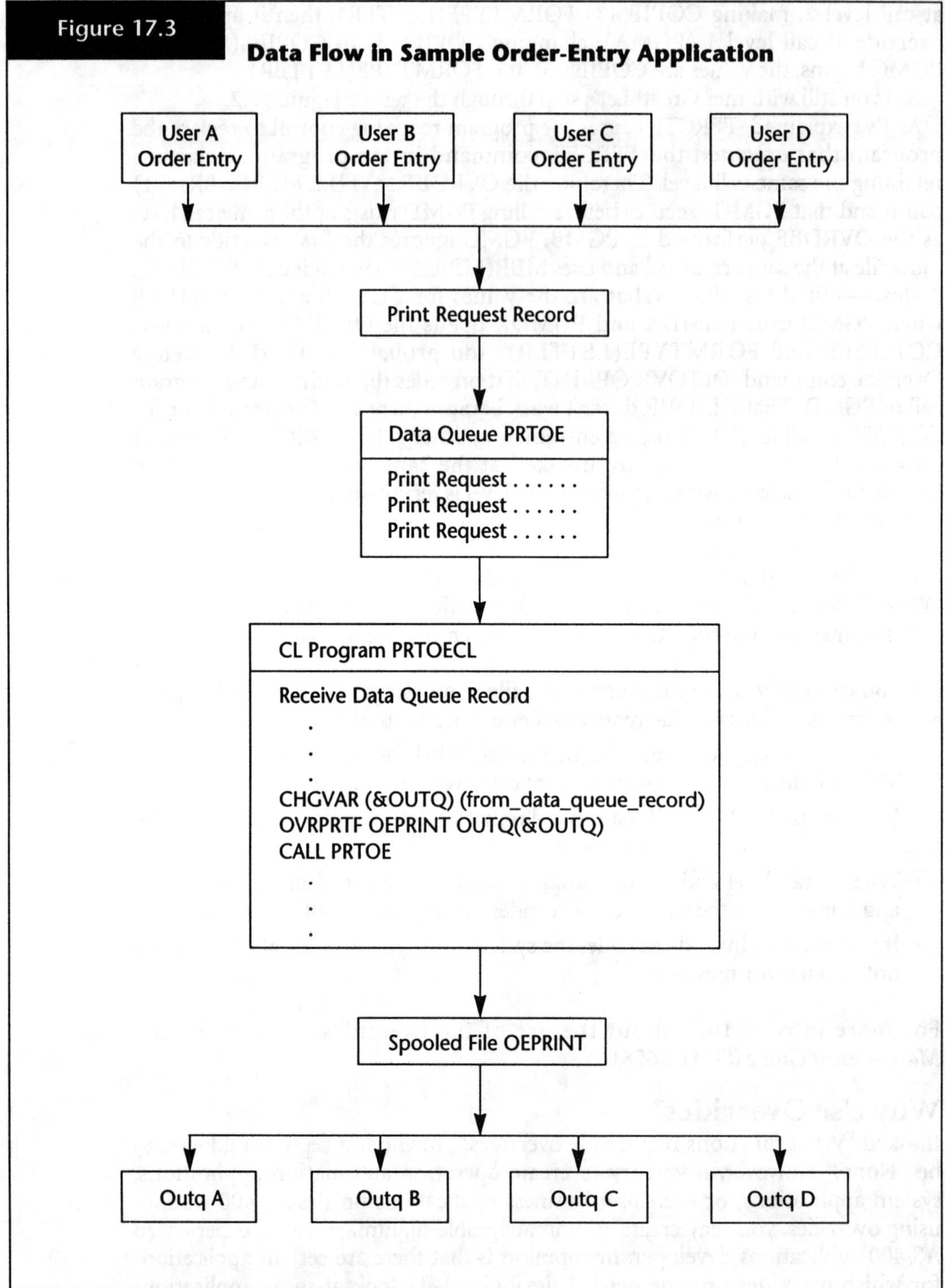

for which overrides provide needed flexibility. Let's look at some applications that would benefit from the use of file overrides.

One situation in which overrides are helpful is when you want to direct output from a batch print program. Figure 17.3 represents the flow of data in an application designed to handle order-entry printing requests in batch mode. Sending print requests to a batch job prevents performance problems that can result from too many users executing interactive print programs simultaneously. Notice that the order entry program first sends a print request to a data queue. The print request contains data that specifies the form to be printed, the order or invoice number, the user requesting the printout, and the name of the output queue that should receive the print job. The CL program uses the output queue name in the OVRPRTF (Override with Printer File) command to direct the output before calling HLL program PRTOE, which generates the output.

Another practical use for file overrides is when you use multiple-member data files. Either physical or logical files may contain multiple data members (the logical file data members do not actually contain data, but represent access paths). If you do not use an override statement before calling an HLL program to access a physical or logical file that contains multiple data members, your program will always open the first member. In the sample program in Figure 17.4, each year's

Figure 17.4

Sample Override for Data Member

```
/*==============================================================*/
/* Program: WRKYRSCL                                            */
/* 1. Prompt user for desired year                              */
/* 2. Construct &MBR variable and check for existence of member */
/* 3. Override database file for member                         */
/* 4. Execute HLL maintenance program                           */
/*==============================================================*/
         .
         .
         .
/* Prompt for &MBR choice */
 PROMPT:     SNDRCVF     FORMAT(PROMPT)

             CHGVAR      VAR(&MBR) VALUE('YR' || &YEAR)

/* Check &MBR from prompt screen. If not found, issue message. */
             CHKOBJ      OBJ(MYLIB/MYFILE) MBR(&MBR)
             MONMSG      MSGID(CPF9801) EXEC(SNDPGMMSG MSGID(CPF9898) +
                           MSGF(QSYS/QCPFMSG) MSGDTA('Member '      +
                           || &MBR |< ' does not exist in file.')   +
                           TOPGMQ(*PRV) MSGTYPE(*ESCAPE))

/* Override file for selected member */
             OVRDBF MYLIB/MYFILE MBR(&MBR)
             CALL   HLLPROGRAM
         .
         .
         .
/* Delete Override */
             DLTOVR MYFILE
             ENDPGM
```

data is stored in a separate data member in the physical and logical files that comprise the application database. When you enter the application via program WRKYRSCL, you can select the year of data you need. WRKYRSCL uses the value in variable &YEAR to construct the correct member name and override the file to the appropriate data member. If that data member does not exist, you receive an error message when your program attempts to open that data member.

File overrides are also useful when you want to tell the system to allow subsequent opens of a file to use the Open Data Path (ODP) created by the OPNQRYF command. When using the OPNQRYF command, you should ensure that the file has the attribute SHARE(*YES) so that subsequent programs will use the ODP created by the OPNQRYF command. If the file attribute is SHARE(*NO), the operating system creates a new data path every time it opens the file. To ensure that SHARE(*YES) is used with OPNQRYF, you can use the following OVRDBF command:

```
OVRDBF FILE(file_name) SHARE(*YES)
OPNQRYF
```

Although you don't have to use overrides to write applications, they do simplify application development by providing the flexibility to change the attributes of system objects at run time.

Chapter 18

File Sharing

by Wayne Madden

You can use the SHARE attribute to optimize application programs

As the father of two young children, I have learned that to maintain peace in the house, my wife and I must either teach our children to share or buy two of everything. Those of you who can identify with this predicament know that in reality peace occurs only when you do a little of both — sometimes you teach, and sometimes you buy.

The AS/400 inherited a performance-related virtue from the S/38 that lets you "teach" your programs to share file resources. I call it a performance-related virtue because the benefit of teaching your programs to share boosts performance for many applications. However, as is the case with children, there will be times when sharing doesn't provide any benefits and, in fact, is more trouble than it's worth. In this chapter, I will focus on the SHARE (Share Open Data Path) attribute and how you can use it effectively in your applications.

You may already be familiar with the general concept of file sharing, a common feature for many operating systems that lets more than one program open the same file. When each program opens the file, a unique set of resources is established to prevent conflict between programs. This type of file sharing is automatic on the AS/400 unless you specifically prevent it by allocating a file for exclusive operations (using the ALCOBJ (Allocate Object) command). The SHARE attribute does not control this automatic function.

On the AS/400, SHARE is a file attribute. It goes beyond normal file sharing to let programs *within the same job* share the open data path (ODP) established when the file was originally opened in the job. This means that programs share the file status information (i.e., the general and file-dependent I/O feedback areas), as well as the file pointer (i.e., a program's current record position in a file). As we further examine the SHARE attribute, you will see that this type of

Figure 18.1

Physical File TEST

Record 1
Record 2
Record 3
Record 4
Record 5
Record 6
Record 7
Record 8

sharing enhances modular programming performance, but that you must manage it effectively to prevent conflicts between programs.

The SHARE attribute is valid for database, source, device, distributed data management, and save files. You can establish the SHARE attribute or modify it for a file using any of the CRTxxxF (Create File), CHGxxxF (Change File), or OVRxxxF (Override with File) commands. The valid values are *YES and *NO. If SHARE(*NO) is specified for a file, each program operating on that file in the same job must establish a unique ODP.

Sharing Fundamentals

While sharing ODPs can be a window to enhancing performance, doing so can also generate programming errors if you try to share without understanding a few simple fundamentals. The first fundamental pertains to open options that programs establish.

When a program opens a file, the options specified on the OPNDBF (Open Data Base File) command or by the high-level language definition of the file determine the open options. The open options are *INP (input only), *OUT (output only), and *ALL (input, output, update, and delete operations). These options are significant when you use shared ODPs. If you specify SHARE(*YES) for a file, the initial program's open of the file must use all the open options required for any subsequent programs in the same job. For example, if PGMA opens file TEST (specified with SHARE(*YES)) with the open option *INP (for input only), and then PGMB, which requires the open option *ALL (for an update or delete function) is called, PGMB will fail.

Besides sharing open options, programs also share the file pointer, a capability that is both powerful and problematic. Figure 18.1 displays the eight records that exist in file TEST. In Figures 18.2 and 18.3 are RPG programs TESTRPG1 and TESTRPG2, respectively, which alternately read a record in file TEST. After TESTRPG1 reads a record, it calls TESTRPG2, which then reads a record in file TEST. TESTRPG2 calls TESTRPG1, which reads another record, and so on. Both programs use print device file QPRINT to generate a list of the records read.

When the SHARE attribute for both file TEST and file QPRINT is SHARE(*NO), the output generated appears as displayed in Figure 18.4. Each

Figure 18.2

RPG Program TESTRPG1

```
*... ... 1 ... ... 2 ... ... 3 ... ... 4 ... ... 5 ... ... 6 ... ... 7

     *****************************************************************
     *  TESTRPG1 - Test Program 1                                    *
     *             For the purpose of testing SHARE(*YES *NO) attr   *
     *****************************************************************
     *
    FTEST    IF  E                    DISK
    FQPRINT  O   F     132      OF     PRINTER
     *
    C                    READ TEST                     99
     *
    C           *IN99    DOWEQ'Ø'
     *
    C                    EXCPTDTL
     *
    C                    CALL 'TESTRPG2'
     *
    C                    READ TEST                     99
    C                    END
     *
    C                    MOVE '1'       *INLR
    C                    RETRN
     *
    OQPRINT  E  1             DTL
    O                         FIELD
```

Figure 18.3

RPG Program TESTRPG2

```
*... ... 1 ... ... 2 ... ... 3 ... ... 4 ... ... 5 ... ... 6 ... ... 7

     *****************************************************************
     *  TESTRPG2 - Test Program 2 (called by TESTRPG1)               *
     *             For the purpose of testing SHARE(*YES *NO) attr   *
     *****************************************************************
     *
    FTEST    IF  E                    DISK
    FQPRINT  O   F     132      OF     PRINTER
     *
    C                    READ TEST                     99
     *
    C           *IN99    IFEQ 'Ø'
    C                    EXCPTDTL
    C                    END
     *
    C                    RETRN
     *
    OQPRINT  E  1             DTL
    O                         FIELD
```

program reads all eight records because each program uses a unique ODP. If you change file TEST or override it to specify SHARE(*YES), the programs generate the lists displayed in Figure 18.5. Each program reads only four records, because the programs share the same ODP. Finally, if you also change or override the attribute of file QPRINT to be SHARE(*YES), the output appears as shown in

Figure 18.4

Output when SHARE(*NO) Is Specified for Files TEST and QPRINT

QPRINT splnbr 1 (TESTRPG1)	QPRINT splnbr 2 (TESTRPG2)
Record 1 Record 2 Record 3 Record 4 Record 5 Record 6 Record 7 Record 8	Record 1 Record 2 Record 3 Record 4 Record 5 Record 6 Record 7 Record 8

Figure 18.5

Output when SHARE(*YES) Is Specified for File TEST

QPRINT splnbr 1 (TESTRPG1)	QPRINT splnbr 2 (TESTRPG2)
Record 1 Record 3 Record 5 Record 7	Record 2 Record 4 Record 6 Record 8

Figure 18.6. Both programs share print file QPRINT and, while each program reads only four records, the output is combined in a single output file.

One common misconception is that using SHARE(*YES) alters the way in which the database manager performs record locking — a conclusion you could easily reach if you confuse record locking with file locking. It is true that when you specify SHARE(*YES), file locking is handled differently than when you specify SHARE(*NO); when you specify SHARE(*YES), the first open establishes the open options. Thus, if the first open of a file with SHARE(*YES) uses option *ALL, every program using that file obtains a SHRUPD (Shared Update) lock on that file. This lock occurs even when a particular program normally opens the file with *INP open options.

Record locking, on the other hand, is not controlled by the open options, but by the RPG compiler. The program compiler determines which locks are needed for any input operations in the program and creates the object code to make them happen during program execution. Thus, programs perform record locking on files with SHARE(*YES) the same way they perform record locking on files with SHARE(*NO). Let me stress that this fact alone does not prevent the problems you must address when you write multiple programs to perform with files having SHARE(*YES) in an on-line update environment. But record locking, in and of itself, is not a serious concern. The real hazard is that because

Figure 18.6 **Output when SHARE(*YES) Is Specified for Files TEST and QPRINT**

```
QPRINT splnbr 1 (TESTRPG1 and TESTRPG2 sharing QPRINT)
```

Record 1
Record 2
Record 3
Record 4
Record 5
Record 6
Record 7
Record 8

SHARE(*YES) lets programs share the file pointer, programs can easily become confused about which record is actually being retrieved, updated, or output if you fail to write the programs so they recognize and manage the shared pointer.

The following example illustrates this potential problem. PGMA first reads file TEST for update purposes. Then PGMA calls PGMB, which also reads file TEST for update. If PGMB ends before performing the update, the file pointer remains positioned at the record read by PGMB. If PGMA then performs an update, PGMA updates the values of the current record variables (from the first read in PGMA) into the record PGMB read because *that is where the file pointer is currently positioned.* While you would never purposely code this badly, you might accidentally cause the same problem in your application if you fit program modules together without considering the current value of the SHARE attribute on the files.

The moral of the story is this: When calling programs that use the same file, always reposition the file pointer after the called program ends, unless you are specifically coding to take advantage of file pointer positioning within those applications.

Sharing Examples

The most popular use of the SHARE attribute is to open files at the menu level when users frequently enter and exit applications on that menu. Figure 18.7 illustrates a simple order-entry menu with five options, each of which represents a program that uses one or more of the described files. If SHARE(*NO) is defined for each file, then each time one of these programs is called, an ODP is created for each program file. If users frequently switch between menu options, they experience delays each time a file is opened.

The coding example in Figure 18.8 provides a solution to this problem. First, the OVRDBF (Override with Database File) command specifies SHARE(*YES) for each file identified. Then, OPNDBF opens each file with the maximum open options required for the various applications. The overhead required to open the files affects the menu program only. When users select an option on the menu,

Figure 18.7

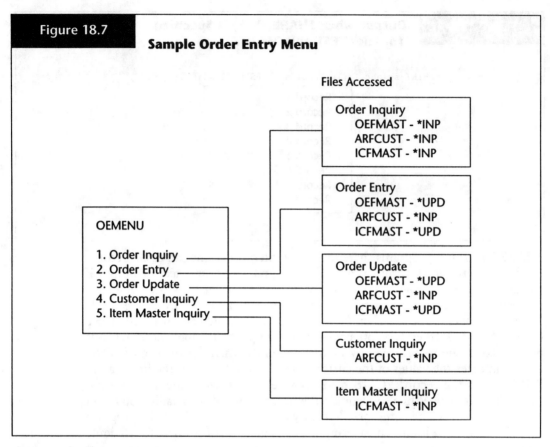

Sample Order Entry Menu

Files Accessed

OEMENU

1. Order Inquiry
2. Order Entry
3. Order Update
4. Customer Inquiry
5. Item Master Inquiry

Order Inquiry
OEFMAST - *INP
ARFCUST - *INP
ICFMAST - *INP

Order Entry
OEFMAST - *UPD
ARFCUST - *INP
ICFMAST - *UPD

Order Update
OEFMAST - *UPD
ARFCUST - *INP
ICFMAST - *UPD

Customer Inquiry
ARFCUST - *INP

Item Master Inquiry
ICFMAST - *INP

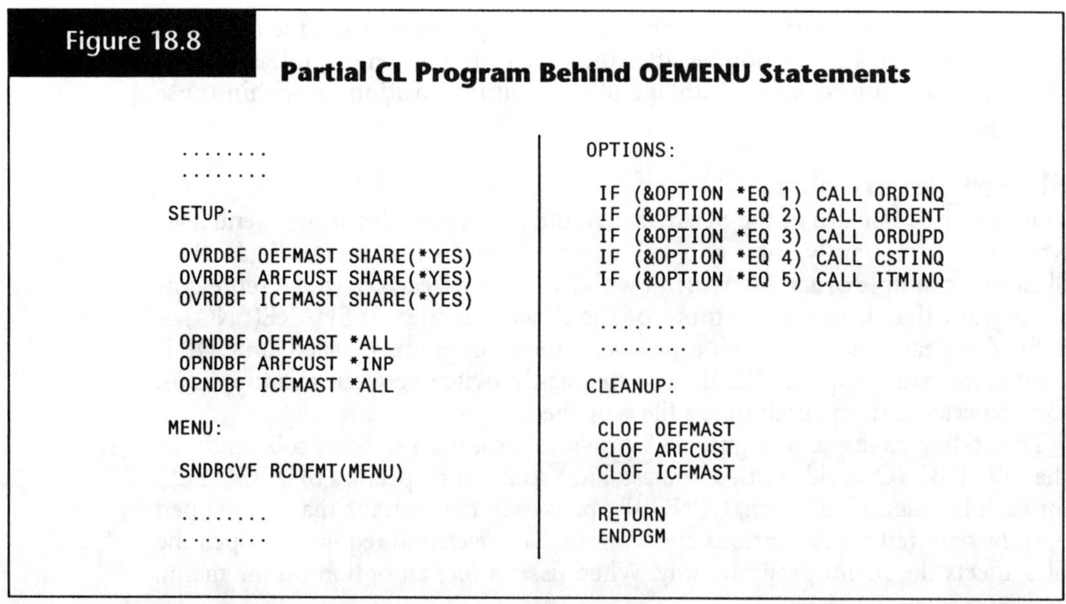

Figure 18.8

Partial CL Program Behind OEMENU Statements

```
 ........
 ........

SETUP:

 OVRDBF OEFMAST SHARE(*YES)
 OVRDBF ARFCUST SHARE(*YES)
 OVRDBF ICFMAST SHARE(*YES)

 OPNDBF OEFMAST *ALL
 OPNDBF ARFCUST *INP
 OPNDBF ICFMAST *ALL

MENU:

 SNDRCVF RCDFMT(MENU)

 ........
 ........

OPTIONS:

 IF (&OPTION *EQ 1) CALL ORDINQ
 IF (&OPTION *EQ 2) CALL ORDENT
 IF (&OPTION *EQ 3) CALL ORDUPD
 IF (&OPTION *EQ 4) CALL CSTINQ
 IF (&OPTION *EQ 5) CALL ITMINQ

 ........
 ........

CLEANUP:

 CLOF OEFMAST
 CLOF ARFCUST
 CLOF ICFMAST

 RETURN
 ENDPGM
```

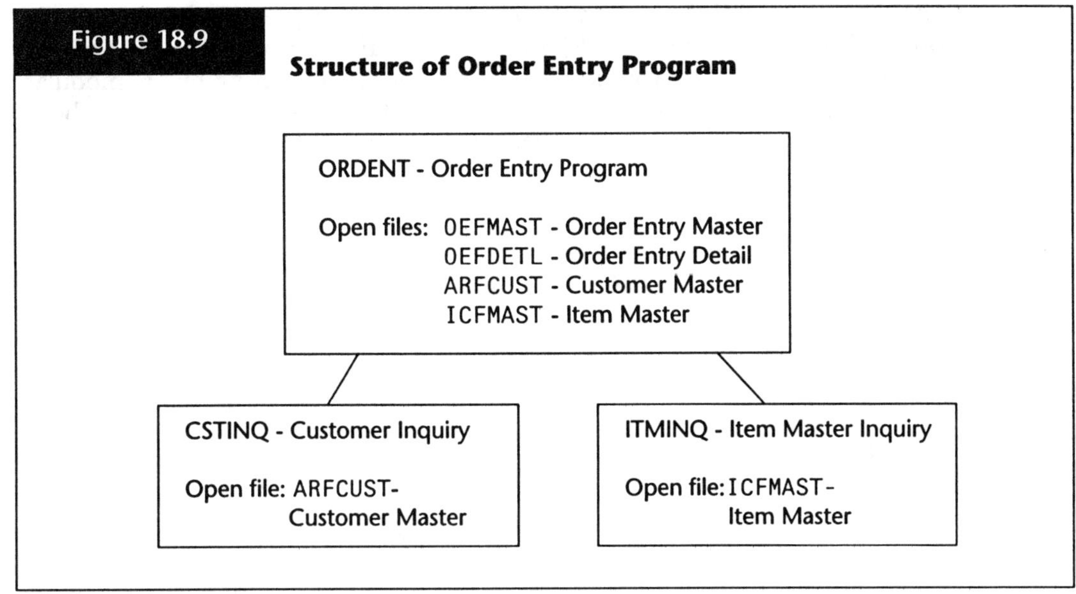

Figure 18.9 **Structure of Order Entry Program**

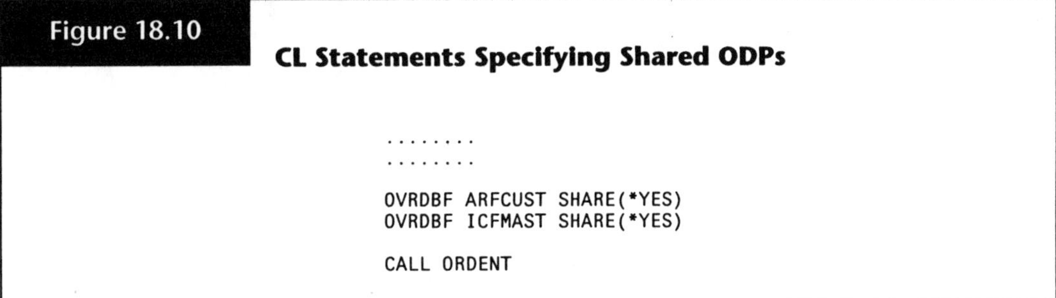

Figure 18.10 **CL Statements Specifying Shared ODPs**

```
........
........

OVRDBF ARFCUST SHARE(*YES)
OVRDBF ICFMAST SHARE(*YES)

CALL ORDENT
```

the respective program need not open the file, and thus the programs are initiated more quickly. Remember, however, to plan carefully when using SHARE to open files, keeping in mind the above-mentioned guidelines about placing the file pointer.

The SHARE attribute also comes in handy when you write applications that provide on-line inquiries into related files. Figure 18.9 outlines an order-entry program that opens several files and that lets the end user call a customer inquiry program or item master inquiry program to look up specific customers or items. Either program uses a file already opened by the initial program. By including the statements in Figure 18.10 in a CL program that calls the order-entry program, you can ensure that the ODP for these files is shared, reducing the time needed to access the two inquiry programs.

There is no doubt that SHARE is a powerful attribute. Unfortunately, the power it provides can introduce errors (specifically, the wrong selection of records due to file pointer position) unless you understand it and use it carefully. SHARE(*YES) can shorten program initiation steps and can let programs share vital I/O feedback information. If you're using batch programs that typically open files, process the records, and then remain idle until the next night, SHARE(*YES) will buy you nothing. But if you're considering highly modular programming designs, SHARE(*YES) is a must. For more information about SHARE, see IBM's *Database Guide* (SC41-9659) and *Control Language Reference* (SC41-0030).

Chapter 19

Relational Database Principles

by Paul Conte

A relational DBMS can help you design better applications and take advantage of database facilities

According to some estimates, more than 80 percent of a typical high-level language (HLL) program is taken up with code related to file access — including definition, retrieval, selection, and updating of records — and with the editing of input data for valid values. Less than 20 percent of the code is concerned with calculations and transformations of data after it is read as input and before it is written as output. This is an extensive imbalance, but there is an additional problem with writing code for file access and editing — the same code often is repeated in different programs. This repetitive coding of "housekeeping" functions is not only an expensive component of software development and maintenance, but it is also error prone. Taken together, the large proportion of code not directly related to the main function of an application system and the repetition of this code throughout the system are obstacles to higher productivity in application development. But a quest that began more than 20 years ago is leading to a brighter tomorrow for application development.

In the late 1960s systems designers looked for a way to reduce the 80 percent chunk of nonproblem-oriented application code by having the systems software automatically handle many of the record specification, file access, and field editing functions, thus freeing application programmers to concentrate on the computations and manipulations of the data. The various systems developed as a result of this quest are known collectively as "database management systems" (DBMSs). Since their first appearance, DBMSs have had a dramatic impact on data processing. As a result, more and more database functions are being added to minicomputers, including the AS/400. Thus, it is becoming increasingly important that applications be designed with the use of DBMS facilities in mind.

For AS/400 sites, even though the full range of DBMS functions may not be available yet, well-planned HLL applications can be implemented so they can take advantage of both present and forthcoming DBMS facilities. As an additional benefit, applications designed for relational DBMSs will be better structured even if they use standard files.

This chapter will help you understand the components of a relational DBMS (so you can make use of the components as they become available) and will help you incorporate relational database concepts into your application design. After taking a brief look at the general notion of a DBMS, I'll describe the relational database model — the approach IBM and many other vendors have settled on as the most powerful.

Conventional File System vs. DBMS

The impact of the conventional file system approach on record keeping software is substantial because programs are dependent on the physical way in which data is stored. In some cases, this includes device-type dependence, although in most modern file systems, a good measure of device-type independence has been achieved through HLL and operating system control language facilities. Nevertheless, all nondatabase systems (and even many nonrelational database systems) are dependent on the way records are stored in the file (i.e., their physical sequence, record links, or indexes) and on the way fields are laid out in the record (i.e., their location, type, and length).

This physical data dependence requires programmers to waste time declaring the same field, record, and file information in every program. (Although this task is aided by use of the RPG/COPY, COBOL COPY, or PL/I INCLUDE facilities, it remains a programmer, not a system, responsibility.) Even more costly than the original coding is the required change to the source code in all programs that use a file if any change is made to the physical storage (i.e., adding a field, changing a field's length, or splitting files). This change is necessary even if the programs don't use any of the modified items, such as fields with revised lengths.

A DBMS, on the other hand, attempts to free programs from physical data dependence. Central to this facility is the ability to define to the system an "entity" about which you wish to store "properties." Entities are represented by different constructs and have various names, depending on the specific DBMS being considered — "record types," "segments," "relations," and "tables" are a few of the terms used. (An entity in a conventional file system usually would be represented by a file). What these alternative constructs have in common is that they all represent a distinguishable object of some sort, whether the object is concrete (e.g., a customer) or is abstract (e.g., an AS/400 job). If "customer" is an example of a specific entity, the customers' names and addresses are "properties" for the customer entity. A "property" is known as a "field" in a conventional file system (and in many DBMSs as well). A property is simply some piece of information about an entity.

So far it may appear that a DBMS offers no earth-shattering improvement over the records and fields of an ordinary file. But for a nondatabase file, every program must contain the layout of fields in a record, while a DBMS provides a "Data

Definition Language" (DDL) that is used to define both entities and properties (including record layouts) in a system dictionary (also known as a catalogue or directory). Thus, a DBMS permits a program to reference a property by name (e.g., CUST_NAME) without a programmer-coded specification of where the actual field-level data is stored. (Keep in mind that the degree to which current commercial DBMSs achieve physical data independence, or any of the other concepts that I discuss, varies greatly. While some products hardly merit classification as a DBMS, I describe here the facilities found in many systems.)

In the best case, with a DBMS, the storage of a property can be changed (e.g., its length or location within a physical (disk) record can be changed), and programs that use the property will continue to execute properly with no revisions. Removing the physical aspects of a field from a program's code removes a significant amount of work, especially in system maintenance; it also removes a significant source of errors.

Besides requiring specification of the record layout in every program, a conventional file system also requires that every add or update program include code to check for legitimate values in the fields before a record is written. This validation typically is implemented by a series of conditional tests (IF AGE > 15..., IF ACTTYP = 'A' OR 'B' OR 'C'...) on values entered on a display for interactive updating or in a transaction record read by a batch program. Not only is this code repeated (possibly with slight variations) in many programs, but also, when the tests are directed at input values (i.e., precalculation or pretransformation values) rather than at a record's output values at the time of a file update, it is still possible, due to a program error, to write an invalid record to the file. Thus, most field editing code in a conventional file system is both cumbersome to maintain and not wholly effective at guaranteeing the integrity of the data.

DBMSs address this problem by allowing the DDL to be used to specify integrity constraints in the system dictionary. The integrity constraints that can be specified vary among the different DBMSs. At a minimum, they usually include range checks ("between 1 and 50") or allowable values ("A" or "B" or "C"). More complex constraints may be specifiable, as well. Examples include relationships between fields for the same record (EMPDAT > BTHDAT) or inter-record relationships (an ORDNBR value in an order detail record must exist as an ORDNBR value in exactly one order header record). The DBMS, which handles all database updating, generally checks these constraints when a record is written to the database. If a constraint is not met, the update does not occur and an error is signalled. Specifying integrity in a central dictionary helps immensely in speeding implementation and in achieving improved quality of the organization's data.

Only in recent years, however, have many DBMSs offered much in the way of built-in integrity support. It is a complex function to implement in the systems software, and many developers feared it would require too much machine resource (i.e., CPU cycles and memory) to execute in a cost-effective manner. The current trend, though, is based on the recognition that system-provided integrity checking is less expensive than invalid corporate data. And with developments in hardware and systems software, better DBMSs can not only outperform custom HLL code, but also reduce application development and maintenance costs.

At a level above the field level, a conventional file system leaves it to each program to implement relationships between records. So if a program needs an order header record, a customer information record, and a set of order line-detail records, the program must know which files to access and how to retrieve the appropriate records. Conventional file systems use two common methods to relate records: They use fields to store the relative record numbers of related records (in the same file or in different files), and they use matching values in common fields to associate records (e.g., having an order number field in both the order header record and the order line-detail record). Whichever method is used, in a conventional file system the access strategy required to retrieve related records is reimplemented in every program that uses a relationship between records.

But in a DBMS, "relationships" also can be defined in the dictionary using the DDL. Thus, an order header entity might be defined as the "parent" of an order line-detail entity, which is the "child." The implementation of this relationship is (ideally) hidden from the program. The program does not know whether relative record number pointers or indexes are being used; for that matter, the program doesn't know whether one, two, or more files are used to store the data. The DBMS provides the "logical" I/O operations such as "get first child," "get next sibling," "update current," and "get all records with specific property." So in defining relationships, as in defining entities and properties, the DBMS DDL provides program independence from the physical data.

A DBMS that provides only a DDL capability for specifying entities, properties, and integrity constraints is useful, but it is not what is considered "full-function." To be a "full-function" DBMS, the system also must have a set of system-provided manipulations that can be performed on the data. The manipulative part of a DBMS generally provides functions equivalent to HLL I/O operations. That is, at least the following manipulations usually are possible: Retrieve (Get, Fetch, Read), Insert (Put, Add, Write), Delete, and Update. These manipulations may operate on one or more records at a time, depending on the DBMS system. What distinguishes the DBMS manipulations from conventional file I/O operations is the way in which the target of the action is specified. In a conventional file system, the I/O operation must be targeted at a specific record in the file using either an explicit record number, an explicit key value, or a "read next" that implicitly targets a record based on the relative record number or key of the previous record. A DBMS, on the other hand, usually supports access by field contents, regardless of whether the field is a key (e.g., "get next course with course — status = 'OPEN' "). And based on relationships in the dictionary, a DBMS can retrieve related records without explicit targeting (e.g., "get first student for this course" or "get first joined student and course").

The functions available in a specific DBMS are included in its "Data Manipulation Language" (DML). The power, consistency, and ease of use of a particular DBMS's DML is an important determinant of how useful it will be in complex application systems. If the DML is well-implemented in the DBMS, it can reduce significantly the number of source code statements necessary to implement application functions.

DBMSs vary in how much they provide the application developer. The best are powerful, highly dynamic, and easy to use; and most importantly, they succeed in substantially reducing the proportion of code that is not "problem-oriented." DBMSs also vary in the underlying model of the entities, the relationships between entities, and the types of manipulations that can be performed on the entities. Thus far in the history of DBMSs, four models have been used: hierarchic, network (also known as CODASYL), inverted list, and relational. Both the hierarchic and network models are based on explicit links between records of the same type ("sibling" links) or between records of different types (where one is the "parent" and one is the "child"). The major difference between the two is that the hierarchic model allows a "child" to have only one "parent" (just as in any familiar form of hierarchy, such as an organization chart), while the network model allows a record type to be the "child" of any number of "parent" record types (for example, in the case where a "course" record type can be the "child" of both an "instructor" record type and a "student" record type).

Both the hierarchic and the network DBMS approaches have fallen into disfavor because they, like conventional file systems, require a knowledge of how the entities are physically structured — that is, which entities have explicit links to each other. These explicit links not only require that the programmer write procedural code to "navigate" the database along the link pathways, but they also make the database relatively static; new or modified link types are not always easy to incorporate once the database has gone into production.

A third alternative, the inverted-list model, is really little more than a conventional file system with enhanced file index facilities to aid in record retrieval. Another way of viewing the inverted-list model is as the relational model with no high-level relational manipulations because records in different files are related by the values in fields (rather than by pointers), but retrieval is still done by single-record read and write operations. As such, the inverted list is of interest not so much because of its particular approach but rather because a DBMS based on the inverted list model can be extended naturally to a relational DBMS by adding relational operators and integrity rules. This is of particular importance to AS/400 sites, because with each new release of OS/400 the AS/400 is being extended from an inverted-list DBMS to a relational DBMS.

The Relational Database Model

The foundation of that relational DBMS toward which the AS/400 is moving is the relational database model, which has become a standard for both IBM and much of the rest of the industry. The relational database model was first introduced in the paper "A Relational Model of Data for Large Shared Data Banks," which Edgar Codd published in June 1970. Since this paper, the relational model has been developed extensively, and a number of DBMS products are based on it. IBM offers DB2 for S/370 MVS users and SQL/DS for S/370 VM/CMS and DOS/VSE users; Oracle Corporation offers Oracle for IBM S/370, S/88, VAX, and PCs; Relational Technology, Inc., offers Ingres for a wide variety of UNIX systems.

Unlike hierarchic, network, and inverted-list DBMSs, which are not based on a formal underlying database model, relational DBMSs all stem from the well-defined foundation of the relational database model. In the following sections, I provide an overview of this model by examining the three major parts: data structure, data integrity, and data manipulation.

Data Structure

The data structure portion of the relational database model defines the form for representing data. Most basic to this form is the concept of a "relation." Figure 19.1 shows the composition of a relation, which looks like what is commonly called a "table," and for the most part it can be treated that way. That is, a relation can be thought of as having columns that lay out properties ("attributes," in relational nomenclature) and rows that hold specific instances of the entities ("tuples," in relational nomenclature) being stored in the table. To be more precise, however, a relation has two parts — the "heading" and the "body." The "heading" is an unordered set of attributes. In Figure 19.1, the PEOPLE relation's heading is the set of attributes (SSN, NAME, BTHDAT); I also could have said the heading is the set of attributes (BTHDAT, SSN, NAME) because a set has no specific ordering of its elements. The "body" of the relation is a set of tuples (each tuple appears as a row in Figure 19.1). Each tuple in the PEOPLE relation represents information about a single person; that is, each tuple is an instance of the PEOPLE entity. Formally, each tuple is a set of attribute-and-value pairs. The tuple in Figure 19.1 identified by SSN value 123-45-6789 is actually the following set of pairs: (<SSN: 123-45-6789>, <NAME: 'SMITH'>, <BTHDAT:4/9/65>). Or I could have said the tuple is the following set of pairs: (<NAME:'SMITH'>,<SSN: 123-45-6789 >, < BTHDAT: 4/9/65 >). Again, sets are not ordered. Because the values in a tuple are not ordered, a value is always paired with the appropriate attribute that serves as a label; thus, you can keep track of the meaning of all the values in all the tuples in a relation.

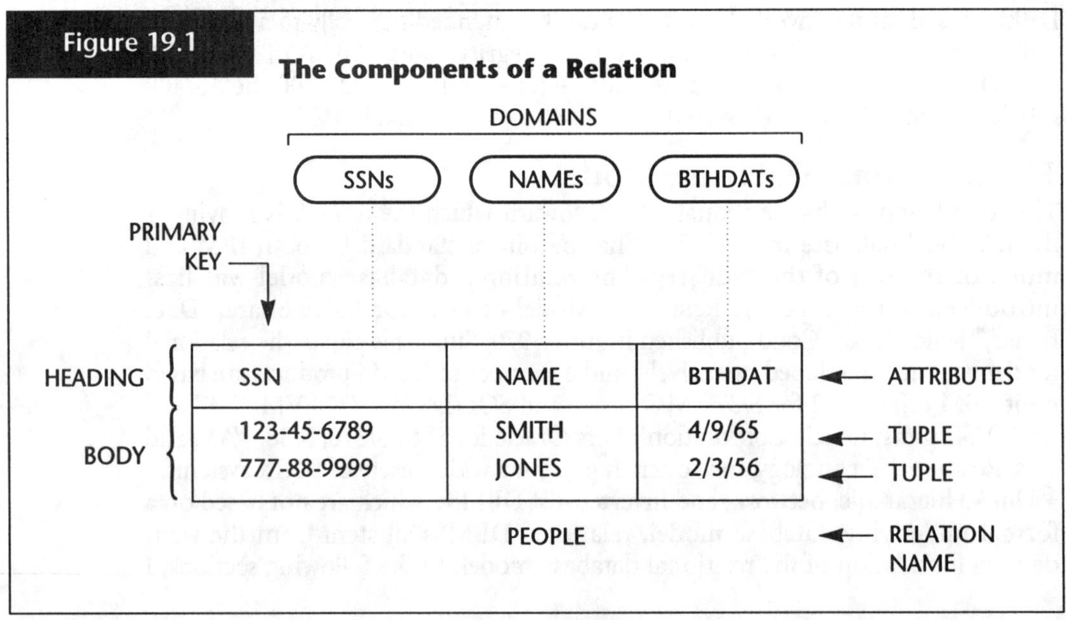

Figure 19.1 The Components of a Relation

At this point, you may wonder why something so simple as the row-column structure of a table must become as complex as a "set of attribute-and-value pairs." Because an unordered, labeled representation of data is used, the relational model can reference all values by name rather than by some physical mechanism such as the position of the column in a table. This distinction is not a minor one — it is one of the breakthroughs in modeling data that the relational approach brought about.

Another distinction between a "table" and a "relation" is that the tuples in a relation have no specific ordering. That is, while it makes sense to refer to the second row in a table, there is no such concept as the "second tuple" in a relation. So how are tuples referenced, if not by a row number? Every tuple in a relation can be referenced by specifying values for "primary key" attributes. For example, in Figure 19.1, a tuple can be referenced by specifying its SSN attribute value (SSN is thus a "primary key" attribute for the PEOPLE relation). This, of course, requires that a unique combination of attribute values exist for every tuple in a relation, and this requirement is one of the integrity concepts discussed later.

The two concepts of referencing attributes by name and referencing tuples by values provide a data model that has no physical storage concepts associated with the data organization. The same statement cannot be made about the hierarchic, network, or inverted-list DBMS approaches. Thus, the relational database model is the only one that achieves complete physical data independence.

Another fundamental part of data representation in the relational model is the concept of "domain." Simply put, a domain combines two pieces of information: the set (possibly infinite) of allowable values and the semantics (or "meaning") of the values. A domain is not part of a relation, and it stores no particular values. Instead, a domain defines a pool of values that an attribute can have. Every attribute is specified as being "over" a domain. Figure 19.2 shows some simplified examples of domains and attributes defined over the respective domains. These examples point out some interesting and important facets of domains. First, as I just mentioned, domains define allowable values; thus, the attribute EMPL_SALARY can never be negative because it is defined over the domain Salary, which has no negative values. Second, a domain specifies the units of measure. Attributes defined over domains with similar units of measure can be compared or added, but attributes defined over domains with dissimilar units of measure cannot be compared or added meaningfully. Thus, a statement such as "IF HAIR_COLOR = PRODUCT_COLOR," while perhaps an unlikely comparison, is at least possible, whereas "IF HAIR_COLOR = EMPL_SALARY" is not allowed. This type of mismatched comparison may seem obvious, but domains help clarify to the DBMS (and to programmers) more subtle distinctions. For example, in most HLL's a field used to store the number of children in a household (HH_CHILDREN) will be an integer, as will the field to store the number of cars owned by a household (HH_CARS). Neither the RPG, COBOL, nor PL/I compilers cough at a statement such as "TOTAL_POSSESSIONS = HH_CARS + HH_CHILDREN." This statement is probably the result of bad coding, not a medieval social philosophy, and should be prevented. In the

Figure 19.2 **Domains and Attributes**

Domain :	Color Values (Red, Orange, Yellow, Green, Blue, Indigo, Violet...)
Attributes:	PRODUCT_COLOR HAIR_COLOR
Domain :	Salary Range (0 through 100,000,000) Units Dollars/year
Attributes:	EMPL_SALARY CONTRACTOR_SALARY
Domain :	Wages Range (0 through 100,000) Units Dollars/hour
Attributes:	EMPL_WAGES CONTRACTOR_WAGES
Domain :	Weight Range (0 through 100,000,000) Units Pounds
Attributes:	SHIPPING_WT EMPL_WT
Domain :	Children Range (Integers >= 0) Units People
Attribute :	HH_CHILDREN
Domain :	Cars Range (Integers >= 0 Units Cars
Attribute :	HH_CARS
Domain :	Units Range (Integers) Units Unitless
Attribute :	UNIT_COUNT

relational database model, these two attributes could not be added because they are from different domains.

What if you really do want to add such dissimilar units? In that case, you use a "mapping" function — for example a function, UNIT_CVT, that is defined to convert (i.e., "map") any integer value to a "unitless" value. The required statement then becomes "UNIT_COUNT = UNIT _CVT(HH_CARS) + UNIT_CVT (HH_CHILDREN)." A more common example of required mapping would be from annual salary values to hourly wages or vice versa. In this case, the numerator (i.e., dollars) for both units of measure is identical. This identity is precisely the cause of a typical HLL programming error in adding fields such as EMPL_SALARY and EMPL_WAGES without converting either. The concept of domains allows system detection of invalid or questionable comparisons or computations.

Another point to be made about a "relation" is that a database relation (unlike the mathematical notion of relation) cannot have sets as values for an attribute. Every attribute value in a tuple must be a single element drawn from the underlying domain. Figure 19.3 shows the distinction between a mathematical relation (shown in table format) and a database relation. Note that restructuring a mathematical relation that has sets of values into a database relation is a trivial operation of repeating values for some attributes.

The operation of repeating values introduces another facet of a relational database. By definition, a database relation is in what is called "first normal form" (or 1NF), which simply means that there are no sets as attribute values. Because a relation is in 1NF, all of the referencing and manipulative operations of the relational model can be performed on it. However, a 1NF relation may not be the ideal form for representing data. A relation in 1NF can store information redundantly, leading to undesirable inconsistency in the database. Figure 19.4 shows a 1NF relation with redundant storage of WAREHOUSE_ADDRESS. Figure 19.5 shows the 1NF relation split into two relations that eliminate the WAREHOUSE_ADDRESS redundancy. The process of splitting relations with redundant information storage into two or more relations without the redundancy is a process known as "normalization." There are five main levels of normalization (1NF through 5NF), each level removing one type of information redundancy. (For a more detailed look at normalization, see Chapter 20, "Database Normalization.")

Figure 19.3

Mathematical and Database Relations

PARENT	CHILDREN
SMITH	BUBBA
JONES	BILLY SUSIE FRED
HARRIS	JANICE TOMMY

Mathematical Relation

PARENT	CHILDREN
SMITH	BUBBA
JONES	BILLY
JONES	SUSIE
JONES	FRED
HARRIS	JANICE
HARRIS	TOMMY

Database Relation

Figure 19.4

1NF INVENTORY Relation

PART	WAREHOUSE_NBR	QTY	WAREHOUSE_ADDRESS
167	1	10	1511 Central Ave.
448	1	26	1511 Central Ave.
302	2	18	6803 Alder St.

INVENTORY

Figure 19.5

2NF INVENTORY and WAREHOUSE Relations

PART	WAREHOUSE_NBR	QTY
167	1	10
448	1	26
302	2	18

INVENTORY

WAREHOUSE_NBR	WAREHOUSE_ADDRESS
1	1511 Central Ave.
2	6803 Alder St.

WAREHOUSE

In summary, the data structures of the relational model provide data independence (a separation of the conceptual and physical aspects), and, when viewed (as they normally are) as tables, relations are easy to understand and work with. Relations also put a firm theoretical footing under any DBMS based on them. This combination of the conceptual simplicity and formal definition of relations forms the foundation for the next two parts of the model — data integrity and data manipulation.

Data Integrity

While the data-structure portion of the relational database model defines the form for representing data, the data integrity portion of the model defines mechanisms for ensuring that the stored data is valid. This requires that the attribute values each be valid, that the set of values in a tuple be unique, and that relations known to be interrelated have consistent values within the tuples.

In introducing the concept of "domains" in the previous section, I essentially covered the first form of data integrity — that values for attributes come only from the underlying domain. This concept covers the common HLL implementation technique of checking a value to see that it is within an allowable range or that it is one of a list of allowable values; it also extends the concept to the meaning of the values (e.g., whether units are children or cars). What it does not address is a large group of validity constraints that involve other attribute values in the same tuple (e.g., QTY_SHIP <= QTY_ORDERED) or other tuples (e.g., SUM (LOAN_AMT) <= 10000). These aspects of attribute integrity are included as part of the current state of development of the relational database model; however, they usually are considered an extension of the model rather than a fundamental component of the model, as the concept of "domain" is considered.

The second form of integrity essential to the relational database model is "entity" integrity. This is a fairly straightforward concept — every tuple in a relation must "exist" in the "real world"; therefore, every tuple must be uniquely identifiable. It follows that there can be no completely duplicate tuples (all attribute values identical) in a relation; otherwise, their unique existence is not represented in the database. From this property of uniqueness is derived the principle that there exists in every relation some set of attributes (possibly all the relation's attributes) whose values are never duplicated entirely in any two tuples in the relation (i.e., the set of values for these attributes is unique). If you don't include any superfluous attributes (i.e., ones not needed to guarantee uniqueness) in the set of attributes, the set of attributes can serve as the relation's "primary key." (More than one possible set of attributes may meet the criteria for a primary key; each of these is referred to as a "candidate" key, and one is picked arbitrarily as the primary key.)

The primary key is a minimal set of attributes whose values are unique for all tuples in a relation. Because of this, the primary key forms the only means of addressing a specific tuple in the relational database model. A consequence of the requirement for unique primary key values is that none of the values in a tuple's primary key attributes can be "null" (i.e., missing or unknown). None of the primary key attributes can have a null value because a null value cannot be guaranteed to be unequal to a valid value. Thus, if SSN is the attribute serving as the primary key in the relation PEOPLE and there exists a tuple with SSN = 123-45-6789, another tuple could not have SSN = null, because you can't tell whether null is equal to 123-45-6789. If you can't tell whether the two values are equal, you can't guarantee uniqueness. A similar argument holds for primary keys made up of more than one attribute (i.e. "composite" primary keys), which need all attribute values to guarantee uniqueness and hence cannot have null for any of the attributes in the primary key.

The third, and final, form of integrity fundamental to the relational database model is "referential" integrity. Simply put, referential integrity requires that tuples that exist in separate relations, but that are interrelated, be unambiguously interrelated. Let's look at the warehouse example again to understand referential integrity. In Figure 19.5, two relations are used so a warehouse address can be stored nonredundantly. The WAREHOUSE_NBR is retained as an attribute in both relations, so the WAREHOUSE_NBR value can be used in an INVENTORY tuple to address ("look up") the appropriate WAREHOUSE tuple via its WAREHOUSE_NBR primary key. Thus, the tuples in the two relations are interrelated, based on matching values in the WAREHOUSE_NBR attributes in the two relations.

As I pointed out earlier, the WAREHOUSE_NBR attribute in the WAREHOUSE relation serves as a primary key and can never be null. The WAREHOUSE_NBR attribute in the INVENTORY relation is referred to as a "foreign" key (it addresses "foreign" tuples — ones usually, though not always, outside the same relation). A foreign key value can be all null. That means that its related record is unknown. A foreign key value also can match exactly a primary key value in a related tuple. But a foreign key value cannot have some attribute values present (i.e., at least one attribute value is not null) and not match the primary key value of an existing tuple in the related relation. This requirement says nothing more than that if the foreign key "points" to a related tuple, the tuple must be there. A consequence of this rule is that composite foreign key values cannot be partially null because, by the entity integrity rule, no primary key attribute value can ever be null.

Together, the three integrity rules — attribute, entity, and referential integrity — allow specification of important constraints that a relational DBMS can enforce automatically whenever a database update occurs. These rules "protect" not only the specific values in attributes, but also the identity and interrelationships of tuples as well. A DBMS that provides this level of integrity support lifts a large coding load off the backs of application programmers.

Data Manipulation

But as I stated in the general discussion on DBMS, data representation and integrity rules do not make a complete model. There must be some means of manipulating the data as well. The relational database model defines data manipulations as the relational assignment operation and eight algebraic operations. The assignment operation simply allows the value of some arbitrary expression of relational algebra to be assigned to another relation. For example, REL_C <= REL_A JOIN REL_B, allows the relation REL_C to take on the value (set of tuples) resulting from the join operation performed over tuples in relations REL_A and REL_B. This is analogous to arithmetic assignment in HLL computations.

The eight relational algebraic operations include four standard set operations (union, intersection, difference, and product) and four operations specific to database relations (projection, selection, division, and join). This group of eight operations has the property of algebraic "closure," which means that the result of any of the eight operations is a relation. Thus, the operations can be combined into complex, parenthesized expressions similar to the way ordinary arithmetic expressions can be built up; for example, (REL_A UNION REL_B) TIMES REL_C is a valid relational algebraic expression. Because the operands and results in relational algebra are relations, not simple values or single records, the manipulations provide a very powerful base for database operations. To relate this concept to a conventional file system, think of how much you could accomplish with operations expressed in algebraic form, but which treated entire files (or record subsets) as the operands.

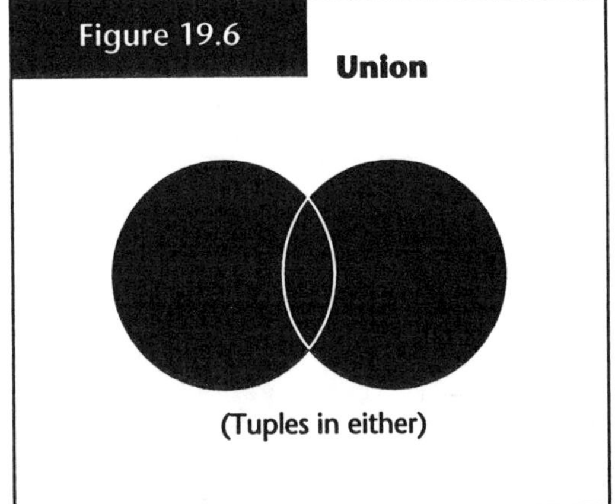
Figure 19.6 **Union**

(Tuples in either)

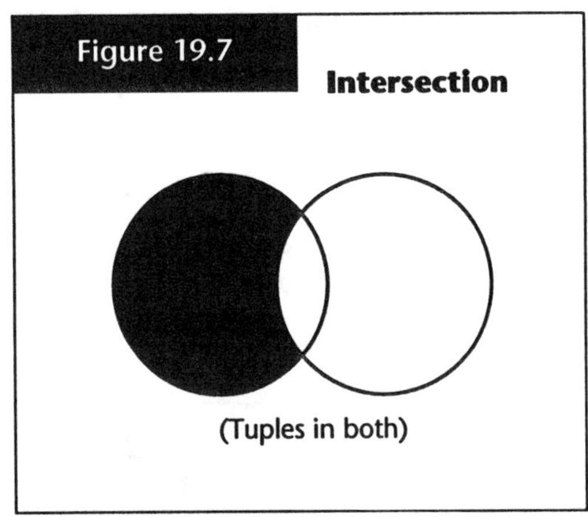
Figure 19.7 **Intersection**

(Tuples in both)

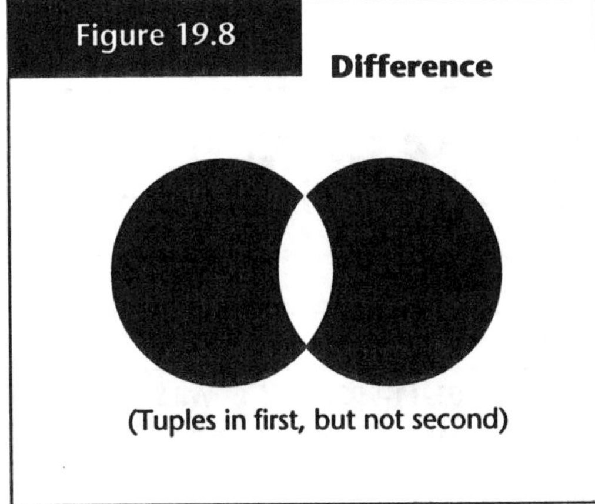
Figure 19.8 **Difference**

(Tuples in first, but not second)

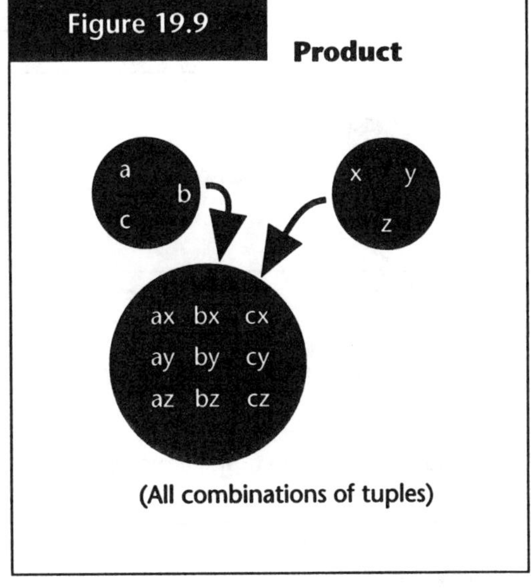

Figure 19.9 **Product**

(All combinations of tuples)

The four relational algebraic operations found in conventional set theory are union, intersection, difference (MINUS) and product (TIMES). Figures 19.6, 19.7, 19.8, and 19.9 show Venn diagrams of these operations. The results of these four operations performed on the sample relations in Figure 19.10 are shown in Figures 19.11, 19.12, 19.13, 19.14, and 19.15. Note that union, intersection, and difference require the two relations to have the same attributes (i.e., they must be "union-compatible"). The product operation can work on dissimilar relations; if one relation has M attributes, and the other has N attributes, the result is a relation with M + N attributes. Also, union, intersection, and product dare "associative" operations — the order of operands does not matter (e.g., A UNION B is equal to B UNION A). The difference operation is not associative as Figures 19.13 and 19.14 show.

In addition to the conventional set operations, four special operations apply only to database relations. Examples of these operations performed on the sample relations in 19.16 are shown in Figures 19.17, 19.18, 19.19, 19.20, 19.21,

Figure 19.10 **Three Relations Used as Operands**

SSN	NAME
123-45-6789 601-11-9999	SMITH WILSON

REL_A

SSN	NAME
145-67-8888 601-11-9999	JONES WILSON

REL_B

COURSE	INSTRUCTOR
MATH 101 PSYCH 203	ALDRIDGE ULRICH

REL_C

Figure 19.11 **REL_A UNION REL_B**

SSN	NAME
123-45-6789 601-11-9999 145-67-8888	SMITH WILSON JONES

(Note that duplicate tuples are dropped)

Figure 19.12 **REL_A INTERSECT REL_B**

SSN	NAME
601-11-9999	WILSON

Figure 19.13 **REL_A MINUS REL_B**

SSN	NAME
123-45-6789	SMITH

(Difference is not associative)

Figure 19.14 **REL_B MINUS REL_A**

SSN	NAME
145-67-8888	JONES

(Difference is not associative)

and 19.22. The project operation (Figures 19.17 and 19.18) eliminates some attributes (columns) from a relation; any resulting duplicate tuples are then

Figure 19.15 **REL_A TIMES REL_C**

SSN	NAME	COURSE	INSTRUCTOR
123-45-6789	SMITH	MATH 101	ALDRIDGE
123-45-6789	SMITH	PSYCH 203	ULRICH
601-11-9999	WILSON	MATH 101	ALDRIDGE
601-11-9999	WILSON	PSYCH 203	ULRICH

Figure 19.16 **Sample Relations**

CUST_NBR	CUST_CITY	CUST_STS	CUST_CREDIT
123	PORTLAND	00	1,000
456	PORTLAND	20	500
789	EUGENE	10	10,000
304	PORTLAND	00	2,000

CUSTOMERS

ORDER_NBR	ORDER_CUST	ORDER_AMT
601	123	2,000
602	789	50
603	123	500
604	198	1,000

ORDERS

COMPANY	VEHICLE
FORD	CAR
FORD	TRUCK
GM	CAR
NISSAN	TRUCK

AUTO_COMPANIES

VEHICLE
CAR

CARS_ONLY

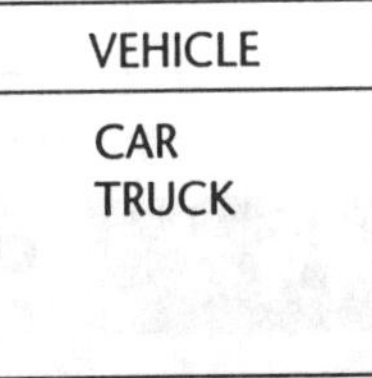

VEHICLE
CAR
TRUCK

CARS_TRUCKS

eliminated. The select operation (19.19) eliminates entire tuples (rows) if they don't satisfy a condition. Note that if I specify "WHERE CUST_NBR = 123," a specific tuple can be selected by its primary key value. The division operation

Figure 19.17 **PROJECT CUSTOMERS [CUST__NBR, CUST__CITY]**

CUST__NBR	CUST__CITY
123	PORTLAND
456	PORTLAND
789	EUGENE
304	PORTLAND

Figure 19.18 **PROJECT CUSTOMERS [CUST__CITY, CUST__STS]**

CUST__CITY	CUST__STS
PORTLAND	00
PORTLAND	20
EUGENE	10

Figure 19.19 **SELECT CUSTOMERS WHERE CUST_CITY = 'PORTLAND'**

CUST__NBR	CUST__CITY	CUST__STS	CUST__CREDIT
123	PORTLAND	00	1,000
456	PORTLAND	20	500
304	PORTLAND	00	2,000

Figure 19.20 **AUTO__COMPANIES DIVIDEBY CARS__ONLY**

COMPANY
FORD
GM

Figure 19.21 **AUTO__COMPANIES DIVIDEBY CARS__TRUCKS**

COMPANY
FORD

Figure 19.22 **CUSTOMERS JOIN ORDERS WHERE CUST__NBR = ORDER__CUST**

CUST__NBR	CUST__CITY	CUST__STS	CUST__CREDIT	ORDER__NBR	ORDER__CUST	ORDER__AMT
123	PORTLAND	00	1,000	601	123	2,000
123	PORTLAND	00	1,000	603	123	500
789	EUGENE	10	10,000	602	789	50

(Figures 19.20 and 19.21) results in all values of an attribute in the first relation that match (in a different attribute) all values in the second relation.

The final special relational algebraic operation is the join. The join is not a primitive operation (i.e., all join operations are equivalent to a product of two relations from which some tuples are then selected); however, its usefulness in interrelating two relations is so great that it is treated as one of the essential set of eight operations. Figure 19.22 provides an example of an "equijoin" where the two relations (CUSTOMERS and ORDERS) are interrelated by equal values in the CUST_NBR and ORDER_CUST attributes. Conditions other than equality can be used to join tuples in two relations; for example, values of two attributes can be tested for "greater-than" or "unequal." (In general, the test used can be any scalar comparison (=, >, > =, < =, etc.). This comparison operator is often referred to by the Greek symbol for *theta*, and thus the generic version of the operation is often called "*theta*-join."

The result of an equijoin always has two attributes with identical values in every tuple (in Figure 19.22, these attributes are CUST_NBR and ORDER_CUST). If one of these unnecessary attributes is dropped from the resulting relation, the equijoin is said to be a "natural" join. The natural join is the join most commonly meant when you see a nonspecific reference to a database "join."

One further variant of the join is possible. Figure 19.22 shows an "inner" join, one in which unmatched tuples are dropped. If, instead of dropping unmatched tuples, you include them and put null in the attributes of the "missing" tuple, you have an "outer" join. If only the first relation's (the one on the left of the JOIN operator) unmatched tuples are paired with nulls, the result is a "left outer join"; a mirror image "right outer join" is also possible.

The eight relational algebraic operations provide a standard by which any DBMS that claims to support "relational" data manipulations can be measured. While a particular DBMS may use a syntax (or fill-in-the-blank menus) different from the syntax of the relational algebra, it must provide equivalent power in manipulating relations without iteration (looping) or recursion. In addition, the relational database model is unique among the various approaches in that it provides for manipulations of entire sets (i.e., relations) of tuples. An example of using a set-at-a-time manipulation would be "Update all students with total-credits > 300, setting academic-year to 'SENIOR.'" The set-at-a-time operations provide a more powerful means of manipulating data than is possible with the record-at-a-time operations available with conventional file system I/O or with the other three types of DBMS. (Keep in mind that a set of tuples can contain a single tuple and, thus, set-at-a-time operations provide both higher level manipulations and record-at-a-time operations.)

Expressions in relational algebra are used not only to retrieve data or create new relations, but also to define a scope for record-at-a-time retrieval and update. The result of a relational algebraic expression can be treated as a "view" relation (rather than a "base" relation — one in which the data is actually stored). Changes to a tuple in a "view" are treated as changes to the underlying tuple in the "base" relation. While a comprehensive discussion of views is beyond the scope of this chapter, the view concept is used to allow single-record retrieval (FETCH NEXT tuple operation) and updating (ADD tuple, DELETE CURRENT tuple, UPDATE CURRENT tuple operations). Single-tuple retrieval and update, because it is part of any DBMS, not just the relational database model, is not treated as one of the fundamental components of the relational model. Nevertheless, it does exist and enables a mixture of set-at-a-time and record-at-a-time (within a specific view) operations when using a relational DBMS to implement an application.

Taken together, the data structure, data integrity, and data manipulation components of the relational database model go a long way toward elevating the application developer out of the role of "housekeeper." The sooner IBM (or third-party vendors) provides "full Function" relational DBMS facilities for the AS/400, the better it will be for programmers and end users.

In the meantime, you can define your files using the concepts of domains and normalized relations. And you can design your HLL programs to preserve the attribute, entity, and referential integrity of the database, as well as to write system specifications and program designs for data manipulation using relational algebraic constructs. The design and implementation structure of applications that use database concepts will show immediate improvement. In addition, if you understand the relational model, you can take advantage of functions currently available (e.g., the AS/400 join logical file). Familiarity with the relational model also will make clear what components of a relational DBMS are available only in limited form on the AS/400 (e.g., the AS/400 join logical file is statically defined rather than defined at execution time) or not present at all (e.g., the AS/400 does not support "referential integrity"). Finally, as new relational DBMS facilities become available on the AS/400, you can incorporate them smoothly into your application systems, thus providing the substantial productivity advantages of a relational database management system.

Chapter 20

Database Normalization

by Paul Conte

Balance fact redundancy with data redundancy to realize the benefits of "normalized" files

If you have been considering the highly touted "relational" model for designing your organization's database but have been put off because the "fully normalized" form of relations appears to require dozens of files where your experience tells you one or two would serve perfectly well, you just need to learn how you can mix "normalization" with a little abnormal, albeit well-controlled, behavior in database design to solve your problems.

First, for those of you who fear that Edgar Codd, the "father of the relational database model," and of whom I am a real admirer, would roundly denounce you if you designed an abnormal file, let me offer some reassurance and some guidance. You always should fully normalize your logical database design; that is, on paper, you should design normalized files. Thus, you remain loyal to, and the full beneficiary of, the many design advantages of the relational model. But because a full-function relational database management system (RDBMS) is not really available on the AS/400, when you implement your database design, you may want to combine some files. In the discussion that follows I review normalization and the five normal forms and then offer specific guidelines for implementing the appropriate level of file normalization or abnormalization to fit your application requirements.

To begin, let's review normalization. Normalizing is a process whereby a single relation (or file) is split into multiple relations (or files) so that "facts" are stored in a regular, nonredundant fashion. Generally, a "fact" is the value of a field (such as birth date) associated with the value of one or more other fields (such as name) that serve as a "primary key" for the entity to which the fact relates. For example, in Figure 20.1 are two records (or two "tuples," in relational nomenclature) for the PEOPLE relation. The values shown represent two "facts":

SMITH (the value in the first field) has a birth date of September 9, 1948 (the value in the second field), and JONES has a birth date of June 3, 1952.

It is important to realize that the objective of normalization is the nonredundant representation (or in the case of disk files, nonredundant storage) of facts, not data. Indeed, normalization often requires that data be stored redundantly if the data is used to interrelate normalized files. Figure 20.2 shows how the value "SMITH" must be repeated for each child in the normalized CHILDREN relation. Counting the three occurrences of "SMITH" in CHILDREN and the single occurrence in PEOPLE, the data — "SMITH" — is redundantly stored four times. But the facts, SMITH's birth date and SMITH's children, are not redundantly stored. For example, between the two files, the fact that BUBBA is a SMITH child is represented only once.

In Figures 20.1 and 20.2, the value "SMITH" had to be repeated because it serves to relate records in the PEOPLE and CHILDREN relations. When used as a value for the NAME field in the PEOPLE relation, "SMITH" serves as the "primary key" value, providing a unique identifying value for that record. When used as values for the PARENT field in the CHILDREN relation, "SMITH" serves as a "foreign key" value. (The term "foreign key" comes from the key field role that "SMITH" plays in PEOPLE, a relation that is "foreign" to — i.e., separate from — CHILDREN.)

The redundant storage of key field data is, perhaps, the most troublesome problem when you use normalized files. With normalized files, it is essential that

Figure 20.1

PEOPLE Relation

NAME	BIRTHDATE
SMITH	09/09/48
JONES	06/03/52

Figure 20.2

CHILDREN Relation

PARENT	CHILD
SMITH	BUBBA
SMITH	HELGA
SMITH	BETTY
JONES	FRED
JONES	ESTER

whenever the value of a primary key field is changed, all occurrences of that value in related foreign key fields (i.e., in other files) be changed immediately. If you use fully normalized files, this might involve dozens of files — leading to a substantial coding task during implementation as well as a runtime execution burden. In the sections that follow, I show how the carefully considered decision to use "abnormal" files — those that are not fully normalized — can reduce the problem of foreign key updating while preserving the major benefits of normalized files.

The Five Normal Forms — A Brief Review

So you can see what rules of normalization you may choose to violate, let me briefly review the five normal forms.

- 1NF - Each data element in the relation is "atomic." No composite values or repeating groups are allowed.
- 2NF - Each data element not part of the primary key is "functionally dependent" on the entire primary key; that is, the "fact" is about the whole entity, not some part of it.
- 3NF - No nonkey data element is "functionally dependent" on another nonkey data element in the record. A change to one of the "facts" in a record doesn't imply a change to one of the other "facts."
- 4NF - Whenever a multivalued "fact" exists in a relation (e.g., one PARENT can have more than one CHILD in the CHILDREN relation), other independent "facts" do not exist in the same relation.
- 5NF - The relation cannot be broken down into relations with smaller records, each with a different primary key, without losing some of the "facts."

If a database design consists entirely of 5NF relations, it is said to be "fully normalized." This form ensures that problems of database inconsistency will not occur because of the redundant storage of facts in a single relation. The fully normalized database, however, implies nothing about the consistency of primary and foreign key values. Instead, rather than implying that these redundantly stored values are consistent, a fully normalized database requires that these redundant values be kept consistent at all times (in relational parlance, this is known as "referential integrity"). Therein lies the rub on the AS/400; the system does not provide an automatic database management facility to keep the primary and foreign key values consistent.

While development plans for the AS/400 are thought to include a system facility for maintaining the consistency of primary and foreign keys, such a facility is not expected to be available in the near future. Thus, database design for AS/400 applications in the foreseeable future must plan for locally implemented mechanisms to change all occurrences of a value wherever it is used as a foreign key whenever the value changes in the file in which it is the primary key. Accordingly, it pays to design a database with a balance between the evils of fact redundancy and the evils of key-field data redundancy.

First Abnormal Form

Let's examine ways to achieve this balance by looking at examples of several "abnormal" forms. First normal form prohibits composite values, but it is often reasonable to behave "abnormally" and allow them. Essential to the first normal form, indeed to the whole notion of a "relation," is the concept of an "atomic" (i.e., indivisible) data element (or field). However, I think it was Max Planck who said, "One person's indivisible atom is another person's composite of protons, electrons, and neutrons." Similarly, a composite data element can violate the letter of the law for 1NF and thereby simplify file design, while still following the spirit of 1NF.

Consider street addresses, phone numbers, and dates as three common examples of composite data elements. To create atomic elements, do you need to split these into separate fields such as house number and street name, or area code and local number, or month, day, and year? Not necessarily.

To derive the best solution requires two steps. First, you must determine whether the composite field represents a single "fact" or several distinct "facts," because you never should lump two distinct facts into the same data element. Consider for a moment a person's street address. It can be considered a single fact if you are using it only for mailing purposes. On the other hand, the address must be treated as at least two distinct facts — the street name and the house number — if you are printing walking lists for door-to-door political handshaking activity because you must list houses on the same side of the street (all odd or all even numbers) in sequence. Thus, anticipating when you will use the entire "fact" and when you will use some component of it is the first determinant of how you should define a data element.

The second determination is how the components of the fact will be used. A birth date, for example, is commonly treated as a single fact. If most of your applications simply display or list the birth date, it should be defined as a single data element. But if many of your applications use year of birth by itself in tests or computations, you may find it easier to define three data elements — birth year, birth month, and birth day. While a high level language (HLL) program would have no difficulty splitting apart a single birth date field, it becomes much more difficult when a package such as Query is used. Thus, assessing the difficulty of decomposing a composite data element versus the difficulty of recombining separate data elements is the second determinant of how you should define a data element.

First normal form also prohibits repeating data elements, but there are also times when repeating data elements — like composite values — are reasonable in spite of the 1NF guidelines. Figure 20.3 shows an unnormalized way to store information about available scholarship funds for four school terms (i.e., fall term, winter term, spring term, and summer term). This simplified case might be used convincingly as an example of why it is helpful to normalize. After all, if you add a fifth term, you have to add a field to every record in the file. And isn't it simpler to calculate fund totals and averages if the amounts are in a single data element, not four? Both of these are valid reasons to use the normalized relations in Figure 20.4.

But as soon as you introduce two relations where you had one, any program that allows changes and deletions of scholarships must handle two files instead of

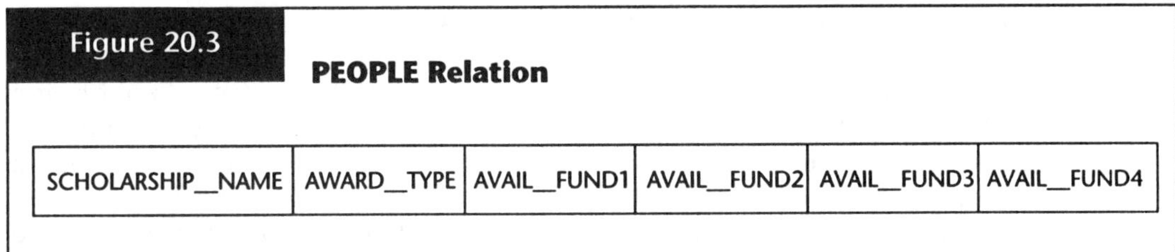

Figure 20.3 **PEOPLE Relation**

SCHOLARSHIP_NAME	AWARD_TYPE	AVAIL_FUND1	AVAIL_FUND2	AVAIL_FUND3	AVAIL_FUND4

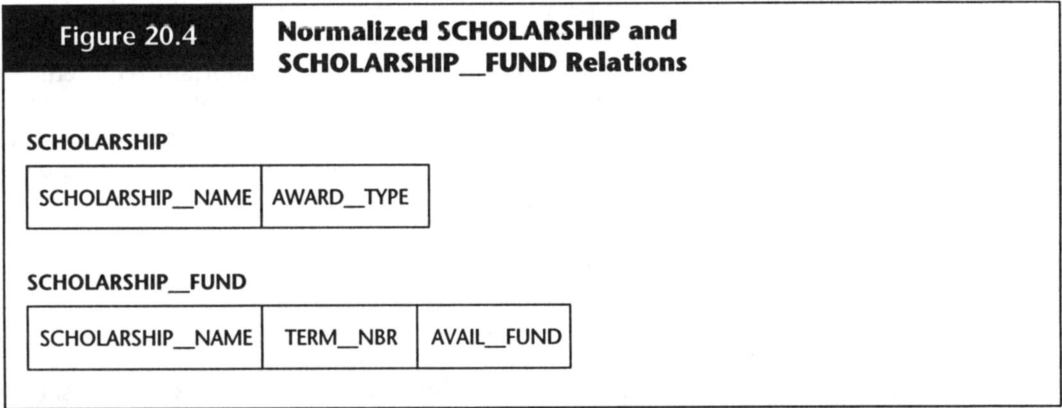

Figure 20.4 **Normalized SCHOLARSHIP and SCHOLARSHIP_FUND Relations**

SCHOLARSHIP

SCHOLARSHIP_NAME	AWARD_TYPE

SCHOLARSHIP_FUND

SCHOLARSHIP_NAME	TERM_NBR	AVAIL_FUND

one. Similarly, while reporting the total available funds has become simpler, reporting totals for one term by award type has become more complex.

If the AS/400 had a full-featured RDBMS you wouldn't have to fret over these implementation concerns. You could implement the relations in 1NF and rely on the RDBMS to use the relational operations "project" and "join" to combine the two relations into whatever form you needed, including one that resembled Figure 20.3. This "view" would be available for both retrieval (a capability implemented on the AS/400) and updating (which is not yet available — i.e., you cannot update a join logical file). But as the AS/400 doesn't have a fully implemented RDBMS, you need to consider the implementation complexity of a multifile approach. At times like this, your guide should be that it is reasonable to use a single file if, and only if, an inherently fixed number of repetitions is to be represented. As with allowing composite values, this definition is application-dependent.

The best example of an inherently fixed number of repetitions is the number of months in the Gregorian year. A good example of an indeterminate number of repetitions is children. In the scholarship example, the number of terms could be treated either way, depending on the school. At many small colleges, a simple academic calendar of four terms remains constant, so the relation can be left abnormal. At my alma mater, on the other hand, the number of terms seems to change every year as "interterm," "early summer term," and other terms are dreamed up, and normalization is a necessity. Do not confuse "inherently fixed number" with "maximum possible." The CHILDREN relation should call to mind the unpleasant surprises in store if you design around a maximum. It would be easier as a parent to find a new house when the maximum is exceeded than it would be as a programmer to revise your software in a similar case.

Are you still nervous about Edgar Codd's reaction? Because you do not have a RDBMS available, even Codd might allow for the preceding well-controlled abnormal behavior that repeats a data element to deal with the difficulties of referential integrity. Furthermore, in the cases presented so far, I have retained functional equivalence to normalized forms. For example, the normalized relations in Figure 20.4 always can be derived by a fixed sequence of projection, join, and union relational operations on the relation in Figure 20.3 (and four "constant" relations providing the four term numbers). In addition, the primary thrust of 1NF is the "shape" of a record type, the most important requirement being that all records in a relation have the same number of data elements. This principle does not allow a variable number of repeating data elements or varying forms of composite data elements, but it can readily admit fixed repeating data elements or fixed composite structures.

Second and Third Abnormal Forms

The second and third normal forms are closely related, the primary difference being whether the disallowed functional dependency is on a portion of a composite primary key (2NF) or on a nonkey data element (3NF). Both will be treated here by discussing an example of "third abnormal form." Figure 20.5 shows a relation, ADDRESS, that in a strict sense is not in third normal form because the CITY and STATE data elements are functionally dependent on the nonkey data element ZIP_CODE. Figure 20.6 shows the data elements reorganized as two relations in third normal form. Which of these is the preferable design?

In most applications, the unnormalized relation in Figure 20.5 is better. Obviously, it has the simplicity of one relation instead of two, but there are more important reasons to use this abnormal form. Most importantly, you may need to store an address for someone who does not provide you with a zip code. While the relational model does allow null values to be represented in nonkey data elements, that won't do you much good in trying to store the person's CITY and STATE. Even if you had a zip code for everyone, you would be required to maintain an up-to-date zip code directory — feasible perhaps, but a responsibility you may prefer to leave to the Postal Service. Finally, what happens if the zip code is entered incorrectly in the normalized ADDRESS relation (Figure 20.6)? Most likely, any mail will be returned.

Now that I've pointed out the problems with the normalized approach, let's examine the abnormal form. This form indeed redundantly stores the "fact" that a specific zip code identifies a specific city and state. But if a mistake occurs, and the city and state are identified with an inconsistently stored zip code, what is the cost? In most cases, the mail with the wrong zip code will be delivered late because the Postal Service will correct the erroneous zip code. But late mail is a much less serious problem than those that could result with the normalized design. The important specific point here is that in many cases, you don't care about the "fact" that a zip code implies a city and state; you care about the "fact" that a person has a specific and complete address. In general, before you use

Figure 20.5 **Unnormalized ADDRESS Relation**

ADDRESS

NAME	STREET_ADDRESS	CITY	STATE	ZIP_CODE

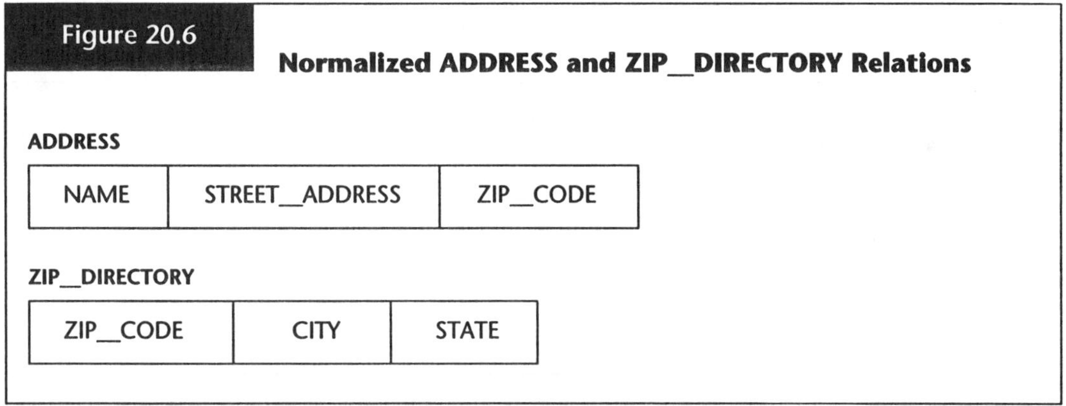

Figure 20.6 **Normalized ADDRESS and ZIP_DIRECTORY Relations**

third normal form, be sure that you always can supply a non-null value for the foreign key field (in Figure 20.6, ZIP_CODE in the ADDRESS relation is the foreign key field) and that you are interested in maintaining the "fact" that led you to consider splitting the single relation in the first place.

Fourth Abnormal Form

Reasonable exceptions to the fourth normal form are not as common as reasonable exceptions to the first three normal forms. They do exist, however. The fourth normal form does not allow multivalued facts to coexist with other independent facts in the same relation. However, when multivalued "facts" exist in the same relation and are independent, but always have the same number of values, they can be represented as a single relation. This situation, though unusual, can occur if you need to track "pooled" resources — for example, if you need to track automobiles and parking spaces for company divisions. Figure 20.7 shows a normalized relation, CAR_POOL, that stores license numbers for all cars in a division's motor pool. Figure 20.7 also shows the normalized relation, PARKING, that stores all parking space numbers available to the division. If there is no association between a car and a specific parking space when they are assigned to a particular division, and if the number of cars and number of parking spaces are not necessarily equal, the database must be designed as in Figure 20.7.

On the other hand, if a car associated with a particular division is assigned to one or more specific parking spaces, (i.e., if the car with license FJC 979 is assigned to parking spaces A18 and B24 when it is associated with the sales

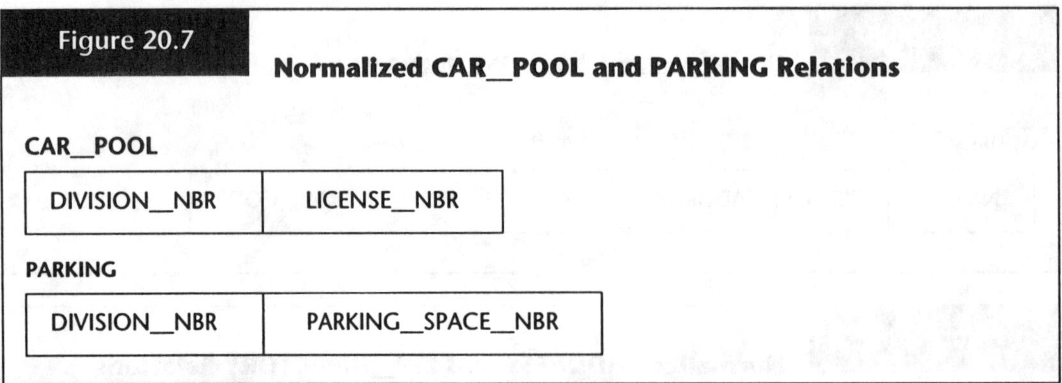

Figure 20.7 Normalized CAR__POOL and PARKING Relations

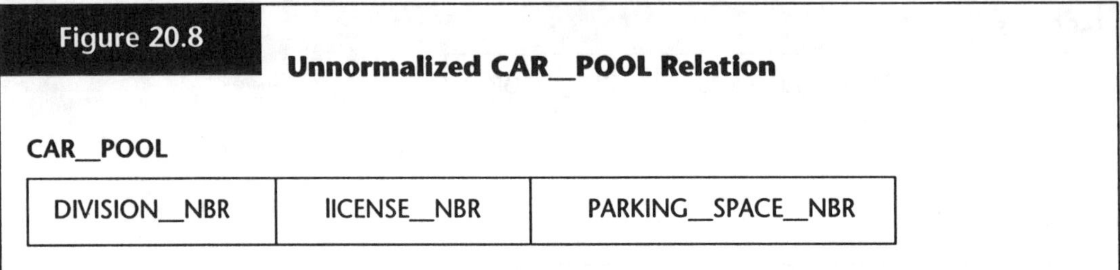

Figure 20.8 Unnormalized CAR__POOL Relation

division), the multivalued facts are not independent and a single relation, as in Figure 20.8, must be used. With interdependent multivalued facts, the single relation in Figure 20.8 is already in fourth normal form.

There is a third possibility, however. If a parking space always is added to the "pool" of cars (and similarly removed) as cars are added and removed from the pool, but a parking space is not associated with a specific car (i.e., any car can park in any space and when the car is assigned to another division it is not necessarily paired with the same parking space), the multivalued "facts" are independent but can nevertheless be represented satisfactorily as the single unnormalized relation in Figure 20.8. The only caution here is that there always must be an identical number of cars and parking spaces.

Most relations in fourth normal form are already in fifth normal form as well. If this is not the case, however, the fourth normal form relation must be split into three or more fifth normal form relations. There is not a "fifth abnormal form."

The examples provided above demonstrate that on the AS/400 effective database file design should incorporate the intent of normalization, but that it is not always necessary, or preferable, to use fully normalized files. During the "logical" (on paper) design of the database, relations should be laid out in a normalized form. At the next stage, implementation design, some relations may be combined into single files. For each occasion on which you consolidate multiple relations into a single file, the design document should include a precise statement of the rationale for the consolidation. This well-disciplined "abnormal" behavior can help you and other implementation programmers lead a more "normal" life.

Chapter 21

Using Join Logical Files

by Frieda Parker

Gain increased productivity, more flexible database design, and improved performance with join logical files

The join operation — the ability to connect records from two files by using the values in the records — is a major piece in the AS/400's relational-like database architecture. Using the OS/400 Join Logical File command, you can create a logical file that joins records from up to 32 physical files. The result is a single logical file record format that can include fields from all the underlying physical file record formats.

While join logical files go a long way toward improving the relational database capabilities of the AS/400, they are not yet a full implementation of relational join. In this chapter, I examine join logical files in depth and point out which relational join capabilities they bring to the AS/400 and which they do not. I also provide a step-by-step account, with examples, of how to create DDS for join logical files. Finally, I discuss implementation considerations relevant to join logical files.

The Concept of a Join

A join is generally defined as the ability to logically concatenate information from records in multiple files based on a relationship between values in the records. An ideal join facility would link files in a single-record format, thus allowing an application program to get all the data from the related records in a single read operation. In addition, with a single-record format join file it is desirable to be able to use any field in the record format as a key or in select/omit criteria, regardless of which underlying physical file the field comes from.

An ideal join also would allow files to be linked by specifying logically related fields, without requiring that those fields be key fields in either the physical file or the resulting join file. For example, suppose a Sales History file is joined to a

Salesman Master file keyed by salesman number. If both the Sales History file and Salesman Master file contain a field for sales territory, an ideal join would allow you to link the files via that field even though it is not the key field in the Salesman Master file, or a key field in the join file.

In addition, an ideal join would allow either an *inner* join or an *outer* join. An inner join includes only records from the two files that match. An outer join includes all records from both the files regardless of whether there is a match; default values are used to fill the fields from the missing record.

A subset of the outer join is a left outer join. A left outer join includes all records from the first file in the join (i.e., the leftmost file), even if no matching records exist in the second file. Records from the second file are included in the join only if a corresponding record exists in the primary file.

In summary, the ideal join facility should:

- Logically link files without using predefined keys
- Allow any field in a join file to be used as a key or for select/omit criteria
- Support inner and outer joins

Characteristics of Join Logical Files

Now that you know the features that the ideal join facility should provide, let's see how the AS/400 join logical file compares. The primary differences between an ideal join and an AS/400 join logical file are that an AS/400 join logical file does not support a full outer join, and it allows only fields contained in the first file (i.e., the "primary file" in AS/400 terminology) to be used as key fields in the join logical file. Here are the characteristics of AS/400 join logical files:

- Join logical files can be based on from two to 32 physical files. (Thus, one AS/400 join logical file actually specifies up to 31 two-file join operations.) These physical files may be in key or arrival sequence, and predefined keys need not be used to link files. The same physical file can be specified as a based-on file more than once, so a file can be joined to itself.
- Join logical files support inner and left outer join only. Outer join is not supported.
- Select/omit criteria can be specified for any field in a join logical file.
- Key fields, if specified, must come from the primary file.
- Join logical files are read-only files and cannot be used to update files.

The benefits of join logical files fall into three categories: Increased productivity, more flexible database design, and improved performance.

- *Increased productivity.* HLL programs that process multiple files for displays and reports can be simplified by using join logical files. Instead of having to open and read several files (or record formats), the program can open a single join logical file so that only one HLL read is required to get all of the data.

- *More flexible database design.* Because join logical files provide more ways to access data in physical files, it is possible for physical files to conform more closely to normalized database design. Greater database normalization means that databases can be designed to further reduce "fact" redundancy. In addition, fully normalized files allow more complex inquiries into the database, although physical files or nonjoin logical files remain the only means of updating the database. Also, because a join logical file can provide access to the database that would otherwise require a database modification, the database is more insulated from changes in program design than before.
- *Improved performance.* Because HLL programs require fewer database read operations (e.g., READ, CHAIN), performance is improved. A single HLL read operation causes multiple VMC (Vertical Microcode) reads, which is more efficient and incurs less overhead than multiple HLL reads. In addition, if a program has fewer open data paths, the job's PAG (Process Access Group) size is reduced, which allows more efficient use of main storage and faster program loading.

Related DDS Keywords

Before you can enjoy the benefits of join logical files, you need to know how to set up the required DDS. The procedure for creating DDS for a join logical file is as follows:

First, you name all the physical files that will be referenced in the join logical file. Next, you create the join specifications — that is, you indicate which fields will interrelate each pair of physical files. Finally, you list all the fields to be included in the join logical file record format.

The DDS to create a join logical file is built around eight keywords. Six of these keywords (JFILE, JOIN, JFLD, JREF, JDUPSEQ, and JDFTVAL) pertain only to join logical files; the other two (DFT and DYNSLT) also are used with physical or nonjoin logical files. Let's look at each of these keywords as they apply to join logical files.

JFILE, a record level keyword, identifies the physical files (up to a maximum of 32) over which the join logical file is built:

```
JFILE([LIBRARY-NAME/]PHYSICAL-FILE-NAME...)
```

At least two file names must be specified, but the file names need not be unique. The first file listed is the primary file and all other files are secondary files. As you will see later, the sequence in which the files are specified can affect the meaning and performance of the join function.

JOIN, a join level keyword, marks the beginning of a join specification. The JOIN keyword specifies which two files are to be linked by the fields named in the JFLD statements that follow the JOIN statement in the DDS. The JOIN statement, which must contain a "J" in position 17 of the DDS, takes the form

```
JOIN(FROM-FILE TO-FILE)
```

A JOIN statement is entered for every join between two of the files named in the JFILE statement. Thus, if two physical files are named, one JOIN statement is used; if three physical files are named, two JOIN statements are required; and so forth. The files may be specified by name or by relative position in the JFILE keyword. For example, the primary file is file number 1, the first secondary file is file number 2, the second secondary file is file number 3, and so on. There always will be one less JOIN statement than the number of files listed in the JFILE statement.

JFLD, a join level keyword, identifies the "from" and "to" fields that will join the pair of physical files specified in the JOIN statement:

```
JFLD(FROM-FIELD TO-FIELD)
```

Files can be joined by any fields that have the same content. If more than one field will join the two files, more JFLD keywords must be specified. At least one JFLD keyword is required for each join specification. The "from" field attributes (type, length, and decimal positions) must exactly match the "to" field attributes. However, this restriction can be circumvented by redefining fields in the logical file format so the fields have matching attributes.

The values of fields included in the JFLD statement determine which records in the secondary files are included in the join logical file. Consider the records contained in the two files shown in Figure 21.1. If the primary file and secondary file are joined only by Customer Number, then all the records shown in the secondary file are included in the join because the values of the Customer Number fields in the secondary file match values of the Customer Number fields in the primary file. If the files are joined by Customer Number and Product Category, only the first and third records in the secondary file are included in the join because only the values in those fields match the values of corresponding fields in the primary file. JOIN and JFLD statements are added until all the join specifications for the join logical file have been given.

JREF, a field level keyword, identifies the physical file from which a field included in the join logical file format is to be retrieved if it exists in more than one based-on physical file:

```
JREF(FILE-NAME) or JREF(FILE-NUMBER)
```

Figure 21.1

Sample Files in a Join Operation

Primary File		Secondary File	
Customer Number	Product Category	Customer Number	Product Category
100	A	100	A
100	B	100	C
101	A	101	A
102	C	101	B
102	D	102	A

The file may be specified by file name or file number (the position the file occupies in the JFILE list of physical files).

JDUPSEQ, a join level keyword, specifies the order in which records with duplicate join fields are retrieved:

```
JDUPSEQ(SEQUENCING-FIELD-NAME [*DESCEND])
```

For example, if the field Order Number joins two files and there are duplicate order numbers in the secondary file, the field Order Date could determine the order in which the duplicate Order Number records are retrieved. The sequencing field name can be in ascending (the default) or descending order. Without this keyword, you have no guarantee in what order records with duplicate field values will be retrieved.

JDFTVAL, a file-level keyword, specifies a left outer join. In other words, if no matching secondary record is found, the record from the primary file still will be included in the join file.

If you don't specify the JDFTVAL keyword, an inner join occurs. When the JDFTVAL keyword is specified and no matching secondary record is found, the secondary fields will contain default values of blanks or zeroes, or the value specified in the DFT keyword in the based-on physical file.

DFT, a field level keyword, specifies a default value for a field:

```
DFT('LITERAL' | NUMERIC-LITERAL |
    X'HEXADECIMAL-LITERAL')
```

The DFT keyword is valid for physical files only, and is used in an input operation to join logical files when all the following are true:

- The JDFTVAL keyword is specified in the join logical file.
- The physical file that has the DFT keyword is a secondary file in the join logical file.
- The input operation occurs, and no matching secondary record is found for the primary record.

DYNSLT, a file-level keyword, causes record selection to occur when a record is retrieved rather than when it is stored. The keyword is valid for logical files only. It does not affect the maintenance of access paths (i.e., the operation of the MAINT parameter in the CRTLF (Create Logical File) command). The DYNSLT keyword is required when you want to specify select/omit fields and any of the following is true:

- When the join logical file has no keys. However, if all the select/omit statements for a join logical file come from a secondary file — but not from more than one based-on physical file — the DYNSLT keyword is optional.
- When the JDFTVAL keyword is specified on join logical files.
- When the select/omit fields in a join logical file come from more than one based-on physical file and one of the following is true:

- The select/omit fields are on the same select or omit statement. For example:

```
S FILEI_FLDI CMP(GT FILE2_FLD2)
```

- The select/omit fields are on a mixture of select and omit statements. For example:

```
O FILEI_FLDI CMP(GT Ø)
S FILE2_FLD2 CMP(EQ 4)
```

- The select/omit fields are on select statements connected by an OR relation. For example:

```
S FILEI_FLDI CMP(GT Ø)
S FILE2_FLD2 CMP(EQ 4)
```

- The select/omit fields are on omit statements connected by an AND relation. For example:

```
O FILEI_FLDI CMP(GT Ø)
FILE2_FLD2 CMP(EQ 4)
```

Dynamic record selection should be considered instead of maintaining an access path when both of the following are true:

- The logical file is used only occasionally as a read-only file and its based-on physical files are updated frequently.
- The logical file contains no large cluster of omitted records (generally, but not always, this is true when the file has a low percentage of omitted records).

Putting Join Logical Files to Work

Now that you are familiar with the keywords required to create the DDS for a join logical file, let's look at three specific coding examples. The examples are based on three physical files: Employee Master, General Ledger Master, and General Ledger Transaction. The DDS for the physical files and the data contained in them are listed in Figures 21.2 through 21.7.

EMPMAS, the Employee Master file, is keyed by employee number. It contains the employee number, employee name, employee title, the manager's employee number, and the employee's pay rate (Figures 21.2 and 21.3). GLMAST, the General Ledger Master file, contains general ledger account numbers. It is keyed by department number and account number (Figures 21.4 and 21.5). GLTRAN, the General Ledger Transaction file, contains accounting journal entries. Each entry includes the general ledger department and account numbers, description, date, type (debit or credit), amount, and a reference number. The reference number is an employee number when appropriate (Figures 21.6 and 21.7).

In our first example, which illustrates an inner join of two files, files GLMAST and GLTRAN are joined so that the general ledger transactions are ordered by general ledger account description. The transactions for each account will appear in amount sequence. Let's look more closely at some of the DDS statements for this join logical file (Figure 21.8):

Figure 21.2

DDS for File EMPMAS

```
A      R EMPFMT
A        EMPNO      7P      TEXT('Employee number')
A        EMPNM     35A      TEXT('Name')
A        ETITL     20A      TEXT('Employee title')
A        EMNGR      7P      TEXT('Manager emp#')
A        EMPRT      7P  2   TEXT('Pay rate')
A      K EMPNO
```

Figure 21.3

Data Contained in File EMPMAS

EMPNO	EMPNM	ETITL	EMNGR	EMPRT
1	Janet Joslyn	President	0	50000.00
2	Mark Chapman	Vice Pres. of Sales	1	45000.00
3	Nicholas Lombardi	Vice Pres. of Marketing	1	45000.00
4	Martha Bane	Vice Pres. of Finance	1	45000.00
5	Dick Franklin	Telemarketing	2	20000.00
6	Dean McMartin	Salesperson	2	25000.00
7	Sally Palmer	Salesperson	2	25000.00
8	Lola Little	Advertising Manager	3	27000.00
9	Robert Dickerson	Marketing Writer	3	23000.00
10	Oliver Gallager	Controller	4	35000.00
11	Susan Howard	A/R Clerk	10	18000.00
12	Mary Martin	A/P Clerk	10	18000.00

Figure 21.4

DDS for File GLMAST

```
A      R GLFMT
A        DPTNO      2S      TEXT('Department')
A        ACTNO      5S      TEXT('Account number')
A        GDESC     35A      TEXT('Description')
A        GTYPE      1A      TEXT('Type')
A      K DPTNO
A      K ACTNO
```

R JOINFMT — This statement specifies the name of the format for the join logical file. A join logical file can have only one format.

Figure 21.5

Data Contained in File GLMAST

DPTNO	ACTNO	GDESC	GTYPE
1	10110	Wage expense	E
1	10120	Insurance expense	E
1	10130	Phone expense	E
1	10140	Travel expense	E
1	10150	Depreciation expense	E
1	10160	Sales commissions	E
1	20110	Sales revenue	R
1	20120	Interest income	R
1	30110	Accounts Receivable	A
1	30120	Office building	A
1	30130	Prepaid insurance	A
1	30140	Prepaid rent	A
1	30150	Computers	A
1	30160	Cash	A
1	30170	Car allowance	A
1	40110	Accounts Payable	L
1	40120	Notes payable	L
1	40130	Wages payable	L
1	40140	Employee reimbursements	L
1	40150	Accrued vacation	L
1	50110	Common Stock	O
1	50120	Owner's equity	O

Figure 21.6

DDS for File GLTRAN

```
A       R TRNFMT
A         DPTNO        2S      TEXT('Department')
A         ACTNO        5S      TEXT('Account number')
A         TDESC       35A      TEXT('Description')
A         TDATE        6S      TEXT('Transaction date')
A         TTYPE        1A      TEXT('Debit/Credit')
A         TAMNT       11P      TEXT('Amount')
A         TREF#        6P      TEXT('Transaction number')
A       K DPTNO
A       K ACTNO
```

JFILE(GLMAST GLTRAN) — This statement specifies the based-on physical files for the join logical file. The first file listed, GLMAST, is the primary file; the second file, GLTRAN, is the secondary file.

J JOIN(GLMAST GLTRAN) — The JOIN keyword, which indicates the start of a join specification, specifies which two files are to be joined. The files may be

Figure 21.7

Data Contained in File GLTRAN

DPTNO	ACTNO	TDESC	TDATE	TTYPE	TAMNT	TREF#
1	10110	Salaries - Joslyn	11586	D	2083.33	1
1	10110	Salaries - Chapman	11586	D	1875.00	2
1	10110	Salaries - Lombardi	11586	D	1875.00	3
1	10110	Salaries - Bane	11586	D	1875.00	4
1	10110	Salaries - Franklin	11586	D	833.00	5
1	10110	Salaries - McMartin	11586	D	1041.66	6
1	10110	Salaries - Palmer	11586	D	1041.66	7
1	10110	Salaries - Little	11586	D	1125.00	8
1	10110	Salaries - Dickerson	11586	D	958.33	9
1	10110	Salaries - Gallager	11586	D	1458.33	10
1	10110	Salaries - Howard	11586	D	750.00	12
1	10110	Salaries - Martin	11586	D	750.00	13
1	10120	Insurance - Joslyn	21086	D	300.00	1
1	10150	Depreciation - computers	31586	D	25000.00	0
1	10160	Commission - Franklin	11586	D	500.00	5
1	10160	Commission - McMartin	11586	D	1000.00	6
1	10160	Commission - Palmer	11586	D	1500.00	7
1	20110	Sales	31586	C	10000.00	0
1	30170	Car allowance - Palmer	20186	D	250.00	7
1	30170	Car allowance - McMartin	20186	D	250.00	6
1	40140	Repayment for supplies	20386	C	15.00	11
1	40150	Vacation - Franklin	20186	C	100.00	5
1	40150	Vacation - McMartin	20186	C	125.00	6
1	40150	Vacation - Palmer	20186	C	125.00	7
1	40160	Income taxes due	30186	C	5000.00	0

specified by file name, as in this example, or by relative position. The first file is the "from" file and the second file is the "to" file. If there are only two based-on physical files, the JOIN keyword can be omitted.

JFLD(DPTNO) / JFLD(ACTNO) — The JFLD keyword specifies which fields in the "from" and "to" files will join the files. If there are multiple fields, as in this example, multiple JFLD keywords are specified. The "from" and "to" fields must have identical attributes, but need not have the same name. The first field must correspond to a field in the "from" file of the previous JOIN keyword and the second file must correspond to the "to" file.

JDUPSEQ(TAMNT) — This statement specifies that if more than one secondary file record matches a primary file record, the records should be retrieved in TAMNT order. In other words, transaction records for each account will be listed in amount order.

JREF(GLMAST) — If fields to be included in the join logical file exist in more than one based-on physical file, the JREF keyword must specify from which file the field is to be retrieved.

Figure 21.8

DDS for an Inner Join of Two Files

```
     A          R JOINFMT
     A                                          JFILE(GLMAST GLTRAN)
     A          J                               JOIN(GLMAST GLTRAN)
     A                                          JFLD(DPTNO DPTNO)
     A                                          JFLD(ACTNO ACTNO)
     A                                          JDUPSEQ(TAMNT)
     A            DPTNO                         JREF(GLMAST)
     A            ACTNO                         JREF(GLMAST)
     A            GDESC
     A            GTYPE
     A            TAMNT
     A            TDATE
     A          K GDESC
```

Figure 21.9

Data Resulting from an Inner Join of Two Files

DPTNO	ACTNO	GDESC	GTYPE	TAMNT	TDATE
1	40150	Accrued vacation	L	100.00	20186
1	40150	Accrued vacation	L	125.00	20186
1	40150	Accrued vacation	L	125.00	20186
1	30170	Car allowance	A	250.00	20186
1	30170	Car allowance	A	250.00	20186
1	10150	Depreciation Expense	E	2500.00	31586
1	40140	Employee reimbursements	L	15.00	20386
1	10120	Insurance expense	E	300.00	21086
1	10160	Sales Commission	E	500.00	11586
1	10160	Sales Commission	E	1000.00	11586
1	10160	Sales Commission	E	1500.00	11586
1	20110	Sales revenue	R	10000.00	31586
1	10110	Wage expense	E	750.00	11586
1	10110	Wage expense	E	750.00	11586
1	10110	Wage expense	E	833.33	11586
1	10110	Wage expense	E	958.33	11586
1	10110	Wage expense	E	1041.66	11586
1	10110	Wage expense	E	1125.00	11586
1	10110	Wage expense	E	1458.33	11586
1	10110	Wage expense	E	1875.00	11586
1	10110	Wage expense	E	1875.00	11586
1	10110	Wage expense	E	1875.00	11586
1	10110	Wage expense	E	2083.33	11586

K GDESC — This statement specifies that the join logical file is to be keyed by general ledger description.

The contents of the join logical file created by the DDS shown in Figure 21.8 are listed in Figure 21.9. In this join logical file, it also would have been possible to concatenate the department and account number fields so that they would print as one field. Concatenated fields must be from the same based-on physical file. The result of a concatenation cannot be used in the JFLD keyword. However, it is possible to use fields in the JFLD keyword that will not appear in the join logical file. In this example, the concatenated version of the department and account number fields could be included without the individual fields being included (Figure 21.10).

In our second example, which illustrates an inner join of three files, the resultant join logical file contains all expense general ledger transactions by employee name. The file includes employee name, employee pay rate, department number, account number, transaction amount, general ledger account description, and type. Again, let's look more closely at some of the DDS statements for this logical file (Figure 21.11):

JFILE(EMPMAS GLTRAN GLMAST) — Three based-on physical files are specified. EMPMAS is the primary file and GLTRAN and GLMAST are secondary files.

JOIN(EMPMAS GLTRAN) / JFLD (EMPNO TREF#) — These join specifications interrelate files EMPMAS and GLTRAN. The reference number field in file GLTRAN sometimes contains an employee number. But fields EMPNO and TREF# have different attributes. To use these fields in one JFLD keyword, one field must be redefined to match the attributes of the other field.

TREF# 7P N — Field TREF# is redefined to have the same attributes as field EMPNO. Because field TREF# is not to be included in the join logical file, it is

Figure 21.10

DDS Showing Concatenation of Two Fields

```
A          R JOINFMT
A                                          JFILE(GLMAST GLTRAN)
A          J                               JOIN(GLMAST GLTRAN)
A                                          JFLD(DPTNO DPTNO)
A                                          JFLD(ACTNO ACTNO)
A                                          JDUPSEEQ(TAMNT)
A            ACCOUNT                       CONCAT(DPTNO ACTNO)
A                                          JREF(GLMAST)
A            GDESC
A            GTYPE
A            TAMNT
A            TDATE
A          K GDESC
```

Figure 21.11

DDS for an Inner Join of Three Files

```
A          R JOINFMT
A                                      JFILE(EMPMAS GLTRAN GLMAST)
A          J                           JOIN(EMPMAS GLTRAN)
A                                      JFLD(EMPNO TREF#)
A          J                           JOIN(GLTRAN GLMAST)
A                                      JFLD(DPTNO DPTNO)
A                                      JFLD(ACTNO ACTNO)
A            EMPNM
A            EMPRT
A              DPTNO                   JREF(GLMAST)
A              ACTNO                   JREF(GLMAST)
A              TAMNT
A              GDESC
A              GTYPE
```

marked as a "neither" field. Thus, it can be redefined for join purposes, but not included in the join logical format.

O GTYPE COMP (NE 'E') — All transactions whose account numbers are not expense accounts are omitted. Note that this selection criterion is based on a field from a secondary file.

The resultant join logical file is shown in Figure 21.12. Because an inner join was specified, if there were employees for which there were no expense transactions (or transactions for which the General Ledger Master file record was missing), they would not have been included in the joined file. If the JDFTVAL keyword had been specified, the employees would have been included in the file; the secondary fields would have defaulted to blanks, zeroes, or the default value specified in the DFT keyword in the physical file.

Our last example illustrates a left outer join of one file to itself. In this case, a join logical file is created that lists employees with a pay rate greater than $20,000 and the names of their managers. The primary file, EMPMAS, provides employee names, and the secondary file, also EMPMAS, provides the name of each employee's manager. The DDS for such a file is shown in Figure 21.13; but again, let's look more closely at specific statements:

DYNSLT — Because this file has no key fields, but does have select/omit criteria, the DYNSLT keyword must be specified.

JDFTVAL — This join logical file specifies a left outer join, so the join will include employees for which no record is found for their manager's employee number. This situation occurs for the company president, Janet Joslyn, because she has no manager. If the JDFTVAL keyword was not specified, the record for Janet would not be included.

JOIN(1 2) / JFLD(EMNGR EMPNO) — The manager employee number from the primary file is used to retrieve from the secondary file the record that contains the name of the employee's manager. In this JOIN statement, the

Figure 21.12

Data Resulting from an Inner Join of Three Files

AEMPNM	EMPRT	DEPTNO	ACCTNO	TAMNT	GDESC	GTYPE
Dean McMartin	25000.00	1	10110	1041.66	Wage expense	E
Dean McMartin	25000.00	1	10160	1000.00	Sales commiss	E
Dick Franklin	20000.00	1	10110	833.33	Wage expense	E
Dick Franklin	20000.00	1	10160	500.00	Sales commiss	E
Janet Joslyn	50000.00	1	10110	2083.33	Wage expense	E
Janet Joslyn	50000.00	1	10120	300.00	Insurance exp	E
Lola Little	27000.00	1	10110	1125.00	Wage expense	E
Mark Chapman	25000.00	1	10110	1875.00	Wage expense	E
Martha Bane	45000.00	1	10110	1875.00	Wage expense	E
Mary Martin	18000.00	1	10110	750.00	Wage expense	E
Nicholas Lombardi	45000.00	1	10110	1875.00	Wage expense	E
Oliver Gallager	35000.00	1	10110	1458.33	Wage expense	E
Robert Dickerson	23000.00	1	10110	958.33	Wage expense	E
Sally Palmer	25000.00	1	10110	1041.66	Wage expense	E
Sally Palmer	25000.00	1	10160	1500.00	Sales commiss	E
Susan Howard	18000.00	1	10110	750.00	Wage expense	E

relative file numbers must be used because the same file (EMPMAS) is both the primary and secondary file.

MNAME RENAME(EMPNM) JREF(2) — Field EMPNM is included from the primary file to list the employee's name. To include the manager's name, field EMPNM from the secondary file must be renamed. In this example, field EMPNM is renamed MNAME.

The contents of the join logical file created by the DDS shown in Figure 21.13 are listed in Figure 21.14.

Implementation Considerations

The preceding examples should put you on the road to implementation of join logical files. But before you experiment with the join operation, you should be aware of a few additional aspects of join logical files.

- By their nature, join logical files can contain only one record format.
- A record format in a join logical file cannot be shared. In other words, the FORMAT keyword is not supported. All fields in a join logical file must be specified in the DDS.
- The ACCPTH keyword is not supported. Implicit access path sharing is done automatically.
- A field defined with the CONCAT keyword cannot be used as a join field (i.e., in the JFLD keyword).
- Commitment control cannot be applied to join logical files.
- Renamed, redefined, and translated fields may be used as join or key fields.

Figure 21.13

DDS for a Left Outer Join of One File

```
A                                          DYNSLT
A                                          JDFTVAL
A          R JOINFMT
A                                          JFILE(EMPMAS EMPMAS)
A          J                               JOIN(1 2)
A                                          JFLD(EMNGR EMPNO)
A            EMPNO                         JREF(1)
A            EMPNM                         JREF(1)
A            EMPRT                         JREF(1)
A            EMNGR                         JREF(1)
A            MNAME                         RENAME(EMPNM) JREF(2)
A          O EMPRT                         COMP(LT 2000)
```

Figure 21.14

Data Resulting from a Left Outer Join of One File

EMP	EMPNM	EMPRT	EMGR	MNAME
1	Janet Joslyn	50000.00	0	
2	Mark Chapman	45000.00	1	Janet Joslyn
3	Nicholas Lombardi	45000.00	1	Janet Joslyn
4	Martha Bane	45000.00	1	Janet Joslyn
5	Dick Franklin	20000.00	2	Mark Chapman
6	Dean McMartin	25000.00	2	Mark Chapman
7	Sally Palmer	25000.00	2	Mark Chapman
8	Lola Little	27000.00	3	N. Lombardi
9	Robert Dickerson	23000.00	3	N. Lombardi
10	Oliver Gallager	35000.00	4	Martha Bane

In addition, you will find it beneficial to understand how a join logical file is used to retrieve records. A discussion of the "odometer" cursor concept, which illustrates how a file cursor is used to read the based-on physical files, will help explain why the sequence in which the files are specified in the JFILE statement is important to the performance of a join logical file. You will see that inefficiently structuring the join logical file can degrade performance severely.

In our discussion of the odometer cursor concept, let's use three files:

- A 2,000-record Customer Master file that contains one record per customer.
- A 100-record Open Order file that contains one record per order. (Assume two orders apiece for 50 customers.)
- A 5,000-record Order Shipments file that contains one record for each shipment on an order. (Assume two shipments for each open order.)

Suppose these three files are joined with the Customer Master file first, the Open Order file second, and the Order Shipment file third. The Customer Master and Open Order files are joined by Customer Number and the Open Order and Order Shipment files are joined by Order Number. The DDS would be as follows:

```
JFILE(CUSTOMERS ORDERS SHIPMENTS)
JOIN (CUSTOMERS ORDERS)
JFLD (CUST# CUST#)
JOIN (ORDERS SHIPMENTS)
JFLD (ORDER# ORDER#)
```

In this case, the join process works this way: The odometer cursor first reads a record from the Customer Master file; next it reads the matching Open Order record (if there is one); and then it reads the matching Order Shipment record. The odometer cursor continues reading all Order Shipment records that match the current Open Order record, then it reads the next Open Order record and all of its Order Shipment records. When all of the Open Order records that match a Customer Master record have been read, the odometer cursor reads the next Customer Master record. The odometer cursor continues this process until all of the Customer Master records have been read.

This process produces 200 records in the resultant join logical file (50 customers x 2 orders x 2 line items = 200 records) and requires 2,300 database reads (2,000 customers + 100 orders + 200 shipments = 2,300 reads).

Now suppose the order of the Open Order and Customer Master files is reversed in the JFILE statement:

```
JFILE(ORDERS CUSTOMERS SHIPMENTS)
JOIN (ORDERS CUSTOMERS)
JFLD(CUST# CUST#)
JOIN(CUSTOMERS SHIPMENTS)
JFLD(CUST# CUST#)
```

In this case, the join file still contains 200 records, but only 400 database reads are required (2 orders x 50 customers x 2 shipments = 200 records, and 100 orders + 100 customers + 200 shipments = 400 reads.)

A good rule to follow is to place the files with the smallest number of records to the left in the JFILE keyword to control the number of reads that the odometer cursor makes. But you must keep in mind how changing the order of files will affect the result of the join, especially considering that only fields from the primary file can be used as keys.

The AS/400 has always had strong database management capabilities. With some work, programmers could develop applications to meet most information needs. Join logical files are one of the AS/400's great strengths in its relational database capabilities. As a result, programmers will find it easier to get information out of the AS/400 and database designers will be able to build more efficient and elegant databases.

Chapter 22

Using Open Query File

by Paul Conte

Use the OPNQRYF command to simplify application development

The AS/400 is touted as a "database machine" and, indeed, it has built into the MI (Machine Interface) architecture a great deal of support for database functions. One of the AS/400's advanced database features is found in its Open Query File (OPNQRYF) command. OPNQRYF extends the AS/400 database functions to high-level language (HLL) application development.

The OPNQRYF command is just a beginning for database-oriented application design. While it does not address important issues such as set-at-a-time updates or an end user-oriented relational query facility, it provides substantial immediate benefits to application programmers and portends well for the future. The OPNQRYF command provides dynamic record selection, "virtual" fields, dynamic join, record aggregation, and more — all from your CL or HLL program. Just as importantly, the command provides IBM or third-party vendors with a firm foundation for more advanced application development facilities.

Without the OPNQRYF command, the database facilities available to application programmers were limited to field definitions (DDS), indexing (keyed access paths), static (compiled) record selection, and record-at-a-time input-output operations. Thus, a simple application to display a set of customer records for customers located in a *user-specified* city required conventional, nondatabase application program logic to get the user-specified city value (from a command parameter or display input field), position the file pointer (e.g., by an RPG SETLL operation), read and select the individual records, move them one at a time to a display file, and finally write the display.

Logical files, even with the DYNSLT (Dynamic Select) keyword, would be little help because selection criteria values still had to be hard-coded in DDS and compiled in the logical file (the DYNSLT keyword only determines when records are selected; that is, whether the selection occurs at the time a record is updated or at the time it is retrieved). Furthermore, records selected through a logical file could be retrieved only in the order of the logical file's access path; alternate sequencing was not possible.

With the highly functional OPNQRYF command, IBM has been able to capitalize on the MI architecture and to deliver significant database facilities to the AS/400 application programmer. In this chapter, I introduce the functions provided by the OPNQRYF command and describe how it can be used to simplify application development.

Before exploring what the OPNQRYF command does, however, let me dispose of some confusion that arises from the command's name. The Open Query File command has nothing to do with the Query report-generator product, other than that both OPNQRYF and Query use the same underlying VMC (Vertical Microcode) support for functions such as dynamic record selection and field mapping. In fact, the OPNQRYF command cannot be used with Query because Query does not use shared-file opens, which the OPNQRYF command requires. In addition, although the OPNQRYF command actually does open a file, an HLL shared file open must follow the command before an application program can use selected records. Thus, the OPNQRYF command does not replace your HLL database file opens; rather it is used, much as an OVRDBF (Override with Database File) command, to modify the results of an HLL file open.

Dynamic Record Selection

The OPNQRYF command, which is executed before an HLL file open, changes what is "viewed" by an HLL program in the same way that a logical file changes what an HLL program "views" of the underlying physical file(s). The major difference is that the OPNQRYF command allows record selection, record ordering, field mapping, and other "view" specifications when the OPNQRYF command is *executed* rather than when a logical file is *compiled.*

For example, an OPNQRYF command can handle the simple case described in the introduction to this chapter by using a CL variable to limit the customer records "viewed" by an HLL program to those customers in a specific city. Figure 22.1 shows how the OPNQRYF command could be used to provide such execution-time (i.e., truly "dynamic") record selection. The CL variable &CITY_INP must be loaded with a value for a city (e.g., "PORTLAND"); the value can be loaded from a command parameter, or by calling another HLL program that prompts for the city name, or by using the SNDUSRMSG (Send User Message) command. The OVRDBF command is used to specify that the CUSTOMER file will be opened as a *shared* file; the shared open enables the HLL program to subsequently access the file through the ODP (Open Data Path) established by the OPNQRYF command and thus take advantage of the record selection specified by the OPNQRYF command's QRYSLT (Query Select) parameter. (In this example, no OVRDBF command would be necessary if the file were created with SHARE(*YES).)

The OPNQRYF command uses the QRYSLT parameter to specify record selection. Record selection is specified as a character string that contains a free-format logical expression with file field names, relational operators, and arithmetic or embedded-character-string expressions. The logical, arithmetic, and embedded-character-string expressions can be fully parenthesized.

In the example in Figure 22.1, the QRYSLT argument is created by concatenating (||) the field name (CUSCTY) and the equal sign with the contents of CL variable &CITY_INP. This type of concatenation allows you to select criteria dynamically; when the OPNQRYF command is executed, the QRYSLT argument is parsed and appropriate VMC instructions are built into the file cursor associated with the ODP. When an HLL program retrieves records through the shared ODP, the VMC instructions test and select the records.

Now let's look at how the OPNQRYF command handles a more complex selection operation. In this example (Figure 22.2), the QRYSLT parameter value is used to select all customers who have a specific product (e.g., &PROD_INP = "SOFTWARE") in their customer name and who have a current balance due (CUSBAL) that exceeds a specified fraction (e.g., &FRAC_INP = 0.3) of the customer's credit limit (CUSCRDLMT).

Figure 22.1

Dynamically Selecting Customers Based on CUSCTY Field

```
DCL      &city_inp       *CHAR  20

/*       Get customer city, using HLL program or SNDUSRMSG       */

OVRDBF   FILE(customer) SHARE(*yes)

OPNQRYF  FILE(customer) QRYSLT('CUSCTY *EQ "' || &city_inp || '"')

CALL     PGM(dspcus)     /* Call HLL to open CUSTOMER file and
                         /* display ALL records.

CLOF     FILE(customer)

DLTOVR   FILE(customer)
```

Figure 22.2

Complex QRYSLT Selection

```
    ... QRYSLT('(%XLATE(CUSNAM QSYSTRNTBL) *CT "'       || +
                &prod inp                               || +
               '") *AND  (CUSBAL > CUSCRDLMT * '        || +
                &frac_inp
               ')')
```

This use of the QRYSLT parameter demonstrates the %XLATE function, used to translate lowercase to uppercase for string matching, and the *CT (contains) operator, used to look for a string value anywhere within a character field. The QRYSLT parameter also demonstrates the use of arithmetic expressions and compound logical tests. Figure 22.3 lists other functions that can be used in selection — and field mapping — expressions.

The OPNQRYF command uses a powerful and simple free-form expression for record selection, unlike the Query report generator's cumbersome fill-in-the-blank select/omit facility. This approach makes complex selection specification

Figure 22.3 **Functions Available for Selection Expressions and "Virtual" Fields**

ABSVAL	Absolute value
ACOS	Arccosine
AND	Logical AND
ANTILOG	Antilogarithm (Base 10)
ASIN	Arcsine
ATAN	Arctangent
ATANH	Inverse hyperbolic tangent
AVG	Average (mean)
COS	Cosine
COSH	Hyperbolic cosine
COT	Cotangent
COUNT	Count
DIGITS	Numeric Value to character
EXP	Exponential
LN	Natural (base e) logarithm
LOG	(base 10) logarithm
MAX	Maximum
MIN	Minimum
OR	Logical OR
NOT	Logical NOT
RANGE	Range (selection expression only)
SIN	Sine
SINH	Hyperbolic sine
SQRT	Square root
SST	Substring
STDDEV	Standard deviation
SUM	Sum
TAN	Tangent
TANH	Hyperbolic tangent
VALUES	Values (selection expression only)
VAR	Variance
WLDCRD	(String) wildcard (selection expression only)
XLATE	Translate
XOR	Logical exclusive OR

easier for both programmers and users. The only significant limitation to the QRYSLT parameter is that it cannot exceed 2,000 characters, the maximum length of any character-type command parameter.

Dynamic Sequencing

An OPNQRYF command also can be used to resequence selected records dynamically. For example, if the CUSTOMER physical file referenced in Figure 22.1 is keyed by CUSNBR (Customer Number), but you want to retrieve and display the selected records by CUSNAM (Customer Name), you can do so by using the KEYFLD parameter in the OPNQRYF command (Figure 22.4). It is not necessary to have a logical file over the CUSTOMER physical file that provides an access path on field CUSNAM. If no appropriate access path exists, the OPNQRYF command selects the records and builds a temporary access path on the selected records.

As you can see, the flexibility of the OPNQRYF command allows you to build a *single* retrieve/display program for the CUSTOMER file and use that program to select and sequence records in countless ways — *without making any program modifications.* The control of the OPNQRYF QRYSLT and KEYFLD parameters can be provided directly to the user or you can front-end these parameters by using menu options.

"Virtual" Fields

Dynamic record selection and sequencing are only two of the functions provided by the OPNQRYF command. Figure 22.5 provides a list of other OPNQRYF parameters and a brief description of their use. Chapter 9 of the *Database Guide* (SC41-9659) provides more details and numerous examples. In the following paragraphs, I'll point out some of the more significant functions and offer a few guidelines for using them.

One of the most useful features of the OPNQRYF command is its ability to "map" fields. The "mapping" of fields is defined in the OPNQRYF command by using the MAPFLD parameter. Field mapping allows you to derive new fields from underlying fields in a physical file. (In relational database terminology, the derived fields are known as "virtual" attributes, and the underlying fields are known as "direct" attributes.) You can create a virtual field from several fields in a single underlying physical file. For example, you can derive a virtual field for the cost (CST) of an item on an order detail line from the underlying physical file fields for the item quantity (QTY), the unit price (UNTPRC), and the discount

Figure 22.4 **Dynamically Resequencing Customers Based on Field CUSNAM**

```
OPNQRYF FILE(customer)                                        +
        QRYSLT('CUSCTY *EQ "' || city_inp || '"')             +
        KEYFLD(cusnam)
```

Figure 22.5

OPNQRYF Command Parameters

FILE	A single file, or multiple files (up to 32) for dynamic join
OPTION	Type(s) of processing (*ALL, *INP, *OUT, *UPD, or *DLT)
FORMAT	A file format for retrieved records, if different from the format of the file specified in FILE parameter
QRYSLT	Selection statement (up to 2,000 characters)
KEYFLD	Key fields (with optional *DESCEND or *ABSVAL ordering)
UNIQUEKEY	Limits retrieved records to first of equal keys (*NONE, *ALL, or number of key fields required to be unique)
JFLD	Join fields
JDFTVAL	Use joined records with default values (*YES, *NO, or *ONLYDFT
JORDER	Order in which files are joined (*ANY or *FILE)
GRPFLD	Grouping fields for summarization
GRPSLT	Selection Statement applied after grouping
MAPFLD	Mapping definition for "virtual" fields
ALWCPYDTA	Allow a copy of the data to occur (*YES or *NO)
OPTIMIZE	Type of optimization (*ALLIO, *FIRSTIO, *MINWAIT)
IGNDECERR	Ignore data decimal errors (*NO, *YES)
OPNID	File open identifier (*FILE or open-id-name)
SEQONLY	Sequential only processing (*YES [record count] or *NO)
COMMIT	Open under commitment control (*YES or *NO)
TYPE	Invocation level for RCLRSC (Reclaim Resources) command processing (*NORMAL or *PERM)
DUPKEYCHK	Return duplicate key feedback (*NO, *YES)

percentage for the item (DSCPCT). The OVRDBF and OPNQRYF commands in Figure 22.6 result in the automatic calculation of the CST virtual field whenever HLL program DSPORDCST reads a record from file ORDDTLCST.

To use field mapping, you normally define a new record format that includes all underlying physical file fields that you want visible to the HLL program and any new virtual fields that you want automatically computed by the ODP. This new record format is defined by using a physical file. Figure 22.7 shows the DDS for ORDDTLCST, a physical file that defines a record format with two underlying physical file fields (ORDNBR and ITMNBR from physical file ORDDTL — Figure 22.8) and one virtual field (CST). File ORDDTLCST is *not* used to contain any data and can be created without any members. HLL program DSPORDCST, used to display order item net cost, must declare ORDDTLCST (*not* ORDDTL) in the RPG/400 file specification or COBOL SELECT statement. The compiler then uses the record format from ORDDTLCST to declare the appropriate fields (ORDNBR, ITMNBR, and CST) and their layout in any record that is read.

Because two files are involved in field mapping — the underlying physical file and the file that defines the resulting record format — you must relate these two files correctly with the OVRDBF and OPNQRYF commands. Thus, in Figure 22.6 the OVRDBF command specifies in the FILE parameter the file that

Figure 22.6 Establishing Field Mapping from an Underlying Physical File

```
/*        Override the HLL program's internal file ORDDTLCST to */
/*        the underlying physical file ORDDTL.                  */

OVRDBF    FILE(orddtlcst)  TOFILE(orddtl)  SHARE(*yes)


/*        Open the underlying physical file, but specify that   */
/*        the record format to be used when records are read    */
/*        is the HLL program's internal format with the virtual  */
/*        field (CST).  Also specify how to compute the virtual */
/*        field.                                                */

OPNQRYF FILE(orddtl)        FORMAT(orddtlcst)
        MAPFLD((CST     'QTY * UNTPRC * (1 - (DSCPCT / 100))'))


CALL    PGM(dspordcst) /* Call HLL to open ORDDTLCST file and */
                       /* display order number, item number,  */
                       /* and net cost for item on this order.*/


CLOF    FILE(orddtl)

DLTOVR  FILE(orddtlcst)
```

Figure 22.7 **Physical File ORDDTLCST — Used to Define Format or "Virtual" Fields**

```
*  ORDDTLCST - Order Detail Cost

        R ORDDTLCST

          ORDNBR     R                  REFFLD(ORDNBR  ORDDTL     )
          ITMNBR     R                  REFFLD(ITMNBR  ORDDTL     )
          CST                 7P 2      TEXT('Cost'                 )
```

Figure 22.8 **Physical File ORDDTL**

```
* ORDDTL - Order Detail

                              UNIQUE
        R ORDDTL

          ORDNBR    R                   REFFLD(ORDNBR  ORDHDR     )
          ITMNBR    R                   REFFLD(ITMNBR  ITEM       )
          QTY                 7P Ø      TEXT('Quantity'           )
          UNTPRC              7P 2      TEXT('Unit price'         )
          DSCPCT              7P 5      TEXT('Discount percent'   )

        K ORDNBR
        K ITMNBR
```

defines the resulting record format, including virtual fields (i.e., the file declared in the HLL program). The OVRDBF command specifies in the TOFILE parameter the underlying physical file and specifies SHARE(*YES). The OVRDBF command redirects the HLL open file operation to the shared ODP, which is set up in the subsequent OPNQRYF command.

The OPNQRYF command defines the relationship between the fields in the underlying physical file and the fields, including virtual fields, in the resulting record format. Thus, the OPNQRYF command specifies in the FILE parameter the underlying physical file and in the FORMAT parameter the file that defines the resulting record format. Note that the OVRDBF and OPNQRYF commands use opposite values in their respective FILE parameters; a general rule is that the OVRDBF FILE parameter's value should be the same as the OPNQRYF FORMAT parameter's value, and the OVRDBF TOFILE parameter's value should be the same as the OPNQRYF FILE parameter's first (and possibly only) value.

The "mapping" of the fields, as I mentioned earlier, is defined by the MAPFLD parameter. If a field in the resulting format has the same name and meaning as a field in the underlying physical file, it does not need to be included in the MAPFLD parameter (e.g., fields ORDNBR and ITMNBR.) But the computations to derive a virtual field, such as CST, must be included in the MAPFLD parameter, as shown in Figure 22.6. The computation can use standard arithmetic or character-string expressions, and the functions listed in Figure 22.3.

After executing an OPNQRYF command to access a format with virtual fields, you should follow the normal practice of closing the file and deleting the file override. As Figure 22.6 shows, the CLOF and DLTOVR FILE parameters' values correspond to the OPNQRYF and OVRDBF FILE parameters, respectively.

When you use numeric virtual fields, you may encounter a problem: division by zero. For example, if a derived field were specified as "income-per-child = gross-income / number-of-children" — MAPFLD((INCPERCHL 'GRSINC / NBRCHL')) — a division-by-zero error would occur for those records with zero children. But if you use the expression '(GRSINC * NBRCHL) / %MAX((NBRCHL * NBRCHL) 0.1)' in the MAPFLD parameter, a default result of zero for INCPERCHL can be calculated and you will not trigger an error.

If NBRCHL is zero, NBRCHL * NBRCHL in the divisor is also zero, and the %MAX function returns 0.1, a valid divisor. In this case, GRSINC * NBRCHL in the dividend is also zero and the final result is 0.0 / 0.1, or zero. If NBRCHL is not zero, the %MAX function returns NBRCHL * NBRCHL, which is divided into GRSINC * NBRCHL. The result is the desired value of GRSINC / NBRCHL. When you use this method, the constant (e.g., 0.1) should be 10-(2d+1) where d is the number of decimal places in the divisor (e.g., NBRCHL has zero decimal places so the constant is 10-1 = 0.1; for a dollar field with two decimal places, you should use 10-5 = 0.00001.) This simple "trick" can avoid a common error with virtual fields.

Dynamic Join

OPNQRYF mapped fields also can be used to create a dynamic join file that takes advantage of OPNQRYF virtual fields and dynamic sequencing. Consider an application that joins order header, order detail, customer, and item records (files ORDHDR, ORDDTL CUSTOMER, and ITEM in Figures 22.9, 22.8, 22.10, and 22.11). The selection is based on a customer city value input by the user; the sequencing is by customer name, order number, and item number — a mixture of primary and secondary file fields; and a virtual field (CST) is calculated from underlying fields in the physical file.

With the OPNQRYF command, a dynamic join file is set up much like a single file with mapped fields. First you create a physical file (*not* a join logical file) to define the resulting record format (see ORDFULDTL in Figure 22.12.) Then you can write an HLL program that references this physical file.

To use the dynamic join file, an OVRDBF is used in Figure 22.13 to redirect the physical file that defines the resulting format (i.e., ORDFULDTL) to the *primary* (i.e., first) file in the dynamic join (e.g., ORDHDR). Next the OPNQRYF command specifies all the underlying physical files in the FILE parameter; the first of these is the primary file. The JFLD parameter defines the field correspondence between pairs of files that are joined.

Figure 22.9

Physical File ORDHDR

```
*   ORDHDR - Order Header

                             UNIQUE
          R ORDHDR
            ORDNBR           7P Ø    TEXT('Order number'      )
            CUSNBR     R             REFFLD(CUSNBR  CUSTOMER )
            ORDDAT           8P Ø    TEXT('Order date (YMD)' )

          K ORDNBR
```

Figure 22.10

Physical File CUSTOMER

```
*   CUSTOMER - Customer description

                                 UNIQUE
          R CUSTOMER

            CUSNBR            7P Ø  TEXT('Customer number'    )
            CUSNAM           5ØA    TEXT('Customer name'      )
            CUSCTY           2ØA    TEXT('Customer city'      )
          K CUSNBR
```

Figure 22.11

Physical File ITEM

```
*   ITEM - Item description

                                  UNIQUE
          R ITEM

            ITMNBR           7P Ø    TEXT('Item number'       )
            ITMDSC          5ØA      TEXT('Item description'  )

          K ITMNBR
```

Note that field names are qualified with a file name by using the syntax "file-designator/field-name." A similar syntax is used in the definition of mapped fields — both those mapped without modification (but which must be specified

Figure 22.12 **Physical File ORDFULDTL Used to Define Format for Dynamic Join File**

```
*  ORDFULDTL - Order Full Detail

  R ORDFULDTL

    ORDNBR     R           REFFLD(ORDNBR  ORDHDR    )
    CUSNBR     R           REFFLD(CUSNBR  ORDHDR    )
    ORDDAT     R           REFFLD(ORDDAT  ORDHDR    )
    ITMNBR     R           REFFLD(ITMNBR  ORDDTL    )
    QTY        R           REFFLD(QTY     ORDDTL    )
    UNTPRC     R           REFFLD(UNTPRC  ORDDTL    )
    DSCPCT     R           REFFLD(DSCPCT  ORDDTL    )
    CST             7P 2   TEXT('Cost'              )
    CUSNAM     R           REFFLD(CUSNAM  CUSTOMER  )
    CUSCTY     R           REFFLD(CUSCTY  CUSTOMER  )
    ITMDSC     R           REFFLD(ITMDSC  ITEM      )
```

if the field name occurs in more than one underlying physical file) and those that are virtual fields.

As with a format for mapped fields from a single underlying physical file, an HLL program opens the file that defines the resulting record format for a dynamic join file. The shared ODP established by the OPNQRYF command will join and resequence the records at execution time. Field mapping and resequencing on secondary file fields can result in a temporary copy of the data, but the VMC routines used by the OPNQRYF command attempt to minimize both file accesses and duplication of data.

After the dynamic join file has been used, it is closed with a CLOF that references the primary file. Last, a DLTOVR command should be executed for the file that defines the resulting format (e.g., ORDFULDTL).

Group Fields

The final way that mapped fields add flexibility to application implementation is with "group" fields, a special type of virtual field set up by using the GRPFLD (Group Field) parameter. Group fields provide automatic data aggregation such as counts, totals, and averages. The process for using group fields is the same as that for other virtual fields; a physical file is used to define the resulting format and the OPNQRYF MAPFLD parameter is used to define how the group fields are calculated.

Figure 22.14 shows the DDS for physical file ORDITMSUM, which defines a format that contains a count of the different items included in each order, the total number of items ordered, and the average unit price for the items ordered. The OPNQRYF command in Figure 22.15 includes a MAPFLD parameter that uses the functions %COUNT, %SUM, and %AVG to specify how the group fields are calculated. The GRPFLD keyword specifies how the aggregation will be

Figure 22.13 **Dynamically Joining Four Files With Record Selection and Ordering**

```
DCL     &city inp       *CHAR  20

/*      Get desired customer city ....                          */

/*      Override the HLL program's internal file ORDFULDTL to */
        the primary file for the join (ORDHDR).                 */

OVRDBF  FILE(ordfuldtl)  TOFILE(ordhdr)  SHARE(*yes)

/*      Open ALL underlying physical files that are involved  */
/*      in the join, but specify that the record format to be */
/*      used when record are read is the HLL program's        */
/*      internal format with all joined fields and the virtual*/
/*      field (CST).  Also specify how to join the records,   */
/*      how to select and order them, and how to calculate the*/
/*      virtual field.

OPNQRYF FILE(ordhdr orddtl customer item)  FORMAT(ordfuldtl)      +
        QRYSLT('CUSCTY *EQ "' || city_inp || '"')                 +
        KEYFLD(CUSNAM ORDNBR ITMNBR)                              +
        JFLD((ORDHDR/ORDNBR ORDDTL/ORDNBR)                        +
            (ORDHDR/CUSNBR CUSTOMER/CUSNBR)                       +
            (ORDDTL/ITMNBR ITEM/ITMNBR))                          +
        MAPFLD((ORDNBR ORDHDR/ORDNBR)                             +
             (CUSNBR ORDHDR/CUSNBR)                               +
             (ITMNBR ORDDTL/ITMNBR)                               +
             (CST   'QTY * UNTPRC * (1 - (DSCPCT / 100))'))

CALL    PGM(dspfulord) /* Call HLL to open ORDFULDTL file and  */
                       /* display full order details by        */
                       /* customer name for selected city.     */

CLOF        FILE(ordhdr)

DLTOVR FILE(ordfuldtl)
```

done. In this case, the grouping is done for each order number (ORDNBR). When HLL program DSPITMSUM reads records from file ORDITMSUM, each record will contain the desired aggregate values for a single order number.

The GRPSLT (Group Select) keyword allows record selection *after* an aggregate record is calculated; in this example, only aggregates with three or more items on an order will be selected. GRPSLT operates like QRYSLT, but QRYSLT selects records before aggregation and GRPSLT selects records after aggregation.

Figure 22.14 **Physical File ORDITMSUM — Used to Define Format for "Group" Fields**

```
*   ORDITMSUM - Order Item Summary

          R ORDITMSUM

            ORDNBR      R                   REFFLD(ORDNBR  ORDDTL     )
            ITMCNT              7P Ø        TEXT('Item count'         )
            QTYTOT              7P Ø        TEXT('Quantity total      )
            UNTPRCAVG           7P 2        TEXT('Unit price avg.'    )
```

Figure 22.15 **Using "Group" Fields**

```
/*      Override the HLL program's internal file ORDITMSUM to */
/*      the underlying physical file ORDDTL.                  */

OVRDBF  FILE(orditmsum)  TOFILE(orddtl)  SHARE(*yes)

/*      Open the underlying physical file, but specify that   */
/*      the record format to be used when records are read    */
/*      is the HLL program's internal format with the group   */
/*      fields.  Also specify how to compute the group fields.*/

OPNQRYF FILE(orddtl)       FORMAT(orditmsum)                  +
        GRPFLD(ordnbr)     KEYFLD(ordnbr)                     +
        MAPFLD((ITMCNT       '%COUNT')                        +
               (QTYTOT       '%SUM(QTY)')                     +
               (UNTPRCAVG   '%AVG(UNTPRC)'))                  +
        GRPSLT('ITMCNT >= 3')

CALL    PGM(dspitmum)   /* Call HLL to open ORDITMSUM file and */
                        /* display order number, item count,   */
                        /* total quantity, and average unit    */
                        /* price for each order.               */

CLOF    FILE(orddtl)

DLTOVR  FILE(orditmsum)
```

Additional Considerations

However you use the OPNQRYF command, note that it must be executed *before* the HLL file open. But it is not necessary to go in and out of your HLL application program to change selection or ordering specifications because QCMDEXC can be called to execute the OPNQRYF command from an HLL program.

Note also that the file opened by an OPNQRYF command should be closed with a CLOF (Close File) command once the current use is over. Because the file is shared, it can inadvertently affect subsequent file opens if left open. By using a four-step cycle — get the selection and sequencing requirements, execute the OPNQRYF command, execute an HLL program to process the current "view," execute CLOF — you can allow a user to retrieve records with different selection and sequencing without ever exiting the application program.

As the examples have shown, you now can use a single display (or print) program to handle many different requests for selection, sequencing, and virtual field calculations. But the previous examples only serve to introduce the OPNQRYF command; the command provides many other flexible and useful features, including file update capability (except for join files or records with group fields) and parameters to optimize performance. The functions provided by the OPNQRYF command offer the AS/400 truly *dynamic* support for relational database manipulations.

Chapter 23

SQL Embedded Statements

by Paul Conte

Bring the power of SQL to your applications through the use of embedded statements

SQL's data manipulation language (DML) provides powerful operations that can retrieve or update sets of records for each statement, and it is this "set-at-a-time" capability that makes SQL such a useful tool in building applications. It is by using SQL's "other mode" — embedded statements, that you can bring the power of SQL to your applications.

Embedded SQL statements are not entered directly, but must be coded in, or processed by, a high-level language (HLL) program. SAA currently defines RPG II, COBOL 85, C, and FORTRAN 77 as the four SQL *host* languages — HLLs that support embedded SQL. (On the AS/400, host language support for SQL/400 is available with the RPG/400 option of RPG/400, with the COBOL 85 option of COBOL/400, and with PL/I.)

The DBMS handles embedded SQL by a two-step process outlined in Figure 23.1. The first step creates two objects: an executable HLL program and a database management system (DBMS) *application plan.* During this step, the entire host program source code, including embedded SQL statements, is processed by a *precompiler* that translates the SQL statements to host language variable declarations and external program calls. The precompiler passes its translated output to a host language compiler that creates an executable HLL program. The precompiler also passes SQL statements to a DBMS component, called *Bind,* which creates executable routines collectively referred to as the *application plan.* The DBMS stores the application plan routines in a private area of its catalogue for use at execution time. (On the AS/400, the application plan access routines are stored in the program object.)

The second step occurs when the host program is executed. At each point in the program where a SQL operation (e.g., an UPDATE statement) is specified, a

Figure 23.1

SQL Processing for Embedded Statements

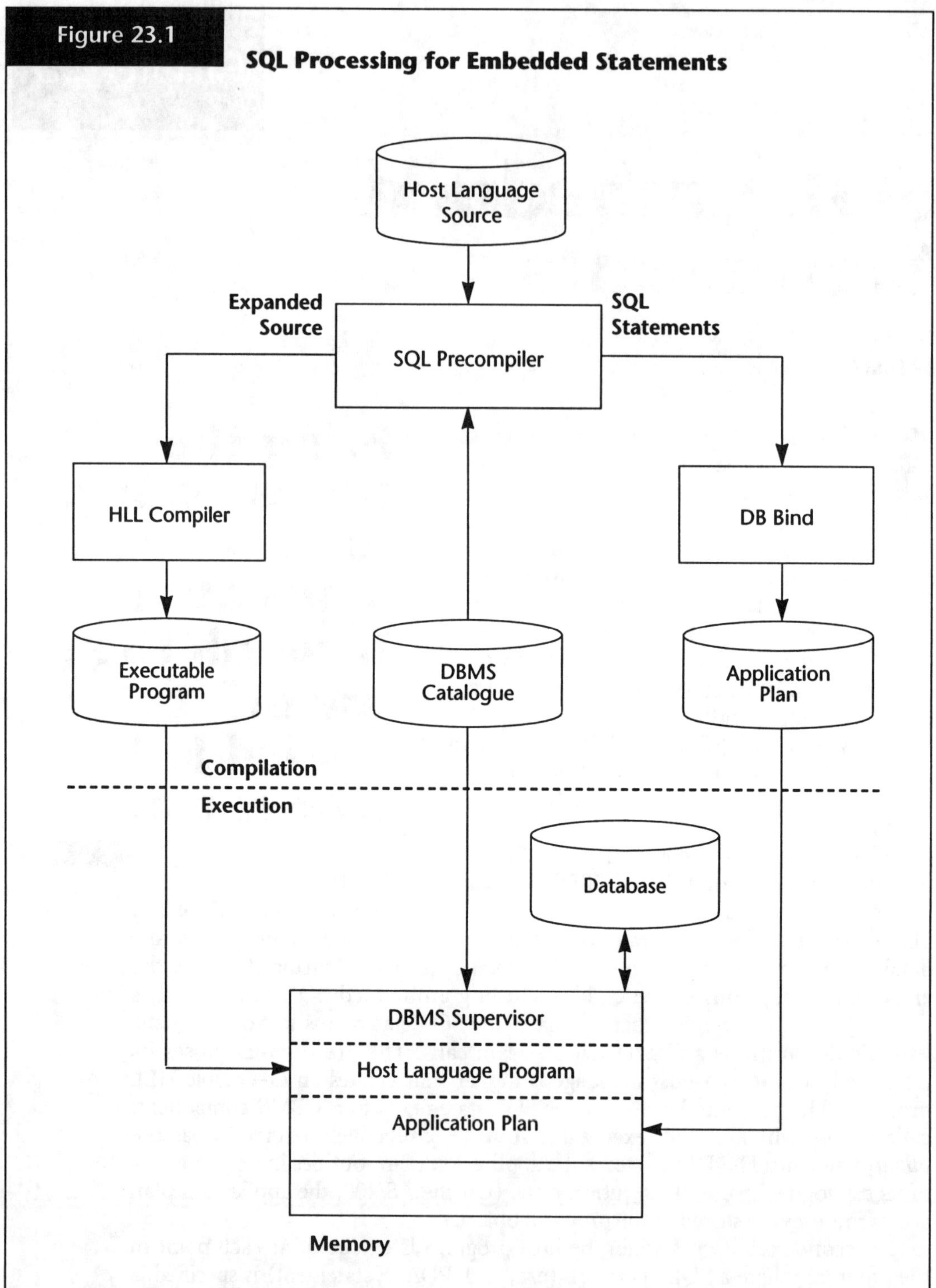

HLL call transfers control to the DBMS, which uses a routine from the program's application plan to access table data. Arguments supplied with the call provide the DBMS routines with values for retrieval search conditions and column updates. The DBMS returns its results in parameters specified in the call.

Embedded SQL statements fall into three classes:

- "Static" operations that don't involve cursors
- "Dynamic" operations that don't involve cursors
- Operations that involve cursors

Figure 23.2 provides a quick reference to the SQL DML statements that you can use as embedded statements, and in the following sections, I sketch the three classes of embedded statements.

Static Operations That Don't Involve Cursors

In "static" operations, the *structure* of the SQL statement (but not necessarily the values to be tested or set) is known at precompile time. In a host language program, you can embed a static SELECT statement that returns a *single* row, or

Figure 23.2

SQL Data Manipulation Language Statements

Statements that can be used ad hoc (interactively) or embedded in an HLL program

DELETE	Delete one or more rows from a table
INSERT	Insert one or more rows into a table
SELECT	Retrieve one or more rows into a result table
UPDATE	Update the values of one or more columns in one or more rows of a table

Statements that can be used only embedded in an HLL program

BEGIN DECLARE SECTION	Mark the beginning of a host variable declaration section
CLOSE	Close a SQL cursor
DECLARE CURSOR	Define a SQL cursor
DESCRIBE	Retrieve the description of the result columns of a prepared SQL statement
END DECLARE SECTION	Mark the end of a host variable declaration section
EXECUTE	Execute a prepared SQL statement
EXECUTE IMMEDIATE	Prepare and execute a SQL statement
FETCH	Retrieve values of a single row from a SQL cursor into host variables
INCLUDE	Insert SQL control area declarations into host program
OPEN	Ready a SQL cursor to be used to retrieve values with a FETCH statement
PREPARE	Prepare a SQL statement for execution
WHENEVER	Define exception handling action

you can embed static *multirow* UPDATE, DELETE, or INSERT statements. For example, you can include the following statement in a COBOL 85 program's PROCEDURE DIVISION to retrieve a single customer's name and discount:

```
EXEC SQL
SELECT  NAME, DISC
 INTO   :CUST-NAME,
        :CUST-DISC:CUST-DISC-NULL
 FROM   CUST
 WHERE  CUSTID = :CUST-ID
END-EXEC.
```

The EXEC SQL and END-EXEC keywords delimit the embedded SQL statement. (RPG/400 uses /EXEC SQL and /END-EXEC as delimiters.) Figure 23.3 shows the structure for an embedded SELECT, which has a form similar to an *ad hoc* SELECT. An embedded SELECT adds the INTO clause that lists the host variables that receive the results and drops the GROUP BY and ORDER BY clauses. The host variables are denoted by a colon (:) as their first character. SQL doesn't support multirow, noncursor SELECTs because the number of rows that a SELECT returns must be known *before* host variable memory is allocated to receive the results, and memory must be allocated before the SELECT is executed. The only way to satisfy this circular requirement is to limit the result table to a single row.

You must declare any host variable used in a SQL statement in a section of your program bracketed by BEGIN DECLARE and END DECLARE as in the following example:

```
DATA DIVISION.
WORKING-STORAGE SECTION.
  .. Non-SQL program variable declarations ..
    EXEC SQL
     INCLUDE SQLCA
    END-EXEC.
    EXEC SQL
     BEGIN DECLARE SECTION
    END-EXEC.

Ø1  CUST-ID         PIC S9(9)       COMP-4.
Ø1  CUST-NAME       PIC  X(3Ø).
Ø1  CUST-DISC       PIC S9(1)V9(4) COMP-3.
Ø1  CUST-DISC-NULL  PIC S9(4)       COMP-4.

  .. Other SQL host variable declarations ..

    EXEC SQL
     END DECLARE SECTION
    END-EXEC.
```

Figure 23.3

Embedded SELECT Statement Structure

```
SELECT     select list
 INTO      host variable list
 FROM      table(s)
 WHERE     search condition
```

A host variable must have a data type and size compatible with its corresponding column's definition. In this example, the host variable CUST-ID is declared as a COBOL full-word binary data item with no decimal places so it corresponds to the integer column CUSTID. Similarly, host variable CUST-DISC is a packed decimal data item with the same precision and decimal positions as column DISC.

For columns that can have null values, you optionally can specify an *indicator* with the host variable, using the format :VARIABLE:INDICATOR. In the previous SELECT example, :CUST-DISC:CUST-DISC-NULL specifies that indicator CUST-DISC-NULL should be set to a negative value if the DISC column for the retrieved row is null. If the retrieved value of DISC is not null, CUST-DISC-NULL will be non-negative. You also can use negative host indicator variables in update statements to set column values to null.

The sample SQL host variable declarations above show how to declare a SQL *communication area.* (Don't be confused by the term "communication" area — the area is just for feedback from the DBMS and has nothing to do with telecommunications or distributed databases.) The INCLUDE SQLCA statement causes the precompiler to insert the record structure shown in Figure 23.4 into the host program's declarations. During execution, the DBMS updates this SQL communication area after every operation.

The most important variable in the communication area is SQLCODE, which the DBMS sets to zero for successful completion, to a positive number for an exception condition (e.g., +100 means the last available row has been fetched via a cursor), or to a negative number for an error. You can test this variable after any SQL statement.

As an alternative, you can specify a SQL WHENEVER statement to establish implicit tests and actions that the SQL precompiler automatically places after every SQL statement. For example, the following statement places the equivalent of an IF SQLCODE < 0 GO TO ERR- ON-SQL after every SQL statement:

```
EXEC SQL
 WHENEVER SQLERROR GO TO ERR-ON-SQL
END-EXEC.
```

A WHENEVER statement can test three conditions:

- NOT FOUND is equivalent to SQLCODE = +100
- SQLERROR is equivalent to SQLCODE < 0
- SQLWARNING is equivalent to SQLCODE > 0 AND SQLCODE < > +100

Figure 23.4

SQLCA Structure (COBOL Version)

```
01   SQLCA.
     05 SQLCAID       PIC X(8).
     05 SQLCABC       PIC S9(9) COMP-4.
     05 SQLCODE       PIC S9(9) COMP-4.
     05 SQLERRM.
        49 SQLERRML   PIC S9(4) COMP-4.
        49 SQLERRMC   PIC X(70).
     05 SQLERRP       PIC X(8).
     05 SQLERRD       OCCURS 6 TIMES
                      PIC S9(9) COMP-4.
     05 SQLWARN.
        10 SQLWARN0   PIC X(1).
        10 SQLWARN1   PIC X(1).
        10 SQLWARN2   PIC X(1).
        10 SQLWARN3   PIC X(1).
        10 SQLWARN4   PIC X(1).
        10 SQLWARN5   PIC X(1).
        10 SQLWARN6   PIC X(1).
        10 SQLWARN7   PIC X(1).
     05 FILLER        PIC X(8).
```

Data Item	Contents
SQLCAID	'SQLCA'
SQLCABC	136 (Size in bytes of SQLCA)
SQLCODE	Return code set after SQL operation
SQLERRML	Length of SQLERRMC
SQLERRMC	Error message substitution values
SQLERRP	Diagnostic information (e.g., module name)
SQLERRD	Array of 6 values for operation feedback (e.g., SQLERRD(3) is number of updated rows)
SQLWARN0	'W' iff any of SQLWARN1-7 are 'W'
SQLWARN1	'W' iff string column truncated
SQLWARN2	'W' iff null values eliminated from column function
SQLWARN3	'W' iff more columns than host variables
SQLWARN4	'W' iff prepared UPDATE or DELETE has no WHERE clause
SQLWARN5-7	System dependent
FILLER	System dependent

The only two actions you can specify with a WHENEVER statement are CONTINUE (i.e., ignore the condition) and GO TO. Generally, at the beginning of your program, you can place a single WHENEVER, as shown in the previous example, to trap otherwise undetected errors. But because you cannot specify procedure names in a WHENEVER statement, explicit

SQLCODE tests after SQL statements provide better control and program structure than WHENEVER statements.

The syntax rules for static embedded update statements (UPDATE, DELETE, INSERT) that don't involve cursors are similar to those for the SELECT, except that an update statement's WHERE clause can specify a set of records because nothing is retrieved into host variables. The following three simple examples show how to use static embedded updates.

The first example sets the discount for all customers in a user-input city to a user-input value:

```
EXEC SQL
 UPDATE CUST
  SET   DISC = :INPUT-DISC
  WHERE CITY = :INPUT-CITY
END-EXEC.
```

The second example deletes customers whose total orders are less than a user-input amount:

```
EXEC SQL
 DELETE
  FROM  CUST C
  WHERE :INPUT-TOTAMT >
        (SELECT SUM(TOTAMT)
          FROM  ORDHDR O
          WHERE O.CUSTID = C.CUSTID)
END-EXEC.
```

The final example inserts a new customer using user-input values:

```
EXEC SQL
 INSERT
  INTO  CUST (CUSTID, NAME, CITY, DISC)
  VALUES     (:INPUT-CUSTID,
              :INPUT-NAME,
              :INPUT-CITY,
              :INPUT-DISC:DISC-NULL)
END-EXEC.
```

Note in this last example that if the user does not input a discount, the host program should set the null indicator variable, :DISC-NULL, to a negative number (using an HLL statement such as MOVE -1 TO DISC-NULL) before executing the INSERT. When :DISC-NULL is negative, the DBMS sets the DISC column to null; otherwise the DBMS sets DISC to the value of :INPUT- DISC.

Dynamic Operations That Don't Involve Cursors

In "dynamic" SQL operations, the structure of the SQL statement is known only at execution time. SQL dynamic embedded statements let you construct a string that is a SQL statement, prepare the string for execution, and execute it. This

SQL facility is somewhat analogous to the QCMDEXC program, which executes a string that is a CL command. You might find this facility useful if you want one host language program to support a wide variety of updates yet want to carefully control database updates. A host language program either can use string operations (with HLL statements) to build the SQL statement from non-SQL user inputs or can let the user enter an *ad hoc* SQL statement and check the statement before passing it to the DBMS for execution.

Let's look at a simple example that could be executed using a static embedded statement but that illustrates how you execute dynamic statements.

```
MOVE "UPDATE CUST SET DISC = 0"
      TO STMT-STRING.
EXEC SQL
 PREPARE UPDSTMT FROM :STMT-STRING
END-EXEC.

IF   SQLCODE = 0
     EXEC SQL
      EXECUTE UPDSTMT
     END-EXEC
ELSE PERFORM ERROR-ON-PREPARE.
```

The first statement is a COBOL statement that assigns a string containing a SQL UPDATE statement to the host variable STMT-STRING. (STMT-STRING must be declared between SQL BEGIN DECLARE and END DECLARE SECTION statements.) The second statement is a SQL PREPARE statement that invokes SQL precompile and bind modules to parse the string and create an executable access routine with the SQL *statement name* UPDSTMT. The third statement is a combination of COBOL and SQL that first tests SQLCODE to see whether the string contains a valid SQL statement. If the string is valid, it is executed with a SQL EXECUTE statement, thereby setting all customers' discounts to zero.

The SQL PREPARE statement performs, during program execution, functions that the precompiler performs during precompilation — generating code that can be called later to execute the specified operation. Once a dynamic statement is prepared, it can be executed multiple times in the same program execution (more precisely, in the same unit of recovery) without being prepared again. If you want to execute a dynamic statement just once, you can use the EXECUTE IMMEDIATE statement, which combines PREPARE and EXECUTE but does not save the executable access routine.

Dynamic statements can contain SELECT, UPDATE, DELETE, and INSERT statements, as well as data definition language (DDL) statements such as CREATE TABLE, CREATE VIEW, and CREATE INDEX. SAA SQL, however, allows a prepared SELECT statement to be used only with a DECLARE CURSOR statement (discussed in next section) and even then, it is fully supported only in C. (C programs also can use a SQL DESCRIBE statement to get a list of the column names, types, and lengths in the result table of a prepared SELECT statement.) The restrictions on dynamic SELECTs aren't as limiting as they might seem. *Ad hoc* SELECTs are a more straightforward way to handle flexible retrieval anyway, and dynamic statements are more commonly used for updates.

Dynamic update statements follow essentially the same rules as *ad hoc* update statements, with the one additional feature of *parameter markers.* When you prepare a dynamic statement, you can put question marks (?) in the statement string as placeholders to be replaced by the contents of a host variable when the statement is executed. A parameter marker can appear almost anywhere that a host variable can appear in a static embedded statement. When you execute a prepared statement that contains parameter markers, you list host variables that supply the values to take the place of the parameter markers. For example, the following statements let you supply the discount and city values when a dynamic statement is executed:

```
MOVE "UPDATE CUST SET DISC = ?
      WHERE CITY = ?" TO STMT-STRING.
EXEC SQL
  PREPARE UPDSTMT FROM :STMT-STRING
END-EXEC.

IF   SQLCODE = 0
     EXEC SQL
      EXECUTE UPDSTMT
       USING  :INPUT-DISC, :INPUT-CITY
     END-EXEC
ELSE PERFORM ERROR-ON-PREPARE.
```

Although this example is so simple it could just as easily be done with a static statement, dynamic SQL lets you build "on the fly" strings with different SQL statement clauses, table names, column names, and parameter markers. You then can prepare the statement once and execute it repeatedly supplying different values each time. There is one little wrinkle, however. When you execute a COMMIT WORK or ROLLBACK WORK, the DBMS destroys all prepared statements and you must re-execute their respective PREPARE statements before you can execute them again. This process doesn't limit the flexibility of dynamic SQL, but — because many major applications should use commit/rollback — it does diminish the potential performance benefit from separating statement preparation and execution into two steps. In many cases, you'll find a single EXECUTE IMMEDIATE the simpler approach and just as efficient as PREPARE and EXECUTE.

Static and dynamic embedded SQL statements let you use host language programs to update your database in a variety of ways. But static and dynamic SQL statements alone don't let you retrieve a set of records for display or one-by-one updating. The mechanism that bridges SQL's set-at-a-time retrieval and host languages' record-at-a-time retrieval is the *cursor.*

Operations That Involve Cursors

A SQL cursor is an object that provides dynamic addressability to a selected set of database rows. A SQL cursor is analogous to OPNQRYF. You use a cursor by defining it, opening it, fetching rows from it, and closing it, in much the same way you use OPNQRYF.

To define a cursor, you place a DECLARE CURSOR statement in your host language program. A DECLARE CURSOR includes a SELECT that defines the set of rows to be accessed via the cursor. For example, the following cursor declaration defines a table with customer name and discount columns and that includes a subset of customer rows based on their city:

```
EXEC SQL
  DECLARE CURSOR CUSTCITY FOR
   SELECT NAME, DISC
    FROM  CUST
    WHERE CITY = :SELECT-CITY
 END-EXEC.
```

The DECLARE CURSOR is not an executable statement but is processed by the precompiler to generate an access routine in the application plan. The SELECT essentially defines a view that you can use for row-at-a-time retrieval in the host program. The cursor's WHERE clause can name host variables (e.g., :SELECT-CITY) that supply scalar values for the search condition at the time the cursor is opened.

To access rows using this view, the cursor must first be opened. The following COBOL assignment and three SQL statements show the basic steps to use a cursor:

```
MOVE "PORTLAND" TO SELECT-CITY.

EXEC SQL  OPEN  CUSTCITY  END-EXEC.
EXEC SQL
 FETCH CUSTCITY
  INTO :CUST-NAME, :CUST-DISC
END-EXEC.
EXEC SQL  CLOSE CUSTCITY  END-EXEC.
```

In this example, the COBOL MOVE puts a value in the host variable used in the cursor's search condition. The SQL OPEN dynamically identifies the rows that satisfy the search condition (i.e., customers in Portland) and positions the cursor before the first row (if any). The SQL FETCH advances the cursor to the next row after the pointer position and places values from the columns specified in the cursor declaration (i.e., NAME, DISC) into host variables specified in the FETCH (i.e., :CUST-NAME, :CUST-CITY). The SQL CLOSE closes the current cursor making it unusable until it is reopened. After it's closed, a cursor can be reopened with different values supplied for search condition host variables, thus retrieving a different set of rows. (Note that changing host variables while a cursor is open does *not* affect the set of rows until the cursor is closed and reopened.)

Normally, the FETCH statement is inside a host-language loop that iterates over the selected set. The DBMS signals end-of-set by setting SQLCODE to +100. As with other embedded SQL statements, FETCH errors cause SQLCODE to be set to a negative value.

Because FETCH has only a "next" row capability, it isn't very flexible. There are no "previous," "first," "last," or "nth" row options. If you want to re-retrieve a row, you must close the cursor, reopen it, and fetch rows until you get the one you want. Accordingly, you'll find you often need to combine cursor access with static, single-row operations that specify a row by its primary key.

You also can update rows retrieved via a cursor by using a special form of the WHERE clause in UPDATE and DELETE statements. To update a row, you first must position the cursor on it by using a FETCH. Then, as in the following example, you can replace column values with host variable values using an UPDATE with WHERE CURRENT OF:

```
EXEC SQL
 FETCH CUSTCITY
  INTO :CUST-NAME, :CUST-DISC
END-EXEC.

COMPUTE CUST-DISC = CUST-DISC * 1.01.

EXEC SQL
 UPDATE CUST
  SET   DISC = :CUST-DISC
  WHERE CURRENT OF CUSTCITY
END EXEC.
```

An UPDATE via a cursor names the same table or updatable view specified in the FROM clause of the DECLARE CURSOR (e.g., CUST) and references the cursor name in the WHERE clause. To be updatable, a cursor declaration must include a FOR UPDATE clause such as the following:

```
EXEC SQL
 DECLARE CURSOR CUSTCITY FOR
  SELECT NAME, DISC
   FROM  CUST
   WHERE CITY = :SELECT-CITY
   FOR UPDATE OF DISC
END-EXEC.
```

The SELECT for an updatable cursor has the same restrictions as the SELECT for updatable views.

To remove the current row of a cursor, you can enter:

```
EXEC SQL
 DELETE FROM CUST
  WHERE CURRENT OF CUSTCITY
END-EXEC.
```

Because SQL offers just a primitive FETCH and because there can be row lock conflicts between update cursors and other embedded SQL statements in the same program, you'll find cursors have two primary applications: batch updates and loading arrays in interactive programs.

In many batch-update programs, SQL's FETCH and UPDATE provide an adequate structure for sequentially processing a selected set of rows. In interactive programs, on the other hand, you often need to present a set of rows to the users and let them enter updates. To post these updates you must update a row no longer pointed to by the cursor, thus requiring a noncursor, embedded UPDATE. The simplest approach to this program structure is to fill an array using a read-only cursor, display the array using presentation services, and update any changed rows using a static UPDATE or DELETE. You also need to consider an appropriate protocol to handle concurrent updating. For many SQL applications, the read-copy-validate-update approach provides a way to minimize interjob lock conflicts and avoid lost updates.

Blue Skies and Sunshine?

SAA SQL clearly offers a powerful data manipulation tool, but the question remains whether SQL is good enough to let you kiss your application backlog goodbye. SQL is certainly going to help with your *ad hoc* retrievals because SQL excels as a language for describing *what* you want rather than *how* to get it. True, there are a few rough edges in the way SQL implements some relational operations, but those inconveniences are for the most part surmountable, and SQL is still far better than less expressive vehicles such as the AS/400 Query product. Of course, SQL doesn't provide any display or hard-copy formatting facilities, so you'll need other tools to control how you present the data you retrieve.

Unfortunately, SQL is somewhat hamstrung in its updating capabilities. The problem isn't that the update DML statements aren't powerful enough; rather it's that the DDL is so weak that the update DML is dangerous to use unless you combine it with HLL or application-generator statements to do the integrity checking that should have been included in the DDL to begin with. Until SQL DDL is strengthened, SQL updating cannot be significantly improved.

Because many SQL applications still require host language programs, the SQL cursor is an especially important DML element. Unfortunately, SQL cursors remain essentially the same as when they were first prototyped under System R in IBM's San Jose lab. Several researchers have proposed improvements to cursors: Chris Date has suggested that the cursor allow normal file operations such as "read by key"; Michael Stonebraker, the developer of INGRES, has outlined a database "portal" that extends cursor operations by using dynamic, sequential line numbers to identify rows in a cursor. None of the proposals seem to be making much headway with either the ANSI X3H2 Database Committee or IBM. So if you're an AS/400 programmer who's grown to love using RPG/400 file operations in combination with OPNQRYF, you're going to be unhappy having just the FETCH and UPDATE...CURRENT OF cursor statements.

SAA SQL offers the advantage of standardization, which for multisystem or multivendor organizations can mean substantial development savings. The SAA standard is a hybrid of the ANSI X3.135-1986 standard and IBM's DB2 version of SQL (all three are slightly different, however). Other vendors' products such as Oracle, INGRES, and SYBASE also follow the ANSI and DB2 standards relatively closely. Of course, "relatively" is a relative word. If you're planning applications to run on different systems — IBM's or other vendors' — be sure to check the fine print in their manuals, and check Chris Date's *A Guide to the SQL Standard* (Addison-Wesley, 1987) for an excellent description of ANSI standard SQL, including an extensive critique and a section that compares ANSI standard SQL to DB2.

In balance, SQL may help you increase your productivity, but it isn't going to make your application challenges disappear. It is especially important that you carefully evaluate alternative SQL products — they vary widely in their capabilities, even among IBM's SAA products. Then plan carefully how best to incorporate SQL's facilities into your implementation strategy.

SQL/400 vs. SAA SQL

In the following sections I describe the major differences between SQL/400 and the SAA standard.

Data Definition Language

The SQL/400 statement `CREATE DATABASE persnl` creates a SQL/400 database (`persnl`), which is a library (also named `persnl`) that contains a journal, a journal receiver, and a collection of tables and views that make up the database catalogue. The catalogue contains table, view, column, index, and key definitions.

`CREATE TABLE emp` creates a SQL/400 table (`emp`), which is a physical file object. SQL/400 tables can have 8,000 columns and a maximum row size of 32,766 bytes. SQL/400 column data types do not include DATE and TIME. For all table columns, you must specify NOT NULL or NOT NULL WITH DEFAULT because SQL/400 does not support nulls. If you specify WITH DEFAULT, the system uses blanks for character columns and zero for numeric columns (you cannot choose the default value).

`CREATE [UNIQUE] INDEX` creates a SQL/400 unique or nonunique index that is a logical file with a MAINT(*IMMED) access path. The maximum key length for a SQL/400 index is 120 bytes.

`CREATE VIEW` creates a SQL/400 view that is a logical file.

You can use `LABEL ON emp (empid IS 'Employee ID')` to add labels to columns (e.g., `empid`).

SQL/400 adds nothing to the little that SAA SQL offers for integrity support.

Data Control Language

Although SQL/400 `GRANT` and `REVOKE` statements follow the SAA standard, you still can

Continued

use AS/400 GRTOBJAUT (Grant Object Authority) and RVKOBJAUT (Revoke Object Authority) CL commands with physical and logical file objects to customize table and view authority.

SQL/400 provides commitment control with `COMMIT WORK` and `ROLLBACK WORK`, but SQL/400 uses the AS/400 MI *single* record lock type (exclusive-allow-read) rather than the *two* row lock type (shared, exclusive) used by the other SAA SQL products on the S/370 and OS/2.

Data Manipulation Language

To use *ad hoc* (interactive) SQL/400, you execute the STRSQL (Start SQL) CL command. You then can enter SQL statements on a SQL entry screen. The interactive SQL facility includes a prompter for database, table, and column names. On the STRSQL command, you specify either *NONE, *CHG, or *ALL for the interactive session's commitment control level. If you specify *CHG or *ALL, the maximum number of updated rows for any DML statement is 4,096.

By far the most important difference between SQL/400 and the SAA standard is that SQL/400 does not support *subqueries* (i.e., nested SELECTs). Subqueries aren't just syntactic sugar; they are essential for expressing many of the result tables possible with SQL. For example, SAA SQL — but not SQL/400 — can express the query:

Retrieve all customers who have an order with total amount greater than the average order amount of customers in the same city.

```
SELECT C.CUSTID
 FROM  CUST C
 WHERE EXISTS
      (SELECT *
        FROM  ORDHDR O
        WHERE C.CUSTID = O.CUSTID AND
        O.TOTAMT >
        (SELECT AVG(OX.TOTAMT)
          FROM  CUST CX, ORDHDR OX
          WHERE CX.CITY   = C.CITY AND
           CX.CUSTID = OX.CUSTID) )
```

Developers should be cautious about moving to SQL/400 as an application platform before IBM rectifies this major deficiency in SQL/400's data manipulation language.

SQL/400 adds `SUBSTR` and `LENGTH` scalar functions for character columns, and `DECIMAL`, `DIGITS`, `FLOAT`, and `INTEGER` functions to convert between different column data types. SQL/400 also allows a character concatenation (||) operator in character expressions.

Embedded SQL

The SQL/400 precompilers do not require that host variable declarations be contained

Continued

between BEGIN DECLARE and END DECLARE statements. The SQLCA communication area for statement feedback is automatically generated in RPG/400 programs (similar to the way the file information data structure is built) and does not require an INCLUDE SQLCA.

A typical embedded SQL statement in an RPG III program looks like the following:

```
C/EXEC SQL
C+ SELECT  EMPID,   EMPNAM
C+   INTO  :EMPID, :EMPNAM
C+   FROM   EMP
C+   WHERE  EMPID = 12345
C/END-EXEC.
```

Now that you know the details and the differences of both SAA SQL and SQL/400, you can plan for how best to use SQL in your AS/400 application development.

Chapter 24

Controlling Object Locks

by Paul Conte

Control data and program sharing during critical processing with the ALCOBJ command

What do you do when one user starts end-of-day batch transaction processing and another user, not knowing this, calls an interactive program to add a few last-minute transactions? If your program is not designed to handle this situation, transactions may be lost as they are added behind those already processed. Or what if a programmer decides to delete a program, unaware that a user is running the program? OS/400, high-level languages (HLLs), and system utilities such as DFU provide some object allocation to preserve the integrity of objects being used by a job. But when such automatic allocation fails to meet your requirements, you need to turn to the ALCOBJ (Allocate Object) command to control access to objects during critical processing.

Object allocation occurs when a program such as OS/400 executes a Lock Object machine instruction or when an ALCOBJ command is executed. When you allocate an object during a job, the AS/400 places a "lock" on the object. This lock serves two purposes: The lock guarantees to your job specific types of access to the object and the lock prevents other jobs from having specific types of access to the object. The lock is released when a program executes the Unlock Object machine instruction, when the DLCOBJ (Deallocate Object) command is executed, when the routing step ends, or when the object is deleted.

The type of lock placed on an object governs the way the object is shared among different jobs. This mechanism allows the AS/400 to provide different users a high degree of concurrent access to programs, data, and other objects. While sharing is allowed, the object is protected against simultaneous uses that would conflict; for example, a job cannot delete a file member if another job is currently reading it.

Object allocation differs from object authorization, which is used to protect the security of shared objects. Object authorization allows a user profile specific types of access to an object; this authority generally remains in effect even when no job is active (the exception is the authority that may be "adopted" while a program is executing).

Object allocation, on the other hand, is used to protect the integrity of shared objects. Object allocation grants a specific type of lock to the routing step that requested the allocation; objects are allocated only by active jobs. The allocation remains in effect only while the routing step is active. (For one-step jobs it might be simpler to think of allocating an object to a job rather than to a routing step. Thus, where I use the term "routing step," you can read "job" for most situations.) The ALCOBJ command can be used to

- Prevent a program from being deleted while someone is executing it.
- Allow only one job at a time to execute a program.
- Obtain locks that are not available when you use the default locks obtained by HLLs.
- Guarantee access to a group of required objects before using any one of them.
- Set aside a data area to provide an unduplicated sequence number for control purposes (such as sequencing transactions).

Types of Object Locks

Suppose the automatic allocation provided by a HLL has not obtained restrictive enough locks in one of your applications and you have decided you need to explicitly allocate an object. In doing so, you will, to some degree, "lock" other jobs out of the object — the degree depending upon the kind of lock you obtain. You have five types of locks from which to choose:

- *Exclusive (*EXCL).* Only the routing step holding the lock can use the object. Routing steps in other jobs cannot access the object.
- *Exclusive-allow-read (*EXCLRD).* The routing step that holds the lock can read or update the object, while routing steps in other jobs can only read it.
- *Shared-for-update (*SHRUPD).* The routing step that holds the lock, as well as routing steps in other jobs, can read or update the object.
- *Shared-no-update (*SHRNUP).* The routing step that holds the lock, as well as routing steps in other jobs, can only read the object.
- *Shared-for-read (*SHRRD).* The routing step that holds the lock can only read the object, while routing steps in other jobs can read or update it.

The table in Figure 24.1 summarizes these locks. You can use the table to quickly determine the type of lock to obtain in a given instance. Suppose you have decided to update an object and while you are updating it you want other jobs or routing steps to be able to read the object but not update it. In the left column of the table in Figure 24.1, find "Update." Move across the Update row to

Figure 24.1

Lock Type for Access Control

Your routing step needs this type of access:	Choose this type of lock to allow a routing step in another job the following access:		
	No access	Read only	Update
None, but restrict other jobs	*EXCL	*SHRNUP	(no lock)
Read only	*EXCL	*SHRNUP	*SHRRD
Update	*EXCL	*EXCLRD	*SHRUPD

the "Read Only" column for routing steps in other jobs. The type of lock you need in this instance is *EXCLRD.

Although a lock provides the routing step that holds it a guarantee of access to an object and limits access by routing steps in other jobs, it does not limit subsequent access in the same routing step that holds the lock. For example, a CL program can execute an ALCOBJ command to obtain an *EXCLRD lock on a database file member. Another CL program cannot call an RPG/400 program that opens the locked file member for updating. However, it is possible for the CL program holding the *EXCLRD lock to call an RPG/400 program that updates the file.

When a routing step attempts to obtain a lock, it will be allowed to get the lock unless a routing step in another job already holds a conflicting lock on the same object. The AS/400 ensures proper sharing of an object by preventing conflicting locks. Figure 24.2 shows the types of locks that are allowed if a routing step in another job already holds a lock.

Figure 24.2

Allowable Lock Combinations

If a routing step already has this lock:	A routing step in another job can obtain this lock:				
	*EXCL	*EXCLRD	*SHRUPD	*SHRNUP	*SHRRD
*EXCL					
*EXCLRD					Yes
*SHRUPD			Yes		Yes
*SHRNUP				Yes	Yes
*SHRRD		Yes	Yes	Yes	Yes

A routing step, at different times in its processing, can obtain multiple locks of the same or different type on an object. The system keeps a count of each type of lock placed on an object. Eventually, each of these locks must be released individually, even if they are of the same type. Thus, if at two different points in a routing step a *SHRRD lock is placed on an object, at some point both *SHRRD locks must be released on that object to return the system lock count to zero. Not until the count returns to zero is the *SHRRD lock totally removed from the object.

A routing step can obtain more than one lock with a single ALCOBJ command. Therefore, a group of objects required to complete an operation can be allocated at one time. Often a HLL program will require several files, some for read-only access, others for updating. By allocating the files before calling the HLL program, you can simplify error handling. If explicit allocation is not used, you must either open all files before processing begins so that you are assured of access to them all, or you must use a restart procedure to continue at an interruption point.

Figure 24.3 shows an ALCOBJ command that allocates the following objects: a daily transaction input file that no other job will be allowed to update, a customer name file that will be read, a customer account file that will be updated, and a data area with the last transaction number processed that will be updated and can be read by other jobs. If any one of the locks cannot be obtained, none of the objects will have locks placed on them by this ALCOBJ command. This "all-or-none" approach makes it easy to allocate the set of objects you need before you start to use any of them.

An ALCOBJ command will succeed if all of the requested locks can be obtained. If any of the locks cannot be granted, an escape message (CPF1002) will be sent to the program executing the ALCOBJ command. If the command is in a CL program, you can monitor for this message using the MONMSG command. If a system utility (such as DFU) or a HLL program cannot allocate an object, the utility or HLL exception procedures will handle the problem.

The WAIT(10) parameter in Figure 24.3 specifies that the ALCOBJ command can wait up to 10 seconds for the locks. This wait may be necessary if a routing step in another job has one or more of the objects allocated with a lock that conflicts with the requested lock. If such a conflict exists and the conflicting locks are released within 10 seconds, then this routing step normally gets the locks it has requested (unless a job with a higher dispatching priority also has requested locks on any of the objects).

Figure 24.3

Allocating Several Objects with One ALCOBJ Command

```
ALCOBJ OBJ((DAILY_TRAIN  *FILE    *SHRNUP DAILY_TRAIN)    +
           (CUST_NAME    *FILE    *SHRRD  CUST_NAME  )    +
           (CUST_ACT     *FILE    *SHRUPD CUST_ACT   )    +
           (LST_TRNNBR   *DTAARA  *EXCLRD            ))
       WAIT(10)
```

A routing step also can release more than one lock with a single DLCOBJ command. When the objects in Figure 24.3 are no longer needed, they can be deallocated with the command in Figure 24.4. Generally, for every ALCOBJ command in your CL program, there should be a corresponding DLCOBJ command with the same object list. However, if the job ends when the objects are no longer needed, no DLCOBJ command is necessary. The routing step will end when the job ends and all objects will be deallocated automatically. The use of DLCOBJ for an object that has not been allocated by an ALCOBJ can be dangerous. Deallocating objects that you have not specifically allocated can release locks on device descriptions or internal system locks and cause system malfunctions.

Within a routing step, you may need to change the type of lock you have on an object. You should first obtain the new lock and then release the old lock. This technique prevents a routing step in another job from obtaining a conflicting lock before you obtain the new lock. For example, if you first want to use a file for updating and then just want to read the file, execute the sequence of commands shown in Figure 24.5.

Allocation of Objects by Type

Only certain object types can be allocated using the ALCOBJ command. Figure 24.6 shows these objects and the valid lock types for each. Other object types, such as user profiles, can be locked by the Lock Object machine instruction. Different purposes are served by allocating each of the object types. Let's look at five object types that require special consideration when using the ALCOBJ command:

Data areas: Data areas can be used to provide a unique control number for shared programs. When a program needs a control number, it calls a CL program such as GETCTLNBR shown in Figure 24.7. The CL program first

Figure 24.4

Deallocating Several Objects with One DLCOBJ Command

```
DLCOBJ OBJ((DAILY_TRAN   *FILE    *SHRNUP DAILY_TRAIN)    +
           (CUST_NAME    *FILE    *SHRRD  CUST_NAME  )    +
           (CUST-ACT     *FILE    *SHRUPD CUST_ACT   )    +
           (LST_TRNNBR   *DTAARA  *EXCLRD            ))
```

Figure 24.5

Proper Way to Change a Lock Type

```
ALCOBJ OBJ((MAST_FILE   *FILE   *SHRUPD    MAST_FILE))
   .
   .  Call a program that updates the file.
   .
ALCOBJ OBJ((MAST_FILE   *FILE   *SHRRD     MAST_FILE))
```

Figure 24.6

Allowable Locks Using ALCOBJ Command

Object Type	Lock Type *EXCL	*EXCLRD	*SHRUPD	*SHRNUP	*SHRRD
Data Area	Yes	Yes	Yes	Yes	Yes
Data Queues	Yes	Yes	Yes	Yes	Yes
Device Description	Yes				
File	Yes	Yes	Yes	Yes	Yes
Forms Control Table	Yes	Yes	Yes	Yes	Yes
Library	Yes	Yes	Yes	Yes	
Message Queue	Yes		Yes		
Program	Yes	Yes	Yes		
Session Description	Yes	Yes	Yes	Yes	Yes
Subsystem Description	Yes				

Figure 24.7

CL Program GETCTLNBR

```
PGM       PARM(&CTLNBR_ARG)
DCL       VAR(&CTLNBR_ARG)      TYPE(*DEC) LEN(9 0)
DCLDTAARA DTAARA(CTLNBR)

ALCOBJ    OBJ((CTLNBR *DTAARA *EXCL))      WAIT(60)
RCVDTAARA DTAARA(CTLNBR)
CHGVAR    VAR(&CTLNBR_ARG)                 VALUE(&CTLNBR + 1)
CHGVAR    VAR(&CTLNBR)                     VALUE(&CTLNBR_ARG)
SNDDTAARA DTAARA(CTLNBR)

DLCOBJ    OBJ((CTLNBR *DTAARA *EXCL))

RETURN
ENDPGM
```

places an *EXCL lock on the data area so that no other job can access it. The CL program then receives the data area to get the last number used, increments it by one, updates the data area, and releases the lock. ALCOBJ must be used to place the *EXCL lock on the data area because the RCVDTAARA (Receive Data Area) command only places a *SHRRD lock on the data area. Without the *EXCL lock, another job could read the same control number from the data area before the first job has a chance to update it.

Programs: When a program is called, normally no locks are placed on it. This means that a job can execute or delete the program while it is being executed by another job. Often this is not a desirable situation. Using allocation, you can prevent a program from being deleted while it is in use or let only one job at a time execute the program.

To prevent a program from being deleted, obtain a *SHRRD lock on it. A convenient place to do this is in CL menu programs just before the CALL command is executed. After the program returns to the calling program, it should be deallocated using the DLCOBJ command.

If you want only one job at a time to execute a program, you can implement a controlling CL program that attempts to obtain an *EXCL lock on the desired program before calling it. Because no two jobs can hold an *EXCL lock on the same object at the same time, you can have the calling program monitor for failed allocation of the restricted program and execute a GOTO to branch to a label after the CALL command. At that label you can send a message informing the user that the program is in use and then exit the controlling program.

Device Descriptions: Generally, OS/400 handles necessary device allocations. But if you need to allocate a device description, you should keep the following points in mind. First, the device must be powered on and varied on. Second, the only allowable lock is an *EXCLRD and device descriptions of TYPE(*PEER) cannot be allocated. And finally, when a WAIT parameter is specified for the ALCOBJ command on a device description any value from one second through 14 seconds is treated as a 15-second wait.

Device Files: A device file is a file object type that contains a description of how input data from an external device is to be presented to a program, or how output data from the program is to be presented to the external device. External devices can be display stations, card devices, diskette drives, tape drives, or communications lines. Generally, device files are allocated by OS/400 or a HLL program as needed. HLLs allocate all types of device files with a *SHRNUP lock when they are opened. If a specific device description is allocated when the device file is opened, the device description will be allocated *EXCLRD.

Database Files: An open operation executed on a database file by CL or a HLL will obtain default locks determined by the type of open operation (input, output, input-output). When an open operation is executed on a file, a lock is placed on the file itself, but the locking does not end there. If the file is a physical file, a lock is also placed on the member of the file you are opening, on the access path of the opened member (if it is a keyed file), and on the data of the opened member. If the file is a logical file, a lock is placed on the member of the file you are opening and a lock is placed on one or more of the following: the access path of the opened member, the access path of a member that is sharing its access path with the member you are opening, and the data of all physical file members included in the scope of the logical file member you are opening. If all this seems a bit complex, just remember that when you open a file, you lock the data that is accessed through a member and anything else that is necessary to protect the integrity of related files and members.

By default, CL and HLLs place a *SHRRD lock on the data in input-only physical file members and place a *SHRUPD lock on the data in output-only and input-output physical file members. (PL/I allows you to optionally specify lock types of *EXCL or *EXCLRD in the ENVIRONMENT file attribute.)

You can cause locks other than these defaults to be obtained when a database file is opened by using the OVRDBF (Override with Data Base File) command parameter RCDFMTLCK (Record Format Lock) to specify that a more restrictive lock be placed on a record format when the file is opened. When used with a logical file, this parameter places more restrictive locks on the underlying data in the physical file member. The RCDFMTLCK parameter affects the allocation of the file only when it is opened, not when an ALCOBJ command is used.

If the control provided by CL or a HLL is not sufficient, you can explicitly allocate a file before you open it by executing an ALCOBJ command such as:

```
ALCOBJ OBJ((PRDLIB/MYFILE *FILE *SCHURP MBR__ABC))
```

When this command is executed, if MYFILE is a physical file, the file will get a *SHRRD lock, the member MBR__ABC will get a *SHRRD lock, and the data will get a *SHRUPD lock. Then, when MYFILE is opened, its access path will get a *SHRRD lock, the default lock of an open operation. Default locks on the file, the member, and the data also will be obtained by the open operation. If MYFILE is a logical file, many other locks may be placed on it. The important consideration about these other locks is their effect on jobs trying to access different logical files that may be sharing the same underlying data.

Locks placed on a database file member through the ALCOBJ command or a file-open operation should not be confused with "record locks." File member locks establish, for the entire file member, allowable access methods by routing steps in different jobs. Record locks, on the other hand, restrict access to individual records within a physical file member. A record lock usually is obtained at the beginning of an input-output statement and held until the next input-output statement begins, at which time the first record lock is released. If you use commitment control, which allows processing a group of database records as a single unit, the locks on the records are held from one commitment boundary to the next (e.g., between COMMIT and ROLLBACK statements).

A record lock is held by an open data path (ODP) and without commitment control is similar to the *EXCLRD object lock, in that it lets a locked record be read, but not updated or locked, through another ODP. If all ODPs for a file are in use under commitment control, then the record lock is like an *EXCL object lock in that the locked record cannot be read or updated except through the ODP that holds the lock. An important point to keep in mind is that record locks can conflict within the same routing step (unlike object locks). This conflict can occur if the same physical file record is accessed for updating through separate open data paths — for example, by having opened two logical files at the same time that are over the same physical file member.

Displaying Locks

A time may come when you need to see how objects and database file records are being locked. At that point three commands are available to you: DSPOBJLCK (Display Object Locks), DSPRCDLCK (Display Record Locks), and DSPJOB (Display Job). These commands can help you understand what OS/400 and the HLLs are doing automatically, and also can identify the cause of any failed allocation. IBM's *Control Language Reference* manual (SC41-0030) provides full descriptions of the displays for each command. Let's review the information provided by these displays. If you want to see the locks held on an object by all jobs, use the WRKOBJLCK (Work with Object Locks) command. This command presents a display similar to Figure 24.8.

The status (STS) column on the display can show HELD, WAIT, or REQ. HELD means the lock has been obtained and all locks within the same ALCOBJ command object list have been obtained. WAIT means a routing step in another job already holds a conflicting lock, and this job is waiting for it to be released. REQ means there are no conflicting locks held by other jobs on this particular object, but some other object in the same ALCOBJ object list has not yet received the requested lock. This last status demonstrates the "all-or-none" allocation rule at work.

The Work with Object Locks display in Figure 24.8 usually shows the lock for a database file as *SHRRD, although this is not necessarily the way the data is locked.

If you want to see the locks on the file members, press CF6 from the Work with Object Locks display, and the Work with Member Locks display (Figure 24.9) will be presented. This display shows the data locks for the physical file members.

Figure 24.8

Work with Object Locks Panel

```
                                              System: AS400

Object:    LF_FILE     Library:   TSTDTAPTC      Type:    *FILE-LGL

Type options, press Enter.
  4=End job    5=Work with     8=Work with job locks

Opt   Job          User         Lock      Status
      _GOLDEN      CONTE        *SHRRD      HELD

                                                   Bottom
F3=Exit    F5=Refresh  F6=Work with member locks  F12=Cancel
```

The lock type (Type) column on this screen can have the following values: MBR for the member control block; DATA for the actual data in a physical file member; or ACCPTH for the access path of a keyed file. The lock held for DATA is generally the most useful in determining how the member is being shared.

For logical file members only, use option 9 on the Member Locks display — Shared member locks — to move to the Work with Shared Member Locks display (Figure 24.10). The Work with Shared Member Locks display shows one or more displays with all the other logical or physical file members that have had a lock placed on them because of the locks on the logical file member that you are displaying. This information always includes the data of physical file members within the scope of the logical file member. It also includes logical file members

Figure 24.9

Work with Member Locks Panel

```
                                                   System: AS400
File:    LF_FILE           Library:    TSTDTAPTC     Type:       LGL

Type options, press Enter.
 4=End Job      5=Work with job          8=Work with job locks
 9=Work with shared member locks

Opt  Member      Job        User             Type      Lock      Status  Share
     _LF_MBR_1  GOLDEN     CONTE            MBR       *SHRRD    HELD    YES
     _                                      ACCPTH    *SHRRD    HELD

F3=Exit   F5=Refresh    F12=Cancel
```

Figure 24.10

Work with Shared Member Locks Panel

```
                                                  System:   AS400
Logical member:      LF_MBR_1     File:    LF_FILE    Library:    TSTDTAPTC
Shared file:       PF_FILE      Library:    TSTDTAPTC
Type options, press Enter.
  4=End Job    5=Work with job    8=Work with job locks

Opt   Member           Job          User            Type     Lock       Status
      _PF_MBR_1        GOLDEN       CONTE           DATA      *SHRUPD    HELD
      _PF_MBR_2        GOLDEN       CONTE           DATA      *SHRUPD    HELD

                                                                   Bottom
F3=Exit     F5=Refresh   F12=Cancel
```

that share an access path with the logical file member you are displaying. (Shared access paths are established by the ACCPTH Data Description Specification keyword and the ACCPTHMBR parameter of the CRTLF (Create Logical File) and ADDLFM (Add Logical File Member) commands.)

You use the second command, DSPRCDLCK, to look at the records in a physical file that have locks on them. The Record Locks display (Figure 24.11) shows the status (STS) of all locks, either HELD — the job holds the record lock, or WAIT — the job is waiting for a record lock.

The third command, DSPJOB, leads you to the Display Job Menu. From there, option 12 — Display Locks (if active) — displays the Job Locks display (Figure 24.12), which displays all external locks, both those already held and those for which a job is waiting. From this display you can get further information about object locks through displays similar to those displayed by the DSPOBJLCK command. In addition, you can display information about record locks through displays similar to those displayed by the DSPRCDLCK command.

You also can use the System Request key to interrupt an interactive program and then select System Request Menu option 3 — Display Current Job — to get to the Display Job Menu and from there to the Job Locks display. This display can provide insight into how OS/400 and HLLs are locking objects. When you see that they are not providing the exact type of sharing you want, then it is time to try the ALCOBJ and DLCOBJ commands.

While OS/400 and HLLs take care of most of the necessary object allocation on the AS/400, many complex applications will require specific control of data and program sharing. A traditional solution is to provide written procedures to tell the operator to make sure that the program about to be run will not interfere with other jobs on the system. But with an understanding of object allocation, you can automate this control, writing it into the program instead of including it

Figure 24.11

Display Member Record Locks Panel

```
                                                          System:   AS400

 File . . . . . . . . . :    PF_FILE        Member . . . . . . . : PF-MBR-2
   Library  . . . . . . :  TSTDTAPTC
   Record                                                      Lock
   Number   Job             User         Number     Status      Type
        1   GOLDEN          CONTE        019739     HELD
        1   GOLDEN

                                                          Bottom
 Press Enter to continue.

 F3=Exit   F5=Refresh  F12=Cancel
```

Figure 24.12

Work with Job Locks Panel

```
                                                    System: AS400
Job:    GOLDEN         User:  CONTE          Number:  019859

Job Status: ACTIVE
Type options, press Enter.
 5=Work with job member locks     8=Work with object locks

Opt   Object      Library     Type            Lock    Status Locks
      _BIRDMAN    PRDMSC      *MSGQ           *EXCL   HELD
      _CONTE      QSYS        *USRPRF         *SHRRD  HELD
      _GOLDEN     QSYS        *DEVD           *EXCLRD HELD
      _                                       *EXCLRD HELD
      _                                       *EXCLRD HELD
      _LF_FILE    TSTDTAPTC   *FILE-LGL       *SHRRD  HELD   YES
      _PRDCBL     QSYS        *LIB            *SHRRD  HELD
      _PRDCLP     QSYS        *LIB            *SHRRD  HELD
      _PRDCMD     QSYS        *LIB            *SHRRD  HELD
      _PRDDTA     QSYS        *LIB            *SHRRD  HELD
      _PRDMSC     QSYS        *LIB            *SHRRD  HELD
      _QCBL       QSYS        *LIB            *SHRRD  HELD
                                                     More...
F3=Exit   F5=Refresh  F10=Display job record locks F12=Cancel
F16=Job Menu
```

in run books or other operations documentation. Using the ALCOBJ and DLCOBJ commands can “unlock” one more of the AS/400’s advanced application support facilities.

Chapter 25

Concurrent File Updating

by Paul Conte

These guidelines will help you write applications that are 100% reliable

The AS/400 architecture is specifically designed for database applications, right? Right. The AS/400 lets you write an interactive program as if it were for use by a single person, yet it allows many people to use the program simultaneously, right? Right. So it follows that any AS/400 interactive program that updates a database file should work correctly whether it is in use by one person or by several people, right? Wrong! If you are using high-level language (HLL) interactive programs to update AS/400 databases, chances are that under certain conditions these programs will not execute properly when more than one person uses them at the same time. Because of the way HLL programs control record locking, interactive HLL programs may block other interactive jobs from reading database records for display; they may cause batch jobs to fail; and they may lose changes made to database records.

Do these possibilities — especially the possibility of lost changes — sound so disastrous as to be unbelievable? To convince yourself that they can occur, try the following tests on a couple of your HLL application programs used to update a database file:

- Test A — *Simultaneous single-record update.* For this test, you need an interactive program that allows updating of one database record at a time. Most programs of this type first prompt for a record key and then retrieve and display the record to allow changes.

To conduct the test, sign on to two jobs. Call the program in the first job. Retrieve for update the record with key *x* (where *x* is some appropriate key value). Then call the same program in the second job, and retrieve the record with the same key *x*. Did the program in the second job find the record locked? Perhaps all you wanted to do in the second job was look at record *x*, yet the retrieval of record *x* in the first job blocked retrieval of the record in the second job.

The typical application works around this problem by having separate menu options for "display" and for "update" access to the database. But this solution forces a user to bounce back and forth between the menu and the display/update program to display records that another job has retrieved for updating. In an interactive job that displays a single record at a time, this is inconvenient, but not disastrous. The next test demonstrates a more serious problem.

- Test B — *Simultaneous interactive and batch update.* For this test you need an interactive update program like the one used for Test A. In addition, you need a batch program that retrieves for updating all records from the same file. The batch program might be used in an accounts aging process or in the processing of a transaction file where a transaction record that has been applied successfully to the master file is updated with a new "status" field. First use the interactive program to retrieve for update the first database record that the batch program will read. Then start the batch program in a separate job. Did the batch program abnormally terminate because it could not read the record? Or is it still there waiting for the interactive program to finish with the record? Let's hope a person using the interactive program doesn't retrieve a record and go to lunch with the record still displayed. If this happens, your midday batch jobs face real trouble.

The common solution to this problem is to run batch update jobs only at night, when no interactive jobs are accessing the data. While this solution may fit an organization's normal work schedule, it is more an awkward way around the problem than a satisfactory solution to it. The next test presents a problem that cannot be worked around.

- Test C — *Simultaneous subfile record and single record update.* This third test is tough to pass. You need two different interactive programs that update the same file. The first program must retrieve two or more records at a time and display them in a subfile. The user must be able to update any of the displayed records. The second program, like the one used for Tests A and B, must allow updating of a single record at a time.

To conduct the test, sign on to two jobs. In the first job, call the subfile program and use it to retrieve a set of records for updating. In the second job, call the single-record program and use it to retrieve the first record displayed in the other job's subfile (this record will be referred to as "record *x*").

While still in the second job, change a single field in the displayed record (i.e., record *x*). For example, if this is a "customer account" file, you might change the "credit limit" field from $500 to $700. Press Enter so the change takes effect. Then return to the first job and change a *different* field in the same record *x*, which is displayed in the subfile. For example, change the "mailing address city" field from "EUGENE" to "PORTLAND." Do not change the "credit limit" field. Press Enter so the change takes effect.

You now have changed both the "credit limit" and the "mailing address city" in record *x*. Let's take a look at the results. Using either job, reretrieve record *x*. Does the "credit limit" field have the correct new value of $700? Or is it the old value of $500? If it is $700 and if you passed Tests A and B, you can skip the rest of the article; your programs are properly handling simultaneous updating.

However, if your programs failed one or more of the tests, don't rush out to trade in your AS/400 for another system. That the AS/400 is not at fault becomes apparent when you try the same three tests using DFU applications instead of HLL programs. You will find that DFU handles all three tests properly. The fault is not with the AS/400 but with the standard input/output (I/O) approach taken by RPG/400, COBOL, and PL/I.

The Basics of Simultaneous Updating

Before exploring the weakness with the HLL approach to I/O and a technique for countering that weakness, I must digress for a moment to review the basic update cycle for both batch and interactive programs. This review provides a foundation for showing how the HLL attempt to solve problems inherent in simultaneous updating actually gives rise to the problems the three tests illustrated.

Let's first review the batch update cycle, which is usually:

1. Retrieve a database record.
2. Compute new values as functions of retrieved values.
3. Update the database record.

The normal interactive update cycle is a little more complex:

1. Retrieve a database record (or group of records for subfiles).
2. Display the record(s).
3. Wait until a user enters changes.
4. Read the revised record(s) from display.
5. Update the database record(s).

Both cycles work fine as long as a database record is accessed by only one job at a time during the update cycle. But what happens if you move these basic cycles to a shared environment and two jobs attempt to update the same record at the same time? Then, even the simple batch cycle can present problems. With the basic update cycle in a shared environment, the following sequence of events results in the loss of the database changes made by Job A:

1. Job A retrieves record *x*.
2. Job B retrieves record *x*.
3. Job A computes new values for record *x*.
4. Job A updates record *x*.
5. Job B computes new values for record *x* (using the original values retrieved in Step 2).

6. Job B updates record *x* (overlaying the revised record x and erasing the changes made by Job A).

The solution to this problem is to add record locking to the retrieval step (Step 1) of the basic update cycle to prevent lost record changes. The revised batch update cycle then becomes:

1. Retrieve a database record and lock it.
2. Compute new values as functions of retrieved values.
3. Update the database record and release the record lock.

A similar revision can be made to the interactive update cycle. Then during the retrieval step in either cycle, if the desired record cannot be retrieved because another job has a lock on it, the program can wait until the lock is released or can execute exception-handling code.

Problems Caused by Record Locking

This modified update cycle is the one normally used in HLL programs. All HLL programs *automatically* obtain a record lock when a read occurs to a file opened for *update*. A record lock is automatically released when an update operation occurs or another read is done to the file opened for update.

Locking a record when it is first retrieved, as HLLs do, works well enough when only batch programs are involved because the compute and update steps (Steps 2 and 3) usually are completed in a matter of seconds. If two batch jobs attempt to update the same record, the second retrieval attempt must wait until the first job completes its compute and update steps, but this brief wait usually does not adversely affect the second job.

However, if one of the contending programs is an interactive program, HLL automatic record locking hinders proper handling of simultaneous updating. During the wait step in the interactive update cycle (Step 3), the program waits for a user to enter changes. Any record lock obtained in Step 1 is kept for the duration of the "think time" in Step 3. If the user is eating lunch instead of thinking, a record may be locked much longer than another job's maximum record-wait time. The second job receives a "record is locked" I/O status after the wait time expires. The second job then must execute exception-handling code, which is usually termination if the second job happens to be a batch job. The indefinite duration of the record lock is what caused the problems observed in Tests A and B.

The problem of losing changes to database records, which was demonstrated with Test C, can occur even with HLLs' use of automatic record locking because only the *last* record in a subfile is usually locked. Unless commitment control is in use, neither OS/400 nor the HLLs allow a job to hold more than one record lock at a time for one database ODP (open data path). When an OS/400 "get for update" operation is attempted, any previous record lock is released. Thus, when a subfile is loaded, usually only the last record displayed, which is also the last record retrieved, has a record lock. Locks on all other records have been released. This puts us back to square one with subfiles — no protection is provided against other jobs that update records displayed in the subfile. Because OS/400 does not support multiple record locks except with commitment control, record locking is not a viable solution to the "lost record change" problem when subfiles are used.

A Viable Solution

Both the problem of cross-job interference by long duration record locks and the problem of lost record changes can be solved with a refinement to the *interactive* update cycle. (No revision is required for the batch update cycle because it does not involve long duration locks and does not use subfiles.) The refinement still uses record locks but holds them for only brief record-validation and record-updating steps. The refined update cycle prevents loss of updates by using multiple copies of each database record retrieved.

Figure 25.1 shows (in pseudo code) the algorithm for the new interactive update cycle. The essential mechanism of this algorithm is that a copy is made of

Figure 25.1

Interactive Update Algorithm

```
/*  ──────────────────────────────  Mnemonics  ──────────────────────────────  */
/*                                                                             */
/*  array-size                    The maximum number of elements in the        */
/*                                arrays. Equal to 1 for single records or     */
/*                                equal to subfile size for record sets.       */
/*  false                         Logical value.                               */
/*  io-ok                         File status indicating successful I/O.       */
/*  null                          The 'no-value-present' special value.        */
/*                                Usually blanks, zero, or Hexadecimal '00'.   */
/*  record-locked                 File status indicating record locked by      */
/*                                another ODP (usually another job).           */
/*  record-not-found              File status indicating end of file           */
/*                                (sequential access) or invalid key (keyed    */
/*                                and relative access).                        */
/*  record-size                   The number of bytes in the database record.  */
/*  true                          Logical value.                               */

/*  ──────────────────────────────  Variables  ──────────────────────────────  */
/*                                                                             */

/*  Variable      Array                                                        */
/*  Name          Size          Type       Length           Comment            */
/*  ─────────     ──────────    ───────    ─────────────    ───────────────    */

DCL array_cnt                   DECIMAL    (2)              /* Actual number   */
                                                            /* of records in   */
                                                            /* org_rcd array.  */
DCL chg_pnd       (array-size)  LOGICAL                     /* Array of flags  */
                                                            /* for pending     */
                                                            /* record changes. */
DCL cur_rcd                     CHARACTER  (record-size)    /* Current record. */
DCL file_status                 CHARACTER                   /* File status     */
                                                            /* set by system   */
                                                            /* after each I/O  */
                                                            /* operation.      */
DCL i                           DECIMAL    (2)              /* Loop index.     */
```

Figure 25.1 Continued

Figure 25.1

Interactive Update Algorithm *Continued*

```
DCL io_rrn                          DECIMAL    (9)                /* Relative record    */
                                                                  /* number set by      */
                                                                  /* system.            */
DCL org_rcd       (array-size)  CHARACTER  (record-size)          /* Array of           */
                                                                  /* original rcds.     */
DCL quit                          LOGICAL                         /* Loop control.      */
DCL rcd-rrn       (array-size)  DECIMAL    (9)                    /* Array of           */
                                                                  /* relative record    */
                                                                  /* numbers of         */
                                                                  /* original rcds.     */
DCL rvs_rcd                       CHARACTER  (record-size)        /* Revised record.    */
DCL set_done                      LOGICAL                         /* A set of           */
                                                                  /* records is         */
                                                                  /* done.              */

/*  ——————————————————————  Functions  ——————————————————————     */

FUNCTION RCDKEY (record)                   /* Returns the key value from     */
                                           /* the character variable         */
                                           /*                                */

/*  ——————————————————————  Procedure  ——————————————————————     */
quit         <— false

WHILE ( quit)
 BEGIN
      .
      .
      .
/*  Write/read display file to get identification of next record           */
/*  or set of records. This may be a prompt for key value(s), a            */
/*  Roll key, etc. During this process, the user may enter a               */
/*  function key to signal that quit should be set true.                   */
      .
      .
      .
 IF   ( quit)
  BEGIN
  array_cnt   <— 0
  file_status <— io-ok
      .
      .
      .
/*  Position file record pointer for first read. This may be an            */
/*  RPG/400 SETGT or SETLL operation or a COBOL START verb.                */
      .
      .
      .
  FOR i = 1 TO array-siz WHILE (file_status = io-ok)
   BEGIN
Ⓐ  READ NEXT FILE RECORD INTO org_rcd(i) WITHOUT LOCK

   IF (file_status = io-ok)
    BEGIN
    array_cnt  <— array_cnt + 1
    rcd_rrn(i) <— io_rrn
    chg_pnd(i) <— false
    ENDIF
   ENDFOR
   CASE
```

Figure 25.1 Continued

Figure 25.1

Interactive Update Algorithm *Continued*

```
      BEGIN
      ((array_cnt   = 0)      AND (file_status = record-not-found))
       BEGIN
       SNDMSG 'No records(s) found'
       set_done <— true
       END()
      ((array_cnt   = 0)      AND (file_status   = record-not-found))
       BEGIN
       SNDMSG 'Error occurred, no record(s) could be retrieved'
       set_done <— true
       END()
      ((file_status = io-ok) OR (file_status = record-not-found))
       BEGIN
       set_done <— false
       END()
      (OTHERWISE)
       BEGIN
       SNDMSG 'Error occurred, records were partially retrieved'
       set_done <— false
       END()
      ENDCASE
     ENDIF
    WHILE (( quit) AND ( set_done))
     BEGIN
     set_done <— true
     FOR i = 1 TO array_cnt
      BEGIN
      IF (chg_pdn(i))
       BEGIN
       REWRITE PREVIOUS DISPLAY RECORD TO DISPLAY
       /*   Use the previous iput from the display or leave the          */
       /*   subfile record unchanged.                                     */
       ENDIF
      ELSE
       BEGIN
       WRITE FROM org_rcd(i)  TO DISPLAY
       /*   Use subfiles for sets of records. Null records are not        */
       /*   displayed and are not input capable.                          */
       ENDELSE
      chg_pnd(i) <— false
      ENDFOR
       .
       .
       .
  /*   If subfiles are used, the subfile is displayed and read at         */
  /*      this point.
       .
       .
       .
     FOR i = TO array_cnt
      BEGIN
      READ FROM DISPLAY TO rvs_rcd
      /* Use subfile record number (i) for sets of records.              */
Ⓑ     IF (rvs_rcd   = org_rcd(i))
       BEGIN
Ⓒ      READ FILE RECORD USING RCDKEY (org_rcd(i)) INTO cur_rcd WITH LOCK
       /*   This read could use relative access instead of keyed access;  */
       /*   in this case it would have USING rcd_rrn(i).                  */
       CASE
        BEGIN
```

Figure 25.1 Continued

Figure 25.1 **Interactive Update Algorithm** *Continued*

```
        (file_status = record-not-found)
         BEGIN
         SNDMSG 'Subfile record number ' || i || ' has been deleted,          +
                changes ignored.'
         org_rcd(i) <— null
         END()
        (file_status = record-locked)
         BEGIN
         SNDMSG 'Subfile record number ' || i || ' is in use, changes         +
                still pending.'
         chg_pnd(i) <— true
         set_done   <— false
         END()
        (file_status = io-ok)
         BEGIN
(D)      IF (cur_rcd = org_rcd(i))
          BEGIN
(E)       UPDATE FILE RECORD USING RCDKEY (org_rcd(i)) FROM rvs_rcd
          /*   This update could use relative access instead of keyed        */
          /*   access; in this case it would be USING rcd_rrn(i).            */
          org_rcd(i) <— rvs_rcd
          rcd_rrn(i) <— io_rrn
          ENDIF
         ELSE
          BEGIN
(F)       RELEASE FILE RECORD LOCK USING RCDKEY (cur_rcd)
  (G)     SNDMSG 'Subfile record number ' || i || ' has been changed         +
                 by another job. Reenter changes.'
          org_rcd(i) <— cur_rcd
          rcd_rrn(i) <— io_rrn
          set_done   <— false
          ENDELSE
         END()
        (OTHERWISE)
         BEGIN
         SNGMDG 'Subfile record number ' || i || ' had IO error on           +
                retrieval. Changes ignored.'
         END()
        ENDCASE
       ENDIF
      ENDFOR
     ENDWHILE
    ENDWHILE
```

each database record when it is first retrieved. The original record retrieval occurs *without record locks* (A, Figure 25.1). The record copy is used later in the algorithm to determine whether the user actually changed the record on the display (B). If a user changes a field in the record (e.g., changes "credit limit" from $500 to $700), the database record is re-retrieved, this time *with a record lock* (C); the newly retrieved record is compared to the copy of the record as it was originally retrieved (D). This comparison determines whether another job has changed the record after it was first retrieved. If the original and re-retrieved records are identical, the update occurs using the revised record (E). If the original and the re-retrieved record are different, the update does not occur. Instead the record lock is released (F), the user is presented with a new version of the record, and a message is issued indicating that the record has been changed by another job and that the user's update has been ignored (G).

The algorithm in Figure 25.1 includes statements necessary to permit use of relative record access instead of keyed access for re-retrievals and updates. Relative record access improves the algorithm's performance because read and update operations by relative record number are substantially faster than read and update operations by record key. Relative record access also improves the algorithm's function because relative record access provides more accurate feedback to the user. If a record's key fields have been changed by another job, using keyed access to re-retrieve the record can result in the "Record has been deleted since retrieval" condition, even if the record still exists, albeit with changed key fields. But if relative record access is used, a record whose key fields have been changed by another job still can be found during the re-retrieval because the record is in the same relative location in the file. In this case, the user will be notified with the more accurate "Record has been changed since retrieval" condition.

The algorithm in Figure 25.1 works not only for interactive programs that display a single record but also for interactive programs that display a set of records (as in a subfile). The implementation for a subfile requires that instead of a single structure to keep a copy of the record as it was originally retrieved, an array with one element for each retrieved record be used. The subfile itself serves as an array of the user-modified version of the records. A single-record structure is still adequate to temporarily hold the re-retrieved record for comparison with an element in the array of original records.

The array of originally retrieved records should contain the same number of elements as the subfile size. For this reason, SFLPAG (Subfile Page) equal to SFLSIZ (Subfile Size), and roll up/roll down should be handled by the program, not by OS/400. (For a discussion of subfile techniques and the Roll keys see Part Five: Workstation Programming.)

Interactive programs using the algorithm in Figure 25.1 pass the three tests at the beginning of the article. Unfortunately, implementing the algorithm in RPG/400, COBOL, or PL/I is not as simple as it may appear. Granted, statements in the algorithm such as `"array_cnt  Ø"` or `"FOR  i  =  I  TO  array_cnt"` can be implemented using appropriate statements in any of the HLLs. However, implementing such statements as `"READ NEXT FILE RECORD INTO org_rcd(i) WITHOUT LOCK"` is not simple because obtaining a record lock is not controlled by an option of the HLL read operation. Instead, in HLLs multiple-read statements are required, and it is necessary to open the file twice, once for input only (which lets a HLL retrieve a record without a record lock) and once for update (which causes a HLL to retrieve a record with a record lock). The file opens should be "shared" opens so that the same ODP is used. Shared opens are specified by using the OVRDBF (Override with Data Base File) command with the SHARE(*YES) parameter before the HLL file opens.

To point you in the right direction, Figures 25.2 and 25.3 show the RPG/400 and COBOL code for implementing the algorithm's "read without lock" and "read with lock" operations. In both languages, the file is defined twice: first as an input file and second as an update file. After the files are open, it is a matter of

Figure 25.2

RPG/400 Code for READ Operations With Optional Lock

```
The AS/400 filename is SMPFIL. The record format name is SMPFMT.

OS/400 command required for compiling RPG code when AS/400 file is to have RPG file name
UPDFIL

    OVRDBF     FILE(UPDFIL)   TOFILE(SMPFIL)

RPG/400 source

*... ... 1 ... ... 2 ... ... 3 ... ... 4 ... ... 5 ... ... 6 ... ... 7

     FSMPFIL  IF  E           K        DISK                  UC
     FUPDFIL  UF  E           K        EDISK             A   UC
     F            SMPFMT                          DRENAMEUPDFMT
         .
         .
         .
     C                        OPEN SMPFIL
     C                        OPEN UPDFIL
         .
         .
         .
         SMPKEY must be defined as a KLIST with the key fields of SMPFIL
         .
         .
         .
      *  Read without lock:
      *
     C            SMPKEY   CHAINSMPFIL
      *
      *  Read with lock:
      *
     C            SMPKEY   CHAINUPDFIL
```

chaining to the input file to retrieve a record without a lock or chaining to the update file to retrieve a record with a lock.

Because RPG/400 requires unique file names, the second file specification in Figure 25.2 uses an RPG file name that is not the same as the OS/400 file name. An OVRDBF command associates this RPG file name with the same OS/400 file specified in the first file specification. In addition, the second file specification renames the record format to preserve uniqueness. COBOL straightforwardly manages two internal files as the same OS/400 file because the SELECT statement binds the internal and external names.

If you choose to use relative record access, a *third* shared file open, using relative record access for updating, is required. You cannot simply replace the keyed access for updating with relative record access for updating. The keyed access is still necessary because new records must be added to the file using a write operation to the file opened for keyed access. This third access is implemented with code similar to that shown in Figures 25.2 and 25.3 for the keyed access for updating. In addition, the relative record number from the program's I/O feedback area must be saved when a record is first retrieved. If a subfile is used, an array is necessary to store all the subfile's relative record numbers.

Figure 25.3

COBOL Code for READ Operations With Optional Lock

```
The AS/400 filename is SAMPLEFILE. The record format name is also SAMPLEFILE.

 ENVIRONMENT       DIVISION.
     .
     .     Other ENVIRONMENT DIVISION statements.
     .
 INPUT-OUTPUT      SECTION.
 FILE-CONTROL.

     SELECT                         INPUT-FILE
          ASSIGN        TO          DATABASE-SAMPLEFILE
          ORGANIZATION  IS          INDEXED
          ACCESS MODE   IS          DYNAMIC
          RECORD KEY    IS          EXTERNALLY-DESCRIBED-KEY
          STATUS        IS          FILE-STATUS.

     SELECT                         UPDATE-FILE
          ASSIGN        TO          DATABASE-SAMPLEFILE
          ORGANIZATION  IS          INDEXED
          ACCESS MODE   IS          DYNAMIC
          RECORD KEY    IS          EXTERNALLY-DESCRIBED-KEY
          STATUS        IS          FILE-STATUS.

 I-O-CONTROL.      SAME RECORD AREA FOR
                   INPUT-FILE
                   UPDATE-FILE

    .
    .
    .
DATA               DIVISION.
FILE               SECTION.
*    Note: The 01 levels for the FD's below actually reference
*    the same internal storage when the file opens are shared.
*    After either READ statement in the PROCEDURE DIVISION below,
*    the record that was read can be referred to as INPUT-RCD.

FD   INPUT-FILE.
     LABEL RECORDS ARE STANDARD.

01   INPUT-RCD.

     COPY DDS-ALL-FORMATS OF SAMPLEFILE.

FD   UPDATE-FILE.
     LABEL RECORDS ARE STANDARD.

01   UPDATE-RCD.

     COPY DDS-ALL-FORMATS OF SAMPLEFILE.
     .
     .
     .
PROCEDURE DIVISION.
     .
     .
     .
    OPEN INPUT   INPUT-FILE.
    OPEN I-O     UPDATE-FILE.
     .
     .
```

Figure 25.3 Continued

Figure 25.3 **COBOL Code for READ Operations With Optional Lock** *Continued*

```
       .
*      Read without lock:

       READ INPUT-FILE.
       .
       .
       .
*      Read with lock.

       READ UPDATE-FILE.
```

Just as neither RPG/400 nor COBOL has a "read without lock" or a "read with lock" operation, neither has a "release record lock" I/O operation such as is needed if the re-retrieved record is different from the original record (F, Figure 25.1). A lock can be released in a HLL, however, by executing an unsuccessful read operation to the file opened for update. The read can be forced to fail by using an invalid key.

While the algorithm presented applies to interactive programs that let users update either a single record at a time or sets of independent records, it does not apply to programs that involve simultaneous update of multiple interrelated records or "change all" programs.

In conclusion, you have on the one hand the AS/400, which provides advanced database facilities and numerous aids to interactive programming. But on the other hand, there remain problems in using those advanced facilities with HLL programs — problems that a conscientious application programmer must consider carefully. Although errors due to simultaneous record updating may occur infrequently, the results can range from troublesome job failures to serious loss of record changes. Most AS/400 installations probably would prefer that the chance of such errors be eliminated altogether. Third-party software developers in particular will want to design their products for 100 percent reliability. The guidelines in this chapter can help programmers achieve that desired goal.

Chapter 26

Using Data Queues

by Brian Gordon

Use data queues to pass data between jobs efficiently and quickly

Data queue processing is the fastest, most efficient means to pass data between jobs or programs. It is also one of the AS/400's least used and least understood data management features. This chapter will introduce you to AS/400 data queue processing, discuss data queue's primary benefits, provide several practical examples illustrating the use of data queues, and conclude with several important factors you should consider as you evaluate the value of data queues in your situation.

What Is a Data Queue?

A data queue is an AS/400 object used to transfer data between programs. Like a file, entries can be added to and retrieved from a data queue. Data queue entries can be retrieved in either sequential or keyed sequence. Unlike a file, however, entries are automatically removed as they are retrieved. The attributes of a data queue are specified at the time the data queue is created and cannot be changed. As with any AS/400 object, AS/400 security controls data queue access. One unique feature of data queues, however, is the effect of the Allocate Object (ALCOBJ) command. Even when a data queue is allocated for exclusive use, other jobs may still read and write to the data queue. While this may seem to create a new set of problems to contend with, it actually provides more management control over application contention.

Another unique data queue attribute is the way performance is affected by the number of entries placed on the data queue. As entries are added, a forward link list (series of pointers from one entry to the next) is searched to find the "end" of the queue. The greater the number of entries on the data queue, the longer it takes to access those entries. The *CL Programmers Guide* (SC41-8077) recommends keeping the number of entries to 100 or less for best performance. Because data queues are used for communicating between jobs rather than for permanently storing data, this is not a serious limitation.

Some additional notes on the internals of data queue processing relate to the way storage is used. It is important to understand that as entries are retrieved the disk storage is not freed. This means that a data queue will never decrease in size — something you need to consider when designing applications that use data queues. More specifically, housekeeping logic is required to delete and re-create a data queue as needed.

Maximum entry length, one of the parameters specified when a data queue is created, determines the amount of storage used for each data queue entry. The amount of storage required for each entry is equal to the maximum entry length *specified*, regardless of the *actual* length of that entry. IBM developers in Rochester recommend keeping the overall size of the data queue to 32K or less, which allows the entire data queue to reside within the Process Access Group (PAG). Keeping the data queue within the PAG helps to reduce application paging and to improve overall performance.

Data Queue Benefits

The primary use of data queue processing is to provide a means of communication between jobs. While jobs can mean programs executing on separate processors, including non-OS/400 systems such as DOS, Windows, or OS/2, in this context jobs refers to different programs or functions on the AS/400. Figure 26.1 provides an overview of how data queue processing works.

Based on how often a program is used and the number of jobs concurrently requesting the services, data queue processing can provide a significant reduction in system overhead. An important feature of data queue processing is the way a data queue can be used to allow one program to retrieve and process entries that have been placed on the queue by one or more separate programs. This feature can be used to allow a single job to provide services for multiple jobs executing concurrently. For example, in a program that requires 12 open data files, with four sessions using this program, there will be 48 opens, 48 closes, and 48 open data paths (ODPs) to manage. By changing to a data queue approach, this could be reduced to 12 opens and 12 ODPs to manage. Multiple interactive jobs could use a data queue as the means to send a print request to a background job as shown in Figure 26.2. The single background job can also allocate to the needed system resources to avoid unnecessary paging. This improves performance by eliminating online batch processing while still retaining all the required functionality.

Data queues also make online programs easier to maintain and make the addition of complex online facilities more manageable. By implementing this approach, it becomes much easier — in fact, almost automatic — to manage resources. For example, resource contention (files and other objects) is automatically reduced. It is practical to allocate memory and processor time to a specific function. If the volume of work to be performed exceeds the ability of a single job, you can have multiple background jobs active servicing the same data queue. When more than one job is waiting to retrieve an entry from the same data queue, the job with the highest priority will receive the entry. For the sake of

Figure 26.1

Data Queue Processing

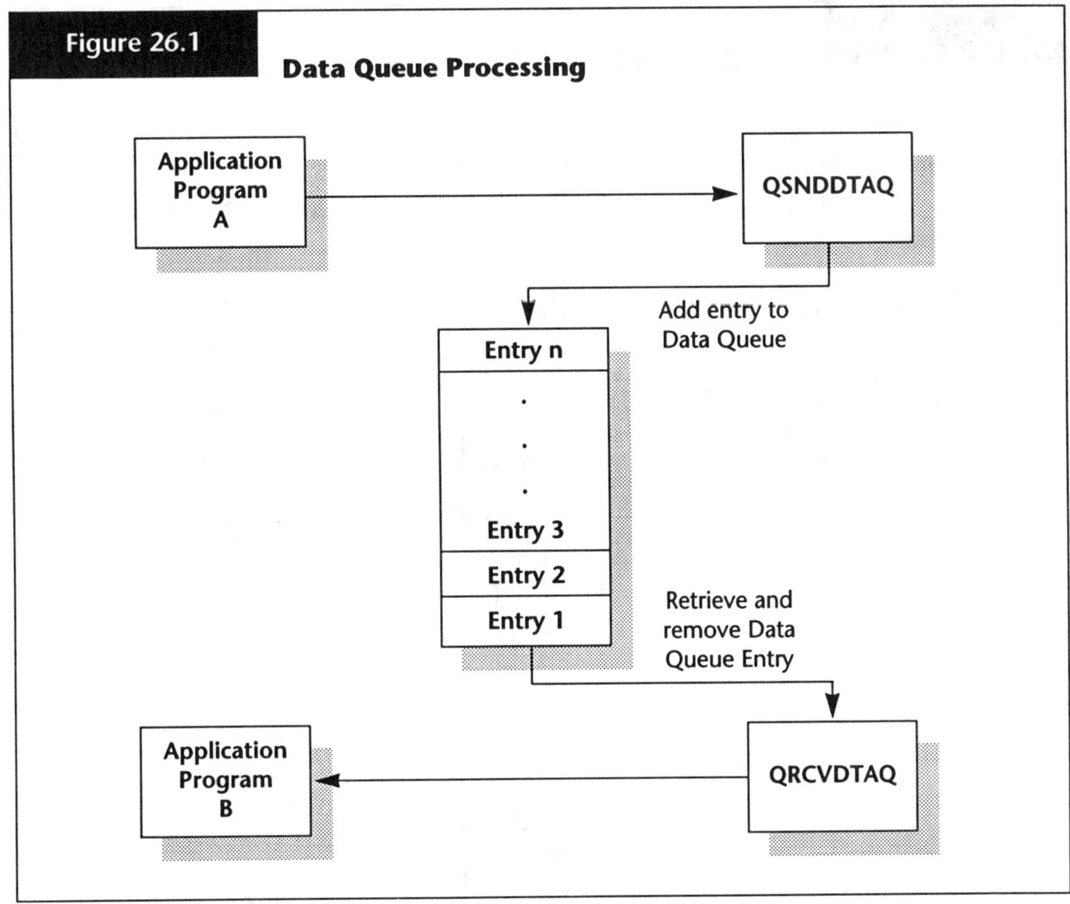

consistent processing, data queue processing can be implemented to use a single job for a given task. No matter where the task is required within the application, it will always be performed in a consistent manner. This also reduces maintenance requirements.

Figure 26.2 demonstrates how data queues can be used for synchronous (or one-way) processing. The interactive program does not have to wait to continue until completion of the print processing. In addition, any overhead associated with creating the requested report is limited to a single copy of the program. This is in contrast to incorporating the logic and overhead into multiple interactive sessions.

Data queues provide the means to implement a cooperative processing application using IBM-supplied APIs (Application Programming Interfaces) — for example, on a programmable workstation (PWS) to write to and read from an AS/400 data queue. A PWS program uses the functions in much the same way an AS/400 HLL program uses an API. Figure 26.3 shows an example in which data queues are used for a cooperative processing application. Note that once an entry is added, the entry is identical to any other data queue entry and is processed accordingly.

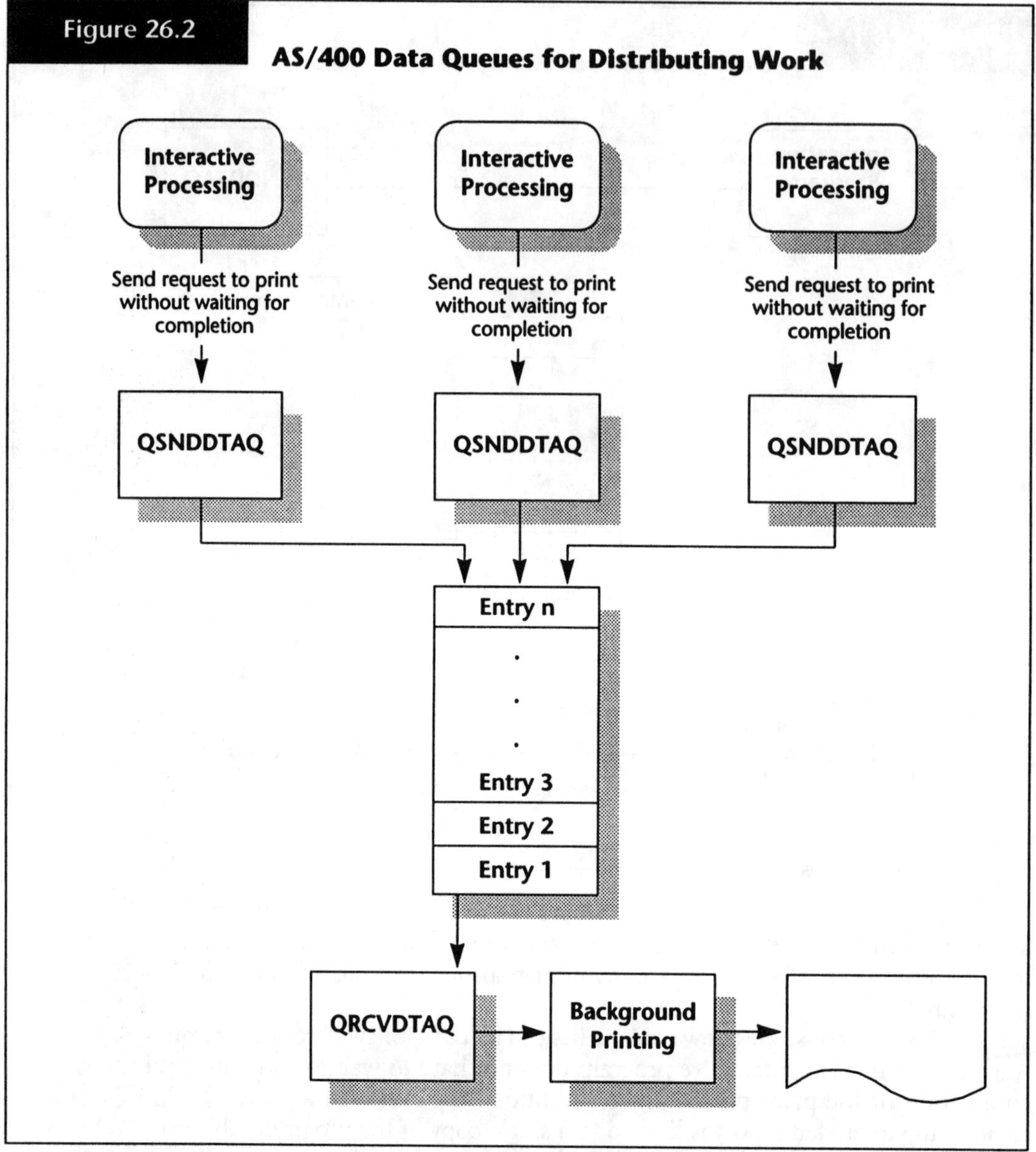

The steps required to use data queues from a PWS are first to translate the content of the entry from ASCII to EBCDIC and then add the entry to the data queue. Both of these functions are performed using IBM-supplied APIs. When you retrieve an entry, the sequence of events is reversed: The entry is retrieved and then translated.[1]

[1]While developing a C language PWS program may be outside the skill set of most AS/400 RPG programmers, IBM certainly put data queue processing within the reach of an experienced C programmer. IBM provides sample PC programs in the PC Support tools folder (QIWSTOOL) for use with the PC Support APIs.

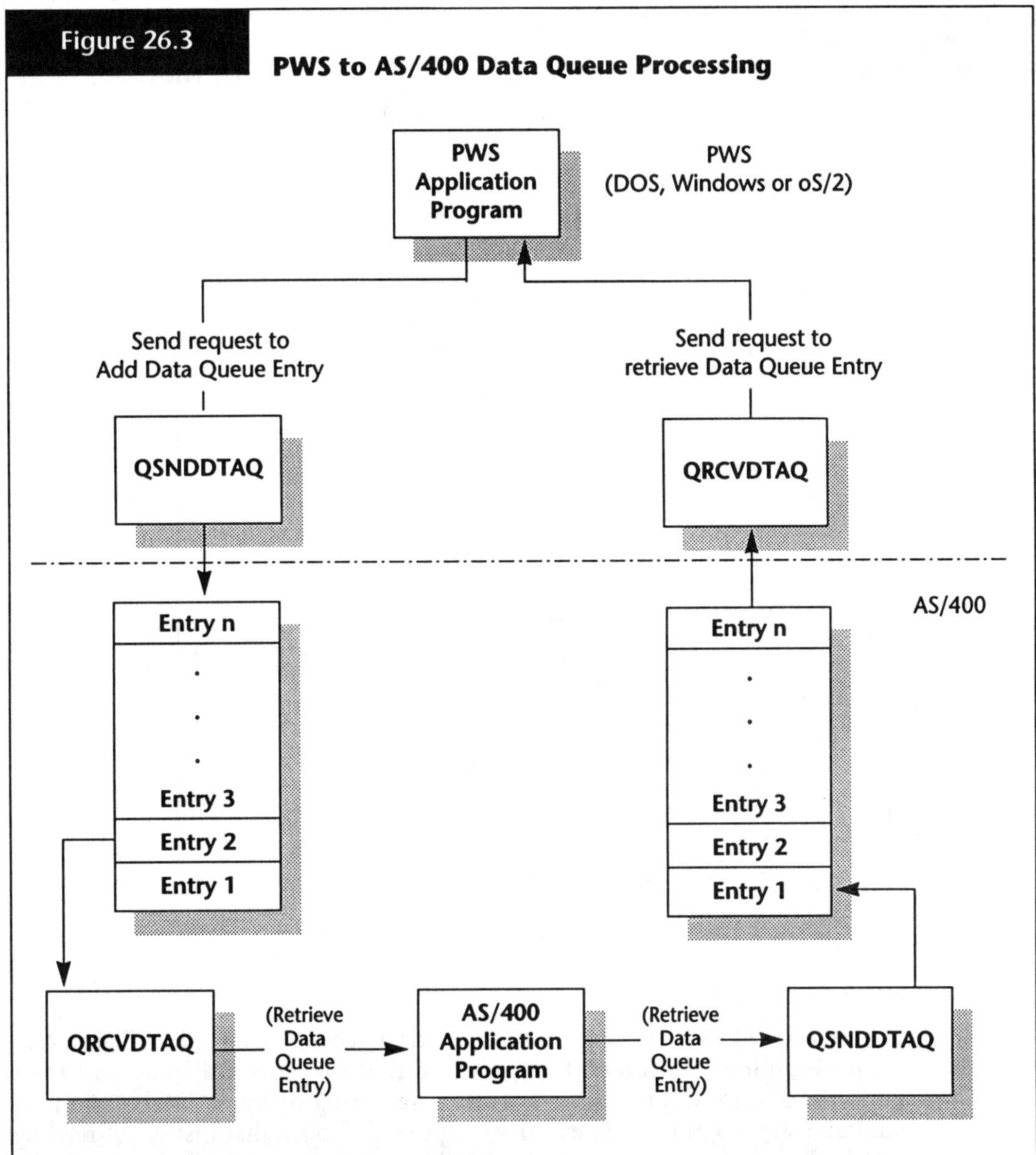

Data queues also can provide a vehicle for developing event-driven programs, such as an interactive program that must report progress on a background process while accepting data input. One means of writing the code for such a program would be to read the display (properly coded so it does not wait if input is not available) and then retrieve another object, such as a data area, for the status of the background process. Using data queues in this application could simplify the logic significantly. As Figure 26.4 illustrates, the background job and the Display file could both add entries to the same data queue. In this way, the

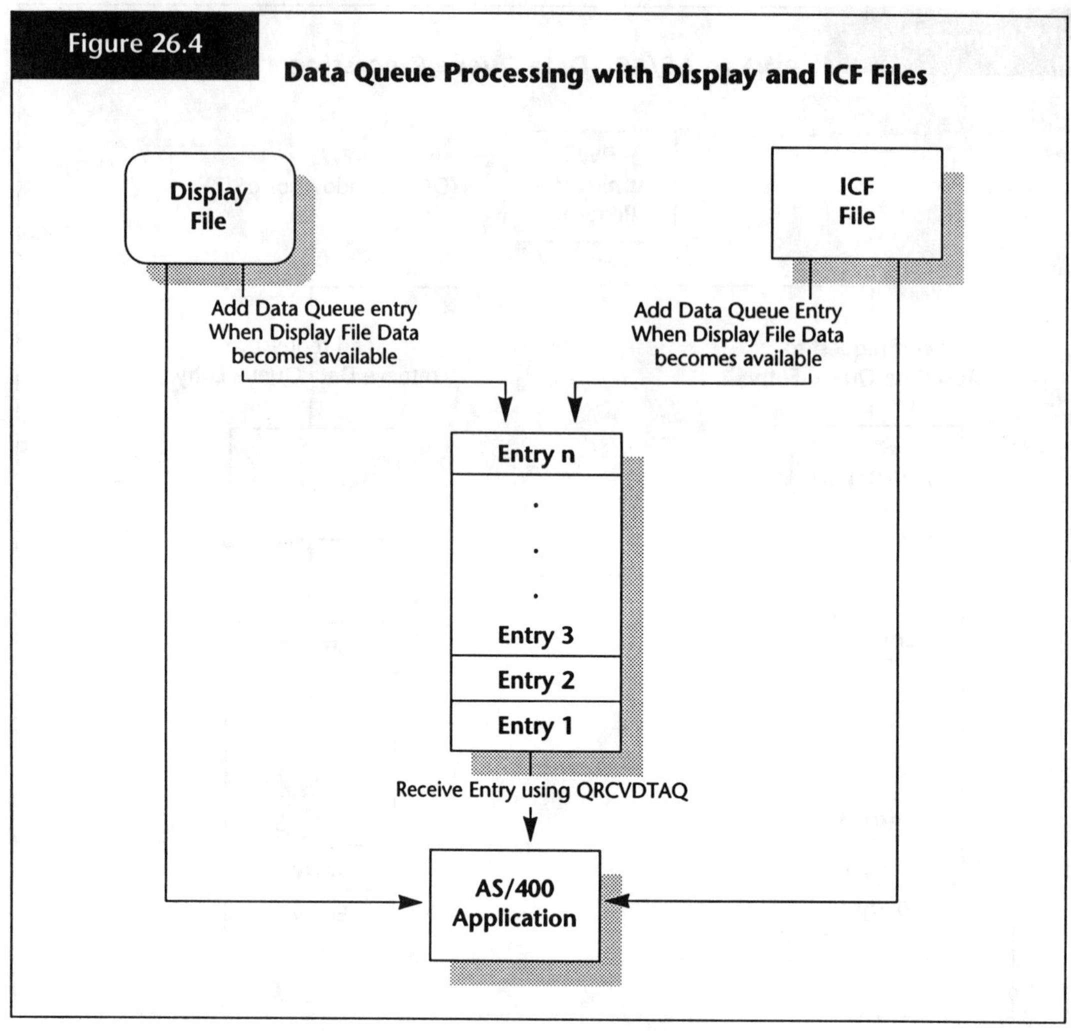

Figure 26.4
Data Queue Processing with Display and ICF Files

program would look to a single source (the data queue) for direction. Figure 26.5 is an example of an interactive program that presents a display and then periodically refreshes the display without requiring operator intervention. In addition, the program must exit if F3 is pressed. Notice that instead of reading the display file (to check for a function key), the data queue is monitored for both the refresh data (background job status) and the operator request. Once a display file entry is received, the display file is read to check for F3. Also notice that a wait time of -1 is specified. This causes the program to wait indefinitely for an entry to become available. It is important to note that in the DDS the INVITE keyword must be active when the format is written to the display. The following command is used to create the associated display file:

```
CRTDSPF FILE(QGPL/STATUS) SRCFILE(QDDSSRC)                    +
        DTAQ(QGPL/PROGRESS) DFRWRT(*NO)
```

Figure 26.5

Receive Data Queue Entries from Display File

```
FSTATUS  CF     E      WORKSTN
I* DATA STRUCTURE TO RECEIVE DATA QUEUE ENTRY
I*
IDSENT       DS                              80
I                                         1  10 DSTYPE
I                                         1   52DSCOMP
C* PRESENT INITIAL DISPLAY
C*
C           *INKC     DOUEQ*ON
C                     WRITESTATUS01
C*
C* RETRIEVE NEXT DATA QUEUE ENTRY
C*
C                     CALL 'QRCVDTAQ'
C                     PARM 'PROGRESS'QNAME  10
C                     PARM 'QGPL'    LIB    10
C                     PARM 80        FLDLEN  50
C                     PARM           DSENT
C                     PARM -1        WAIT    50
C*
C* REFRESH DISPLAY IF ENTRY IS UPDATE INFORMATION
C* (FROM ANOTHER JOB PROCESSING IN BACKGROUND, ETC)
C* OR READ DISPLAY FILE TO CHECK FOR F3 IF ENTRY IS
C* FROM DISPLAY FILE DATA MANAGEMENT
C*
C           DSTYPE    CASEQ'*DSPF'   SRDSPF
C                     CAS            SRUPDT
C                     END
C*
C                     END
C*
C* PROCESS A DISPLAY FILE ENTRY
C*
C           SRDSPF    BEGSR
C                     READ STATUS                  90
C                     ENDSR
C*
C* PROCESS AN ENTRY FROM BACKGROUND PROCESSING
C* (COPY PERCENT COMPLETE STATUS TO DISPLAY)
C
C           SRUPDT    BEGSR
C                     Z-ADDDSCOMP    WSCOMP
C                     ENDSR
```

DDS for Example Display File

```
A          R STATUS01
A                                        INVITE
A                                        CF03
A                                    1  3'Processing is'
A            WSCOMP         2  50    1 17EDTWRD(   .  )
A                                    1 24'percent complete'
```

The DTAQ and DFRWRT parameters are the significant ones. The DTAQ parameter specifies the name of the data queue to receive an entry when a function key is pressed on the display. The DFRWRT parameter causes the display to be presented without waiting for a read request.

When you use a data queue with a display file or ICF file, the data queue entry that is specified on the CRTDSPF, CHGDSPF, OVRDSPF, CRTICFF, CHGICFF, or OVRICFF command must have a length of at least 80 characters. This is because the display file or ICF file entry that is put on the data queue is 80 characters in length. The portion of the entry relevant to this example is the first 10 bytes. The entry in these positions will be "*ICFF" for an ICF file or "*DSPF" for a display file. The remaining information in the entry is used to uniquely identify which file placed the entry on the data queue. The application program illustrated in Figure 26.4 must process data from both an AS/400 display file and ICF (Intersystem Communication Function) file. Instead of alternately testing each file for input, a single data queue is monitored using the QRCVDTAQ program. When data becomes available from either the display file or ICF file, an entry is placed on the data queue (by Display File or ICF File Management). Once the data becomes available, the application performs a read to the appropriate file. A complete description of the display file or ICF file data queue entry is contained in the *Data Management Guide* (SC41-9658).

The final and most significant benefit from the application of data queue technology is the ability to implement a client/server architecture. When you consider the ease with which entries can be added to and retrieved from a data queue in OS/400, OS/2, and DOS environments, the possibilities are astounding. Keeping in mind that the origination point of a data queue is of no concern to the program that processes the entry, it is easy to visualize the possibilities. For example, the same program that processes requests via data queue entries can be used to service both PWS and AS/400 requests. This means that when you start to add cooperative features to an application, you can use a single program to process requests for both environments. Data queues are an excellent means to implement a cooperative architecture that includes a Graphical User Interface (GUI). Data queue processing provides a means to develop an application that is much easier to write than an APPC application and less restrictive than reading and writing a display file buffer.

Commands and Programs that Use Data Queues

OS/400 supplies several commands and programs that allow AS/400 applications to work with data queues and their contents. The following is a description of the OS/400 commands and programs that use data queues, as well as examples showing their use. Note that while the examples are given in RPG, these programs can be called from any AS/400 High-Level Language (HLL), including CL.

CRTDTAQ — Create Data Queue. The CRTDTAQ command is used to create a data queue and is the only place to specify certain operational attributes of a data queue. For example, if keyed access to a data queue will be used, then the SEQ(*KEYED) parameter must be specified as part of the CRTDTAQ command. Additionally, it is only possible to obtain information about the sender of a data queue entry if the data queue is created with the parameter of SENDERID(*YES) specified.

The following command creates a data queue named MYDTAQ in library MYLIB:

```
CRTDTAQ DTAQ(MYLIB/MYDTAQ) MAXLEN(30) FORCE(*NO) SEQ(*KEYED)   +
        KEYLEN(15) SENERID(*YES)
```

The maximum length of an entry that can be added to this data queue is 30 bytes. To avoid the additional overhead of writing the data queue to auxiliary storage each time an entry is added or removed, a value of *NO is specified for the FORCE parameter.

The order in which entries are retrieved from a data queue is determined by the SEQ parameter. The possible values are *FIFO for First-In-First-Out retrieval, *LIFO for Last-In-First-Out processing or *KEYED for indexed access. In the example above, the KEYLEN parameter value is required because the sequence is specified as keyed. The value of 15 means that the key provided for each entry added or retrieved can be up to 15 bytes long.

The value *YES for the SENDERID parameter means the sender ID (qualified job name and sender's "current" user profile) is attached to each entry added to the data queue. This sender information is then available to be received along with the actual data queue entry.

DLTDTAQ — Delete Data Queue. DLTDTAQ is the command used to remove a data queue from the system. The following example deletes the data queue MYDTAQ from MYLIB:

```
DLTDTAQ  DTAQ(MYLIB/MYDTAQ)
```

QSNDDTAQ — Send Data Queue Entry. If you were to think of a data queue in terms of a database file, the QSNDDTAQ program would be equivalent to a database write operation. As the name implies, the QSNDDTAQ program is used to send an entry to a data queue. The parameters used on the CALL include the name of the data queue to receive the entry, the entry value, and optionally the "key" for the entry. Figure 26.6 presents a basic RPG program that reads data from a display file and then sends an entry to a data queue. The values of the WAELEN (Entry length) and WSKLEN (Key length) parameters are restricted by the MAXLEN and KEYLEN parameters specified on the CRTDTAQ command. The key and key-length parameters are only allowed if the data queue is created with the SEQ(*KEYED) parameter. In addition, if the data queue was created as a keyed data queue, then the key-length parameter value must match the length on the CRTDTAQ command. While an application will typically know the attributes of a data queue (entry length, key length, etc.) in advance, it is possible to determine these attributes dynamically. This is done using the system program QMHQRDQD, which is documented in the "Using Data Queues" section of the *CL Programmers Guide* (SC41-8077).

QCLRDTAQ — Clear Data Queue. The QCLRDTAQ program is used to clear all of a specific data queue's entries. The program in Figure 26.6 also provides an option to clear the data queue (remove all currently existing entries) before sending the new entry. The values of the WSDTAQ and WSQLIB parameters specify the name and library of the data queue to be cleared. It is important to note that when a data queue is cleared the disk storage is not freed. This means that after successfully executing the QCLRDTAQ program, no entries are available for the QRCVDTAQ program to retrieve, but the size of the data queue

Figure 26.6

RPG Program to Send Data Queue Entry

```
FSNDDQE  CF  E                    WORKSTN
C* RETRIEVE OPERATOR INPUT
C*
C         *INKC     DOUEQ*ON
C                   EXFMTSEND01
C*
C* CLEAR data queue BEFORE SENDING
C* NEW ENTRY (IF REQUESTED BY OPERATOR)
C*
C          WSCLR     IFEQ 'Y'
C                   CALL 'QCLRDTAQ'
C                   PARM           WSDTAQ
C                   PARM           WSQLIB
C                   END
C*
C* SEND DATA QUEUE ENTRY
C*
C                   CALL 'QSNDDTAQ'
C                   PARM           WSDTAQ
C                   PARM           WSQLIB
C                   PARM 30        WAELEN  50
C                   PARM           WSDATA
C                   PARM           WSKLEN
C                   PARM           WSKEY
C                   END
C*
C                   SETON                     LR
```

DDS for Example Display File

```
A                                          DSPSIZ(24 80 *DS3)
A                                          CF03
A          R SEND01
A                                      1 24'Send Data Queue Entry'
A                                      3  3'Data Queue name  . . .'
A            WSDTAQ        10A  B  3 28
A                                      4  5'Library  . . . . . .'
A            WSQLIB        10A  B  4 28
A                                      5  3'Data to send . . . . .'
A            WSDATA        30A  B  5 28
A                                      6  3'Entry key  . . . . . .'
A            WSKEY         15A  B  6 28
A                                      7  5'Key length . . . . .'
A            WSKLEN          3  0B  7 28
A                                      8  3'Clear Data Queue . . .'
A            WSCLR           1A  B  8 28
A                                      8 63'Y-Yes,N-No'
```

has not changed. The DLTDTAQ and CRTDTAQ commands must be used to rebuild a data queue if the intention is to reset its size.

QRCVDTAQ — Receive Data Queue Entry. Once again relating data queues to database operations, the QRCVDTAQ program would be comparable to a database read operation. The parameter values for the QRCVDTAQ program include the name of the data queue from which to retrieve an entry and the field to receive the entry value. Other optional parameters can be used to specify keyed access for retrieval and to specify whether or not to include information about the sender of the entry. The example program in Figure 26.7 retrieves an entry from a data queue based on input from a display file. The display file input includes the name of the data queue, a key value and key relationship, and an option for whether or not to retrieve sender information. The length of the field to receive the data queue entry value (WSDATA) is 256 bytes. This means that the data queue must have been created with a MAXLEN parameter of 256 bytes or less. After returning from the CALL, the WAELEN parameter will contain a value specifying the actual length of the entry retrieved. In the event an entry is not retrieved, WAELEN will be set to zero. Again, the key field parameters are only valid if the data queue was

Figure 26.7 RPG Program to Retrieve Data Queue Entry

```
FRCVDQE  CF  E                    WORKSTN
C* RETRIEVE OPERATION INPUT
C*
C           *INKC     DOUEQ*ON
C                     EXFMTRECV01
C*
C* IF SENDER ID IS TO BE RETRIEVED THEN
C* SET LENGTH PARAMETER TO INCLUDE COMPLETE ID
C*
C           WSISND    IFEQ 'Y'
C                     Z-ADD44        WASLEN
C                     ELSE
C                     Z-ADD*ZERO     WASLEN
C                     END
C*
C* RETRIEVE DATA QUEUE ENTRY
C*
C                     CALL 'QRCVDTAQ'
C                     PARM           WSDTAQ
C                     PARM           WSQLIB
C                     PARM           WAELEN  50
C                     PARM           WSDATA
C                     PARM           WSWAIT
C                     PARM           WSORDR
C                     PARM           WSKLEN
C                     PARM           WSKEY
C                     PARM           WASLEN  30
C                     PARM           WASNDR 44
C                     END
C                     SETON                    LR
```

Figure 26.7 Continued

Figure 26.7 **RPG Program to Retrieve Data Queue Entry** *Continued*

DDS for Example Display File

```
A                                        DSPSIZ(24 80 *DS3)
A                                        CF03
A          R RECV01
A                                    1 28'Receive Data Queue Entry'
A                                    3  3'Data Queue name   . . .'
A            WSDTAQ        10A  B    3 28
A                                    4  5'Library  . . . . . .'
A            WSQLIB        10A  B    4 28
A                                    5  3'Wait time  . . . . . .'
A            WSWAIT         5  0B    5 28
A                                    6  3'Key length . . . . . .'
A            WSKLEN         3  0B    6 28
A                                    7  3'Entry key  . . . . . .'
A            WSKEY         15A  B    7 28
A                                    8  5'Relationship . . . .'
```

created with the parameter SEQ(*KEYED). The possible values for the relationship parameter (WSORDR) are: GT (greater than), LT (less than), NE (not equal), EQ (equal), GE (greater than or equal), and LE (less than or equal). The wait parameter (WSWAIT) is used to determine what action the QRCVDTAQ program should take if a data queue entry is not readily available. A positive value represents the number of seconds to wait for an entry; a value of zero will cause control to be returned immediately; and a negative value will instruct the program to wait until an entry becomes available. One final point relates to the sender ID parameters. These parameters are allowed only for a data queue that has been created with the SENDERID(*YES) parameter. If sender information is requested, the qualified job name and "current" user profile (from the job that added the entry) will be returned in the format shown in Figure 26.8.

Figure 26.8 **Sender ID Format**

From	To	Format	Description
1	4,0	Packed	Value specified for SENDER ID LENGTH parameter
5	8,0	Packed	Actual length of SENDERID parameter
9	18	Character	Job name (Sending Data Queue entry)
19	28	Character	User ID (Sending Data Queue entry)
29	34,0	Zoned	Job number (Sending Data Queue entry)
35	44	Character	Current User Profile (Sending Data Queue entry)

Detailed Transaction Example

While the first part of this chapter provides a conceptual foundation for how data queue processing works, the second part presents a more detailed example of an on-line transaction processing application. This example comes from a commercial shop floor control application. Figure 26.9 provides an overview of this application. In this example, a data-entry screen is used to request input from the operator. The transaction is sent to a background program via a data queue for validation and updating. The background program then returns the completion status and message via a data queue. As Figure 26.9a shows, the significant components used in this transaction include the following:

- *Transaction Entry Program* — an AS/400 program that uses a display file to request input from an operator. Once the input is received, a data queue entry is submitted for background processing. The program waits for a completion message (received via data queue) and presents the message to the operator.
- *Inbound "Public" Data Queue* — a single data queue used by any transaction entry program to request the service of the background program.
- *Background Program* — where all the validation and file updates take place. This program retrieves entries from the inbound data queue in FIFO (First-In-First-Out) sequence. The appropriate validation and update processing are performed and then a completion message is sent to the requesting program. The background processing program is an RPG program initiated by an autostart job entry. Figure 26.9b illustrates the data structures that are used to read the Transaction Request data queue (DSTRAN) and write to the Transaction Completion data queue (DSCOMP).
- *"Private" Completion Data Queue* — Each transaction entry session has its own private data queue. The name of the data queue is unique and is passed to the background program as a data element in the input data queue entry. The purpose of this data queue is for the background program to send and the transaction entry program to receive a completion message.

Transaction Logic

The processing used in the data queue transaction approach is very similar to a conventional AS/400 application. The data is entered and validated, files are updated, and a completion or error message is displayed to the operator. Unlike the conventional approach, however, the processing is divided between multiple jobs — not just multiple programs. A detailed explanation of each step in the processing of a sample transaction follows. The code for each step is included in Figures 26.10a through 26.10g where appropriate.

Step 1. *Data Entry (Transaction Entry Program)* (Figure 26.10a). Using a standard AS/400 display file, the execute format (EXFMT) operation is used to present a display and subsequently request operator input. The input consists of a lot number and lot quantity. A message line is used to display completion or error messages.

Figure 26.9a

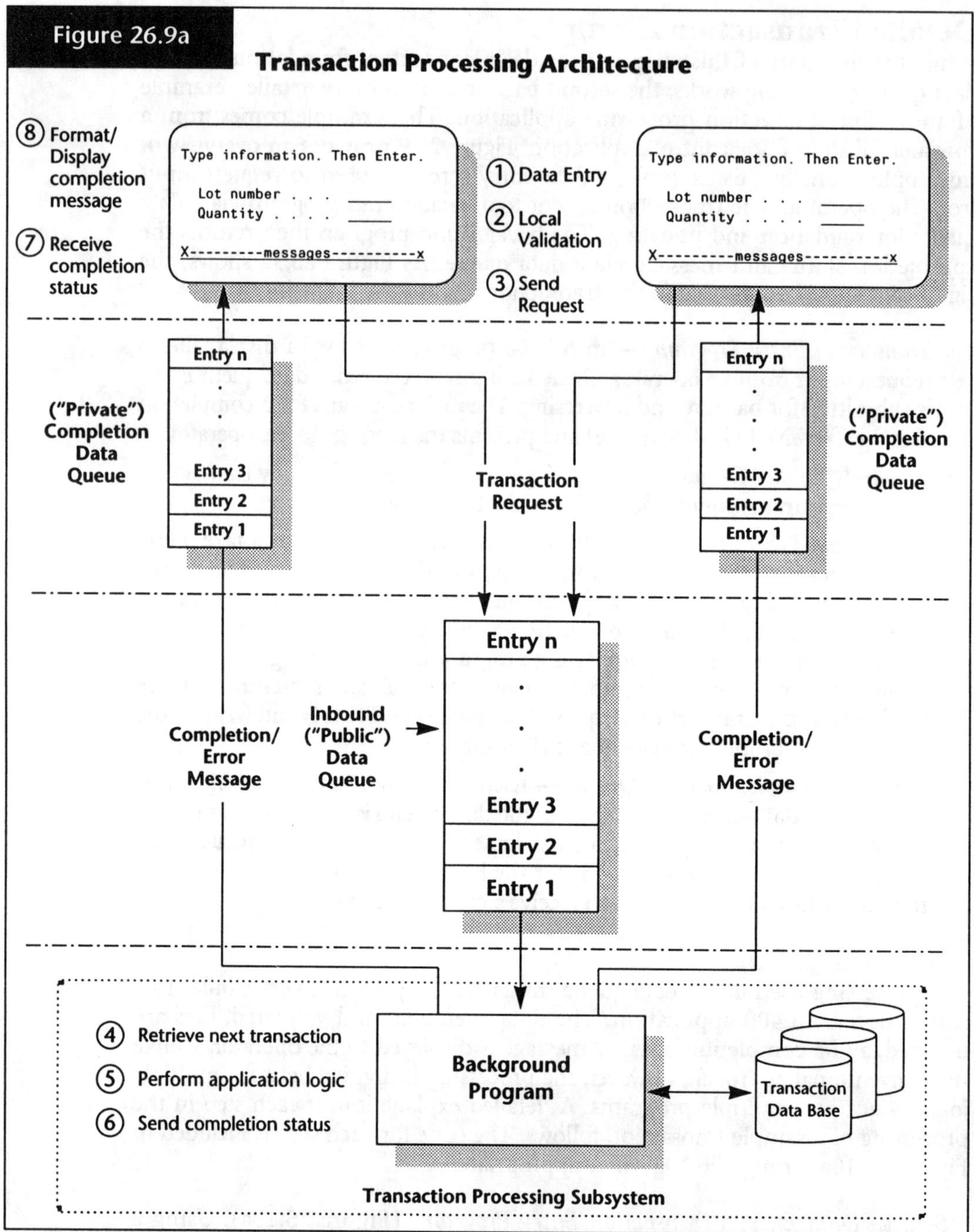

Step 2. *Local Validation (Transaction Entry Program)* (Figure 26.10b). Prior to submitting the transaction request, a certain level of validation is performed. In this example only the most obvious errors are edited (e.g., lot number not

Figure 26.9b

Background Processing Program

```
FLOTMAST UF  E            K         DISK
E                      MSG      1    3 75
I*   TRANSACTION INFORMATION DATA STRUCTURE
I*
IDSTRAN       DS
I                                          1   10 DSDTAQ
I                                         11   20 DSQLIB
I                                         21   30 DSLOT
I                                         31   370DSQTY
I*   TRANSACTION COMPLETION INFORMATION
I*
IDSCOMP       DS
I                                          1    1 DSSTAT
I                                          2   76 DSMSG
I                                         77   80 DSFLD
```

Figure 26.10a

Step (1) — Data Entry

```
C* DISPLAY DATA ENTRY SCREEN
C* AND REQUEST OPERATOR INPUT
C*
C                      EXFMTSCREEN1                 99
C*
C           *INKC      IFEQ *ON
C                      SETON                      LR
C                      RETRN
C                      END
C*
C* CLEAR MESSAGE LINE AND RESET
C* FOR NEXT TRANSACTION
C*
C                      MOVE *BLANKS   WSMSG
C                      MOVE *OFF      *IN
```

entered). While the specific level of validation required will vary between applications, some basic guidelines exist. First, if the editing requires significant or complex logic (logic that otherwise would be performed in a subprogram), leave it to the background program. Second, if the validation requires an open file, it is also best to leave that to the background program. In both cases, this helps control system overhead. Remember that there will be multiple jobs executing the transaction entry program, but only one job executing the background program, which means you can reduce the overall number of file opens, closes, and open data paths. In the conventional approach, all the editing would be contained in a single section of the logic. Dividing the edit logic in the data queue approach avoids the additional overhead of sending and receiving

Figure 26.10b

Step (2) — Local Validation

```
C* PERFORM LOCAL VALIDATION PRIOR
C* TO SUBMITTING TRANSACTION REQUEST
C*
C*   LOT NUMBER IS A REQUIRED ENTRY
C*
C            WSLOT     IFEQ *BLANKS
C                      MOVELMSG,1     WSMSG
C                      END
```

data queue entries to catch the most common errors. In practice, this type of editing can be accomplished using display file keywords.

Step 3. *Send Transaction Request (Transaction Entry Program)* (Figure 26.10c). Once the data entry values have passed local edits, the request is submitted for comprehensive editing and update processing. This is accomplished by copying the transaction-specific values to a data structure, then setting variables common to all transactions. Next, the program QSNDDTAQ is called to add an entry to the inbound transaction data queue. Like adding records to a program-described file, a data structure is used to define each of the subfields contained in the data queue entry. Each subfield used is defined as follows:

DSDTAQ data queue Name is the name of the data queue to be used for receiving completion messages. The name is unique to each session executing the transaction entry program.

DSQLIB data queue Library Name is the name of the library that contains the completion message data queue.

DSLOT Lot Number is the value entered on the display.

DSQTY Lot Quantity is the value entered on the display.

The sequence for sending the transaction request is to clear the completion data queue, add a transaction request entry to the inbound data queue, and then receive the completion status from the completion data queue. It is important to clear the completion data queue before sending the transaction request to ensure that the completion message received is the one associated with this request. It is also necessary to clear the completion data queue because a previous session may have ended abnormally (after the transaction request was sent and before the completion message was retrieved). In this example the completion entry is only used to display an operator message and can therefore be ignored by future transactions. If other processing were dependent on the completion entry, a different approach would be required.

At this point the differences between data queue processing and a conventional approach become more obvious. The conventional approach would be either to call a subprogram or to execute an internal subroutine for this processing.

Figure 26.10c

Step (3) — Send Transaction Request

```
C* COPY TRANSACTION SPECIFIC FIELD VALUES
C* TO THE TRANSACTION DATA STRUCTURE
C*
C                     MOVELWSLOT     DSLOT
C                     Z-ADDWSQTY     DSQTY
C*
C* THE FOLLOWING CODE IS USED TO INITIALIZE
C* FIELD VALUES WHICH ARE COMMON TO ALL
C* TRANSACTIONS AND THEN SEND A TRANSACTION
C* REQUEST BY ADDING AN ENTRY TO THE INBOUND
C* DATA QUEUE.
C*
C* NOTE THAT "TRNCMP01" IS HARD-CODED IN ORDER TO KEEP
C* THIS EXAMPLE SIMPLE.  IN PRACTICE, THIS WOULD BE A
C* VARIABLE AND MUST BE THE NAME OF A DATA QUEUE WHICH
C* IS UNIQUE TO EACH SESSION.
C*
C                     MOVEL'TRNCMP01'DSDTAQ
C                     MOVEL'*LIBL'   DSQLIB
C*
C                     CALL 'QCLRDTAQ'
C                     PARM           DSDTAQ
C                     PARM           DSQLIB
C*
C                     CALL 'QSNDDTAQ'
C                     PARM 'TRNREQ'  WADTAQ 10
C                     PARM '*LIBL'   WAQLIB 10
C                     PARM 37        WALEN   50
C                     PARM           DSTRAN
```

Step 4. *Retrieve Next Transaction (Background Program)* (Figure 26.10d). This processing can be equated to retrieving the next record from a transaction file. In this case, the IBM-supplied program QRCVDTAQ is called to retrieve the next entry from the inbound data queue. Note that the wait time is set to 30 seconds to allow the program to periodically test for a request to end. The entry is retrieved into a data structure so the request is immediately available for processing.

Step 5. *Perform Application Logic (Background Program)* (Figure 26.10e). All the editing and validation are performed at this point, followed by file update processing. The logic is unique to the application.

Step 6. *Send Transaction Completion Status/Message (Background Program)* (Figure 26.10f). Once all the transaction logic has been completed, the result is returned to the requesting program. This is accomplished by returning an entry to the requesting program's private data queue using the program QSNDDTAQ. The name of that data queue was provided as part of the input transaction request. The completion data returned consists of a status code (DSSTAT), an identifier for the field in error (DSFLD), and the message text (DSMSG). The text will be either the completion message or the error message, as appropriate. The use of each data structure subfield is as follows:

Figure 26.10d

Step (4) — Retrieve Next Transaction

```
C* THE FOLLOWING CODE WILL FIRST TEST FOR A
C* REQUEST TO END THIS PROGRAM AND THEN RETRIEVE
C* RETRIEVE THE NEXT AVAILABLE DATA QUEUE ENTRY
C* FROM THE INBOUND data queue. IF AN ENTRY IS NOT
C* AVAILABLE THE PROGRAM WILL WAIT FOR UP TO 30
C* SECONDS FOR AN ENTRY TO BECOME AVAILABLE.
C*
C          WALEN     DOUGT*ZERO
C                    SHTDN                   LR
C*
C          *INLR     IFEQ *ON
C                    RETRN
C                    END
C*
C                    CALL 'QRCVDTAQ'
C                    PARM 'TRNREQ'  WADTAQ 10
C                    PARM '*LIBL'   WAQLIB 10
C                    PARM           WALEN   50
C                    PARM           DSTRAN
C                    PARM 30        WAWAIT  50
C                    END
C*
```

DSSTAT Transaction Status is used to determine the status of the transaction. A value of "P" means the transaction posted (completed successfully). A value of "E" means an error was detected.

DSFLD If an edit error is found, this field contains the identifier for the field in error. This value is used by the transaction entry program to determine where to position the cursor.

DSMSG This is the text of the message to present.

Step 7. *Receive Transaction Completion Status/Message (Transaction Entry Program)* (Figure 26.10g). The last action taken by this program was to send a request for a transaction. The program enters a loop that will be ended only by retrieving an entry from its completion message data queue.

To avoid having the operator think the program is "stuck," a wait time is used on the CALL to QRCVDTAQ. If the wait time expires before an entry becomes available, a message is displayed to keep the operator informed. The operator then has the opportunity to take the appropriate action if the background program is not active. This logic is unique to data queue processing. It also addresses a potential problem created by the need to have a secondary job active in order to continue. While the example shows a very simple solution (tell the operator a problem exists and expect him to resolve it), there are more robust solutions available. For example, logic could be added to start the background job if it is not active.

Figure 26.10e

Step (5) — Perform Application Logic

```
C* THE FOLLOWING PROGRAM CODE WILL FIRST VALIDATE
C* THE LOT NUMBER BY RETRIEVING A RECORD FROM THE
C* LOT MASTER FILE. IF THE RECORD IS FOUND AND THE
C* QUANTITY IS VALID THE RECORD IS UPDATED, OTHERWISE
C* THE FIELD-IN-ERROR VALUE IS UPDATED AND A MESSAGE
C* IS PREPARED TO BE RETURNED.
C*
C          DSLOT     CHAINLOTMAST              90
C          *IN90     IFEQ *ON
C                    MOVEL'LOT '    DSFLD
C                    MOVE 'E'       DSSTAT
C                    MOVELMSG,1     DSMSG
C                    ELSE
C*
C          DSQTY     IFLE *ZERO
C                    MOVEL'QTY '    DSFLD
C                    MOVE 'E'       DSSTAT
C                    MOVELMSG,2     DSMSG
C                    ELSE
C*
C                    Z-ADDDSQTY     LOTQTY
C                    UPDATLOTMASTR
C*
C                    MOVE 'P'       DSSTAT
C                    MOVELMSG,3     DSMSG
C                    END
C                    END
```

Figure 26.10f

Step (6) — Send Completion Status

```
C* ONCE THE TRANSACTION HAS BEEN COMPLETED OR
C* REJECTED THE FOLLOWING CODE IS USED TO SEND
C* THE STATUS BACK TO THE REQUESTING PROGRAM.
C*
C*
C                    CALL 'QSNDDTAQ'
C                    PARM           DSDTAQ
C                    PARM           DSQLIB
C                    PARM 80        WALEN
C                    PARM           DSCOMP

** MSG -- PROGRAM RETURN MESSAGES
Invalid lot number, record not found
New lot quantity must be greater than zero
Lot updated.
```

Step 8. *Format Message for Presentation to Operator.* The final step in the transaction cycle is to present the completion or error status to the operator. This is done by copying the return variables to display file variables and setting on the

Figure 26.10g

Step (7) — Receive Completion Status

```
     C* AFTER THE REQUEST IS SENT A RESPONSE IS RECEIVED BY
     C* RETRIEVING AN ENTRY FROM THE COMPLETION DATA QUEUE.
     C*
     C           WALEN     DOUGT*ZERO
     C                     CALL 'QRCVDTAQ'
     C                     PARM           DSDTAQ
     C                     PARM           DSQLIB
     C                     PARM           WALEN
     C                     PARM           DSCOMP
     C                     PARM 30        WAWAIT  50
     C*
     C* IF TIME-OUT OCCURRED THEN PRESENT DISPLAY TO NOTIFY
     C* OPERATOR A PROBLEM EXISTS.
     C*
     C* NOTE:  DISPLAY FILE MUST HAVE DFRWRT(*NO) SPECIFIED
     C* FOR THIS TO FUNCTION PROPERLY.
     C*
     C           WALEN     IFEQ *ZERO
     C                     WRITESCREEN2
     C                     END
     C                     END
     C*
     C* AFTER RECEIVING THE COMPLETION STATUS
     C* COPY THE MESSAGE TEXT TO THE DISPLAY FILE
     C* AND SET ANY REQUIRED DISPLAY ATTRIBUTE
     C* INDICATORS.
     C*
     C                     MOVELDSMSG     WSMSG
     C*
     C           DSSTAT    IFEQ 'E'
     C           DSFLD     COMP 'LOT '                    50
     C           DSFLD     COMP 'QTY '                    51
     C                     END

  ** MSG -- PROGRAM MESSAGES
  Lot number must be entered
```

appropriate display attribute indicators. The processing then continues back at step one where the execute format operation (EXFMT) is used to present the updated display file.

The single most important point about the overall architecture described in this example is that *all of the information required to complete a transaction is contained within a single data queue entry.* This means all processing required to complete a transaction may be performed without the need to synchronize multiple data queue entries. This does not mean, however, that a transaction must be limited to the size of a single data queue entry. A practical approach to sending a variable volume of data is to include a pointer (key to a work file or name of a private or keyed data queue) in the transaction request.

Considerations for Using Data Queues

As you examine the value of using data queues, your first consideration will be the complexity of this approach, which is new for most of us and generally more complicated than a self-contained RPG program. There are more pieces to manage, which introduces more room for error. However, once development is complete, the ongoing maintenance is significantly reduced, performance is improved, and room for application growth is expanded.

A second consideration that primarily affects the debugging cycle is the lack of visibility into the contents of a data queue. When a file is used for an input source, commands can be used to view or alter the input. Since an entry is automatically removed when it is retrieved, there is no practical approach for performing similar functions with a data queue.

Housekeeping is also required if you use data queues. The size of a data queue should be kept to a minimum for performance purposes. This can require extra program logic to clear or delete and rebuild data queues, plus the additional program logic to initially create the data queues.

Perhaps the single most important consideration is that, in many cases, an application will need to be designed for data queue processing from the beginning. Even though converting an existing program to use data queues should be as simple as dividing the data entry from the edit and update logic, attempting to retrofit an existing system may not be practical. It all depends on the structure of the existing program(s).

Additional information on data queues is available in Chapter 3 of the *CL Programmers Guide* (SC41-8077). Refer to the *PC Support/400 API Reference* manual (SC41-8254) for details on accessing data queues from a PWS.

THE DEVELOPMENT PLATFORM

Chapter 27

Using PDM

by Jeffrey Pisarczyk and Michael Otey

PDM is the AS/400 programmer's best friend

IBM has designed Programming Development Manager (PDM) to help you manage your AS/400 program development environment. PDM provides an interface to the AS/400 operating system and lets you display, browse, duplicate, rename, change or delete libraries, objects, and file members. The PDM interface is both easy to use and powerful. PDM presents you with a list of AS/400 objects and lets you perform actions on those objects by selecting from the list of available options or command keys. While PDM provides a number of built-in shortcuts, you can also customize PDM to meet your needs. In this chapter, we will cover the basics of using PDM as well as show you how to take advantage of some of the advanced features of the PDM environment.

PDM's "Work with" Options

All PDM "work with" functions (i.e., work with libraries, objects, and members) look and operate similarly to each other (see Figure 27.1 for the "Work with Libraries Using PDM" panel). At the top of the panel, the list type is indicated (i.e., library, object, or member, depending on whether you are working with libraries, objects, or members); *LIBL indicates you are working with the list of libraries in your current job library list. If you are working with list types *ALL or *ALLUSR, you can change this parameter to create a new list using the F17 (subset) Function key without dropping back to the main PDM menu. (Press the F24 Function key to see what other function keys are available, including F17.) PDM's F17 function allows you to specify a subset of objects that PDM displays for you (see Figure 27.2 for a subset library list).

Immediately below the list-type parameter appears the option legend — the operations you can perform on the items on the list. Each option has a numeric identifier that identifies an action. PDM is not limited to these predefined options. In addition to the IBM-supplied options, PDM allows user-defined

Figure 27.1

Work with Libraries Using PDM (WRKLIBPDM)

```
                      Work with Libraries Using PDM

List type . . . . . . .    *LIBL_____

Type options, press Enter.
  2=Change                    3=Copy        5=Display        7=Rename
  8=Display description       9=Save        10=Restore       12=Work with ...

Opt  Library     Type        Text
__   QSYS        *PROD-SYS   System Library
__   QHLPSYS     *PROD-SYS
__   QUSRSYS     *PROD-SYS
__   QPDA        *PROD-PRD
__   GLLIB       *PROD-USR   General Ledger
__   GLLIB15     *TEST-USR   General Ledger v1.5
__   QTEMP       *TEST-USR
__   QIWS        *PROD-USR
__   QGDDM       *PROD-USR
                                                                   More...
Parameters or command
===> ________________________________________________________________________
F3=Exit          F4=Prompt               F5=Refresh           F6=Add to list
F9=Retrieve      F10=Command entry       F23=More options     F24=More keys
```

Figure 27.2

Subset Library List

```
                   Subset Library List

Type choices, press Enter.

  Library . . . . . . .    *ALL______    *ALL, name, *generic*

  Library type . . . . .   *ALL______    *ALL, *PROD, *TEST

  Text . . . . . . . . .   *ALL___________________________________________





F3=Exit         F5=Refresh          F12=Cancel
```

options (user-defined options are covered in detail in Chapter 29). Below the option definitions is PDM's item list area. Here, PDM presents items in a single-column, 9- or 17-line (full-screen mode) list, giving you a long description of each item and fewer items per screen than POP. The bottom of the panel displays an

Figure 27.3

PDM Main Menu

```
                 AS/400 Programming Development Manager (PDM)

Select one of the following:

     1. Work with libraries
     2. Work with objects
     3. Work with members

     9. Work with user-defined options




Selection or command
===> ________________________________________________________________

F3=Exit        F4=Prompt        F9=Retrieve        F10=Command entry
F12=Cancel     F18=Change defaults
```

optional function-key legend. After you've mastered the option and function-key definitions, you can switch to full-screen mode, which trades the option and function-key legends for more space in which to display eight additional item lines.

Running PDM

You can run PDM from its own application menu, or you can call specific portions directly from a command prompt. The easiest way to familiarize yourself with PDM is to access it through the menu interface by running the STRPDM command. The PDM main menu (Figure 27.3) offers you four different options: work with libraries (WRKLIBPDM), work with objects within a library (WRKOBJPDM), work with members within a file (WRKMBRPDM), and work with user-defined options.

WRKLIBPDM (Figure 27.1) is different from both WRKOBJPDM and WRKMBRPDM because it serves a dual purpose: first, to work on a list of libraries and second, to work on a library list. A list of libraries is a sequential list of all libraries on your system or a subset of those libraries. Some of the list options and function keys differ, depending on the list type you choose. In contrast, a library list is an OS/400 job attribute that specifies the libraries to search whenever a program tries to find an object. When a program requests an object, OS/400 first determines the object type by usage and then looks for the object name of that type, searching each library in the library list from top to bottom. With library lists, you do not have to qualify each object name with its corresponding library name.

WRKOBJPDM (Figure 27.4) has two additional options not found in WRKLIBPDM or WRKMBRPDM and one option it shares with WRKMBRPDM. Option "15=Copy file" appears only in WRKOBJPDM and is valid for objects

Figure 27.4

Work with Objects Using PDM (WRKOBJPDM)

```
                         Work with Objects Using PDM

Library . . . . .   QUSRSYS___        Position to . . . . . . . .   _____
                                      Position to type  . . . . .   _____

Type options, press Enter.
  2=Change        3=Copy         4=Delete       5=Display       7=Rename
  8=Display description          9=Save         10=Restore      11=Move ...

Opt  Object       Type           Attribute      Text
__   QAALERT      *FILE          PF-DTA         Data base file for alerts processing
__   QAALHLSN     *FILE          LF             Logical file for alerts processing
__   QAALRCLC     *FILE          LF             Logical file for alerts processing
__   QAALRSCN     *FILE          LF             Logical file for alerts processing
__   QAALRSCT     *FILE          LF             Logical file for alerts processing
__   QAALSOC      *FILE          PF-DTA         Data base file for SOC processing
__   QAEABKMT     *FILE          PF-DTA         System Delivered Education Bookmark F
__   QAEACRSI     *FILE          PF-DTA         System Delivered Education Course Ind
                                                                             More...
Parameters or command
===> ____________________________________________________________________________
F3=Exit             F4=Prompt                F5=Refresh              F6=Create
F9=Retrieve         F10=Command entry        F23=More options        F24=More keys
```

of type *FILE. Option "16=Run" also appears only in WRKOBJPDM and is valid for object types *CMD, *PGM, and *QRYDFN. Option "18=Change using DFU" appears in both WRKOBJPDM and WRKMBRPDM. It is valid for object type *FILE with attributes of PF-DTA, LF, and DDMF, and for DFU programs (object type of *PGM, attribute of DFU).

PDM's WRKMBRPDM command is used to manipulate source and procedure members. WRKMBRPDM (Figure 27.5) lets you work with members of two physical file types: data physical files (object type *FILE with PF-DTA attribute) and source physical files (object type *FILE with PF-SRC attribute). Some of the PDM options available differ, depending on the type of physical file, data or source, with which you are working. Option 18 (change with DFU), which is available with data physical files, is not a valid option with source physical files. The edit, print, compile, and change-with-SDA options available when working with source physical files are not valid options when working with a data physical file.

Advanced Features

You will like the integrated user-defined options built into PDM. PDM has a 2-byte option field and supplies, at last count, 20 substitution parameter types. When executed, the user-created command string is parsed, and these substitution parameters are replaced with their corresponding values. In the example in Figure 27.6, user option SD prompts the STRDBRDR (Start Database Reader) command. As user option SD is executed, &L is replaced with the library name

Figure 27.5

Work with Members Using PDM (WRKMBRPDM)

```
                         Work with Members Using PDM

File . . . . . .   QCLSRC____
  Library . . . .  WORKLIB___             Position to . . . . .   __________

Type options, press Enter.
  2=Edit          3=Copy        4=Delete        5=Display       6=Print
  7=Rename        8=Display description         9=Save          13=Change text ...

Opt  Member       Type          Text
__   AP0010C      CLP_______    Audit report on daily entries__________________
__   ATTNPGM      CLP_______    ATTN pgm for group jobs________________________
__   CAMON        CLP_______    message monitor________________________________
__   CHGPRTFC     CLP_______    Find/then change print files on System_________
__   CL0010C      CLP_______    Chg security on selected files_________________
__   CLCMPSRC     CLP_______    check source last change dates in version libs____
__   COMPC        CLP_______    Compare_2_files_up_to_1024_in_length___________
__   CONFIG       CLP_______    _______________________________________________
                                                                        More...
Parameters or command
===> ___________________________________________________________________________
F3=Exit           F4=Prompt                 F5=Refresh            F6=Create
F9=Retrieve       F10=Command entry         F23=More options      F24=More keys
```

Figure 27.6

Example User-Defined PDM Option

```
?STRDBRDR FILE(&L/&F) MBR(&N) MSGQ(*REQUESTER)
```

containing the member, &F is replaced with the file name containing the member, and &N is replaced with the selected item name (for more information about the user-defined options in PDM, read Chapter 28, "Customizing PDM").

Another useful feature of PDM is its ability to perform text searches from the PDM list panel. For instance, Figure 27.7 shows the use of the search option from the WRKOBJPDM panel. Pressing F23 (More Options) on the initial WRKOBJPDM display brings up several additional options which includes option "25=Find String...". Entering a 25 in the option field before the selected object will cause the panel shown in Figure 27.8 to be displayed. This panel allows you to specify the search parameters. In this case, the string "CALL PGMA" will be searched for in all members of the QCLSRC file in library TESTLIB.

Using PDM in conjunction with SEU will also help speed you through the edit/compile/list cycle by providing a central work environment. Using options 2 and 14 of the WRKMBRPDM panel allow you to invoke the editor and the compiler from the PDM member list. Option 2 performs a STRSEU command

Figure 27.7

Use of Search Option from WRKOBJPDM Panel

```
                         Work with Objects Using PDM

 Library . . . . .   TESTLIB___        Position to . . . . . . . .   __________
                                       Position to type  . . . . .   __________

 Type options, press Enter.
   12=Work with              13=Change text          15=Copy file
   16=Run                    18=Change using DFU     25=Find string ...

 Opt  Object       Type         Attribute    Text
 25   QCLSRC       *FILE        PF-SRC       Default source data base file for CL
 __   QCMDSRC      *FILE        PF-SRC       Default source data base file for cmd
 __   QDDSSRC      *FILE        PF-SRC       Default source data base file for DDS
 __   TALLYA       *FILE        PF-DTA       Tally Header File
 __   TALLYB       *FILE        PF-DTA       Tally Detail File
 __   CVTBIN2      *CMD                      Command for to convert 2 binary
 __   RTVSBSJOB    *CMD                      Retreive the Subsystem Jobs

                                                                          Bottom
Parameters or command
===> ___________________________________________________________________________
F3=Exit          F4=Prompt              F5=Refresh             F6=Create
F9=Retrieve      F10=Command entry      F23=More options       F24=More keys
```

Figure 27.8

PDM Find String Panel

```
                              Find String

Type choices, press Enter.

  Find . . . . . . . . . . . . . .   CALL PGMA______________________________
    From column number . . . . . .   1______    1 - *RCDLEN
    To column number . . . . . . .   *RCDLEN    1 - *RCDLEN
    Kind of match  . . . . . . . .   2          1=Same case, 2=Ignore case

  Option . . . . . . . . . . . . .   5____      *NONE, Valid option
    Prompt . . . . . . . . . . . .   N          Y=Yes, N=No
  Print list . . . . . . . . . . .   N          Y=Yes, N=No
  Print records  . . . . . . . . .   N          Y=Yes, N=No
    Number to find . . . . . . . .   *ALL_      *ALL, number
    Print format . . . . . . . . .   *CHAR__    *CHAR, *HEX, *ALTHEX
    Mark record  . . . . . . . . .   Y          Y=Yes, N=No
    Record overflow  . . . . . . .   1          1=Fold, 2=Truncate
  Find string in batch . . . . . .   N          Y=Yes, N=No
  Parameters . . . . . . . . . . .   __________________________________________

F3=Exit              F5=Refresh           F12=Cancel          F16=User options
F18=Change defaults
```

for the selected member while option 14 performs the appropriate CRTxxxPGM command. (The create command that is started will vary with the type. For example, if the member type is RPG, then the CRTRPGPGM command will be run.) After selecting option 2 to start SEU, you will find several additional features to aid you in your program development cycle. The powerful, split-screen browse ability of SEU means you no longer suffer excessive neck strain from compile listings on your right, SEU on your left, and the "what's that error, find that line" eyeball aerobics. Pressing F15 during your SEU editing session will display the panel shown in Figure 27.9. Selecting option "2=Spool File" will put SEU in split-screen mode (with your source member at the top of your screen and the compile listing on the bottom). You can then scan for errors by entering "F *ERR" on the SEU command line and search through the spooled compile. In addition, you benefit when SEU/400 finds a compile error and displays the error message at the bottom of the panel. You move the cursor down to the message and press the Help key, and second-level text for the error message appears. SEU/400 lets you copy lines of code from the spooled-file split screen back into the source member. After the code has been modified, you can exit SEU and compile the member using option 14 on the WRKMBRPDM panel. As you can see, the combination of PDM and SEU provide a very functional work environment. PDM allows you to launch the compiler and the editor from the member list panel while SEU allows you to change the source member and diagnose the compiler listing.

Figure 27.9

SEU Browse/Copy Panel

```
                         Browse/Copy Options

Type choices, press Enter.

  Selection . . . . . . . . . . .   2              1=Member
                                                   2=Spool file
                                                   3=Output queue
  Copy all records  . . . . . . .   N              Y=Yes, N=No
  Browse/copy member  . . . . . .   RTVSBSJOBC     Name, F4 for list
    File  . . . . . . . . . . . .     QCLSRC____   Name, F4 for list
      Library . . . . . . . . . .       TESTLIB___ Name, *CURLIB, *LIBL

  Browse/copy spool file  . . . .   RTVSBSJOBC     Name, F4 for list
    Job . . . . . . . . . . . . .     RTVSBSJOBC   Name
      User  . . . . . . . . . . .       MIKEO_____ Name, F4 for list
      Job number  . . . . . . . .       *LAST_     Number, *LAST
    Spool number  . . . . . . . .     *LAST        Number, *LAST, *ONLY

  Display output queue  . . . . .   QPRINT____     Name, *ALL
    Library . . . . . . . . . . .     *LIBL_____   Name, *CURLIB, *LIBL

F3=Exit        F4=Prompt          F5=Refresh        F12=Cancel
F13=Change session defaults       F14=Find/Change options
```

Other useful PDM features include the ability to automatically duplicate an option for the entire PDM list. Using "F13=Repeat", PDM will save you from the tedious manual keying that would otherwise be required to perform an option on multiple members. To display the member's date instead of its type, you can press "F14=Display date" and the last change date of the members will be displayed instead of the member's type. To sort the PDM list based on the date, press "F15=Sort date" and the list will be sorted from the last changed member to the first.

PDM is the AS/400 programmer's best friend. It provides a central development environment plus many useful tools to aid in the manipulation of AS/400 libraries, files, and members. While this chapter serves to introduce some of the key features of PDM, its many features go far beyond this coverage. The best way to learn about PDM is through exploration.

Chapter 28

Customizing PDM

by Carol-Ann Doucher

Enhance and extend PDM by using PDM defaults and creating your own options

The AS/400 Programming Development Manager (PDM) provides programmer tools to facilitate application development and object management. PDM, which is available in IBM's Application Development Tools licensed program, has features that make it easy to work with objects. These features include lists of objects you can work with to simplify development and maintenance; an interface to other AS/400 application development tools, such as the Source Entry Utility (SEU), the Screen Design Aid (SDA), the Data File Utility (DFU); and options for object manipulation, such as editing and compiling a source member and executing a program. But PDM's most exciting feature is that you can enhance and extend PDM functions to suit your own needs by customizing its defaults and options.

PDM and Application Development

PDM makes application development easy by displaying lists of libraries, objects, and members. (Figure 28.1 shows a sample list display.) These lists let you look up the name of a member, for example, and request an operation on the member directly from the PDM screen. You need not know the command name or parameter keywords. On the basis of the object or member type, PDM constructs the proper command and fills in the necessary parameters, saving you the time you would spend looking up and typing parameters. When you display a list of members, you can place the cursor next to a member and choose an option (e.g., edit). PDM lets you edit the member and then returns you to the PDM screen so you can choose another option. When you return to the PDM screen, the cursor location is unchanged, so you can type a different option for the same member. You also can type options for more than one member at a time.

Figure 28.1

Sample List-Display Panel

```
                     Work with Members Using PDM
File  . . . . . .   SRCFILE                 Position to . . . . .
  Library . . . .   MAPLIB

Type options, press Enter.
  2=Edit         3=Copy        4=Delete         5=Display        6=Print
  7=Rename       8=Display description          9=Save           13=Change text

Opt  Member      Type         Text
     ALBMAP      RPG          Map of Alberta
     ALLPROV     CLP          Map of all provinces
     BCMAP       RPG          Map of British Columbia
     MANMAP      RPG          Map of Manitoba
     MAPMENU     MNU          Map Menu
     MAPPRT      PRTF         Printer file for all maps
     MAPSCRNS    DSPF
     NBMAP       RPG          Map of New Brunswick
                                                                     More...
Parameters or command
===>
F3=Exit          F4=Prompt           F5=Refresh          F6=Create
F9=Retrieve      F12=Previous        F23=More options    F24=More keys
```

The PDM list options also let you access AS/400 application development tools. For example, you can access SDA by typing 17 (Option 17 means Change Using SDA) in the option field beside a source member with display file data description specifications (DDS) or SDA menu source. Then, according to member type (i.e., DSPF or MNU), PDM calls the appropriate function in SDA to change the source. You can access DFU by typing Option 18 (Change Using DFU) beside a data physical file. PDM then calls DFU to create a temporary program to let you change your file.

You might have thousands of members in a file; displaying them all would be time consuming and would result in a long, hard-to-use list. Instead, you can view part of a list by using the PDM subset feature. (Figure 28.2 shows a subset screen.) You can select subsets based on item type (i.e., library, object, or member). Another screen then lets you select smaller subsets based on combinations of specific characters in the library, object, or member name. For example, you can show all names starting with the characters ABC, all names ending with ABC, all names including ABC in any position, or all names starting with A and ending with B. You also can choose a subset based on member type (e.g., RPG, COBOL, PL/I), the date the member was last changed, or the descriptive text.

PDM efficiently renames and copies, as well. When you select several members to rename, PDM groups them on one screen (Figure 28.3). PDM lists the selected members in two columns. The first column lists the selected members' current names. The second column is for the new names, but the current names appear in this column as the default value until you type over them to rename

Figure 28.2

Subset Panel

```
                         Subset Member List
Type choices, press Enter.

  Member . . . . . . .   *MAP          *ALL, generic*, name

  Member type  . . . .   RPG           *ALL, *BLANK, type

  From date  . . . . .   01/01/00      Earliest date to include

  To date  . . . . . .   12/31/99      Latest date to include

  Text . . . . . . . .   *ALL

F3=Exit  F5=Refresh     F12=Previous
```

Figure 28.3

Rename Panel

```
              Rename Members
     File . . . . . . . :    SRCFILE
       Library . . . . . :     MAPLIB

To rename member, type New Name, press Enter.

Member         New Name                    Member         New Name
ALABAMA        ALABAMA                     INDIANA        INDIANA
ALASKA         ALASKA                      IOWA           IOWA
ARIZONA        ARIZONA                     KANSAS         KANSAS
ARKANSAS       ARKANSAS                    KENTUCKY       KENTUCKY
CALIFORNIA     CALIFORNIA                  LOUISIANA      LOUISIANA
COLORADO       COLORADO                    MAINE          MAINE
CONNECTICT     CONNECTICT                  MARYLAND       MARYLAND
DELAWARE       DELAWARE                    MASS           MASS
FLORIDA        FLORIDA                     MICHIGAN       MICHIGAN
GEORGIA        GEORGIA                     MINNESOTA      MINNESOTA
HAWAII         HAWAII                      MISSISSIPP     MISSISSIPP
IDAHO          IDAHO                       MISSOURI       MISSOURI
ILLINOIS       ILLINOIS                    MONTANA        MONTANA
                                                                   More...
F3=Exit    F5=Refresh     F12=Previous     F19=Submit to batcha
```

the members. Thus, if you want to change only one character to rename a member, you need not retype the entire name. The same procedure applies to copying: PDM displays all members selected for copying. You can copy to the same file and library the members currently are in simply by giving the members new names. You also can copy all chosen members to a different file and library by typing the file and library names once. PDM copies all the members selected.

Changing PDM Defaults

PDM's development environment contains just the start of what you can do with PDM. You can enhance and tailor the PDM environment to your own needs by using the change-defaults function and creating your own options to use on the lists PDM displays.

Function key F18 (Change Defaults) is available from many PDM screens. When you press F18, PDM shows the change-defaults screen (Figure 28.4), from which you can alter the way PDM compiles or runs your programs (e.g., in batch or interactively), change the look of PDM screens, and tell PDM which of your personal options to use (e.g., call a commonly used command or display a personalized menu).

Compile defaults: The first five fields on the change-defaults screen let you change your compile environment when using Option 14 (Compile on the Work with Members Using PDM screen). The changes you can make include choosing the library where the objects will be created when the compile is complete. You also can indicate whether the compile is in batch or interactive. You can also tell PDM what to do when it begins a compile and finds that the object to be created already exists. You can let PDM automatically replace the object without informing you first, or you can have PDM show a warning screen that lets you decide whether to replace the existing object or cancel the compile.

Screen defaults: Another use for the change-defaults display is to tailor PDM screens. The display's last field lets you specify full-screen mode. Typing Y (for Yes) in this field causes all PDM list screens to list additional libraries, objects, and members. Because PDM makes screen space for the additional list items by

Figure 28.4

Change Defaults Panel

```
                              Change Defaults
Type choices, press Enter.

Object library . . . . . . .  *SRCLIB       *CURLIB, *SRCLIB, name
Replace object . . . . . . .  N             Y=Yes, N=No

Compile in batch . . . . . .  Y             Y=Yes, N=No
Run in batch . . . . . . . .  Y             Y=Yes, N=No
Job description  . . . . . .  QBATCH        Name, *USRPRF
  Library  . . . . . . . . .  *LIBL         *CURLIB, *LIBL, name

Change type and text . . . .  Y             Y=Yes, N=No

Option File  . . . . . . . .  QAUOOPT       Name
  Library  . . . . . . . . .  QGPL          *CURLIB, *LIBL, name
Member . . . . . . . . . . .  QAUOOPT       Name

Full screen mode . . . . . .  N             Y=Yes, N=No


F3=Exit   F5=Refresh   F12=Previous
```

removing instruction lines, the list of available options, and the list of available function keys, you should choose this screen only when you know the PDM options and function keys. By using the Help key, you can get general help text that explains how to return to the usual list screen.

The Work with Members Using PDM screen lets you input the member type and descriptive text directly into the list area. This screen (shown in Figure 28.1) is convenient when you change the type and text frequently, but not when you want to type options in the list: The cursor jumps to the type field instead of to the next option field. You can use the Change Type and Text field on the Change Defaults screen to solve this problem. If you change this field to N (for No), PDM removes the input fields for the type and text and makes typing options in the member list easy.

User options: Finally, the change-defaults display has fields in which you can type the name of the file that contains your personal PDM list options. PDM comes with an option file called QAUOOPT in QGPL. To create your own options file, use PDM to copy QAUOOPT. List the objects starting with QAUO* in library QGPL, and then type Option 3 (Copy) beside the QAUOOPT file. This process copies the file to your own library. After you finish, change the name of your option file and library on the Change Defaults screen. Now you have your own option file, to which you can add useful options.

Creating Your Own PDM List Options

There are many reasons for having your own options that work on the PDM list displays. For example, you might want an option to call a system command you use frequently, or you might want to perform on a specific list item an action not available through PDM. In some cases, you might want to call the same commands the PDM options call, but set some parameters differently. You might need options to create new objects, libraries, or members to add to your lists. Or you might want an option to run your own applications or to display a menu you have created.

Abbreviated commands: User-defined options in PDM are handy for executing commonly used system commands. Without PDM, many programmers create short forms of IBM commands by creating a CL program to execute the IBM command and then creating a short, personally meaningful command to call the CL program. PDM makes abbreviating a command much easier than the old method. From any PDM list screen, you can press F16 (User Options) or take Option 9 to display a list of all options in your personal file (specified on the Change Defaults display). To create a new option, just press F6 (Create). Then you can type in a two-character option code and a command to be executed when you use the option code on a PDM list.

For example, the screen in Figure 28.5 shows the option and command you type to create an option to display your messages. After you create this option, each time you type DM in the Opt column of any PDM list, PDM executes the DSPMSG (Display Messages) command. It is faster to type the option in the list, where the cursor usually is, than to move the cursor to the command line and type the entire command.

Figure 28.5

Sample Option and Command for Displaying Messages

```
                    Create User-Defined Option

Type option and command, press Enter.
  Option . . . . . . . . .   DM    Option to create

  Command . . . . . . . . .  DSPMSG


F3=Exit    F4=Prompt    F12=Previous
```

The screen in Figure 28.6 shows other examples of abbreviated command options. Note that you can include comments as part of the command.

Create options with substitution variables: You can use your abbreviated command options on any list item. You can type your options anywhere in the list's Opt column, and they always behave the same way. You can create options that you then can type next to a particular item on the list to perform an operation on that item.

For example, let's look at the PDM command to edit the authority of objects in the list. Figure 28.7 shows the PDM EA option that's used to edit an object authority. The command to edit an object's authority is EDTOBJAUT, and the required parameters are the object name and the object type. You convey the parameters to the command by using the appropriate PDM substitution variables, which consist of an ampersand (&) followed by a single character. PDM defines these substitution variables. (See Figure 28.8 for a complete list of PDM substitution variables and their meanings.) Before executing the command, PDM replaces all the substitution variables with the correct information for the object you want to edit.

A word of warning: PDM always considers an ampersand as denoting a substitution variable. If you follow an ampersand with any character other than a valid substitution-variable character (e.g., N, T, L, O), the resulting combination is not a valid substitution variable, and you get an error message. Thus, you cannot use ampersands in PDM except as substitution variables.

In the example in Figure 28.7, PDM replaces substitution variable &L with the name of the library containing the object (the library displayed). PDM replaces the &N parameter with the name of the list item; in this case, because an object list is displayed, PDM replaces &N with the name of the object beside which you typed the EA option. Finally, the &T parameter picks up the object type for the object beside which you typed the EA option. Many other substitution parameters are available in PDM, including object attribute, member date, descriptive text, and some of the defaults on the Change Defaults display. For a detailed description of defaults, press Help on the command field when you create a user-defined option.

When developing applications, programmers often edit a member, compile the member, and then run the program to test the changes. Using PDM, you edit and

Figure 28.6

Sample Short-Form Command Options

```
Option  . . . . .   DM
Command . . . . .   DSPMSG
```

Figure 28.7

Sample Option and Command for Editing Object Authority

```
                          Work with User-Defined Objects

File  . . . . . .   QAUOOPT                 Member . . . . .
  Library . . . .     QGPL

Type options, press Enter.
  2=Change          4=Delete          5=Display

Opt  Option         Command
     EA             EDTOBJAUT OBJ(&L/&N) OBJTYPE(&T)




                                                                      More...
Parameters or command
===>
F3=Exit             F4=Prompt              F5=Refresh          F6=Create
F9=Retrieve         F10=Command Entry                          F24=More keys
```

compile from a member list, but you run the program from an object list. An easy alternative is to create your own option to run a program from the member list. Figure 28.9 shows such an option.

You can replace the &O substitution variable with the name of the object library from the Change Defaults display. If you want the object created in the same library the member is in, use &L as the substitution variable.

PDM replaces the &N variable with the name of the member beside which you typed the C option. So the created object's name is the same as the source member's. If you give a program a name different from the member's, you must type the actual name in place of &N (e.g., CALL LIBAA/PGMBB). Or you can use a concatenated name: If the member is AAA, and the program is AAAPGM, the command could be CALL &O/&NPGM.

Change parameters: In some situations, PDM supplies a command but does not provide the parameters you need. In this case, you could use the PDM option, press F4 (Prompt) to show the command's prompt screen, and then fill in the desired parameters. But you must follow this procedure every time you use the PDM option. Instead, you can create your own options to execute the same commands as PDM, but permanently set your own parameters.

Figure 28.8

PDM Substitution Variables

Parm	Meaning	Description
&A	Object attribute	If you are working with objects, &A is replaced by the object attribute from the list. If you are working with libraries or members, &A is replaced by *NULL.
&B	List type	If you are working with a library list (*LIBL,*USRLIBL), &B is replaced by X. If you are working with a list of libraries (*ALL,*ALLUSR), &B is replaced by L. If you are working with a list of objects, &B is replaced by O. If you are working with a list of members, &B is replaced by M.
&C	Option	&C is replaced by the user-defined option code.
&D	Member change date	If you are working with members, &D is replaced by the date the member was last changed. The value will be in the configured format just as it appears if the date is displayed on the list. Otherwise, &D is replaced by *NULL. You may need to use this variable in single quotation marks (for example, '&D') because the date may contain a slash (/), which is used as an operator.
&E	Run in batch	&E is replaced by *YES if Y is specified in the "Run in Batch" prompt on the PDM defaults. If N is specified, &E will be *NO.
&F	File name	If you are working with members, &F is replaced by the name of the file that contains these members. Otherwise, &F is replaced by *NULL.
&G	Job description library	&G is replaced by the job description library from the PDM defaults screen.
&H	Job description name	&H is replaced by the job description name from the PDM defaults screen.
&J	Job description	&J is replaced by the job description value from the Change Defaults display in the format library/job description. The job description is qualified by the library name.
&L	Library name	If you are woking with libraries, &L is replaced by QSYS. If you are working with objects or members, &L is replaced by the name of the library that contains these objects or members.
&N	Item name	&N is replaced by the name of the item in the list beside which the option was typed.
&O	Object	&O is replaced by the object library from the Change Defaults display.

Figure 28.8 Continued

Figure 28.8

PDM Substitution Variables *Continued*

Parm	Meaning	Description
&P	Compile in batch	&P is replaced by *YES if Y is selected for the "Compile in Batch" prompt on the PDM defaults display. If N is selected, &P will be *NO.
&R	Replace object	&R will be replaced by *YES if Y is entered in the "Replace object" prompt on the PDM defaults display. If N is specified &R will be *NO.
&S	Item type without '*'	If you are working with libraries, &S is replaced by LIB. If you are working with objects, &S is replaced by the object type without the asterisk (*). If you are working with members, &S is replaced by the member type as it appears in the list.
&T	Item type with '*'	If you are working with libraries, &T is replaced by *LIB. If you are working with objects or members, &T is replaced by the object or member type as it appears in the list.
&U	User defined options file	&U is replaced by the name of the user defined options file specified in the PDM defaults.
&V	User defined options library	&V is replaced by the name of the user defined options file library specified in the PDM defaults display.
&W	User defined options member	&W is replaced by the name of the user defined options file member specified in the PDM defaults display.
&X	Item text	&X is replaced by the text (in single quotation marks) of the item beside which the option was typed.

Figure 28.9

Option to Run a Program from a Member List

```
Option . . . . .   C
Command  . . . .   CALL &O/&N
```

Suppose you follow a convention that all your program objects have descriptive text that indicates the source file containing the program source. You can comply with such a convention when you use PDM by creating your own option to set this text when you compile a member. Figure 28.10 shows how to create such an option.

PDM fills in the substitution parameters for the particular member beside which you type this option. PGM(&O/&N) creates a program in the object library from the change-defaults display and gives the program the same name as the source member. SRCFILE(&L/&F) is the name of the library and file

Figure 28.10

Option for Descriptive Text When Compiling

```
Option . . . . .   RP
Command . . . . .  CRTRPGPGM PGM(&O/&N)
                            SRCFILE(&L/&F)
                            SRCMBR(&N)
                            TEXT('Source file is &F')
```

containing the member to be compiled. SCRMBR(&N) picks up the name of the member in the list next to which you typed the RP option. The TEXT parameter contains the &F substitution variable, so the name of the source file for the member becomes part of the text.

When PDM expands this command, it may look like this:

```
CRTRPGPGM
     PGM(OBJLIB/PGMAA)                                    +
     SRCFILE(LIBYY/FILEXX)                                +
     SRCMBR(PGMAA)                                        +
     TEXT('Source file is                                 +
     FILEXX')
```

You can make this command more generic so it applies to compilers other than RPG:

```
Command: CRT&TPGM PGM(&O/&N)
```

You just change the command name from CRTRPGPGM to CRT&TPGM, but keep the same parameters as in the previous example. PDM replaces the &T parameter with the member type from the list. When the member type is CBL (for Cobol), the command becomes CRTCBLPGM. When the member type is PLI, the command becomes CRTPLIPGM. The only member type that does not work is CLP, because the command is CRTCLPGM, not CRTCLPPGM.

You can create the same kind of option for compiling members into files rather than programs with the following command:

```
Command:  CRT&T FILE(&O/&N)                              +
               SRCFILE(&L/&F)                            +
               SRCMBR(&N)
```

When the member type is DSPF, the command becomes CRTDSPF. When the member type is PRTF, the command becomes CRTPRTF.

Creating objects to add to your list: With user-defined options, you also can create new libraries, objects, and members. For example, you can create an option to create a DFU program.

```
Option:  DF
Command:  STRDFU OPTION(2)
```

When you type Option DF on a list screen, PDM calls DFU to create a DFU program. The displayed screen shows the name of the last DFU program you created, so you can change the name as you desire.

When you display a list of members in a source physical file using PDM, the F6 (Create) key creates a new member by calling SEU. If you want to use SDA instead of SEU, you can create the following option:

```
Option:   SC
Command:   STRSDA OPTION(1)
             SRCFILE(&L/&F)
               ??SRCMBR()
```

This option calls SDA to design a new screen. You type the option on a PDM member list so PDM can fill in the &L and &F parameters with the library and file name where you want the member created. Because you have not specified the new member's name, the command contains two question marks in front of the SRCMBR parameter. When you type the SC option, PDM shows a prompt screen with only the SRCMBR parameter. You then type the new member's name and go into SDA to design the new screen.

You can change the command slightly to design a menu instead of a screen:

```
Option:   MN
Command:   STRSDA OPTION(2)
               ??SRCMBR()
```

You do not need the SRCFILE parameter because the AS/400 keeps all menu source in QMENUSRC, which SDA creates.

Call programs and menus: Finally, you can call programs and display menus with user-defined options. By calling CL programs, you greatly expand user-defined options. One option can execute several commands if the option runs a CL program that then executes the commands. For example, you can create an option to edit, compile, and then run a program:

```
Option:   ER
Command:   CALL LIBYY/EDITRUN
```

The CL program EDITRUN calls SEU to edit, calls the correct compiler, and finally issues the CALL command to run the program.

You should check the list of substitution variables available through PDM. You can use these variables to pass parameters to your CL program. One useful substitution variable is &B for the list type. PDM replaces &B with one of four characters (i.e., X for a library search list, L for a library, O for an object, M for a member), depending on which type list you are working from. Thus, you can have a CL program that calls different commands depending on the kind of list you are using.

You also can have an option to display your own menus:

```
Option:   XX
Command:   GO LIBYY/MENUXX
```

You use the MN option to call SDA. Then you can create option XX to display the menu. The menu can include all the commands you execute frequently. Instead of creating one user-defined option for each command, you can call the individual commands by selecting an option from the menu.

PDM is a step toward integrating SEU, SDA, DFU, and advanced printer functions in one application development environment on the AS/400. The creative possibilities PDM offers let you adapt or extend your environment to suit your needs. Because of its flexibility, PDM helps you manage application development and enhance your productivity. The user-defined options discussed here are only the beginning — the possibilities for new ideas are endless.

Chapter 29

CL Programming Techniques

by Wayne Madden

Master a few classic techniques to raise your CL programming to an art form

Since the inception of CL on the S/38 in the early eighties, programmers have been collecting their favorite and most useful CL techniques and programs. Over time, some of these have become classics. In this chapter, we'll visit three timeless programs and five techniques essential to writing classic CL.

The five techniques are:

- Error/exception message handling
- String manipulation
- Outfile processing
- IF-THEN-ELSE and DO groups
- OPNQRYF (Open Query File) command processing

When I consider the CL programs I would label as classic, I find these techniques being employed to some degree.

You may recognize the classic programs we'll visit as similar to something you have created. They provide functions almost always needed and welcomed by MIS personnel at any AS/400 installation. If you are new to the AS/400, I guarantee you will get excited about CL programming after you experience the power of these tools. And if you are an old hand at CL, you may have missed one of these classics.

These programs are useful and the techniques valid on the S/38 as well, although some of the details will be different (e.g., the syntax of qualified object names and some outfile file and field names).

Classic Program #1: Changing Ownership

If you ever face the problem of cleaning up ownership of objects on your system, you will find the CHGOBJOWN (Change Object Owner) command quite useful. You will also quickly discover that this command works for only one object at a time. That means you must identify the objects that will have a new owner and

Figure 29.1

Command: CHGOWN

```
/*==================================================================*/
/* AS/400                                                           */
/* Command Name: CHGOWN                                             */
/* Description : Change Ownership for Objects                       */
/*==================================================================*/

            CMD   PROMPT( 'Change Ownership of Objects' )

            PARM  KWD( OBJ )                                         +
                  TYPE( Q1 )                                         +
                  MIN( 1 )                                           +
                  PROMPT( 'Object or *generic name:' 1 )

            PARM  KWD( NEWOWN )                                      +
                  TYPE( *NAME )                                      +
                  LEN( 10 )                                          +
                  MIN( 1 )                                           +
                  PROMPT( 'New owner:' 3 )

            PARM  KWD( OBJTYPE )                                     +
                  TYPE( *CHAR )                                      +
                  LEN( 8 )                                           +
                  RSTD( *YES )                                       +
                  DFT( *ALL )                                        +
                  VALUES( *ALRTBL *AUTL    *CFGL    *CHTFMT          +
                          *CLD    *CLS     *CMD     *COSD            +
                          *CSPMAP *CSPTBL  *CTLD    *DEVD            +
                          *DTAARA *DTADCT  *DTAQ    *EDTD            +
                          *FCT    *FILE    *FNTRSC  *FORMDF          +
                          *GSS    *JOBD    *JOBQ    *JRN             +
                          *JRNRCV *LIB     *LIND    *MENU            +
                          *MODD   *MSGF    *MSGQ    *OUTQ            +
                          *OVL    *PAGSEG  *PGM     *PNLGRP          +
                          *PRDDFN *QRYDFN  *RCT     *SBSD            +
                          *SCHIDX *SPADCT  *SSND    *S36             +
                          *TBL    *USRPRF )                          +
                  SPCVAL( ( *ALL ) )                                 +
                  PROMPT( 'Object type:' 2 )

            PARM  KWD( CUROWNAUT )                                   +
                  TYPE( *CHAR )                                      +
                  LEN( 7 )                                           +
                  RSTD( *YES )                                       +
                  DFT( *REVOKE )                                     +
                  VALUES( *REVOKE  *SAME )                           +
                  PROMPT( 'Current owner authority:' 4 )
```

Figure 29.1 Continued

Figure 29.1

Command: CHGOWN *Continued*

```
Q1:          QUAL  TYPE( *GENERIC )                                          +
                   LEN( 10 )                                                 +
                   DFT( *ALL )                                               +
                   SPCVAL( ( *ALL ) )

             QUAL  TYPE( *NAME )                                             +
                   LEN( 10 )                                                 +
                   DFT( *LIBL )                                              +
                   SPCVAL( ( *ALL )       ( *ALLUSR )      ( *CURLIB )+
                           ( *LIBL )      ( *USRLIBL ) )                     +
                   PROMPT( 'Library name:' )
```

then enter the CHGOBJOWN command for each of those objects. Or is there another way? When the solution includes the repetitious use of a CL command, you can almost always use a CL program to improve or automate that solution. To that end, try this first classic CL program, CHGOWNCPP.

CHGOWNCPP demonstrates three of the fundamental CL programming techniques: *message monitoring*, *string handling*, and *outfile processing*. Let's take a quick look at how the program logic works and then examine how each technique is implemented.

Program Logic. When you execute the command CHGOWN (Figure 29.1), it invokes the command-processing program CHGOWNCPP (Figure 29.2). A program-level message monitor traps any unexpected function check messages caused by unmonitored errors during program execution. If it encounters an unexpected function check message, the MONMSG (Monitor Message) command directs the program to continue at the RSND_LOOP label.

The CHKOBJ (Check Object) command verifies that the value in &NEWOWN is an actual user profile on the system. If the CHKOBJ command can't find the user profile on the system, a MONMSG command traps CPF9801. If this happens, an escape message is then sent to the calling program using the SNDPGMMSG command, and the CPP terminates.

The DSPOBJD (Display Object Description) command generates the outfile QTEMP/CHGOWN based on the values for variables &OBJ and &OBJTYPE received from command CHGOWN. The program then processes the outfile until message CPF0864 ("End of file") is issued.

For each record in the outfile, the CPP executes a CHGOBJOWN command to give ownership to the user profile specified in variable &NEWOWN. The variables &ODLBNM and &ODOBNM contain the object's library and object name, obtained from fields in the outfile file format QLIDOBJD. The value in variable &CUROWNAUT specifies whether the old owner's authority should be revoked or retained. When the CHGOBJOWN command is successful, the program sends a completion message to the calling program's message queue and reads the next record from the file. If the CHGOBJOWN command fails, the

Figure 29.2

CL Program: CHGOWNCPP

```
/*===================================================================*/
/* IBM AS/400                                                        */
/* Program name: CHGOWNCPP                                           */
/* Purpose: Change ownership of object(s)                            */
/*===================================================================*/

             PGM PARM(&OBJ &NEWOWN &OBJTYPE &CUROWNAUT)

/* Command Variables */
             DCL &OBJ       *CHAR  20
             DCL &NEWOWN    *CHAR  10
             DCL &OBJTYPE   *CHAR   8
             DCL &CUROWNAUT *CHAR   7

/* Work variables */
             DCL &MSGDTA    *CHAR 256
             DCL &MSGF      *CHAR  10
             DCL &MSGFLIB   *CHAR  10
             DCL &MSGID     *CHAR   7
             DCL &OBJNAM    *CHAR  10
             DCL &OBJLIB    *CHAR  10

/* Declare file */
             DCLF FILE(QADSPOBJ)
/* Program-level monitor message */
             MONMSG CPF9999 EXEC(GOTO RSND_LOOP)

/* Check to make sure &NEWOWN is valid user profile */
             CHKOBJ OBJ(QSYS/&NEWOWN) OBJTYPE(*USRPRF)
             MONMSG CPF9801 EXEC(DO)
               SNDPGMMSG MSGID(CPF9898)                          +
                         MSGF(QSYS/QCPFMSG)                      +
                         MSGDTA('User profile ' || &NEWOWN       +
                          |< ' does not exist')                  +
                         MSGTYPE(*ESCAPE)
             ENDDO

/* Break &OBJ qualified name into two work variables */
Ⓐ            CHGVAR &OBJNAM %SST(&OBJ 1 10)
             CHGVAR &OBJLIB %SST(&OBJ 11 10)

/* Display object description to database file */
             DSPOBJD OBJ(&OBJLIB/&OBJNAM)  +
                     OBJTYPE(&OBJTYPE)     +
                     DETAIL(*FULL)         +
                     OUTPUT(*OUTFILE)      +
                     OUTFILE(QTEMP/CHGOWN)
/* Override to System File QADSPOBJ to the current outfile */
```

Figure 29.2 Continued

Figure 29.2

CL Program: CHGOWNCPP *Continued*

```
             OVRDBF FILE(QADSPOBJ) TOFILE(QTEMP/CHGOWN)

/* Receive file records (loop till end) */
 RCD_LOOP:   RCVF RCDFMT(QLIDOBJD)
             MONMSG CPF0864 EXEC(GOTO FINISH)

             CHGOBJOWN OBJ(&ODLBNM/&ODOBNM)  +
                       OBJTYPE(&ODOBTP)      +
                       NEWOWN(&NEWOWN)       +
                       CUROWNAUT(&CUROWNAUT)

             SNDPGMMSG MSGID(CPF9898)                            +
                       MSGF(QSYS/QCPFMSG)                        +
                       MSGDTA('Ownership of object ' || &ODLBNM  +
                        |< '/' || &ODOBNM |< ' changed to user ' +
                        || &NEWOWN)                              +
                       MSGTYPE(*COMP)
             GOTO RCD_LOOP


/* Resend error messages to calling program */
 RSND_LOOP:  RCVMSG RMV(*YES)          +
                    MSGDTA(&MSGDTA)    +
                    MSGID(&MSGID)      +
                    MSGF(&MSGF)        +
                    MSGFLIB(&MSGFLIB)
             MONMSG CPF9999 EXEC(GOTO RSND_END)
             IF (&MSGID = ' ') GOTO RSND_END /* no more messages */
             SNDPGMMSG MSGID(&MSGID)           +
                       MSGF(&MSGFLIB/&MSGF)    +
                       MSGDTA(&MSGDTA)         +
                       MSGTYPE(*DIAG)
             MONMSG CPF9999 EXEC(GOTO RSND_END)
             GOTO RSND_LOOP

 RSND_END:   SNDPGMMSG MSGID(CPF9898)                        +
                       MSGF(QSYS/QCPFMSG)                    +
                       MSGDTA('Operation ended in error. See +
                         previously listed messages')        +
                       MSGTYPE(*COMP)

/* Program cleanup. */
 FINISH:     RETURN
             ENDPGM
```

(B) [marks the highlighted MSGF/MSGDTA/MSGTYPE lines of the first SNDPGMMSG]

error message causes a function check, and the program-level message monitor passes control to the RSND_LOOP label. (Note: The CUROWNAUT parameter does not exist on the S/38 CHGOBJOWN command, so you would need to eliminate it, along with variable &CUROWNAUT in CHGOWNCPP. See Appendix A for the complete source for the CHGOBJOWN tool.)

After all records have been read, the next RCVF command generates error message CPF0864, and the command-level message monitor causes the program to branch to the FINISH label. The RSND_LOOP label is encountered only if an unexpected error occurs. This section of the program is a loop to receive the unexpected error messages and resend them to the calling program's message queue.

The Techniques

Message Monitoring. The first fundamental technique we will examine is error/exception message handling. Monitoring for system messages within a CL program is a technique that both traps error/exception conditions and directs the execution of the program based on the error conditions detected. The CL MONMSG command provides this function. Program CHGOWNCPP uses both command-level and program-level message monitoring.

A command-level message monitor lets you monitor for specific messages that might occur during the execution of a single command. For instance, in program CHGOWNCPP, `MONMSG CPF9801 EXEC(DO)` immediately follows the CHKOBJ command to monitor specifically for message CPF9801 ("Object not found"). If CPF9801 is issued as a result of the CHKOBJ command, the message monitor traps the message and invokes the EXEC portion of the MONMSG command — in this instance, a DO command.

Another example in the same program is the MONMSG command that comes immediately after the RCVF statement. If the RCVF command causes error message CPF0864, the message monitor traps the error and invokes the EXEC portion of that MONMSG — in this instance, `GOTO FINISH`.

What happens if an error occurs on a command and there is no command-level MONMSG to trap the error? If there is also no program-level MONMSG for that specific error message, the unexpected error causes function check message CPF9999, and if no program-level MONMSG for CPF9999 exists, the program ends in error.

A program-level message monitor is a MONMSG command placed immediately after the last declare statement in a CL program. In our program example, there is a program-level `MONMSG CPF9999 EXEC(GOTO RSND_LOOP)`. This MONMSG handles any unexpected error since all errors that are unmonitored at the command level eventually cause a function check. For instance, if the CHGOBJOWN command fails, an error message is issued that then generates function check message CPF9999. The program-level MONMSG traps this function check, and the EXEC command instructs the program to resume at label RNSD_LOOP and process those error messages.

For more information on monitoring messages, see the AS/400 manual *Control Language Programmer's Guide* (SC41-8077), or Appendix E of the AS/400 manual *Control Language Reference, Volume 1* (SC41-9775-2).

String Handling. Another fundamental technique program CHGOWNCPP employs is string manipulation. The program demonstrates two forms of string handling — substring manipulation and concatenation. The first is the %SST (Substring) function. (%SST is a valid abbreviated form of the function %SUBSTRING — both perform the same job.) The %SST function, which returns to the program a portion of a character string, has three arguments: the name of the variable containing the string, the starting position, and the number of characters in the string to extract.

For instance, when the command CHGOWN passes the argument &OBJ to the CL program, the variable exists as a 20-character string containing the object name in positions 1 through 10 and the library name in positions 11 through 20. The CL program uses the %SST function in the CHGVAR (Change Variable) command (A in Figure 29.2) to extract the library name and object name from the &OBJ variable into the &OBJNAM and &OBJLIB variables.

The second form of string handling in this program is concatenation. The control language interface supports three distinct, built-in concatenation functions:

- *CAT (||): Concatenate — concatenates two string variables end to end;
- *TCAT (|<): Trim and concatenate — concatenates two strings after trimming all blanks off the end of the first string;
- *BCAT (|>): Blank insert and concatenate — concatenates two strings after trimming all blanks off the end of the first string and then adding a single blank character to the end of the first string.

To see how these functions work, let's apply them to these variables (where ƀ designates a blank):

```
&VAR1 *CHAR 10
VALUE('Johnƀƀƀƀƀ') and
&VAR2 *CHAR 10 VALUE('Doeƀƀƀƀƀƀƀ')
```

The results of each operation are as follows:

```
&VAR1 || &VAR2 = JohnƀƀƀƀƀƀDoe
&VAR1 |< &VAR2 = JohnDoe
&VAR1 |> &VAR2 = John Doe
```

The SNDPGMMSG command (B in Figure 29.2) uses concatenation to build a string for the MSGDTA (Message Data) parameter. Notice that you can use a combination of constants and program variables to construct a single string during execution. The only limitation is that variables used with concatenation functions must be character variables because they will be treated as strings for these functions. You must convert any numeric variables to character variables before you can use them in concatenation.

If the variables &ODLBNM, &ODOBNM, and &NEWOWN in the SNDPGMMSG command contain the values MYLIB, MYPROGRAM, and USERNAME, respectively, the SNDPGMMSG statement generates the message "Ownership of object MYLIB/MYPROGRAM granted to user USERNAME."

Outfile Processing. The final fundamental technique demonstrated in program CHGOWNCPP is how to use an outfile. You can direct certain OS/400 commands to send output to a database file instead of to a display or printer. In this program, the DSPOBJD command generates the outfile QTEMP/CHGOWN. This file contains the full description of any objects selected.

The file declared in the DCLF (Declare File) command is QADSPOBJ, the system-supplied file in library QSYS that serves as the externally defined model for the outfile generated by the DSPOBJD command. (Note: To get a list of the model outfiles provided by the system, you can execute the command `"DSPOBJD QSYS/QA* *FILE"`.) Because file QADSPOBJ is declared in this program, the program will include the externally defined field descriptions when you compile it, allowing it to recognize and use those field names during execution.

The next step in using an outfile in this program is actually creating the contents of the outfile using the DSPOBJD command. DSPOBJD uses the object name and type passed from command CHGOWN to create outfile QTEMP/CHGOWN. The outfile name is arbitrary, so I make a practice of giving an outfile the same name as the command or program that creates it.

The program then executes the OVRDBF (Override with Database File) command to specify that the file QTEMP/CHGOWN is to be accessed whenever a reference is made to QADSPOBJ. This works because QTEMP/CHGOWN is created with the same record format and fields as QADSPOBJ. Now when the program reads record format QLIDOBJD in file QADSPOBJ, the actual file it reads will be QTEMP/CHGOWN.

These three fundamental CL techniques give you a good start in building your CL library, and the "Change Owner of Object(s)" tool is definitely handy. You may have discovered the CHGLIBOWN (Change Library Owner) tool in library QUSRTOOL. (For more details about library QUSRTOOL, see Appendix A.) This IBM-provided tool offers a similar function.

Classic Program #2: Delete Database Relationships

Our second classic program features a utility that's a real timesaver: the "Delete Database Relationships" tool provided by command DLTDBR and CL program DLTDBRCPP. DLTDBR uses the same three fundamental techniques described above and adds a fourth: the IF-THEN clause. Let's take a quick look at the program logic and then discuss the IF-THEN technique.

Program Logic. When you execute command DLTDBR (Figure 29.3), the command-processing program DLTDBRCPP (Figure 29.4) is invoked. As in CHGOWNCPP, a program-level MONMSG handles unexpected errors.

The DSPDBR (Display Database Relations) command generates an outfile based on the file you specify when you execute the command DLTDBR. The CPP then processes this outfile until message CPF0864 ("End of File") is issued.

Figure 29.3

Command: DLTDBR

```
/*---------------------------------------------------------------------*/
/* AS/400                                                              */
/* Command Name: DLTDBR                                                */
/* Description : Delete Database Relations (dependent files)          */
/*---------------------------------------------------------------------*/

             CMD    PROMPT( 'Delete Database Relations' )

             PARM   KWD( FILE )                                        +
                    TYPE( Q1 )                                         +
                    MIN( 1 )                                           +
                    PROMPT( 'File or *generic name:' )

Q1:          QUAL   TYPE( *GENERIC )                                   +
                    LEN( 10 )                                          +
                    DFT( *ALL )                                        +
                    SPCVAL( ( *ALL ) )

             QUAL   TYPE( *NAME )                                      +
                    LEN( 10 )                                          +
                    DFT( *LIBL )                                       +
                    SPCVAL( ( *ALL )      ( *ALLUSR )    (*CURLIB) +
                            ( *LIBL )     ( *USRLIBL ) )               +
                    PROMPT( 'Library name:' )
```

For each record in the outfile, the program performs two tests as decision mechanisms for program actions. Both tests check whether or not the record read is a reference to a physical file (&WHRTYP = &PFTYPE). If the file is not a physical file, the program takes no action for that record; it just reads the next record. The first test (A in Figure 29.4) determines whether dependencies exist for this physical file. &WHNO represents the total number of dependencies. If &WHNO is equal to zero, there are no dependencies for this file, and the program sends a message (using the SNDPGMMSG command) to that effect.

The second test (B) checks whether &WHNO is greater than zero. If it is, the record represents a dependent file, and you can delete the file name specified in variables &WHRELI (dependent file library) and &WHREFI (dependent file name) with the DLTF (Delete File) command.

When the DLTF is successful, the program sends a completion message to the calling program's message queue. The GOTO RCD_LOOP command sends control to the RCD_LOOP label to read the next record. If the DLTF command fails, the error message causes a function check, and the program-level message monitor directs the program to resume at the RSND_LOOP label.

After all records have been read, the RCVF command generates error message CPF0864, and the command-level message monitor causes the program to branch to the FINISH label, where the program ends. As with the first program, you will encounter the RSND_LOOP label only if an unexpected error occurs.

Figure 29.4

CL Program: DLTDBRCPP

```
/*===============================================================*/
/* IBM AS/400                                                    */
/* Program name: DLTDBRCPP                                       */
/* Purpose: Delete database relationships for selected files     */
/*===============================================================*/

             PGM PARM(&FILE)

/* Command variables */
             DCL &FILE    *CHAR  20

/* Work variables */
             DCL &FILELIB *CHAR  10
             DCL &FILENAM *CHAR  10
             DCL &MSGDTA  *CHAR 256
             DCL &MSGF    *CHAR  10
             DCL &MSGFLIB *CHAR  10
             DCL &MSGID   *CHAR   7
             DCL &PFTYPE  *CHAR   1  VALUE('P') /* Code for *PF file */

/* Declare file */
             DCLF FILE(QADSPDBR)

/* Program-level monitor message */
             MONMSG CPF9999 EXEC(GOTO RSND_LOOP)

/* Break &FILE qualified name into two work variables */
             CHGVAR &FILENAM %SST(&FILE 1 10)
             CHGVAR &FILELIB %SST(&FILE 11 10)

/* Load selected records to outfile using DSPDBR command */
             DSPDBR FILE(&FILELIB/&FILENAM) +
                    OUTPUT(*OUTFILE)        +
                    OUTFILE(QTEMP/DLTDBR)

/* Override to System File QADSPDBR format for RPG program */
             OVRDBF FILE(QADSPDBR) TOFILE(QTEMP/DLTDBR)

/* Receive file records (loop till end) */
 RCD_LOOP:   RCVF RCDFMT(QWHDRDBR)
             MONMSG CPF0864 EXEC(GOTO FINISH)

/* Physical file, but no dependencies */
```

Figure 29.4 Continued

Figure 29.4

CL Program: DLTDBRCPP *Continued*

```
Ⓐ             IF (&WHRTYP = &PFTYPE *AND &WHNO = Ø) DO
                SNDPGMMSG MSGID(CPF9898)                                +
                          MSGF(QSYS/QCPFMSG)                            +
                          MSGDTA('No dependencies exist for physical +
                            file ' || &WHRLI |< '/' || &WHRFI)          +
                          MSGTYPE(*INFO)
              ENDDO

/* Physical file, with dependencies */
Ⓑ             IF (&WHRTYP = &PFTYPE *AND &WHNO > Ø) DO
                DLTF FILE(&WHRELI/&WHREFI)
                SNDPGMMSG MSGID(CPF9898)                                +
                          MSGF(QSYS/QCPFMSG)                            +
                          MSGDTA('File ' || &WHRELI |< '/' || &WHREFI +
                            |< ' dependent upon physical file ' ||     +
                            &WHRLI |< '/' || &WHRFI |< ' deleted')     +
                          MSGTYPE(*COMP)
              ENDDO

              GOTO RCD_LOOP

/* Resend error messages to calling program */
 RSND_LOOP:  RCVMSG RMV(*YES)            +
                    MSGDTA(&MSGDTA)      +
                    MSGID(&MSGID)        +
                    MSGF(&MSGF)          +
                    MSGFLIB(&MSGFLIB)
             MONMSG CPF9999 EXEC(GOTO RSND_END)
             IF (&MSGID = ' ') GOTO RSND_END
             SNDPGMMSG MSGID(&MSGID)             +
                       MSGF(&MSGFLIB/&MSGF)      +
                       MSGDTA(&MSGDTA)           +
                       MSGTYPE(*DIAG)
             MONMSG CPF9999 EXEC(GOTO RSND_END)
             GOTO RSND_LOOP

 RSND_END:   SNDPGMMSG MSGID(CPF9898)                          +
                       MSGF(QSYS/QCPFMSG)                      +
                       MSGDTA('Operation ended in error. See +
                         previously listed messages')          +
                       MSGTYPE(*COMP)

/* Program cleanup. */
 FINISH:     RETURN
             ENDPGM
```

The Technique

IF-THEN-ELSE and DO Groups. The IF-THEN clause lets you add decision support to your CL coding via the IF command, which has two parameters: COND (the conditional statement) and THEN (the action to be taken when the condition is satisfied). A simple IF-THEN statement would be

```
IF COND(&CODE = 'A') THEN(CHGVAR VAR(&CODE) VALUE('B'))
```

In this example, if the value of variable &CODE is A, the CHGVAR command changes that value to B. To create code that is easier to read and interpret, it is usually best to omit the use of the keywords COND and THEN. The above example is much clearer when written as

```
IF (&CODE = 'A') CHGVAR VAR(&CODE) VALUE('B')
```

Conditions can also take more complex forms, such as

```
IF ((&CODE = 'A' *OR &CODE = 'B') *AND (&NUMBER = 1))              +
GOTO CODEA
```

This example demonstrates several conditional tests. The *OR connective requires at least one of the alternatives — `(&CODE = 'A')` or `(&CODE = 'B')` — to be true to satisfy the first condition. The *AND connective then requires that `(&NUMBER = 1)` also be true before the THEN clause can be executed. If both conditions are met, the program executes the GOTO command. (For more information about how to use *AND and *OR connectives, see Chapter 2 of the AS/400 manual *Control Language Programmer's Guide.*)

The ELSE command provides additional function to the IF command. Examine these statements:

```
IF  (&CODE = 'A') CALL PGMA
ELSE              CALL PGMB
```

The program executes the ELSE command if the preceding condition is false.

You can also use the IF command to process a DO group. Examine the following statements:

```
IF (&CODE = 'A') DO
  CALL PGMA
  CALL PGMB
  CALL PGMC
ENDDO
```

If the condition in the IF command is true, the program executes the DO group until it encounters an ENDDO.

The DO command also works with the ELSE command, as this example shows:

```
IF (&CODE = 'A') DO
  CALL PGMA
  CALL PGMB
  CALL PGMC
```

```
  ENDDO
  ELSE DO
    CALL PGMD
    CALL PGME
    CALL PGMF
  ENDDO
```

For more information about IF and ELSE commands, see the AS/400 manual *Control Language Reference*, Volume 4 (SC41-9778) or the *Control Language Programmer's Guide*.

Classic Program #3: List Program-File References

The third and final fundamental technique we will examine is the "Display Program References" tool, where we stand face-to-face with one of the most powerful influences on CL programming — the one and only OPNQRYF (Open Query File) command. As this program demonstrates, this classic technique is one of the richest and most powerful tools available through CL. Let's take a quick look at the program logic for this tool, provided via the LSTPGMREF (List Program References) command and the LSTPRCPP CL program. Then we can take a close look at the OPNQRYF command.

Program Logic. When you execute command LSTPGMREF (Figure 29.5), the command-processing program LSTPRCPP (Figure 29.6) is invoked. LSTPRCPP uses the DSPPGMREF (Display Program References) command to generate an outfile based on the value you entered for the PGM parameter. The outfile LSTPGMREF then contains information about the specified programs and the objects they reference.

Notice that this program does not use the DCLF statement. There is no need to declare the file format because the program will not access the file directly. You will also notice that the program uses the OVRDBF command, but the SHARE(*YES) parameter has been added. Because a CL program cannot send output to a printer, LSTPRCPP must call a high-level language (HLL) program to print the output. The OVRDBF is required so the HLL program, which references file QADSPPGM, can find outfile QTEMP/LSTPGMREF. The override must specify SHARE(*YES) to ensure that the HLL program will use the Open Data Path (ODP) created by the OPNQRYF command instead of creating a new ODP and ignoring the work the OPNQRYF has performed. Files used with OPNQRYF require SHARE(*YES).

After the DSPPGMREF command is executed, file LSTPGMREF contains records for program-file references as well as program references to other types of objects. The next step is to build an OPNQRYF selection statement in variable &QRYSLT that selects only *FILE object-type references and optionally selects the particular files named in the FILE parameter. LSTPRCPP uses IF tests to construct the selection statement. Then the CPP determines the sequence of records desired (based on the value entered for the OPT parameter in the LSTPGMREF command) and uses the OPNQRYF command to select the records and create access paths that will allow the HLL program to read the records in the desired sequence.

Figure 29.5

Command: LSTPGMREF

```
/*---------------------------------------------------------------*/
/* AS/400                                                        */
/* Command Name: LSTPGMREF                                       */
/* Description : List Program-File References                    */
/*---------------------------------------------------------------*/

             CMD   PROMPT( 'List Program-File References' )

             PARM  KWD( FILE )                                    +
                   TYPE( *GENERIC )                               +
                   DFT( *ALL )                                    +
                   SPCVAL( ( *ALL ) )                             +
                   PROMPT( 'File or *generic name:' )

             PARM  KWD( PGM )                                     +
                   TYPE( Q1 )                                     +
                   PROMPT( 'Program or *generic name:' )

             PARM  KWD( OPT )                                     +
                   TYPE( *CHAR )                                  +
                   LEN( 1 )                                       +
                   RSTD( *YES )                                   +
                   DFT( *FILE )                                   +
                   SPCVAL( ( *FILE F )  ( *PGM P ) )              +
                   PROMPT( '*FILE or *PGM sequence:' )

 Q1:         QUAL  TYPE( *GENERIC )                               +
                   LEN( 10 )                                      +
                   DFT( *ALL )                                    +
                   SPCVAL( ( *ALL ) )

             QUAL  TYPE( *NAME )                                  +
                   LEN( 10 )                                      +
                   DFT( *LIBL )                                   +
                   SPCVAL( ( *ALL )     ( *ALLUSR )    ( *CURLIB )+
                           ( *LIBL )    ( *USRLIBL ) )            +
                   PROMPT( 'Library name:' )
```

The CL program then calls HLL program LSTPRRPG to print the selected records (I haven't provided code here — you will need to build your own version based on your desired output format). The outfile will appear to contain only the selected records, and they will appear to be sorted in the desired sequence.

The Technique

The OPNQRYF Command. Without a doubt, one of the more powerful commands available to CL programmers is the OPNQRYF command. OPNQRYF uses the same system database query interface SQL uses on the AS/400. The command provides many functions, including selecting records and establishing keyed access paths without using an actual logical file or DDS. These two basic functions are the bread-and-butter classic techniques demonstrated in program LSTPRCPP.

Record selection is accomplished with OPNQRYF's QRYSLT parameter. If you know the exact record selection criteria when you write the program, filling in the QRYSLT parameter is easy, and the selection string will be compiled with the program. But the real strength of ONPQRYF's record selection capability is that you can construct the QRYSLT parameter at runtime to match the particular user requirements specified during execution. Program LSTPRCPP demonstrates both the compile-time and runtime capabilities of OPNQRYF.

When you write program LSTPRCPP, the requirement to include only references to physical files is a given. Therefore, you can use the statement `CHGVAR VAR(&QRYSLT) VALUE('WHOBJT = "F"')` to initially provide a value for &QRYSLT to satisfy that requirement. The &FILE value is unknown until execution time, so the code must allow this selection criteria to be specified dynamically. First, what are the possible values for the FILE parameter on command LSTPGMREF?

- You may specify a value of *ALL. If you do, you should not add any selection criteria to the QRYSLT parameter. The &QRYSLT value would be

  ```
  'WHOBJT = "F"'
  ```

- You may specify a generic value, such as IC* or AP??F*. If you enter a generic value, the CL program must determine that &FILE contains a generic name and then use OPNQRYF's %WLDCRD (wildcard) function to build the appropriate QRYSLT selection criteria. The %WLDCRD function lets you select a group of similarly named objects by specifying an argument containing a wildcard (e.g., * or ?). For instance, if you wanted to select all files beginning with the characters IC, you would use the argument IC*. An example of the &QRYSLT variable for this generic selection would be

  ```
  'WHOBJT = "F" *AND WHFNAM = %WLDCRD("IC*")'
  ```

- You may specify an actual file name. If you do, the CL program must first determine that fact and then simply use the compare function in OPNQRYF to build the value for the QRYSLT parameter. An example for this &QRYSLT variable would be

  ```
  'WHOBJT = "F" *AND WHFNAM = "FILE_NAME"'
  ```

Examining the program, you will see that it performs a series of tests on the variable &FILE to determine how to build the QRYSLT parameter. If *ALL is the value for &FILE, all other IF tests are bypassed, and the program continues. If the program QCLSCAN finds the character * in the string &FILE, it uses the %WLDCRD function to build the appropriate QRYSLT parameter. If the program does not find *ALL and does not find a * in the name, the value of &FILE is assumed to represent an actual file name, and the program compares the value of &FILE to the field WHFNAM for record selection. Obviously, the power of the QRYSLT parameter is in the hands of those who can successfully build the selection value based on execution-time selections.

Figure 29.6

CL Program: LSTPRCPP

```
/*===================================================================*/
/* IBM AS/400                                                        */
/* Program name: LSTPRCPP                                            */
/* Purpose: List program file references - CPP for LSTPGMREF command */
/*===================================================================*/

             PGM PARM(&FILE &PGM &OPT)

/* Command variables */
             DCL &FILE     *CHAR   10
             DCL &PGM      *CHAR   20
             DCL &OPT      *CHAR    1

/* Variable work fields */
             DCL &PGMNAM   *CHAR   10
             DCL &PGMLIB   *CHAR   10
             DCL &MSGDTA   *CHAR  256
             DCL &MSGF     *CHAR   10
             DCL &MSGFLIB  *CHAR   10
             DCL &MSGID    *CHAR    7
             DCL &FILESEQ  *CHAR    1  VALUE('F') /* file sequence */
             DCL &PGMSEQ   *CHAR    1  VALUE('P') /* program sequence */
             DCL &QRYSLT   *CHAR  256

/* Variables used with QCLSCAN */
             DCL &STRLEN   *DEC   (3 0) VALUE(10)
             DCL &STRPOS   *DEC   (3 0) VALUE(1)
             DCL &PATTERN  *CHAR    1  VALUE('*')
```

Figure 29.6 Continued

The second basic bread-and-butter technique is using OPNQRYF to build a key sequence without requiring additional DDS. Program LSTPRCPP tests the value of &OPT to determine whether the requester wants the records listed in *FILE (file library/file name) or *PGM (program library/program name) sequence. The appropriate OPNQRYF statement is executed based on the result of these tests (see A in Figure 29.6).

When &OPT is equal to &FILESEQ (which was declared with the value F), the OPNQRYF statement sequences the file using the field order of WHLNAM (file library), WHFNAM (file name), WHLIB (program library), WHPNAM (program name). When &OPT equals &PGMSEQ (declared with the value P), the key fields are in the order WHLIB, WHPNAM, WHLNAM, WHFNAM. No DDS is required. The HLL program called to process the opened file can provide internal level breaks based on the option selected.

For more information concerning the use of the OPNQRYF command with database files, refer to the *Control Language Reference, Volume 4,* or *Database Guide* (SC41-9659).

Figure 29.6

CL Program: LSTPRCPP *Continued*

```
             DCL &PATLEN   *DEC  (3 0) VALUE(1)
             DCL &TRNSLTE *CHAR     1  VALUE('0')
             DCL &TRIM    *CHAR     1  VALUE('0')
             DCL &WILD    *CHAR     1  VALUE(' ')
             DCL &RESULT  *DEC  (3 0) VALUE(0)

/* Program-level monitor message */
             MONMSG CPF9999 EXEC(GOTO RSND_LOOP)

/* Break &PGM qualified name into two work variables */
             CHGVAR &PGMNAM %SST(&PGM 1 10)
             CHGVAR &PGMLIB %SST(&PGM 11 10)

/* Display program references to database file */
             DSPPGMREF PGM(&PGMLIB/&PGMNAM)       +
                       OUTPUT(*OUTFILE)           +
                       OUTFILE(QTEMP/LSTPGMREF)

/* Override system format to database file and SHARE(*YES) for OPNQRYF */
             OVRDBF     FILE(QADSPPGM)            +
                        TOFILE(QTEMP/LSTPGMREF)   +
                        SHARE(*YES)

/* First set the &QRYSLT to select only *FILE type objects. */
             CHGVAR &QRYSLT ('WHOBJT = "F"')
/*-------------------------------------------------------------------*/
/* Determine &FILE selection and build &QRYSLT appropriately        */
/*    If &FILE  = *ALL, do nothing.                                  */
/*    If &FILE ^= *ALL, then scan for '*' in &FILE                   */
/*       IF '*' found, then build generic search using %WILDCARD     */
/*       If '*' not found, then search for actual &FILE              */
/*-------------------------------------------------------------------*/

             IF (&FILE *NE '*ALL') (DO)
               CALL PGM(QCLSCAN) PARM(&FILE &STRLEN &STRPOS +
                             &PATTERN &PATLEN &TRNSLTE &TRIM &WILD +
                             &RESULT)
               IF (&RESULT *GT 0) DO
                  CHGVAR &QRYSLT (&QRYSLT |< ' *AND WHFNAM = +
                    %WLDCRD("' || &FILE |< '")')
               ENDDO
               ELSE DO
                  CHGVAR &QRYSLT (&QRYSLT |< ' *AND WHFNAM = "' +
                    || &FILE |< '"')
               ENDDO
             ENDDO
```

Figure 29.6 Continued

Figure 29.6

CL Program: LSTPRCPP *Continued*

```
/*---------------------------------------------------------------------*/
/* Perform OPNQRYF Command                                             */
/* If &OPT = &FILESEQ, OPNQRYF sequences file in reference file seq */
/* If &OPT = &PGMEQ,   OPNQRYF sequences file in program seq          */
/*---------------------------------------------------------------------*/

              IF (&OPT = &FILESEQ) DO
                 OPNQRYF FILE(QADSPPGM)                                   +
                         QRYSLT(&QRYSLT)                                  +
                         KEYFLD((WHLNAM) (WHFNAM) (WHLIB) (WHPNAM))
              ENDDO

Ⓐ /* OPNQRYF sequences database file in *PGM sequence */
              IF (&OPT = &PGMSEQ) DO
                 OPNQRYF FILE(QADSPPGM)                                   +
                         QRYSLT(&QRYSLT)                                  +
                         KEYFLD((WHLIB) (WHPNAM) (WHLNAM) (WHFNAM))
              ENDDO

/* Call RPG program to print the list from file QTEMP/LSTPGMREF */
              CALL       PGM(LSTPRRPG) PARM(&FILE &PGM &OPT)

/* Complete, no errors. */
              GOTO FINISH

/* Resend error messages to calling program */
 RSND_LOOP:   RCVMSG RMV(*YES)           +
                     MSGDTA(&MSGDTA)     +
                     MSGID(&MSGID)       +
                     MSGF(&MSGF)         +
                     MSGFLIB(&MSGFLIB)
              MONMSG CPF9999 EXEC(GOTO RSND_END)
              IF (&MSGID = ' ') GOTO RSND_END
              SNDPGMMSG MSGID(&MSGID)          +
                        MSGF(&MSGFLIB/&MSGF)   +
                        MSGDTA(&MSGDTA)        +
                        MSGTYPE(*DIAG)
              MONMSG CPF9999 EXEC(GOTO RSND_END)
              GOTO RSND_LOOP

 RSND_END:    SNDPGMMSG MSGID(CPF9898)                        +
                        MSGF(QSYS/QCPFMSG)                    +
                        MSGDTA('Operation ended in error. See +
                          previously listed messages')        +
                        MSGTYPE(*COMP)

/* Program cleanup. */
 FINISH:      RETURN
              ENDPGM
```

Chapter 30

CL Programming Style

by Wayne Madden

Code your CL programs in clear, simple, flowing, and consistent lines

The key to creating readable, maintainable code is establishing and adhering to a set of standards about how the code should look. Standards give your programs a consistent appearance — a style — and create a comfortable environment for the person reading and maintaining the code. They also boost productivity. Programmers with a consistent style don't think about how to arrange code; they simply follow clearly defined coding standards, which become like second nature through habit. And programmers reading such code can directly interpret the program's actions without the distraction of bad style. Good coding style transcends any one language. It's a matter of professionalism, of doing your work to the best of your abilities and with pride.

Although most CL programs are short and to the point, a *consistent* programming style is as essential to CL as it is to any other language. When I started writing CL, I used the prompter to enter values for command parameters. Today, I still use the prompter for more complex commands or to prompt for valid values when I'm not sure what to specify. The prompter produces a standard of sorts. Every command begins in column 14, labels are to the left of the commands, and the editor wraps the parameters onto continuation lines like a word processor wraps words when you've reached the margin. While using the prompter is convenient, code generated this way can be extremely difficult to read and maintain.

Let's look at CL program CVTOUTQCL (Figure 30.1), which converts the entries of an output queue listing into a database file. Another application can then read the database file and individually process each spool file (e.g., copy the contents of the spool file to a database file for saving or downloading to a PC). Without a program such as CVTOUTQCL, you would have to jot down the name

Figure 30.1

CL Program CVTOUTQCL — Version 1

```
/* Program CVTOUTQCL */
             PGM        PARM(&OUTQ &OUTFILE)
/* Work Variables */
             DCL        VAR(&OUTQ) TYPE(*CHAR) LEN(20)
             DCL        VAR(&OUTFILE) TYPE(*CHAR) LEN(20)
             DCL        VAR(&MSGDTA) TYPE(*CHAR) LEN(256)
             DCL        VAR(&MSGF) TYPE(*CHAR) LEN(10)
             DCL        VAR(&MSGFLIB) TYPE(*CHAR) LEN(10)
             DCL        VAR(&MSGID) TYPE(*CHAR) LEN(7)
             DCL        VAR(&RTNTYPE) TYPE(*CHAR) LEN(2)
             DCL        VAR(&MSG_FLAG) TYPE(*LGL) LEN(1) VALUE('0')
             DCL        VAR(&RTNCODE) TYPE(*CHAR) LEN(1) VALUE('0')
             DCL        VAR(&FL1EXIST) TYPE(*LGL) LEN(1) VALUE('0')
             DCL        VAR(&FL2EXIST) TYPE(*LGL) LEN(1) VALUE('0')
/* Program-level monitor message */
             MONMSG     MSGID(CPF9999) EXEC(GOTO CMDLBL(GLOBAL_ERR))
/* Validation and setup */
/* Check for the Outq Object. */
             CHKOBJ     OBJ(%SST(&OUTQ 11 10)/%SST(&OUTQ 1 10)) +
                          OBJTYPE(*OUTQ)
             MONMSG     MSGID(CPF9801) EXEC(DO)
             SNDPGMMSG  MSGID(CPF9898) MSGF(QSYS/QCPFMSG) +
                          MSGDTA('Output queue' *BCAT %SST(&OUTQ 11 +
                          10) *TCAT '/' *CAT %SST(&OUTQ 1 10) *BCAT +
                          'not found') TOPGMQ(*SAME) MSGTYPE(*DIAG)
             CHGVAR     VAR(&MSG_FLAG) VALUE('1')
             GOTO       CMDLBL(CLEAN_UP)
             ENDDO
/* Set up work file in QTEMP. */
             CHGVAR     VAR(&FL1EXIST) VALUE('1')
             CHKOBJ     OBJ(QTEMP/DSPOUTQ) OBJTYPE(*FILE)
             MONMSG     MSGID(CPF9801) EXEC(CHGVAR VAR(&FL1EXIST) +
                          VALUE('0'))
             IF         COND(&FL1EXIST) THEN(CLRPFM +
                          FILE(QTEMP/DSPOUTQ))
             ELSE       CMD(DO)
             CRTPF      FILE(QTEMP/DSPOUTQ) RCDLEN(132)
             CHGVAR     VAR(&FL1EXIST) VALUE('1')
             ENDDO
             OVRDBF     FILE(DSPOUTQ) TOFILE(QTEMP/DSPOUTQ)
/* Create outfile named in &outfile variable */
             CHGVAR     VAR(&FL2EXIST) VALUE('1')
             CHKOBJ     OBJ(%SST(&OUTFILE 11 10)/%SST(&OUTFILE 1 10)) +
                          OBJTYPE(*FILE)
             MONMSG     MSGID(CPF9801) EXEC(CHGVAR VAR(&FL2EXIST) +
                          VALUE('0'))
             IF         COND(&FL2EXIST) THEN(CLRPFM +
                          FILE(%SST(&OUTFILE 11 10)/%SST(&OUTFILE 1 +
                          10)))
             ELSE       CMD(DO)
             CRTDUPOBJ  OBJ(QACVTOTQ) FROMLIB(KWMLIB) OBJTYPE(*FILE) +
                          TOLIB(%SST(&OUTFILE 11 10)) +
                          NEWOBJ(%SST(&OUTFILE 1 10))
```

Figure 30.1 Continued

Figure 30.1

CL Program CVTOUTQCL — Version I *Continued*

```
              CHGVAR     VAR(&FL2EXIST) VALUE('1')
              ENDDO
              OVRDBF     FILE(QACVTOTQ) TOFILE(%SST(&OUTFILE 11 +
                           10)/%SST(&OUTFILE 1 10))
/*  Override spool file to HOLD(*YES). QPRTSPLQ is spoool file */
/*    created by WRKOUTQ OUTPUT(*PRINT).                       */
              OVRPRTF    FILE(QPRTSPLQ) SCHEDULE(*IMMED) HOLD(*YES)
              WRKOUTQ    OUTQ(%SST(&OUTQ 11 10)/%SST(&OUTQ 1 10)) +
                           OUTPUT(*PRINT)
/*  Copy the spool file to disk file DSPOUTQ.            */
/*  Override the declared disk file to the one in QTEMP. */
              CPYSPLF    FILE(QPRTSPLQ) TOFILE(QTEMP/DSPOUTQ) +
                           SPLNBR(*LAST)
              DLTSPLF    FILE(QPRTSPLQ) SPLNBR(*LAST)
              MONMSG     MSGID(CPF3303 CPF3344) /* file not found or +
                           no longer on system */
              CALL       PGM(CVTOUTQR) PARM(&RTNCODE)
              MONMSG     MSGID(CPF0006) EXEC(DO)
              SNDPGMMSG  MSGID(CPF9898) MSGF(QSYS/QCPFMSG) +
                           MSGDTA('Call to program CVTOUTQR ended in +
                           error') TOPGMQ(*SAME) MSGTYPE(*DIAG)
              CHGVAR     VAR(&MSG_FLAG) VALUE('1')
              GOTO       CMDLBL(CLEAN_UP)
              ENDDO
              IF         COND(&RTNCODE = '1') THEN(DO)
              SNDPGMMSG  MSGID(CPF9898) MSGF(QSYS/QCPFMSG) MSGDTA('No +
                           entries found in output queue' *BCAT +
                           %SST(&OUTQ 11 10) *TCAT '/' *CAT +
                           %SST(&OUTQ 1 10)) TOPGMQ(*SAME) +
                           MSGTYPE(*DIAG)
              CHGVAR     VAR(&MSG_FLAG) VALUE('1')
              GOTO       CMDLBL(CLEAN_UP)
              ENDDO
              IF         COND(&RTNCODE = '0') THEN(SNDPGMMSG +
                           MSGID(CPF9898) MSGF(QSYS/QCPFMSG) +
                           MSGDTA('Output queue' *BCAT %SST(&OUTQ 11 +
                           10) *TCAT '/' *CAT %SST(&OUTQ 1 10) *BCAT +
                           'entries converted') MSGTYPE(*COMP))
              GOTO       CMDLBL(CLEAN_UP)
/* Program level MONMSG detected, flag for messages. */
GLOBAL_ERR:   IF         COND(&MSG_FLAG) THEN(DO) /* To protect from +
                           error looping */
              SNDPGMMSG  MSGID(CPF9898) MSGF(QSYS/QCPFMSG) +
                           MSGDTA('Error in message handling process +
                           detected during a program failure.  See +
                           joblog for details') MSGTYPE(*ESCAPE)
              MONMSG     MSGID(CPF0000) EXEC(RETURN)
              ENDDO
              CHGVAR     VAR(&MSG_FLAG) VALUE('1')
/* Perform any program cleanup operations. */
 CLEAN_UP:    IF         COND(&FL1EXIST) THEN(DLTF FILE(QTEMP/DSPOUTQ))
/* Error handling - resend messages to calling program          */
/*    IF &msg_flag, then error messages are in queue to be sent. */
```

Figure 30.1 Continued

Figure 30.1

CL Program CVTOUTQCL — Version I *Continued*

```
RSND_BGN:     IF          COND(&MSG_FLAG) THEN(DO)
RSND_RPT:     RCVMSG      RMV(*YES) MSGDTA(&MSGDTA) MSGID(&MSGID) +
                            RTNTYPE(&RTNTYPE) MSGF(&MSGF) +
                            MSGFLIB(&MSGFLIB)
              MONMSG      MSGID(CPF0000) EXEC(GOTO CMDLBL(RSND_END))
              IF          COND(&MSGID = ' ') THEN(GOTO +
                            CMDLBL(RSND_END)) /* no more messages */
              IF          COND(&RTNTYPE = '02' *OR &RTNTYPE = +
                            '15') THEN(DO)
              SNDPGMMSG   MSGID(&MSGID) MSGF(&MSGFLIB/&MSGF) +
                            MSGDTA(&MSGDTA) MSGTYPE(*DIAG)
              MONMSG      MSGID(CPF0000) EXEC(GOTO CMDLBL(RSND_END))
              ENDDO
              GOTO        CMDLBL(RSND_RPT)
 RSND_END:    SNDPGMMSG   MSGID(CPF9898) MSGF(QSYS/QCPFMSG) +
                            MSGDTA('Operation ended in error.  See +
                            previously listed messages') MSGTYPE(*ESCAPE)
              MONMSG      MSGID(CPF0000) EXEC(GOTO CMDLBL(FINISH))
              ENDDO
/* End of program */
FINISH:       RETURN
              ENDPGM
```

of each output queue entry and enter each name into the CPYSPLF (Copy Spool File) command or any other command you use to process the entry.

Now compare the code in Figure 30.1 to the version of CVTOUTQCL shown in Figure 30.2. The programs' styles are dramatically different. Figure 30.1's code is crowded and difficult to read, primarily because of the CL prompter's default layout. In addition, this style lacks elements such as helpful spacing, code alignment, and comments that help you break the code down into logical, readable chunks. Figure 30.2's code is much more readable and comprehensible. An informative program header relates the program's purpose and basic functions. The program also features more attractive code alignment, spacing that divides the code into distinct sections, indentation for nested DO-ENDDO groups, and mnemonic variable names. (See Appendix D for the complete CVTOUTQ Command and CPP, and full implementation details.) Let's take a closer look at the elements responsible for Figure 30.2's clarity and some coding guidelines you can use to produce sharp CL code with a consistent appearance.

Write a descriptive program header

If the first source statement in your CL program is the PGM statement, something's missing. All programs, including CL programs, need an introduction. To create a stylish CL program, first *write a program header that describes the program's purpose and basic function.*

Figure 30.2

CL Program CVTOUTQCL — Version 2

```
/*===================================================================*/
/*   Program name :  CVTOUTQCL                                        */
/*   Program type :  CPP  -  for command CVTOUTQ                      */
/*   Author name..:  Wayne Madden                                     */
/*   Date created :  March 1, 1992                                    */
/*                                                                    */
/*   Purpose......:  Convert output queue list of entries to an       */
/*                   externally described database file.              */
/*                                                                    */
/*   Program Summary                                                  */
/*   --------------------------------------------------------------- */
/*   1. Verify existence of selected outq named in &i_ql_outq         */
/*   2. Create work files.                                            */
/*   3. WRKOUTQ of output queue to OUTPUT(*PRINT)                     */
/*   4. Copy the spool file of above step to flat file DSPOUTQ        */
/*   5. Use HLL program CVTOUTQR to convert spool file entry records  */
/*        found in DSPOUTQ to the externally described outfile        */
/*        named in &i_ql_outf.                                        */
/*                                                                    */
/*                                                                    */
/*   Revision Summary                                                 */
/*   --------------------------------------------------------------- */
/*   Wayne Madden    03/01/92    Modify escape message handling to    */
/*                               ensure cleanup operations performed. */
/*                                                                    */
/*===================================================================*/

   PGM  PARM( &i_ql_outq  /* IN Output queue name (qualified)     */ +
              &i_ql_outf  /* IN Outfile name (qualified)          */ +
            )

/* Incoming Parameters from command CVTOUTQ                          */

   DCL  &i_ql_outq    *CHAR   20
   DCL  &i_ql_outf    *CHAR   20

/* Work variables for incoming parameters                            */

   DCL  &outq         *CHAR   10
   DCL  &outqlib      *CHAR   10
   DCL  &outfile      *CHAR   10
   DCL  &outflib      *CHAR   10

/* Work variables for message handling                               */

   DCL  &msgdta       *CHAR  256
   DCL  &msgf         *CHAR   10
   DCL  &msgflib      *CHAR   10
   DCL  &msgid        *CHAR    7
   DCL  &rtntype      *CHAR    2
/* General work variables                                            */

   DCL  &f11exist     *LGL     1  VALUE('0')
```

Figure 30.2 Continued

Figure 30.2

CL Program CVTOUTQCL — Version 2 *Continued*

```
  DCL  &fl2exist    *LGL     1  VALUE('0')
  DCL  &io_rtncode  *CHAR    1  VALUE('0')
  DCL  &msg_flag    *LGL     1  VALUE('0')

/* Work variables for defining mnemonics                           */

  DCL  &@blanks     *CHAR    1  VALUE(' ')
  DCL  &@diag       *CHAR    2  VALUE('02')
  DCL  &@escape     *CHAR    2  VALUE('15')
  DCL  &@false      *LGL     1  VALUE('0')
  DCL  &@rtn_norec  *CHAR    1  VALUE('1')
  DCL  &@rtn_ok     *CHAR    1  VALUE('0')
  DCL  &@true       *LGL     1  VALUE('1')

/* Program-level monitor message                                   */

  MONMSG CPF9999 EXEC(GOTO GLOBAL_ERR)

/* Create actual work variables from qualified name parameters     */

  CHGVAR  &outq     (%SST(&i_ql_outq 1 10))
  CHGVAR  &outqlib  (%SST(&i_ql_outq 11 10))

  CHGVAR  &outfile  (%SST(&i_ql_outf 1 10))
  CHGVAR  &outflib  (%SST(&i_ql_outf 11 10))

/*=================================================================*/
/* Validation and setup                                            */
/*=================================================================*/

/* Check for the Outq Object.                                      */

  CHKOBJ OBJ(&outqlib/&outq) OBJTYPE(*OUTQ)
  MONMSG CPF9801 EXEC(DO)
    SNDPGMMSG MSGID(CPF9898)                                    +
              MSGF(QSYS/QCPFMSG)                                +
              MSGDTA('Output queue' |>                          +
                     &outqlib       |<                          +
                     '/'            ||                          +
                     &outq          |>                          +
                     'not found')                               +
              TOPGMQ(*SAME)                                     +
              MSGTYPE(*DIAG)
    CHGVAR &msg_flag &@true
    GOTO CLEAN_UP
  ENDDO

/* Set up work file in QTEMP.                                      */

  CHGVAR &fl1exist &@true
  CHKOBJ OBJ(QTEMP/DSPOUTQ) OBJTYPE(*FILE)
  MONMSG CPF9801 EXEC(DO)
    CHGVAR &fl1exist &@false
```

Figure 30.2 Continued

Figure 30.2

CL Program CVTOUTQCL — Version 2 *Continued*

```
  ENDDO
  IF (&fl1exist) DO
    CLRPFM QTEMP/DSPOUTQ
  ENDDO
  ELSE DO
    CRTPF FILE(QTEMP/DSPOUTQ) RCDLEN(132)
    CHGVAR &fl1exist &@true
  ENDDO
  OVRDBF  FILE(DSPOUTQ) TOFILE(QTEMP/DSPOUTQ)

/* Create outfile named in &outfile and &outflib variables          */

  CHGVAR &fl2exist &@true
  CHKOBJ OBJ(&outflib/&outfile) OBJTYPE(*FILE)
  MONMSG CPF9801 EXEC(DO)
    CHGVAR &fl2exist &@false
  ENDDO
  IF (&fl2exist) DO
    CLRPFM &outflib/&outfile
  ENDDO
  ELSE DO
    CRTDUPOBJ OBJ(QACVTOTQ)                                        +
              FROMLIB(KWMLIB)                                      +
              OBJTYPE(*FILE)                                       +
              TOLIB(&outflib)                                      +
              NEWOBJ(&outfile)
    CHGVAR &fl2exist &@true
  ENDDO
  OVRDBF FILE(QACVTOTQ) TOFILE(&outflib/&outfile)


/*  Override spool file to HOLD(*YES). QPRTSPLQ is spoool file       */
/*    created by WRKOUTQ OUTPUT(*PRINT).                             */

  OVRPRTF FILE(QPRTSPLQ) SCHEDULE(*IMMED) HOLD(*YES)
  WRKOUTQ &outqlib/&outq OUTPUT(*PRINT)

/*  Copy the spool file to disk file DSPOUTQ.                        */
/*  Override the declared disk file to the one in QTEMP.             */

  CPYSPLF FILE(QPRTSPLQ) TOFILE(QTEMP/DSPOUTQ) SPLNBR(*LAST)
  DLTSPLF FILE(QPRTSPLQ) SPLNBR(*LAST)
  MONMSG (CPF3303 CPF3344) /* file not found or no longer on system */


/*=================================================================*/
/* Call HLL program CVTOUTQR to perform data conversion             */
/*      &io_rtncode values:   'Ø' = successful operation            */
/*                            '1' = no spool file entries found     */
/*=================================================================*/

  CALL CVTOUTQR PARM( &io_rtncode  /* IN/OUT return code        */ +
                    )
```

Figure 30.2 Continued

Figure 30.2

CL Program CVTOUTQCL — Version 2 *Continued*

```
  MONMSG CPF0006 EXEC(DO)
    SNDPGMMSG MSGID(CPF9898)                                              +
              MSGF(QSYS/QCPFMSG)                                          +
              MSGDTA('Call to program CVTOUTQR ended in error')           +
              TOPGMQ(*SAME)                                               +
              MSGTYPE(*DIAG)
    CHGVAR &msg_flag &@true
    GOTO CLEAN_UP
  ENDDO

  IF (&io_rtncode = &@rtn_norec) DO
    SNDPGMMSG MSGID(CPF9898)                                              +
              MSGF(QSYS/QCPFMSG)                                          +
              MSGDTA('No entries found in output queue' |>                +
                     &outqlib                           |<                +
                     '/'                                ||                +
                     &outq)                                               +
              TOPGMQ(*SAME)                                               +
              MSGTYPE(*DIAG)
    CHGVAR &msg_flag &@true
    GOTO CLEAN_UP
  ENDDO

  IF (&io_rtncode = &@rtn_ok) DO
    SNDPGMMSG MSGID(CPF9898)                                              +
              MSGF(QSYS/QCPFMSG)                                          +
              MSGDTA('Output queue'       |>                              +
                     &outqlib             |<                              +
                     '/'                  ||                              +
                     &outq                |>                              +
                     'entries converted')                                 +
              MSGTYPE(*COMP)
  ENDDO

  GOTO CLEAN_UP

/*===================================================================*/
/* Program level MONMSG detected, flag for messages.                 */
/*===================================================================*/
GLOBAL_ERR:
  IF (&msg_flag) DO  /* To protect from error looping */
    SNDPGMMSG MSGID(CPF9898)                                              +
              MSGF(QSYS/QCPFMSG)                                          +
              MSGDTA('Error in message handling process ' ||              +
                'detected during a program failure.'      |>              +
                'See joblog for details')                                 +
              MSGTYPE(*ESCAPE)
    MONMSG CPF0000 EXEC(RETURN)
  ENDDO
  CHGVAR &msg_flag &@true

/*-------------------------------------------------------------------*/
/* Perform any program cleanup operations.                           */
```

Figure 30.2 Continued

Figure 30.2

CL Program CVTOUTQCL — Version 2 *Continued*

```
/*--------------------------------------------------------------------*/

CLEAN_UP:
  IF (&fl1exist) DLTF QTEMP/DSPOUTQ

/*====================================================================*/
/* Error handling - resend messages to calling program               */
/*    IF &msg_flag, then error messages are in queue to be sent.     */
/*====================================================================*/

RSND_BGN:
  IF (&msg_flag) DO

    RSND_RPT:
      RCVMSG RMV(*YES)                                                +
             MSGDTA(&msgdta)                                          +
             MSGID(&msgid)                                            +
             RTNTYPE(&rtntype)                                        +
             MSGF(&msgf)                                              +
             MSGFLIB(&msgflib)
      MONMSG CPF0000 EXEC(GOTO RSND_END)
      IF (&msgid = &@blanks) GOTO RSND_END /* no more messages */
      IF (&rtntype = &@diag *OR &rtntype = &@escape) DO
        SNDPGMMSG MSGID(&msgid)                                       +
                  MSGF(&msgflib/&msgf)                                +
                  MSGDTA(&msgdta)                                     +
                  MSGTYPE(*DIAG)
        MONMSG CPF0000 EXEC(GOTO RSND_END)
      ENDDO
      GOTO RSND_RPT

    RSND_END:
      SNDPGMMSG MSGID(CPF9898)                                        +
                MSGF(QSYS/QCPFMSG)                                    +
                MSGDTA('Operation ended in error. ' ||                +
                  'See previously listed messages')                   +
                MSGTYPE(*ESCAPE)
      MONMSG CPF0000 EXEC(GOTO FINISH)

  ENDDO

/*====================================================================*/
/* End of program                                                     */
/*====================================================================*/

FINISH:
  RETURN
  ENDPGM
```

Figure 30.2's program header provides the basic information a programmer needs to become familiar with the program's purpose and function. An accurate introduction helps programmers who later work with your programs feel more comfortable as they debug or enhance your code.

The program header begins with the program's name, followed by the author's name and the date created. An essential piece of the program header is the "program type," which identifies the type of code that follows. CL program types include the CPP (command processing program), the VCP (validity checking program), the CPO (command prompt override program), the MENU (menu program), and the PROMPT (prompter). You may use other categories or different names to describe the types of CL programs. But whatever you call it, you should identify the type of program you are writing and label it appropriately in the header.

Another important part of the introduction is a description of what the program does. State the program's purpose concisely, and, in the program summary, outline the basic program functions to familiarize the programmer with how the program works. You should detail the summary only in terms of what happens and what events occur (e.g., building a file or copying records). A good program header also includes a revision summary, featuring a list of revisions, the dates they were made, and the names of those who made them.

If you don't have a standard CL program header, create a template of one in a source member called CLHEADER (or some other obvious name) and copy the member into each CL program. Fill in the current information for each program, and remember to maintain the information as part of the quality control checks you perform on production code. While an up-to-date program header is valuable, an outdated one can be misleading and harmful.

Format your programs to aid understanding

Determining where to start each statement is one of the most basic coding decisions you can make. If you're used to prompting each CL statement, your first inclination would be to begin each one in column 14. While you should use prompting when necessary to enter proper parameter values, the resulting alignment of commands, keywords, and values creates code that is difficult, at best, to read and maintain. Over the years, I've collected several guidelines about where to place code and comments within CL programs.

For starters, *begin all comments in column 1, and make comment lines a standard length.* Beginning comments in column 1 gives you the maximum number of columns in which to type the comment. And establishing a consistent comment line-length (i.e., the number of spaces between the beginning "/*" and the closing "*/") makes the program look neat and orderly.

Comments should also stand out in the source. In Figure 30.2, a blank line precedes and follows each comment line to make it more visible. Notice that comments describing a process are boxed-in by lines of special characters (I use the "-" character). Nobody wants to read code in which comments outnumber program statements. But descriptive (not cryptic) comments that define and describe the program's basic sections and functions are helpful road signs.

A second guideline is to *begin all label names in column 1 on a line with no other code (or at the appropriate nesting level, if located within an IF-THEN or IF-THEN-ELSE construct).* Labels in CL programs serve as targets of GOTO statements. The AS/400 implementation of CL requires you to use GOTO statements to perform certain tasks that other languages can accomplish through a subroutine or a DO WHILE construct. Because labels provide such a basic function, they should clearly reveal entry points into specific statements. Starting a label name in column 1 and placing it alone on the line helps separate it from subsequent code. Notice in Figure 30.2 how you can quickly scan down column 1 and locate the labels (e.g., GLOBAL_ERR, CLEAN_UP, RSND_BGN). However, notice the placement of labels RSND_RPT and RSND_END (at B and C). Instead of beginning these two labels in column 1, I indented them to the expected nesting level to promote comprehension of the overall process. The code following the indented labels remains indented to help the labels stand out and to make the IF-THEN construct more readable.

To offset command statements from comments and labels, *start commands in column 3*. Beginning commands in column 3 — rather than the prompter's default starting column (14) — gives you much more room to enter keywords and values. It also gives you more room to arrange your code.

The exception to this guideline concerns using the DO command as part of an IF-THEN or IF-THEN-ELSE construct. To help identify what code is executed in a DO group, I recommend that you *indent the code in each DO group*. A simple indented DO-ENDDO group might appear as follows:

```
IF ("condition") DO
  CL statement
  CL statement
ENDDO
```

A multilevel set of DO-ENDDO groups, including an ELSE statement, might appear like this:

```
IF ("condition") DO
  IF ("condition") DO
    CL statement
    CL statement
    IF ("condition") DO
      CL statement
    ENDDO
  ENDDO
  ELSE DO
    CL statement
    CL statement
  ENDDO
ENDDO
```

Notice that the IF and ENDDO statements — and thus the logic — are clearly visible.

Simplify and align command parameters

When you use the prompter to enter values for command parameters, Source Entry Utility (SEU) automatically places the selected keywords and values into the code. Several simple guidelines can greatly enhance the way commands, keywords, and values appear in your CL programs. First, omit the following common keywords when using the associated commands:

Command	Keyword
DCL	VAR, TYPE, LEN
CHGVAR	VAR, VALUE
IF	COND, THEN
ELSE	CMD
GOTO	CMDLBL
MONMSG	MSGID

The meanings of the parameter values are always obvious by position. Thus, the keywords just clutter up your code. The following statements omit unneeded keywords:

```
DCL  &outq  *CHAR  10
CHGVAR &outq (%SST(&i_ql_outq 1 10))
IF (&flag) GOTO FINISH
GOTO RSND_RPT
```

By starting commands in column 3 and following the indentation guidelines, you can type most commands on one line. But when you must continue the command to another line, you have several alternatives, as Figure 30.3 shows. The first alternative is to use the "+" continuation symbol, indent a couple of spaces on the next line, and continue entering command keywords and values. This is the simplest way to continue a command but the most difficult to read. The second alternative is to place as many keywords and values as possible on the first line and arrange the continuation lines so the additional keywords and values appear as columns under those on the first line. Although this option may be the easiest to read, creating the alignment is a major headache. The third alternative is simply to place each keyword and associated value on a separate line. This method is both simple to implement and easy to read. Thus, a second guideline is to *place the entire command on one line when possible; otherwise, place the command and first keyword on the first line and each subsequent keyword on a separate line, using the* "+" *continuation symbol.*

A third guideline is to *align the command and its parameters in columns when you repeat the same single-line command statement.* This rule of thumb applies when you have a group of statements involving the same command. The DCL statement is a good example. Normally, one or more groups of DCL statements appear at the beginning of each CL program to define variables the program uses. Figure 30.2 shows how placing the DCL statement and parameter values in columns creates more readable code. This alignment rule also applies to multiple CHGVAR (Change Variable) commands.

While you can apply the above rules to most commands, the IF command may require special alignment consideration. If the *IF statement won't fit on a single line, use the DO-ENDDO construct.* For example, the IF statement

Figure 30.3

Options for Arranging Parameters

```
/*==================================================================*/
/* Option 1 - Parameter arrangement - wrap to next line             */
/*==================================================================*/

RSND_RPT:
    RCVMSG RMV(*YES) MSGDTA(&msgdta) MSGID(&msgid) RTNTYPE(&rtntype) +
      MSGF(&msgf) MSGFLIB(&msgflib)
    MONMSG CPF0000 EXEC(GOTO RSND_END)
    IF (&msgid = ' ') GOTO RSND_END /* no more messages   */
    IF (&rtntype = &@diag *OR &rtntype = &@escape) DO
      SNDPGMMSG MSGID(&msgid) MSGF(&msgflib/&msgf) MSGDTA(&msgdta) +
MSGTYPE(*DIAG)
    MONMSG CPF0000 EXEC(GOTO RSND_END)
    ENDDO
    GOTO RSND_RPT


/*==================================================================*/
/* Option 2 - Parameter arrangement - wrap and align in columns     */
/*==================================================================*/

RSND_RPT:
    RCVMSG RMV(*YES)          MSGDTA(&msgdta) MSGID(&msgid)          +
           RTNTYPE(&rtntype) MSGF(&msgf)     MSGFLIB(&msgflib)
    MONMSG CPF0000 EXEC(GOTO RSND_END)
    IF (&msgid = ' ') GOTO RSND_END /* no more messages */
    IF (&rtntype = &@diag *OR &rtntype = &@escape) DO
      SNDPGMMSG MSGID(&msgid)   MSGF(&msgflib/&msgf)                 +
                MSGDTA(&msgdta) MSGTYPE(*DIAG)
    MONMSG CPF0000 EXEC(GOTO RSND_END)
    ENDDO
    GOTO RSND_RPT


/*==================================================================*/
/* Option 3 - Parameter arrangement - one on each line              */
/*==================================================================*/

RSND_RPT:
    RCVMSG RMV(*YES)                                                 +
           MSGDTA(&msgdta)                                           +
           MSGID(&msgid)                                             +
           RTNTYPE(&rtntype)                                         +
           MSGF(&msgf)                                               +
           MSGFLIB(&msgflib)
    MONMSG CPF0000 EXEC(GOTO RSND_END)
    IF (&msgid = ' ') GOTO RSND_END /* no more messages */
    IF (&rtntype = &@diag *OR &rtntype = &@escape) DO
      SNDPGMMSG MSGID(&msgid)                                        +
                MSGF(&msgflib/&msgf)                                 +
                MSGDTA(&msgdta)                                      +
                MSGTYPE(*DIAG)
      MONMSG CPF0000 EXEC(GOTO RSND_END)
    ENDDO
    GOTO RSND_RPT
```

```
IF (&fl2exist) CRTDUPOBJ OBJ(QACVTOTQ)                              +
  FROMLIB(KWMLIB) OBJTYPE(*FILE)                                    +
  TOLIB(&outlib) NEWOBJ(&outfile)
```

should be written

```
IF (&fl2exist) DO
  CRTDUPOBJ OBJ(QACVTOTQ)                                           +
            FROMLIB(KWMLIB)                                         +
            OBJTYPE(*FILE)                                          +
            TOLIB(&outlib)                                          +
            NEWOBJ(&outfile)
ENDDO
```

This construction implements guidelines discussed earlier and presents highly accessible code.

Align, shorten, and simplify for neatness

One of the most common symptoms of poor CL style is a general overcrowding of code. Such code moves from one statement to the next without any thought to organization, spacing, or neatness. The result looks more like a blob of commands than a flowing stream of clear, orderly statements. To save yourself and others the eyestrain of trying to read a jumble of code, follow these suggestions for clean, crisp CL programs:

Align all "+" continuation symbols so they stand out in the source code. In Figure 30.2, I've aligned all "+" continuation symbols in column 69. Not only does alignment give your programs a uniform appearance, but it also clearly identifies commands that are continued on several lines. I use the "+" symbol instead of the "-" for continuation because the "+" better controls the number of blanks that appear when continuing a string of characters. Both symbols include as part of the string blanks that immediately precede or follow the symbol on the same line. But when continuing a string onto the next line in your source, the "+" symbol ignores blanks that precede the first nonblank character in the next record. The "-" continuation symbol includes them.

Use blank lines liberally to make code more accessible. Spacing between blocks of code and between comment lines and code can really help programmers identify sections of code, distinguish one command from another, and generally "get into" the program. Blank lines don't cost you processing time, so feel free to space, space, space.

*Use the shorthand symbols ||, |<, and |> instead of the corresponding *CAT, *TCAT, and *BCAT operatives.* Concatenation can be messy when you use a mixture of strings, variables, and the *CAT, *BCAT, and *TCAT operators. The shorthand symbols shorten and simplify expressions that use concatenation keywords and commands, and clearly identify breaks between strings and variables.

Highlight variables with distinct, lowercase names

An essential part of CL style concerns how you use variables in your programs. I don't have any hard-and-fast rules, but I do have some suggestions. First, consider the names you assign variables. *Give program parameters distinct names that identify them as parameters.* In Figure 30.2, the two parameters processed by the CPP are `&i_ql_outq` and `&i_ql_outf`. The "`i_`" in the names tells me both parameters are input-only ("`io_`" would have indicated a return variable). The "`ql_`" tells me the parameters' values are qualified names (i.e., they include the library name).

When program CVTOUTQCL calls program CVTOUTQR, it uses parameter `&io_rtncode` (A in Figure 30.2). The prefix indicates the parameter is both an input and an output variable, and the rest of the name tells me program CVTOUTQR will return a value to the calling program.

A second guideline concerns variables that contain more than one value (e.g., a qualified name or the contents of a data area). You should *extract the values into separate variables before using the values in your program.* In Figure 30.2, input parameter `&i_ql_outq` is the qualified name of the output queue. Later in the program, you find the following two statements:

```
CHGVAR &outq      (%SST(&i_ql_outq 1 10))
CHGVAR &outqlib   (%SST(&i_ql_outq 11 10))
```

These two statements divide the qualified name into separate variables. The separate variables let you code a statement such as

```
CHKOBJ OBJ(&outqlib/&outq) OBJTYPE(*OUTQ)
```

instead of

```
CHKOBJ OBJ(%SST(&i_ql_outq 11 10)/                        +
           %SST(&i_ql_outq 1 10))                         +
       OBJTYPE(*OUTQ)
```

You should also *define variables to represent frequently used literal values.* For example, define values such as `'x'`, `' '`, and `'0'` as variables `&@x`, `&@blanks`, and `&@zero`, and then use the variable names in tests instead of repeatedly coding the constants as part of the test condition. This guideline lets you define all of a program's constants in one set of DCL statements, which you can easily create and maintain at the start of the program source. In addition, notice the difference between the following statements:

```
IF (&value = ' ') DO
IF (&value = &@blanks) DO
```

You can more easily digest the second statement because it explicitly tells you what value will result in execution of the DO statement. You may find that defining frequently used variables not only improves productivity, but also promotes consistency as programmers simply copy the variable DCL statements into new source members.

A final guideline concerning variables is to *type variable names in lowercase.* The lowercase variable names contrast nicely with the uppercase commands/parameters. Although typing the names in lowercase may not be easy using SEU, the contrast in type will greatly improve the program's readability.

Compare Figure 30.1 with Figure 30.2 again. Which code would you like to encounter the next time you examine a CL program for the first time? I hope you can use these guidelines to create a consistent CL style from which everyone in your shop can benefit. Remember, when you're trying to read a program you didn't write, appearance can be everything.

Summary of CL Style Guidelines

- Write a program header that describes the program's purpose and basic function.
- Begin all comments in column 1, and make comment lines a standard length.
- Begin all label names in column 1 or at the appropriate nesting level (if located within an IF-THEN or IF-THEN-ELSE construct), and put them on a line with no other code.
- Start CL commands in column 3.
- Indent the code in each DO group.
- Omit the following common keywords when using the associated commands:

Command	Keyword
DCL	VAR, TYPE, LEN
CHGVAR	VAR, VALUE
IF	COND, THEN
ELSE	CMD
GOTO	CMDLBL
MONMSG	MSGID

- Place the entire command on one line when possible; otherwise, place the command and first keyword on the first line and each subsequent keyword on a separate line, using the "+" continuation symbol.
- Align commands and keywords in columns when you repeat the same single-line command statement.
- If the IF statement won't fit on a single line, use the DO-ENDDO construct.
- Align all "+" continuation symbols so they stand out in the source code.
- Use blank lines liberally to make code more accessible.
- Use the shorthand symbols | |, |<, and |> instead of the *CAT, *TCAT, and *BCAT operatives.
- Give program parameters distinct names that identify them as parameters.
- Extract values from multiple-value variables into separate variables before using the values in your program.
- Define variables to represent frequently used literal values.
- Type variable names in lowercase.

Chapter 31

RPG Programming Style

by Richard M. Rubin

Follow these rules for clear code to save time testing and maintaining programs

We all know him. Johnny B. Hacker, the programmer who, like Johnny B. Goode on the guitar, is a virtuoso on the coding keyboard, but whose reading and writing skills were arrested shortly after kindergarten. He can't interpret user requirements, and his documentation (if it exists) requires translation into some natural human language to make sense out of it. But give him a set of specifications, and he'll have a working program five times faster than anybody else around.

Working code, however, is only the minimum requirement for a successful program. It means that you were able to communicate with the machine. Yet a program must not only work, but work correctly. In other words, what you tell the machine to do must correspond to the requirements of the system the program is a part of. Moreover, the code should clearly convey to the reader the task it is performing; for a program's code is both the means by which you generate instructions to a machine and an instrument for letting other human beings know how you implemented the program's specifications.

The skills needed to code clearly are similar to those needed to write clearly. Good writing comes from more than a feeling for words and what words can do: A sense for grammar, clarity of diction, and orderly presentation of ideas require logical as well as verbal skills. Programming, on the other hand, is not merely an exercise of the logical faculties. Some say that programming is essentially logic or mathematics and that the essence of programming is a series of maneuvers performed on a set of symbols. However, to perform these logical or mathematical maneuvers, you must first translate user or system requirements into the appropriate symbols, and this preliminary task of translation is not trivial. Making logical connections and communicating clearly with people are different functions requiring different skills, but both are necessary to good programming.

This should not be taken to mean only that specifications should be explicit before coding begins or that programs should be well documented. Code itself should be written with an eye toward making it as easy to follow as possible. If Johnny B. Hacker's lightning code is hard for others to decipher, then his coding speed rapidly loses its advantage at testing and maintenance time.

Code for Clarity

Consider Figure 31.1, a pair of RPG calculation specifications I found in a program I was maintaining. Forget for a moment that it is best to avoid indicators. Forget even the absurdity of using one group of indicators to store the values of another group. Stop reading and try to follow these C-specs.

How quickly did you realize that the purpose of these lines is to put the values of indicators 9, 10, and 11 into indicators 27, 28, and 29? Could you tell at first glance? It surely would have been easier had the programmer coded as in Figure 31.2. Figure 31.1 saved only one line of code and that was at the cost of clarity.

Now consider the single C-spec in Figure 31.3. This line employs a widely used technique for converting a six-digit date from month-day-year format to year-month-day. It works because the result field is a six-digit integer, so unwanted digits are truncated at both the right and the left. Multiply 032591 by 10000.01, and you get 0325910325.91. But as everything to the right of the decimal and to the left of the first 9 is truncated, you are left with 910325. It is clever, isn't it? Compact, too. But if you weren't in on the technique, would you know why this off-the-wall multiplication was sitting in the middle of a program? Isn't the code in Figure 31.4 better? Yes, this improvement requires two extra lines of code, but at least the code says what it doing.

These examples point out the first three guidelines for writing code that is easy to read and maintain:

Figure 31.1

Obscure Indicator Setting

```
*... ... 1 ... ... 2 ... ... 3 ... ... 4 ... ... 5 ... ... 6 ... ... 7

     C                          MOVEA*IN,Ø9     X3        3
     C                          MOVEAX3         *IN,27
```

Figure 31.2

Clear Indicator Setting

```
*... ... 1 ... ... 2 ... ... 3 ... ... 4 ... ... 5 ... ... 6 ... ... 7

     C                          MOVE *INØ9      *IN27
     C                          MOVE *IN1Ø      *IN28
     C                          MOVE *IN11      *IN29
```

Figure 31.3

Unintuitive Date Conversion Trick

```
*... ... 1 ... ... 2 ... ... 3 ... ... 4 ... ... 5 ... ... 6 ... ... 7

     C          DTMDY     MULT 10000.01  C@YMD   60
```

Figure 31.4

Clearer Date Conversion

```
*... ... 1 ... ... 2 ... ... 3 ... ... 4 ... ... 5 ... ... 6 ... ... 7

     C          4         SUBSTDTMDYA:1  C@MDA   4
     C          2         SUBSTDTMDYA:5  C@YYA   2
     C          C@YYA     CAT  C@MDA     C@YMDA  6
```

Code should reveal its purpose, not hide it

Don't try to force a program into fewer lines of code at the expense of clarity

Avoid clever programming tricks

Efficiency vs. Clarity

At this point, someone is sure to ask, "Isn't Figure 31.3 more efficient?" The answer is no. Even if the answer were yes, the code in Figure 31.4 is preferable. Kernighan and Plauger, in *The Elements of Programming Style*, emphasize the importance of clarity over and over:

"Write clearly — don't sacrifice clarity for efficiency."

"Make it right before you make it faster."

"Keep it right when you make it faster."

"Make it clear before you make it faster."

"Don't sacrifice clarity for small gains in efficiency."

This drum-like repetition is warranted. In his essay "A Case Against the GOTO," W.A. Wolf wrote a sentence that should flash in your head any time you are tempted to spend a few hours (or even minutes) to save a few microseconds: "More computing sins are committed in the name of efficiency (without necessarily achieving it) than for any other single reason — including blind stupidity."

This is not to say that you can ignore all performance considerations. The amount of database I/O can sometimes make the difference between acceptable and unbearable response time. But you should understand which considerations are important and which are trivial. Here are some considerations you should definitely *not* allow to interfere with producing readable code:

- whether a Z-ADD is as efficient as a MOVE
- whether a MOVEL is as efficient as a MOVE
- whether a MOVE is as efficient as an IF
- whether code in subroutines is as efficient as code in the mainline
- whether CAS groups are as efficient as IF-ELSE constructions
- where to place subroutines for maximum efficiency

A Real Case Study

Let us look now at a section of code (Figure 31.5) from the same program. This program has been in use for several years and is therefore well past initial debugging. It is not a particularly complex program; and for the most part, it does its job. It is an interactive update program for a master file (in this case, a location master in a gas measurement system). The program uses two screens (SCR10 and SCR20), the first for entering the key field values and the second for displaying or entering all the non-key fields of the record identified by the values entered on the first screen. The first screen (the key screen) lets the user choose, by means of function keys, one of four modes of action: display, add, change, and delete.

The code is not impossible to follow — it could have been much worse — but it nevertheless presents several problems for the maintenance programmer trying to understand how it works. I have included the code's documentation

Figure 31.5

Poor Indicator Usage and Internal Documentation

```
 *... ... 1 ... ... 2 ... ... 3 ... ... 4 ... ... 5 ... ... 6 ... ... 7

     C*   Chain to operator master w/operator no entered.                 *
(A)  C          KEY1      CHAINLOCMSTRF               50
     C*                                                                   *
     C*   Make sure that if attempting to add a location that it          *
     C* doesn't already exist, if so issue error message.                 *
     C* Also for a delete make sure that it is not in the meter master.   *
(B)  C          *IN61     IFEQ ON                                ADD mode
     C          *IN50     IFEQ OFF                               Already Exists?
     C                    MOVE ON        *IN30                   >YES
     C                    END                                    50,off
(C)  C                    ELSE                                   09,on
     C*                                                                   *
     C*   Make sure that if attempting to modify/delete a location that   *
     C* it does exist, if not issue error message.                        *
(D)  C          *IN50     IFEQ ON
     C                    MOVE ON        *IN31
     C                    ELSE                                   50,on
     C          *IN63     IFEQ ON
     C          KEY1      SETLLMTRMSTRA                   33
(E)  C                    END                                    11,on
     C                    END                                    50,on
     C*                                                                   *
     C                    END                                    09,on
```

just as it appeared — even though the focus of this chapter is the clarity of code itself — if only to emphasize that documentation is no substitute for a clearly written program and to show that partial or incorrect documentation can be more of a hindrance than a help.

Indicator Usage and Meaningful Names

The code in Figure 31.5 edits the values entered on the key screen. The programmer attempted to clarify the code by substituting the variables ON and OFF for the constants '1' and '0'. ON and OFF were initialized to '1' and '0', respectively, at the start of the program. (Recent versions of RPG/400 support *ON and *OFF figurative constants instead of requiring the use of programmer-defined variables.) The technique of letting variables contain constant values is a good one and should be encouraged, but the readability problem the programmer alleviated was trivial (is it really that hard to remember what '1' and '0' mean?), and he ignored the more fundamental problem posed by those notorious remnants of RPG's past, the indicators. Line B in Figure 31.5 has a comment telling us that *IN61 means "ADD Mode." The next line reminds us that, if *IN50 is off, a record has been found that matches the key field values the user entered. The following line turns *IN30 on.

Moving to the code that follows the first ELSE (D), things get somewhat more confusing. We have to remember (there is no comment to help us this time) that *IN50 being on means no record was found back at A and that no record is bad because we're not in add mode (you have to *have* a record to display, change, or delete it). By now we've gone through two negations (one of which is signaled by an indicator in the ON state, so perhaps it's three negations) to figure out what is happening. The comment ("Make sure that if attempting to modify/delete a location that it does exist") attempts to state things positively, but probably confuses the situation more because it fails to mention that we might be in display mode. The comment on the first ELSE statement (C) doesn't help, either: "09,on." Does the comment mean that *IN09 is on or not on? And what difference does it make? *IN09 doesn't even appear in this part of the code!

Next, *IN63 appears out of the blue without comment. What does it mean? A few moments of reflection might enable you to realize that the next line, which is executed if *IN63 is on, determines whether the key field values are found in some other file, and therefore must be a referential integrity check for the use of the location as a foreign key in another file. Checking whether key field values occur elsewhere in the database should always be done before changing those key field values or before deleting the record that contains them. Because the program is not proposing to change key field values at this moment, but is merely trying to determine whether it may continue with a selected operation, you might (correctly) conclude that the purpose of the referential check is to prohibit an invalid deletion, and therefore that *IN63 must be the delete indicator. This conclusion is supported rather obliquely by the comment on the END statement that is paired with line E. The comment says "11,on." If you are a student of RPG archaeology, you would know that on the S/38, Command key 11 is the standard function key for deletion, and you might guess that somehow this comment alludes to that function key. The misplaced comment just before line B verifies this conclusion. All this confusion about what the code in Figure 31.5 does leads to another rule:

Make the meaning of the code jump out

Yes, you can figure this code out. But understanding code should not require detective work or archaeology. The problem with indicators is that it is easy to confuse them and hard to tell what they mean, even when they are well documented, which is not the case here. The difficulty with indicators is just an instance of a more general problem that is not restricted to RPG: confusing variable names.

Use variable names that are easily distinguished

RPG's six-character limit makes it especially hard to invent names that are, at the same time, consistently derived, easy to understand, and hard to confuse. Indicators only make things worse and call for another rule:

Use indicators only when they are absolutely necessary (i.e., for I/O operations and testing the result of a LOKUP operation)

Some of the indicators in Figure 31.5 are not necessary at all. A hint of what to do comes earlier in the program immediately after reading the first screen. Figure 31.6 shows that not only does the program set indicators 60 to 63 on or off in response to different function keys, it also moves the word 'DISPLAY', 'ADD', 'CHANGE', or 'DELETE' to a variable called ACTION. The programmer defined ACTION in the display file to show the user what mode the program is in. He also could have used ACTION in place of *IN61 and *IN63 in Figure 31.5, as shown in Figure 31.7. This substitution uses one clearly named variable that has four values to replace four arbitrarily assigned variables, each with two values (indicators 60 to 63; we haven't seen it yet, but two more modes need to be handled explicitly).

Use variable names that convey their meaning

In Figure 31.7, I've eliminated the interlinear comments and cleaned up the end-of-line comments so as to focus on the code itself. (In practice, it is an excellent idea to write the comment lines *before* you write any code.) Figure 31.7 is already more readable than Figure 31.5, but it has a way to go yet. Hard-coding constants like '   ADD' is dangerous, especially if a constant is used more than once, as it is here (the constant '   ADD' is copied into ACTION in Figure 31.6 and checked in Figure 31.7). Did you notice that the first occurrence of the constant above has one less blank than the second occurrence? Couldn't you easily mistype one of them if you were entering this code?

Don't hard-code quoted character constants into the main body of your program; instead, use named constants or variables initialized at the start of the program

Figure 31.6

Block of Code After First Screen Read

```
*... ... 1 ... ... 2 ... ... 3 ... ... 4 ... ... 5 ... ... 6 ... ... 7

     C           *IN08     IFEQ ON
     C                     MOVEA'1000'    *IN60
     C                     MOVE ' DISPLAY'ACTION
     C                     ELSE                            08,ON
     C           *IN09     IFEQ ON
     C                     MOVEA'0100'    *IN,60
     C                     MOVE '     ADD'ACTION
     C                     ELSE                            09,ON
     C           *IN10     IFEQ ON
     C                     MOVEA'0010'    *IN,60
     C                     MOVE '  CHANGE'ACTION
     C                     ELSE                            10,ON
     C           *IN11     IFEQ ON
     C                     MOVEA'0001'    *IN,60
     C                     MOVE '  DELETE'ACTION
     C                     ELSE                            11,ON
     C*                                                             *
     C           *IN02     CASEQON        FRESH
     C           *IN25     CASEQON        SCR10
     C                     CAS            SCR20
     C                     END                             CASxx
     C*                                                             *
     C                     END                             08,on
     C                     END                             09,on
     C                     END                             10,on
     C                     END                             11,on
```

To let the compiler trap missing characters and misspellings, you should use variables to hold constant values, as was done with the variables ON and OFF. RPG/400 provides explicitly for named constants; but even if you are using a version of RPG without this feature, you can create your own equivalent of named constants by putting a value into a variable in an initialization routine and leaving that variable unchanged in the rest of the program. It's a good idea to use some naming convention to help distinguish variables that contain constants from those that are actually subject to change. Let's start the names of constants (or variables containing constants) with the @ character, and define and initialize four of them, as in Figure 31.8.

Assuming ACTION is 10 characters long, can you see any other problem with Figure 31.7? Comparisons made using the IF operation begin on the left, but the MOVE operation used to put a value into ACTION starts on the right. Suppose the program were in add mode. Although Figures 31.6 and 31.7 use the same constant, i.e., '   ADD', when you compare ADD preceded by five blanks to ACTION in Figure 31.7, you see that ACTION contains ADD preceded by seven blanks. The comparison fails, and either an existing record goes undetected or the non-existence of a record is erroneously flagged as an error. In other words, the code in Figure 31.7 does not work correctly. If you should "keep it right when

Figure 31.7

Improved Readability Using a Meaningful Variable

```
*... ... 1 ... ... 2 ... ... 3 ... ... 4 ... ... 5 ... ... 6 ... ... 7

     C*
     C           KEY1      CHAINLOCMSTRF             50
     C*
     C           ACTION    IFEQ '     ADD'                 ADD mode
     C           *IN50     IFEQ OFF                        Rcd found
     C                     MOVE ON        *IN30
     C                     END                             50,off
     C                     ELSE                            Not ADD
     C*
     C           *IN50     IFEQ ON                         Rcd not found
     C                     MOVE ON        *IN31
     C                     ELSE                            Rcd found
     C*
     C           ACTION    IFEQ '  DELETE'                 DELETE mode
     C           KEY1      SETLLMTRMSTRA               33
     C                     END                             DELETE mode
     C                     END                             50,on
     C*                                                            *
     C                     END                             ADD mode
     C*                                                           *
```

Figure 31.8

Named Constants Instead of Literal Constants

```
*... ... 1 ... ... 2 ... ... 3 ... ... 4 ... ... 5 ... ... 6 ... ... 7
     I                    '     ADD'       C         @ADD
     I                    '  CHANGE'       C         @CHG
     I                    '  DELETE'       C         @DLT
     I                    ' DISPLAY'       C         @DSP
```

you make it faster," you should certainly keep it right when you make it clearer. Because ACTION is ten characters long, you must replace literal constants with named constants, as shown in Figure 31.9, not merely as protection against possible keying errors, but for the code to work at all.

Change indicators into readable variables as soon as possible

We can help minimize the use of *IN50 (the "location not found" indicator) by using a variable called LOCFND in conjunction with two additional named constants, @TRUE and @FALSE, which are initialized to '1' and '0', respectively, at the start of the program.

Using Clear Code Structure

Using our guidelines the code has been restructured and the new version of the code now looks like Figure 31.9. By replacing the program mode and location-

Figure 31.9

Replacing Constants with Named Constants

```
*... ... 1 ... ... 2 ... ... 3 ... ... 4 ... ... 5 ... ... 6 ... ... 7

     C*
     C             KEY1      CHAINLOCMSTRF            50
     C    50                 MOVE @FALSE    LOCFND  1
     C   N50                 MOVE @TRUE     LOCFND
     C*                                                                *
     C             ACTION    IFEQ @ADD                     ADD mode
     C             LOCFND    IFEQ @TRUE                    Rcd found
     C                       MOVE ON        *IN30          Error
     C                       END                           Rcd found
 Ⓐ   C                       ELSE                          Not ADD
     C*
     C             LOCFND    IFEQ @FALSE                   Rcd not found
     C                       MOVE ON        *IN31          Error
     C                       ELSE                          Rcd found
     C*
     C             ACTION    IFEQ @DLT                     DELETE mode
     C             KEY1      SETLLMTRMSTRA               33Error if 33on
     C                       END                           DELETE mode
     C                       END                           Rcd not found
     C*                                                                *
     C                       END                           ADD mode
     C*                                                                *
```

found indicators with the variables ACTION and LOCFND, we were also able to see and correct structural problems with this code. Translate Figure 31.9 into English: *When the specified action is "add," signal an error if the location has been found. When the action is other than "add," signal an error if the location has not been found; otherwise, if the action is "delete," check whether the location is present in the meter master and, if it is, signal an error.*

The logic gets especially hard to follow in the second sentence, which corresponds to the code that starts on line A in Figure 31.9. The problem is that the test for record-not-found is presented as an alternative to a test for add mode, and that the alternative to the test for record-not-found is a test for delete mode. Why mix tests for unrelated conditions? Apparently, the programmer decided to take a shortcut. Seeing that failure to find a record is an error in three modes of action, he decided to combine the tests and, as only delete mode had any additional tests, let that follow in the event that a record is in fact found. The problem with coding this way is that you cannot see that, in this routine, the program has four distinct modes of action. The new code in Figure 31.10 shows the remedy.

Correct structural problems that obscure the purpose of the code

While the program in Figure 31.10 has twice the lines of executable code as our original program in Figure 31.5, it is many times more clear. We've eliminated all indicators in the main body of the code except the screen error indicators (originally 30, 31, and 33, and now 30 to 34). (There is a better way to display error

Figure 31.10

Improved Structure

```
*... ... 1 ... ... 2 ... ... 3 ... ... 4 ... ... 5 ... ... 6 ... ... 7

     C*
     C          KEY1      CHAINLOCMSTRF                 50
     C    50              MOVE @FALSE    LOCFND  1
     C   N50              MOVE @TRUE     LOCFND
     C*                                                                  *
     C          ACTION    IFEQ @ADD                         ADD mode
     C          LOCFND    IFEQ @TRUE                        Rcd found
     C                    MOVE ON        *IN30              Error
     C                    END                               Rcd found
     C                    ELSE                              Not ADD
     C*
     C          ACTION    IFEQ @CHG                         CHANGE mode
     C          LOCFND    IFEQ @FALSE                       Rcd not found
     C                    MOVE ON        *IN31              Error
     C                    END                               Rcd not found
     C                    ELSE                              Not CHANGE
     C*
     C*
     C          ACTION    IFEQ @DLT                         DELETE mode
     C          LOCFND    IFEQ @FALSE                       Rcd not found
     C                    MOVE ON        *IN32              Error
     C                    ELSE                              Rcd found
     C          KEY1      SETLLMTRMSTRA                   33Error if 33on
     C                    END                               Rcd not found
     C                    ELSE                              Not DELETE
     C*
     C          ACTION    IFEQ @DSP                         DISPLAY mode
     C          LOCFND    IFEQ @FALSE                       Rcd not found
     C                    MOVE ON        *IN34              Error
     C                    END                               Rcd not found
     C*                                                                  *
     C                    END                               DISPLAY mode
     C                    END                               DELETE mode
     C                    END                               CHANGE mode
     C                    END                               ADD mode
     C*                                                                  *
```

messages — a CL subprogram and a message subfile — but for our purposes here, the indicators serve adequately to let the display file know which message to show.)

Communication from One Part of a Program to Another

The use of error indicators to communicate with the screen is one thing, but having them serve in another role as well — communicating from one part of the program to another — is bound to lead to further confusion. Look at Figure 31.11, which contains the section of the original program that immediately follows Figure 31.5. Here the indicator values from 30 to 49 are put into a 20-byte character variable (IN20 — not *IN20!), which is then compared to another 20-byte variable (OFF20) that has been initialized to zeroes. (Note that the meaning of

Figure 31.11

Continuation of Old Program

```
 *... ... 1 ... ... 2 ... ... 3 ... ... 4 ... ... 5 ... ... 6 ... ... 7

        C*   Make sure that no errors occured,  if not prepare the indica-   *
        C* tors for format GM913020, which accepts the fields for the        *
        C* location master record.                                           *
Ⓐ       C                    MOVEA*IN,30    IN20                              *
 Ⓑ      C          IN20      IFEQ OFF20                                       *
        C                    MOVEA'01'      *IN,25                            *
        C*                                                                    *
        C*    The following two lines will turn on the indicators that       *
        C* will tell the SCR20 what operation is being performed.            *
Ⓒ       C                    MOVEA*IN,09    X3      3                         *
 Ⓓ      C                    MOVEAX3        *IN,27                            *
        C*                                                                    *
                       .
                       .
                       .
             [many lines of codes initializing screen fields in ADD mode
              or moving database fields to screen fields in other modes]

                       .
                       .
        C                    END                            30-49,off        *
```

IN20 and OFF20 are not clear from the code itself.) The comment says "Make sure that no errors occurred," but the code must be deciphered to understand how it makes sure no errors have occurred and requires considerable checking to verify that it actually does that. A simpler method would be to use a variable called ERRFND and check its value. Figure 31.10 would then look like Figure 31.12, and lines A and B in Figure 31.11 could be replaced with the C-spec in Figure 31.13.

Communicate clearly between parts of the program

Figure 31.12 has one other change. If ACTION contains none of the four modes, the program issues an error message. Yes, this should be impossible; the original code (Figure 31.5) assumed that if the program was not in ADD mode, it was in one of the other three modes. Nevertheless, you should check for all logically possible conditions in order to trap program bugs. Had Figure 31.12 used quoted constants (as in Figure 31.7) instead of @ADD, @CHG, @DLT, or @DSP, the error message would be issued (because no quoted RPG constant can match the right-justified, 10-byte variable ACTION).

Notice that each END statement in Figure 31.12 has a comment showing which IF statement it goes with. Suppose you were to add another mode of action (e.g., edit meters at a location). You would have to remember to put another END statement in the right place with an appropriate comment. Maintenance like this would be easier if Figure 31.12 were reorganized to use a CAS group and a set of subroutines (see Figure 31.14). Indeed, the whole

Figure 31.12 **Restructured Using Meaningful Variable ERRFND for Communication**

```
*... ... 1 ... ... 2 ... ... 3 ... ... 4 ... ... 5 ... ... 6 ... ... 7

     C* Initialize error found flag.
     C                    MOVE @FALSE    ERRFND  1
     C* Retrieve location.
     C          KEY1      CHAINLOCMSTRF             50
     C  50                MOVE @FALSE    LOCFND  1
     C  N50               MOVE @TRUE     LOCFND
     C*
     C* ADD mode
     C          ACTION    IFEQ @ADD                         ADD mode
     C*         If location found, signal error.
     C          LOCFND    IFEQ @TRUE                        Rcd found
     C                    MOVE ON        *IN30              Error
     C                    MOVE @TRUE     ERRFND
     C                    ENDIF                             Rcd found
     C                    ELSE                              Not ADD mode
     C*
     C* CHANGE mode
     C          ACTION    IFEQ @CHG                         CHANGE mode
     C*         If location not found, signal error.
     C          LOCFND    IFEQ @FALSE                       Rcd not found
     C                    MOVE ON        *IN31              Error
     C                    MOVE @TRUE     ERRFND
     C                    ENDIF                             Rcd not found
     C                    ELSE                              Not CHANGE mode
     C*
     C* DELETE mode
     C          ACTION    IFEQ @DLT                         DELETE mode
     C*         If location not found, signal error.
     C          LOCFND    IFEQ @FALSE                       Rcd not found
     C                    MOVE ON        *IN32              Error
     C                    MOVE @TRUE     ERRFND
     C                    ELSE                              Rcd found
     C*         If location found in meter master, signal error.
     C          KEY1      SETLLMTRMSTRA                   33(Rcd fnd = 33on)
     C  33                MOVE @TRUE     ERRFND
     C                    ENDIF                             Rcd not found
     C                    ELSE                              Not DELETE mode
     C*
     C* DISPLAY mode
     C          ACTION    IFEQ @DSP                         DISPLAY mode
     C* If location not found, signal error.
     C          LOCFND    IFEQ @FALSE                       Rcd not found
     C                    MOVE ON        *IN34              Error
     C                    MOVE @TRUE     ERRFND
     C                    ENDIF                             Rcd not found
     C                    ELSE                              Not DISPLAY mode
     C*
     C* Mode not found - error
     C                    MOVE ON        *IN35
     C                    MOVE @TRUE     ERRFND
     C*
```

Figure 31.12 Continued

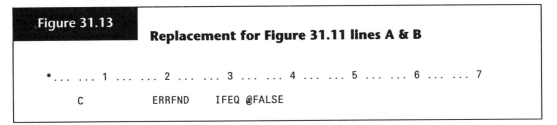

Figure 31.12 **Restructured Using Meaningful Variable ERRFND for Communication** *Continued*

```
*... ... 1 ... ... 2 ... ... 3 ... ... 4 ... ... 5 ... ... 6 ... ... 7
     C                    ENDIF                           Mode error
     C                    ENDIF                           DISPLAY mode
     C                    ENDIF                           DELETE  mode
     C                    ENDIF                           CHANGE  mode
     C                    ENDIF                           ADD     mode
     C*                                                                *
```

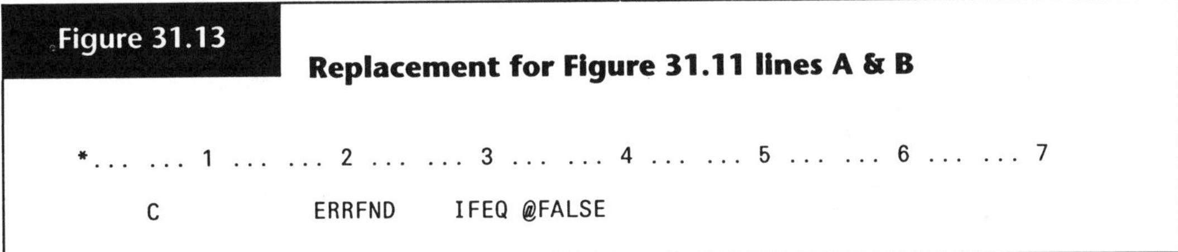

Figure 31.13 **Replacement for Figure 31.11 lines A & B**

```
*... ... 1 ... ... 2 ... ... 3 ... ... 4 ... ... 5 ... ... 6 ... ... 7

     C           ERRFND    IFEQ @FALSE
```

program might be better off if it were reorganized, but that's another issue. The topic here is clarity, and Figure 31.12 is clear enough for most purposes.

Clean Up After Yourself

Look again at Figure 31.11. Lines C and D are the lines of code we first saw in Figure 31.1. The comment says that indicators 27 to 29 are used to tell another part of the program which mode of action the program is in. You might infer from this comment that *IN27 will be on if (and only if) the action is ADD. Your inference would be wrong. A subroutine that processes the entries on the second screen contains the code shown in Figure 31.15.

You can discern the function of this case group only if you know, first, that *IN27 is defined in the display file, by means of the CHANGE keyword, as the indicator that comes on when a user enters something on the screen, and second, that the misnamed UPDATE routine trebles as an add and delete routine. If indicator 27 is set on in Figure 31.11, it doesn't affect processing because the indicator will be reset in accordance with the user's action before the program even looks at it. This doesn't mean that lines C and D are harmless. They are junk. Or at least partial junk — who knows what depends on indicators 28 and 29? Lines C and D were left in the program by a programmer who either didn't know what he was doing, but got the program to work anyway, or who left old code lying around because it didn't affect the result. Either case should be unacceptable simply, if nothing else, as a matter of professional pride; but no maintenance programmer should have to spend time figuring what lines C and D do or don't do.

Clean up your mess — don't leave code that does nothing in a program

Figure 31.14

Replacing IF Logic with the CAS Statement

```
*... ... 1 ... ... 2 ... ... 3 ... ... 4 ... ... 5 ... ... 6 ... ... 7

     C* Initialize error found flag.
     C                    MOVE @FALSE    ERRFND  1
     C*
     C* ADD mode
     C          ACTION    CASEQ @ADD     S1ØADD             ADD mode
     C          ACTION    CASEQ @CHG     S1ØCHG             CHANGE mode
     C          ACTION    CASEQ @DLT     S1ØDLT             DELETE mode
     C          ACTION    CASEQ @DSP     S1ØDSP             DISPLAY mode
     C                    CAS            S1ØERR             mode error
     C                    ENDCS
     C*
     C*-----------------------------------------------------------------
     C*  Edit key screen in ADD mode
     C*    Input:  KEY1 (location key fields)
     C*-----------------------------------------------------------------
     C          S1ØADD    BEGSR                             ADD mode
     C* Determine if location exists
     C                    EXSR CHKLOC                       Check loc
     C*         Input:  KEY1 (location key fields)
     C*         Output: LOCFND (location found - true or false)
     C*
     C*         If location found, signal error.
     C          LOCFND    IFEQ @TRUE                        Loc found
     C                    MOVE @TRUE     ERRFND
     C                    MOVE ADDERR    MSGID
     C                    CALL 'ERRMSGC'
     C                    ENDIF                             Loc found
     C                    ENDSR
     C*
     C*-----------------------------------------------------------------
     C*  Edit key screen in CHANGE mode
     C*    Input:  KEY1 (location key fields)
     C*-----------------------------------------------------------------
     C          S1ØCHG    BEGSR                             CHANGE mode
     C* Determine if location exists
     C                    EXSR CHKLOC                       Check loc
     C*         Input:  KEY1 (location key fields)
     C*         Output: LOCFND (location found - true or false)
     C*
     C*         If location not found, signal error.
     C          LOCFND    IFEQ @FALSE                       Loc not found
     C                    MOVE @TRUE     ERRFND
     C                    MOVE CHGERR    MSGID
     C                    CALL 'ERRMSGC'
     C                    ENDIF                             Loc not found
     C                    ENDSR
     C*
     C*-----------------------------------------------------------------
     C*  Edit key screen in DELETE mode
     C*    Input:  KEY1 (location key fields)
     C*-----------------------------------------------------------------
```

Figure 31.14 Continued

Figure 31.14

Replacing IF Logic with the CAS Statement *Continued*

```
*... ... 1 ... ... 2 ... ... 3 ... ... 4 ... ... 5 ... ... 6 ... ... 7
     C           S10DLT    BEGSR                          DELETE mode
     C* Determine if location exists
     C                     EXSR CHKLOC                    Check loc
     C*          Input:  KEY1 (location key fields)
     C*          Output: LOCFND (location found - true or false)
     C*
     C*          If location not found, signal error.
     C           LOCFND    IFEQ @FALSE                    Loc not found
     C                     MOVE @TRUE     ERRFND
     C                     MOVE DLTERR    MSGID
     C                     CALL 'ERRMSGC'
     C                     ELSE                           Loc found
     C*
     C*  Determine if any meter record contains the location keys
     C                     EXSR CHKMTR                    Check meter
     C*          Input:  KEY1 (location key fields)
     C*          Output: MTRFND (meter found - true or false)
     C*
     C*          If location found in meter master, signal error.
     C           MTRFND    IFEQ @TRUE                     Meter found
     C                     MOVE @TRUE     ERRFND
     C                     MOVE MTRERR    MSGID
     C                     CALL 'ERRMSGC'
     C                     MOVE @TRUE     ERRFND
     C                     ENDIF                          Meter found
     C                     ENDIF                          Loc not found
     C*
     C                     ENDSR
     C*
     C*------------------------------------------------------------------
     C*  Edit key screen in DISPLAY mode
     C*    Input:  KEY1 (location key fields)
     C*------------------------------------------------------------------
     C           S10DSP    BEGSR                          DISPLAY mode
     C* Determine if location exists
     C                     EXSR CHKLOC                    Check loc
     C*          Input:  KEY1 (location key fields)
     C*          Output: LOCFND (location found - true or false)
     C*
     C*          If location not found, signal error.
     C           LOCFND    IFEQ @FALSE                    Loc not found
     C                     MOVE @TRUE     ERRFND
     C                     MOVE DSPERR    MSGID
     C                     CALL 'ERRMSGC'
     C                     ENDIF                          Loc not found
     C                     ENDSR
     C*
     C*------------------------------------------------------------------
     C*  Mode Error
     C*------------------------------------------------------------------
     C           S10ERR    BEGSR                          mode error
     C                     MOVE MODERR    MSGID
```

Figure 31.14 Continued

Figure 31.14

Replacing IF Logic with the CAS Statement *Continued*

```
*... ... 1 ... ... 2 ... ... 3 ... ... 4 ... ... 5 ... ... 6 ... ... 7
     C                    CALL 'ERRMSGC'
     C                    ENDSR
     C*----------------------------------------------------------------
     C*  Check Location
     C*----------------------------------------------------------------
     C*                                                                *
     C          CHKLOC    BEGSR
     C          KEY1      SETLLLOCMSTR                  50(Rcd fnd = 50on)
     C  N50               MOVE @FALSE    LOCFND  1
     C   50               MOVE @TRUE     LOCFND
     C                    ENDSR
     C*----------------------------------------------------------------
     C*  Check Meter
     C*----------------------------------------------------------------
     C          CHKMTR    BEGSR
     C          KEY1      SETLLMTRMSTRA                 33(Rcd fnd = 33on)
     C  N33               MOVE @FALSE    MTRFND  1
     C   33               MOVE @TRUE     MTRFND
     C                    ENDSR
```

Figure 31.15

Part of Screen-Processing Subroutine

```
*... ... 1 ... ... 2 ... ... 3 ... ... 4 ... ... 5 ... ... 6 ... ... 7

     C          *IN27     CASEQON        UPDATE
     C          *IN63     CASEQON        UPDATE
     C                    END                             CASxx
```

The Quest for Clarity

If you think I have spent an inordinate amount of time on what started out as 14 lines of code (and ended up as 38), I will say in response only that the quest for clarity is unending, and we've only begun. Alert readers will notice other problems with the code shown that I haven't even commented on.

Summary of RPG Style Guidelines

General Rules

- Code should reveal its purpose, not hide it.
- Don't try to force a program into fewer lines of code at the expense of clarity.
- Avoid clever programming tricks.
- Make the meaning of the code jump out.
- Don't sacrifice clarity for small gains in efficiency.
- Use variable names that are easily distinguished.
- Use variable names that convey their meaning.
- Don't hard-code quoted character constants into the main body of your program. Instead, use named constants or variables initialized at the start of the program.
- Correct structural problems that obscure the purpose of the code.
- Communicate clearly between parts of the program.
- Clean up your mess — don't leave code that does nothing in a program.

RPG-Specific Rules

- Use indicators only when they are absolutely necessary (i.e., for I/O operations and testing the results of a LOKUP operation).
- Change indicators into readable variables as soon as possible.
- Don't use indicators to communicate from one part of the program to another.
- Avoid the inherently obscure features of RPG (e.g., the RPG logic cycle or the COMP operation).

Chapter 32

COBOL Programming Style

by Gerry Kaplan

Follow these style tips to gain clear and readable COBOL code

Developing computer software is as much an art as composing classical music, creating theater, and writing literature. Programmers are as proud of their programs as actors are of fine performances. One point, though, puts programming into a different league: A program is generally inherited by another programmer, whereas a performance becomes a memory. Programmers who write clean, efficient, and easy-to-understand programs are respected and appreciated by their peers.

Since its inception, COBOL has provided the industry with a self-documenting, business-oriented programming language. Due to language shortcomings (e.g., nested IF statements), COBOL programs in the past often became spaghetti-like and difficult to follow. Within the past decade, however, COBOL has undergone extensive plastic surgery, resulting in a language that's more powerful than ever and making it easier to write clearer structured programs. When writing programs in COBOL/400 — as with any language — you should keep certain guidelines in mind that will lead to clearer, more efficient code. The style tips I present here are not the final word — you must find your own style — but these guidelines help me create code that's readable and maintainable.

Establish a good set of standards

Before starting any application development process — even before designing the screens and reports — you should establish a good set of standards. As an example, the AS/400's default COBOL source physical file for native AS/400 programs is QCBLSRC. Establishing a standard that includes using this name lets you use the COPY statement without having to specify a source physical file name. Consider using all the default names, such as QDDSSRC for the file definitions, QCLSRC for CL programs, and QCMDSRC for commands. Or you could subdivide QDDSSRC into QDDSSRC for physical and logical files, QPRTF for printer files, and QDSPF for display files. One benefit of starting all source physical files with Q is that they all appear next to each other in the WRKOBJPDM (Work with Objects Using PDM) display, making it easy to shift among them without a lot of searching.

Equally important are the naming standards you follow for files, records, and fields. Try to avoid using different names for the same data in different records. If you don't intend to externally describe your files to RPG/400 programs, use the entire 10 characters DDS allows for record and field names. A common practice is to use the first two or three characters of a field name to indicate from what file the field comes. Although this tactic easily identifies a field's owner, it prevents the use of the MOVE CORRESPONDING phrase. Instead, try to use generic names as much as possible. In place of INVCSTNBR as the customer number in the invoice file, for example, use just CSTNBR. Establish the initial definition of CSTNBR in a field-reference file, and you'll never have to define it explicitly again throughout the whole software system. Establishing the field-reference file takes almost no time to do up front and can save enormous amounts of time when you must make global modifications (e.g., extend the customer number size). If multiple files within the same program reference CSTNBR, you will need to use the OF qualifier:

```
MOVE CSTNBR OF CUST-RCD TO fieldname.
```

By the way, using the same name does not cause the variable to occupy the same storage location, as in RPG.

If 10-character field names aren't long enough, use the field-level ALIAS keyword in the DDS. The ALIAS keyword lets you use long names common to COBOL and still maintain compatibility with other languages such as RPG/400.

Another common standard is to assign to the record format the same name as the file. For example, if the file is CSTMST, the record format name is also CSTMST.

Establish a good set of indicator standards, and place them in a COPY book (perhaps labeled INDICDEF). A useful idea is to code the entire indicator array in this copy book (Figure 32.1). This way your program does not have to declare the indicator area or which indicators do what. Just COPY INDICDEF and everything will be set up for you in your program.

Once you've established the indicator assignments, assign short and descriptive names to them and set up indicator constants like those in Figure 32.1. Avoid using keyboard legends such as F3; instead, use something more meaningful, like FK-EXIT. Then you can turn indicators on and off by name instead of by number. For example, you can code

```
SET IND-ON(I-SFLEND) TO TRUE
```

instead of

```
SET IND-ON(54) TO TRUE
```

Figure 32.1

Indicator COPY Book

```
SEQNBR*...+....1....+....2....+...3....+....4....+....5....+....6.

         01  INDIC-AREA.
             03  EACH-IND OCCURS 99 TIMES PIC 1 INDICATOR 1.
                 88 IND-OFF VALUE B"0".
                 88 IND-ON  VALUE B"1".

         01  INDIC-USAGE.
             03  FK-HELP                           PIC 99 VALUE 01.
             03  FK-FK1FK2                         PIC 99 VALUE 02.
             03  FK-EXIT                           PIC 99 VALUE 03.
             03  FK-PROMPT                         PIC 99 VALUE 04.
             03  FK-REFRESH                        PIC 99 VALUE 05.
             03  FK-CREATE                         PIC 99 VALUE 06.
             03  FK-BACKWARD                       PIC 99 VALUE 07.
             03  FK-FORWARD                        PIC 99 VALUE 08.
             03  FK-ACTIONS                        PIC 99 VALUE 10.
             03  FK-CANCEL                         PIC 99 VALUE 12.
             03  FK-TOP                            PIC 99 VALUE 17.
             03  FK-BOTTOM                         PIC 99 VALUE 18.
             03  FK-PRINT                          PIC 99 VALUE 21.
             03  FK-MORE-OPTIONS                   PIC 99 VALUE 23.
             03  FK-MORE-KEYS                      PIC 99 VALUE 24.
             03  FK01-ENABLE                       PIC 99 VALUE 25.
             03  FK02-ENABLE                       PIC 99 VALUE 26.
             03  FK03-ENABLE                       PIC 99 VALUE 27.
             03  FK04-ENABLE                       PIC 99 VALUE 28.
             03  FK05-ENABLE                       PIC 99 VALUE 29.
             03  FK06-ENABLE                       PIC 99 VALUE 30.
             03  FK07-ENABLE                       PIC 99 VALUE 31.
             03  FK08-ENABLE                       PIC 99 VALUE 32.
             03  FK09-ENABLE                       PIC 99 VALUE 33.
             03  FK10-ENABLE                       PIC 99 VALUE 34.
             03  FK11-ENABLE                       PIC 99 VALUE 35.
             03  FK12-ENABLE                       PIC 99 VALUE 36.
             03  FK13-ENABLE                       PIC 99 VALUE 37.
             03  FK14-ENABLE                       PIC 99 VALUE 38.
             03  FK15-ENABLE                       PIC 99 VALUE 39.
             03  FK16-ENABLE                       PIC 99 VALUE 40.
             03  FK17-ENABLE                       PIC 99 VALUE 41.
             03  FK18-ENABLE                       PIC 99 VALUE 42.
             03  FK19-ENABLE                       PIC 99 VALUE 43.
             03  FK20-ENABLE                       PIC 99 VALUE 44.
             03  FK21-ENABLE                       PIC 99 VALUE 45.
             03  FK22-ENABLE                       PIC 99 VALUE 46.
             03  FK23-ENABLE                       PIC 99 VALUE 47.
             03  FK24-ENABLE                       PIC 99 VALUE 48.
             03  I-DISABLE-PAGEUP                  PIC 99 VALUE 49.
```

Figure 32.1 Continued

Figure 32.1

Indicator COPY Book *Continued*

```
            03  I-DISABLE-PAGEDOWN             PIC 99 VALUE 50.
            03  I-SFLDSPCTL                    PIC 99 VALUE 51.
            03  I-SFLDSP                       PIC 99 VALUE 52.
            03  I-SFLCLR                       PIC 99 VALUE 53.
            03  I-SFLEND                       PIC 99 VALUE 54.
            03  I-SFLNXTCHG                    PIC 99 VALUE 55.
            03  I-SFLINZ                       PIC 99 VALUE 56.
            03  I-MSGSFLEND                    PIC 99 VALUE 57.
            03  I-OVERLAY                      PIC 99 VALUE 58.
            03  I-PROTECT-INPUT                PIC 99 VALUE 59.
            03  I-PUTOVR                       PIC 99 VALUE 60.
            03  I-INZINP                       PIC 99 VALUE 61.
            03  I-ERASEINP                     PIC 99 VALUE 62.
            03  I-OUTPUT                       PIC 99 VALUE 63.
            03  I-OPT-ERROR                    PIC 99 VALUE 70.
            03  I-POSN-CRSR                    PIC 99 VALUE 71.
```

Fill in the IDENTIFICATION DIVISION

Considered by many as pointless typing, the IDENTIFICATION DIVISION has hidden benefits that show up later in the program's life. Use at least the AUTHOR and DATE-WRITTEN keywords, which help you track down information about the program's origin. For compiled listings, use DATE-COMPILED because the compiler fills in the date. Brief comments describing the program and its function within a job stream are also helpful. And you can keep a modification log in this division as well.

Make file names clear and reasonable

The INPUT-OUTPUT section of the ENVIRONMENT DIVISION is where you identify files to the program. One naming convention that simplifies the readability of the code is to use the suffixes -FILE and -RCD: filename-FILE, filename-RCD. If the file is a customer file, for example, you might use the names CUST-FILE for the file name and CUST-RCD for its associated record. This also makes coding easier when reading and writing to the files.

In the ENVIRONMENT DIVISION, you indicate to the system how you will deal with indicators for your display and printer files. One method, using the INDARA keyword in the DDS, enables your program to maintain its own indicator array, while the default method blends the indicators right in with the data fields — each taking up one byte. To take advantage of the INDARA keyword, you must code your assignment names with the -SI suffix. A COBOL assignment name consists of device-file-attribute; SI is the optional attribute part. For instance, the select clause might read

```
SELECT DISP-FILE  ASSIGN TO WORKSTATION-CSTMNTFM-SI.
```

Use COPY DDS- statements whenever possible

When setting up the FD file entries in the DATA DIVISION, try to match the record name to the file name as closely as possible. The CUST-FILE and CUST-RCD relationship demonstrates this point. You should, however, avoid the DDS-ALL-FORMATS when describing external display and printer files. When the ALL-FORMATS option is specified, each record format "overlays" (redefines) the other in a common record buffer area. Each time a record is read from the display, any previous contents of any other display screens becomes corrupt. For this reason, it is easier to specify a generic buffer big enough to hold the largest record in the file (not hard to estimate).

In the WORKING-STORAGE section, use the COPY DDS-recname-I (or -O or -I-O) command to copy each record's input and output buffer to separate areas. Although this method requires more memory, it relieves the program of the burden of maintaining data from previously displayed screens. At any given time, the program can use

```
MOVE CORR input-record TO output-record
```

to move all fields from the input buffer to the output buffer.

In addition, you can design the program to handle "refresh" or "restore" options similar to those of most OS/400 functions. If the user types data into fields and then presses "F5=Refresh," you can simply redisplay the same output record without moving the input data to it.

Use the LIKE keyword whenever possible

The LIKE keyword defines one field with the same length and attributes as another field. If you need temporary variables to hold data from a data file or a display file, you declare the temporary variable name to be LIKE the variable name found in the display file. To illustrate the power of using the LIKE keyword, assume you have a field named CUSTNBR defined in a file as 6 characters and a temporary holding field named SAVE-CUSTNBR defined as PIC X(6) in your program. Suppose that sometime later, you expand the CUSTNBR to 8 characters. You must go through every program and find variables used for holding CUSTNBR and change them to 8. However, if you use the declaration

```
01 SAVE-CUSTNBR  LIKE CUSTNBR OF PRIMARY-REC
```

changing the definition of SAVE-CUSTNBR would not be necessary, because it defines its length based on the CUSTNBR field in the file.

Use 88-level conditionals

One of COBOL's most underused features is its ability to SET variables to predefined values and then test those values based on variable names instead of on constants. People commonly set up flags in programs to declare a variable in WORKING-STORAGE (with names such as END-OF-FILE-FLAG) and then, within the program, move a character constant into the variable. Later, the variable is compared (using the EQUAL test) against another constant. The use

Figure 32.2

Use of 88-Level Conditionals

```
01 END-OF-FILE-FLAG          PIC X.
READ CUST-FILE
   AT END
MOVE "Y" TO END-OF-FILE-FLAG
   NOT AT END
MOVE "N" TO END-OF-FILE-FLAG
END-READ.
IF END-OF-FILE-FLAG EQUAL "Y"
   PERFORM blah blah blah
END-IF

as opposed to

01   EOF-FLAG                 PIC X VALUE "N".
     88 NOT-EOF-CUSTFILE            VALUE "N".
     88 EOF-CUSTFILE                VALUE "Y".
READ CUST-FILE
   AT END
SET EOF-CUSTFILE TO TRUE
   NOT AT END
SET NOT-EOF-CUSTFILE TO TRUE
END-READ
IF EOF-CUSTFILE
   PERFORM blah blah blah
END-IF
```

of 88 conditionals makes the code much more clear to read and understand, as seen in Figure 32.2.

Make readability a goal

COBOL programs are, for the most part, free-form (except for specified areas A and B). Periods indicate the end of a sentence (i.e., a logical step). Use them. Many programmers omit periods when they don't have to use them. Don't. This practice, combined with nested IF statements, can make the program difficult to maintain, especially if revising the code results in moving statements around.

Use proper indentation. Most programmers use three or four spaces to indent lines. If you are prone to writing massive IF structures and multiple in-line PERFORMs, you might find that you run out of room more quickly using four spaces. I generally use three to avoid having to break a single sentence onto two lines. And anything more than four spaces makes the code look erratic.

You should align all statements that are at the same level. Don't stagger the lines when there's no logical reason for doing so. Figure 32.3 demonstrates the difference between poorly and well indented code.

Good variable names also help make a program easier to read and understand. Use single-character variable names such as I or X only for a simple loop that has a limited scope and life. If you need an index variable for a more complex loop, call it IDX or something similar.

Figure 32.3

Examples of Indented Code

Poorly indented code:

```
READ-CUSTOMER-PARA.
    PERFORM GET-CUST-KEY
      PERFORM CHECK-FOR-DETAIL-RECORDS
        IF DETAIL-RECORDS-EXIST
           PERFORM PROCESS-DETAILS
              MOVE NEW-BALANCE TO CURRENT-BALANCE
           END-IF.
```

Well indented code:

```
READ-CUSTOMER-PARA.
    PERFORM GET-CUST-KEY.
    PERFORM CHECK-FOR-DETAIL-RECORDS.
    IF DETAIL-RECORDS-EXIST
        PERFORM PROCESS-DETAILS
        MOVE NEW-BALANCE TO CURRENT-BALANCE
    END-IF.
```

Controversy has always surrounded paragraph-numbering conventions. Experienced programmers tend to number their paragraphs (e.g., 0100-MAIN-PARA) because numbering helps to locate a particular paragraph quickly, especially if the source is large. While numbering can cause problems when you have to add paragraphs, you can alleviate the problems by leaving expansion room in your numbering scheme. Thus, your paragraphs in sequence might be

```
1000-xxxxxxxxxx
1100-xxxxxxxxxx
1200-xxxxxxxxxx
      .
      .
      .
```

Then you can always later insert in sequence

```
1150-xxxxxxxxxx
```

As a general rule, also try to keep paragraphs to no more than one page in length. If a paragraph is considerably longer than one page, you can probably break it down into smaller paragraphs.

Avoid using the GO TO phrase as much as possible. COBOL/400 has enough structured verbs to handle almost any programming requirement. GO TO verbs, if used at all, should be used only for aborting after critical errors are encountered during runtime.

Always use the END-IF statement

With these pointers in mind, let's examine some of the new COBOL verbs and see how they can help improve your COBOL code. IF now has its counterpart, END-IF, letting you nest your IF statements without having to use the NEXT SENTENCE clause. Here's an example:

```
IF BAL-DUE GREATER THAN CREDIT-LIMIT
   PERFORM REJECT-CHARGE-REQUEST
ELSE
   PERFORM ACCEPT-CHARGE-REQUEST
END-IF.
```

Because the END-IF statement is nonexecutable, it does not affect the performance of your program; therefore, you should always use it. If you don't use it, you are relying on a period to terminate the IF scope. Using the END-IF also makes it easier to add lines before the end of the scope, whereas with just the period, you would have to move the period to the end of the new sentences.

Simplify with the EVALUATE verb and PERFORM and END-PERFORM statements

If you have a problem with nested IF statements, EVALUATE is for you. As a general rule, if an IF statement has more than two conditions, EVALUATE may be a better choice. Consider the IF statement versus its EVALUATE counterpart in Figure 32.4. Clearly, the code with EVALUATE is easier to understand and modify when additional conditions arise. If you are not familiar with the EVALUATE verb, refer to the *COBOL/400 Reference Summary* (SC09-1380) or the *COBOL/400 User's Guide* (SC09-1383).

When you want to repeat a block of code in COBOL, that block of code no longer has to reside in a separate paragraph that gets PERFORMed. The block can immediately follow the PERFORM statement. The two segments of code in Figure 32.5 illustrate the difference between the way you used to have to treat a repeat block of code and the new method.

Use MOVE CORRESPONDING when moving large blocks of variables

Although labeled dangerous by some, proper use of the MOVE CORRESPONDING verb can be extremely powerful. It can also save you many unnecessary lines of code (not to mention a lot of typing). If variable names from files are kept generic (CUSTNAM instead of INVCSTNAM and GLCSTNAM), you can do large moves from file to file with one sentence. For debugging purposes, the compiler will generate a list of which field names are being moved.

READ and WRITE with care

One problem that frequently arises in COBOL programs that READ and WRITE a lot to various files is the occurrence of file I-O verbs within the exception block of another file I-O. This problem is usually caused by the need for a period

Figure 32.4

IF vs. EVALUATE

```
IF MEMBER-TYPE EQUAL GOLD-MEMBER
   PERFORM ACCEPT-CHARGE-REQUEST
ELSE
   IF FRILL-CHARGE
      PERFORM REJECT-CHARGE-REQUEST
   ELSE
     IF FOOD-CHARGE
        PERFORM ACCEPT-CHARGE-REQUEST
     ELSE
        PERFORM CONTACT-SERVICE-REP
     END-IF
   END-IF
END-IF.


EVALUATE MEMBER-TYPE ALSO CHARGE-TYPE
  WHEN GOLD-MEMBER ALSO ANY            PERFORM ACCEPT-CHARGE-REQUEST
  WHEN NORMAL-MEMBER ALSO FRILL-CHARGE PERFORM REJECT-CHARGE-REQUEST
  WHEN NORMAL-MEMBER ALSO FOOD-CHARGE  PERFORM ACCEPT-CHARGE-REQUEST
  WHEN OTHER                           PERFORM CONTACT-SERVICE-REP
END-EVALUATE.
```

Figure 32.5

Use of PERFORM and END-PERFORM

```
OLD-METHOD-PARA.
    PERFORM CLEAR-INDICATOR-PARA VARYING INDX FROM 1 BY 1
       UNTIL INDX GREATER THAN 5Ø.

CLEAR-INDICATOR-PARA.
    SET IND-ON(INDX) TO TRUE.



NEW-METHOD-PARA.
    PERFORM VARYING INDX FROM 1 BY 1 UNTIL INDX GREATER THAN 5Ø
       SET IND-ON(INDX) TO TRUE
    END-PERFORM.
```

within the scope of the READ or WRITE verb. Look at Figure 32.6. This code won't work because the first PERFORM is seen as a continuation of the AT EOP clause. The PERFORM will get executed only if the EOP (end of page) condition occurs. You also cannot put a period after WRITE-HEADERS because that would not only terminate the AT EOP clause but also the WRITE and READ clauses. A better way to code this paragraph is shown in Figure 32.7.

Figure 32.6

Code that Needs a Scope Terminator

```
READ CUST-FILE
   INVALID KEY
      WRITE ERROR-RCD AFTER ADVANCING 1 LINE
         AT EOP PERFORM WRITE-HEADERS
      PERFORM AFTER-WRITING-TO-THE-PRINTER PROCESSING
```

Figure 32.7

Code with Scope Terminators

```
READ CUST-FILE
   INVALID KEY
      WRITE ERROR-RCD AFTER ADVANCING 1 LINE
         AT EOP PERFORM WRITE-HEADERS
      END-WRITE
      PERFORM AFTER-WRITING-TO-THE-PRINTER PROCESSING
END-READ
```

For this reason, the END-READ, END-WRITE, and END-REWRITE keywords were conceived. The NOT condition was also added for more flexibility. Previously, programs were written to set on a flag if a record was not found. Then that flag would be tested to determine whether a particular block of code should be executed. This flag is no longer needed. The first segment of code in Figure 32.8 demonstrates the use of the END terminator for a READ statement.

Using these keywords can also help when you're designing a program that steps through all records in a file and takes an action for each one, as shown in the second code segment in Figure 32.8.

It is not unusual for a program to require from the same file data for displaying as well as modifying. During regular displaying of data on the screen, it is essential that the data not be locked from other users. When the user decides to modify something for a given record, the record should then be locked to avoid other programs' access. Previously, the only way to do this was to open the same file twice, once for input only and once for updating, or to open the file in I-O mode and do an immediate REWRITE after reading a record. Now, you can open a single file in I-O mode, and the READ can specify whether to lock the record. The READ WITH NO LOCK will read a record without locking it from other users.

Use CALL to isolate in external programs functions common to your system

The COBOL CALL verb enables one program to dynamically call another one. Earlier, I recommended that paragraphs be short and concise. If 100 programs in your system require, say, a tenant's current balance, it makes sense that a

Figure 32.8

Use of the END Terminator

```
READ CUST-FILE
   INVALID KEY
      WRITE CUST-RCD
         INVALID KEY CONTINUE
      END-WRITE
   NOT INVALID KEY
      REWRITE CUST-RCD
         INVALID KEY CONTINUE
      END-REWRITE
END-READ.


SET NOT-EOF-CUSTFILE TO TRUE.
PERFORM UNTIL EOF-CUSTFILE
   READ CUST-FILE NEXT RECORD
      AT END
         PERFORM END-OF-FILE PROCESSING
      NOT AT END
         PERFORM EACH-RECORD-PROCESSING
   END-READ
END-PERFORM.
```

program that receives a tenant's key as its parameter could return the tenant's balance (as well as any other important information) to the calling program. Using external program calls affects performance most on the first execution of the CALL; once the CALL has been completed, the called program remains in memory for subsequent calls. Even though a CALL affects performance, the cost of a CALL rarely is so great that it outweighs the advantages of separate programs. Use CALLed programs for retrieving account balances, formatting dates, validating fields found in many programs — any functions that are common to multiple programs.

COBOL has come a long way since its inception. What used to be a somewhat cumbersome and strict language has become more flexible and permissive of today's structured techniques. These new capabilities, along with the guidelines presented in this chapter, can help make your programs easier to understand and maintain.

Summary of COBOL Style Guidelines

- Establish a good set of standards.
- Fill in the IDENTIFICATION DIVISION.
- Make file names clear and reasonable.
- Use COPY DDS- statements whenever possible.
- Use the LIKE keyword whenever possible.
- Use 88-level conditionals.
- Make readability a goal.
- Always use the END-IF statement.
- Simplify with the EVALUATE clause and PERFORM and END-PERFORM statements.
- Use MOVE CORRESPONDING when moving large blocks of variables.
- READ and WRITE with care.
- Use CALL to isolate in external programs common functions to your system.

Chapter 33

Using the Integrated Debugger

by Jon Vote

Keep your programs pest-free with AS/400 debug commands

The AS/400 debug facility, a special environment for finding and eradicating program bugs, gives you powerful tools for diagnosing problems in your programs. You can momentarily stop program execution at any statement, display or change variable values, trace program flow over any range of statements, or step through program statements one at a time as they execute. If you do not already use the AS/400 debug commands, learning and using them can speed your production considerably.

You can use the debug facility either interactively or in batch. Your approach will probably differ depending on the mode you use. I limit this discussion to interactive debugging, which is probably the more widely used of the two. Figure 33.1 summarizes the AS/400 debug commands. In this chapter, I will discuss the most useful commands.

The Debug Environment

To begin an interactive debug session, execute the STRDBG (Start Debug) command (Figure 33.2 shows the command syntax of the STRDBG command). The parameters of this command control the attributes of the debug environment (also known as the debug mode). The PGM parameter lets you specify up to 10 programs to place into debug mode. The DFTPGM parameter determines the program to be debugged for other debug commands that specify *DFTPGM on their PGM parameter.

You cannot update production files while you're in debug mode unless you explicitly tell OS/400 otherwise via the UPDPROD parameter. Although this feature may give you some peace of mind, use caution: Even though you cannot update or remove members from a production library, you can still delete production files. Copying the necessary production files into a test library is the safest way to debug and test your programs.

Figure 33.1

AS/400 Debug Command Overview

DEBUG ENVIRONMENT COMMANDS

ADDPGM (Add Program): Adds up to 10 programs to the debug environment.

CHGDBG (Change Debug): Changes the parameter values of the STRDBG command (i.e., changes the attributes of the debug environment).

DSPDBG (Display Debug): Displays the current attributes of debug mode, including the invocation stack and the programs being debugged.

ENDCBLDBG (End COBOL Debug): Deactivates COBOL source language debugging statements.

ENDDBG (End Debug): Ends a debugging session. Any breakpoints or traces that were initiated in debug will no longer be in effect.

STRCBLDBG (Start COBOL Debug): Activates COBOL source language debugging statements.

STRDBG (Start Debug): Begins a debug session, specifies the attributes of the debug environment, and adds up to 10 programs to debug mode. Once you have started a debug session, you can use any of the other debugging commands.

RMVPGM (Remove Program): Removes up to 10 programs from debug mode.

TRACE COMMANDS

ADDTRC (Add Trace): Tells OS/400 to trace the flow of the program for the range of statements that you specify.

CLRTRCDTA (Clear Trace Data): Clears all trace data from any previous trace command.

DSPTRC (Display Trace): Displays all traces that are currently defined for the programs being debugged.

DSPTRCDTA (Display Trace Data): Displays the statements traced by the most recent trace operation and displays the program variables within that range of statements.

RMVTRC (Remove Trace): Removes all or part of the traces that you specified in any ADDTRC commands. (Removing a trace does not erase the trace data.)

BREAKPOINT AND VARIABLE COMMANDS

ADDBKP (Add Breakpoint): Inserts a breakpoint that stops program execution momentarily at the line number(s) you specify. You can enter other debug commands at a breakpoint.

CHGPGMVAR (Change Program Variable): Changes the value of any variable used in a program being debugged.

DSPBKP (Display Breakpoints): Displays currently set breakpoint locations for up to 10 programs.

DSPPGMVAR (Display Program Variable): Displays the value of any variable used in the program being debugged.

RMVBKP (Remove Breakpoint): Removes the breakpoint(s) that you specify.

RSMBKP (Resume Breakpoint): Causes a program to continue processing after it has stopped at a defined breakpoint.

Note: All commands except STRDBG are valid only in debug mode.

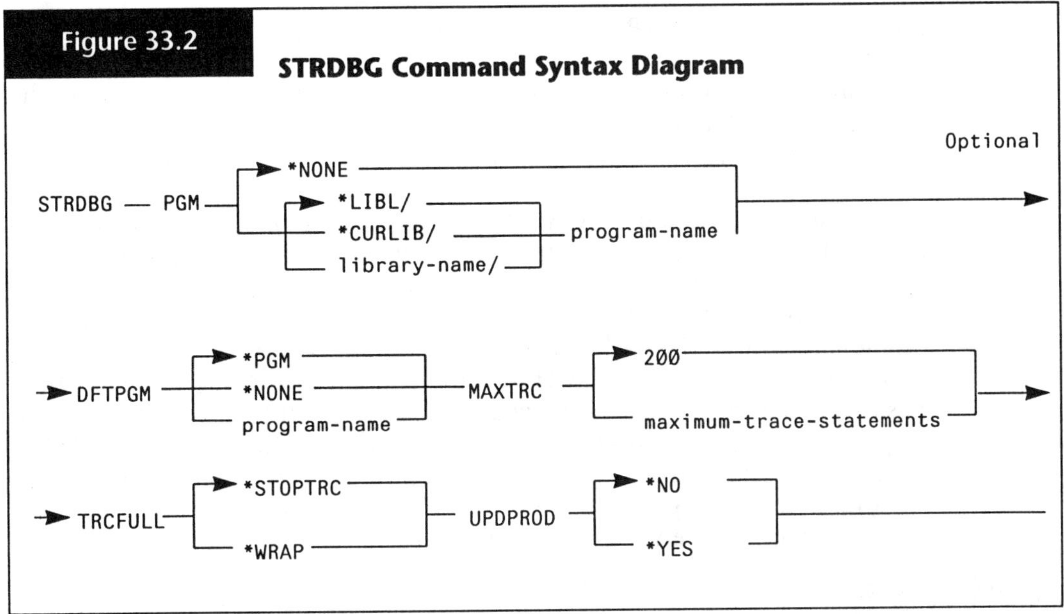

While in debug mode, you can execute any OS/400 command — including other debug commands — whenever you have access to a command line. You can change the programs being debugged with the ADDPGM (Add Program) and RMVPGM (Remove Program) commands, which add and remove programs from debug mode, respectively. You can change any STRDBG parameter (and thus change the attributes of the debug environment) with the CHGDBG (Change Debug) command. To end a debug session, use the ENDDBG (End Debug) command.

Tracing

The debug mode's trace functions let you track a program's execution and display the results. You can specify up to five ranges of program statements to trace. When you execute the program in debug mode, the system records the execution sequence of traced statements and, optionally, the value of specified program variables every time a traced statement is executed. Tracing is especially useful for debugging infinite loops because you can quickly pinpoint where the loops occur.

Two STRDBG parameters, MAXTRC and TRCFULL, control the trace functions. The MAXTRC parameter sets the maximum number of trace statements that can be put into the job's trace file (the default is 200). Once the maximum is reached, the system determines what to do next based on the TRCFULL parameter. The default is *STOPTRC; for interactive programs, *STOPTRC halts program execution and returns control to your terminal. You can continue to execute the program statement by statement, and the trace file will expand to contain new entries. The alternative to *STOPTRC is *WRAP, which causes tracing to continue even after the maximum has been reached. The additional trace statements wrap to the beginning of the trace file and overwrite the original data. *WRAP comes in handy when you need to see only the final data from the trace.

To single-step through your program, specify MAXTRC(1), which causes the system to reach the maximum and return control to you after each statement. (This technique can often help you figure out old RPG II code with complicated combinations of indicators.)

You initiate a program trace with the ADDTRC (Add Trace) command (the syntax of the ADDTRC command is shown in Figure 33.3). ADDTRC's STMT parameter lets you limit tracing to up to five sections of code that you specify by first and last statement number. The PGMVAR parameter lets you specify up to 10 variables to trace for each section of code. If any of those variables are string variables, you can use the START and LEN parameters to specify the starting position and length of a substring whose value you want to record. You can also display those variables in hexadecimal by specifying *HEX for the OUTFMT parameter. During a trace, variable values appear in the trace data at their initial occurrence in the program, and thereafter only when their values change, unless you specify otherwise via the OUTVAR parameter. The last parameter, PGM,

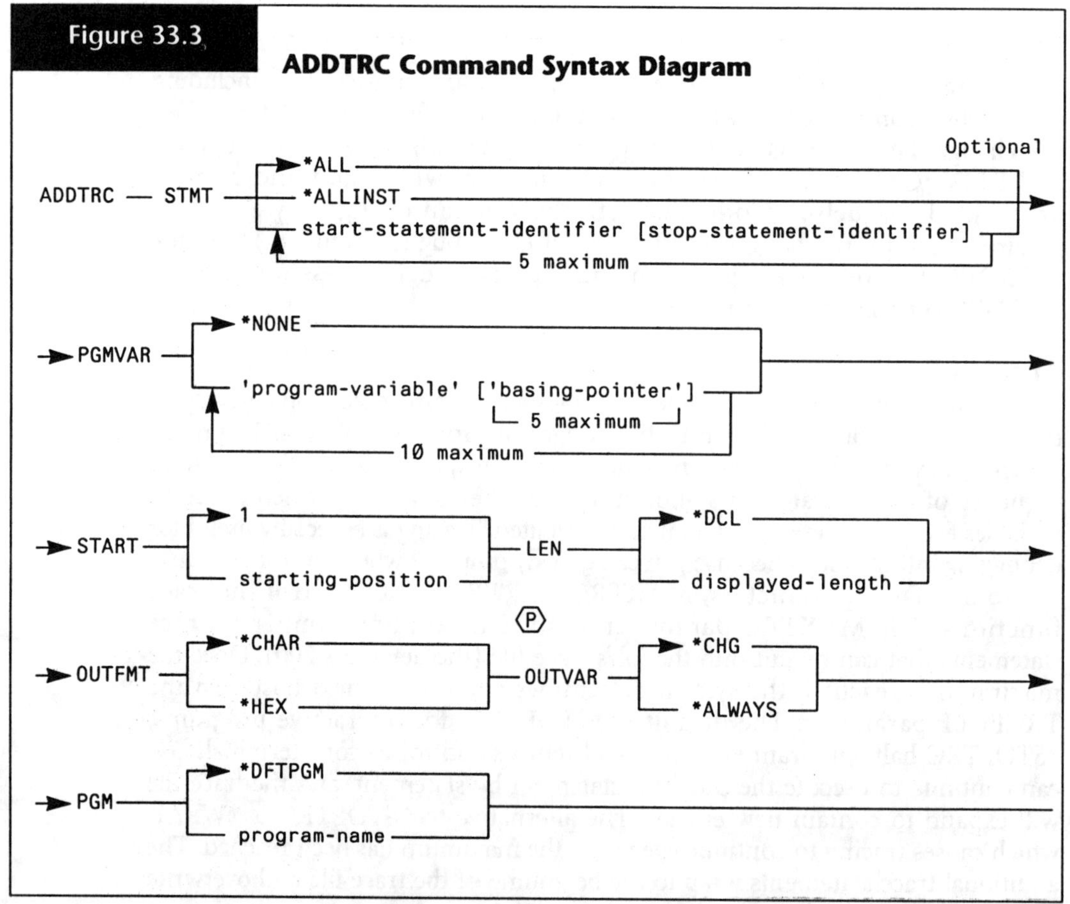

does not require a value unless you are debugging multiple programs and the program you want to trace is not the default.

To view the trace data, use the DSPTRCDTA (Display Trace Data) command. If you want to discard the traced data, you can do so with the CLRTRCDTA (Clear Trace Data) command. To end all or part of a trace, use the RMVTRC (Remove Trace) command.

Breakpoints and Variables

One of the most versatile of your debugging options is setting breakpoints in your program. A breakpoint stops a program at the statement specified and returns control to you. When a program being executed in debug mode encounters a breakpoint, the program stops *before* the statement is executed and shows you the breakpoint display. The breakpoint display shows you which breakpoint has been reached and, optionally, the current value of specified program variables. You can cancel the program by pressing F3, continue program execution by pressing Enter, or obtain a command entry screen by pressing F10.

To set up a breakpoint, use the ADDBKP (Add Breakpoint) command (Figure 33.4 shows the syntax of the ADDBKP command). The STMT parameter

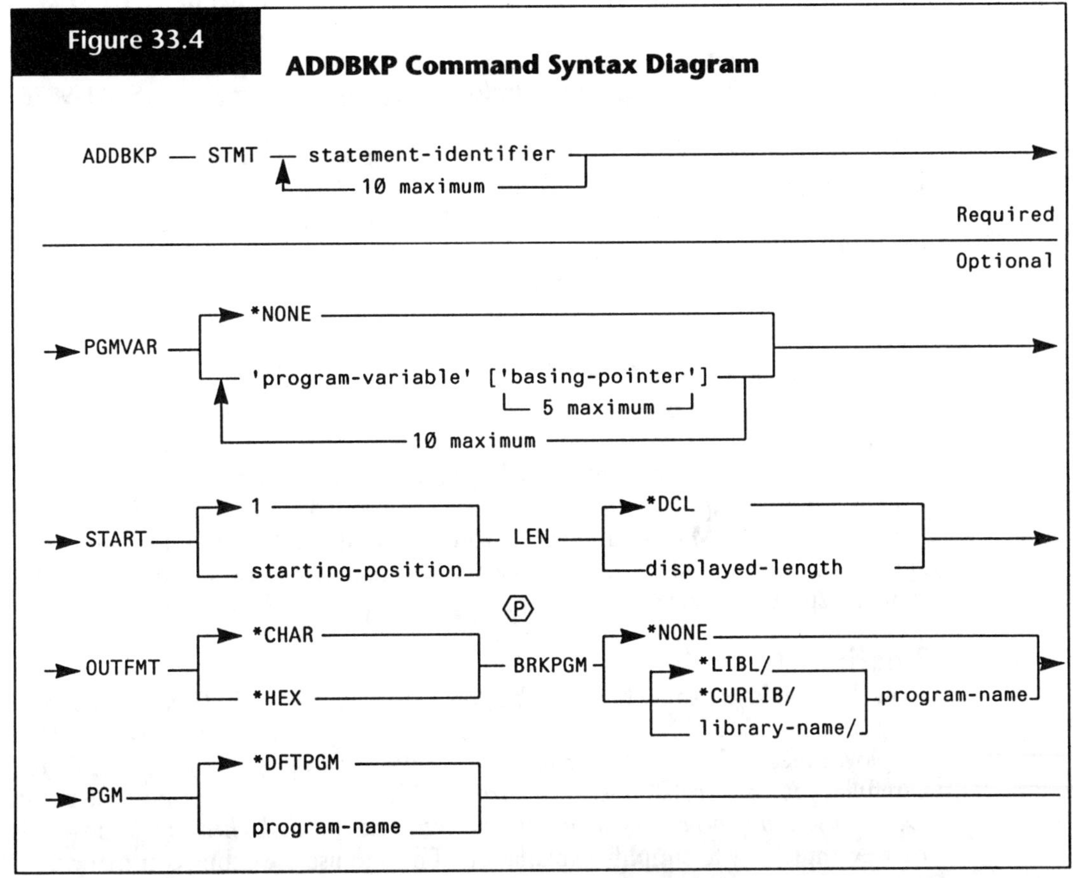

Figure 33.4
ADDBKP Command Syntax Diagram

lets you specify the statement or statements at which you want to set a breakpoint. You can set up to 10 breakpoints at any one time. For an RPG or CL program, the statement numbers correspond to the line numbers in the source member, but without the decimal point SEU adds. For example, to set a breakpoint at statement 50.00, you would specify STMT(5000). For COBOL programs, you need a compile listing because ADDBKP uses the compiler line numbers, not the source member line numbers.

In many cases, displaying the values of program variables at a breakpoint can help you find problems. ADDBKP's PGMVAR parameter lets you specify up to 10 variables whose values will be displayed at each breakpoint. If you want to display different variables at each breakpoint, you must execute a separate ADDBKP command for each breakpoint and specify different PGMVAR values for each command.

Specifying RPG variables in the PGMVAR parameter is straightforward. But for CL programs, for COBOL variables longer than six characters, or for variables containing characters not allowed in RPG variables, you must place single quotes around each variable name.

In most cases, you need to specify only the STMT and PGMVAR parameters with the ADDBKP command. But, like the ADDTRC command, ADDBKP also has START, LEN, and OUTFMT parameters. The BKPPGM parameter, which is valid only for batch processing, specifies a program to be called when a breakpoint is reached (see the *Control Language Reference* manual (SC41-9776) for more details).

Two helpful debug commands that you can use when your program stops at a breakpoint are DSPPGMVAR (Display Program Variable) and CHGPGMVAR (Change Program Variable). DSPPGMVAR lets you view the contents of variables not specified on the ADDBKP command. CHGPGMVAR lets you change a program variable's contents on the fly. With this command, you can often fix bugs that you discover at a breakpoint, and then continue the program to check for more problems. For example, if a breakpoint display shows a garbage value in the key for a CHAIN operation, you could use CHGPGMVAR to load the key with a valid value and then continue the program to look for other problems. This command is especially useful for new development work, in which you often discover multiple bugs on your early test runs.

Removing breakpoints is easy: Just use the RMVBKP (Remove Breakpoint) command. The STMT parameter lets you remove the last breakpoint (when you specify an asterisk), all breakpoints (when you specify *ALL), or any breakpoint that you specify by line number.

Reality Check

Now that you know some basics, let's apply them to a partial RPG earnings report program, EMPEARN (Figure 33.5). (Figures 33.6 and 33.7 show the DDS for the employee master file and the earnings file, respectively.) If you look at EMPEARN carefully, you can probably see the errors, which brings up an important point: *Do not use debug processing as an alternative to careful desk checking.* I chose this easy example only to simplify explanation of how to use the debug commands.

Figure 33.5

Partial RPG Program for Debugging

```
*... ... 1 ... ... 2 ... ... 3 ... ... 4 ... ... 5 ... ... 6 ... ... 7

*****************************************************************
** - EMPLOYEE EARNINGS REPORT                                    *
*****************************************************************
**
**   FILE 1 : EMPLOYEE MASTER FILE
**
FFILE1   IF  E                    DISK
**
** - FILE 2 : EMPLOYEE EARNINGS FILE
**
FFILE2   UF  E           K        DISK
**
** - MONTH PARAMETER
**
C           *ENTRY    PLIST
C                     PARM           MNTH    2
**
** - KEY FOR EARNINGS FILE
**
C           KEY       KLIST
C                     KFLD           MONTH
C                     KFLD           EMP#
C**
C** - GET THE FIRST RECORD
C**
C                     READ FILE1F                   90
C**
C** - LOOP WHILE RECORD FOUND
C**
C           *IN90     DOWEQ'0'
C**
C** - CHAIN TO THE EARNINGS RECORD
C**
C           KEY       CHAINFILE2F               91
C**
C** - PROCESS THE RECORD
C**
C  N91                EXSR PROCSS
C**
C** - GET THE NEXT RECORD FROM THE MASTER FILE
C**
C                     READ FILE1F                   91
C                     END                             WHILE
**
C                     SETON                     LR
```

EMPEARN is a straightforward data-in/data-out report program. It does not use the RPG cycle; rather, it accesses the input file via a READ loop. Let's suppose that EMPEARN is a batch program you are testing interactively on a small test file. During testing, you find that subroutine PROCSS (which we don't need to

Figure 33.6

DDS for Employee Master File

```
*... ... 1 ... ... 2 ... ... 3 ... ... 4 ... ... 5 ... ... 6 ... ... 7

     ****************************************************************
     ** - EMPLOYEE MASTER FILE                                      *
     ****************************************************************
     A          R FILE1F
     A            EMP#           9            TEXT('EMPLOYEE NUMBER')
     A            EMPNME        30            TEXT('EMPLOYEE NAME')
```

Figure 33.7

DDS for Earnings File

```
*... ... 1 ... ... 2 ... ... 3 ... ... 4 ... ... 5 ... ... 6 ... ... 7

     ****************************************************************
     ** - EMPLOYEE EARNINGS FILE                                    *
     ****************************************************************
     A          R FILE2F
     A            MONTH          2
     A            EMP#           9
     A            GROSS$         7  2
```

see for this example) apparently is never called. Furthermore, you seem to enter the DOW loop (line 30.00 on Figure 33.5), but never leave it.

You first decide to verify your suspicion that the program never calls subroutine PROCSS, so you set a breakpoint at statement 38.00 and specify indicator 91 (which conditions the call) for display. You then start debug mode with the command

```
STRDBG PGM(EMPEARN)
```

and set the breakpoint with

```
ADDBKP STMT(3800)                                                 +
       PGMVAR(*IN91)
```

Now you run the program. When statement 38.00 is about to execute, you get a breakpoint display (Figure 33.8) that shows indicator 91 with a value of 1, which indicates no hit (i.e., the program tried to access a record, but failed to find one and turned off the indicator). So you decide to look at the CHAIN key that failed to get a hit. Looking at the KLIST statement in the source, you see that the key consists of MONTH and EMP#. To look at these variables, you press F10 to get a command entry screen and enter:

```
DSPPGMVAR PGMVAR((MONTH EMP#)
```

Figure 33.8

Sample Breakpoint Display

```
                         Display Breakpoint

Statement/Instruction . . . . . . . . . :  3800 /0065
Program . . . . . . . . . . . . . . . . :  EMPEARN
Recursion level . . . . . . . . . . . . :  1
Start Position  . . . . . . . . . . . . :  1
Format  . . . . . . . . . . . . . . . . :  *CHAR
Length  . . . . . . . . . . . . . . . . :  *DCL

Variable  . . . . . . . . . . . . . . . :  *IN91
  Type  . . . . . . . . . . . . . . . . :  CHARACTER
  Length  . . . . . . . . . . . . . . . :  1
  '1'



Press Enter to continue

F3=Exit Program   F10=Command Entry
```

You get the program variable display (Figure 33.9) and see the cause of the problem. EMP# contains a value, but MONTH is blank. Looking at the PARM statement in the RPG program, you see that the variable name is MNTH, not MONTH. You either need to change the PARM to MONTH or add a MOVE statement to initialize MONTH with the value in MNTH. Because you cannot continue until you fix this problem, you press F3 once to return to the breakpoint display and again to cancel the program.

At this point, you could modify and recompile the program. Instead, you decide to fix the CHAIN key and see what other problems you can find. You enter:

```
ADDBKP STMT(3400)
```

to stop the program just before the chain operation. Running the program again, you reach the breakpoint for statement 34.00 and press F10 to get a command entry screen. Now you set MONTH to a valid value with

```
CHGPGMVAR PGMVAR(MONTH)                                     +
          VALUE('06')
```

This time, when the program breaks at statement 38.00, you get the breakpoint display and see that indicator 91's value is 0, as it should be.

So far so good; you have fixed the problem that prevented the call to PROCSS — but you still have an infinite DOW loop. Because the terminating condition for the loop is the value of indicator 90, you set up a trace to see what happens to the indicator in the loop. (Again, in this simple case, you probably already see

Figure 33.9

Sample Program Variable Display

```
                  Display Program Variables

Program . . . . . . . . . . . . . . . . . : EMPEARN
Recursion level . . . . . . . . . . . . . : 1
Start Position  . . . . . . . . . . . . . : 1
Format  . . . . . . . . . . . . . . . . . : *CHAR
Length  . . . . . . . . . . . . . . . . . : *DCL

Variable  . . . . . . . . . . . . . . . . : MONTH
  Type  . . . . . . . . . . . . . . . . . : CHARACTER
  Length  . . . . . . . . . . . . . . . . : 2
  '  '
Variable  . . . . . . . . . . . . . . . . : EMP#
  Type  . . . . . . . . . . . . . . . . . : CHARACTER
  Length  . . . . . . . . . . . . . . . . : 9
  '101000010'

Press Enter to continue.

F3=Exit   F12=Cancel
```

what is wrong, but this approach to tracing is the same that you would use with a more complex problem.)

First, you get rid of all the breakpoints because you no longer need them. You could specify each breakpoint to remove with the command

```
RMVBKP STMT(3400 3800)
```

but it would save some typing to enter

```
RMVBKP STMT(*ALL)
```

Also, to reduce the clutter in the trace display, let's limit the trace to the statements in the loop and exclude a trace of the PROCSS subroutine by entering:

```
ADDTRC STMT(3000 4300)                                    +
       PGMVAR(*IN90)
```

Press F3 to exit the command entry screen, and the program continues.

After a few minutes, the trace data file fills up (we have not modified the STRDBG command's MAXTRC parameter from the default value of 200), and you get a "trace full" display. Pressing F10 gives you a command entry screen, and you enter:

```
DSPTRCDTA
```

to view the trace data.

Figure 33.10

Sample Trace Data Display

```
                    Display Trace Data

     Statement/
ProgramInstruction              Recursion level          Sequence number
EMPEARN3000                          1                               403

Start Position  . . . . . . . . . . . . . . : 1
Length  . . . . . . . . . . . . . . . . . . : *DCL
Format  . . . . . . . . . . . . . . . . . . : *CHAR

Variable  . . . . . . . . . . . . . . . . . : *IN90
  Type  . . . . . . . . . . . . . . . . . . : CHARACTER
  Length  . . . . . . . . . . . . . . . . . : 1
  '0'

     Statement/
ProgramInstruction              Recursion level          Sequence number
EMPEARN4300                          1                               404
EMPEARN3000                          1                               405
EMPEARN4300                          1                               406
EMPEARN3000                          1                               4 +
```

Looking at the trace data display (Figure 33.10), you see that the initial value for indicator 90 is 0. Browsing through the display, you see that the value for indicator 90 never changes — thus, the infinite loop. Taking another look at the program, you see the problem. You used the wrong indicator for the second read to FILE1F. The indicator (line 42.00 in Figure 33.5) should be 90, not 91. Changing the indicator should fix the infinite DOW loop. Now you can end the trace with the RMVTRC command and continue debugging. Or, having diagnosed the problems you set out to address, you can simply exit debug mode with the ENDDBG command, fix the mistakes in the source code, and recompile the program.

Try It, You'll Like It

The OS/400 debug commands help you locate and correct program problems quickly and painlessly. Although this chapter only scratches the surface, you should find what you need to know to get started. The *Control Language Programmer's Guide* (SC41-8077) provides more specifics on the debug commands. Try them — you'll wonder how you ever got along without them!

Section V

CONSTRUCTING COMMANDS

Chapter 34

Command Principles

by Douglas T. Parrish

Tailor functions of the AS/400 to meet your unique operating characteristics

Once in a while it just makes sense to sit back and take a close look at some rather "taken-for-granted" items on the AS/400. Take AS/400 commands, for example. You use them every day, but do you really understand why IBM engineers designed the AS/400 command processor the way they did?

The AS/400 command processor is unique among IBM systems — and if you understand how it works, you can streamline applications to your heart's content and your shop's needs. For instance, commands can replace some prompt screens and the programs that display them. IBM-supplied commands can be modified to take the "right" defaults for your shop. And a command's validity-checking program can increase your control over the system by restricting options that cause confusion or delay.

The designers of OS/400 wanted to provide a high-level interface to all system functions, and they chose commands to implement this support rather than job streams, procedures, or OCL/JCL — the methods other systems use in an attempt to provide this support. Several criteria determined the development of the command concept.

First, it was important that commands be meaningful. Verb and object abbreviations were standardized to identify action and the objects of that action uniquely. The command name, therefore, became the description of the action to be performed on the desired object. For example, WRK became the abbreviation for Work with, and OUTQ became the abbreviation for Output Queue. WRKOUTQ is obviously the command to Work with Output Queue. To a first-time AS/400 user the abbreviations may seem foreign, but once the logic is learned, it is easy to understand and use most of the system commands.

Second, it was decided that a command should allow entry and front-end validity checking of the parameter data. A prompting function was made available to assist the operator with entry of parameters and their associated values. This function reduces the need for constant access to a command syntax manual.

Third, the command should pass parameters to a program in the proper sequence and format. The passing of parameters occurs only if all required parameters are entered and parameter syntax requirements are met. A translation feature also converts words more meaningful to people into a form more acceptable to programs.

Fourth, all system functions, including future user-designed applications, should be able to take advantage of commands as a high-level method of requesting a program to be executed. In fact, you should be able to incorporate all commands into a program. On many older systems, commands could not be placed into a program. This is the case with the S/34 and S/36, for example.

Command Objects

The command processor relies on three basic objects whenever a command is executed: a Command object, a Command Processing Program (CPP), and an optional Validity Checking Program (VCP). Together, the trio provides the information the command processor requires.

The command object is created by entering Command Definition Statements into a source file, usually QCMDSRC. There are six different command definition statements: CMD (command), PARM (parameter), ELEM (element), QUAL (qualifier), DEP (dependencies), and PMTCTL (Prompt Control).

The two most significant statements are CMD and PARM. The CMD statement defines the title of the command. PARM statements define each parameter, its attributes, and some of its validity-checking requirements. ELEM specifies parameters that are lists of elements. QUAL specifies parameters that are qualified values, such as object name and its qualifying library. DEP statements define specialty error checking — the results of two or more interdependent parameters. PMTCTL statements provide control over conditional prompting.

The CPP (Command Processing Program) and VCP (Validity Checking Program) are program objects. They can be of any type: RPG/400, COBOL/400, CL, PL/I, or even REXX. The CPP is the program that will be called as a result of the successful entry of any required command parameters. The CPP is a required object. When a command is created, the CPP name must be specified. The CPP, however, does not have to exist when a command is created; it can be generated later. Of course, if a command is executed for which a CPP does not exist, an error occurs. A different CPP can be specified by using the CHGCMD (Change Command) command.

The VCP is a slightly different animal. Its purpose is to provide extended error checking — more than what the command itself is equipped to supply. The VCP can be specified when the command is created or specified afterward using the CHGCMD command. The VCP is called after all command-defined validity checking has been performed and before the CPP is called. If the VCP finds an error, it signals the command processor and can even cause a unique error message to be displayed.

The VCP can be written to validate command parameters by performing extensive cross-checking, especially checking that might require access to a database file or data area for verification. For each error encountered in the VCP, you should program a diagnostic message to be sent with text that describes the error condition. The message can be free-form or predefined in a message file. After all diagnostic messages have been sent, an escape message, CPF0002, should be sent from message file QCPFMSG, located in library QSYS. This action informs the command analyzer that a VCP error has occurred. The diagnostic messages are displayed by the command prompter to assist the operator with problem correction. (The relationships between the command, CPP, and VCP are discussed in IBM's *CL Programmer's Guide*, SC41-8077, in the chapter on defining commands.)

Command Processor Flow

Once the command, CPP, and VCP (if required) have been created and the command is executed, the following steps occur:

Step 1. The command string is checked for validity using definitions found in the command object. If the command is found to be in error, an exception message is signaled. If the command is valid, interparameter checks are performed as defined in the command. Again, if an error occurs, an exception message is sent.

Step 2. If specified, the user-defined VCP is called and passed the command parameter values. If errors are found, escape message CPF0002 sent.

Step 3. If no errors exist, control is transferred to the CPP, which is also passed the parameter list.

Commands and Your Application Programs

By studying commands and the command processor, it is possible to understand just how you can implement commands to handle the "front-end" requirements of your application programs. For instance, I believe that commands can and should be used to eliminate or augment the need for prompt screens in many application programs. Commands are easier to code, and they provide error checking and parameter translation.

When using commands in lieu of prompt screens, a programmer can take advantage of the same functions that IBM-supplied commands use. Consider some of the problems inherent in the use of prompt screens. The typical implementation uses a prompt-screen display file and a "front-end" program — a CL program that displays the prompt screen and then either calls another program (RPG, for example) interactively or submits one to batch. The interactive or batch program then processes the parameters entered at the prompt screen and performs the work.

Commands, on the other hand, eliminate the need for "front-end" programs and the associated prompt screen display file. Commands also can be executed interactively or submitted to batch. The system programs QCMDEXC and

QCMDCHK allow the use of all command features in your application programs for menus and special processes.

Another benefit of using commands with your programs is that the user sees a common interface with the machine, whether using IBM-supplied commands or the application commands. The command keys are the same, the prompt functions identical. Users feel most at ease when they use something that is consistent.

Parameter Translation from the Command Definition

A unique use of application commands is for parameter translation or substitution. Assume for a moment that an example financial program, G/L Account Balance Display, requires the operator to enter a fiscal year via a prompt screen.

Instead of using a prompt screen, you could code a command to default the year parameter to *CURRENT. Using features already built into the command processor, the *CURRENT default value can be translated into the proper value for the current fiscal year, if the user does not modify the default value. If a different year is required, the user can enter the necessary value. The command source for this technique is shown in Figure 34.1. Note, however, that when the fiscal year changes, it is necessary to change the command source and re-create the command. In the parameter translation described below, the need to change the command when the year changes is avoided by having the current year accessed from disk.

Parameter Translation from the VCP

Another method of parameter translation can be performed by the VCP. This technique is based on a VCP's ability to modify parameters, even though they may have been specified differently by the user. If the VCP encounters no errors (i.e., no CPF0002 message is sent), the modified parameters are passed to the CPP.

Using the above financial application example, let's modify the command source to translate *CURRENT into the value of zero (Figure 34.2). Then code a VCP to check for a zero value in the year field. If a zero is found, the VCP will consult a data area to determine the current fiscal year. This determination also could be the result of a database control file or some other exotic logic applicable to your system. The VCP would then place the now-determined fiscal year value into the year field and terminate. The program-determined value will be passed

Figure 34.1 **Command Using Parameter Translation from the Command Definition**

```
CMD       PROMPT('G/L Account Balance Display')
PARM      KWD(YEAR) TYPE(*DEC) LEN(2 Ø)       +
            DFT('*CURRENT')                   +
            SPCVAL(('*CURRENT' 85))           +
            PROMPT('Fiscal year or *CURRENT')
```

Figure 34.2

Command Using Parameter Translation from the VCP

```
Command Source

      CMD        PROMPT('G/L Account Balance Display')
      PARM       KWD(YEAR) TYPE(*DEC) LEN(2 0)         +
                   DFT('*CURRENT')                     +
                   SPCVAL(('*CURRENT' 0))              +
                   PROMPT('Fiscal year or *CURRENT')

VCP Source

      PGM        PARM(&YEAR)
      DCL        VAR(&YEAR) TYPE(*DEC) LEN(2 0)
      IF         COND(&YEAR *NE 0) THEN EXEC(RETURN)
      RTVDTAARA DTAARA(GLLIB/GLYEAR 1 2) RTNVAR(&YEAR)
      ENDPGM
```

to the application program (G/L Account Balance Display in our example). The possibilities for this type of parameter translation are endless.

Modification of IBM-Supplied Commands and Parameters

Understanding commands also allows you to modify IBM-supplied commands. In some situations it is advantageous to tailor IBM-supplied commands and parameters to your specific situation. For instance, some IBM commands are unmanageable because they offer too many options to inexperienced operators. It is possible to force default values and not even present some parameters to the user.

There are three ways to modify IBM-supplied commands: using the CHGCMDDFT command, re-entering a replacement command source and re-creating the command, or using the VCP translation method explored earlier. Using the CHGCMDDFT is definitely the simplest method, but it can only modify the default parameter values that the original command requires. The CHGCMDDFT command cannot alter the actual command prompts. Re-entering a replacement command source does give you the capability of altering the command prompts as well as the default values and valid responses. However, re-entry of the source involves solving the riddle of how the source actually looks.

Writing a VCP for an IBM-supplied command is a less flexible but useful way to modify or enforce command parameters. The fact that IBM does not use VCPs for any of its own commands offers the programmer an opportunity to modify the command by writing a program and, using the CHGCMD (Change Command) command with the proper authority, specify the VCP to be used by the command.

To use this technique, you still need to know the command's parameters and the parameters' relative positions, lengths, and types. Most of the parameters are straightforward. And although some parameter lists can become quite tricky, they too can be worked out. A general discussion of parameter lists and their formats can be found in the *AS/400 CL Programmer's Guide* (SC41-8007).

As an example, suppose that you do not want a user to execute the Display Library (DSPLIB) command with the value *ALL, which causes the command to display all libraries. If selected, DSPLIB *ALL ties up the system for too long a time. Using a VCP can restrict the use of *ALL in the command parameters.

The DSPLIB command has two parameters: LIBRARY and OUTPUT. LIBRARY has a length of 10 and OUTPUT a length of one. A VCP written to exclude the value of *ALL would look like Figure 34.3. Note that if &LIB is not *ALL, control is returned to the command analyzer. If it is *ALL, then a diagnostic message is sent to identify the problem and an escape message follows to signal an error. To implement this example, enter the CL program source code into a member that could be called DSPLIBVCP. Then create the program into QGPL or any other library you wish and perform the following Change Command:

```
CHGCMD CMD(QSYS/DSPLIB) VLDCKR(QGPL/DSPLIBVCP)
```

A second example involves restricting an IBM-supplied command. You might want to restrict the RGZPFM (Reorganize Physical File Member) command from being performed for selected files because those files should not be reorganized or because they contain so many records that the process would take a long time to perform. Such an example is demonstrated in Figure 34.4.

The RGZPGM command uses six parameters. For our example, the first parameter, the qualified file name (library/file name), is the most important. The VCP tests for the specification of a file called FILEA in library QGPL. If such a file has been specified as one that isn't to be reorganized, then a diagnostic message is sent, followed by escape message CPF0002, which terminates the VCP. To implement this example, enter the CL program source code into a member that could be called RGZPFMVCP. Then create the program into QGPL or any other library you wish and perform the following Change Command:

Figure 34.3

Do Not Allow *ALL for DSPLIB Command

```
PGM       PARM(&LIB &OUTPUT)
DCL       VAR(&LIB) TYPE(*CHAR) LEN(10)
DCL       VAR(&OUTPUT) TYPE(*CHAR) LEN(1)
IF        COND(&LIB *NE '*ALL') THEN EXEC(RETURN)
SNDPGMMSG MSG('*ALL OPTION NOT ALLOWED FOR LIB     +
                   PARAMETER') MSGTYPE(*DIAG)
SNDPGMMSG MSGID(CPF0002) MSGF(QSYS/QCPFMSG)        +
            MSGTYPE(*ESCAPE)
ENDPGM
```

Figure 34.4

Restrict Files from Reorganization (RGZPFM)

```
PGM        PARM(&FILE &MBR &SRCOPT &SRCSEQ          +
               &KEYFILE &RCDFMT)
DCL        VAR(&FILE) TYPE(*CHAR) LEN(2Ø)
DCL        VAR(&MBR) TYPE(*CHAR) LEN(1Ø)
DCL        VAR(&SRCOPT) TYPE(*CHAR) LEN(1)
DCL        VAR(&SRCSEQ) TYPE(*CHAR) LEN(1)
DCL        VAR(&KEYFILE) TYPE(*CHAR) LEN(3Ø)
DCL        VAR(&RCDFMT) TYPE(*CHAR) LEN(1Ø)
IF         COND(&FILE *EQ 'FILEA     QGPL      ')   +
           THEN EXC(DO)
SNDPGMMSG MSG('REORGANIZATION OF QGPL/' || &FILE |+
           NOT ALLOWED.') MSGTYPE(*DIAG)
SNDPGMMSG MSGID(CPFØØØ2) MSGF(QSYS/QCPFMSG)         +
           MSGTYPE(*ESCAPE)
ENDDO
ENDPGM
```

```
CHGCMD CMD(QSYS/RGZPFM) VLDCKR(QGPL/RGZPFMVCPL)
```

Your imagination is the limit when it comes to uses of validity-checking programs attached to IBM-supplied commands. Some programmers would rather avoid modifying IBM-supplied commands because installation of the next release of OS/400 will destroy any modifications. However, simply keeping a small CL program in a source member, which can reproduce all of your changes, makes modification after installation of the next release manageable.

Your ability to tailor functions of the AS/400 to meet your unique operating characteristics lies in your ability to master the command processor and its concepts. Adding commands to your application programs can be an important step toward integration of those applications with the operating system. Sometimes we all need to slow the program development pace for just one minute and ponder in detail just how the AS/400 works. That minute of thought may save hours of programming.

Chapter 35

Creating Commands

by Douglas T. Parrish

Writing your own commands can enhance the capability of your application programs

All AS/400 users are familiar with CL commands. From the users' perspective, everything executed by the system is requested by some form of command. There are commands to create and delete objects (CRTPF, DLTF); there are commands to start and terminate subsystems (STRSBS, ENDSBS); and there is a command to power down the system (PWRDWNSYS). There is even a command to create other commands (CRTCMD).

You can create commands to execute any application program, whether it's written in CL, RPG/400, COBOL, or REXX. These commands are processed just like IBM-supplied commands. Commands can be written to take advantage of the prompter, syntax checking, and multiple list functions of the AS/400.

User-generated commands, when compared to prompt screens, offer several advantages. One advantage is the continuity of command processing. Once an operator learns the prompter functions, then all IBM and user-generated commands are processed in the same way. Moreover, when executing programs that require the passing of parameters, a user command can prompt for, and syntax check, the entries.

It's important to understand the AS/400 command processor and how to create commands. Let's create a simple command as an example. Assume that we have a program called PGMA, and that this program requires two parameters: company number and period ending date. if we were to call this program, the command string might look like this (remember that CALL is also a command):

```
CALL PGM(PGMA) PARM(01 070183)
```

Now let's create a simple command, CMDA, to prompt for these parameters. The source for this command might look like this:

```
CMD       PROMPT('COMMAND TO CALL PGMA')
PARM      KWD(COMPANY) TYPE(*DEC) LEN(2 0) RANGE(01) MIN(1)     +
          PROMPT('COMPANY NUMBER')
PARM      KWD(ENDING) TYPE(*DATE) MIN(1)                        +
          PROMPT('PERIOD ENDING DATE')
```

As shown in our example, the first source statement for any command must be CMD. The PROMPT parameter is the text that will appear at the top of the screen when the command is prompted.

A PARM statement must exist for each parameter that will be passed to the receiving program. The PARM statement also has associated parameters that define and qualify the PARM statement. For instance, in our first PARM statement, KWD(COMPANY) specifies that COMPANY is the keyword for the parameter being passed to the program. In addition, MIN(1) indicates that a value must be entered for COMPANY (i.e., it is a required parameter).

Using Qualified Names

Qualifiers are most commonly used on the AS/400 to further define or "qualify" an object (i.e., to specify the library to which an object belongs). A qualified name consists of the name of a library followed by the name of an object delimited by a forward slash. For example, LIBA/PGM001 specifies that PGM001 is qualified by LIBA, the library to which PGM001 belongs.

Processing Qualified Names with Commands

Let's assume we have a program that requires a qualified object name as a parameter. It would be possible to pass the data as two 10-byte parameters or as a qualified name. The first method would require a command with two PARM statements to define each parameter. The latter requires only one PARM statement and allows the names to be delimited by a forward slash, which is more consistent with OS/400.

We can write a command to process the qualified name. First, qualified names are defined by using the QUAL statement and an associated PARM statement. The PARM statement requires reference to a labeled QUAL group (which is placed after all the PARM statements). The source, for example, might look like this:

```
      PARM     KWD(OBJECT) TYPE(Q01)                          +
               PROMPT('Object name')
Q01   QUAL     TYPE(*NAME)
      QUAL     TYPE(*NAME)PROMPT('Library name')
```

Notice in our example that the PARM statement parameter TYPE(Q01) refers to the first QUAL statement, which establishes the relationship. The QUAL statements must be in the order in which they occur in the qualified name. In this case, the first QUAL statement refers to the object name and the second to the library name.

The first QUAL statement must be one of the following types:

*NAME
*GENERIC
*CHAR
*INT2
*INT4

The prompt text for the first part of the qualified name is entered on the PARM statement. The first QUAL statement cannot have a prompt. The prompt for each qualifier is entered on its appropriate QUAL statement. Syntax checking for each part of the qualified name is entered on the QUAL statement. Exceptions to this include SNGVAL since it refers to the entire qualified parameter, not just a particular portion. SNGVAL is coded on the PARM statement.

A qualified name is not passed to your command processing program with the slash delimiter, but is passed positionally in a contiguous field, and formatted by type. In our example, the qualified name is passed as a 20-byte field; the first 10 bytes (remember that *NAME is 10 bytes by default) are the first QUAL statement and the next 10 bytes are the second QUAL statement. TYPE(*NAME) is left-adjusted and padded on the right with blanks.

If PGM001 was entered for the name and LIBA was entered for the qualifier, the 20-byte field passed into your program would look like this:

```
00000000001111111111
12345678901234567890
PGM001    LIBA
```

In our example, the receiving field of our program must be defined with a length of 20. Assuming that the command processing program is CL, it might look like this:

```
PGM     PARM(&OBJ)
DCL     VAR(&OBJ) TYPE(*CHAR) LEN(20)
```

To process the qualified name in a CL program, use the %SST (substring) function. If the command processing was to check for existence, you might code:

```
CHKOBJ OBJ(%SST(&OBJ 11 10)/%SST(&OBJ 1 10)) OBJTYPE(*FILE)
```

Creating Command Validity Checkers

There are two types of validity checking: command syntax checking and a validity checker program. Syntax checking uses the VALUE, SPCVAL, SNGVAL, and RANGE syntax keywords of the PARM, QUAL and ELEM command definition statements. Syntax checking also can be performed using the DEP statement and is used to check for parameter dependencies.

If a parameter's validity can be affected by the values of one or more other parameters, you can use the DEP statement. You can assign a message ID to a DEP statement to be issued if the dependency is not true. If no message ID is entered, the command processor issues a message stating that "A REQUIRED

DEPENDENCY HAS NOT BEEN SATISFIED." (Try that one on your operators!) Use a message ID whenever possible. The DEP statement must be placed after all the PARM statements it refers to.

Syntax checking cannot be used to verify the existence of objects or to test for something programmable. If you have this need, a validity checking program (commonly known as a VCP) is required.

A validity checker is a program you can write for preprocessing command parameters. If you write a validity checker for a command, you must specify the VCP's name in the VLDCHK parameter of the CRTCMD command. Change command (CHGCMD) may be used to add it later, if necessary. The VCP is called only if the parameters pass the syntax checks in the command itself.

When the validity checker discovers an error, it should send a diagnostic message to the command processor notifying it of the problem. This message must be followed immediately by escape message CPF0002. The diagnostic message must also have a special format: That is, the first message substitution parameter must exist and must be four zeros. This four-character area is reserved for use by the command processor.

In our example, let's create a message to indicate that an object does not exist. Assume that a message file, USRMSGF, exists in LIBA.

```
ADDMSGD MSGID(USR1001) MSGF(LIBA/USRMSGF)                              +
        MSG('Object &3/&2 is missing.')                                +
        FMT((*CHAR4)(*CHAR 10)(*CHAR 10))
```

Notice that three substitution parameters are specified (FMT keyword). The first is the reserved space; the second and third are the object name and its qualifier, respectively. The first parameter is not used in the message text.

The validity checker will send this as a diagnostic message followed by an escape message if the object is not found. This might be coded as:

```
CHKOBJ     OBJ(%SST(&OBJ 11 10)/%SST(&OBJ 1 10)) OBJTYPE(*FILE)
MONMSG     MSGID(CPF0000) EXEC(DO)
SNDPGMMSG MSGID(USR1001) MSGF(LIBA/USRMSGF)                            +
           MSGDTA('0000' *CAT &OBJ) MSGTYPE(*DIAG)
SNDPGMMSG MSGID(CPF0002) MSGF(QSYS/QCPFMSG)                            +
           MSGTYPE(*ESCAPE)
ENDDO
```

The MSGDTA parameter of the SNDPGMMSG (Send Program Message) command contains the concatenation of a four-byte zero field and the object-name variable (&OBJ). It is not necessary to use %SUBSTRING since the 20-byte field will be separated by the message itself. The escape message immediately follows. CPF0002 is a special message and must be used. It is found in the QSYS/QCPFMSG message file. Remember that sending an escape message will terminate the validity checker, making it unnecessary to explicitly return to the command processor.

Upon receipt of the diagnostic/escape message pair, the command processor will display the diagnostic message at the bottom of the screen (if the command has been prompted).

Creating Command Parameter Lists

With some commands, a parameter can accept more than one entry. This is usually indicated by two parameter input lines and the words "+ for more." This is called a *simple list.* A list allows more than one entry for a parameter. In a simple list, all entries have the same attributes: A *mixed list* allows each list element to be different.

An example of a simple list can be found in the DSPOBJD (Display Object Description) command. The OBJTYPE (Object Type) parameter allows more than one value to be entered. When prompted, the command looks like the example in Figure 35.1. If a "+" is entered into either the first or second input field for OBJTYPE, the panel shown in Figure 35.2 is displayed.

If the entries *FILE, *CMD, *PGM and *JOBD are entered, the command will look like the example in Figure 35.3. The command processor will pass those four entries to the command processing program QLIDOBJD, the OS/400 program that displays the requested object descriptions.

Creating Your Own List Parameters

The key to understanding lists is to examine how the command parameter is defined and how entries are passed into a receiving program.

For example, let's define a command that calls a program to print inventory balances. Assume that the print program is written in RPG and that the command will request from one to 10 items to print. Let's call the parameter ITEM. The item number is defined as seven alphanumeric characters. To make things interesting, assume that *ALL can be specified, which would request the print program to list all items.

Figure 35.1

Display Object Description (DSPOBJD) Panel

```
          Display Object Description (DSPOBJD)
Type choices, press Enter.
Object . . . . . . . . . . . . . ________     Name, generic*, *ALL
  Library  . . . . . . . . . . .   *LIBL____  Name, *LIBL, *USRLIBL...
Object type  . . . . . . . . . . ________     *ALL, *ALRTBL, *AUTL...
               + for more values
Detail . . . . . . . . . . . . . *BASIC__     *BASIC, *FULL, *SERVICE
Output . . . . . . . . . . . . . *_______     *, *PRINT, *OUTFILE


                                                     Bottom
F3=Exit  F4=Prompt   F5=Refresh  F12=Cancel   F13=How to use this display
F24=More
```

Figure 35.2

Specify More Values for Parameter OBJTYPE Panel

```
              Specify More Values for Parameter OBJTYPE

 Type choices, press Enter.

 Object type . . . . . . . . . . .   _______
                                     _______
                                     _______
                                     _______
                                     _______
                                     _______
                                     _______
                                     _______
                                     _______
                                     _______
                                     _______
                                     _______
                                     _______
                                     _______
                                     _______
                                     _______
                                     _______
                                     _______
                                     _______
                                     _______
                   More...
 F3=Exit   F4=Prompt   F5=Refresh   F12=Cancel   F13=How to use this display
 F24=More keys
```

Figure 35.3

Specify More Values for Parameter OBJTYPE Panel with Entries Included

```
              Specify More Values for Parameter OBJTYPE

 Type choices, press Enter.

 Object type . . . . . . . . . .   *FILE____
                                   *CMD_____
                                   *PGM_____
                                   *JOBD____
                  More...
 F3=Exit   F4=Prompt   F5=Refresh   F12=Cancel   F13=How to use this display
 F24=More keys
```

The parameter definition statement, PARM, for this parameter would look like this:

```
PARM KWD(ITEM) TYPE(*CHAR) LEN(7)                           +
     SNGVAL((*ALL)) MIN(01) MAX(10)                         +
     PROMPT('Item numbers or *ALL')
```

On the parameter definition statement (PARM) for ITEM, the minimum number of parameter entries is coded as MIN(01). Since up to 10 entries are allowed, the maximum number of parameter entries is coded as MAX(10). MIN(01) specifies that one parameter is required. This combination of MIN(01) and MAX(10) parameters informs the command processor that at least one entry is required and that up to 10 may be specified.

The maximum possible number of elements in a list cannot exceed 300. Therefore, when you are defining your own commands, remember that MAX (300) is the largest allowed value when defining a list.

When the command is created and prompted, the ITEM parameter looks like this:

```
Item numbers or *ALL      ITEM       R        __________
                          + for more          __________
```

Notice that the ITEM parameter definition contains SNGVAL(*ALL), which indicates that *ALL is a single list value. If *ALL is entered, the command processor will allow no other list element to be specified. This is enforced by the command processor.

When the command is executed, and if proper values are entered, the command processor will pass entries to the command processing program. In this case, the command will pass the entries on to the RPG program.

The List Parameter String

The command processor passes list elements preceded by a 2-byte binary counter that indicates the number of elements passed. If one element was entered for our example, the print program would be passed a 9-byte string (one element times 7 bytes for each element, plus 2 bytes for the counter).

The field or data structure defined in the RPG program to receive the list must be as large as the maximum number of elements multiplied by the element length, plus two. This insures that all entries are received.

In our example, the RPG program must have a field or data structure with a length of 72 (10 elements times 7 bytes for each element, plus 2 bytes for the counter). The elements are passed as seven-character values that are left-justified and padded with blanks.

Assume that three item numbers are entered: PX12-A, FR985 and TT01. The passed string would have the following format:

Bytes	Contents	
01-02	X'0003'	(three elements passed)
03-09	PX12-A	
10-16	FR985	
17-23	TT01	

Processing Lists in RPG Programs

The easiest way to process a simple list is with a data structure and an array. In this print program, the parameter list could be handled in this way:

```
*... ... 1 ... ... 2 ... ... 3 ... ... 4 ... ... 5 ... ... 6
     E                   L        10  7
     IDSLIST  DS
     I                                        B        1   20COUNT
     I                                                 3  72 L
     C           *ENTRY    PLIST
     C                     PARM               DSLIST
```

An array, L, is defined as 10 elements of seven characters each. A data structure, DSLIST, is defined as 72 bytes with two subfields: COUNT, a 2-byte binary field, and the array L. DSLIST, which is referenced on the input parameter list.

In our example, if the aforementioned elements were entered into the parameter input fields, COUNT would contain a value of 3. Element 1 of array L would be PX12-A, element 2 would contain FR985 and element 3 would contain TT01. Our program could then print the requested numbers by executing a loop similar to that shown in Figure 35.4.

If the single value entry of *ALL was entered, the command processor would ensure that it was the only list element and pass it to our print program, which could take appropriate action if element 1 of array L was equal to *ALL (Figure 35.5).

A Word of Caution

A special note needs to be made here. If you use multiple parameters, junk data used to pad the list string could contain the entries for the parameters that follow the list. If you were to blank out the array elements past the desired elements (starting with position COUNT + 1), those following parameters would also be blanked since they address space that was blanked. A way to avoid this is by defining a field other than the array as a subfield to the list data structure. Then move (MOVEA) this field into the array. Once the data is moved, you can blank the elements. If no elements are passed (in the case of an optional list), then the counter bytes are set to X'0000'.

List Within Lists

In some cases a command parameter can be defined as a list consisting of elements, each of which is another list. The second list may have elements that are a third list,

Figure 35.4

RPG Logic to Process List Entries

```
*... ... 1 ... ... 2 ... ... 3 ... ... 4 ... ... 5 ... ... 6
     C*
     C*  RETRIEVE ITEM MASTER RECORDS (FOR EACH LIST ELEMENT)
     C*  ----------------------------------------------------
     C                     DO COUNT       X        30
     C             L,X     CHAINITEMFILE              91
     C                     EXCEPT
     C                     END
```

Figure 35.5

Test for the Single Value of *ALL

```
*... ... 1 ... ... 2 ... ... 3 ... ... 4 ... ... 5 ... ... 6
     C*
     C*   FIRST LIST ELEMENT IS *ALL
     C*   --------------------------
     C              L,1       IFEQ'*ALL'
     C*
     C*   READ ITEM RECORDS UNTIL *IN91 TURNS ON (END-OF-FILE)
     C*   ----------------------------------------------------
     C              *IN91     DOUEQ'1'
     C                        READ ITEMFILE                 91
     C              *IN91     IFEQ '0'
     C                        EXCPT
     C                        END
     C                        END
     C*
     C*   FIRST LIST ELEMENT NOT *ALL
     C*   ---------------------------
     C                        ELSE
     C*
     C*   RETRIEVE ITEM MASTER RECORDS (FOR EACH LIST ELEMENT)
     C*   ----------------------------------------------------
     C                        DO COUNT       X        30
     C              L,X       CHAINITEMFILE             91
     C              *IN91     IFEQ '0'
     C                        EXCPT
     C                        END
     C                        END
     C*
     C                        END
```

and so on. In these cases, the parameter string passed to the program remains the same in concept, but not in format.

To facilitate the process, the command processor passes list displacement information that indicates exactly where each list is located. At the start of each list are bytes that indicate the number of elements in the list (or the number of lists if the elements can be a list). If you become confused, read the section on "Defining Lists Within Lists" in the Defining Commands chapter of IBM's *AS/400 CL Programmer's Guide* (SC41-8077).

The need for lists within lists is probably not great, although the capability is there if needed. I have used lists within lists very successfully, and they add a nice touch for command execution.

AS/400 commands are a very powerful tool, and writing your own commands can enhance the capability of your application programs. By using lists you increase the power of those commands.

Chapter 36

Command Performance: Return Variables

by Paul Conte

Increase the power of your CL programs by creating your own commands that use return variables

AS/400 commands are powerful and flexible tools for controlling system operations. The AS/400 command set is also extensible — that is, you can create new commands that address your particular processing needs. (For basic information on creating commands, see Chapter 35, "Creating Commands.") Most locally created commands include parameters that allow you to *supply* a value (e.g., you may have created a command to do your daily incremental backups, and you may supply the reference date as a parameter value). But what about *retrieving* values from the system via a command parameter? For example, with a command that retrieves names of all the jobs currently executing in your interactive subsystems, your end-of-day operations could send those jobs a break message to sign off.

Several IBM-supplied commands (e.g., the RTVSYSVAL — Retrieve System Value, RTVJOBA — Retrieve Job Attributes, and RTVGRPA — Retrieve Group Attributes commands) retrieve values for a CL program via "return variables" that receive *output* from the command processing program (CPP) rather than supply *input* values to the CPP. Being familiar with IBM commands that use return variables, you may want to create your own commands with return variables. This chapter shows you how to define an AS/400 command parameter as a return variable and provides two useful commands as examples. The first example is a RTVSBSJOB (Retrieve Subsystem Jobs) command that returns, via CL return variables, information about selected jobs. The second example, the CVTTYP command, converts a job-type code to a job type description. This command is used by the RTVSBSJOB command.

The RTVSBSJOB Command

The RTVSBSJOB command returns, in CL variables, lists of job names and other job attributes from selected jobs. The two input parameters for command RTVSBSJOB are a list of subsystems and a user name; output parameters are two single-value return variables that contain the count of jobs meeting the subsystem and user criteria and six list-type return variables that contain the job information for the selected jobs. There is one list-type return variable for each of the job attributes (i.e., subsystem name, job name, job user name, job number, job type, and job status).

Both input and output parameters are coded in the command definition for the RTVSBSJOB command (Figure 36.1). The first two parameters, SBS (subsystem name) and USER (user name), are input parameters; their coding is similar to the coding of parameters in any command definition. Specifically, parameter SBS is declared as a list of 10-character names, with a maximum of 50 names. The single value *ALL also can be specified, and *ALL is the default value. Thus, you can retrieve the jobs within a list of specified subsystems, or all jobs known to the system. The USER parameter is declared as a single-value parameter with a special value of *ALL (the value *ALL is the default). Thus, you can retrieve the jobs either for a single user or for all users (but note that the SBS and USER parameters are conjunctive criteria — both criteria must be satisfied for a job to be retrieved).

Figure 36.1

The RTVSBSJOB Command Definition

```
/* RTVSBSJOB                                                          */
/*                                                                    */
/*  Use the following command to create the RTVSBSJOB command in      */
/*  library PRDEXC:                                                   */
/*                                                                    */
/*  CRTCMD     CMD(prdexc/rtvsbsjob)  PGM(rtvsbsjobc)         +       */
/*             SRCFILE(cmdsrc)        VLDCKR(rtvsbsjobv)      +       */
/*             ALLOW(*ipgm *bpgm)                             +       */

CMD        PROMPT('Retrieve Subsystem Jobs')

PARM       sbs          *name  10                                   +
                        MAX(50)                                     +
                        SNGVAL((*ALL))                              +
                        DFT(*ALL)                                   +
                        EXPR(*yes)                                  +
                        PROMPT('Subsystem name(s):')

PARM       user         *name  10                                   +
                        SPCVAL((*ALL))                              +
                        DFT(*ALL)                                   +
                        EXPR(*yes)                                  +
                        PROMPT('User whose jobs to display:')

PARM       totjobcnt *dec  ( 5 0)                                   +
```

Figure 36.1 Continued

Figure 36.1

The RTVSBSJOB Command Definition *Continued*

```
                          RTNVAL(*yes)                                   +
                          PROMPT('CL var for total job count:')

PARM        lstjobcnt *dec  ( 5 Ø)                                       +
                          RTNVAL(*yes)                                   +
                          PROMPT('CL var for list job count:')

PARM        sbsl          *char   1                                      +
                          RTNVAL(*yes)                                   +
                          VARY(*yes)                                     +
                          PROMPT('CL var for subsystem list:')

PARM        jobnaml       *char   1                                      +
                          RTNVAL(*yes)                                   +
                          VARY(*yes)                                     +
                          PROMPT('CL var for job name list:')

PARM        jobusrl       *char   1                                      +
                          RTNVAL(*yes)                                   +
                          VARY(*yes)                                     +
                          PROMPT('CL var for job user list:')

PARM        jobnbrl       *char   1                                      +
                          RTNVAL(*yes)                                   +
                          VARY(*yes)                                     +
                          PROMPT('CL var for job number list:')

PARM        jobtypl       *char   1                                      +
                          RTNVAL(*yes)                                   +
                          VARY(*yes)                                     +
                          PROMPT('CL var for job type list:')

PARM        jobstsl       *char   1                                      +
                          RTNVAL(*yes)                                   +
                          VARY(*yes)                                     +
                          PROMPT('CL var for job status list:')
```

The program segment shown in Figure 36.2 illustrates how these input parameters may be used. In this use of the RTVSBSJOB command, three values are specified for the subsystem parameter: two subsystem names (QINTER, QCMN, and QSPL). The USER parameter is specified as *ALL. In this example, the RTVSBSJOB command retrieves information about all users' jobs currently in subsystem QINTER, QCMN, or in QSPL, jobs in subsystem QCMN, or on an output queue.

Return-Variable Parameters

The output (i.e., return-variable) parameters in the command definition (Figure 36.1), are declared with the RTNVAL(*YES) option. The first two return variables, TOTJOBCNT and LSTJOBCNT, are declared as five-digit, packed-decimal parameters. They each receive a single value. TOTJOBCNT contains the total number of jobs retrieved using the criteria specified in parameters SBS and USER;

Figure 36.2

Example Program That Uses the RTVSBSJOB Command

```
PGM
/* Declare character variables to hold lists of up to 199 entries.   */

DCL  &jobnam_lst *CHAR 1990                   /* Job name       list  */
DCL  &jobnbr_lst *CHAR 1194                   /* Job number     list  */
DCL  &jobsbs_lst *CHAR 1990                   /* Job subsystem list  */
DCL  &jobsts_lst *CHAR  796                   /* Job status     list  */
DCL  &jobtyp_lst *CHAR  597                   /* Job type       list  */
DCL  &jobusr_lst *CHAR 1990                   /* Job user       list  */

/* Declare decimal variables to receive counts.                      */

DCL  &lst_jobcnt *DEC     5                   /* List  job count      */
DCL  &tot_jobcnt *DEC     5                   /* Total job count      */

/* Declare temporary variables to demonstrate getting an entry out   */
/* of a list.                                                         */

DCL  &cur_jobnam *CHAR   10                   /* Job name entry       */
DCL  &cur_jobnbr *CHAR    6                   /* Job number entry     */
DCL  &cur_jobsts *CHAR    4                   /* Job status entry     */
DCL  &cur_sbsnam *CHAR   10                   /* Subsystem name entry*/

DCL  &bgn_bytidx *DEC     5                   /* Beginning byte index*/
DCL  &n          *DEC     5                   /* Nth entry            */


/* Retrieve the job and subsystem information.                        */

RTVSBSJOB    SBS(qinter qcmn qspl) USER(*all)                           +
             TOTJOBCNT(&tot_jobcnt) LSTJOBCNT(&lst_jobcnt)              +
             SBSL(&jobsbs_lst)      JOBNAML(&jobnam_lst)                +
             JOBUSRL(&jobusr_lst)   JOBNBRL(&jobnbr_lst)                +
             JOBTYPL(&jobtyp_lst)   JOBSTSL(&jobsts_lst)


/* Reference the first job name.                                      */

CHGVAR       &cur_jobnam  %SST(&jobnam_lst  1  10)

/* Reference the Nth subsystem name.                                  */

CHGVAR       &bgn_bytidx  (((&N - 1) * 10) + 1)

CHGVAR       &cur_sbsnam  %SST(&jobsbs_lst  &bgn_bytidx  10)

/* Reference the 11th job status.                                     */

CHGVAR       &cur_jobsts  %SST(&jobsts_lst  41 4)

/* Reference the last job number.                                     */

CHGVAR       &bgn_bytidx  (((&lst_jobcnt - 1) * 6) + 1)
CHGVAR       &cur_jobnbr  %SST(&jobnbr_lst  &bgn_bytidx  6)

RETURN
ENDPGM
```

LSTJOBCNT contains the number of job entries put in the lists specified by the other return variables (e.g., SBSL). TOTJOBCNT will be greater than LSTJOBCNT if more jobs are retrieved than can be put in the list-type return variables.

The other return variables (i.e., SBSL through JOBSTSL) contain lists of character values. These list-type return parameters are declared as variable-length character strings by specifying the VARY(*YES) option. They are declared as variable-length parameters because command RTVSBSJOB can be called by a variety of CL programs, and within these programs the variables used to receive the job information lists may be declared with different sizes.

Each list-type return variable is declared with a *minimum* size of one byte and, as with any CL variable, these list-type parameters are limited to a maximum length of 9,999 bytes. The layout of the list-type return variables is determined by how the CPP puts list entries into the variable-length character string. In this example, the CPP RVTSBSJOBC laces list entries into the character string with no extra blanks added. Because each entry in the list of subsystem names (SBSL) and in the list of job names (JOBNAML) is 10 bytes, these lists can contain no more than 999 entries. (At 10 bytes each, 999 entries require 9,990 bytes; as discussed below, the command analyzer adds a 2-byte header to a variable length character string when it is passed to the CPP — thus, 9,992 bytes is required). In the unlikely event that more than 999 jobs meet the selection criteria specified in the SBS and USER parameters, the "extra" jobs will not appear on the list-type return variables.

Not all the list-type return variables contain 10-byte entries. Parameter JOBNBRL contains 6-byte entries; parameter JOBTYPL contains 3-byte entries, and JOBSTSL contains 4-byte entries. Because the entries in these parameters are less than 10 bytes each, they could possibly contain more than 999 elements. But the information for these "extra" jobs would not be complete because no corresponding entry could be placed in the SBSL or JOBNAML lists. So that all lists contain comparable data, command RTVSBSJOB forces each list to have the same number of entries. For example, suppose the calling program's variable for the job names list is large enough to hold 10 job names, but the variable for the job numbers list is large enough to hold 15 job numbers. The command limits both return variables to only 10 entries (the number of entries in the job names list); any excess bytes in the job number variable will be blank.

When list-type return variables are declared as variable-length character strings, the command analyzer puts a 2-byte binary length field at the beginning of the character variable passed to the CPP. (For return variables, the length field contains the length of the CL variable supplied by the CL program executing the command). Thus, if a 50-character CL program return variable is specified for parameter SBSL, the CPP is passed a variable (actually an address of a variable) that should be treated as a 52-byte character variable that has the binary value +50 in the first two bytes. Bytes three through 52 are the locations into which the list entries should be placed. The 2-byte length header is *not* returned to the CL program that invokes the command; the command analyzer strips this header off before returning to the CL program, and the list returned to the CL program begins in the first byte of the CL program return variable. (The RTVSBSJOB command uses parameter LSTJOBCNT to return the number of entries placed in the lists to the CL program).

Note that the 2-byte *length* header for a variable length character return variable is *not* the same as the 2-byte *count* header the command analyzer puts at the beginning of a non-return variable list parameter (e.g., SBS) that allows more than one value to be entered. Even though both headers are 2-byte binary numbers, the header of a variable-length, character-return variable states the variable's length in bytes while the header of a list parameter states the number of entries entered for the parameter.

Creating the Command and Its CPP

After you have entered the source for command RTVSBSJOB, you must execute a CRTCMD (Create Command) command. For commands with return variables, you must specify ALLOW(*IPGM *BPGM) (or just one of the two special values) to restrict use of the command to a CL program. A command that includes return variables cannot be used interactively, in a database job, or with QCMDEXC, because CL program variables must be referenced when the CPP is executed.

When a command is created, a CPP also must be specified; for the RTVSBSJOB command, program RTVSBSJOBC (Figure 36.3) is the designated CPP. Commands also can have an associated validity checking program to trap erroneous input before the CPP is invoked. The validity checking program for command RTVSBSJOB, program RTVSBSJOBV, will be described in Chapter 37 and it guarantees that duplicate subsystem names are not entered for the SBS parameter. The command creation specifies this validity checking program in the VLDCKR(RTVSBSJOBV) parameter. (Command RTVSBSJOB can be created without a validity checking program by specifying VLDCKR(*NONE) when the command is created.)

The CPP for a command with return variables is not greatly different from the CPP for a command without return variables. The only difference is the assignment of the return-variable values and the necessary determination of which parameters are specified by the calling CL program.

Program RTVSBSJOBC (Figure 36.3) declares program parameters that correspond to the command parameter definitions. For example, `&sbs_prm` corresponds to the command's SBS input parameter and `&jobsbs_lst` corresponds to the command's SBSL return variable. CPP variables for variable-length return variables (e.g., `&jobsbs_lst`) are declared with the maximum length (9,999 bytes).

Program RTVSBSJOBC also declares several logical variables that correspond to the return variables. Each logical variable indicates whether or not its corresponding parameter is actually specified by the calling program. Program RTVSBSJOBC must keep track of which parameters are actually specified by the invoking program because some parameters may be omitted. For example, if you want only a list of the job users, your CL program that invokes command RTVSBSJOB might not define variables to receive job status or job type.

The logical variables are initialized to "true", and then an attempt is made to reference each return variable. If a return variable is not present, the system sends escape message MCH3601 to program RTVSBSJOBC. By monitoring for message MCH3601, the CPP can set the corresponding logical variable to "false" if the

Figure 36.3

RTVSBSJOBC Command Processing Program

```
/*   RTVSBSJOBC                                                      */
/*-------------------------------------------------------------------*/
/*  Abstract: Command Processing Program (CPP) for RTVSBSJOB:        */
/*            Retrieve subsystem job information.                    */
/*-------------------------------------------------------------------*/
/* Written by Paul Conte                                             */
/* Modified by Michael Otey for V2.R2 compatibility                  */
/*-------------------------------------------------------------------*/

PGM                                                                    +
PARM(                                                                  +
     &sbs_prm      /* IN     Subsystem (name(s), *ALL)               */+
     &usr_prm      /* IN     User name (name or  *ALL)               */+
     &tot_jobcnt   /*    OUT Total jobs associated with subsystem(s)*/+
     &lst_jobcnt   /*    OUT Number of jobs put in following lists   */+
     &jobsbs_lst   /*    OUT String for job subsystem list           */+
     &jobnam_lst   /*    OUT String for job name      list           */+
     &jobusr_lst   /*    OUT String for job user      list           */+
     &jobnbr_lst   /*    OUT String for job number    list           */+
     &jobtyp_lst   /*    OUT String for job type      list           */+
     &jobsts_lst   /*    OUT String for job status    list           */+
    )

DCL  &all         *CHAR   10 ('*ALL      ')   /* Mnemonic              */
DCL  &not_fnd     *DEC     1 (0)              /* Mnemonic              */
DCL  &errcnt      *DEC     7 (0)              /* Error count           */
DCL  &esc_rcved   *LGL     1 ('1')            /* Escape msg. received*/
DCL  &false       *LGL     1 ('0')            /* Mnemonic              */
DCL  &fst_entidx  *DEC     5 ( 1 )            /* Mnemonic - index 1  */
DCL  &fst_lstbyt  *DEC     5 ( 3 )            /* The first byte in a */
                                              /* list variable. It is*/
                                              /* after the two-byte  */
                                              /* length field.       */
DCL  &jobnam_lst *CHAR 9999                   /* Job name       list  */
DCL  &jobnam_usd *LGL     1                   /* Parameter is used    */
DCL  &jobnbr_lst *CHAR 9999                   /* Job number     list  */
DCL  &jobnbr_usd *LGL     1                   /* Parameter is used    */
DCL  &jobsbs_lst *CHAR 9999                   /* Job subsystem list   */
DCL  &jobsbs_usd *LGL     1                   /* Parameter is used    */
DCL  &jobsts_lst *CHAR 9999                   /* Job status     list  */
DCL  &jobsts_usd *LGL     1                   /* Parameter is used    */
DCL  &jobtyp_lst *CHAR 9999                   /* Job type       list  */
DCL  &jobtyp_usd *LGL     1                   /* Parameter is used    */
DCL  &jobusr_lst *CHAR 9999                   /* Job user       list  */
DCL  &jobusr_usd *LGL     1                   /* Parameter is used    */
DCL  &lst_jobcnt *DEC     5                   /* List  job count      */
DCL  &lstcnt_usd *LGL     1                   /* Parameter is used    */
DCL  &max_int     *DEC     5 VALUE(99999)     /* Max integer mnemonic*/
DCL  &min_lstcnt *DEC     5                   /* Minimum of all lists*/
DCL  &msgdta      *CHAR  512                  /* Message data          */
DCL  &msgdtalen   *DEC     5                  /* Message data length */
DCL  &msgid       *CHAR    7                  /* Message data          */
DCL  &nam_entsiz *DEC     5 VALUE(10)         /* Job name entry size */
DCL  &nbr_entsiz *DEC     5 VALUE( 6)         /* Job nbr. entry size */
DCL  &rcd_cnt     *DEC     5                  /* Input record count  */
```

Figure 36.3 Continued

Figure 36.3

RTVSBSJOBC Command Processing Program *Continued*

```
DCL  &sbs_cnt     *DEC     5                  /* Subsystem count       */
DCL  &sbs_entidx  *DEC     5                  /* Sbs. list entry idx   */
DCL  &sbs_entsiz  *DEC     5 VALUE(10)        /* Job sbs. entry size   */
DCL  &sbs_prm     *CHAR  502                  /* Subsystem parameter   */
                                              /* list of up to 50      */
                                              /* names or special      */
                                              /* values, or *ALL       */
DCL  &sbs_arg     *CHAR   10                  /* Subsystem parameter   */
DCL  &sts_entsiz  *DEC     5 VALUE( 4)        /* Job sts. entry size   */
DCL  &tmp_bgnidx  *DEC     5                  /* Temporary string      */
                                              /* begin index           */
DCL  &tmp_binlen  *CHAR    2                  /* Temporary binary      */
DCL  &tmp_lstcnt  *DEC     5                  /* Temporary list count*/
DCL  &tot_jobcnt  *DEC     5                  /* Total job count       */
DCL  &totcnt_usd  *LGL     1                  /* Parameter is used     */
DCL  &true        *LGL     1 VALUE('1')       /* Mnemonic              */
DCL  &typ_entsiz  *DEC     5 VALUE( 3)        /* Job type entry size   */
DCL  &usr_entsiz  *DEC     5 VALUE(10)        /* Job user entry size   */
DCL  &usr_prm     *CHAR   10                  /* User parameter        */
DCL  &type        *CHAR    3                  /* Type description      */

DCLF wrkactp

/*-----------------------------------------------------------------*/

/* Handle CPF and MCH messages that are not specifically monitored  */

MONMSG (cpf9999) EXEC(GOTO proc_end)

/*--------   BEGIN PROCEDURE   ------------------------------------*/


/* Initialize that all parameters had a variable supplied in the    */
/* command.  When the return values are initialized, these will be  */
/* be set to false if the variable is not present.                  */

CHGVAR    &totcnt_usd &true
CHGVAR    &lstcnt_usd &true
CHGVAR    &jobsbs_usd &true
CHGVAR    &jobnam_usd &true
CHGVAR    &jobusr_usd &true
CHGVAR    &jobnbr_usd &true
CHGVAR    &jobtyp_usd &true
CHGVAR    &jobsts_usd &true


/* Initialize the minimum count of list entries to a high value so  */
/* the first list with any entries will reset it.                   */

CHGVAR    &min_lstcnt &max_int

/* Initialize the count of how many entries have been read from the */
/* file and the temporary count of how many are put in the list.    */

CHGVAR    &rcd_cnt    0
```

Figure 36.3 Continued

Figure 36.3

RTVSBSJOBC Command Processing Program *Continued*

```
CHGVAR     &tmp_lstcnt 0

/* Initialize the return values and determine the string lengths.   */

CHGVAR     &tot_jobcnt 0
MONMSG     (mch3601)    EXEC(CHGVAR &totcnt_usd &false)

CHGVAR     &lst_jobcnt 0
MONMSG     (mch3601)    EXEC(CHGVAR &lstcnt_usd &false)

CHGVAR     &tmp_binlen %SST(&jobsbs_lst 1 2)
MONMSG     (mch3601)    EXEC(CHGVAR &jobsbs_usd &false)

IF         (&jobsbs_usd)                                             +
            CALL      SETSBJVAR (&jobsbs_lst  &sbs_entsiz  &min_lstcnt)

CHGVAR     &tmp_binlen %SST(&jobnam_lst 1 2)
MONMSG     (mch3601)    EXEC(CHGVAR &jobnam_usd &false)

IF         (&jobnam_usd)                                             +
            CALL      SETSBJVAR (&jobnam_lst  &nam_entsiz  &min_lstcnt)

CHGVAR     &tmp_binlen %SST(&jobusr_lst 1 2)
MONMSG     (mch3601)    EXEC(CHGVAR &jobusr_usd &false)

IF         (&jobusr_usd)                                             +
            CALL      SETSBJVAR (&jobusr_lst  &usr_entsiz  &min_lstcnt)

CHGVAR     &tmp_binlen %SST(&jobnbr_lst 1 2)
MONMSG     (mch3601)    EXEC(CHGVAR &jobnbr_usd &false)

IF         (&jobnbr_usd)                                             +
            CALL      SETSBJVAR (&jobnbr_lst  &nbr_entsiz  &min_lstcnt)

CHGVAR     &tmp_binlen %SST(&jobtyp_lst 1 2)
MONMSG     (mch3601)    EXEC(CHGVAR &jobtyp_usd &false)

IF         (&jobtyp_usd)                                             +
            CALL      SETSBJVAR (&jobtyp_lst  &typ_entsiz  &min_lstcnt)


CHGVAR     &tmp_binlen %SST(&jobsts_lst 1 2)
MONMSG     (mch3601)    EXEC(CHGVAR &jobsts_usd &false)

IF         (&jobsts_usd)                                             +
            CALL      SETSBJVAR (&jobsts_lst  &sts_entsiz  &min_lstcnt)

/* Reset the minimum list count if no lists were present.          */

IF        (&min_lstcnt  = &max_int)  (CHGVAR  &min_lstcnt 0)


/* Use QUSRTOOL command CVTWRKACT to produce a list of active jobs  */
```

Figure 36.3 Continued

Figure 36.3

RTVSBSJOBC Command Processing Program *Continued*

```
TAATOOL/CVTWRKACT OUTLIB(QTEMP)

OVRDBF    FILE(wrkactp) TOFILE(qtemp/wrkactp) POSITION(*START)

/* Loop across the file and move fields to parameter lists          */

READ_BGN:

RCVF      DEV(*file)
          MONMSG  (cpf0864) EXEC(GOTO read_end)
          MONMSG  (cpf0000) EXEC(GOTO proc_end)

/* Check the sbs. to see if the record should be included.  If there*/
/* was only one sbs. specified, all records are included.  Otherwise*/
/* the list must be searched.                                       */

CHGVAR   &sbs_arg %SST(&sbs_prm &fst_lstbyt &sbs_entsiz)

IF       (&sbs_arg *= &all)                                         +
          DO
          CALL  FNDLSTELM (&sbs_prm    &sbs_entsiz   &ajsbs         +
                          &fst_entidx &sbs_entidx)
          IF   (&sbs_entidx = &not_fnd) GOTO read_bgn/* Skip record   */
          ENDDO

/* Check the user parm to see if the record should be included. If  */
/* *ALL was not specified then the user parm must match the record. */

IF       (&usr_prm *= &all)                                         +
          DO
          IF  (&usr_prm *= &ajusr) GOTO read_bgn    /* Skip record   */
          ENDDO

CHGVAR    &rcd_cnt  (&rcd_cnt + 1)

/* If the lists are not already full, add this to them and bump the */
/* count.                                                           */
IF       (&rcd_cnt <= &min_lstcnt)                                  +
          DO
          CHGVAR &tmp_lstcnt (&tmp_lstcnt + 1)

          IF (&jobsbs_usd)                                          +
             DO
             CHGVAR &tmp_bgnidx                                     +
                  (((&tmp_lstcnt - 1) * &sbs_entsiz) + &fst_lstbyt)
             CHGVAR %SST(&jobsbs_lst &tmp_bgnidx &sbs_entsiz)  &ajsbs
             ENDDO

          IF (&jobnam_usd)                                          +
             DO
             CHGVAR &tmp_bgnidx                                     +
                  (((&tmp_lstcnt - 1) * &nam_entsiz) + &fst_lstbyt)
```

Figure 36.3 Continued

Figure 36.3 RTVSBSJOBC Command Processing Program *Continued*

```
            CHGVAR %SST(&jobnam_lst &tmp_bgnidx &nam_entsiz)  &ajjob
            ENDDO

         IF (&jobusr_usd)                                             +
            DO
            CHGVAR &tmp_bgnidx                                        +
                   (((&tmp_lstcnt - 1) * &usr_entsiz) + &fst_lstbyt)
            CHGVAR %SST(&jobusr_lst &tmp_bgnidx &usr_entsiz)  &ajusr
            ENDDO

         IF (&jobnbr_usd)                                             +
            DO
            CHGVAR &tmp_bgnidx                                        +
                   (((&tmp_lstcnt - 1) * &nbr_entsiz) + &fst_lstbyt)
            CHGVAR %SST(&jobnbr_lst &tmp_bgnidx &nbr_entsiz)  &ajjobn
            ENDDO

         IF (&jobtyp_usd)                                             +
            DO
            CVTTYP &ajtype &ajsubt &type
            CHGVAR &tmp_bgnidx                                        +
                   (((&tmp_lstcnt - 1) * &typ_entsiz) + &fst_lstbyt)
            CHGVAR %SST(&jobtyp_lst &tmp_bgnidx &typ_entsiz)  &type
            ENDDO

         IF (&jobsts_usd)                                             +
            DO
            CHGVAR &tmp_bgnidx                                        +
                   (((&tmp_lstcnt - 1) * &sts_entsiz) + &fst_lstbyt)
            CHGVAR %SST(&jobsts_lst &tmp_bgnidx &sts_entsiz)  &ajsts
            ENDDO

         ENDDO

GOTO     read_bgn

READ_END:

/* Return the total (i.e. record) count and the list count.         */

IF       (&totcnt_usd)  (CHGVAR &tot_jobcnt  &rcd_cnt)

IF       (&lstcnt_usd)  (CHGVAR &lst_jobcnt  &tmp_lstcnt)


/* Successful completion; indicate that no escape message received. */

CHGVAR   &esc_rcved &false

/*--------   END   PROCEDURE   -------------------------------------*/
```

Figure 36.3 Continued

Figure 36.3

RTVSBSJOBC Command Processing Program *Continued*

```
PROC_END:       /* Procedure end.  Clean up objects and resend any     */
                /* escape messages.                                    */

/* The following use of &errcnt protects against a loop caused by     */
/* global message monitoring.                                          */

IF          (&errcnt > 0) (GOTO exit)
CHGVAR       &errcnt       (&errcnt + 1)


/* If escape message received, resend it.                              */

IF    (&esc_rcved)                                                     +
      DO
      RCVMSG     MSGTYPE(*excp)          MSGDTA(&msgdta)               +
                 MSGDTALEN(&msgdtalen) MSGID(&msgid)
                 MONMSG (cpf0000) EXEC(GOTO exit)

      SNDPGMMSG MSGID(&msgid)            MSGF(qcpfmsg)                 +
                 MSGDTA(%SST(&msgdta 1 &msgdtalen))                    +
                 MSGTYPE(*escape)
                 MONMSG (cpf0000) EXEC(GOTO exit)
      ENDDO

/*--------   EXIT  PROGRAM     -------------------------------------*/

EXIT:
RETURN
ENDPGM
```

return variable is not present. Then, by checking the value of these logical variables, the program limits subsequent return variable references to only those return variables actually specified in the command invocation.

Before the CPP can assign values to the return variables, it must initialize the variable-length return variables to blanks and calculate the maximum number of entries the return variables can hold. Program RTVSBSJOBC calls CL program SETSBJVAR (Figure 36.4) to perform these tasks for each of the list-type return variables.

Program SETSBJVAR determines the number of elements a list can hold based on the variable's length and the length of the list entries for that variable. The program obtains the variable's length from the 2-byte header. However, this header is expressed in binary format, so program SETSBJVAR uses the %BIN function of the CHGVAR command to convert the binary number to packed-decimal format. Program SETSBJVAR then compares the number of entries that will fit in the current list to the number of entries that will fit in the smallest list encountered thus far. The size of the smallest list (i.e., the list that can contain the fewest entries) dictates the usable size of all the lists, so program SETSBJVAR resets the minimum if a list's size is lower than the current minimum.

After initialization of the return variables is complete, program RTVSBSJOBC executes the QUSRTOOL CVTWRKACT command to produce an output file for the active jobs on the system. If the subsystem and user parameters do not contain the special value of *ALL, the outfile records must be tested for the desired subsystem and user names. Program RTVSBSJOBC performs these tests in a loop (Figure 36.3), calling program FNDLSTELM (Figure 36.5) to determine whether the given record's subsystem name appears in parameter SBS's list of subsystem

Figure 36.4

SETSBJVAR CLP Subprogram for RTVSBSJOB Command

```
/*   SETSBJVAR                                                        */
/*===================================================================*/
/*  Abstract: A subroutine called by RTVSBSJOBC to initialize a      */
/*            list variable to blanks and to set the minimum count   */
/*            of items that any list can hold.                       */
/*-------------------------------------------------------------------*/
/*  Written by Paul Conte                                            */
/*  Modified by Michael Otey for V2.R2 Compatiblity                  */
/*-------------------------------------------------------------------*/

PGM                                                                    +
PARM(                                                                  +
     &lst_var      /* IN/OUT List variable, a character variable    */+
                   /*        with the length in first two bytes     */+
     &ent_siz      /* IN     Character size of one list entry       */+
     &min_jobcnt   /* IN/OUT Minimum number of entries allowed by   */+
                   /*        any list                                */+
     )

DCL  &ent_siz    *DEC     5                   /* Entry size          */
DCL  &lst_len    *DEC     5                   /* List length         */
DCL  &lst_var    *CHAR 9999                   /* List variable       */
DCL  &max_lstlen *DEC     5 VALUE(9997)       /* Maximum list size   */
DCL  &min_jobcnt *DEC     5                   /* Minimum    job count */
DCL  &tmp_jobcnt *DEC     5                   /* Temporary job count */
DCL  &tmp_len    *CHAR    2                   /* Temporary length    */
                                              /* in two-byte binary  */

/*-------------------------------------------------------------------*/

/* Handle CPF and MCH messages that are not specifically monitored   */

MONMSG (cpf9999) EXEC(GOTO error)

/*-------   BEGIN PROCEDURE   ---------------------------------------*/

/* Convert the two-byte binary length to a packed decimal length    */
/* The maximum size is 9997, to allow for the two-byte header       */

CHGVAR     &tmp_len   %SST(&lst_var 1 2)
CHGVAR     &lst_len   %BIN(&tmp_len)
IF        (&lst_len > &max_lstlen)  (CHGVAR &lst_len  &max_lstlen)
```

Figure 36.4 Continued

Figure 36.4 **SETSBJVAR CLP Subprogram for RTVSBSJOB Command** *Continued*

```
/* Blank out the return variable                                         */

CHGVAR     %SST(&lst_var 3 &lst_len)      ' '

/* Reset the minimum number of job entries.  The number of entries       */
/* that can go in a list is determined by dividing the length by the*/
/* size of one entry in the list, then truncating.                       */

CHGVAR     &tmp_jobcnt  (&lst_len / &ent_siz)

IF        (&tmp_jobcnt < &min_jobcnt) (CHGVAR &min_jobcnt &tmp_jobcnt)

GOTO       exit     /* Normal return                                     */

/*--------    ERROR EXIT -------------------------------------------*/

ERROR:

SNDPGMMSG  MSGID(cpf9898) MSGF(qsys/qcpfmsg) MSGTYPE(*escape)          +
           MSGDTA('Subroutine SETSJBVAR failed.')
MONMSG    (cpf0000)

EXIT:
RETURN
ENDPGM
```

names. The user parameter &usr_prm is tested against the record's user name &ajusr to determine if there is a match.

Program FNDLSTELM loops across a list parameter from the first entry specified by the program parameter &bgn_entidx until a matching entry is found or until the last entry in the list has been checked. Note that FNDLSTELM subroutine parameter &lst_var is a character variable with the format of a command multivalue list parameter (i.e., with a 2-byte *count* header), and that program FNDLSTELM uses the %BIN function to convert the binary count to a packed-decimal variable (&lst_cnt) used to limit the loop.

If the record meets the SBS and USER parameter criteria, program RTVSBSJOBC increments the total count of selected records (Figure 36.3); if there is room to put this entry in the list return variables, program RTVSBSJOBC moves the record's fields to the appropriate substrings of each list return variable that is present. When processing the substring for the job type list (&job_typist), the CVTTYP command (Figure 36.6) is called to convert the job type (&ajtype) and job subtype (&ajsubt) codes in the CVTWRKACT outfile to the more familiar descriptions that are seen the WRKACTJOB display. the CVTTYPC command processing program (Figure 36.7) takes the job type and subtype codes as input parameters and uses a return variable to pass the job type description back to the

Figure 36.5 FNDSTELM CLP Subprogram for RTVSBSJOB Command

```
/*   FNDLSTELM                                                          */
/*=====================================================================*/
/*  Abstract: A subroutine to see if a specified character variable */
/*            is found as an element in a list.                      */
/*---------------------------------------------------------------------*/
/*  Written by Paul Conte                                               */
/*  Modified by Michael Otey for V2.R2 Compatiblity                     */
/*---------------------------------------------------------------------*/

PGM                                                                    +
PARM(                                                                  +
     &lst_var      /* IN    List variable, a character variable   */+
                   /*       with the number of entries in first   */+
                   /*       two bytes.                            */+
     &ent_siz      /* IN    Character size of one list entry      */+
     &ent          /* IN    Character entry to be found           */+
     &bgn_entidx   /* IN    Beginning entry index                 */+
     &ent_idx      /*    OUT Index of found entry (Ø if not found) */+
    )

DCL  &bgn_entidx *DEC     5                  /* Beginning entry indx*/
DCL  &ent        *CHAR 9997                  /* Entry to be found   */
DCL  &ent_idx    *DEC     5                  /* Index of found entry*/
                                             /* (Ø if not found)    */
DCL  &ent_siz    *DEC     5                  /* Entry size          */
DCL  &fst_lstbyt *DEC     5 VALUE( 3)        /* The first byte in a */
                                             /* list variable. It is*/
                                             /* after the two-byte  */
                                             /* count  field.       */
DCL  &tmp_bin    *CHAR    2                  /* Temporary Binary    */
DCL  &lst_cnt    *DEC     5                  /* Number of entries   */
DCL  &lst_len    *DEC     5                  /* List char. length   */
DCL  &lst_var    *CHAR 9999                  /* List variable       */
DCL  &max_lstlen *DEC     5 VALUE(9997)      /* Maximum list length */
DCL  &tmp_bytidx *DEC     5                  /* Beginning byte index*/
DCL  &tmp_entidx *DEC     5                  /* Entry index         */

/*---------------------------------------------------------------------*/

/* Handle CPF and MCH messages that are not specifically monitored  */

MONMSG (cpf9999) EXEC(GOTO error)

/*--------   BEGIN PROCEDURE   -------------------------------------*/

/* Initialize to not found, set to true if found.                    */

CHGVAR      &ent_idx   Ø


/* Set the number of entries.                                        */
CHGVAR      &tmp_bin   %SST(&lst_var 1 2)
CHGVAR      &lst_cnt   %BIN(&tmp_bin)
```

Figure 36.5 Continued

Figure 36.5 **FNDSTELM CLP Subprogram for RTVSBSJOB Command** *Continued*

```
/* Adjust to the subroutine maximum                                    */

CHGVAR     &lst_len  (&lst_cnt * &ent_siz)

IF         (&lst_len > &max_lstlen)                                     +
            DO
            CHGVAR &lst_len  &max_lstlen
            CHGVAR &lst_cnt (&lst_len / &ent_siz)
            ENDDO


/* Return if entry size is not in range 1 to list_length.             */

IF        ((&ent_siz < 1       )  *or                                   +
           (&ent_siz > &lst_len))                                       +
            GOTO exit


/* Look for the item starting with the beginning entry in the list   */

CHGVAR     &tmp_entidx     &bgn_entidx
CHGVAR     &tmp_bytidx  (((&bgn_entidx - 1) * &ent_siz) + &fst_lstbyt)

LOOPBGN:

IF         (&tmp_entidx > &lst_cnt)  (GOTO loopend)

IF         (%SST(&ent      1          &ent_siz)  =                      +
            %SST(&lst_var &tmp_bytidx &ent_siz))                        +
            DO
            CHGVAR &ent_idx &tmp_entidx
            GOTO   loopend
            ENDDO

CHGVAR     &tmp_entidx  (&tmp_entidx + 1       )
CHGVAR     &tmp_bytidx  (&tmp_bytidx + &ent_siz)

GOTO       loopbgn

LOOPEND:

GOTO       exit    /* Normal return                                   */

/*--------   ERROR EXIT --------------------------------------------*/

ERROR:

SNDPGMMSG  MSGID(cpf9898) MSGF(qsys/qcpfmsg) MSGTYPE(*escape)          +
           MSGDTA('Subroutine FNDLSTELM failed.')
MONMSG    (cpf0000)

EXIT:
RETURN
ENDPGM
```

calling program. After the loop finishes, program RTVSBSJOBC sets the total and list job count return variables, if they are present in the calling program.

When command RTVSBSJOB completes, the CL program that invoked the command has the desired job information retrieved in its program variables in an easily available format for programs that control the operation of the system. (You can use the %SST function to retrieve information about specific jobs, as shown in Figure 36.2.) As commands RTVSBSJOB and CVTTYP illustrate, adding a return variable parameter to a command is straightforward, and by using the techniques shown in this article, you can extend the power of your CL programs substantially to retrieve whatever type of information you need.

Figure 36.6

CVTTYP Command Definition

```
/*   CVTTYP                                                                */

/*   This command returns a value in the variable for TYPE parameter;*/
/*   the  command must be created with ALLOW(*IPGM *BPGM).              */

CMD          PROMPT('Convert Type Code to Job Type')

PARM         typcod       *CHAR     1                                      +
                                              MIN(1)                       +
                                              PROMPT('Job Type Code:')
PARM         subcod       *CHAR     1                                      +
                                              MIN(1)                       +
                                              PROMPT('Job Subtype:')

PARM         type         *CHAR     3                                      +
                                              RTNVAL(*yes)                 +
                                              MIN(1)                       +
                                              PROMPT('Job Type (3) var:')
```

Figure 36.7

CVTTYPC Command Processing Program

```
/*   CVTTYPC                                                           */
/*--------------------------------------------------------------------*/
/*  Abstract: CPP for CVTTYP Command                                   */
/*            Converts CVTWRKACT type code to longer description      */
/*--------------------------------------------------------------------*/
/* Written by Michael Otey                                             */
/*--------------------------------------------------------------------*/

PGM                                                                    +
PARM(                                                                  +
         &i_typcod       /* IN     Job Type Code                        */+
         &i_subtyp       /* IN     Job Subtype                          */+
```

Figure 36.7 Continued

Figure 36.7

CVTTYPC Command Processing Program *Continued*

```
        &o_type            /*     OUT Job Type Variable                          */+
        )

  DCL  &i_typcod       *CHAR     1                 /* Type Code from CVTWRKACT*/
  DCL  &i_subtyp       *CHAR     1                 /* Subtype from CVTWRKACT  */
  DCL  &o_type         *CHAR     3                 /* Type Description        */

  /* Type Codes */
  DCL  &a              *CHAR     1 'A'                        /* Mnemonics*/
  DCL  &b              *CHAR     1 'B'
  DCL  &i              *CHAR     1 'I'
  DCL  &w              *CHAR     1 'W'
  DCL  &r              *CHAR     1 'R'
  DCL  &s              *CHAR     1 'S'
  DCL  &x              *CHAR     1 'X'
  DCL  &m              *CHAR     1 'M'

  /* Subtype Codes */
  DCL  &d              *CHAR     1 'D'
  DCL  &e              *CHAR     1 'E'
  DCL  &t              *CHAR     1 'T'
  DCL  &j              *CHAR     1 'J'
  DCL  &p              *CHAR     1 'P'
  DCL  &blank          *CHAR     1 ' '

  /* Type Descriptions */
  DCL  &asj            *CHAR     3 'ASJ'           /* Autostart               */
  DCL  &bch            *CHAR     3 'BCH'           /* Batch                   */
  DCL  &bci            *CHAR     3 'BCI'           /* Batch immediate         */
  DCL  &evk            *CHAR     3 'EVK'           /* Evoked                  */
  DCL  &int            *CHAR     3 'INT'           /* Interactive             */
  DCL  &mrt            *CHAR     3 'MRT'           /* Multiple requestor      */
  DCL  &pj             *CHAR     3 'PJ '           /* Prestart Job            */
  DCL  &pdj            *CHAR     3 'PDJ'           /* Print driver job        */
  DCL  &rdr            *CHAR     3 'RDR'           /* Reader                  */
  DCL  &sys            *CHAR     3 'SYS'           /* System                  */
  DCL  &sbs            *CHAR     3 'SBS'           /* Subsystem Monitor       */
  DCL  &wtr            *CHAR     3 'WTR'           /* Writer                  */
  /*-----------------------------------------------------------------------*/
  /* Handle CPF and MCH messages that are not specifically monitored      */

  MONMSG (cpf9999) EXEC(GOTO error)

  /*--------   BEGIN PROCEDURE   -------------------------------------*/


  IF       (&i_typcod = &a)                                              +
           DO
                   CHGVAR &o_type &asj
                   RETURN
           ENDDO


  IF       (&i_typcod = &b)                                              +
           DO
```

Figure 36.7 Continued

Figure 36.7

CVTTYPC Command Processing Program *Continued*

```
                IF      (&i_subtyp = &blank)                                  +
                        DO
                                CHGVAR &o_type &bch
                                RETURN
                        ENDDO

                IF      (&i_subtyp = &d)                                      +
                        DO
                                CHGVAR &o_type &bci
                                RETURN
                        ENDDO

                IF      (&i_subtyp = &e)                                      +
                        DO
                                CHGVAR &o_type &evk
                                RETURN
                        ENDDO

                IF      (&i_subtyp = &t)                                      +
                        DO
                                CHGVAR &o_type &mrt
                                RETURN
                        ENDDO

                IF      (&i_subtyp = &j)                                      +
                        DO
                                CHGVAR &o_type &pj
                                RETURN
                        ENDDO
        ENDDO

IF      (&i_typcod = &i)                                                      +
        DO
                CHGVAR &o_type &int
                RETURN
        ENDDO


IF      (&i_typcod = &w)                                                      +
        DO
                IF      (&i_subtyp = &blank)                                  +
                        DO
                                CHGVAR &o_type &wtr
                                RETURN
                        ENDDO

                IF      (&i_subtyp = &p)                                      +
                        DO
                                CHGVAR &o_type &pdj
                                RETURN
                        ENDDO
        ENDDO
```

Figure 36.7 Continued

Figure 36.7

CVTTYPC Command Processing Program *Continued*

```
IF       (&i_typcod = &r)                                          +
         DO
                 CHGVAR &o_type &rdr
                 RETURN
         ENDDO


IF       ((&i_typcod = &s) *OR (&i_typcod = &x))                   +
         DO
                 CHGVAR &o_type &sys
                 RETURN
         ENDDO


IF       (&i_typcod = &m)                                          +
         DO
                 CHGVAR &o_type &sbs
                 RETURN
         ENDDO



IF       (&i_typcod = &w)                                          +
         DO
                 CHGVAR &o_type &wtr
                 RETURN
         ENDDO

/* No match */
CHGVAR &o_type &blank
RETURN

/*--------   ERROR EXIT -------------------------------------------*/
ERROR:

SNDPGMMSG  MSGID(cpf9898) MSGF(qsys/qcpfmsg) MSGTYPE(*escape)       +
                 MSGDTA('Command CVTTYP failed.')
MONMSG     (cpf0000)

EXIT:
RETURN
ENDPGM
```

Chapter 37

Validity Checking Programs

by Paul Conte

VCPs provide better protection and fewer required tasks in the command processing program

Among the AS/400 commands' greatest advantages are the consistent interface and parameter checking provided by the command analyzer. One way the command interface aids programmers and users is by providing feedback about parameter syntax errors before the command processing program (CPP) is invoked. This early feedback is especially helpful when command prompting is used. Command parameter checking also eases the development of programs because most syntax rules for a parameter can be specified with a simple set of rules in the command definition, rather than with procedural code in the CPP.

But sometimes the CL command definition facilities do not provide a way to specify a necessary rule for a parameter; for example, you cannot specify that a list parameter must not contain duplicate values. One alternative for enforcing such a rule is to code a test in the CPP and send an escape message if the rule is violated. Sending an escape message from the CPP, however, not only bypasses the consistent interface provided by the command analyzer's rule checking, but it also provides error feedback to the user after the command has begun processing rather than at the time the command analyzer checks the command's syntax.

Both of these disadvantages can be overcome by using a validity-checking program (VCP) to implement command parameter rules that cannot be specified using built-in CL command-definition facilities. A VCP is a program called by the command analyzer before the CPP is called. The VCP notifies the command analyzer of parameter rule violations. The command analyzer handles VCP-detected errors in a manner consistent with other syntax errors (e.g., by displaying an error message on the command prompt display).

To check the validity of a command's input parameters with a VCP, you must create a program to act as the VCP and you must identify this program when you create (or change) the command.

Creating the VCP

Creating a VCP is straightforward, but you must follow a few rules so that the VCP will function properly. These rules include properly defining the VCP parameters and properly sending program messages to notify the command analyzer of any error condition.

The RTVSBSJOB (Retrieve Subsystem Jobs) command, shown in Figure 37.1, includes a list parameter (SBS) that should be checking to ensure that the list contains no duplicate subsystem values. The necessary checking is included in CL program RTVSBSJOBV (Figure 37.2), the VCP for command RTVSBSJOB. Program RTVSBSJOBV is invoked after the command analyzer determines that the input parameters to command RTVSBSJOB meet the criteria specified in the command definition. The VCP's parameters (Figure 37.2) must correspond to the command's parameters and should be identical to the CPP's parameters. By defining the parameters in this way, the VCP can map the command's parameters properly.

To test for duplicate names in parameter SBS, VCP RTVSBSJOBV determines the number of elements listed in SBS. RTVSBSJOBV then loops across the list (C) and calls program FNDLSTELM (See Chapter 36, "Return Variables," for a more detailed description of these programs), to determine whether a subsystem name appears more than once in the list. As is true for any VCP, if program RTVSBSJOBV finds an erroneous condition (i.e., a duplicate subsystem name), the program must communicate this error to the command analyzer by sending program messages.

VCPs must send two types of messages to communicate an error condition: one or more diagnostic messages and a final escape message. RTVSBSJOBV sends a diagnostic message for each repeated subsystem name. You can base the diagnostic message on a user-defined message description, such as USR9191 in this example (Figure 37.3 shows the ADDMSGD (Add Message Description) command to define this message); or you can base the message on an ad hoc message description by using the IBM-supplied CPD0006 message description.

Figure 37.1

RTVSBSJOB Command Definition

```
/* RTVSBSJOB                                                          */
/*                                                                    */
/*  Use the following command to create the RTVSBSJOB command in     */
/*  library PRDEXC:                                                   */
/*                                                                    */
/*  CRTCMD      CMD(prdexc/rtvsbsjob)  PGM(rtvsbsjobc)             + */
/*              SRCFILE(cmdsrc)        VLDCKR(rtvsbsjobv)          + */
/*              ALLOW(*ipgm *bpgm)                                 + */
```

Figure 37.1 Continued

Figure 37.1

RTVSBSJOB Command Definition *Continued*

```
CMD         PROMPT('Retrieve Subsystem Jobs')

PARM        sbs         *name  10                                  +
                        MAX(50)                                    +
                        SNGVAL((*ALL))                             +
                        DFT(*ALL)                                  +
                        EXPR(*yes)                                 +
                        PROMPT('Subsystem name(s):')

PARM        user        *name  10                                  +
                        SPCVAL((*ALL))                             +
                        DFT(*ALL)                                  +
                        EXPR(*yes)                                 +
                        PROMPT('User whose jobs to display:')

PARM        totjobcnt *dec   ( 5 0)                                +
                        RTNVAL(*yes)                               +
                        PROMPT('CL var for total job count:')

PARM        lstjobcnt *dec   ( 5 0)                                +
                        RTNVAL(*yes)                               +
                        PROMPT('CL var for list job count:')

PARM        sbsl        *char   1                                  +
                        RTNVAL(*yes)                               +
                        VARY(*yes)                                 +
                        PROMPT('CL var for subsystem list:')

PARM        jobnaml     *char   1                                  +
                        RTNVAL(*yes)                               +
                        VARY(*yes)                                 +
                        PROMPT('CL var for job name list:')

PARM        jobusrl     *char   1                                  +
                        RTNVAL(*yes)                               +
                        VARY(*yes)                                 +
                        PROMPT('CL var for job user list:')

PARM        jobnbrl     *char   1                                  +
                        RTNVAL(*yes)                               +
                        VARY(*yes)                                 +
                        PROMPT('CL var for job number list:')

PARM        jobtypl     *char   1                                  +
                        RTNVAL(*yes)                               +
                        VARY(*yes)                                 +
                        PROMPT('CL var for job type list:')

PARM        jobstsl     *char   1                                  +
                        RTNVAL(*yes)                               +
                        VARY(*yes)                                 +
                        PROMPT('CL var for job status list:')
```

Figure 37.2 **RTVSBSJOBV Validity Checking Program for RTVSBSJOB**

```
/*   RTVSBSJOBV                                                       */
/*--------------------------------------------------------------------*/
/*  Abstract: Validity Checking  Program (VCP) for RTVSBSJOB:         */
/*            Retrieve subsystem job information.                     */
/*            Checks for duplicates in SBS  parameter                 */
/*--------------------------------------------------------------------*/

PGM                                                                     +
PARM(                                                                   +
     &sbs_prm      /* IN     Subsystem (name(s), *ALL, *JOBQ, *OUTQ)*/+
     &usr_prm      /* IN     User name (name or  *ALL)              */+
     &tot_jobcnt   /*    OUT Total jobs associated with subsystem(s)*/+
     &lst_jobcnt   /*    OUT Number of jobs put in following lists  */+
     &jobsbs_lst   /*    OUT String for job subsystem list          */+
     &jobnam_lst   /*    OUT String for job name      list          */+
     &jobusr_lst   /*    OUT String for job user      list          */+
     &jobnbr_lst   /*    OUT String for job number    list          */+
     &jobtyp_lst   /*    OUT String for job type      list          */+
     &jobsts_lst   /*    OUT String for job status    list          */+
    )

DCL  &cur_sbs    *CHAR   10                   /* Current sbs. name   */
DCL  &cur_sbsidx *DEC     5                   /* Current sbs. entry  */
DCL  &dup_sbs    *LGL     1                   /* Duplicate sbs. exist*/
DCL  &dup_sbsidx *DEC     5                   /* Duplicate entry idx */
DCL  &errcnt     *DEC     7 VALUE( 0 )        /* Error count         */
DCL  &esc_rcved  *LGL     1 VALUE('1')        /* Escape msg. received*/
DCL  &false      *LGL     1 VALUE('0')        /* Mnemonic            */
DCL  &fst_lstbyt *DEC     5 VALUE( 3 )        /* The first byte in a */
                                              /* list variable. It is*/
                                              /* after the two-byte  */
                                              /* length field.       */
DCL  &jobnam_lst *CHAR 9999                   /* Job name      list  */
DCL  &jobnbr_lst *CHAR 9999                   /* Job number    list  */
DCL  &jobsbs_lst *CHAR 9999                   /* Job subsystem list  */
DCL  &jobsts_lst *CHAR 9999                   /* Job status    list  */
DCL  &jobtyp_lst *CHAR 9999                   /* Job type      list  */
DCL  &jobusr_lst *CHAR 9999                   /* Job user      list  */
DCL  &lst_jobcnt *DEC     5                   /* List  job count     */
DCL  &msgdta     *CHAR  512                   /* Message data        */
DCL  &msgdtalen  *DEC     5                   /* Message data length */
DCL  &msgid      *CHAR    7                   /* Message data        */
DCL  &msgpad     *CHAR    4 VALUE('0000')     /* Padding for diag.   */
                                              /* msgs. to command    */
                                              /* analyzer            */
DCL  &tmp_bin    *CHAR    2                   /* Temp Binary field   */
DCL  &nxt_sbsidx *DEC     5                   /* Next sbs. entry idx */
DCL  &sbs_cnt    *DEC     5                   /* Subsystem count     */
DCL  &sbs_entsiz *DEC     5 VALUE(10)         /* Subsystem entry size*/
DCL  &sbs_prm    *CHAR  502                   /* Subsystem parameter */
                                              /* list of up to 50    */
                                              /* names or special    */
```

Figure 37.2 Continued

Figure 37.2 RTVSBSJOBV Validity Checking Program for RTVSBSJOB *Continued*

```
                                                 /* values, or *ALL      */
DCL  &tmp_bgnidx *DEC     5                      /* Temporary string     */
                                                 /* begin index          */
DCL  &tot_jobcnt *DEC     5                      /* Total job count      */
DCL  &true       *LGL     1 VALUE('1')           /* Mnemonic             */
DCL  &usr_prm    *CHAR   10                      /* Job user parameter   */

/*-------------------------------------------------------------------*/

/* Handle CPF and MCH messages that are not specifically monitored   */

MONMSG (cpf0000 mch0000) EXEC(GOTO proc_end)

/*---------------   BEGIN PROCEDURE   ------------------------------*/

/* Initialize that no duplicate user has been found yet.  Set to     */
/* true if duplicate is found.                                        */

CHGVAR    &dup_sbs  &false

/* Convert the count of list elements.  Then loop, looking for       */
/* duplicates.                                                        */
CHGVAR    &tmp_bin (%SST(&sbs_prm 1 2))
CHGVAR    &sbs_cnt (%BINARY(&tmp_bin))
CHGVAR    &cur_sbsidx  1

LOOP_BGN:

IF       (&cur_sbsidx >= &sbs_cnt)     (GOTO loop_end)

CHGVAR    &nxt_sbsidx   (&cur_sbsidx + 1)

CHGVAR    &tmp_bgnidx (((&cur_sbsidx - 1) * &sbs_entsiz) + &fst_lstbyt)

CHGVAR    &cur_sbs   %SST(&sbs_prm &tmp_bgnidx &sbs_entsiz)

CALL      FNDLSTELM (&sbs_prm    &sbs_entsiz   &cur_sbs            +
                     &nxt_sbsidx &dup_sbsidx)

IF        (&dup_sbsidx  > 0)                                       +
          DO
          SNDPGMMSG MSGID(usr9191) MSGF(usrmsgf)  +
                    MSGDTA(&msgpad || &cur_sbs) MSGTYPE(*diag)
          CHGVAR    &dup_sbs  &true
          ENDDO


CHGVAR    &cur_sbsidx  (&cur_sbsidx + 1)

GOTO      loop_bgn

LOOP_END:
```

Figure 37.2 Continued

Figure 37.2 **RTVSBSJOBV Validity Checking Program for RTVSBSJOB** *Continued*

```
/* If a duplicate was found, send the CPF0002 escape message to      */
/* the command analyzer. This exits validity checking program.       */

IF        (&dup_sbs)                                                  +
            DO
            SNDPGMMSG  MSGID(cpf0002) MSGF(qcpfmsg) MSGTYPE(*escape)
            ENDDO

/* Successful completion; indicate that no escape message received. */

CHGVAR    &esc_rcved &false


/*---------------   END   PROCEDURE   ------------------------------*/


PROC_END:      /* Procedure end.  Resend any escape message.          */

/* The following use of &errcnt protects against a loop caused by    */
/* global message monitoring.                                         */

IF          (&errcnt > 0) (GOTO exit)
CHGVAR       &errcnt      (&errcnt + 1)


/* If escape message received, resend it as diagnostic, then send    */
/* CPF0002 to command analyzer.                                       */

IF    (&esc_rcved)                                                    +
      DO
      RCVMSG     MSGTYPE(*excp)          MSGDTA(&msgdta)              +
                 MSGDTALEN(&msgdtalen) MSGID(&msgid)
      MONMSG    (cpf0000)                EXEC(GOTO exit)

      SNDPGMMSG MSGID(&msgid)            MSGF(qcpfmsg)                +
                 MSGDTA(%SST(&msgdta 1 &msgdtalen))                   +
                 MSGTYPE(*diag)
      MONMSG    (cpf0000)                EXEC(GOTO exit)

      SNDPGMMSG MSGID(cpf0002)           MSGF(qcpfmsg)                +
                 MSGTYPE(*escape)
      MONMSG    (cpf0000)                EXEC(GOTO exit)
      ENDDO

/*---------------   EXIT   PROGRAM   -------------------------------*/

EXIT:
RETURN
ENDPGM
```

Figure 37.3 ADDMSGD Command for VCP RTVSBSJOBV Diagnostic Message

```
ADDMSGD MSGID(usr9191) MSGF(prdmsc/usrmsgf)                              +
        MSG('User name &2 is duplicated in list.')                       +
        SECLVL('Each user name can only be specified once in the list +
        of job''s users. &2 is specified more than once. Remove or cor+
        rect duplicate names.')
        SEV(40)         FMT((*CHAR 4) (*CHAR 10))
```

Regardless of the message description used, the message data must begin with four "pad" characters; and if no other message data is used, the fourth position must not be blank. The simplest approach is to create the message data as the concatenation of two strings. The first string is a four-character pad (in Figure 37.2, &msgpad contains "0000"). (The pad characters are necessary because the first four character positions of the message data are reserved for the command analyzer.) The second character variable string contains the data that should be substituted in the diagnostic message text (in Figure 37.2, &cur_sbs is the duplicated subsystem name). The resulting message data is referenced as two substitution variables, &l and &2, defined in the FMT parameter of the ADDMSGD command (Figure 37.3). The FMT parameter in Figure 37.3 demonstrates how substitution variable &t is defined for the pad characters and how substitution variable &2 is defined for a 10-character subsystem name. Because substitution variable &l refers to the four bytes reserved for the command analyzer, only &2 is used in the MSG and SECLVL parameters.

If the VCP sends any diagnostic messages, it must also send a final escape message. This escape message must use message description CPF0002, the signal the command analyzer expects when the VCP detects an error. If the command analyzer receives escape message CPF0002, the CPP is not invoked until the user corrects the error.

After you create a validity-checking program, you need to identify it as such. To identify the VCP, you specify the VCP with the VLDCKR (Validity Checker) keyword of either the CRTCMD (Create Command) or the CHGCMD (Change Command) command (see the beginning comment section in Figure 37.1 for the CRTCMD command that identifies RTVSBSJOBV as the VCP for command RTVSBSJOB).

VCP Invocation

The command analyzer provides users with feedback about VCP-detected errors, but the timing of the feedback depends on whether or not CL variables are used in the command. When CL variables are used as command parameters (e.g., in the case of RTVSBSJOB, which requires CL variables as return variables), the VCP is not invoked until the command is executed. Validity checking cannot be performed until the CL variables have values assigned to them.

For commands that do not use CL variables as parameters, the VCP provides immediate feedback during prompting. For example, consider command SAVALLCHG (Save All Changed Objects), a locally written command designed to simplify the creation of daily incremental backups. (The command definition is shown in Figure 37.4.) The CPP (which is not shown) executes the DSPOBJD (Display Object Description) command to produce an outfile that contains library names. The CPP then loops over the outfile, executing a SAVCHGOBJ (Save Changed Object) command for every user library. The command includes a VOL parameter for the operator to specify a list of tape volumes for the backup. Obviously, the tape volume list should not include duplicates, and the VCP SAVALLCHGV (Figure 37.5) checks this condition.

Figure 37.4

SAVALLCHG Command Definition

```
/*  SAVALLCHG                                                           */
/*                                                                      */
/*  Use the following command to create the SAVALLCHG command in        */
/*  library PRDEXC:                                                     */
/*                                                                      */
/*  CRTCMD      CMD(prdexc/savallchg)  PGM(savallchgc)          +       */
/*              SRCFILE(cmdsrc)        VLDCKR(savallchgv)               */

CMD         PROMPT('Save All Changed Objects')

PARM        vol         *char  6                                        +
                        MIN(1)                                          +
                        MAX(10)                                         +
                        FULL(*yes)                                      +
                        PROMPT('Tape volume ID''s:')

PARM        refdate     *DATE                                           +
                        DFT(*SAVLIB)                                    +
                                                                        +
                        /* Note that the date special value is MMDDYY */+
                        /* in the command, but will be CYYMMDD in the */+
                        /* Command Processing Program.                */+
                                                                        +
                        SPCVAL((*NORMAL 010101) (*SAVLIB  010201))      +
                        MIN(0)                                          +
                        PROMPT('Save if changed after date:')

PARM        expdate     *DATE                                           +
                        DFT(*NORMAL)                                    +
                                                                        +
                        /* Note that the date special value is MMDDYY */+
                        /* in the command, but will be CYYMMDD in the */+
                        /* Command Processing Program.                */+
                                                                        +
                        SPCVAL((*NORMAL 010101) (*PERM    010201))      +
                        MIN(0)                                          +
                        PROMPT('File expiration date:')
```

Figure 37.5 **SAVALLCHGV Validity Checking Program for SAVALLCHG**

```
/*   SAVALLCHGV                                                      */
/*===================================================================*/

/*  Abstract: Validity Checking  Program (VCP) for SAVALLCHG:        */
/*            Save all changed objects.                              */

/*            Checks for duplicates in VOL parameter                 */

/*-------------------------------------------------------------------*/

PGM                                                                   +
PARM(                                                                 +
     &vol_lst       /* IN     Volume list up to 10 volume ID's       */+
     &refdat        /* IN     Save if changed on or after this date  */+
     &expdat        /* IN     Expiration date for files.             */+
    )


DCL  &cur_vol     *CHAR   10                     /* Current volume ID    */
DCL  &cur_volidx  *DEC     5                     /* Current volume entry*/
DCL  &dup_vol     *LGL     1                     /* Duplicate vol. exist*/
DCL  &dup_volidx  *DEC     5                     /* Duplicate vol. idx   */
DCL  &errcnt      *DEC     7 VALUE(0)            /* Error count          */
DCL  &esc_rcved   *LGL     1 VALUE('1')          /* Escape msg. received*/
DCL  &expdat      *CHAR    7                     /* EXPDATE parameter    */
DCL  &false       *LGL     1 VALUE('0')          /* Mnemonic             */
DCL  &fst_lstbyt  *DEC     5 VALUE( 3 )          /* The first byte in a */
                                                 /* list variable. It is*/
                                                 /* after the two-byte   */
                                                 /* length field.        */
DCL  &msgdta      *CHAR  512                     /* Message data         */
DCL  &msgdtalen   *DEC     5                     /* Message data length */
DCL  &msgid       *CHAR    7                     /* Message data         */
DCL  &msgpad      *CHAR    4 VALUE('0000')       /* Padding for diag.    */
                                                 /* msgs. to command     */
                                                 /* analyzer             */
DCL  &nxt_volidx  *DEC     5                     /* Next vol. entry idx */
DCL  &refdat      *CHAR    7                     /* REFDATE parameter    */
DCL  &tmp_bgnidx  *DEC     5                     /* Temporary string     */
                                                 /* begin index          */
DCL  &true        *LGL     1 VALUE('1')          /* Mnemonic             */
DCL  &tmp_bin     *CHAR    2                     /* Temp binary          */
DCL  &vol_cnt     *DEC     5                     /* Volume count         */
DCL  &vol_entsiz  *DEC     5 VALUE( 6)           /* Volume entry size    */
DCL  &vol_lst     *CHAR   62                     /* Volume parameter - a*/
                                                 /* list of up to 10     */
                                                 /* tape volume ID's     */

/*-------------------------------------------------------------------*/

/* Handle CPF and MCH messages that are not specifically monitored   */

MONMSG (cpf0000 mch0000) EXEC(GOTO proc_end)
```

Figure 37.5 Continued

Figure 37.5 **SAVALLCHGV Validity Checking Program for SAVALLCHG** *Continued*

```
/*---------------   BEGIN PROCEDURE   ------------------------------*/

/* Initialize that no duplicate volume has been found yet.  Set to  */
/* true if duplicate is found.                                       */

CHGVAR     &dup_vol  &false


/* Convert the count of list elements.  Then loop, looking for      */
/* duplicates.                                                       */

CHGVAR     &tmp_bin   %SST(%vol_1st 1 2)

CHGVAR     &vol_cnt   &tmp_bin

CHGVAR     &cur_volidx  1


LOOP_BGN:

IF        (&cur_volidx >= &vol_cnt)     (GOTO loop_end)

CHGVAR     &nxt_volidx   (&cur_volidx + 1)

CHGVAR     &tmp_bgnidx (((&cur_volidx - 1) * &vol_entsiz) + &fst_lstbyt)

CHGVAR     &cur_vol   %SST(&vol_lst &tmp_bgnidx &vol_entsiz)

CALL       FNDLSTELM (&vol_lst    &vol_entsiz   &cur_vol             +
                      &nxt_volidx &dup_volidx)

IF         (&dup_volidx  > Ø)                                         +
           DO
           SNDPGMMSG MSGID(usr9361)              MSGF(prdmsc/usrmsgf)  +
                     MSGDTA(&msgpad || &cur_vol) MSGTYPE(*diag)
           CHGVAR    &dup_vol  &true
           ENDDO

CHGVAR     &cur_volidx  (&cur_volidx + 1)

GOTO       loop_bgn

LOOP_END:


/* If a duplicate was found, send the CPFØØØ2 escape message to     */
/* the command analyzer. This exits validity checking program.      */

IF        (&dup_vol)                                                  +
           DO
           SNDPGMMSG  MSGID(cpfØØØ2) MSGF(qcpfmsg) MSGTYPE(*escape)
```

Figure 37.5 Continued

Figure 37.5 **SAVALLCHGV Validity Checking Program for SAVALLCHG** *Continued*

```
          ENDDO

/* Successful completion; indicate that no escape message received. */

CHGVAR    &esc_rcved &false

/*---------------   END   PROCEDURE   ----------------------------*/


PROC_END:     /* Procedure end.  Resend any escape message.          */

/* The following use of &errcnt protects against a loop caused by    */
/* global message monitoring.                                        */

IF         (&errcnt > 0) (GOTO exit)
CHGVAR      &errcnt      (&errcnt + 1)


/* If escape message received, resend it as diagnostic, then send    */
/* CPF0002 to command analyzer.                                      */

IF   (&esc_rcved)                                                     +
       DO
       RCVMSG     MSGTYPE(*excp)         MSGDTA(&msgdta)              +
                  MSGDTALEN(&msgdtalen) MSGID(&msgid)
       MONMSG    (cpf0000)               EXEC(GOTO exit)

       SNDPGMMSG MSGID(&msgid)           MSGF(qcpfmsg)                +
                  MSGDTA(%SST(&msgdta 1 &msgdtalen))                  +
                  MSGTYPE(*diag)
       MONMSG    (cpf0000)               EXEC(GOTO exit)

       SNDPGMMSG MSGID(cpf0002)          MSGF(qcpfmsg)                +
                  MSGTYPE(*escape)
       MONMSG    (cpf0000)               EXEC(GOTO exit)
       ENDDO

/*---------------   EXIT   PROGRAM     ----------------------------*/

EXIT:
RETURN
ENDPGM
```

SAVALLCHGV executes similarly to the VCP RTVSBSJOBV and uses another user-defined message description (Figure 37.6) to send diagnostic messages to the command analyzer. But unlike RTVSBSJOBV, SAVALLCHGV is invoked when command SAVALLCHG is prompted as long as no CL variables are entered as command parameters. Because the command analyzer invokes SAVALLCHGV during prompting, duplicate volume ID names are discovered before the backup begins. Figure 37.7 shows the command prompt display and the VCP diagnostic

Figure 37.6 **ADDMSGD Command for VCP SAVALLCHGV Diagnostic Message**

```
ADDMSGD MSGID(usr9361) MSGF(prdmsc/usrmsgf)                              +
        MSG('Tape volume ID &2 is duplicated in list.')                  +
        SECLVL('Each tape volume ID can only be specified once in the +
        list of tapes. &2 is specified more than once. Remove or corre+
        ct duplicate tape volume IDs.')
        SEV(40)          FMT((*CHAR 4) (*CHAR 10))
```

Figure 37.7 **Prompt for Command SAVALLCHG with Diagnostic Messages**

```
        Save All Changed Objects (SAVALLCHG) Prompt

Enter the following:
  Tape volume ID's:                  VOL        R    TAP001
                                                     TAP002
                                                     TAP002
                                                     TAP004
                                                     TAP005
                                     + for more      TAP004
  Save if changed after date:        REFDATE    P    *SAVLIB
  File expiration date:              EXPDATE    P    *NORMAL


 Tape volume ID TAP002 is duplicated in list.                            +
 Tape volume ID TAP004 is duplicated in list.
```

messages sent when duplicate tape volumes are entered for the SAVALLCHG command. If the operator enters duplicate tape volumes, he or she must correct the tape volume list before the command analyzer will invoke the CPP.

Among the many possible uses for VCPs are such functions as checking for the existence of objects and proper authority to access them, checking that a required batch function has completed before allowing interactive file access, checking the time of day to restrict resource-consumptive commands, or checking complex relationships between parameters. VCPs are easy to write and can be shared or "cloned" for similar commands. A VCP's benefits include earlier, more user-friendly feedback for the person entering the command, better protection for the CPP, and fewer tasks to be accomplished in the CPP. Because the VCP is written in CL or an HLL, you can expand the command's parameter-checking facilities to cover practically any situation you're likely to run into.

Chapter 38

Designer Commands

by Nicholas Knowles

Commands are excellent interfaces for both programmers and "power users"

I recently came across some interesting new computer jargon: "drim," "flatch," and "globby." Before I tell you what they mean, I'd like you to answer the following questions. First, what are the plurals of a drim, a flatch, and a globby? Second, what are the past tenses of the verbs to drim, to flatch, and to globby?

For the plurals you probably guessed "drims," "flatches," and "globbies," respectively. For the verbs you probably hazarded "drimmed," "flatched," and "globbied" (unless your knowledge of Old English drove you toward the less regular "dram" or "flutch"). In doing so, you used a number of different rules. For instance, "to form a plural, add an 's,' unless the word ends in 'y,' in which case replace the 'y' with an 'i' and add 'es;' or, if the word ends with 'ch,' add an 'es' instead of an 's.'" Furthermore, you probably used those rules quite unconsciously and would have to think twice to explain why you did what you did. You have generalized these rules in the course of learning English and can now apply them without thinking to generate new usages.

Now, if I tell you that a drim is a new object type IBM is going to introduce in Release 9.9 of OS/400, can you tell me what will be the CL command to delete the object? The answer, of course, is DLTDRM. How would I move a drim from one library to another? Quick as a single-user E70, you reply, "MOVOBJ OBJTYPE(*DRIM)." And if I also tell you that a globby is a type of drim, just as an RPG program is a type of program, what then is the command to create a globby? CRTGLBDRM would be a good guess, though you might not be quite so sure about the mnemonic (GLO, GLB, GLY?). Next, what is the source type for a globby and in what source file does it reside? The answers — as I saw when I snooped at Release 9.9 in Rochester — are GLB and QGLBSRC, respectively. I also learned in Rochester that "to flatch" is a new process that you will be able to perform on any object type (including drims), the result of which will depend on the property of each object type. What then will be the commands to flatch programs and drims? In picoseconds, you reply, "FLCPGM and FLCDRM," respectively.

My point here, of course, is that CL also has a set of rules, most of which you pick up intuitively in the course of learning CL, using the same language acquisition mechanisms you use to learn natural languages. In fact, CL is particularly good in this respect: As command languages go, CL is remarkable for its lack of ambiguity and for its consistency, simplicity, and even elegance, all of which make it easy to learn. Furthermore, CL comes with a good, simple notation — the command syntax diagram — and can be used to extend itself. CL includes a set of command definition statements (e.g., CMD, PARM, ELEM, QUAL, DEP, PMTCTL) that you can use to define your *own* commands.

There are good reasons for using your own CL commands to invoke your applications. Commands are robust and allow a "layered" (i.e., slow and fast path) interface, and the prompts can be translated easily into other natural languages. But the consistency — and the "transfer of learning" that consistency can give your users — is justification alone. Consistency gives your users the ability to generalize successfully from what they know to cover new cases as they arise. You can use commands — and get the benefits — not only to invoke utilities that work on OS/400 system object types, but also to front-end your own applications. For instance, if your system has customers, products, and orders, you might have commands to create, delete, change, or work with customers, products, and orders.

However, to obtain the benefits of transfer of learning, you must ensure that your commands are consistent with CL conventions, both implicit and explicit. You must be consistent with both the syntax and the semantics of CL. Keeping the syntax — the allowed words, word order, and relationships between words — consistent is fairly straightforward: It did not take long for most of us to realize that programs are always PGMs, job descriptions are always JOBDs, and create is always CRT. (So automatic does this become, in fact, that we may even adopt OS/400 words in normal speech, so that conversation becomes peppered with "pugums" (PGM), "job-dees" (JOBD), and "crits" (CRT), as in "my CRTPGM just failed because the JOBD had the wrong INLIBL.")

Maintaining the semantics — the meaning of the commands in relation to the underlying model world on which they operate — is a more subtle process, but nonetheless of paramount importance. If you look at IBM's SAA Common User Access (CUA) standards, you will see that they emphasize the user's conceptual model of the application. (For details about the CUA standards, see the *Systems Application Architecture, Common User Access Basic Interface Design Guide*, IBM publication SC26-4583, and the *Systems Application Architecture, Common User Access Advanced Interface Design Guide*, publication SC26-4582.) Fundamental to this conceptual model is a decomposition of the user interface into *objects* and *actions* of standard types that are combined in simple and consistent ways.

This chapter discusses some design principles you should use to create commands consistent with CL and with the OS/400 conceptual model (Figure-38.1 summarizes the factors that make for consistency). The chapter also attempts to set down many of the basic syntactic rules for using and combining

Figure 38.1

Factors Leading to Consistency in CL Commands

Semantic Consistency
- Choice of design objects
- Choice of verbs/actions
- Choice of parameters

Syntactic Consistency
- Choice of mnemonics
- Command names
- Command parameter keywords
- Order of command parameters
- Command parameter values
- Required parameters for commands
- Text on command prompts

the command names, parameters, and special values of the CL command language. I begin with the semantic considerations, proceed to the syntactic, and finish off with a few tips on actually coding commands.

The Semantics of Command Design

To understand the semantics — the meanings of commands — we must consider the context within which they operate. Underpinning the consistent user interface that OS/400 presents to the user is an implicit conceptual model that provides a basis for understanding what is going on. The conceptual model states, for example, that an object always resides within a library but may be moved from one library to another. The conceptual model is central to the effective use of the machine, and any new CL commands you add should be consistent with the conceptual model.

To follow the conceptual model when writing your own commands involves more than just following CL's surface features, such as which verbs you use and the order in which you place parameters. In a sense, all these syntactical points are merely cosmetic. What really matters is achieving the relationship between the command and the conceptual model — in particular, being clear as to which type of action is being performed on which type of object.

As an analogy, here are some English imperative phrases that, although syntactically correct, do not make *literal* sense because they violate the regular conceptual model of the real world:

Move the time to the order
Delete Henry immediately
Eat software crookedly

Or, to quote Noam Chomsky's famous example of a well formed (i.e., syntactically correct) but semantically meaningless sentence:

Colorless green ideas sleep furiously.

You may, of course, find a metaphoric or metonymic meaning for these statements, but that takes you into the realms of poetry or humor rather than programming. Remember the famous "missing" CL command DLTUSR (Delete User), with its popular parameter, OPTION(*IMMED)? An equivalently maladroit CL command would be STROBJ (Start Object). "But how can an object be a process?" you immediately ask. MOVLIB (Move Library) would be equally silly in the context of a single machine (but not if we extended our conceptual model to cover multiple networked S/38s or AS/400s).

Objects Are Simple

Our starting point, then, in designing a command should be to ask, "What is the underlying operand or design object?" The answer might be an existing OS/400 system software entity (e.g., a source member, job, user profile), or it might be a new entity that makes up part of an extended conceptual model (e.g., a list, a customer, or a product). If you use an existing software entity, you should rigorously follow CL conventions for the entity type, such as the parameter keyword and any use of qualifiers — e.g., JOB(name/user/number). When you add your own entity, you should decide which existing entity the new object is most similar to and then design to be consistent with the chosen type. In either case, you should aim to have a limited number of object types that are intuitively familiar to the user. As Ludwig Wittgenstein said in his *Tractatus*: "Objects are simple."

In designing a command, it is above all important to be clear about the entity with which you are dealing. Is it an OS/400 object (e.g., a file)? A definition of an object (e.g., a file description)? A repeating entry within the definition (e.g., the member names of a file)? The contents of the object (e.g., data)? Is it a process that you are are starting, stopping, suspending, releasing, or otherwise altering?

Having chosen your object, you should then decide the action. You should try to equate the action your command invokes to one of the standard operations performed by the system commands. Does the action create or delete the object? Does it invoke an interactive program to edit the object's details? Does it initiate a batch process?

Figure 38.2 shows my attempt to draw a picture of part of the conceptual model for OS/400. Things (objects) reside within a context (a library), and each thing may have a definition part as well as a content part — a distinction it is vital to keep clear. Contexts (e.g., QSYS library) are themselves things residing within the world (i.e., the system). Processes (i.e., jobs) may also exist within the system and may be associated with things.

Notice that particular CL verbs and verb pairs may only be used in certain senses. Some verbs, like CHG, WRK, and DSP, can be used on things or lists of things at any level, and not only on permanent objects, but also on other entities, such as processes (e.g., work with jobs). Others, like CRT/DLT or ADD/RMV, may only be used on a particular type of software entity. So, for example, you may create or delete an object (e.g., a program, a file, a subsystem description), but you cannot create or delete a member or a subsystem entry — you must add or remove them.

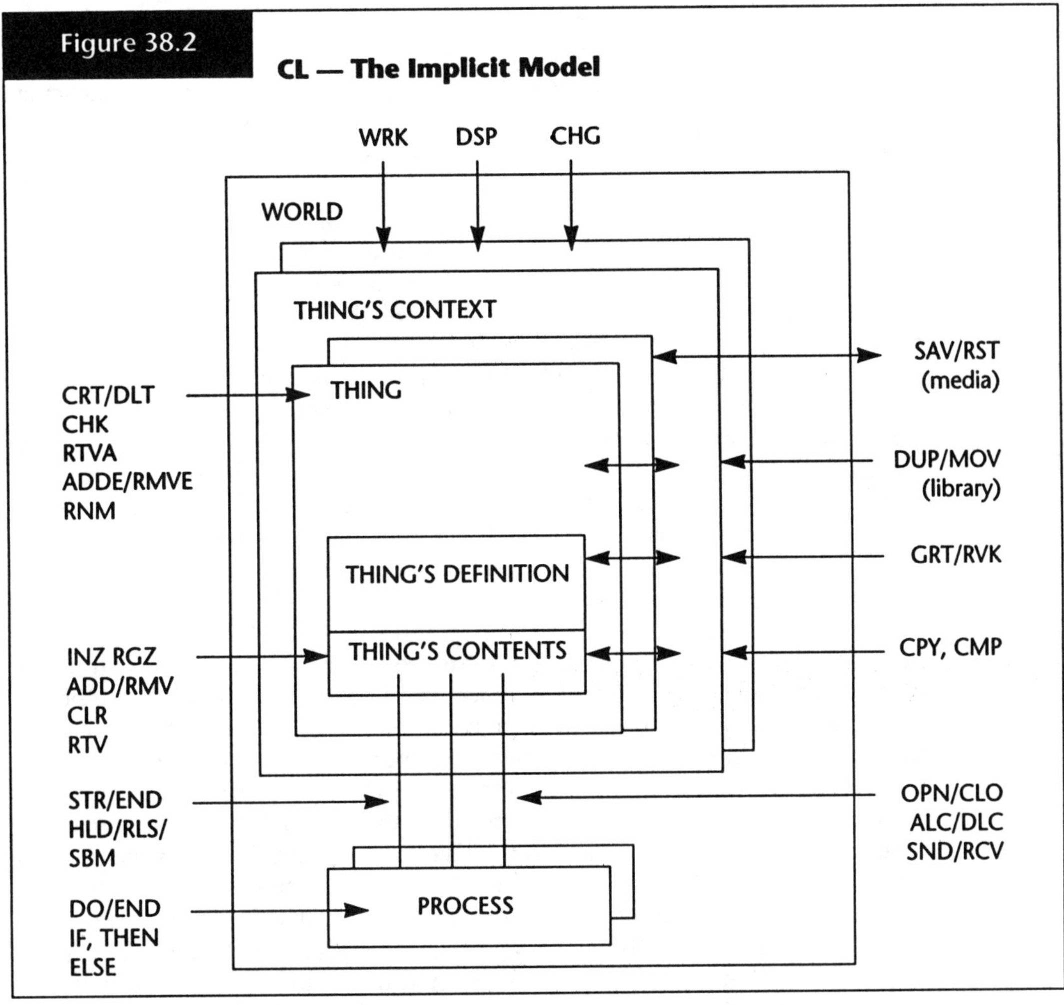

Along the top of Figure 38.2 appear some of the verbs that apply at any level. Examples of verbs that apply at a particular level are shown down the sides. On the left are simple verbs that work on a single subject, and on the right are the "transitive" verbs that require you to specify additional objects. By placing our new objects in the conceptual model, we can rationalize why we *create* a drim, but *add* a member of type globby.

What might following the OS/400 conceptual model mean in practice? Consider a simple order entry system with product, customer, and order "objects." You might decide that because each object has a unique identifier (product number, customer number, and order number, respectively), it is a design object in its own right and should be created or deleted. An order item or a customer address, on the other hand, might exist only within the context of a particular order or customer: They should therefore be added to or removed from the appropriate objects.

Actions Speak Louder than Words

Having decided what you are operating on, you can consider the operations you perform. As Figure 38.2 shows, CL commands use particular verbs in particular senses. Figure 38.3 gives some of the rules for using CL verbs.

It is interesting to observe that two-thirds of the 400 or more OS/400 commands are constructed using a vocabulary of just 10 verbs (CRT, CHG, DLT, ADD, RMV, DSP, WRK, CPY, STR, END). Thus, a user need remember very little to be able to invoke a wide range of functions (and consequently the range of meaning within the operating system world is quite restricted). It is also interesting that the main changes made to OS/400 CL over S/38 CL have been to refine semantic consistency in areas where CPF failed to distinguish clearly (e.g., the difference between change, edit, and work with) or failed to see the common concept (e.g., between start/begin and end/terminate/cancel).

Another observation we can make is that some verbs have a single subject (e.g., CHGDTAARA (Change Data Area)); others, although they can still be considered to have a single main subject, involve additional objects in ancillary roles. For example, CHGOBJOWN (Change Object Owner) requires you to specify a user profile as well as the name of the object whose owner is to be changed. This difference is analogous to the distinction between simple English verbs, which require only a subject (e.g., "John runs") and transitive ones, which have both subject and object (e.g., "John hits the ball"). However, within our conceptual model, both subject and object must be entities of particular types.

Providing that you choose your design objects correctly, these same conceptual primitives should suffice for most of your applications — and for different user interfaces. The users' fundamental perception of using a computer by requesting operations upon objects will hold up whether they do so through a command or by using a mouse to click on an icon. This object/action principle is the unifying tenet of IBM's SAA CUA standard. In either case, you should restrict yourself to simple primitive operations that can be used on more than one type of object.

It is important to keep the meanings of commands as simple and as primitive as possible. Although the temptation is sometimes to add as many optional extra features as possible to make the commands more "powerful," a command should operate on only one conceptual model entity and should carry out only one type of operation on the entity. For example, a rename command should be concerned only with changing the name of an object, not with changing its other attributes, like ownership; a delete command should name only the named object or objects, not any associated parent objects. However, if there are dependencies between the objects, then you must consider their implications on the meaning of delete (e.g., you would prevent the deletion of a physical file if logical files depended on it). If the dependent objects are subservient, you should delete them. If not, you should either block the deletion or provide an option to transfer the dependency (e.g., the DLTUSRPRF (Delete User Profile) command gives you the option of changing the ownership of any objects owned by the profile being deleted).

Figure 38.3

Some Rules for Using CL Verbs

For semantic consistency, when using CL verbs you should:

- Use existing verbs wherever possible — i.e., avoid introducing new verbs for actions that are synonymous with existing conceptual operations. For example, change, update, maintain, alter, edit, and modify can all be represented either as Edit (EDT), if the process invokes an interactive update, or Change (CHG), if it does not.
- Preserve the OS/400 distinction between verbs that operate on objects and verbs that operate on the *contents* of objects. For example, MOV/DUP are used to copy or duplicate between contexts; CPY is used to copy or duplicate within a context.

  Thus you would create/delete a file, but add/remove a file member; create/delete a subsystem description, but add/remove a routing entry within it; create/delete a drim, but add/remove a drim globby; create/delete an order, but add/remove an order item.

Object	**Content**
CRT	ADD
DLT	RMV
DUP	CPY

- Follow the OS/400 distinction between operating on an object and operating on the *description* of an object — e.g., DSPSBS (Display Subsystem) versus DSPSBSD (Display Subsystem Description), DSPGLB (Display Globby) versus DSPGLBD (Display Globby Description).
- Preserve the OS/400 distinction between working interactively on a list of entities (WRK verb) and working interactively on the attributes or contents of an individual entity (EDT verb) or invoking an interactive tool, such as an editor (STR verb).
- Follow the OS/400 distinctions in using pairs of antonymous mnemonics (i.e., pairs of verbs with opposite meanings). For example,

AS400	**Function**
CRT/DLT	To create/delete an entity.
ADD/RMV	To add/remove data within an entity.
STR/END	To begin/end a functional mode.
STR/END	To start/end a process.
STR/END	To start/terminate a process.
SND/RCV	To send/receive data.
HLD/RLS	To hold/release a process.
SAV/RST	To save/restore an object.
OPN/CLO	To open/close a function.
ALC/DLC	To allocate/de-allocate.
GRT/RVK	To grant/revoke a property.
CHG/RTV	To set/retrieve an attribute.
APY/RMV	To apply/remove a property.
FLC/DFL	To flatch/deflatch.

One area that is important to keep simple is the use of work management attributes. Because it is generally preferable to control work management values through the job, you should avoid adding parameters that specify work management attributes (e.g., job priority, switch settings, output queue) to your commands unless the command is specifically concerned with the initialization of a job (e.g., your own version of the SBMJOB (Submit Job) command) or with changing the properties of a job or a work management object. For example, say you have a Print Orders command that produces a print file. It is generally more flexible to have the print file obtain all of its parameters (e.g., output queue, number of copies) from the job rather than having COPIES and OUTQ parameters on the command. Where it is useful to have an override on a particular command, you should make the default value *JOB.

The Naming of Parts

Having sorted out the fundamental design objects, we can move on to the syntax — the rules governing the words we use and the order in which we use them.

The starting point for considering CL syntax is the command name itself. CL command names should always have the form Verb/Noun Phrase, where Verb is a mnemonic for a verb representing an action and Noun Phrase is either a simple mnemonic for a design object name — e.g., CHGJOB (Change Job), FLCDRM (Flatch Drim) or a design object name preceded by an adjective — e.g., WRKACTJOB (Work with Active Jobs), WRKUSRJOB (Work with User Jobs). Such a usage corresponds to the sentence structure of the simple English imperative mood — the sentence form used to give orders (e.g., "Do this," "Stop that"), which is very appropriate for a command language.

Things to Remember About Mnemonics

CL uses mnemonics extensively to provide concise but recognizable command names and keyword names (e.g., WRK for work, PGM for program). CL is generally systematic in the way it forms mnemonics. (Figure 38.4 shows the 76 verbs used in OS/400 commands. All but five follow one of the three simple rules shown.) Although most CL mnemonics can be explained by a simple set of rules, there are a fair number of exceptions. (Why is it CLeaR, but CLOse instead of CLoSe? Why CaNceL, but ConVerT (instead of CNV)? Why TransFeR, ReorGaniZe, DUPlicate?)

Ideally each mnemonic is unique — it represents only one eligible word. One reason for some of the inconsistencies in the way CL mnemonics are formed is that the convention emphasizes the beginning of words — which means that finding unique mnemonics can be difficult. Certain English word beginnings are very common because of the use of Latin-derived prefixes (e.g., In-, Co-, Un-, De-, Re-). I once asked one of the developers of the original CL command language how they had arrived at the three-letter (plus or minus two) mnemonic system. He said that they had at first tried to use a two-letter system (which was adequate for the number of distinctions to be made), but when they started combining them, they wound up with a lot of rude-looking four-letter words — Create Application was one example he gave. On the whole, we have to regard the choice

Figure 38.4

OS/400 Verb Mnemonics

The following table shows the mnemonics for OS/400 verbs and analyzes them by rule (Y is treated as a consonant):

Key

Rule 0 Use all letters or use first syllable in full.

Rule 1 Use first three significant consonants (if word begins with vowel, include it).

Rule 2 Use first two significant consonants plus the last significant consonant.

Rule * Irregular

Verb	Rule Used	Verb	Rule Used
ADD	0	MoDeL	1,2
ALloCate	1	MONitor	0
ANSwer	1,0	MOVe	1,2,0
ANalyZe	2	MeRGe	1,2
APplY	2	OPeN	1,2
ASK	0	OVeRride	1
CALL	0	PAGinate	0
CHanGe	2	POSition	0
CHecK	2	PRinT	2
CLOse	0	PoWeR	1,2
CLeaR	1,2	ReCLaim	1
CoMPare	1	ReCeiVe	1,2
CaNceL	2	ReorGaniZe	*
CiPHer	1	ReLeaSe	1,2
CoPY	1,2	ReMoVe	1,2
CReaTe	1,2	ROLL	0
ConVerT	*	RePLace	1
DeCLare	1	ReRouTe	1,2
DeaLloCate	1	ReSuMe	1,2
DeLeTe	1,2	ReSTore	1
DeLaY	1,2	ReTurN	2
DuMP	1,2	ReTrieVe	2
DO	0	RUN	1,2
DiSPlay	1	ReVoKe	1,2
DUPlicate	0	SAVe	0
EDiT	1,2	SuBMit	1
ENCipher	1	SET	0
END	0	SIGN	0
EXTract	1	SeLecT	2
FILe	1,2	SeND	1,2
ForMaT	*	STaRt	1
GENerate	0	TransFeR	*
GO	0	TRaCe	1,2
GRanT	2	UPDate	1,3
HoLD	1,2	VeriFY	*
INitiliaZe	2	VaRY	1,2
LiNK	1,2	WAIT	0
LOaD	1,2	WoRK	1,2

Figure 38.5

How to Form CL Mnemonics

- Always use any appropriate existing CL mnemonic wherever possible, both for verbs (e.g., CRT, DSP, CPY) and for entities (e.g., PGM, OBJ, DTAARA). Appendix F of the AS/400 *Control Language Reference* manuals (SC41-0030) provides a complete list of keywords.
- If no appropriate mnemonic exists, attempt to form one by taking the first phonetically significant consonant on each syllable (e.g., ProGraM, ComMuNications, ReNaMe, MoDeL, DRiM), unless the word begins with a vowel, in which case include the vowel (e.g., OBJect, AUThority, ALloCate, ANSwer).
- If the mnemonic you form is already in common use, try using the last significant syllable phoneme instead (e.g., CoMmanD, ReTrieVe).
- If the word is short (e.g., JOB, DO, GO), use it in full.

of CL mnemonics, like English orthography itself, as a somewhat arbitrary process, albeit one that has been validated by extensive usability testing. However, for what it is worth, Figure 38.5 shows my rules for forming mnemonics.

For obvious practical reasons, the names of user-defined commands should not conflict with existing OS/400 commands, nor with any commands that IBM may introduce into OS/400 in the future. But what if your command is semantically equivalent to an existing command? For instance, you might have a generic Move Object command that does what the CL MOVOBJ command does, but on lots of objects at a time: The most meaningful name is still MOVOBJ. To use a different noun (e.g., MOVOBJS) would be to make a distinction that CL does not bother with anywhere else (i.e., whether a command may run on one entity only, or on many entities generically). The solution I use on all my commands is a prefix letter (Y) that does not meaningfully combine with the verb: it is quite clear what YMOVOBJ, YCHGOBJOWN, YFLCGLB do. If you adopt this approach, you should choose a letter that will not be confused with the first letter of a mnemonic — no OS/400 commands begin with B, J, K, N, Y, or Z.

Command Parameters

Having decided how the command fits into the conceptual model and named it accordingly, let's consider its parameters.

You will recall that a globby is a type of drim that you will be able to create from source under Release 9.9 of OS/400. What do the parameters for the CRTGLBDRM (Create Globby Drim) command look like and why?

When you consider the actual parameters of the command, the semantics again are relevant, especially for ordering the parameters. Because we regard all commands as operating on a design object, you should place the parameters that identify the subject of the command — i.e., those that provide the subject's unique name — before all others. Any other parameters that identify semantically important objects should follow. For example, STRSEU (Start SEU) has the operand, identified by the FILE and MEMBER parameters, first; CHGJOB has the JOB name parameter first; and CHGOBJOWN first has the parameters specifying the name and type of the object whose ownership is to be changed, followed by the name of the new owner.

Having placed the subject first and any secondary subject next, you should optimize the remaining parameters for frequency of use — that is, place the parameters most likely to change before those that are unlikely to change. On the AS/400, you should use the PMTCTL (Prompt Control) keyword on the PARM command definition statement to hide ancillary parameters from the initial prompt displays. If you specify *PMTRQS for the PMTCTL keyword, the parameters will be displayed automatically after the main parameters when the user presses F10.

Other ordering rules are:

- Place all required — i.e., mandatory (MIN(1)) — parameters before any nonrequired parameters.
- When TEXT and OUTPUT parameters are present, they should normally be placed after all other parameters.
- On the AS/400, which supports conditional prompting, parameters that control the prompting of other parameters should appear before the ones they control.

In normal circumstances, all of these rules work together. Thus our CRTGLBDRM command has the actual operand — the globby name as a required parameter — first, followed by the semantically related object — the source file and member names, followed by the less important attributes (e.g., SAAFLAG), and finishing up with TEXT:

```
CRTGLBDRM DRIM(object-name) SRCFILE(QGLBSRC) SRCMBR(*DRIM)     +
          GENLVL(10) SAAFLAG(*NOFLAG) AUT(*CHANGE)             +
          TEXT(*SRCMBRTXT)
```

Choosing CL Command Parameters

What guidelines should you follow in choosing parameters? The first rule is that universal rule of systems design — "keep it simple." Keep the number of parameters to a minimum. Furthermore, the parameters of a command should be orthogonal: Each parameter should represent the values of only one variable. For example, rather than having four values for an OUTPUT parameter representing different combinations of output detail and output device (e.g., *PRT, *DSP, *PRTDTL, *DSPDTL), use two parameters: OUTPUT (*, *PRINT) and DETAIL (*FULL, *BASIC).

Many commands will have a number of required parameters. For example, create, change, and delete commands should always require the identifiers of the objects that are to be created, changed, or deleted, respectively. For "transitive" commands, both subject and object are required. Generally only these parameters, which identify the operand, need to be mandatory; you should provide default values for all other parameters.

Commands to be run in batch should not have optional parameters that invoke functions requiring interactive intervention; all of the facilities of a command should be usable in all circumstances. For example, you might have a PRTCSTORD (Print Customer Orders) command for which the main parameter is CST — the identifier of the customer whose orders are to be printed. If the command is intended for batch use, you should not allow the user to specify a value such as CST(*SELECT) to obtain an interactive inquiry of existing customers. Instead, a separate Work with Customers command should provide an interactive display and let the user take a selection action against the customers to invoke the PRTCSTORD command. On the AS/400, you can explicitly state the execution environment by means of the MODE parameter of the CRTCMD (Create Command) command. Figure 38.6 shows some rules for choosing parameters and parameter keywords.

As well as being consistent in the way you name and order parameters, you should be consistent in your use of values, especially special values for command parameters. Special values are the reserved words (e.g., *YES, *NO) that represent special actions to be taken. Figure 38.7 shows the OS/400 conventions concerning the use of special values.

Where a parameter is optional, it is important to use a "visible default" so as to be explicit about what will happen. Rather than allowing the optional parameter to take a blank value, use a "visible" special value of *ALL, *NONE, or *BLANK to specify the meaning of the default value.

Figure 38.6

Rules for CL Command Parameter Keywords

- Use existing standard CL keywords for entities and attributes (e.g., FILE, PGM, DTAARA, OUTPUT, TEXT) whenever possible. Do not use variants of existing words (e.g., FL, FIL, PROGRAM, OUTPT, TXT). Appendix F of the AS/400 *Control Language Reference* manuals (SC41-0030) lists all of the CL keywords.
- Entities identified within the context of another entity should be given qualified names where the qualifier is the containing entity. Use existing OS/400 syntax order whenever possible. For instance,
  - LIB/FILE MBR
  - JOBNBR/USER/JOB
- Keywords that identify operands should be in the singular (e.g., FILE, not FILES), even when a list of objects is allowed (e.g., as for SAVOBJ).
- If an entity type occurs more than once as a command parameter, distinguish between instances by an appropriate prefix on the keyword (e.g., FROMFILE, TOFILE, FROMLIB, TOLIB). If the verb copies between contexts, use FROM and TO as prefixes on the respective instances of the entities (e.g., CPYF FROMFILE TOFILE). If the verb changes or renames a property of the entity, use NEW as a prefix on the second reference (e.g., CHGOBJOWN NEWOWN(new_owner) or RNMOBJ OBJ(object_name) NEWOBJ(new_object_name)).

Figure 38.7

Rules for CL Command Parameter Special Values

- A special value indicates a function or default action. Special values for command parameters should always begin with an asterisk (e.g., *ALL, *PRINT, *NONE, *YES, *NO). Explicit values (e.g., the default name of a file to be used, such as QTXTSRC) should not begin with an asterisk.
- Do not use *N as a special value. *N is reserved as the null value for the CL command parser.
- Use existing OS/400 special values where possible. Some of these follow.

Special Value	Meaning
*ALL	All values
*ALLUSR	All user values
*CURRENT	Current values
*	Current value, especially job
*JOB	Use value from invoking job
*JOBD	Use job description value
*FIRST	Start at first value found
*LAST	Continue until last value found
*PRINT	Direct output to printer (AS/400)
*LIBL	Current job's library list
*NO	No or false
*NOMAX	No limit on number of instances
*PRV	Use previous value
*SAME	Use existing value
*USER	Use value from user profile
*USRLIBL	User library list
*YES	Yes or true

- Where a special value relates to another parameter, the special value should be derived from the keyword for the based-on parameter. For example:

```
FILE(file_name)   MBR(*FILE)

JOBD(job_description_name)   OUTQ(*JOBD)
```

- If you must supply a default name for a library in which to create objects, use the special value *CURLIB on AS/400 commands. For example:

```
UCRTPF FILE(X.QGPL)

UCRTPF FILE(*CURLIB/X)
```

Finally, for ease of use, you should generally default to the most commonly required value. For example, when copying a file, you usually want the TOMBR name to be the same as the FROMMBR name:

```
CPYSRCF FROMFILE(BERNARD) TOFILE(DAVE) FROMMBR(ARIC)          +
  TOMBR(*FROMMBR) MBROPT(*REPLACE)
```

Command Prompt Text

You should also strive for consistency in the prompt text on commands. Figure 38.8 shows some rules for CL command parameter text. Although prompt text is in one sense only cosmetic, it nonetheless contributes to the users' perception of consistency, and you should always use the same text with the same parameter keyword, avoid abbreviations, and take care with capitalization. For example, for an AS/400 LIB parameter, the text should use "Library," not variously "Library," "Library name," "Name of library," and "Lib name."

For consistency, it is a good idea to use a message file to define your prompt text. Message files let you reuse the same standard text in many places — and they reduce the amount of work needed to translate an application.

Coding Commands

You can implement most of the command definition conventions I've described in a very straightforward manner by using the CL command definition statements (for more information about command definition statements, see the *Application System/400 Programming: Control Language Reference, Volume 1* (SC41-0030)). Having got the main features of your commands correct, you should note that there are a number of additional standards to follow when coding commands so as to be consistent with OS/400. Some of these follow.

- When entering commands using the QCMD program, you may type in parameters positionally (i.e., without keywords) up to a specified point. This positional limit is specified by the MAXPOS parameter on the CRTCMD command. You should use the MAXPOS keyword if you know or suspect that it will be necessary to add a parameter later, and that the new parameter will need to precede one of the existing parameters.

Figure 38.8

Rules for CL Command Parameter Test

- Prompt text for AS/400 command titles should be in mixed case. For instance:

```
'Display Object List'
```

- Prompt text for AS/400 command parameters should use mixed case and not end with a colon (the compiler will automatically add trailing dots). For instance:

```
'Member name'
```

- For AS/400 command parameter prompts, show allowed values in the CHOICE text.
- If a parameter is returned to the calling program (i.e., RTNVAL(*YES) is specified for it), include the length of the variable in the prompt text:

```
'Cl Var. for menu name:     (10)'
'Cl Var. for length:       (5.0)'
```

- Prompt text should normally be stored in an external message file to enable easy translation.

- If the values allowed for a parameter are conditional on the value entered for another parameter, you should use the CL Dependent Definition (DEP) statement to cross-check the values. On the AS/400 you can use the PMTCTL keyword to direct the prompting of the second parameter.
- If there is more than one value or special value for a command parameter, specify the most important values first so that they appear first in the CHOICE text, which appears on the right side of AS/400 commands.
- If the parameter specifies an object whose use should be cross-referenced (e.g., a file, program, or data area), specify the object use on the PARM and ELEM command definition statements using the FILE, PGM, or DTAARA keywords. This specification ensures that the output of the OS/400 DSPPGMREF (Display Program References) command is correct. Figure 38.9 shows examples of coding command cross-reference information.

Use of PRODLIB on Commands

On the AS/400 you can specify a product library (PRODLIB) on each command. The named library is added automatically to the invoking job's library list when the command is called. You can therefore ensure that the command processing program (CPP) and other required objects are present in the library list. If the command resides in the same library as the other product objects, it may not be necessary to specify a PRODLIB.

You should specify PRODLIB for a command

- if the command is likely to be called by a qualified call (i.e., without the CPP already being present in the library list),
- if the command requires objects in a second product library — i.e., in a library other than the one in which the command will reside (the second product library should be named as the PRODLIB), or
- if the command calls a program or command that may modify the library list so as to remove the library containing the command from the invoking job's library list.

Figure 38.9

Coding Command Cross-Reference Information

```
/*H:   1. Data area name.              */
       PARM KWD(DTAARA) TYPE(*NAME) DTAARA(*YES) PROMPT(YYD0001)

/*H:   2. Program name.                */
       PARM KWD(PGM) TYPE(*GENERIC) PGM(*YES) PROMPT(YYP0001)

/*H:   3. Qualified file name.         */
       PARM KWD(FILE) TYPE(FL) PROMPT(YYF1001) FILE(*IN)

FL:    QUAL TYPE(*NAME) DFT(QTXTSRC)                      /* File */
       QUAL TYPE(*NAME) PROMPT(YYL0001) /* Library */ +
                          DFT(*LIBL) SPCVAL((*LIBL))
```

Note that once you specify a product library, it is cumbersome to use the library list to access alternative versions of the command. Therefore, you should not use PRODLIB during testing.

Command Processing Programs

The CL command definition statements are tailor-made to allow you to define commands concisely and consistently. However, not quite all of a command's standard behavior comes from the command definition. The program the command calls must also follow certain conventions.

A CPP is the program to which a command hands control once it has validated the entry parameters. CPPs are normal CL (or other HLL) programs to which some extra considerations should be applied:

- You should ensure that your CPPs handle processing and messages in a manner consistent with standard CL command use. In particular, the processing a command invokes should generally be regarded as a single unit of work — that is, as a unitary operation that either runs or fails as a whole.
- Processing should use the CHKOBJ (Check Object) command (a relatively fast operation) to check for the presence of all required objects and the authorization to use those objects before changing any data or objects. Prechecking the required objects helps ensure that the command runs cleanly: Either it functions completely, or not at all.
- If function errors occur in a CPP, the CPP should trap and retransmit them to the invoking program, rather than causing an interrupt requiring user intervention. The CPP should send an escape message, preceded by diagnostic messages when appropriate to help the user diagnose the cause of the fault. Figure 38.10 shows sample error-handling code.
- CPPs should send a completion message, which should contain substitution data if relevant. You should couch the message in terms of the operation that has just been performed (e.g., "Drim FRED deleted"). The substitution data should be as specific as possible.
- CPPs should remove irrelevant messages from the program message queue. Thus, the effect of examining the log is to see only messages that relate sensibly to the requested operation. You can remove irrelevant messages by using the OS/400 RCVMSG (Receive Message) command, as Figure 38.11 shows.
- CPPs that process generic lists of items should be structured so that the CPP receives a diagnostic or a completion message for each item processed (e.g., "Object &1/&2 not found - ignored."). The CPP should also send an overall completion or escape message (e.g., "&1 objects successfully processed, &2 errors.") to the program that invokes the command so the user can determine which items the command has actually processed.

Command Validity Checking Programs

A validity checking program (VCP) is a user-defined subprogram that can be associated with a user-defined command. The OS/400 command prompter calls

Figure 38.10

Sample Code to Resend an Escape Message

```
/*H:  Ø.  GLOBAL ERROR MONITOR                                      */
            DCL VAR(&MSGID) TYPE(*CHAR) LEN(7)
            DCL VAR(&MSGDTA) TYPE(*CHAR) LEN(132)
            DCL VAR(&MSGF) TYPE(*CHAR) LEN(1Ø)
            DCL VAR(&MSGFLIB) TYPE(*CHAR) LEN(1Ø)
            MONMSG (CPFØØØØ YYYØØØØ) EXEC(GOTO ERROR)
             : :
             : :
            RETURN
/*H: 99.  ERROR HANDLING                                            */
ERROR:      RCVMSG    MSGTYPE(*EXCP) MSGDTA(&MSGDTA) MSGID(&MSGID) +
                          MSGF(&MSGF) MSGFLIB(&MSGFLIB)
            MONMSG CPFØØØØ
            SNDPGMMSG  MSGID(&MSGID) MSGF(&MSGFLIB/&MSGF) +
                          MSGTYPE(*ESCAPE)   MSGDTA(&MSGDTA)
           MONMSG CPFØØØØ
            GOTO ENDPGM
ENDPGM
```

Figure 38.11

CL Code to Remove Irrelevant Error Messages

```
CHKOBJ OBJ(QTEMP/WORK) OBJTYPE(*FILE)
MONMSG MSGID(CPF98Ø1) EXEC(DO) /* Create if not found */
   RCVMSG    MSGTYPE(*EXCP) RMVMSG(*YES) /* Suppress msg   */
   CRTPF FILE(QTEMP/WORK) RCDLEN(8Ø)
ENDDO
```

the VCP before handing control over to the CPP. A VCP can carry out additional user-defined validation of the command parameters. (For details about writing VCPs, see Chapter 37.) Your use of VCPs should also be consistent with that of OS/400 system-supplied commands:

- VCPs should perform only limited validation. For instance, VCPs are useful for cross-checking parameters that you cannot check with the CL DEP command definition statement or the REL keyword on the PARM command definition statement. Under normal circumstances, parameter cross-checking is necessary only when checking the components of lists and qualified names.
- VCPs should not check for the existence of objects or other entities, nor should VCPs invoke selection functions. The reason for this rule is that the VCP is invoked whenever the OS/400 command prompter or syntax checker is invoked for the command, even if the command is not executed. You should use validity checkers to ensure that the command is called with a

Figure 38.12

Sample VCP Error-Handling Code

```
/*H: 99.   ERROR HANDLING */
 ERROR:      RCVMSG      MSGTYPE(*EXCP) MSG(&MSG)
 SNDMSG:     SNDPGMMSG   MSGID(CPD0006) MSGF(QCPFMSG) MSGDTA('0000' +
                         || &MSG) MSGTYPE(*DIAG)
             SNDPGMMSG   MSGID(CPF0002) MSGF(QCPFMSG) MSGTYPE(*ESCAPE)
```

legitimate combination of parameters, not to check whether the command will execute successfully in a particular instance.

- VCPs should resend diagnostics using the standard CPF or OS/400 message (i.e., CPD0006 in QCPFMSG).
- If the validity check fails, the errors should be retransmitted to the invoking program (i.e., the command prompter) as diagnostics, and an escape message (CPF0002) should be sent to return control. Figure 38.12 shows sample error-handling code.

Commands are excellent interfaces for both programmers and "power users." Even if your users use only menus and interactive displays, you can use commands behind the scenes: Commands can perform a valuable role as design and system building components. The discipline of decomposing your application design into objects and well-defined operations upon those objects can both clarify your thinking and clarify the common principles. Commands also provide an effective framework for documenting a system: You can use OS/400-style command diagrams to document the available options concisely and unambiguously.

Chapter 39

UIM Help for Commands

by Bryan Meyers

Create help text for your application display files and custom commands with IBM's User Interface Manager

If you've gotten very far into programming the AS/400, you've probably dabbled in user-defined commands. Even with hundreds of CL commands at your disposal, you're likely to have found the need to personalize some of them for your installation, or to create a whole new command that does something none of IBM's commands do. Or maybe you have built an application that's entirely based on user-defined commands. Too bad you couldn't help your users use it.

User-defined commands use the same familiar interface and syntax as IBM-supplied commands, including the command prompt screen, positional and keyword parameters, and validity checking. The one thing that's been blatantly missing in user-defined commands, however, is the ability to create help text for them. IBM's commands have comprehensive help screens that guide you well enough through the use of the command that you usually don't need any more documentation to use them effectively. But for your own carefully crafted commands, users who go looking for help get only the disappointing message, "Help key not allowed."

One of the functions AS/400 programmers have most persistently asked for since the machine's introduction has been the ability to create help displays for user-defined commands. With OS/400 Version 2, that request has been answered. The User Interface Manager (UIM) IBM uses to display online help windows is now available for you to use in applications and user-defined commands. All the functions IBM designed into its system's help interface, including cursor-sensitive help, extended help, index search, windows, and hypertext linking, are now easy to incorporate into your application display files and custom commands.

SAA defines two types of help displays: contextual and extended. *Contextual help* is cursor-sensitive help, meaning the information displayed is specific for a section of the display. For example, if you position the cursor on the "Customer Name" field on a screen and press Help, contextual help provides instructions for using the customer name field. *Extended help* describes the entire display, including the purpose of the program or command that displays the screen. In addition, extended help should include all the contextual help for the display. SAA prescribes two methods for displaying extended help. The user can move the cursor to an area of the display that isn't covered by contextual help (usually the title of the display), and press Help. Or, if the user is already displaying contextual help, he or she can press F2 to display extended help.

From the start, the AS/400 has supported two methods of defining help information for application displays: help records and help documents. *Help records* are display file formats defined using Data Description Specifications (DDS). *Help documents* are OfficeVision/400 documents that contain help labels, which are special document instruction tags that support online help text. Both methods present full-screen help displays when the user presses the Help key.

Help Panel Groups

With Version 2, OS/400 introduced easy access to a third type of help display, *help panel groups.* A panel group is a unique AS/400 object — sort of a turbo-charged display file. Panel groups are not new; they were just inaccessible before V2R1. The panel group is the means by which IBM presents most of the operating system displays you see on the AS/400, including menus, list panels, and help displays. Starting with V1R3, the system began displaying help text in windowed sections of the display, leaving appropriate portions of the underlying screen uncovered. That's done with panel groups. The UIM is the operating system function that displays panel groups and automatically handles window sizing and positioning, scrolling, and screen consistency among the various components of an application (including the SAA "More..." and "Bottom" standard).

Which help method is best? Each has its own unique characteristics, but UIM's panel groups have distinct advantages over help records and help documents. Most notably, panel groups are the only way you can implement help for user-defined commands. In addition, when you use panel groups, OS/400 automatically positions and sizes your help windows. Panel groups offer hypertext linking (which I describe later), and they are the only practical means of providing an index search function within help. These advantages and the ease with which you can define panel groups make UIM an ideal vehicle for implementing help for both individual commands and entire applications.

To create help panel groups for your own commands, you need to learn how to use UIM. I'll take you through some examples based on the WRKOBJUSG (Work with Object Usage) user-defined command. Once you understand the concepts used in building the help files for each of these elements, you'll be able to apply them to your own commands and programs.

Creating a Panel Group

Creating a panel group is simple enough. You start by entering UIM source statements into a source file member, using SEU type PNLGRP. Then you compile the member with the new CRTPNLGRP (Create Panel Group) CL command. *Voila!* (That's French for "Wow, is this ever easy!") A panel group is born.

As with any language, UIM source has a unique syntax you must follow to ensure your panel group works properly. The bulk of the source specifications consists simply of the help text information. To format and identify the help text, you use UIM *tags*, special character sequences that tell the UIM compiler how to treat the marked text. Some tags, known as *markup tags*, are used to format, highlight, and organize your help text. For example, `:HP1.` and `:EHP1.` are the UIM panel markup tags used to demarcate underlined text. So the UIM statement

```
:HP1.This is underlined text.:EHP1.
```

is displayed in a help panel as

```
This is underlined text.
```

Other UIM tags define the text's role on the help screen, such as whether it is a comment or module name or the help text itself.

UIM tags always begin with a colon and end with a period. Most tags work in pairs (e.g., `:HP1.` for the beginning of an underlined phrase and `:EHP1.` for the end). The *Guide to Programming Displays* (SC41-0011) describes the extensive UIM tag language.

Help For Your Commands

Figure 39.1 shows the UIM code required to create WRKUSGHLP, the help panel group for WRKOBJUSG. Every panel group starts with a `:PNLGRP.` tag and ends with an `:EPNLGRP.` tag, which are analogous to the PGM and ENDPGM commands in a CL program. Within a panel group you may have one or more help modules, identified by a `:HELP.` tag at the start of each module and an `:EHELP.` tag at the end (A and D in Figure 39.1), similar to RPG's BEGSR and ENDSR. Easy enough? *Wunderbar!* (That's German for "Wow, is this ever easy!")

The first help module defined in Figure 39.1, WRKOBJUSG, contains the extended help for the command. This is the overall help that appears when a user who is working at the command prompt screen positions the cursor on a word other than one of the parameters and then presses Help. It is also the extended help users get by pressing F2 (Extended help) when they are displaying cursor-sensitive, contextual help. Figure 39.2 shows the extended help window.

When you create the command that uses help text, you specify the panel group name in the HLPPNLGRP parameter and the name of the extended-help module in the HLPID parameter. So to create the WRKOBJUSG command, you would key

```
CRTCMD CMD(WRKOBJUSG) PGM(WRKUSG1) HLPPNLGRP(WRKUSGHLP)        +
       HLPID(WRKOBJUSG)
```

Figure 39.1

UIM Source Specification

```
*...+... 1 ...+... 2 ...+... 3 ...+... 4 ...+... 5 ...+... 6 ...+... 7...+... 8

*****************************************************************
*
*      Panel group . .    WRKUSGHLP - Help for WRKOBJUSG command
*
*      SEU member type :   *PNLGRP
*
*      Create command  :   CRTPNLGRP PNLGRP(WRKUSGHLP)
*
*****************************************************************
:PNLGRP.
*****************************************************************
Ⓐ :HELP. NAME=WRKOBJUSG.
Ⓑ Work with object usage - Help
:P.
The Work with object usage (WRKOBJUSG) command shows a list of objects
in a library, along with object usage information for each object.
:P.
The object name, type attributes, last date used, number of days used,
reset date, object size, and text of each object are shown.  From this
list several object-oriented options can be performed.
:P.
This command was originally described in "Working out with WRKOBJUSG,"
Ⓒ :CIT.NEWS 3X/400,:ECIT. February, 1991.
Ⓓ :EHELP.
*****************************************************************
*
*      OBJ parameter - Help Text
*
:HELP NAME='WRKOBJUSG/OBJ'.
OBJ (Object) - Help
Ⓔ :XH3.OBJ (Object)
:P.
Specifies the name and library of the objects that are listed on the
Work with object usage display.
:P.
This is a required parameter.
:P.
The possible values are:
Ⓕ :PARML.
:PT.:PK.*ALL:EPK.
:PD.
All objects are listed that are of the type specified on the
:LINK PERFORM='DSPHELP WRKOBJUSG/OBJTYP'.
Object type
:ELINK.
prompt (OBJTYP parameter).
:PT.:PV.generic*-object-name:EPV.
:PD.
Specify the generic name of the objects to be listed.  A generic name
is a character string that consists of one or more characters followed
by an asterisk (*).
:PT.:PV.object-name:EPV.
:PD.
Specify the name of the object to be listed.
Ⓖ :EPARML.
:XH3.Library
:P.
Specifies the name of the library containing the object(s) to be
listed.
```

Figure 39.1 Continued

Figure 39.1

UIM Source Specification *Continued*

```
*...+... 1 ...+... 2 ...+... 3 ...+... 4 ...+... 5 ...+... 6 ...+... 7 ...+... 8

:EHELP.
***********************************************************************
*
*      OBJ parameter - Help Text
*
:HELP NAME='WRKOBJUSG/OBJTYP'.
OBJTYP (Object type) - Help
:XH3.OBJTYP (Object type)
:P.
Specifies which type of objects are listed.
:P.
The possible values are:
:PARML.
(H) :PT.:PK DEF.*ALL:EPK.
:PD.
All objects are listed that have the specifed object name.
:PT.:PV.object-type:EPV.
:PD.
Specify the object type for objects to be listed, such as command
(*CMD), program (*PGM) or file (*FILE).  For a complete list of the
object types available, position the cursor on the :HP2.Object
type:EHP2. prompt (OBJTYP parameter), and press F4.
:EPARML.
:EHELP.
:EPNLGRP.
```

Figure 39.2

Extended Help Window

```
                     Work with object usage (WRKOBJUSG)
 ..........................................................................
 :                      Work with object usage - Help                     :
 :                                                                        :
 :      The Work with object usage (WRKOBJUSG) command shows a list of    :
 :      objects in a library, along with object usage information for each:
 :      object.                                                           :
 :                                                                        :
 :      The object name, type attributes, last date used, number of days  :
 :      used, reset date, object size, and text of each object are shown. :
 :      From this list several object-oriented options can be performed.  :
 :                                                                        :
 :      This command was originally described in "Working out with        :
 :      WRKOBJUSG," NEWS 3X/400, February, 1991.                          :
 :                                                                        :
 :   OBJ (Object)                                                         :
 :                                                                        :
 :      Specifies the name and library of the objects that are listed on the :
 :      Work with object usage display.                                   :
 :                                                              More...   :
 :   F3=Exit help       F10=Move to top   F11=Search index   F12=Cancel   :
 :   F13=User support   F14=Print help                                    :
 ..........................................................................
```

UIM will create a title for each help window by adding " - Help" to the end of the text in the command description. If you want a different title, you can specify it on the line immediately following the `:HELP.` tag in the UIM source (B in Figure 39.1).

Each `:P.` markup tag identifies the beginning of a new paragraph, which is separated from the others in the help window by a blank line. UIM automatically formats all lines within a paragraph to fit into the window. For example, the source lines

```
:P.This is
a sample line
of help text.
```

might appear as

```
This is a sample line of help text.
```

depending on the width of the window. UIM also automatically wraps lines to accommodate narrow windows. Note that comment lines, which do not appear in the compiled panel group, are indicated by .* in columns 1 and 2 of the source.

In addition to the extended help, you should create contextual help text for each command parameter. UIM formats the contextual help within a window, automatically giving it a size and location that usually will not cover the original parameter on the underlying screen. The help module WRKOBJUSG/OBJ in Figure 39.1 contains the specific help text for the OBJ parameter. You link the help modules to their parameters by using the following syntax in your panel group source code:

```
:HELP NAME='help-identifier/parameter-name'.
```

The help identifier must be identical to the name of the extended help module, and the parameter name in the help module must match the parameter name in the command. Note that you must enclose the name in single quotation marks whenever you use a slash as a separator, and a period is required at the end of the statement.

Now you've learned the basics about creating help screens for user-defined commands. To summarize the source contents:

```
:PNLGRP.
:HELP NAME='command-name'.
:P.Extended help text for command
:EHELP.
:HELP NAME='help-identifier/parameter-name'.
:P.Contextual help text for parameter
:EHELP.
:EPNLGRP.
```

Are you still with me? *Eureka!* (Greek: "Wow, is this ever easy!")

Details, Details!

In addition to sizing and locating windows automatically, UIM helps consistently format and present the help text using special markup tags. We've already touched upon the :HP1. underlining tag, and the :P. paragraph tag, but many more tags are available.

At C in Figure 39.1, the :CIT. and :ECIT. markup tags surrounding "NEWS 3X/400" indicate the title of a publication. This text will be underlined automatically when you display or print it. By using a special easy-to-remember tag, UIM makes it easy to maintain a standard for publication citations in help text.

There are also special tags for various headings and titles. For example, the :XH3. tag (E in Figure 39.1) identifies OBJ (Object) as an extended heading, which appears as a subheading in the extended help window (Figure 39.2) and as a title within the parameter's contextual help window (Figure 39.3). There are four extended heading tags.

- :XH1. indicates centered text and underlined, boldfaced type;
- :XH2. indicates left justification, underlining and boldface;
- :XH3. indicates left justification and boldface;
- :XH4. indicates left justification and underlining.

Like the citation tags, the extended heading tags are used to enforce consistency.

The WRKOBJUSG/OBJ help module in Figure 39.1 contains a list of parameter values between the :PARML. (F) and :EPARML. (G) tags. This list describes the

Figure 39.3

Contextual Help Window

```
                    Work with object usage (WRKOBJUSG)

 Type choices, press Enter.

 Object . . . . . . . . . . . . .  __________    Name, generic*, *ALL
   Library  . ..............................................................
 Object type    :                OBJ (Object) - Help                      :
                :                                                         :
                :  Specifies the name and library of the objects that are :
                :  listed on the Work with object usage display.          :
                :                                                         :
                :  This is a required parameter.                          :
                :                                                         :
                :  The possible values are:                               :
                :                                                         :
                :  *ALL                                                   :
                :      All objects are listed that are of the type specified :
                :      on the _ Object type prompt (OBJTYP parameter).    :
                :                                                         :
                :                                                More...  :
                :  F2=Extended help  F10=Move to top   F11=Search index   :
 F3=Exit   F4=  :  F12=Cancel        F20=Enlarge       F24=More keys      :
 F24=More keys  :                                                         :
                :..........................................................
```

valid values for the WRKOBJUSG command's OBJ parameter. You precede each value on a list with a :PT. (parameter term) tag so that, on screen, the value will be boldfaced. You also describe each value with a paragraph, starting with a :PD. (parameter description) tag, and include additional paragraphs, as necessary, using the :P. tag. If your parameter values are also programming keywords (such as special values) or variables, you can mark them with the special :PK. or :PV. tags, and their names will show up boldfaced.

Similar coding appears for the OBJTYP parameter list toward the end of the source specification. H in Figure 39.1 indicates the OBJTYP default value (*ALL) with the :PK DEF. tag. This value is boldfaced and underlined when the help panel appears on screen (Figure 39.4).

Using Hypertext Links

The :LINK. and :ELINK. tags in the OBJ parameter value list define a hypertext link. Hypertext, as AS/400 help panels employ it, is a means of linking help modules together by their common words or phrases. To ensure the modules' usefulness, make sure a clear and logical relationship exists between the hypertext reference phrase (the phrase the user needs more information on) and the linked help module. For example, you wouldn't link the phrase "RPG calculations" with a definition of MI microcode.

When you define a hypertext reference phrase in a panel group, that phrase appears highlighted on a help panel to indicate that more information is available about it. The reference phrase in Figure 39.1 ("Object type") is highlighted and

Figure 39.4

Contextual Help Window

```
                     Work with object usage (WRKOBJUSG)

Type choices, press Enter.

Object . . . . . . . . . . . . .   __________    Name, generic*, *ALL
  Library  . . . . . . . . . . .    __________   Name
Object type  . . . . . . . . . .   *ALL______    *ALL, *CMD, *DTAARA, *FILE...
              ...........................................................
              :                OBJTYP (Object type) - Help              :
              :                                                         :
              :  Specifies which type of objects are listed.            :
              :                                                         :
              :  The possible values are:                               :
              :                                                         :
              :  *ALL                                                   :
              :      All objects are listed that have the specifed object :
              :      name.                                              :
              :                                                         :
              :  object-type                                            :
              :                                                More...  :
              :  F6=Viewed topics   F10=Move to top   F11=Search index  :
F3=Exit   F4= :  F12=Cancel         F20=Enlarge       F24=More keys     :
F24=More keys :                                                         :
              :.........................................................:
```

underlined when it appears in the Object help panel window (Figure 39.3). To see additional information for "object type," the user tabs the cursor to the reference phrase and presses Enter, and the object type help screen is displayed (Figure 39.4). Pressing F12 (Cancel) returns the user to the previous panel, and pressing F6 (Viewed topics) displays a list of previously displayed help panels the user can choose to review.

Future Expeditions

To stretch your knowledge of UIM, you might also find it useful to study the sample help text for a user-defined command in QUSRTOOL's QATTUIM file (member T0011CHL). There's a lot of unexplored function in this new feature, and it's all there for the learning. *Radical, dudes!* (American: "Wow, this is really easy!)

Section VI

WORKSTATION PROGRAMMING

Chapter 40

User Interface Design

by J. H. Botterill

Master, and then apply, the principles of AS/400 user interface design

Before you examine design details and apply them in the creation of your own panels and dialogues, you need to understand the principles behind the design. These principles can help you design consistent menu, entry, and list panels, as well as special application-specific panels (e.g., a panel for laying out a warehouse) that fit with the AS/400 application interface.

This chapter addresses the thinking that underlies the design of the AS/400 user interface. The principles discussed here can help you make design decisions and can give you a better understanding of the specifics involved in creating AS/400 workstation programs.

Consistency

One primary way to make an interface easy to learn is by assuring consistency. Consistency lets users learn techniques once and apply them repeatedly throughout an application. Each use reinforces what the users have learned, further develops the users' conceptual model of the application, and increases their confidence in that mental picture of the application's workings. In addition, consistency significantly reduces the time users require to infer the way to interact with an application. When a new application is consistent with other applications with which users are familiar, the time users need to learn the new application decreases. Furthermore, users feel comfortable moving among consistent applications because users need little time to adjust to a different application and experience little frustration.

Consistency does not mean the interface must not change with time. Neither Common User Access (CUA) nor the AS/400 user interface claims this type of consistency because it excludes improvement and eventually makes the interface obsolete and noncompetitive. CUA and the AS/400 interface definition are sets of rules that at any given time describe a consistency of style and interaction for applications. These rules are intended to evolve as technology expands and users from different backgrounds are addressed.

This evolution will be intentionally designed to let applications developed on different versions of CUA or of the AS/400 harmoniously co-exist. Users will be able to move easily to new versions as existing techniques are improved or new features are added. An example is adding command lines to menus that did not previously support this feature. Numeric selection on the menus would continue to function, and the command lines would be available on the new version, but not on applications that had not been upgraded. Another example of this sort of evolution can be found in the OS/400 EUI (Enhanced User Interface) implementation. When used in conjunction with the InfoWindow II terminals, EUI extends the traditional 5250 data stream by providing features like pop-up windows, selection fields, and scroll bars. For example, on an InfoWindow II display, a program using EUI can display a screen window with continuous-line window borders, radio buttons, and scroll bars all complying to the graphical CUA guidelines developed in 1989. However, when the same program is run on a traditional 5250 display, the existing 5250 display attributes and characters will be displayed. CUA provides the backdrop for this consistency while still progressing as technology evolves.

Although consistency can result in an interface that is easier to learn than an inconsistent interface, consistency does not ensure that the interface is easy to use and can increase user productivity. An interface must also be well designed. Several principles come into play to accomplish a good design. The first of these principles is *object orientation.*

Object Orientation

One of the most valuable principles in designing a user interface is to focus users' attention on the objects important to the users. Objects are the items users know about and work with in their daily jobs. In an inventory application, the objects might be parts, customers, and warehouses. In an automotive application, the objects might be cars, parts, orders, and customers. An office application might include such objects as documents, folders, and mail. You should focus users' attention on the objects they concentrate on every day and want to work with. This focus leads users into an efficient object-action interaction flow.

In a text-based user interface, you can represent an object with a name and some set of descriptive attributes. In a graphics interface, you can represent an object with a name and an icon. The computer interface should let users identify the objects that exist, and monitor and manage the data associated with them. Until they see the objects that exist, the users are likely to be unable to identify the object and decide what to do with it. After seeing an object, users want to simply point to the object and designate the action they want to perform on that object.

Once users' attention is properly focused on the required objects, the next step is to ensure that users can easily and quickly perform necessary actions on the objects. One way to provide this ability is by supporting an object-action flow.

Object-Action Flow

A primary AS/400 interface design consideration is the way users request actions. As a rule, users can request an action in one of two ways. The first way is to identify the desired action or task and then designate the object on which to perform that action. This approach, the conventional task orientation, is called *action-object orientation.* The second way is for users to identify the object of the action first and then designate the action they want the application to perform. This approach is called *object-action orientation.* The flows for each of these two approaches are shown in Figure 40.1.

To accommodate users' individual preferences, you can support both approaches, as AS/400 products do. However, because the object-action approach provides many productivity and ease-of-use benefits, this method should be the primary one supported in your applications, and support for the action-object method should be optional. The "Work with" List Panel is the cornerstone of the AS/400's object-action orientation (Figure 40.2).

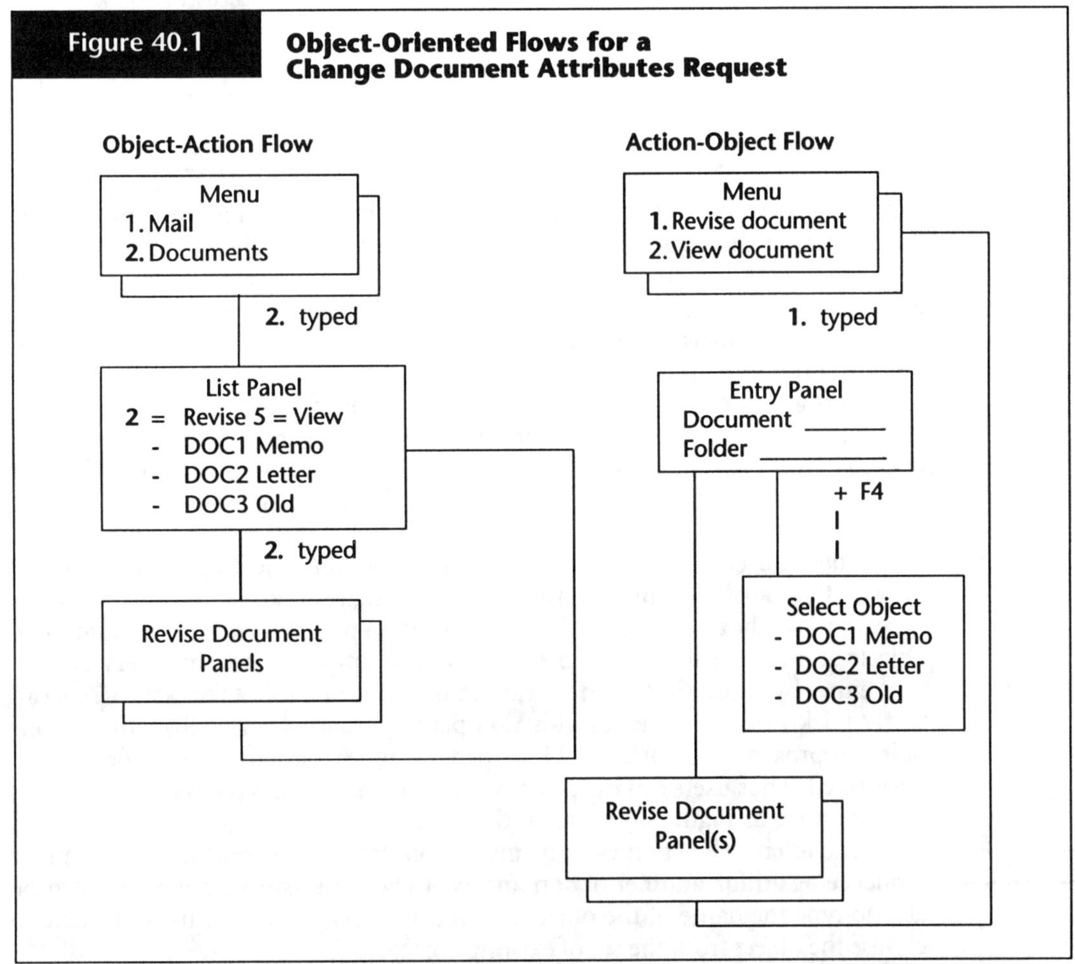

Figure 40.1 **Object-Oriented Flows for a Change Document Attributes Request**

Figure 40.2

Sample Work with List Panel

```
                         Work with Documents

Type options (and Document), press Enter.
  1=Create    2=Edit      3=Copy    4=Delete    5=View       6=Print

Option    Document   Document Description                 Revised    Type
 ___      ________
 ___      INVENTOR   Inventory for warehouse              10/22/87   DOCUMENT
 ___      INVENTSM   Inventory summary                    3/24/87    DOCUMENT
 ___      LETTER1    Letter to ABC CORP                   12/01/87   MEMO
 ___      LETTER2    Memo to J R Scruttle                 12/03/87   MEMO
 5_       LETTER3    Memo to J R Scruttle                 12/04/87   MEMO
 ___      LETTER6    Letter to Rundle Price               9/5/87     MEMO
 ___      MEMOJHB    Memo to J H Bottle                   10/28/87   MEMO
 ___      MONTHLY    Monthly accounting summary           12/01/87   DOCUMENT
 ___      MONTHLYD   Monthly detail for November          12/02/87   DOCUMENT
 ___      OLDMONTH   Last Month's detail - Oct            11/02/87   DOCUMENT
 ___      REPORTYE   Year end report                      11/30/87   DOCUMENT
                                                                      More...
Parameters or command
===> ______________________________________________________________________

F3=Exit    F4=Prompt    F5=Refresh    F12=Cancel
```

To support the object-action approach, you should provide a menu that lets the user select the desired type of object. As Figure 40.1 shows, when the user selects an object type, the application should display a list panel of the requested objects. From this point, the user can request the required actions directly and repeatedly. Only when a requested action needs qualification by the choice of options should the application present entry panels.

Object-action orientation has several advantages. Users can see an object before they decide which actions they want. The name and key attributes appear in each object's list entry. In addition, users can conveniently switch to a different action after seeing the object, without leaving the panel that shows the object or list of objects. Users can point to the name of the object, rather than having to remember and correctly type the name. (The action-object approach can also provide this capability through the prompt dialogue action, but an extra step is necessary.) Without leaving the list, users also can perform an action on multiple objects and can perform multiple actions on multiple objects in a very natural way, either by requesting them all at once or in a sequence of requests. Users can work quickly because the object-action path is usually shorter than the action-object approach — the list-of-objects panel reappears after each set of actions is performed. Thus users can quickly enter additional action requests.

In contrast, as Figure 40.1 shows, the action-object approach returns users to the menu after each action is performed. From there, they must follow the entire sequence again for another action and deal with at least one entry panel to be able to type the name of the object and (optionally) a selection list to be able to choose the object from the set of existing objects.

If you support the action-object approach, you should provide a menu that allows task selection. An entry panel (see Figure 40.3 for a sample entry panel) should follow the menu after the user chooses the task (i.e., makes the action-object choice). The entry panel lets users type the name of the desired object and any other options.

In case the user does not recall what objects are available, the application should let users request a selection list panel (Figure 40.4) by using the prompt common dialogue action (i.e., the F4 key) when the cursor is on the object-name entry field. Such a list lets the user select the object from a list, rather than having to key a name from memory.

Not only must users be focused on the objects they need to work with and be able to perform actions on these objects, but users must also feel comfortable with the interface. They should not have to rely on memory or rote learning to use the interface. One way to help users is to provide choices they can recognize and from which they can make the necessary selection.

Recognize and Select

Recognize and select is also fundamental to AS/400 user interface design. Because recognition is easier than recall and selection is easier than keying, a user interface should, when possible, present users with choices from which to select. You should not require users to remember and type a name or command. Menus are a standard way to capitalize on this design approach because they list object types and actions (or high-level groupings of them) and let the user select by choice number. EUI (Enhanced User Interface) also includes CUA-element extensions that define selection fields that make use of the recognize-and-select principle. Graphical selection fields include menu bars, pull-downs, single-choice selection fields/lists, multiple-choice selection fields/lists, and push-buttons.

Figure 40.3

Sample Entry Panel

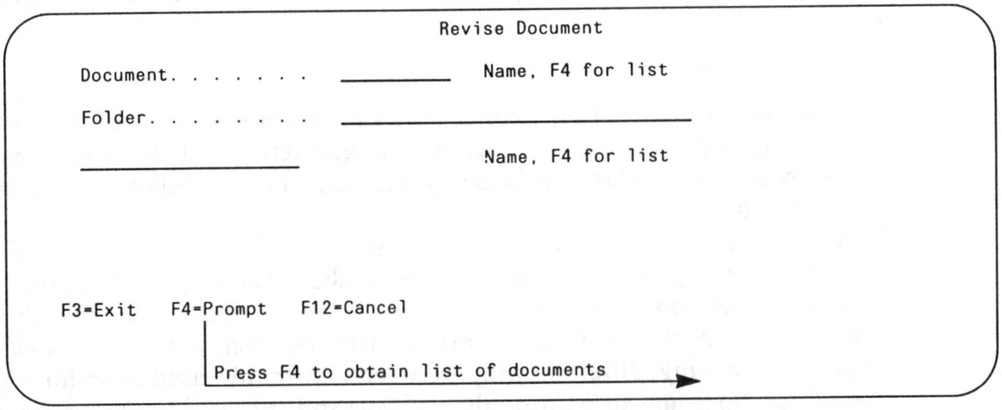

```
                         Revise Document

   Document. . . . . . .   ________     Name, F4 for list

   Folder. . . . . . . .   ________________________

   _______________                      Name, F4 for list



 F3=Exit    F4=Prompt    F12=Cancel
            |
            |Press F4 to obtain list of documents
            |__________________________________________>
```

Figure 40.4

Selection List Resulting from Prompt Dialogue Action

```
                         Select Document

Type options, press Enter.
  1=Select   5=View

Option   Document   Subject                                Revised    Type
  _      INVENTOR   Inventory for warehouse                10/22/87   DOCUMENT
  _      INVENTSM   Inventory summary                      3/24/87    DOCUMENT
  1      LETTER1    Letter to ABC CORP                     12/01/87   MEMO
  _      LETTER2    Memo to J R Scruttle                   12/03/87   MEMO
  _      LETTER6    Letter to Rundle Price                 9/5/87     MEMO
  _      LETTER7    Letter to Rundle Price                 9/5/87     MEMO
  _      MEMOJHB    Memo to J H Bottle                     10/28/87   MEMO
  _      MONTHLY    Monthly accounting summary             12/01/87   DOCUMENT
  _      MONTHLY2   Monthly accounting summary             12/01/87   DOCUMENT
  _      MONTHLYD   Monthly detail for November            12/02/87   DOCUMENT
  _      OLDMONTH   Last Month's detail - Oct              11/02/87   DOCUMENT
  _      REPORTYE   Year end report                        11/30/87   DOCUMENT
  _      REPORTYE   Year end report                        11/30/87   DOCUMENT
  _      REPORTAD   Advanced report                        9/5/87     MEMO
                                                                       More...
F12=Cancel
```

The AS/400 "Work with" list panel uses this approach in two ways. First, the panel lists objects with other information that aids recognition (e.g., an in-stock date and a text description). The users select the desired object to perform an action on. Second, a list of supported actions appears across the top of the list panel, each with its assigned numeric action option (e.g., 2=Change, 3=Copy, 4=Delete, 5=Display). The user need only recognize the desired action and key the appropriate action option next to the desired object to identify the object and the action to perform on it. Users need not key the object name or action. The action option simultaneously selects the object and the desired action.

Entry panels can also use recognition by showing the list of choices to the right of each entry field that has a small set of choices. For example:

```
Type style... __ 1=Bold 2=Elite 3=Pica
```

When the set of choices is long or varies in length (like a list of document names), users can choose the prompt dialogue action (F4) to request a list panel. By showing the list of objects to select from, this panel allows recognition and selection.

Both inexperienced and advanced users can benefit from recognize and select. It frees both user groups from having to remember or look up information they need to do their job and lets them accomplish their work easily and quickly. To give advanced users functions that match their skill level, you can use another approach, *layering*: differentiating between commonly used functions and special functions and structuring the dialogue so the special functions are not obtrusive (i.e., they are not visible on the basic panel) but are never more than a keystroke away.

Layering

The AS/400 user interface uses layering to address the reality that users frequently need only a small portion of an application's functions. The remaining functions are for special cases. For new and day-to-day users, such special-case functions can detract from an interface's simplicity and flow and can make an application difficult to learn. With layering, you can avoid these problems and streamline the user interface while providing good support for the special situations.

Let's look at some practical ways of applying layering. On a menu, you can assign unique option numbers to commonly used actions and put the options in a clear and visible position at the top of the list of choices. You can group special-case options under a single choice that follows the others. For example, a parts inventory application menu might include four common options and a fifth that provides access to a menu of special-case options. The text for the special option should clearly specify its special or restricted purpose. The main menu might include:

1. Work with parts
2. Enter part
3. Ship parts
4. Display parts inventory
5. Perform special parts inventory maintenance

Option 5 would present the Special Parts Inventory Maintenance Menu, which might contain the following options:

1. Back up parts inventory
2. Restore saved parts inventory
3. Handle lost parts
4. Print detailed parts inventory activity

On an entry panel, you can use layering by providing a function key to retrieve advanced functions and by putting only the commonly used choices on the base panel. This setup shows the new user a simple entry panel that asks the essential questions (e.g., which printer, what page spacing, how many copies, and how many pages). The experienced user can then press a function key to get advanced function prompts (e.g., special fonts, multipart paper, and special security measures) that many users do not use or understand. On the AS/400, users press the F10 key, labeled "Additional parameters," to request advanced function parameters.

On list panels, two types of layering might be appropriate: layering the columns of information and layering the actions supported. The columns of information shown initially should be the ones that meet the usual needs. You should support a function key (e.g., F11=Archive information) to provide additional columns of information that users need only occasionally. The initial set of action options across the screen top should be the commonly used actions; users can request another set of less commonly used options by pressing F23=More options.

You can layer options without regard for numbering (as OS/400 products do) to maintain numbering consistency across list panels for similar actions, regardless of whether they are general or advanced. For example, Create is a commonly used action for a document but may be an advanced action in a warehouse inventory management application. On the document list, the usual actions might be:

```
1=Create 2=Change 5=Display 6=Print
```

The less commonly used options available by pressing F23 might be:

```
4=Delete 9=Save 10=Restore
```

On an inventory list, the commonly used actions might be:

```
2=Change 5=Display 6=Print
```

while the less commonly used options might be:

```
1=Create 4=Delete 9=Save 10=Restore
```

You can use the same approach for function keys in the function key area by using F24=More keys to access the other groups of active function keys.

You will likely find other application-specific situations in which you can apply layering to create an interface that efficiently supports novice, intermediate, and special advanced users. To assist users who use deeper levels of your interface, you can support fastpaths.

Fastpaths

In contrast to layering, which helps the novice and occasional user, fastpaths let the experienced user move directly to a desired action or object. Besides providing speed, fastpaths can prevent frustration by letting experienced users avoid intermediate steps. Fastpaths can take various forms.

One form is a shortcut for handling a portion of the task the user is currently working on. An example is letting users key the name of an object rather then making them scroll to it. The input-capable top list entry on some AS/400 list panels uses this method.

Another example is supporting the direct entry of a qualifying option to bypass prompting for it. This method is sometimes referred to as "answer ahead." Some AS/400 Work-with panels support a "Parameters or command" field that gives users the answer-ahead option. When the user keys an option next to a list entry that usually requires an entry panel to finish the specification, the user can key the values into the "Parameters or command" field in command syntax and bypass the entry panel.

Another form of fastpath is one for requesting a new function. One example is letting users request a task by means of a command line on an application panel without having to exit the current function or application. In the midst of working on a function that requires a file of data, the user can enter a CPYF (Copy File) command to copy an existing file.

A further example is letting the user go directly to a particular menu by entering its name, rather than going through a sequence of menus. The Go command supports this fastpath (e.g., Go MYOFFICE takes the user directly to the menu entitled MYOFFICE).

You can support a function key to provide a fastpath to commonly needed functions. For example, in the Interactive Data Definition Utility (IDDU), F22 allows easy movement from Work with Data Base Files to Work with Data Dictionaries.

With a fastpath, users can interrupt the current task to do something else, rather than having to exit the application, do the task, and then return. In your application, you can define an Attention key program users can invoke by pressing the Attention key. This program can support common application functions, such as query inventory or checking a calendar, that users frequently need while working with the application.

Providing a Context for the User

No matter how users get to a function, it is important that you give them enough contextual information to let them know that they have arrived at the function they wanted. You can accommodate users of all skill levels by making sure they always know where they are in an application and how to navigate to where they want to go. You can provide confirmation with such "where-am-I" information in several ways.

One way is to make sure the title of the current panel corresponds to the text of the selected action, whether a menu option, list panel action option, or function key. Another way is to be certain the panel ID in the upper left corner of a menu corresponds to the name users can give the Go command to get to the menu (e.g., Go MYOFFICE). Menu bars provide yet another way of providing context to the user. The available options are listed in the menu bar while the contents of the screen remain visible below the menu bar.

A further way to provide confirmation is to ensure that identifying information appears below the title in the information area and to give the source of the information and any necessary criteria. For example, to display the contents of a particular area of a warehouse, the panel title and information area shown in Figure 40.5 could appear.

An additional way is to use a pop-up window over the base panel when a step is meaningful only in the context of the base panel. This approach keeps the

Figure 40.5

Sample Panel Title and Information Area

```
                         Warehouse Inventory

Warehouse:  ELKGROVE    Area: A15    Part type: Barrels
```

background information in view while focusing the user on a subtask within that context. An example is the spellcheck function in the AS/400 Office document editor. A pop-up window of alternative spellings, instead of a new full panel, appears next to the misspelled word. In this way, context is maintained, and the misspelled word need not be repeated in the window because the word is still visible and highlighted. A recent update to the QUSRTOOL library contains a windows function that shows how to do such windowing in Data Description Specifications (DDS).

When users feel secure that they can find their way around in an interface, know where they are, and understand what the interface presents to them, the users are more comfortable with the application. By encouraging a feeling of confidence, you can help users to be more productive.

Grouping

Another way to help users of all skill levels is by using *grouping*: presenting related pieces of information in groups. The AS/400 interface uses grouping to make the interface easy to understand by helping the user associate like items and learn them as a group, rather than having to learn each item individually. Users more easily remember groups, which are fewer in number, than individual items.

Two ways of communicating grouping are alignment and separation. By aligning columns of like items and using blank lines to separate groups of items, you can take advantage of both methods to communicate relationships, clarify function, and facilitate scanning.

You can find several examples of grouping on the AS/400. On entry panels, a separate column aligns the prompts, entry fields, and descriptive text and makes these elements stand out as distinct from each other. Blank separator lines separate contextual information, instructional information, data, and function-key descriptions on all panel types. In addition, blank lines separate and align groups of entry fields or menu options within the panel body area, so these fields or options stand out and users can quickly scan them. (See Figure 40.3 for a sample entry panel.)

Menu bars and pull-down menus are examples of EUI graphical elements that take advantage of the grouping principle. The major categories of function are displayed on the menu bar, while pull-down menus group together the functions that are related to each area. Selecting an option from the menu bar displays a pull-down menu that contains all of the related actions for that option conveniently grouped together.

The design approaches to the AS/400 user interface discussed in this chapter provide a foundation on which you can build your applications' interfaces to make them consistent with other AS/400 software, new PS/2 software, and with the future direction of IBM Systems Application Architecture (SAA) systems. You will be able to extend such consistency to comply with new methods of interaction as CUA grows and as new SAA tools are provided.

Chapter 41

Creating Standard AS/400 Panels

by Carson Soule

Use Data Description Specifications to create AS/400-compliant menu panels

In Chapter 40, J. H. Botterill explains how to design entry and information panels so they comply to AS/400 standards. In this chapter, I supply the DDS for creating these two panel types so you can implement the AS/400 standard quickly and easily in your shop.

Menu Panels

A menu panel is the first one users typically see after they sign on and the last panel to appear before they sign off. A menu is also the first panel most applications display. Because menus are so prominent, menu panel design is a key part of the Common User Access (CUA) component of Systems Application Architecture (SAA). Consequently, if you want to make your applications' user interfaces comply with CUA standards and resemble AS/400 interface panels, the first step might be to model your menu panels on CUA standards.

On the AS/400, you can choose among three ways of creating programmer-defined native menus. You can use the Screen Design Aid (SDA) facility to create your menu's message and display files automatically; you can create your own message and display files (either through SDA or directly from the Data Description Specifications — DDS); or you can write your own menu driver programs.

When you use AS/400 native SDA's Design Menus option to create a menu panel, the system generates the source code for the menu in two members in the source file QMENUSRC. The first member contains (in the form of S/36 SFGR (Screen Format Generator) specifications) the display file (i.e., a definition of the menu panel as it will appear on the screen). The second member contains (in the format of a S/36 message member) the commands that execute when a user makes a menu selection (i.e., the command text). The system gives both members the same name as the menu, but the second member's name has a suffix of QQ. (Note that the S/36 environment uses the same naming conventions, but the names are followed by ##.)

With menus SDA creates, the system puts the DDS for the display file into the QTEMP library in a file named DDSmenuname. (For an example of the DDS the SDA Design Menus option creates, see Figure 41.1.) From there, the DDS is compiled into a display file with the same name as the menu. The system uses the command text to create a message file with the same name as the menu and then executes the CRTMNU (Create Menu) command to create the menu.

The system can prompt the CRTMNU command, and several options are available for menu panels. One option lets you select a short command line instead of the default long line. Another option lets you choose whether or not to display function keys. Note that the SDA default is to display function keys, but the CRTMNU command defaults to nondisplay.

You can use the GO (Go to Menu) command from any command line to display the menu. However, for the menu to be displayed, the menu object, the display file, and the message file must all exist.

The second way to create programmer-defined native menus is by first using system commands instead of the SDA Design Menus option to create a display file and a message file and then executing the CRTMNU command. You can create the display file through SDA or directly through DDS. The panel must have the same name as the display file and should define only lines 1 through 20 to leave room for the message, function key, and command areas at the bottom of the screen. Chapter 10 of the *Control Language Programmer's Guide* (SC41-8077) provides a detailed description of the DDS and message file rules.

The third alternative for creating a menu is to write a program that displays the menu and handles the menu requests and the optional command line. OS/400 menus support several features not available to menus you create from display files (e.g., support for F23, which you press to designate a particular menu as the base menu; system-name display on the title line; subfile processing for multiple pages of menu options; and option numbers greater than 24). Thus, the only way you can implement your own OS/400-consistent menu panel is to write a program. You use the CRTMNU command to create a menu and specify the type *PGM. Then you use the GO command, which determines that the menu is type *PGM and calls your menu-driver program.

By creating a program menu, you can bypass the system menu driver and thus have complete control over your menu. For example, you can omit a command line in favor of a selection field and support subfiles to allow more than 12 menu options in one column. You can also provide special command keys to suit your application.

You should create a *PGM-type menu to call menu-driver programs that you write on the AS/400. This way, you can access your program menus with the GO command. For information about the parameters the GO command passes to your program, see the CRTMNU command in the *Control Language Reference* and the *CL Programmer's Guide*, Chapter 10.

Figure 41.1

DDS for SDA Design Menus Option

```
*... ... 1 ... ... 2 ... ... 3 ... ... 4 ... ... 5 ... ... 6 ... ... 7 ... ... 8 ...

     A*ØIGC ØDS4
     A                                      DSPSIZ(*DS3 *DS4)
     A                                      USRDSPMGT CHGINPDFT INDARA
     A* FREE  FORM MENU
     A                                      PRINT(QSYSPRT)
     A          R NWSATN
     A                                      DSPMOD(*DS3)
     A                                      LOCK
     A                                      SLNO(Ø1)
     A                                      CLRL(*ALL)
     A                                      ALWROL
     A                                      CFØ3
     A                                      HELP HOME
     A                                      HLPRTN
     A            WSID           2    0 Ø1Ø78
     A            MNUID         1Ø    0 Ø1ØØ2
     A                                 Ø1Ø2Ø'NEWS 3X/4ØØ Attention Key Menu    -
     A                                           '
     A                                      DSPATR(HI)
     A                                 19ØØ2'Selection or command'
     A                                 Ø3ØØ2'Select one of the following:'
     A                                 Ø5ØØ7'1.'
     A                                 Ø5Ø11'Work with your spool files (WRKSPL-
     A                                      F)'
     A                                 Ø6ØØ7'2.'
     A                                 Ø6Ø11'Work with a printer''s spool files-
     A                                       (WRKSPLF SELECT(*ALL printer))'
     A                                 Ø7ØØ7'3.'
     A                                 Ø7Ø11'Work with your jobs (WRKUSRJOB)'
     A                                 Ø8ØØ7'4.'
     A                                 Ø8Ø11'Work with a job queue (WRKJOBQ)'
     A                                 Ø9ØØ7'5.'
     A                                 Ø9Ø11'Display your job log (DSPJOBLOG)'
     A                                 1ØØØ7'6.'
     A                                 1ØØ11'Display your messages (DSPMSG)'
     A                                 11ØØ7'7.'
     A                                 11Ø11'Display system inquiry messages (D-
     A                                      SPMSG *SYSOPR MSGTYPE(*INQ))'
     A                                 12ØØ7'8.'
     A                                 12Ø11'Work with active jobs (WRKACTJOB)'
     A                                 14ØØ6'12.'
     A                                 14Ø11'End Job (SIGNOFF *NOLIST)'
     A          R #HØØØØ
     A                                      DSPMOD(*DS3)
     A                                      LOCK
     A                                      SLNO(Ø1)
     A                                      CLRL(*ALL)
     A                                      ALWROL
     A                                      CFØ3
     A                                      HELP HOME
     A                                      HLPRTN
     A            WSID           2    0 Ø1Ø78
     A            MNUID         1Ø    0 Ø1ØØ2
     A                                 Ø1Ø2Ø'NEWS 3X/4ØØ Attention Key Menu Hel-
     A                                      p Text'
     A                                      DSPATR(HI)
```

Figure 41.1 Continued

Figure 41.1

DDS for SDA Design Menus Option *Continued*

```
*... ... 1 ... ... 2 ... ... 3 ... ... 4 ... ... 5 ... ... 6 ... ... 7 ... ... 8 ...
     A                                  03001'Help test for the entire menu.'
     A                                  03033'This help text will be displayed w-
     A                                       hen the HELP'
     A                                  04001'key is pressed and a valid option -
     A                                       is not on the command line.'
     A          R #H0101
     A                                       DSPMOD(*DS3)
     A                                       LOCK
     A                                       SLNO(01)
     A                                       CLRL(*ALL)
     A                                       ALWROL
     A                                       CF03
     A                                       HELP HOME
     A                                       HLPRTN
     A            WSID           2    0 01078
     A            MNUID         10    0 01002
     A                                  01020'NEWS 3X/400 Attention Key Menu Hel-
     A                                       p Text'
     A                                       DSPATR(HI)
     A                                  03001'Option 1.'
     A                                  03012'Work with your spool files (WRKSPL-
     A                                       F).'
     A                                  03051'This option will display all'
     A                                  04001'spool files created with your user-
     A                                        ID.'
     A                                  04041'It calls the system command WRKSPL-
     A                                       F.'
     A                                  05001'For help with the WRKSPLF command,-
     A                                        key WRKSPLF on the command line an-
     A                                       d press'
     A                                  06001'help.'
     A          R #H0202
     A                                       DSPMOD(*DS3)
     A                                       LOCK
     A                                       SLNO(01)
     A                                       CLRL(*ALL)
     A                                       ALWROL
     A                                       CF03
     A                                       HELP HOME
     A                                       HLPRTN
     A            WSID           2    0 01078
     A            MNUID         10    0 01002
     A                                  01020'NEWS 3X/400 Attention Key Menu Hel-
     A                                       p Text'
     A                                       DSPATR(HI)
     A                                  03001'Option 2.'
     A                                  03012'Work with a printers spool files.'
     A                                  03047'This option will display all of'
     A                                  04001'the spool files created with your -
     A                                       user ID.'
     A                                  04045'It calls the system command WRKSPL-
     A                                       F selecting spool files for all use-
     A                                       rs on the OUTQ for printer PRT01.'
     A                                  05069'A command'
     A                                  06001'prompt screen is displayed to allo-
     A                                       w you to override the printer name.'
     A                                  06072'For help with the WRKSPLF command,-
```

Figure 41.1 Continued

Figure 41.1

DDS for SDA Design Menus Option *Continued*

```
*... ... 1 ... ... 2 ... ... 3 ... ... 4 ... ... 5 ... ... 6 ... ... 7 ... ... 8 ...
     A                                            key WRKSPLF on the command line an-
     A                                          d press help.'
     A          R #H0303
     A                                          DSPMOD(*DS3)
     A                                          LOCK
     A                                          SLNO(01)
     A                                          CLRL(*ALL)
     A                                          ALWROL
     A                                          CF03
     A                                          HELP HOME
     A                                          HLPRTN
     A            WSID           2    0 01078
     A            MNUID         10    0 01002
     A                                      01020'NEWS 3X/400 Attention Key Menu Hel-
     A                                          p Text'
     A                                          DSPATR(HI)
     A                                      03001'Option 3.'
     A                                      03012'Work with your jobs (WRKUSRJOB).'
     A                                      03046'This option will display jobs on'
     A                                      04001'the system initiated with your use-
     A                                          r ID.'
     A                                      04042'This includes your current interac-
     A                                          tive job(s), submitted or evoked jo-
     A                                          bs and completed jobs with printed -
     A                                          output still on a spool file.'
     A                                      06016'This option calls the system comma-
     A                                          nd WRKUSRJOB.'
     A                                      06067'For help with the WRKUSRJOB comman-
     A                                          d, key WRKUSRJOB on the command lin-
     A                                          e and press help.'
     A          R #H0404
     A                                          DSPMOD(*DS3)
     A                                          LOCK
     A                                          SLNO(01)
     A                                          CLRL(*ALL)
     A                                          ALWROL
     A                                          CF03
     A                                          HELP HOME
     A                                          HLPRTN
     A            WSID           2    0 01078
     A            MNUID         10    0 01002
     A                                      01020'NEWS 3X/400 Attention Key Menu Hel-
     A                                          p Text'
     A                                          DSPATR(HI)
     A                                      03001'Option 4.'
     A                                      03012'Work with a job queue (WRKJOBQ).'
     A                                      03046'This option will display jobs on'
     A                                      04001'the QBATCH job queue.'
     A                                      04024'This does not include jobs that ar-
     A                                          e currently executing. A command pr-
     A                                          ompt screen is displayed to allow y-
     A                                          ou to override the job queue to'
     A                                      06001'be displayed.'
     A                                      06016'This option calls the system comma-
     A                                          nd WRKJOBQ.'
     A                                      06063'For help with the WRKUSRJOB comman-
     A                                          d, key WRKUSRJOB on the command lin-
```

Figure 41.1 Continued

Figure 41.1

DDS for SDA Design Menus Option *Continued*

```
*... ... 1 ... ... 2 ... ... 3 ... ... 4 ... ... 5 ... ... 6 ... ... 7 ... ... 8 ...
     A                                          e and press help.'
     A          R #H0505
     A                                          DSPMOD(*DS3)
     A                                          LOCK
     A                                          SLNO(01)
     A                                          CLRL(*ALL)
     A                                          ALWROL
     A                                          CF03
     A                                          HELP HOME
     A                                          HLPRTN
     A            WSID           2    0 01078
     A            MNUID         10    0 01002
     A                                      01020'NEWS 3X/400 Attention Key Menu Hel-
     A                                          p Text'
     A                                          DSPATR(HI)
     A                                      03001'Option 5.'
     A                                      03012'Display your job log (DSPJOBLOG).'
     A                                      03047'This option will display your'
     A                                      04001'job''s log.'
     A                                      04013'This includes messages generated b-
     A                                          y your job since you signed on.'
     A                                      05001'By pressing F10, you can see the -
     A                                          low level messages generated by you-
     A                                          r job.'
     A                                      06001'This option calls the system comma-
     A                                          nd DSPJPBLOG.'
     A                                      06052'For help with the DSPJOBLOG'
     A                                      07001'command, key DSPJOBLOG on the comm-
     A                                          and line and press help.'
     A          R #H0606
     A                                          DSPMOD(*DS3)
     A                                          LOCK
     A                                          SLNO(01)
     A                                          CLRL(*ALL)
     A                                          ALWROL
     A                                          CF03
     A                                          HELP HOME
     A                                          HLPRTN
     A            WSID           2    0 01078
     A            MNUID         10    0 01002
     A                                      01020'NEWS 3X/400 Attention Key Menu Hel-
     A                                          p Text'
     A                                          DSPATR(HI)
     A                                      03001'Option 6.'
     A                                      03012'Display your messages (DSPMSG).'
     A                                      03045'This option will display your'
     A                                      04001'messages.'
     A                                      04012'This includes messages sent to you-
     A                                          r user ID and messages sent to'
     A                                      05001'your workstation.'
     A                                      05020'By pressing F13, you can remove th-
     A                                          e messages from the queue. This opt-
     A                                          ion calls the system command DSPMSG-
     A                                          .'
     A                                      06049'For help with the DSPMSG'
     A                                      07001'command, key DSPMSG on the command-
     A                                            line and press help.'
```

Figure 41.1 Continued

Figure 41.1

DDS for SDA Design Menus Option *Continued*

```
*... ... 1 ... ... 2 ... ... 3 ... ... 4 ... ... 5 ... ... 6 ... ... 7 ... ... 8 ...
     A          R #H0707
     A                                          DSPMOD(*DS3)
     A                                          LOCK
     A                                          SLNO(01)
     A                                          CLRL(*ALL)
     A                                          ALWROL
     A                                          CF03
     A                                          HELP HOME
     A                                          HLPRTN
     A            WSID           2    0 01078
     A            MNUID         10    0 01002
     A                                     01020'NEWS 3X/400 Attention Key Menu Hel-
     A                                          p Text'
     A                                          DSPATR(HI)
     A                                     03001'Option 7.'
     A                                     03012'Display system inquiry messages (D-
     A                                          SPMSG).'
     A                                     03055'This option will display'
     A                                     04001'all inquiry messages on the QSYSOP-
     A                                          R message queue.'
     A                                     04053'This option calls the system comman-
     A                                          d DSPMSG.'
     A                                     05020'For help with the DSPMSG command, -
     A                                          key DSPMSG on the command'
     A                                     06001'line and press help.'
     A          R #H0808
     A                                          DSPMOD(*DS3)
     A                                          LOCK
     A                                          SLNO(01)
     A                                          CLRL(*ALL)
     A                                          ALWROL
     A                                          CF03
     A                                          HELP HOME
     A                                          HLPRTN
     A            WSID           2    0 01078
     A            MNUID         10    0 01002
     A                                     01020'NEWS 3X/400 Attention Key Menu Hel-
     A                                          p Text'
     A                                          DSPATR(HI)
     A                                     03001'Option 8.'
     A                                     03012'Work with active jobs (WRKACTJOB).'
     A                                     03048'This option will display all jobs r-
     A                                          unning on the system.'
     A                                     04025'It is used to monitor system func-
     A                                          tions and'
     A                                     05001'performance.'
     A                                     05015'This option calls the system comma-
     A                                          nd WRKACTJOB.'
     A                                     05066'For help with'
     A                                     06001'the WRKACTJOB command, key WRKACTJ-
     A                                          OB on the command'
     A                                     06054'line and press help.'
     A                                     08001'WARNING:'
     A                                     08011'excessive use of this command can -
     A                                          negatively impact performance.'
```

Setting Up the Menu Panel

Fortunately, the rules for a CUA-compliant menu panel are clear. When you have chosen the method you want to use to create your menus, you will have no trouble determining how to set up the panel: You simply follow CUA rules. According to CUA, a menu panel consists of title, instruction, body, command (or alternatively, a selection field in the body area), function key, and message areas. The rules for laying out each of these areas are well defined and apply to display menus as well as program menus.

First, let's look at the DDS for a native display-file menu created through SDA. For example, the SDA Design Menus option's DDS in Figure 41.1 supports the *NEWS 3X/400* Attention key menu in Figure 41.2. Note that the record name is the same as the menu name, and user display management (USRDSPMGT) and an indicator area (INDARA) are specified as required record-level keywords for display-file menus. You should also use the LOCK keyword to prevent the keyboard from unlocking before the command line appears. The HELP and Help Return (HLPRTN) keywords support the Help function.

Following CUA rules, the panel's title area contains a panel ID, in this case the menu name, and a title. A two-character workstation ID field is defined in position 78 in keeping with the S/36 convention, but because two characters are not enough for an AS/400 workstation ID, native menus must have blanks in these fields.

Because DDS-defined menus do not support roll keys, the menu body area consists of up to 12 options in a single column, instead of the CUA standard of 99 scrollable options. As CUA dictates, you skip unused option numbers and

Figure 41.2

***NEWS 3X/400* Attention Key Menu**

```
NWSATN                 NEWS 3X/400 Attention Key Menu
Select one of the following:
      1.  Work with your spool files (WRKSPLF)
      2.  Work with a printer's spool files (WRKSPLF SELECT(*ALL printer))
      3.  Work with your jobs (WRKUSRJOB)
      4.  Work with a job queue (WRKJOBQ)
      5.  Display your job log (DSPJOBLOG)
      6.  Display your messages (DSPMSG)
      7.  Display system inquiry messages (DSPMSG *SYSOPR MSGTYPE(*INQ))
      8.  Work with active jobs (WRKACTJOB)

     12.  End Job (SIGNOFF *NOLIST)



Selection or command
===>____________________________________________
F3=Exit   F4=Prompt   F9=Retrieve   F12=Cancel
F13=User support      F16=Main menu
```

show a gap in the sequence by using a single blank line. To be consistent with OS/400 menus, you should give the End-job option the number 90. But because display file menus support only up to 24 menu options, by convention you use option 12 for End job on display file menus.

DDS-defined menus do not support subfiles for scrolling or data fields for options, so the panel body area consists of a single set of constants defined on lines 5 through 16. Line 19 contains the constant "Selection or command:" as a prompt for the command area.

You cannot define the command, function-key, and message areas in DDS. The system's menu-driver routine supplies these areas as separate panels in display file QSYS/QDSPMNU. The options are MENULN (menu with a long command line and no command area), MENUSN (short line, no command area), MENULY (long line with a command area), and MENUSY (short line with a command area). You can see the effect of defining these areas as separate panels when you press the Enter key at any menu: The command area flickers as it is redisplayed.

Help panels follow the menu panel in the DDS as separate panels named #H*xxyy*, where *xx* is the first option number and *yy* is the last option number to which the panel applies. Record #H000 is general help for the menu and is displayed when the user presses Help without selecting a menu option.

Now let's look at setting up program menus. You write your menu program and then use the CRTMNU command, specifying type *PGM. No other options are required, but you can specify the current and product libraries, which the system then automatically adds to your library list when you use the GO command to display your menu and invoke your program. The CRTMNU command creates a menu object that points to your menu-driver program. This program, which displays the menu and processes the selection and command keys, has three parameters: the menu name, the menu library name, and a return code. Activating your program menu by using the GO command invokes the menu-driver program.

The *CL Programmer's Guide* (SC41-8077) contains a sample CL program to drive a simple menu. The QUSRTOOL example tools library provides a more sophisticated menu program: member CMDLINE in file QATTINFO (For more information about QUSRTOOL, see Appendix A). Figure 41.3 shows programmer-written DDS for the menu in Figure 41.2. I selected the field names and indicators for compatibility with the program in QUSRTOOL. The record-level keyword OVERLAY prevents the screen from being cleared before the menu is displayed.

The title, instruction, and body areas are the same as in the display file menu's DDS (Figure 41.1). But with the program-menu approach, in addition to these areas, you can define the command, function key, and message areas.

The command area, with a length of 153 characters, is displayed on lines 20 and 21, starting in position 7. This definition is consistent with display-file menus that use a long command line. The CMD field is conditioned with CHECK(LC) to allow lowercase and DSPATR(PC) to position the cursor at the CMD field. (The program in QUSRTOOL uses indicator 90 to control this attribute.)

Figure 41.3

DDS for *NEWS 3X/400* Attention Key Menu

```
*... ... 1 ... ... 2 ... ... 3 ... ... 4 ... ... 5 ... ... 6 ... ... 7
     A                                      DSPSIZ(*DS3 *DS4)
     A                                      PRINT
     A          R PROMPT
     A                                      OVERLAY
     A                                      CF03(93 'Exit')
     A                                      CF04(94 'Prompt')
     A                                      CF09(99 'Retrieve')
     A                                      CF12(92 'Cancel')
     A                                      LOCK
     A                                      SLNO(01)
     A                                      CLRL(*ALL)
     A                                      ALWROL
     A                                  01002'NWSATN'
     A                                  01020'NEWS 3X/400 Attention Key Menu    -
     A                                          '
     A                                      DSPATR(HI)
     A                                  19002'Selection or command
     A                                  03002'Select one of the following:'
     A                                      COLOR(BLU)
     A                                  05007'1.'
     A                                  05011'Work with your spool files (WRKSPL-
     A                                      F)'
     A                                  06007'2.'
     A                                  06011'Work with a printer''s spool files-
     A                                         (WRKSPLF SELECT(*ALL printer))'
     A                                  07007'3.'
     A                                  07011'Work with your jobs (WRKUSRJOB)'
     A                                  08007'4.'
     A                                  08011'Work with a job queue (WRKJOBQ)'
     A                                  09007'5.'
     A                                  09011'Display your job log (DSPJOBLOG)'
     A                                  10007'6.'
     A                                  10011'Display your messages (DSPMSG)'
     A                                  11007'7.'
     A                                  11011'Display system inquiry messages (D-
     A                                      SPMSG *SYSOPR MSGTYPE(*INQ))'
     A                                  12007'8.'
     A                                  12011'Work with active jobs (WRKACTJOB)'
     A                                  14006'12.'
     A                                  14011'End Job (SIGNOFF *NOLIST)'
     A                                  1 35'Screen Title'
     A                                  19  2'Selection or command'
     A                                  20  2'--->'
     A            CMD          153   B 20  7
     A                                      CHECK(LC)
     A  90                                  DSPATR(PC)
     A                                  22  2'F3-Exit    F4-Prompt    F9-Retrieve -
     A                                      F12-Cancel'
     A                                      COLOR(BLU)
     A          R MSGSFL                    SFL
     A                                      SFLMSGRCD(24)
     A            KEYVAR                    SFLMSGKEY
     A            PGMNAM                    SFLPGMQ
     A          R MSGCTL                    SFLCTL(MSGSFL)
     A                                      SFLSIZ(2)
     A                                      SFLPAG(1)
```

Figure 41.3 Continued

Figure 41.3

DDS for *NEWS 3X/400* Attention Key Menu *Continued*

```
     A  88                                  SFLDSP
     A  88                                  SFLDSPCTL
     A  88                                  SFLEND
     A N88                                  SFLCLR
```

The function key area is on line 22. This area uses the record-level keywords CF03, CF04, CF09, and CF12 to define function keys F3=Exit, F4=Prompt, F9=Retrieve, and F12=Cancel, respectively. The function key area of the program in QUSRTOOL does not support the F13=User support or F16=Main menu function keys that appear on the display-file menu.

The message area, which is implemented as a message subfile, is displayed on line 24. Using a message subfile is consistent with display-file menus and lets the program display all messages generated by commands executed from the menu. This method also lets the program display a plus sign (+) when more messages are available to display after the first message.

You define the message subfile in the MSGSFL record. The position is line 24 in the SFLMSGRCD keyword. The program supplies the message key variable and the menu program name in fields KEYVAR and PGMNAM, respectively. These fields are associated with the subfile that contains the SFLMSGKEY and SFLPGMQ keywords, which the message subfile requires. The MSGCTL record defines the subfile control record. The keywords define the initial subfile size (SFLSIZ(2)) as two messages and the number of lines to display (SFLPAG(1)) as one.

The subfile clear keyword (SFLCLR) is conditioned on indicator 88. When the subfile control record is displayed with indicator 88 on, the message display is cleared. When indicator 88 is off, the subfile control record and the subfile are displayed. As a result, the message appears on line 24 with a plus sign (+) on the right when more messages are in the subfile.

Creating menus on the AS/400 can be confusing, because each environment's menu panels are based on different sets of underlying code. In addition, you can choose among three alternative methods just to create native menu panels. However, once you choose a method and follow CUA guidelines for panel layout, you can provide your users with a consistent interface and protect them from the confusion beneath the surface.

List Panels

List panels display a list of choices or objects. You can select an object (e.g., a document) from a displayed list and specify an action (e.g., delete) to perform on the chosen object. The AS/400 user interface uses list panels extensively.

You construct AS/400-compliant list panels, such as the sample in Figure 41.4, by using a subfile as the panel body. Figure 41.5 provides the DDS for the panel in Figure 41.4.

Figure 41.4

Sample AS/400-Compliant List Panel

```
*******************************************************************************
*                                Work with Documents                          *
*                                                                             *
* Type options (and Document), press Enter.                                   *
*   1=Create    2=Revise    3=Copy    4=Delete    5=View      6=Print         *
*                                                                             *
* Option    Document   Subject                            Revised    Type     *
*  ___      ________                                                          *
*   BB      00000000   000000000000000000000000000000     66/66/66   0000000000 *
*   BB      00000000   000000000000000000000000000000     66/66/66   0000000000 *
*   BB      00000000   000000000000000000000000000000     66/66/66   0000000000 *
*   BB      00000000   000000000000000000000000000000     66/66/66   0000000000 *
*   BB      00000000   000000000000000000000000000000     66/66/66   0000000000 *
*   BB      00000000   000000000000000000000000000000     66/66/66   0000000000 *
*   BB      00000000   000000000000000000000000000000     66/66/66   0000000000 *
*   BB      00000000   000000000000000000000000000000     66/66/66   0000000000 *
*   BB      00000000   000000000000000000000000000000     66/66/66   0000000000 *
*   BB      00000000   000000000000000000000000000000     66/66/66   0000000000 *
*   BB      00000000   000000000000000000000000000000     66/66/66   0000000000 *
*   BB      00000000   000000000000000000000000000000     66/66/66   0000000000 *
*   BB      00000000   000000000000000000000000000000     66/66/66   0000000000 *
*   BB      00000000   000000000000000000000000000000     66/66/66   0000000000 *
*                                                                             *
* F3=Exit   F4=Prompt   F5=Refresh   F12=Cancel                               *
*                                                                             *
*******************************************************************************
```

Subfiles consist of a subfile record and a subfile control record. In Figure 41.5, the SFL keyword identifies the subfile record, which defines the portion of the screen that is scrollable. The subfile must contain at least one displayable field. The fields defined in the subfile specify which line on the display is the first line of the subfile page. The subfile contains the Option field as an output/input field and the Document, Subject, Revised, and Type fields as output only. You specify these fields to display on line 8 — the subfile's first line.

The subfile record must immediately precede the subfile control record, which the SFLCTL keyword identifies. SFLCTL defines the panel title, the instruction area, and the input-capable top list entry. (The title and column headings appear in high intensity for consistency with AS/400 list panels.)

In addition, to define the subfile, the subfile control record contains several keywords: subfile size (SFLSIZ), subfile page (SFLPAG), subfile display (SFLDSP), subfile display control (SFLDSPCTL), and subfile clear (SFLCLR). (Several optional keywords for such functions as initialize, drop, roll value, line, and record number are also available.)

SFLSIZ specifies the number of records that comprise the subfile's total initial size. In Figure 41.5, SFLSIZ sets the subfile length to an expected maximum size of 14 records.

Figure 41.5

DDS for Sample AS/400-Compliant List Panel

```
.. ... 1 ... ... 2 ... ... 3 ... ... 4 ... ... 5 ... ... 6 ... ... 7 ... ... 8 ...

     A                                      DSPSIZ(24 80 *DS3)
     A                                      CHGINPDFT(UL)
     A                                      MSGLOC(24)
     A                                      PRINT

     A          R SFL                       SFL
     A                                      KEEP
     A            WOPT           2A  B  8  4TEXT('Option')
     A                                      VALUES('1' '2' '3' '4' '5' '6' ' ')
     A                                      DSPATR(HI)
     A            WDOC           8   O  8 12TEXT('Document')
     A            WSBJ          30   O  8 23TEXT('Subject')
     A            WRVSDT         6  0O  8 56TEXT('Revised')
     A                                      EDTCDE(Y)
     A            WTYP          10   O  8 67TEXT('Type')

     A          R SFLCTL                    SFLCTL(SFL)
     A                                      SFLSIZ(0014)
     A                                      SFLPAG(0014)
     A                                      CF03(03 'F3=Exit')
     A                                      CF04(04 'F4=Prompt')
     A                                      CF05(05 'F5=Refresh')
     A                                      CF12(12 'F12=Cancel')
     A                                      ROLLUP(25)
     A                                      ROLLDOWN(26)
     A                                      KEEP
     A                                      OVERLAY
     A  41                                  SFLDSP
     A N42                                  SFLDSPCTL
     A  42                                  SFLCLR
     A                                  1 31'Work with Documents'
     A                                      DSPATR(HI)
     A                                  3  2'Type options (and Document), pres-
     A                                      s Enter.'
     A                                      COLOR(BLU)
     A                                  4  4'1=Create'
     A                                      COLOR(BLU)
     A                                  4 15'2=Revise'
     A                                      COLOR(BLU)
     A                                  4 26'3=Copy'
     A                                      COLOR(BLU)
     A                                  4 35'4=Delete'
     A                                      COLOR(BLU)
     A                                  4 46'5=View'
     A                                      COLOR(BLU)
     A                                  4 58'6=Print'
     A                                      COLOR(BLU)
     A                                  6  2'Option'
     A                                      DSPATR(HI)
     A                                  6 12'Document'
     A                                      DSPATR(HI)
     A                                  6 23'Subject'
     A                                      DSPATR(HI)
     A                                  6 56'Revised'
     A                                      DSPATR(HI)
     A                                  6 67'Type'
```

Figure 41.5 Continued

Figure 41.5

DDS for Sample AS/400-Compliant List Panel *Continued*

```
.....1.......2.......3.......4.......5.......6.......7.......8...
     A                                      DSPATR(HI)
     A            WOPTT          2A  B  7  4TEXT('Option')
     A                                      DSPATR(HI)
     A                                      VALUES('1' '2' '3' '4' '5' '6' ' ')
     A            WDOCT          8A  B  7 12TEXT('Document')
     A                                      DSPATR(HI)
     A  60                                  ERRMSG('Object already exists as do-
     A                                      cument.' 60)

     A          R CMDLIN
     A            WSFEND         7   O 22 70TEXT('More... / Bottom')
     A                                      DSPATR(HI)
     A                                 23  2'F3=Exit'
     A                                      COLOR(BLU)
     A                                 23 12'F4=Prompt'
     A                                      COLOR(BLU)
     A                                 23 24'F5=Refresh'
     A                                      COLOR(BLU)
     A                                 23 37'F12=Cancel'
     A                                      COLOR(BLU)
```

SFLPAG determines the number of records you can display at one time. In Figure 41.5, SFLPAG sets the subfile page at 14 lines, so the subfile displays on lines 8 through 21.

SFLDSP determines when the application displays the subfile record. SFLDSP is conditioned on an indicator. Following IBM's requirements, when this indicator (in this example, indicator 41) is on, the subfile is displayed.

The subfile display control (SFLDSPCTL) and subfile clear (SFLCLR) keywords are conditioned on indicator 42 in Figure 41.5. As IBM prescribes, when the designated indicator (here, 42) is on, the subfile is cleared and the subfile control record is not displayed. When the indicator is off, the subfile control record is displayed.

You describe the command and function key areas in the record format CMDLIN. This format also includes a field to contain the words "Bottom" or "More...", depending on whether more objects are available for display. The program must supply this field instead of using the standard subfile end (SFLEND) keyword, which uses a plus sign (instead of "More...") to indicate that additional subfile records are available. It is possible to use the AS/400 standards "Bottom" and "More..." only if you bypass much of the subfile's automatic roll handling. To ensure that "Bottom" and "More..." appear at the correct times and that control returns to your program, it must clear the subfile and determine what records to display when the users press the roll keys.

To help you create AS/400-compliant list panels, Figure 41.6 shows the DDS for the *pro forma* list panel shown in Figure 41.7. This example contains the standard options and generic fields for the subfile record. A separate record supplies the "Bottom" and "More." You can quickly copy this DDS and modify it

Figure 41.6

DDS for *Pro Forma* List Panel

```
.. ... 1 ... ... 2 ... ... 3 ... ... 4 ... ... 5 ... ... 6 ... ... 7 ... ... 8 ...

     A                                      DSPSIZ(24 80 *DS3)
     A                                      CHGINPDFT(UL)
     A                                      MSGLOC(24)
     A                                      PRINT

     A          R SFL                       SFL
     A                                      KEEP
     A            WOPT           2A  B  8  4TEXT('Option')
     A                                      VALUES('1' '2' '3' '4' '5' '6' '7' -
     A                                      '8' ' ')
     A                                      DSPATR(HI)
     A            WOBJ           8   O  8 12TEXT('Object')
     A            WCLM          52   O  8 24TEXT('Columns')

     A          R SFLCTL                    SFLCTL(SFL)
     A                                      SFLSIZ(0200)
     A                                      SFLPAG(0011)
     A                                      CF03(03 'F3-Exit')
     A                                      CF04(04 'F4-Prompt')
     A                                      CF05(05 'F5-Refresh')
     A                                      CF12(12 'F12-Cancel')
     A                                      ROLLUP(25)
     A                                      ROLLDOWN(26)
     A                                      KEEP
     A                                      OVERLAY
     A  41                                  SFLDSP
     A N42                                  SFLDSPCTL
     A  42                                  SFLCLR
     A                                  1 32'Center Title Here'
     A                                      DSPATR(HI)
     A                                  3  2'Type options (and Object), press -
     A                                      Enter.'
     A                                      COLOR(BLU)
     A                                  4  4'1-Create'
     A                                      COLOR(BLU)
     A                                  4 15'2-Change'
     A                                      COLOR(BLU)
     A                                  4 26'3-Copy'
     A                                      COLOR(BLU)
     A                                  4 35'4-Delete'
     A                                      COLOR(BLU)
     A                                  4 46'5-Display'
     A                                      COLOR(BLU)
     A                                  4 58'6-Print'
     A                                      COLOR(BLU)
     A                                  4 68'7-Rename'
     A                                      COLOR(BLU)
     A                                  5  4'8-Detail'
     A                                      COLOR(BLU)
     A                                  6  2'Option'
     A                                      DSPATR(HI)
     A                                  6 12'Object'
     A                                      DSPATR(HI)
     A                                  6 24'Column fields'
     A                                      DSPATR(HI)
     A            WOPTT          2A  B  7  4TEXT('Option')
```

Figure 41.6 Continued

Figure 41.6

DDS for *Pro Forma* List Panel *Continued*

```
.. ... 1 ... ... 2 ... ... 3 ... ... 4 ... ... 5 ... ... 6 ... ... 7 ... ... 8 ...
     A                                          DSPATR(HI)
     A            WOBJT          8A  B  7 12TEXT('Object')
     A                                          DSPATR(HI)
     A  60                                      ERRMSG('Object already exists.' 60)

     A          R CMDLIN
     A            WSFEND         7   O 22 69DSPATR(HI)
     A                                 23  2'F3-Exit'
     A                                      COLOR(BLU)
     A                                 23 12'F4-Prompt'
     A                                      COLOR(BLU)
     A                                 23 24'F5-Refresh'
     A                                      COLOR(BLU)
     A                                 23 37'F12-Cancel'
     A                                      COLOR(BLU)
```

Figure 41.7

***Pro Forma* List Panel**

```
*****************************************************************************
*                              Center Title Here                            *
*                                                                           *
*  Type options, (and Object), press Enter.                                 *
*    1-Create   2-Change   3-Copy   4-Delete   5-Display   6-Print   7-Rename *
*    8-Detail                                                               *
*  Option    Object      Column fields                                      *
*                                                                           *
*    BB      00000000    0000000000000000000000000000000000000000000000000  *
*    BB      00000000    0000000000000000000000000000000000000000000000000  *
*    BB      00000000    0000000000000000000000000000000000000000000000000  *
*    BB      00000000    0000000000000000000000000000000000000000000000000  *
*    BB      00000000    0000000000000000000000000000000000000000000000000  *
*    BB      00000000    0000000000000000000000000000000000000000000000000  *
*    BB      00000000    0000000000000000000000000000000000000000000000000  *
*    BB      00000000    0000000000000000000000000000000000000000000000000  *
*    BB      00000000    0000000000000000000000000000000000000000000000000  *
*    BB      00000000    0000000000000000000000000000000000000000000000000  *
*    BB      00000000    0000000000000000000000000000000000000000000000000  *
*    BB      00000000    0000000000000000000000000000000000000000000000000  *
*    BB      00000000    0000000000000000000000000000000000000000000000000  *
*    BB      00000000    0000000000000000000000000000000000000000000000000  *
*                                                                           *
*  F3-Exit   F4-Prompt   F5-Refresh   F12-Cancel                            *
*                                                                           *
*****************************************************************************
```

to create list panels for your own applications. Simply supply a title, correct the optional values, and define the actual columns and their headings. You can use Screen Design Aid (SDA) to modify the DDS records and make these adjustments easily.

Entry Panels

Entry panels are one of the most ubiquitous panel types on the AS/400. Entry panels let users enter values, selections, and data and are where data entry occurs. Like AS/400 menu and list panels, entry panels comprise five panel areas: title, instruction, body, function key, and message.

To create the display file for an entry panel, invoke the CRTDSPF (Create Display File) command with RSTDSP(*YES) if you want to save the display file when another display file suspends it. A *YES value lets the user display a second file and then restore the first file (e.g., lets a user request a help panel from an entry panel and then return to the entry panel). To define each component of an entry panel, such as the Specify Print Options panel in Figure 41.8, use Data Description Specifications (DDS).

You code the title, instruction, descriptive text, and function key definitions as constants. Define the input-capable areas (i.e., the entry and selection fields) as fields supplied by the program using the display file. You can use DDS or the program to edit the data the user enters (e.g., if the user enters an option the program doesn't allow, the program or DDS recognizes the error and returns a message to the user). When you want to make a second panel available (e.g., when more options are available than will fit on one panel), condition the "More..." prompt (on the lower right side of the panel) on an indicator.

DDS for the Specify Print Options panel is shown in Figure 41.9. Format-level keywords (e.g., CA03 for F3=Exit) define the function keys available from this panel. Notice that in DDS a CFnn keyword indicates that data is returned to the program when the user presses the function key. A CAnn keyword indicates that

Figure 41.8

Specify Print Options Panel

```
                         Specify Print Options

 Type choices, press Enter.

   Document name . . . . .   __________    Name, F4 for list

   Type style  . . . . . .   _             1=Prestige Elite (12 pitch)
                                           2=Courier (10 pitch)
                                           3=Essay Standard
 4=Essay Bold

   Margin  . . . . . . . .   __            Number of spaces from left
                                           edge of paper (1-20)

   Copies  . . . . . . . .   __            Number of copies (1-99)

   Duplex  . . . . . . . .   _             Y=Yes (print both sides)
                                           N=No (print one side only)
                                                                More...

 F3=Exit   F4=Prompt   F10=Additional parameters   F12=Cancel
```

no data is returned to the program when the user presses the function key. For example, CA03 is the standard F3=Exit. Data is not returned when the user presses this key.

In this DDS, keywords also assign mnemonic indicators to function keys. The user who presses F3 sets on indicator 03, which is much easier for programmers to remember than F3 setting on the default indicator KC that DDS assigns.

CUA conventions recommend assigning standard functions to the function keys (e.g., F3 is Exit, F4 is Prompt), but CUA does not suggest which type of keyword to use (CAnn or CFnn) for a given function key, nor does it advocate any particular indicator usage. These decisions are left to the programmer.

Keywords ROLLUP and ROLLDOWN enable the roll keys, which always return to the program data the user enters. The record-level keyword put override (PUTOVR) is used with the field-level keywords override data (OVRDTA) and override attributes (OVRATR). When the panel is displayed and the user has keyed in data, PUTOVR tells the system to resend to the screen only the fields with new information. For example, if a user keys "4" in the "Type style" field, OVRDTA displays the 4. The rest of the screen remains the same. If for some reason 4 is not a valid option for this program, OVRATR highlights the field, the cursor moves to the field, and an error message is displayed. Again, the rest of the screen is not redisplayed. This technique eliminates screen flicker and reduces the amount of data sent to the workstation.

Default (DFT) is another field-level keyword used with PUTOVR. If the panel is written with no data in a field with an assigned default value, the default value is substituted.

The ERRMSG keyword provides conditioned error messages to the display. (The program sets the conditions or indicators.) If, for example, a user enters an unacceptable value in a field, the field is highlighted, the cursor moves to the field, and an error message appears. The next input operation (i.e., the next time the user presses Enter or a function key) sets off a response indicator with the same number as the conditioning indicator. The highlighting and error message disappear.

Figure 41.10 shows the DDS for the *pro forma* entry panel in Figure 41.11. The *pro forma* entry panel comprises the standard panel areas with a single field defined for entry. You can quickly copy the DDS and modify it to create entry panels for your own applications. Simply supply a title, provide the actual panel body fields and prompts, and change the function keys if necessary. You can use Screen Design Aid (SDA) to make these adjustments easily.

Information Panels

Information panels are the easiest AS/400 panels to define with DDS because they simply display information and respond when a user presses a function key. Information panels comprise four panel areas: title, instruction, body, and function key. Note that the instruction area is at the bottom of the information panel rather than in the usual position above the body text because no action is needed until after the user is finished with the information the panel presents.

Figure 41.9

DDS for Specify Print Options Panel

```
*... ... 1 ... ... 2 ... ... 3 ... ... 4 ... ... 5 ... ... 6 ... ... 7 ...

     A                                      DSPSIZ(24 80 *DS3)
     A                                      MSGLOC(24)
     A                                      PRINT
     A          R RENTRY
     A                                      BLINK
     A                                      CA03(03 'F3 - EXIT')
     A                                      CF04(04 'F4 - PROMPT')
     A                                      CF10(10 'F10 - ADDTL PARMS')
     A                                      CA12(12 'F2 - CANCEL')
     A                                      ROLLUP(25)
     A                                      ROLLDOWN(26)
     A                                      PUTOVR
     A                                  1 24'Specify Print Options'
     A                                      DSPATR(HI)
     A                                  3  2'Type choices, press Enter.'
     A                                       COLOR(BLU)
     A                                  5  4'Document name . . . . .'
     A            DOCNAM        12   B  5 30CHECK(ME)
     A                                      OVRDTA
     A                                      DSPATR(UL)
     A N61                                  DSPATR(HI)
     A  61                                  ERRMSG('Document not found.' 61)
     A                                  5 45'Name, F4 for list'
     A                                  7  4'Type style  . . . . . .'
     A            TYPSTL         1  0B  7 30OVRDTA
     A                                      EDTCDE(1)
     A                                      RANGE(1 4)
     A                                      CHECK(AB)
     A                                      CHANGE(51)
     A                                      DSPATR(UL)
     A N62                                  DSPATR(HI)
     A  62                                  ERRMSG('Invalid type style entered.-
     A                                      ' 62)
     A                                  7 45'1-Prestige Elite (12 pitch)'
     A                                  8 45'2-Courier (10 pitch)'
     A                                  9 45'3-Essay Standard'
     A                                 10 45'4-Essay Bold'
     A                                 12  4'Margin  . . . . . . . .'
     A            MARGIN         2  0B 12 30OVRDTA
     A                                      RANGE(1 20)
     A                                      DFT('6 ')
     A                                      DSPATR(UL)
     A N63                                  DSPATR(HI)
     A  63                                  ERRMSG('Invalid margin starting pos-
     A                                      ition entered.' 63)
     A                                 12 45'Number of spaces from left'
     A                                 13 47'edge of paper (1-20)'
     A                                 15  4'Copies  . . . . . . . .'
     A            COPIES         2  0B 15 30OVRDTA
     A                                      RANGE(1 99)
     A                                      DFT('1 ')
     A                                      DSPATR(UL)
     A N64                                  DSPATR(HI)
     A  64                                  ERRMSG('Invalid number of copies se-
     A                                      lected.' 64)
     A                                 15 45'Number of copies (1-99)'
```

Figure 41.9 Continued

Figure 41.9

DDS for Specify Print Options Panel *Continued*

```
A                                       17  4'Duplex . . . . . . . . .'
A              DUPLEX          1    B 17 30OVRDTA
A                                           VALUES('Y' 'N')
A                                           DFT('Y')
A                                           DSPATR(UL)
A N65                                       DSPATR(HI)
A  65                                       ERRMSG('Invalid duplex value.' 65)
A                                       17 45'Y-Yes (print both sides)'
A                                       18 45'N-No (print one side only)'
A N41                                   19 65'More...'
A                                           OVRATR
A  41                                   20 74'Bottom'
A                                           OVRATR
A                                       21  2'F3-Exit'
A                                       21 12'F4-Prompt'
A                                       21 24'F10-Additional parameters'
A                                       21 52'F12-Cancel'
```

Figure 41.10

DDS for *Pro Forma* Entry Panel

```
*... ... 1 ... ... 2 ... ... 3 ... ... 4 ... ... 5 ... ... 6 ... ... 7 ...

     A                                      DSPSIZ(24 80 *DS3)
     A                                      MSGLOC(24)
     A                                      PRINT
     A          R RENTRY
     A                                      BLINK
     A                                      CA03(03 'F3 - EXIT')
     A                                      CF04(04 'F4 - PROMPT')
     A                                      CA12(12 'F2 - CANCEL')
     A                                      ROLLUP(25)
     A                                      ROLLDOWN(26)
     A                                      PUTOVR
     A                                  1 28'Center Title Here'
     A                                      DSPATR(HI)
     A                                  3  2'Type choices, press Enter.'
     A                                        COLOR(BLU)
     A                                  5  4'Entry field prompt  . .'
     A            ENTFLD        10   B  5 28CHECK(FE)
     A                                      OVRDTA
     A                                      DSPATR(UL)
     A N61                                  DSPATR(HI)
     A  61                                  ERRMSG('Entry filed error.' 61)
     A                                  5 45'Entry field description'
     A                                 23  2'F3-Exit'
     A                                 23 12'F4-Prompt'
     A                                 23 24'F12-Cancel'
```

You can handle an information panel's body area in one of several ways. For example, you can format the text in paragraphs as on a help panel, in columns as on an output-only list panel, or as a fixed set of attributes for one item with a short descriptive label preceding each value.

Figure 41.11

***Pro Forma* Entry Panel**

```
                         Center Title Here

 Type choices, press Enter.

   Entry field prompt . .  __________        Entry field description








 F3=Exit   F4=Prompt   F12=Cancel
```

Figure 41.12

***Pro Forma* Information Panel**

```
                         Center Title Here

 Information field prompt . . . :









 Press Enter to continue.

 F3=Exit   F12=Cancel
```

You can construct any of these information panel types by copying the DDS of the *pro forma* information panel shown in Figure 41.12 and modifying the DDS to suit your needs. (The DDS is in Figure 41.13.) Simply supply a title and the actual panel body text, and change the function keys if necessary. You can use SDA to make these adjustments easily.

The View Document Details panel in Figure 41.14 is an example of an information panel with descriptive labels preceding text segments. DDS for the View Document Details panel appears in Figure 41.15. You code the title, instructions, field prompts, and function key descriptions as constants and define the output field areas as fields the program supplies.

Figure 41.13

DDS for *Pro Forma* Information Panel

```
*... ... 1 ... ... 2 ... ... 3 ... ... 4 ... ... 5 ... ... 6 ... ... 7 ...

     A                                    DSPSIZ(24 80 *DS3)
     A                                    MSGLOC(24)
     A                                    PRINT
     A          R RINFO
     A                                    BLINK
     A                                    CA03(03 'F3 - EXIT')
     A                                    CA12(12 'F2 - CANCEL')
     A                                    PUTOVR
     A                                1 28'Center Title Here'
     A                                    DSPATR(HI)
     A                                3  2'Information field prompt . . . :'
     A            INFFLD        10   0 3 31
     A                                    OVRDTA
     A                                    DSPATR(UL)
     A                                    DSPATR(HI)
     A                               21  2'Press Enter to continue.'
     A                                      COLOR(BLU)
     A                               23  2'F3-Exit'
     A                               23 12'F12-Cancel'
```

Figure 41.14

View Document Details Panel

```
                              View Document Details

  Document . . . . . . . . :    000000000000
  Creation date  . . . . . :    66/66/66

  Document description . . :    0000000000000000000000000000000000000000000
  Subject  . . . . . . . . :    0000000000000000000000000000000000000000000000000
0000000000
  Change formats/
    options  . . . . . . . :    000
  Authors  . . . . . . . . :    000000000000000000000  000000000000000000000
  Keywords . . . . . . . . :    0000000000000000000000000000000000000000000000000
000000000000000000000000000000000000000000000000000000000000000000000000000000
0000000000000000000000000000000000000000000000000
  Document class . . . . . :    00000000000000000
  Print as labels  . . . . :    000



   Press Enter to continue.

   F3-Exit   F12-Cancel
```

Copying the DDS and following the standards presented in Chapter 40 will ensure that your users see consistent, AS/400-compliant screens each time they face a new application.

Figure 41.15

DDS for View Document Details Panel

```
*... ... 1 ... ... 2 ... ... 3 ... ... 4 ... ... 5 ... ... 6 ... ... 7 ...

     A                                      DSPSIZ(24 80 *DS3)
     A                                      MSGLOC(24)
     A                                      PRINT
     A          R RINFO
     A                                      BLINK
     A                                      CA03(03 'F3 - EXIT')
     A                                      CA12(12 'F2 - CANCEL')
     A                                      PUTOVR
     A                                  1 30'View Document Details'
     A                                      DSPATR(HI)
     A                                  3  2'Document . . . . . . . . :'
     A            DOC           12   0  3 31TEXT('Document')
     A                                  4  2'Creation date  . . . . . :'
     A            CRTDAT         6  00  4 31TEXT('Creation date')
     A                                      EDTCDE(Y)
     A                                  6  2'Document description . . :'
     A            DOCDSC        43   0  6 31TEXT('Document description')
     A                                  7  2'Subject  . . . . . . . . :'
     A            FLD004        60   0  7 31
     A                                  9  2'Change formats/'
     A                                 10  4'options  . . . . . . . :'
     A            CHGFMT         3   0 10 31TEXT('Change formats/options')
     A                                 11  2'Authors  . . . . . . . . :'
     A            ATH1          20   0 11 31TEXT('Author 1')
     A            ATH2          20   0 11 54TEXT('Author 2')
     A                                 12  2'Keywords . . . . . . . . :'
     A            KEYWRD       180   0 12 31TEXT('Keywords')
     A                                 15  2'Document class . . . . . :'
     A            DOCCLS        16   0 15 31TEXT('Document class')
     A                                 16  2'Print as labels  . . . . :'
     A            PRTLBL         3   0 16 31TEXT('Print as labels')
     A                                 21  1'Press Enter to continue.'
     A                                      COLOR(BLU)
     A                                 23  1'F3-Exit'
     A                                 23 11'F12-Cancel'
```

Chapter 42

Efficient Workstation Programming

by Marshall Akins

The consistency of standard program routines benefits both programmers and end users

By using a standardized program structure for your workstation programs, you can speed program development, increase user efficiency, and decrease maintenance time simply through familiarity. Common structures also let you clone entire programs or important program sections. On the AS/400, one of the most frequently written workstation programs is a file maintenance program, which lets you retrieve, add (create), update, and delete a file's records. In this chapter, I discuss structured workstation programming techniques by detailing one such program.

Most file maintenance programs function similarly: The user enters a record key, and the program displays the record values. If the record does not exist, the program displays a screen that lets the user add a new record. After changing the existing record or keying data for the new record, the user presses Enter, and the program validates the input. (Input errors vary for every application — e.g., you can check that every field contains information or that the user enters five digits for the zip code.) If errors occur, the program displays appropriate messages and highlights the fields in error. When no errors occur, the program updates the database.

The best way to learn about workstation programming is to look at a real example. The program described is a seminar registration program for the Birmingham, Alabama, Midrange Users Group. You can use this sample program as a guide to writing your own file maintenance programs.

End-User Functions

To get started, let's look at the sample program from the user's point of view. The program uses a badge number as the primary key to file RGPMAS, which contains

Figure 42.1

Screen One

```
11/03/89 18:08:06            Seminar Registration                MRR0020

Badge Number: _____


Enter badge number to change, or
press Enter without a badge number to add





F3=exit
```

Figure 42.2

Screen Two in ADD Mode

```
11/03/89 18:08:12            Seminar Registration          ADD    MRR0020

Badge Number:

First Name:          ____________   Last: ____________

Company Name:        __________________________

Address Line 1:      ______________________

Address Line 2:      ______________________

City:                ______________________  State: __  Zip: _____ ____

Phone:               ___ _______


F3=exit   F12=previous screen   F16=delete record
```

registrant information. The first screen (Figure 42.1) prompts the user for a badge number. Pressing Enter without entering a badge number lets the user add a new record to the file. In this case, the program reads 0 for the badge number, and a new screen (Figure 42.2) prompts the user to enter the name, address, and phone information for the seminar attendee. The user then enters data and presses Enter. When no errors exist, the program checks the data, assigns the next available badge number to the new record, and writes the record to file RGPMAS. A message appears at the bottom of the screen indicating the record was updated, and the new badge number appears in the badge number entry. At this point, the user can change the record fields or press Enter to return to the first screen.

Figure 42.3

Second-Level Error Message

```
                    Additional Message Information

Message ID . . . . . . :   USRØØØ1        Severity . . . . . . :   Ø
Message type . . . . . :   INFO
Date sent . . . . . . . :  11/Ø3/89       Time sent  . . . . . :   1
From program . . . . . :   SNDMSG         Instruction  . . . . :   Ø
To program . . . . . . :   MRRØØ2Ø        Instruction  . . . . :   Ø

Message . . . . :   Badge number record not found.
No record was found for the badge number you entered.  If you wish
to add a new badge number, press Enter without entering a badge number.




Press Enter to continue.

F3=Exit          F1Ø=Display messages in job log          F12=Previous
```

Figure 42.4

Screen Two in UPDATE Mode

```
 11/Ø3/89 18:1Ø:18          Seminar Registration                 UPDATE
MRRØØ2Ø

 Badge Number:          77

 First Name:          BOB____________   Last: SMITH__________

 Company Name:        ABC COMPANY___________________

 Address Line 1:      P O BOX 123______________

 Address Line 2:      4567 MAPLE STREET________

 City:                SMALLTOWN________________   State: AL   Zip: 35215 123_

 Phone:               205 555-1234


 F3=exit   F12=previous screen   F16=delete record

 Record updated, press Enter or make changes
```

Figure 42.5

RGPMAS File Description

File Name: RGPMAS File Type: PHYSICAL

Field Name	Description	Bytes	Length	Type	From
RGBAGE	Badge Number	5	5.0	S	1
RGFRST	First Name	15	A	6	
RGLAST	Last Name	15	A	21	
RGCONO	Company Name	30	A	36	
RGADR1	Address Line 1	25	A	66	
RGADR2	Address Line 2	25	A	91	
RGCITY	City	25	A	116	
RGSTAT	State	2	A	141	
RGZIP	Zip Code	5	5.0	S	143
RGZIP4	Zip Plus 4	4	4.0	S	148
RGAREA	Area Code	3	3.0	S	152
RGPHON	Phone Number	7	7.0	S	155
RGFL01	Flag 1	1	A	162	
RGFL02	Flag 2	1	A	163	
RGFL03	Flag 3	1	A	164	
RGFL04	Flag 4	1	A	165	
RGFL05	Flag 5	1	A	166	
RGMTNO	Maint Number	3	3.0	S	167
RGSTS	Record Status	1	A	170	

Access Path Maint: *IMMED

RGBAGE

When the user enters a badge number on the first screen, the program looks for a record with that key. If the program does not find the record, the message "Badge number not found" appears at the bottom of the screen. The user can display more information about the error message by moving the cursor to the message and pressing the Help key to display second-level text (Figure 42.3).

When the record exists, the program retrieves and displays the record (Figure 42.4), and the user can change the record fields. After the changes, the program redisplays the record with the new data, and a message indicates that the record was updated. This screen lets the user verify the changes, and the message assures the operator that something really happened. The user can then make further changes or press Enter to return to the first screen. When the user changes a record field, the edit and update processes repeat.

The program's final function lets the user delete a record by displaying it and pressing F16. When the user presses F16, the record reappears with all of the fields protected (i.e., the user cannot change them), and a message prompts the user to press F16 again to delete the record. This confirmation lets the operator verify the record selection and the delete.

Figure 42.6

RGPMAS DDS

```
*... ... 1 ... ... 2 ... ... 3 ... ... 4 ... ... 5 ... ... 6 ... ... 7 ...

A*****************************************************************
A*  SEMINAR REGISTRATION FILE                                    *
A*****************************************************************
A
A                                      UNIQUE
A
A          R RGPREC                    TEXT('Registration record')
A
A            RGBAGE         5S 0       COLHDG('Badge' 'Number')
A                                      EDTCDE(Z)
A            RGFRST        15A         COLHDG('First' 'Name')
A            RGLAST        15A         COLHDG('Last' 'Name')
A            RGCONO        30A         COLHDG('Company' 'Name')
A            RGADR1        25A         COLHDG('Address' 'Line 1')
A            RGADR2        25A         COLHDG('Address' 'Line 2')
A            RGCITY        25A         COLHDG('City')
A            RGSTAT         2A         COLHDG('State')
A            RGZIP          5S 0       COLHDG('Zip' 'Code')
A                                      EDTCDE(Z)
A            RGZIP4         4S 0       COLHDG('Zip' 'Plus 4')
A                                      EDTCDE(Z)
A            RGAREA         3S 0       COLHDG('Area' 'Code')
A                                      EDTCDE(Z)
A            RGPHON         7S 0       COLHDG('Phone' 'Number')
A                                      EDTWRD('   -    ')
A            RGFL01         1A         COLHDG('Flag 1')
A            RGFL02         1A         COLHDG('Flag 2')
A            RGFL03         1A         COLHDG('Flag 3')
A            RGFL04         1A         COLHDG('Flag 4')
A            RGFL05         1A         COLHDG('Flag 5')
A            RGMTNO         3S 0       COLHDG('Maint' 'Number')
A                                      EDTCDE(Z)
A            RGSTS          1A         COLHDG('Record' 'Status')
A
A          K RGBAGE
```

Displaying File Records and Messages

Now that you've seen the user end of the program, let's look at what happens under the covers. RGPMAS is the database file for the registration records. Figure 42.5 shows the file's layout, and Figure 42.6 shows the DDS. This file contains all registrant information. The file's primary key is the badge number field, RGBAGE.

For this basic workstation program, I use a display file with two screen formats (shown in Figure 42.1 and Figure 42.2). A special type of subfile, called the program message queue subfile, displays error messages in two lines at the bottom of the screens. Before I talk about the subfile and the program, I will describe the display file the program uses to display the screens.

Display File MRD0020

Figure 42.7 shows the DDS for the display device file MRD0020. Lines 1 and 2 contain the file-level keywords REF and PRINT. File-level keywords are keywords that pertain to the entire file (as opposed to record-level and field-level keywords). The REF keyword specifies that the display file references physical file RGPMAS for specific variable definitions. For example, the definition for the badge number variable RGBAGE is in line 13. The R in column 29 specifies that the display file use the definition of the field RGBAGE in RGPMAS. The other file-level keyword, PRINT, lets the user print the screen with the Print key.

Lines 3 through 22 define SCREEN1 (i.e., the screen shown in Figure 42.1). The specifications define only one command key for this screen — F3 for exiting the program. This display file uses the CF*xx* keyword (*xx* can be 1 through 24) because it returns data to the program — the CA*xx* keyword does not.

The VLDCMDKEY keyword in line 5 turns on indicator 14 when the user presses a valid command key (i.e., F3 for this screen). The OVERLAY keyword lets the program display a record format without erasing the previous screen. The program uses an overlay technique to display the error message screen first and then SCREEN1 or SCREEN2. When you create a display file that uses the OVERLAY keyword, use the CRTDSPF (Create Display File) command with the RSTDSP(*YES) parameter. Coding RSTDSP(*YES) saves the display whenever the program calls another program or displays a break message. The code then restores the screen image when control returns to the program.

Lines 7 through 11 are common to both screen one and screen two. These lines display the date and time in the upper left corner of the screen, the title "Seminar Registration" in the center, and the program name in the upper right corner.

Screen one allows input only for the badge number field RGBAGE (line 13). The CHECK(RB) keyword right-adjusts the badge number in the input variable and blank fills on the left. When the user enters a badge number that does not exist, the DSPATR(RI) keyword displays the number in reverse image, and the DSPATR(PC) keyword positions the cursor at the badge-number field.

The available command key functions (line 4 for screen one and lines 24 through 26 for screen two) appear at the bottom of the screen above the error message area. This display file does not use DDS validity-checking keywords (e.g., VALUES or RANGE) because the RPG program edits the screen input.

Lines 23 through 95 define the second screen format, SCREEN2. This screen uses F3 to exit the program, F12 to exit screen two and return to screen one, and F16 to delete a record. Like screen one, this screen uses VLDCMDKEY and OVERLAY, but uses two additional keywords (CHANGE and RTNDTA) as well.

The CHANGE keyword causes the program to turn on indicator 02 when the modified data tag (MDT) is on. An MDT is an indication that the user pressed a key while the cursor was in a field (i.e., a field has probably been modified). When indicator 02 is on and the user presses Enter, the program checks the screen for errors and updates the record again. When the indicator is off, the program returns to screen one.

The RTNDTA keyword lets the RPG program perform a READ of the screen record without doing a previous write to the screen — a reREAD, if you like.

Figure 42.7

DDS for Display File MRD0020

```
*... ... 1 ... ... 2 ... ... 3 ... ... 4 ... ... 5 ... ... 6 ... ... 7 ...

0001 A                                            REF(*LIBL/RGPMAS)
0002 A                                            PRINT
0003 A          R SCREEN1
0004 A                                            CF03
0005 A                                            VLDCMDKEY(14 'VLDCMDKEY')
0006 A                                            OVERLAY
0007 A                                        1  2DATE
0008 A                                            EDTCDE(Y)
0009 A                                        1 11TIME
0010 A                                        1 31'Seminar Registration'
0011 A            PGMID         10A  O        1 74
0012 A                                        3  2'Badge Number:'
0013 A            RGBAGE    R        B        3 16CHECK(RB)
0015 A  22                                        DSPATR(RI)
0016 A  22                                        DSPATR(PC)
0017 A                                        6  2'Enter badge number to change, or'
0018 A                                        7  2'press Enter without a badge number
0019 A                                             to add'
0020 A                                       21  2'F3=exit'
0021 A
0022 A
0023 A          R SCREEN2
0024 A                                            CF03
0025 A                                            CF12
0026 A                                            CF16
0027 A                                            VLDCMDKEY(14 'VLDCMDKEY')
0028 A                                            CHANGE(02 'CHANGE')
0029 A                                            RTNDTA
0030 A                                            OVERLAY
0031 A                                        1  2DATE
0032 A                                            EDTCDE(Y)
0033 A                                        1 11TIME
0034 A                                        1 31'Seminar Registration'
0035 A            MODE           6A  O        1 67DSPATR(HI)
0036 A            PGMID         10A  O        1 74
0037 A                                        3  2'Badge Number:'
0038 A            RGBAGE    R        O        3 20
0039 A                                        5  2'First Name:'
0040 A            RGFRST    R        B        5 20
0041 A  21                                        DSPATR(MDT)
0042 A  22                                        DSPATR(RI)
0043 A  22                                        DSPATR(PC)
0044 A  33                                        DSPATR(PR)
0045 A                                        5 37'Last:'
0046 A            RGLAST    R        B        5 43
0047 A  23                                        DSPATR(RI)
0048 A  23                                        DSPATR(PC)
0049 A  33                                        DSPATR(PR)
0050 A                                        7  2'Company Name:'
0051 A            RGCONO    R        B        7 20
0052 A  24                                        DSPATR(RI)
0053 A  24                                        DSPATR(PC)
0054 A  33                                        DSPATR(PR)
```

Figure 42.7 Continued

Figure 42.7

DDS for Display File MRD0020 *Continued*

```
*... ...1 ... ...2 ... ...3 ... ...4 ... ...5 ... ...6 ... ...7 ...
A                                  9  2'Address Line 1:'
A            RGADR1    R        B  9 20
A  25                                  DSPATR(RI)
A  25                                  DSPATR(PC)
A  33                                  DSPATR(PR)
A                                 11  2'Address Line 2:'
A            RGADR2    R        B 11 20
A  26                                  DSPATR(RI)
A  26                                  DSPATR(PC)
A  33                                  DSPATR(PR)
A                                 13  2'City:'
A            RGCITY    R        B 13 20
A  27                                  DSPATR(RI)
A  27                                  DSPATR(PC)
A  33                                  DSPATR(PR)
A                                 13 48'State:'
A            RGSTAT    R        B 13 55
A  28                                  DSPATR(RI)
A  28                                  DSPATR(PC)
A  33                                  DSPATR(PR)
A                                 13 60'Zip:'
A            RGZIP     R        B 13 65CHECK(RB)
A  29                                  DSPATR(RI)
A  29                                  DSPATR(PC)
A  33                                  DSPATR(PR)
A            RGZIP4    R        B 13 71CHECK(RB)
A  30                                  DSPATR(RI)
A  30                                  DSPATR(PC)
A  33                                  DSPATR(PR)
A                                 15  2'Phone:'
A            RGAREA    R        B 15 20CHECK(RB)
A  31                                  DSPATR(RI)
A  31                                  DSPATR(PC)
A  33                                  DSPATR(PR)
A            RGPHON    R        B 15 24CHECK(RB)
A  32                                  DSPATR(RI)
A  32                                  DSPATR(PC)
A  33                                  DSPATR(PR)
A                                 21  2'F3-exit'
A                                 21 12'F12-previous screen'
A                                 21 34'F16-delete record'
A
A
A          R MSGREC                    TEXT('MESSAGE SUBFILE DATA')
A                                      SFL
A                                      SFLMSGRCD(23)
A            MSGKEY                    SFLMSGKEY
A            PGMID                     SFLPGMQ
A
A          R MSGCTL                    TEXT('MESSAGE SFL CONTROL')
A                                      OVERLAY
A                                      SFLCTL(MSGREC)
A                                      SFLSIZ(3)
A                                      SFLPAG(2)
```

Figure 42.7 Continued

Figure 42.7 **DDS for Display File MRD0020** *Continued*

```
*... ... 1 ... ... 2 ... ... 3 ... ... 4 ... ... 5 ... ... 6 ... ... 7 ...
0109 A N99                                     SFLDSP SFLDSPCTL
0110 A N99                                     SFLEND SFLINZ SFLCLR
0111 A            PGMID                        SFLPGMQ
```

Because the program uses the same variables when it reads from the registration file and from the display file, the changes the user enters on the screen are lost when the program reads the registration file for an update operation. For this reason, the program must read the screen after a read to the file. (You may find that you understand this process better when I explain the update process in the RPG program.)

Line 35 defines the variable MODE, which the program displays to indicate whether the current information is a new record ADD or an existing record UPDATE (see the upper right corner of Figure 42.2). The rest of the specifications for this record contain variables for the database record.

Each field displayed on the screen has a unique set of indicators to condition the DSPATR keywords. I set aside indicators 21 through 40 for these attributes. Indicator 33 conditions the DSPATR(PR) keyword, which protects all the fields from changes when the user presses F16. When a field's indicator for DSPATR(RI) and DSPATR(PC) is on (i.e., when an error in a field occurs), the field appears in reverse image, and the cursor is positioned on the field. Although the RPG program does not error-check every field, I use an indicator on every input-capable field. This technique saves maintenance time later if I need to edit the fields.

If the user doesn't notice the screen's error indications and presses Enter, the program redisplays the screen and the error message. This redisplay simply ensures that the user notices errors (the user must press a command key to exit a screen with an error). This technique works by turning on the DSPATR(MDT) keyword for RGFRST, the first name field (you can use DSPATR(MDT) for any field). The MDT forces the program to act as though the screen were modified each time the user presses Enter (i.e., the program checks for errors, highlights the error, and displays the error messages). In other words, the technique forces a recheck of any input whenever the program reads the screen after an error.

The Program Message Queue Subfile

A program message queue subfile is an easy way to display error messages. A message queue exists for each program you call, and the program message queue subfile enables you to send messages from a message file to that message queue. The system can also send messages to the message queue for such things as record locks, duplicate keys, and division by zero.

Using a program message queue subfile to display program error messages has many advantages over using an array or the ERRMSG keyword. For instance, you can define the subfile and message file once and use them for many programs. The message file is a reusable system object, and you simply have to clone the subfile code. Reusing both the message file and the subfile simplifies subsequent program coding and gives consistency to your error messages. Another advantage is that you can easily insert variable data into the messages to make them more meaningful to the users. You can also provide second-level text for descriptive information about the message. And finally, a program can send all messages to the screen at once, letting the user scroll through a set of messages and correct them at one time.

I define the subfile in the DDS with the other record formats. To display messages, the program copies the program error messages into the subfile and displays the subfile on the screen.

Lines 98 through 111 in Figure 42.7 compose the subfile. The 10-character variable PGMID is for the name of the program using the subfile. The SFLMSGRCD keyword (line 100) specifies the first line on which the messages appear, and the SFLPAG keyword specifies how many lines appear. SFLSIZ (subfile size) should be one greater than SFLPAG. This is a standard subfile convention that lets the subfile allocate as much space as it needs to display the messages. Thus, the subfile can send all messages to the message queue at once. If you set SFLSIZ equal to SFLPAG, the system only sends the number of records you indicate in SFLSIZ.

Although this code may look complicated, remember that you only need to write it once. After you define your first file with these specifications, you merely have to copy it with SEU for additional files.

To define the program error messages, first create a message file with the IBM-supplied CRTMSGF (Create Message File) command. To add messages to this file, use the ADDMSGD (Add Message Description) command. Figure 42.8 shows the CL commands that create the message file and the messages for this utility. User messages should always begin with the letters USR to distinguish them from IBM messages, which never begin with U.

To retrieve the messages from the message file and send them to the program, use the IBM-supplied SNDPGMMSG (Send Program Message) command. Because you cannot perform this function in RPG, an RPG program must call a CL program and pass parameters that specify which message to send. Figure 42.9 shows CL program SNDMSG, which formats the information from a calling RPG program into a SNDPGMMSG command. After SNDMSG sends the messages, CL program CLRMSGQ (Figure 42.10) clears the messages from the program message queue.

RPG Program MRR0020

Now let's tie everything together in the RPG program. Program MRR0020 (Figure 42.11, page 575) begins with an explanation of the indicators that the program uses. To avoid confusing code, I try to keep indicator use to a minimum and reserve indicators 21 through 40 for communicating with the screen formats.

Lines 55 through 83 show the file specifications and the data structures the program uses. The program starts with specifications for RGPMAS (the file to be maintained) and MRD0020 (the display file). The program uses three data structures. The first (lines 65 and 66) contains the storage location of the AID

Figure 42.8

Program Message File

```
CRTMSGF     MSGF(MIDMSG) TEXT('Message file')
ADDMSGD     MSGID(USR0001) MSGF(MIDMSG) MSG('Badge record +
              not found') SECLVL('No record was found +
              for the badge number you entered.  If you +
              wish to add a new badge number, press +
              Enter without entering a badge number.')
ADDMSGD     MSGID(USR0002) MSGF(MIDMSG) MSG('Data base +
              I-O error, contact data processing +
              department')
ADDMSGD     MSGID(USR0003) MSGF(MIDMSG) MSG('This record +
              was changed by another program, make your +
              changes again')
ADDMSGD     MSGID(USR0004) MSGF(MIDMSG) MSG('First name +
              cannot be blank')
ADDMSGD     MSGID(USR0005) MSGF(MIDMSG) MSG('Last name +
              cannot be blank')
ADDMSGD     MSGID(USR0006) MSGF(MIDMSG) MSG('Company name +
              cannot be blank')
ADDMSGD     MSGID(USR0007) MSGF(MIDMSG) MSG('City name +
              cannot be blank')
ADDMSGD     MSGID(USR0008) MSGF(MIDMSG) MSG('State name +
              cannot be blank')
ADDMSGD     MSGID(USR0009) MSGF(MIDMSG) MSG('Zip code +
              cannot be blank')
ADDMSGD     MSGID(USR0010) MSGF(MIDMSG) MSG('First +
              address line cannot be blank')
ADDMSGD     MSGID(USR0011) MSGF(MIDMSG) MSG('Invalid +
              command key pressed')
ADDMSGD     MSGID(USR0012) MSGF(MIDMSG) MSG('Record +
              updated, press enter or make changes')
ADDMSGD     MSGID(USR0013) MSGF(MIDMSG) MSG('Area code +
              cannot be blank''')
ADDMSGD     MSGID(USR0014) MSGF(MIDMSG) MSG('Phone number +
              cannot be blank')
ADDMSGD     MSGID(USR0015) MSGF(MIDMSG) MSG('Press F16 +
              again to delete this record or press Enter +
              to cancel the delete')
ADDMSGD     MSGID(USR0016) MSGF(MIDMSG) MSG('Delete not +
              allowed, you are in ADD mode')
```

(Attention Identifier) byte. Pressing a command key changes this byte's value, and the program uses the value to determine which command key the user pressed.

The next data structure (lines 71 through 77) contains the mnemonics ON, YES, TRUE, OFF, NO, and FALSE. The program initializes ON, YES, and TRUE to the value 1 (line 648) and initializes OFF, NO, and FALSE to the value 0 (line 649). The program uses these values to compare the status of indicators. Using mnemonic names makes the code more understandable than code without mnemonics (e.g., *IN10 IFEQ ON and ERROR IFEQ FALSE makes more literal sense than *IN10 IFEQ '1' and ERROR IFEQ '0').

The final data structure is the program status data structure, which begins on line 82. Positions one through 10 of this data structure contain the program

Figure 42.9

CL Program SNDMSG

```
PGM         PARM(&MSGNUM &MSGF &MSGDTA)
/*          SEND A PROGRAM MESSAGE TO THE PREVIOUS +
              PROGRAM MESSAGE QUEUE  */

DCL         &MSGNUM *CHAR LEN(7)
DCL         &MSGF   *CHAR LEN(10)
DCL         &MSGDTA *CHAR LEN(50)

MONMSG      MSGID(CPF0000 MCH0000)

SNDPGMMSG   MSGID(&MSGNUM) MSGF(&MSGF) MSGDTA(&MSGDTA)

ENDPGM
```

Figure 42.10

CL Program CLRMSGQ

```
PGM         /*  CLEAR PREVIOUS PROGRAM MESSAGE QUEUE  */

RMVMSG      PGMQ(*PRV) CLEAR(*ALL)

ENDPGM
```

name stored in variable PGMID. Both the display file and the program message queue subfile use PGMID.

Next, I define the data area that holds the last badge number used. The program uses this data area to assign a badge number to a new record. When the user adds a record, the program simply retrieves the data area, adds one to the badge number, and updates the record.

Line 91 defines the maintenance number variable XXMTNO based on the definition of field RGMTNO in RGPMAS. Each of RGPMAS's records contains a RGMTNO field. The program uses this field and XXMTNO to determine when another user changes a record while the first user has it on display. When a user reads a record from RGPMAS, the program adds one to RGMTNO, saves that value in XXMTNO, and releases the lock on the record. If another program reads the record, that program also increments RGMTNO. When the first user tries to update the record then, the program checks RGMTNO's value against XXMTNO. If they do not match, another user has accessed that record while the first user had it on display. This technique prevents a user from deleting someone else's changes.

Keep in mind that your application programs, not your system, control the maintenance number. For this method to work, each program that updates RGPMAS must use the same technique. Because DFU (Data File Utility) does not add one to RGMTNO, you should not use DFU for file maintenance.

Finally, define constants the program uses to determine its mode: ADD, UPDATE, or DELETE.

The program begins processing by executing subroutine INITSR (line 643) to initialize variables and perform housekeeping functions. Lines 659 through 672 initialize the data area BADGE to the highest badge number in the file. Initializing BADGE every time the program runs prevents BADGE from having an inaccurate value due to a system failure. This subroutine retrieves and locks the data area and uses SETLL with *HIVAL to position the file cursor beyond the last record in the file. Then the READP statement reads the last record in the file. If INITSR finds no record, the subroutine sets the data area to zeros. When the record exists, the subroutine moves the badge number to the data area. INITSR releases the lock on the database record by performing a dummy EXCPT operation, and control returns to the program's mainline.

The Mainline

The mainline begins with a DOU loop that executes until the variable EXTPGM equals TRUE (i.e., until the user presses F3). The program writes the subfile control record MSGCTL (defined in Figure 42.7) to display the program message queue subfile's records (none exist at this point). Then the program displays the first screen (SCREEN1) and waits for the user to press Enter or a command key. At this point the user can enter a badge number, press Enter without a badge number, or exit the program.

The program checks indicator 14 (conditioned on the VLDCMDKEY keyword) to determine whether the user pressed a valid command key. If so, the program calls CL program CMDKEY (Figure 42.12, page 587) to determine which command key the user pressed. The RPG program passes CMDKEY the value of the AID byte. CMDKEY converts that hexadecimal value to a numeric value that indicates which command key the user pressed. CMDKEY returns this numeric value in variable CMDKEY. (For information about the AID byte, check the *Data Management Guide*, SC41-9658.)

This technique of determining command keys has several advantages over using command key indicators. One advantage is that using the AID byte reduces the use of indicators. Also, you can use program CMDKEY with any application. This ability lets you "soft code" command key functions. In other words, if you use your applications on different systems, you merely have to modify program CMDKEY, and your programs will respond correctly to the analogous command keys on the different systems.

Remember that program CMDKEY simply returns the numeric number of the command key the user pressed. Your application program defines the function of that command key. When you determine the command key, you can use a CASxx operation in your application program to execute an appropriate subroutine. In this example, the RPG program defines only one option: CF3 invokes subroutine EXIT1 (line 587) to change the value of EXTPGM to TRUE. When the program finds an undefined command key value, it executes subroutine CMDERR (line 607) to send a message to the user.

CMDERR moves message number USR0011 (which indicates the message "Invalid command key pressed") to variable MSGNUM and executes subroutine $ERROR (line 618). Several subroutines call $ERROR to display error messages. $ERROR simply moves TRUE to ERROR to indicate an error has occurred, then executes subroutine $MSG to display the message.

$MSG (line 630) calls CL program SNDMSG and passes the parameters for message number, message file name, and message data. SNDMSG sends the message to the program message queue with the SNDPGMMSG command.

When the user presses Enter instead of a command key, control falls to line 129, and the program executes subroutine INITER (line 377). This subroutine clears the program message queue subfile and sets off the screen attribute indicators (indicators 21 through 40). Because I reserve indicators 21 through 40 for the screen formats, it's safe to turn them off as a set. The subroutine sets off the indicators by moving ZEROS, a 20-character variable of zeros, to the indicator array *IN starting at position 21. Then the subroutine sets variable ERROR to FALSE, and control returns to the mainline.

When the badge number field RGBAGE is greater than zero (i.e., the user entered a badge number in screen one), the program executes subroutine EDIT01 (line 243) to check whether the number is valid.

The subroutine begins by performing a CHAIN operation to RGPMAS. The CHAIN operation sets on indicator 10 when the badge number does not exist. When indicator 10 is on, EDIT01 turns on the reverse image attribute for the field. The subroutine then moves the message number USR0001 to the message number variable and executes subroutine $ERROR. Message USR0001 states, "No record was found for the badge number you entered. If you wish to add a new badge number, press Enter without entering a badge number."

At the time of the CHAIN operation, the record might be locked by another program. If the CHAIN encounters an I/O problem (which is almost always a record lock), the subroutine sets on indicator 11. In this case, EDIT01 moves the message number USR0002 ("Database I-O error, contact data processing department") to MSGNUM and executes $ERROR. Because I use a program message queue subfile, the system inserts a message into the message queue that indicates who has a lock on the record. If you don't use an indicator in positions 56 and 57, the system sends the user a CPF error message on an I/O error.

When neither indicator 10 nor 11 is on, the program successfully retrieved the requested record. To release the record lock, the subroutine executes a dummy EXCPT operation. Control then returns to the mainline.

At line 140, the mainline checks the value of ERROR. When no error exists, the program initializes the screen for an add or update operation. When the badge number is zero (i.e., the user presses Enter without entering a badge number value), the program executes subroutine INIT01 (line 345). This routine simply changes the MODE variable to ADD and erases screen two's field values. When the badge number does not equal zero (i.e., the user enters a badge number), the program executes subroutine INIT02 (line 366), which changes the mode to UPDATE and moves the value of RGMTNO (the maintenance number field) into XXMTNO.

Regardless of the badge number value, the mainline executes subroutine SCREN2 (line 164), which displays the second screen, checks for missing data, and updates, adds, or deletes the database record. SCREN2 begins with a DOU loop that executes until variable EXTPGM or EXTSUB equals TRUE (i.e., until the user presses CF3, CF12, or Enter without making changes). This subroutine displays the program message queue subfile and then screen two.

SCREN2 checks indicator 14 to determine whether the user pressed a valid command key. If so, the program saves the status of indicator 02 (the CHANGE keyword indicator) by moving the value to indicator 21 (line 179). When indicator 02 is on, the move sets on indicator 21. If the user exits the screen, indicator 02's status may change, but when the user returns to the record, the program moves indicator 21's value to indicator 02, which turns it back on. The opposite is true when indicator 02 is off. Essentially, this move saves indicator 02's status if the user exits the record and returns to it.

The subroutine then processes the command key request. When the user presses F3 (Exit), SCREN2 executes subroutine EXIT1, which simply moves TRUE to EXTPGM to end SCREN2 and exit the program. When the user presses F12 (Previous Screen), SCREN2 executes subroutine EXIT2 (line 597), which moves TRUE to EXTSUB to exit the subroutine and return to the mainline. When the user presses CF16 (Delete), the program executes subroutine DELET1 (line 500) to process the delete request.

DELET1 first checks MODE's value. When it is ADD, the program sends an error message to the screen stating that CF16 isn't valid. When MODE is UPDATE, the program changes the MODE variable to DELETE, sets on indicator 33 to protect the fields on the screen, and sends a message to the screen to confirm the deletion. If the user does not press F16 a second time, the program does not delete the record and waits for the user to press Enter.

When the user presses F16 again to verify the deletion, DELET1 executes subroutine DELET2 (line 539). This subroutine first reads the record with a CHAIN to the registration file. The subroutine then checks indicators 10 and 11 to verify the record exists and can be read. If either indicator is on, the subroutine moves the appropriate message number to MSGNUM and executes subroutine $ERROR. When the indicators are off, DELET2 checks the maintenance number field RGMTNO against the maintenance number in XXMTNO.

When no problems exist, the program deletes the record, and control returns to DELET1, which executes subroutine EXIT2 to exit the SCREN2 subroutine. Here, control returns to the mainline, and screen one is displayed. If a problem occurs in deletion, DELET2 executes $ERROR, and control returns to DELET1. DELET1 then executes subroutine INIT02 to change the program mode to UPDATE.

At line 197, the program tests indicator 02. When indicator 02 is off, the user has made no changes to the screen, and the program executes subroutine EXIT2 to exit SCREN2.

When indicator 02 is on, the program processes the screen. SCREN2 first executes subroutine INITER (line 377) to clear the program message queue and set off the screen attribute indicators. Next, the program executes subroutine EDIT02 to check that a value exists for each field. If the user leaves a field blank, the subroutine sets on the indicators for reverse image and cursor position. EDIT02 then moves the appropriate error message number to MSGNUM and executes subroutine $ERROR.

When control returns to subroutine SCREN2 and ERROR equals TRUE, the subroutine sets on indicator 21 to set on the MDT during the next read. When the MDT is on, the next read turns on indicator 02. Indicator 02 forces a check of the input data, and the user must press a command key to exit the screen (pressing Enter redisplays the screen and the error messages).

When no errors exist, the program tests MODE's value. When MODE equals ADD, the program executes subroutine ADD to add the record to RGPMAS. When MODE equals UPDATE, the program executes subroutine UPDATE to update the record in RGPMAS.

Subroutine ADD (line 389) adds a record to file RGPMAS from the data the user supplies on the screen. The subroutine first initializes the database record fields that did not appear on the screen. The next block of code illustrates the method of using a data area to hold the last badge number used. This code first retrieves the data area BADGE. *LOCK locks the data area, preventing any other program from accessing it. The subroutine adds one to the badge number and updates and releases it with an OUT statement. The subroutine moves the badge number to the key field RGBAGE and writes the record to the file.

ADD's next job is to test for an I/O error by checking the I/O error indicator. When indicator 11 is on, a record with the same key may exist in the file. This event is unlikely, but the program checks to be sure. The rest of the code in ADD sends a status message to the user and executes subroutine INIT02 to change the mode of the program to UPDATE. Control then returns to SCREN2 at line 230.

Subroutine UPDATE works much like subroutine DELET2. UPDATE (line 435) first reads the record with a CHAIN to the registration file. This chain reads the information into the same variables the display file uses. The subroutine checks indicators 10 and 11 to verify that the record exists and can be read. UPDATE then checks the maintenance number field RGMTNO against the maintenance number in XXMTNO to see whether another user changed the record.

When UPDATE encounters no errors, the subroutine is ready to update the database record but must first get the display file's variable values back (because of the CHAIN, the variables do not reflect the displayed values). To place the updated values in the variables, the program reREADS the display file record. For this process to work, you must have the RTNDTA keyword in the display file (Line 29 in Figure 42.7). Without this keyword, the program does not accept the user's input.

The subroutine adds one to the maintenance number, moves its value to XXMTNO, and updates the record. Again, if an error occurs during the update, the program sends a message to the screen. Otherwise, the user sees the message "Record updated, press Enter or make changes." Control of the program returns to SCREN2. When the user finishes processing the record, control returns to the mainline, and the process repeats starting on line 105. The program redisplays screen one, and the user can process another record or exit the application.

Now that you've analyzed this program thoroughly, you're on your way to writing your own workstation programs quickly and easily. Once you have the design you want to use, you can create new programs in about an hour; you just have to change file and variable names. For further reference on the techniques this program uses, check *AS/400 Programming: Data Management Guide* (SC41-9658), and *AS/400 Programming: Control Language Programmer's Guide* (SC41-8077).

When you develop standard program routines for your shop, you can develop and maintain application programs without having to reinvent the wheel each time. By using consistent structure, different programmers can write code that looks alike and performs similarly. This consistency benefits your users — and you — at maintenance time.

Figure 42.11

RPG Program MRR0020

```
*... ... 1 ... ... 2 ... ... 3 ... ... 4 ... ... 5 ... ... 6 ... ... 7 ...

F*************************************************************************
F*                                                                       *
F*                         FUNCTION OF INDICATORS                        *
F*                         ----------------------                        *
F*                                                                       *
F*  02 - CHANGE                                                          *
F*  10 - WORK INDICATOR                                                  *
F*  11 - I-O ERROR ON READ                                               *
F*  14 - VLDCMDKEY                                                       *
F*                                                                       *
F*  INDICATORS 21 THRU 40 ARE RESERVED IN THIS PROGRAM FOR               *
F*  SCREEN ATTRIBUTES AND ARE SET OFF AFTER THE SCREEN IS                *
F*  DISPLAYED                                                            *
F*                                                                       *
F*  SCREEN1 INDICATORS                                                   *
F*                                                                       *
F*  21 - SETON MDT                                                       *
F*  22 - BADGE NUMBER INVALID                                            *
F*                                                                       *
F*  SCREEN2 INDICATORS                                                   *
F*                                                                       *
F*  21 - SETON MDT                                                       *
F*  22 - FIRST NAME INVALID                                              *
F*  23 - LAST NAME INVALID                                               *
F*  24 - COMPANY NAME INVALID                                            *
F*  25 - ADDRESS LINE 1 INVALID                                          *
F*  26 - ADDRESS LINE 2 INVALID                                          *
F*  27 - CITY INVALID                                                    *
F*  28 - STATE INVALID                                                   *
F*  29 - ZIP CODE INVALID                                                *
F*  30 - ZIP+4 IS INVALID                                                *
F*  31 - AREA CODE IS INVALID
```

Figure 42.11 Continued

Figure 42.11

RPG Program MRR0020 *Continued*

```
F*  32 - PHONE NUMBER IS INVALID                                  *
F*  33 - PROTECT FIELDS DURING DELETE MODE                        *
F*                                                                *
F*  DATE WRITTEN: MAY 6, 1989        AUTHOR: MARSHALL AKINS       *
F*                                                                *
F*****************************************************************
F*
F*  REGISTRATION FILE RPGMAS (KEYED BY BADGE NUMBER FIELD RGBAGE)
F*
FRGPMAS  UF  E           K        DISK                    A
F*
F*  DISPLAY DEVICE FILE
F*
FMRD0020 CF  E                    WORKSTN      KINFDS INFDS
I*
I*  AID BYTE USED TO DETERMINE WHICH COMMAND KEY WAS PRESSED
IINFDS       DS
I                                         369 369 AID
I*
I*  MNEMONICS FOR CONSTANTS '1' AND '0':
I*    '1' IS YES, ON, AND TRUE.  '0' IS NO, OFF, AND FALSE.
I*
I            DS
I                                           1   1 ON
I                                           1   1 YES
I                                           1   1 TRUE
I                                           2   2 OFF
I                                           2   2 NO
I                                           2   2 FALSE
I*
I* POSITIONS 1 THROUGH 10 OF THE PROGRAM INFORMATION DATA STRUCTURE
I* CONTAIN THE PROGRAM NAME.  THIS FIELD IS DISPLAYED ON THE SCREEN.
I*
I           SDS
I                                           1  10 PGMID
C*
C*  DATA AREA TO HOLD THE LAST BADGE NUMBER USED
C*
C           *NAMVAR   DEFN           BADGE   50
C*
C*  FIELD TO SAVE THE MAINTENANCE NUMBER IN THE RECORD
C*
C           *LIKE     DEFN RGMTNO    XXMTNO
C*
C*  MNEMONICS FOR CONSTANTS 'ADD', 'UPDATE', AND 'DELETE'
C*
C           *LIKE     DEFN MODE      #ADD
C           *LIKE     DEFN MODE      #UPD
C           *LIKE     DEFN MODE      #DEL
C*
C*  EXECUTE HOUSEKEEPING ROUTINE TO INITIALIZE PROGRAM
C*
C                     EXSR INITSR
C*
C*  DISPLAY BADGE NUMBER SELECTION SCREEN
```

Figure 42.11 Continued

Figure 42.11

RPG Program MRR0020 *Continued*

```
C*
C          EXTPGM    DOUEQTRUE
C*
C                    WRITEMSGCTL
C                    EXFMTSCREEN1
C*
C*  IF VLDCMDKEY = TRUE, PROCESS COMMAND KEY REQUEST
C*
C          *IN14     IFEQ TRUE
C*
C                    CALL 'CMDKEY'                10
C                    PARM AID       PARMA   1
C                    PARM           CMDKEY 155
C*
C          CMDKEY    CASEQ3         EXIT1
C                    CAS            CMDERR
C                    END
C*
C*  ELSE (VLDCMDKEY = FALSE), PROCESS RECORD SELECTION SCREEN
C*
C                    ELSE
C*
C*  INITIALIZE PROGRAM MESSAGE QUEUE, ERROR INDICATOR, AND
C*  SCREEN ATTRIBUTE ERROR INDICATORS
C*
C                    EXSR INITER
C*
C*  IF A BADGE NUMBER WAS ENTERED, EDIT IT
C*
C          RGBAGE    IFGT *ZEROS
C                    EXSR EDIT01
C                    END
C*
C*   IF NO ERRORS OCCURRED,
C*      INITIALIZE AND PROCESS SCREEN 2
C*
C          ERROR     IFEQ FALSE
C*
C*  IF BADGE NUMBER IS ZERO,
C*       INITIALIZE FOR AN ADD
C*
C          RGBAGE    IFEQ *ZEROS
C                    EXSR INIT01
C                    ELSE
C*
C*  ELSE (A BADGE NUMBER WAS ENTERED)
C*       INITIALIZE FOR AN UPDATE
C*
C                    EXSR INIT02
C                    END
C*
C                    EXSR SCREN2
C*
C                    END
C                    END
```

Figure 42.11 Continued

Figure 42.11

RPG Program MRR0020 *Continued*

```
C                     END
C*
C                     MOVE ON        *INLR
C*
C******************************************************************
C*   SCREN2  - PROCESS SCREEN2                                    *
C******************************************************************
C*
C           SCREN2    BEGSR
C*
C           EXTPGM    DOUEQTRUE
C           EXTSUB    OREQ TRUE
C*
C                     WRITEMSGCTL
C                     EXFMTSCREEN2
C*
C*  IF VLDCMDKEY = TRUE, PROCESS COMMAND KEY REQUEST
C*
C           *IN14     IFEQ TRUE
C*
C                     MOVE *IN02     *IN21            SAVE MDT
C*
C                     CALL 'CMDKEY'              10
C                     PARM AID       PARMA   1
C                     PARM           CMDKEY 155
C*
C           CMDKEY    CASEQ3         EXIT1
C           CMDKEY    CASEQ12        EXIT2
C           CMDKEY    CASEQ16        DELET1
C                     CAS            CMDERR
C                     END
C*
C*  ELSE (VLDCMDKEY = FALSE), PROCESS FILE MAINTENANCE SCREEN
C*
C                     ELSE
C*
C*  IF SCREEN WAS NOT CHANGED, EXIT THIS SCREEN
C*
C           *IN02     IFEQ OFF
C                     EXSR EXIT2
C                     ELSE
C*
C*  ELSE (DATA FIELDS CHANGED)
C*
C*  INITIALIZE PROGRAM MESSAGE QUEUE, ERROR INDICATOR, AND
C*  SCREEN ATTRIBUTE ERROR INDICATORS
C*
C                     EXSR INITER
C*
C*  ELSE (A BADGE NUMBER WAS ENTERED)
C*       SAVE THE MAINTENANCE NUMBER FIELD
C*
C                     EXSR EDIT02
C*
C*  IF ERRORS WERE FOUND,
```

Figure 42.11 Continued

Figure 42.11 **RPG Program MRR0020** *Continued*

```
C*       SETON INDICATOR FOR MODIFIED DATA TAG (MDT),
C*       WHICH CAUSES THE CHANGE INDICATOR TO COME ON DURING
C*       THE NEXT READ
C*
C*  ELSE (NO ERRORS WERE FOUND),
C*       RETRIEVE DATABASE RECORD
C*
C            ERROR     IFEQ TRUE
C                      MOVE ON        *IN21
C                      ELSE
C*
C            MODE      CASEQ#ADD      ADD
C            MODE      CASEQ#UPD      UPDATE
C            MODE      CASEQ#DEL      DELET2
C                      END
C*
C                      END
C                      END
C                      END
C                      END
C*
C*  INITIALIZE SCREEN FOR NEXT DISPLAY
C*
C                      MOVE FALSE     EXTSUB
C                      EXSR INITER
C*
C                      ENDSR
C*
C*****************************************************************
C*   EDIT01 - EDIT SCREEN1 FIELDS                                *
C*****************************************************************
C*
C            EDIT01    BEGSR
C*
C            RGBAGE    CHAINRGPMAS                1011
C*
C* RECORD NOT FOUND
C            *IN10     IFEQ ON
C                      MOVE ON        *IN22
C                      MOVE 'USR0001' MSGNUM
C                      EXSR $ERROR
C                      ELSE
C*
C* I-O ERROR
C*
C            *IN11     IFEQ ON
C                      MOVE 'USR0002' MSGNUM
C                      EXSR $ERROR
C                      ELSE
C*
C* RECORD FOUND, RELEASE RECORD LOCK
C*
C                      EXCPTDUMMY1
C*
C                      END
```

Figure 42.11 Continued

RPG Program MRR0020 *Continued*

```
C                          END
C*
C                          ENDSR
C*
C*****************************************************************
C*   EDIT02 - EDIT SCREEN2 FIELDS                                *
C*****************************************************************
C*
C              EDIT02      BEGSR
C*
C*  FIRST NAME
C              RGFRST      IFEQ *BLANKS
C                          MOVE ON        *IN22
C                          MOVE 'USR0004' MSGNUM
C                          EXSR $ERROR
C                          END
C*
C*  LAST NAME
C              RGLAST      IFEQ *BLANKS
C                          MOVE ON        *IN23
C                          MOVE 'USR0005' MSGNUM
C                          EXSR $ERROR
C                          END
C*
C*  COMPANY NAME
C              RGCONO      IFEQ *BLANKS
C                          MOVE ON        *IN24
C                          MOVE 'USR0006' MSGNUM
C                          EXSR $ERROR
C                          END
C*
C* ADDRESS LINE1
C              RGADR1      IFEQ *BLANKS
C                          MOVE ON        *IN25
C                          MOVE 'USR0010' MSGNUM
C                          EXSR $ERROR
C                          END
C*
C* CITY
C              RGCITY      IFEQ *BLANKS
C                          MOVE ON        *IN27
C                          MOVE 'USR0007' MSGNUM
C                          EXSR $ERROR
C                          END
C*
C* STATE
C              RGSTAT      IFEQ *BLANKS
C                          MOVE ON        *IN28
C                          MOVE 'USR0008' MSGNUM
C                          EXSR $ERROR
C                          END
C*
C* ZIP CODE
C              RGZIP       IFEQ *ZEROS
C                          MOVE ON        *IN29
```

Figure 42.11 Continued

Figure 42.11 **RPG Program MRR0020** *Continued*

```
     C                         MOVE 'USR0009' MSGNUM
     C                         EXSR $ERROR
     C                         END
     C*
     C* AREA CODE
     C           RGAREA        IFEQ *ZEROS
     C                         MOVE ON        *IN31
     C                         MOVE 'USR0013' MSGNUM
     C                         EXSR $ERROR
     C                         END
     C*
     C* PHONE NUMBER
     C           RGPHON        IFEQ *ZEROS
     C                         MOVE ON        *IN32
     C                         MOVE 'USR0014' MSGNUM
     C                         EXSR $ERROR
     C                         END
     C*
     C                         ENDSR
     C*
     C*****************************************************************
     C*   INIT01 - INITIALIZE SCREEN2 FIELDS FOR AN ADD               *
     C*****************************************************************
     C*
     C           INIT01        BEGSR
     C*
     C                         MOVE #ADD      MODE
     C                         MOVE *BLANKS   RGFRST
     C                         MOVE *BLANKS   RGLAST
     C                         MOVE *BLANKS   RGCONO
     C                         MOVE *BLANKS   RGADR1
     C                         MOVE *BLANKS   RGADR2
     C                         MOVE *BLANKS   RGCITY
     C                         MOVE *BLANKS   RGSTAT
     C                         MOVE *ZEROS    RGZIP
     C                         MOVE *ZEROS    RGZIP4
     C                         MOVE *ZEROS    RGAREA
     C                         MOVE *ZEROS    RGPHON
     C*
     C                         ENDSR
     C*
     C*****************************************************************
     C*   INIT02 - INITIALIZE SCREEN2 FIELDS FOR AN UPDATE            *
     C*****************************************************************
     C*
     C           INIT02        BEGSR
     C*
     C                         MOVE #UPD      MODE
     C                         MOVE RGMTNO    XXMTNO
     C*
     C                         ENDSR
     C*
     C*****************************************************************
     C*   INITER - INITIALIZE MESSAGE QUEUE AND INDICATORS            *
     C*****************************************************************
```

Figure 42.11 Continued

Figure 42.11

RPG Program MRR0020 *Continued*

```
C*
C          INITER    BEGSR
C*
C                    CALL 'CLRPGMQ'
C                    MOVEAZEROS     *IN,21
C                    MOVE FALSE     ERROR
C*
C                    ENDSR
C*
C*****************************************************************
C*   ADD - ADD A DATABASE RECORD                                  *
C*****************************************************************
C*
C          ADD       BEGSR
C*
C*  INITIALIZE FIELDS THAT WERE NOT SHOWN ON THE SCREEN
C*
C                    Z-ADD1         RGMTNO
C                    MOVE *BLANKS   RGFL01
C                    MOVE *BLANKS   RGFL02
C                    MOVE *BLANKS   RGFL03
C                    MOVE *BLANKS   RGFL04
C                    MOVE *BLANKS   RGFL05
C                    MOVE 'A'       RGSTS
C                    MOVE RGMTNO    XXMTNO
C*
C*  GET LAST BADGE NUMBER USED, INCREMENT BY 1,
C*  THEN UPDATE THE DATA AREA
C*
C          *LOCK     IN   BADGE
C                    ADD  1         BADGE
C                    OUT  BADGE
C*
C                    MOVE BADGE     RGBAGE
C*
C                    WRITERGPREC                  11
C*
C*  IF AN I-O ERROR OCCURRED, SEND A BAD MESSAGE
C*
C          *IN11     IFEQ ON
C                    MOVE 'USR0002' MSGNUM
C                    EXSR $ERROR
C                    ELSE
C*
C*     ELSE SEND A MESSAGE TO REASSURE THE USER THAT THE
C*          RECORD WAS UPDATED.  RESET MODE TO 'UPDATE' SO
C*          THAT THE RECORD CAN BE UPDATED.
C*
C                    MOVE 'USR0012' MSGNUM
C                    EXSR $MSG
C                    MOVE 'UPDATE'  MODE
C                    END
C*
C                    ENDSR
C*
```

Figure 42.11 Continued

Figure 42.11

RPG Program MRR0020 *Continued*

```
C*****************************************************************
C*   UPDATE - UPDATE DATABASE RECORD                              *
C*****************************************************************
C*
C          UPDATE    BEGSR
C*
C*  CHAIN TO BADGE RECORD FOR UPDATE
C*
C          RGBAGE    CHAINRGPMAS                 1011
C*
C*  RECORD NOT FOUND (IT USED TO BE THERE)
C          *IN10     IFEQ ON
C                    MOVE 'USR0001' MSGNUM
C                    EXSR $ERROR
C                    ELSE
C*
C*  I-O ERROR
C          *IN11     IFEQ ON
C                    MOVE 'USR0002' MSGNUM
C                    EXSR $ERROR
C                    ELSE
C*
C*  IF THE MAINTENANCE NUMBER IS NOT EQUAL TO THE MAINTENANCE
C*     NUMBER THAT WAS SAVED, SEND A MESSAGE.  SAVE THE NEW NUMBER
C*     AND RELEASE THE RECORD.
C*
C          RGMTNO    IFNE XXMTNO
C                    MOVE 'USR0003' MSGNUM
C                    EXSR $ERROR
C                    MOVE RGMTNO    XXMTNO
C                    EXCPTDUMMY1
C                    END
C*
C                    END
C                    END
C*
C*  IF RECORD WAS FOUND AND MAINTENANCE NUMBER MATCHED,
C*      READ THE SCREEN AGAIN TO GET THE CHANGED FIELDS.
C*      THEN UPDATE THE DATABASE RECORD
C*
C          ERROR     IFEQ FALSE
C*
C                    READ SCREEN2                    10
C*
C                    ADD  1         RGMTNO
C                    MOVE RGMTNO    XXMTNO
C                    UPDATRGPREC                   11
C*
C*  IF AN I-O ERROR OCCURRED, SEND AN ERROR MESSAGE.
C*     ELSE SEND A MESSAGE TO REASSURE THE USER THAT THE
C*          RECORD WAS UPDATED
C*
C          *IN11     IFEQ ON
C                    MOVE 'USR0002' MSGNUM
C                    EXSR $ERROR
```

Figure 42.11 Continued

Figure 42.11

RPG Program MRR0020 *Continued*

```
C                          ELSE
C*
C                          MOVE 'USR0012' MSGNUM
C                          EXSR $MSG
C                          END
C*
C                          END
C*
C                          ENDSR
C*
C*****************************************************************
C*   DELET1 - DELETE KEY WAS PRESSED                              *
C*****************************************************************
C*
C             DELET1       BEGSR
C*
C*  ADD MODE, DELETE IS INVALID
C             MODE         IFEQ #ADD
C                          MOVE 'USR0016' MSGNUM
C                          EXSR $ERROR
C                          ELSE
C*
C*  UPDATE MODE, PROMPT TO PRESS F16 TO DELETE
C             MODE         IFEQ #UPD
C                          MOVE 'DELETE'  MODE
C                          MOVE ON        *IN33
C                          MOVE 'USR0015' MSGNUM
C                          EXSR $MSG
C                          ELSE
C*
C*  DELETE MODE, DELETE RECORD
C             MODE         IFEQ #DEL
C                          EXSR DELET2
C*
C*  IF AN ERROR OCCURRED, SWITCH BACK TO UPDATE MODE.
C*  ELSE EXIT THE ROUTINE TO RETURN TO SCREEN1.
C*
C             ERROR        IFEQ TRUE
C                          EXSR INIT02
C                          ELSE
C                          EXSR EXIT2
C                          END
C*
C                          END
C                          END
C                          END
C*
C                          ENDSR
C*
C*****************************************************************
C*   DELET2 - DELETE DATA BASE RECORD                             *
C*****************************************************************
C*
C             DELET2       BEGSR
C*
```

Figure 42.11 Continued

Figure 42.11

RPG Program MRR0020 *Continued*

```
C           RGBAGE    CHAINRGPMAS                 1011
C*
C* RECORD NOT FOUND
C*
C           *IN10     IFEQ ON
C                     MOVE 'USR0001' MSGNUM
C                     EXSR $ERROR
C                     ELSE
C*
C* I-O ERROR
C*
C           *IN11     IFEQ ON
C                     MOVE 'USR0002' MSGNUM
C                     EXSR $ERROR
C                     ELSE
C*
C*  THE RECORD WAS FOUND.
C*  IF THE MAINTENANCE NUMBER IN THE RECORD IS NOT THE SAME
C*      AS THE NUMBER THAT WAS SAVED, SEND A MESSAGE.
C*  ELSE
C*      DELETE THE RECORD
C*
C           RGMTNO    IFNE XXMTNO
C                     MOVE 'USR0003' MSGNUM
C                     EXSR $ERROR
C                     MOVE RGMTNO    XXMTNO
C                     EXCPTDUMMY1
C                     ELSE
C*
C                     DELETRGPREC                   11
C*
C           *IN11     IFEQ ON
C                     MOVE 'USR0002' MSGNUM
C                     EXSR $ERROR
C                     END
C*
C                     END
C                     END
C                     END
C*
C                     ENDSR
C*
C*****************************************************************
C*   EXIT1 - EXIT PROGRAM REQUEST                                *
C*****************************************************************
C*
C           EXIT1     BEGSR
C*
C                     MOVE TRUE      EXTPGM  1
C*
C                     ENDSR
C*
C*****************************************************************
C*   EXIT2 - EXIT SUBROUTINE REQUEST                             *
C*****************************************************************
```

Figure 42.11 Continued

Figure 42.11

RPG Program MRR0020 *Continued*

```
C*
C           EXIT2     BEGSR
C*
C                     MOVE TRUE      EXTSUB  1
C*
C                     ENDSR
C*
C*****************************************************************
C*   CMDERR - UNDEFINED COMMAND KEY ERROR                         *
C*****************************************************************
C*
C           CMDERR    BEGSR
C*
C                     MOVE 'USRØØ11' MSGNUM
C                     EXSR $ERROR
C*
C                     ENDSR
C*
C*****************************************************************
C*   $ERROR - ERROR ROUTINE                                        *
C*****************************************************************
C*
C           $ERROR    BEGSR
C*
C                     MOVE TRUE      ERROR   1
C*
C                     EXSR $MSG
C*
C                     ENDSR
C*
C****************************************************************
C*  $MSG - SEND A MESSAGE TO THE PROGRAM MESSAGE QUEUE          *
C****************************************************************
C*
C           $MSG      BEGSR
C*
C                     CALL 'SNDMSG'
C                     PARM           MSGNUM  7
C                     PARM 'MIDMSG'  MSGF   1Ø
C                     PARM           MSGDTA 8Ø
C*
C                     ENDSR
C*
C****************************************************************
C*  INITSR - PROGRAM INITIALIZATION                             *
C****************************************************************
C*
C           INITSR    BEGSR
C*
C                     MOVE '1'       ON
C                     MOVE 'Ø'       OFF
C                     MOVE 'ADD'     #ADD
C                     MOVE 'UPDATE'  #UPD
C                     MOVE 'DELETE'  #DEL
C                     MOVE *ZEROS    ZEROS  2Ø
```

Figure 42.11 Continued

Figure 42.11 RPG Program MRR0020 *Continued*

```
C                    MOVEAZEROS     *IN,21
C*
C*  INITIALIZE BADGE DATA AREA TO THE HIGHEST BADGE
C*    NUMBER IN THE FILE
C*
C          *LOCK     IN   BADGE
C*
C          *HIVAL    SETLLRGPMAS
C                    READPRGPMAS                   10
C          *IN10     IFEQ ON
C                    MOVE *ZEROS    RGBAGE
C                    OUT  BADGE
C                    ELSE
C                    Z-ADDRGBAGE    BADGE
C                    OUT  BADGE
C                    EXCPTDUMMY1
C                    END
C*
C                    MOVE *ZEROS    RGBAGE
C*
C                    ENDSR
O*
O*  DUMMY EXCPT OUTPUT TO RELEASE RECORD LOCK
O*
ORGPREC  E                 DUMMY1
```

Figure 42.12 CL Program CMDKEY

```
PGM        PARM(&PARM1 &PARM2)

/*  PARM1 IS THE AID BYTE FROM POSITION 369 OF THE I-O
/*  FEEDBACK, DESCRIBED ON PAGE A-16 OF AS/400 PROGRAMMING:
/*  DATA MANAGEMENT GUIDE, (SC41-9658-0).
/*  PARM2 IS THE VALUE RETURNED TO THE CALLING PROGRAM AS
/*  FOLLOWS:
/*  COMMAND KEYS 1 THRU 24 RETURN VALUES 1 THRU 24
/*  CLEAR - 25, ENTER - 26, HELP - 33, ROLLDOWN - 34
/*  ROLLUP - 35, PRINT - 30, HOME - 31
DCL        VAR(&PARM1) TYPE(*CHAR) LEN(1)
DCL        VAR(&PARM2) TYPE(*DEC)  LEN(15 5)
DCL        VAR(&CMD01) TYPE(*CHAR) LEN(1) VALUE(X'31')
DCL        VAR(&CMD02) TYPE(*CHAR) LEN(1) VALUE(X'32')
DCL        VAR(&CMD03) TYPE(*CHAR) LEN(1) VALUE(X'33')
DCL        VAR(&CMD04) TYPE(*CHAR) LEN(1) VALUE(X'34')
DCL        VAR(&CMD05) TYPE(*CHAR) LEN(1) VALUE(X'35')
DCL        VAR(&CMD06) TYPE(*CHAR) LEN(1) VALUE(X'36')
DCL        VAR(&CMD07) TYPE(*CHAR) LEN(1) VALUE(X'37')
DCL        VAR(&CMD08) TYPE(*CHAR) LEN(1) VALUE(X'38')
```

Figure 42.12 Continued

Figure 42.12

CL Program CMDKEY *Continued*

```
DCL       VAR(&CMDØ9) TYPE(*CHAR) LEN(1) VALUE(X'39')
DCL       VAR(&CMD1Ø) TYPE(*CHAR) LEN(1) VALUE(X'3A')
DCL       VAR(&CMD11) TYPE(*CHAR) LEN(1) VALUE(X'3B')
DCL       VAR(&CMD12) TYPE(*CHAR) LEN(1) VALUE(X'3C')
DCL       VAR(&CMD13) TYPE(*CHAR) LEN(1) VALUE(X'B1')
DCL       VAR(&CMD14) TYPE(*CHAR) LEN(1) VALUE(X'B2')
DCL       VAR(&CMD15) TYPE(*CHAR) LEN(1) VALUE(X'B3')
DCL       VAR(&CMD16) TYPE(*CHAR) LEN(1) VALUE(X'B4')
DCL       VAR(&CMD17) TYPE(*CHAR) LEN(1) VALUE(X'B5')
DCL       VAR(&CMD18) TYPE(*CHAR) LEN(1) VALUE(X'B6')
DCL       VAR(&CMD19) TYPE(*CHAR) LEN(1) VALUE(X'B7')
DCL       VAR(&CMD2Ø) TYPE(*CHAR) LEN(1) VALUE(X'B8')
DCL       VAR(&CMD21) TYPE(*CHAR) LEN(1) VALUE(X'B9')
DCL       VAR(&CMD22) TYPE(*CHAR) LEN(1) VALUE(X'BA')
DCL       VAR(&CMD23) TYPE(*CHAR) LEN(1) VALUE(X'BB')
DCL       VAR(&CMD24) TYPE(*CHAR) LEN(1) VALUE(X'BC')
DCL       VAR(&CLEAR)    TYPE(*CHAR)  LEN(1) VALUE(X'BD')
DCL       VAR(&ENTER)    TYPE(*CHAR)  LEN(1) VALUE(X'F1')
DCL       VAR(&HELP)     TYPE(*CHAR)  LEN(1) VALUE(X'F3')
DCL       VAR(&ROLLDOWN) TYPE(*CHAR)  LEN(1) VALUE(X'F4')
DCL       VAR(&ROLLUP)   TYPE(*CHAR)  LEN(1) VALUE(X'F5')
DCL       VAR(&PRINT)    TYPE(*CHAR)  LEN(1) VALUE(X'F6')
DCL       VAR(&HOME)     TYPE(*CHAR)  LEN(1) VALUE(X'F8')

IF        (&PARM1 *EQ &CMDØ1) DO
CHGVAR    &PARM2 1
RETURN
ENDDO

IF        (&PARM1 *EQ &CMDØ2) DO
CHGVAR    &PARM2 2
RETURN
ENDDO

IF        (&PARM1 *EQ &CMDØ3) DO
CHGVAR    &PARM2 3
RETURN
ENDDO

IF        (&PARM1 *EQ &CMDØ4) DO
CHGVAR    &PARM2 4
RETURN
ENDDO

IF        (&PARM1 *EQ &CMDØ5) DO
CHGVAR    &PARM2 5
RETURN
ENDDO

IF        (&PARM1 *EQ &CMDØ6) DO
CHGVAR    &PARM2 6
RETURN
ENDDO
```

Figure 42.12 Continued

Figure 42.12

CL Program CMDKEY *Continued*

```
IF          (&PARM1 *EQ &CMD07) DO
CHGVAR      &PARM2 7
RETURN
ENDDO

IF          (&PARM1 *EQ &CMD08) DO
CHGVAR      &PARM2 8
RETURN
ENDDO

IF          (&PARM1 *EQ &CMD09) DO
CHGVAR      &PARM2 9
RETURN
ENDDO

IF          (&PARM1 *EQ &CMD10) DO
CHGVAR      &PARM2 10
RETURN
ENDDO

IF          (&PARM1 *EQ &CMD11) DO
CHGVAR      &PARM2 11
RETURN
ENDDO

IF          (&PARM1 *EQ &CMD12) DO
CHGVAR      &PARM2 12
RETURN
ENDDO

IF          (&PARM1 *EQ &CMD13) DO
CHGVAR      &PARM2 13
RETURN
ENDDO

IF          (&PARM1 *EQ &CMD14) DO
CHGVAR      &PARM2 14
RETURN
ENDDO

IF          (&PARM1 *EQ &CMD15) DO
CHGVAR      &PARM2 15
RETURN
ENDDO

IF          (&PARM1 *EQ &CMD16) DO
CHGVAR      &PARM2 16
RETURN
ENDDO

IF          (&PARM1 *EQ &CMD17) DO
CHGVAR      &PARM2 17
RETURN
ENDDO
```

Figure 42.12 Continued

Figure 42.12

CL Program CMDKEY *Continued*

```
IF          (&PARM1 *EQ &CMD18) DO
CHGVAR      &PARM2 18
RETURN
ENDDO

IF          (&PARM1 *EQ &CMD19) DO
CHGVAR      &PARM2 19
RETURN
ENDDO

IF          (&PARM1 *EQ &CMD20) DO
CHGVAR      &PARM2 20
RETURN
ENDDO

IF          (&PARM1 *EQ &CMD21) DO
CHGVAR      &PARM2 21
RETURN
ENDDO

IF          (&PARM1 *EQ &CMD22) DO
CHGVAR      &PARM2 22
RETURN
ENDDO

IF          (&PARM1 *EQ &CMD23) DO
CHGVAR      &PARM2 23
RETURN
ENDDO

IF          (&PARM1 *EQ &CMD24) DO
CHGVAR      &PARM2 24
RETURN
ENDDO

IF          (&PARM1 *EQ &CLEAR) DO
CHGVAR      &PARM2 25
RETURN
ENDDO

IF          (&PARM1 *EQ &ENTER) DO
CHGVAR      &PARM2 26
RETURN
ENDDO

IF          (&PARM1 *EQ &HELP) DO
CHGVAR      &PARM2 33
RETURN
ENDDO

IF          (&PARM1 *EQ &ROLLDOWN) DO
CHGVAR      &PARM2 34
RETURN
ENDDO
```

Figure 42.12 Continued

Figure 42.12

CL Program CMDKEY *Continued*

```
IF          (&PARM1 *EQ &ROLLUP) DO
CHGVAR      &PARM2 35
RETURN
ENDDO

IF          (&PARM1 *EQ &PRINT) DO
CHGVAR      &PARM2 30
RETURN
ENDDO

IF          (&PARM1 *EQ &HOME) DO
CHGVAR      &PARM2 31
RETURN
ENDDO

CHGVAR      &PARM2 0
RETURN

ENDPGM
```

Chapter 43

Windows with DDS

by Bryan Meyers

Bring pop-up windows to your AS/400 easily with DDS windows keywords

In early versions of OS/400 (and in CPF before that), several coding techniques would let 5250 workstations simulate the pop-up windows that have become a familiar part of the PC environment. These fake window techniques were cumbersome to code and difficult to understand, and they didn't always work reliably.

Beginning with V2R1, you can code DDS specs for display windows, using the new DDS windows keywords. Let the operating system take over the display management problems involved with windows; you can concentrate less on the technique and more on the results. And best of all, you can now code subfiles to appear within windows — something that the old techniques never allowed.

In this chapter, I will illustrate the use of the DDS windows keywords by providing an example tool to work with the PDM user-defined options (for more information about defining your own PDM options, see Chapter 28, "Customizing PDM"). There are nearly a thousand possible user-defined options (due to the character combinations available), so you should take some care to be sure the two-character abbreviation is meaningful to you. Otherwise, you'll never be able to remember the option you've so cleverly set up to send E-mail Valentine's Day greetings to every active workstation. To help keep track of my PDM user options, I have written program DSPUDO to display user-defined options. This program displays a scrollable window (Figure 43.1) over any PDM list display, showing you the options you have stored and letting you execute them from the window.

To build this tool, create the following AS/400 objects:

- CL program DSPUDO
- Display file DSPUDOD
- RPG program DSPUDOR

Figure 43.1

User-Defined Options Window

```
                              Work with Members Using PDM

 File  . . . . . .      N3XSRC  :..............................................:
   Library . . . .       N3XLI  :               User-Defined Options           :
                                : Type option, press Enter.                    :
 Type options, press Enter.     :   1=Select                                   :
   2=Edit            3=Copy     :                                              :
   7=Rename          8=Display  : Opt Option Command                           :
                                :  _    C     CALL &O/&N                       :
 Opt  Member         Type       :  _    AL    ADDLIBLE &N                      :
      DSPUDO         CLP        :  _    CC    CHGCURLIB CURLIB(&L)             :
 OP   DSPUDOD        DSPF       :  _    CL    CHGCURLIB CURLIB(&N)             :
      DSPUDOR        RPG        :  _    CD    STRDFU OPTION(2)                 :
      WRKOBJUSG      CMD        :  _    CM    STRSDA OPTION(2) SRCFILE(&L/&F) ??SR:
      WRKUSGD        DSPF       :  _    CS    STRSDA OPTION(1) SRCFILE(&L/&F) ??SR:
      WRKUSGHLP      PNLGRP     :  _    DM    DSPMSG                           :
      WRKUSGHLPD     PNLGRP     :  _    EA    EDTOBJAUT OBJ(&L/&N) OBJTYPE(&T) :
      WRKUSGQ        QMQRY      :  _    GO    GO &L/&N                         :
                                :  _    JL    DSPJOBLOG                        :
 Parameters or command          :                                              :
 ===>                           :                                     More...  :
                                :                                              :
 F3=Exit             F4=Prompt  : F4=Prompt   F5=Refresh   F12=Cancel          :
 F9=Retrieve         F10=Comman :..............................................:
```

After creating these objects, supply PDM with a user-defined option, perhaps OP, which will execute the following CL command:

```
CALL PGM(DSPUDO) PARM('&A' &B                                    +
      &C '&D' '&E' '&F' &G &H                                    +
      '&J' &L &N &O &P &R '&S'                                   +
      '&T' &U &V &W &X)
```

It is important that you do not change the names of the variables (&A, &B, etc.), as these are the predefined names PDM uses (see Chapter 28, "Customizing PDM," for more information about PDM substitution variables). The apostrophes delimiting certain parameters are also critical because these variables can contain characters, such as slashes or spaces, that would confuse the command processor if they were not delimited.

CL program DSPUDO (Figure 43.2) serves as a driver program. PDM's substitution variables pass through it without changes. DSPUDO then performs a file override to the member in which you store your user-defined options (PDM passes this information in the substitution variables &U, &V, and &W) and calls RPG program DSPUDOR, which does the actual work of displaying the window and executing the option.

Window Display Options

The DDS that controls how the window is presented is shown in Figure 43.3. Here are the DDS keywords that handle the window support:

Figure 43.2 **CL Program DSPUDO**

```
/* ****************************************************************** */
/*                                                                    */
/*      Program - DSPUDO - Display user-defined options in PDM        */
/*                                                                    */
/*      To create this object: CRTCLPGM PGM(DSPUDO)                   */
/*                                                                    */
/* ****************************************************************** */
             PGM        PARM(&A &B &C &D &E &F &G &H &J &L &N &O &P +
                          &R &S &T &U &V &W &X)
             DCL        VAR(&A) TYPE(*CHAR) LEN(10)
             DCL        VAR(&B) TYPE(*CHAR) LEN(10)
             DCL        VAR(&C) TYPE(*CHAR) LEN(2)
             DCL        VAR(&D) TYPE(*CHAR) LEN(8)
             DCL        VAR(&E) TYPE(*CHAR) LEN(10)
             DCL        VAR(&F) TYPE(*CHAR) LEN(10)
             DCL        VAR(&G) TYPE(*CHAR) LEN(10)
             DCL        VAR(&H) TYPE(*CHAR) LEN(10)
             DCL        VAR(&J) TYPE(*CHAR) LEN(21)
             DCL        VAR(&L) TYPE(*CHAR) LEN(10)
             DCL        VAR(&N) TYPE(*CHAR) LEN(10)
             DCL        VAR(&O) TYPE(*CHAR) LEN(10)
             DCL        VAR(&P) TYPE(*CHAR) LEN(10)
             DCL        VAR(&R) TYPE(*CHAR) LEN(10)
             DCL        VAR(&S) TYPE(*CHAR) LEN(10)
             DCL        VAR(&T) TYPE(*CHAR) LEN(10)
             DCL        VAR(&U) TYPE(*CHAR) LEN(10)
             DCL        VAR(&V) TYPE(*CHAR) LEN(10)
             DCL        VAR(&W) TYPE(*CHAR) LEN(10)
             DCL        VAR(&X) TYPE(*CHAR) LEN(50)
             OVRDBF     FILE(QAUOOPT) TOFILE(&V/&U) MBR(&W)
             CALL       PGM(DSPUDOR) PARM(&A &B &C &D &E &F &G &H &J +
                          &L &N &O &P &R &S &T &U &V &W &X)
             ENDPGM
```

- WINDOW
- WDWBORDER
- RMVWDW
- USRRSTDSP

WINDOW is a record-level keyword that defines a record format as a window, and describes its size and location. For most purposes, this is the only keyword necessary to design a window. In the DDS source, I define a window on the screen with an upper-left corner at row 2, column 30 (B in Figure 43.3):

```
WINDOW(2 30 21 47)
```

The window has 21 lines and 47 usable columns *within its borders.* The starting position can also be represented with program variables, which let you change the position of the window on the screen. But the window must be a fixed size. Any field positions you specify in this record format must be relative to the window's

Figure 43.3

Display File DSPUDOD

```
    *...+... 1 ...+... 2 ...+... 3 ...+... 4 ...+... 5 ...+... 6 ...+... 7 ...+
         A*************************************************************
    A*
    A*     DSPF - DSPUDOD - Display user-defined options in PDM
    A*
    A*     To create this object: CRTDSPF DSPF(DSPUDOD)
    A*
    A*****************************************************************
    A                                      DSPSIZ(24 80 *DS3
    A                                             27 132 *DS4)
    A                                      ALTPAGEUP
    A                                      ALTPAGEDWN
    A                                      PAGEDOWN
    A                                      PAGEUP
    A                                      CA03
    A                                      CF04
    A                                      CA05
    A                                      CA12
    A                                      PRINT
Ⓐ  A          R DUMMY                    ASSUME
    A                                  1  2' '
    A          R HEADER
Ⓑ  A                                      WINDOW(2 30 21 47)
    A                                      WDWBORDER((*COLOR BLU) +
Ⓒ  A                                                (*DSPATR HI) +
    A                                                (*CHAR '+-+||+-+'))
Ⓓ  A                                      RMVWDW
Ⓔ  A                                      USRRSTDSP
    A                                  1 15'User-Defined Options'
    A                                      DSPATR(HI)
Ⓕ  A                                  3  1'Type option, press Enter.'
    A                                      COLOR(BLU)
    A                                  4  3'1=Select'
    A                                      COLOR(BLU)
    A                                  6  1'Opt Option Command'
    A                                      DSPATR(HI)
    A          R SUBFIL                   SFL
    A            SFLCOM       250A  H
    A            SFLSEL         1A  B  7  2
    A  95                                  DSPATR(ND)
    A  95                                  DSPATR(PR)
    A            SFLOPT         2A  O  7  5
    A            SFLCMD        36A  O  7 12
    A          R SUBCTL                   SFLCTL(SUBFIL)
Ⓖ  A                                      WINDOW(HEADER)
    A                                      BLINK OVERLAY
    A                                      SFLSIZ(11)
    A                                      SFLPAG(11)
    A N93                                  SFLDSP
    A N93                                  SFLDSPCTL
    A  93                                  SFLINZ
    A N94                             18 41'More...'
    A                                      DSPATR(HI)
    A  94                             18 41' Bottom'
    A                                      DSPATR(HI)
```

Figure 43.3 Continued

Figure 43.3

Display File DSPUDOD *Continued*

```
*...+... 1 ...+... 2 ...+... 3 ...+... 4 ...+... 5 ...+... 6 ...+... 7 ...+
A                                   19  1'Error(s) occurred in command.'
A                                         DSPATR(HI)
A N96                                     DSPATR(ND)
A                                   20  1'F4=Prompt   F5=Refresh
A                                           F12=Cancel
A                                         COLOR(BLU)
```

starting position, after allowing for attribute bytes on either side of the left and right borders. For example, at F in Figure 43.3, the instruction line starts in row 3, column 1 within the window; on the entire display screen, this position is actually row 5, column 32.

If you plan to display more than one record format within a window — as will be the case with subfiles — use the form of the WINDOW keyword shown at B in Figure 43.3 for the first format and the following form of the WINDOW keyword for the subsequent formats:

```
WINDOW(format-name)
```

The format name must correspond to the format in which you originally defined the window. In Figure 43.3 section G, I specify that the formats HEADER and SUBCTL occupy the same window.

The optional WDWBORDER keyword (C) lets you define the characters and attributes that form the borders of your window. The WDWBORDER statement takes the following form:

```
WDWBORDER((*COLOR value)                                     +
          (*DSPATR value-list)                               +
          (*CHAR + 'characters'))
```

The string following the *CHAR parameter identifies the characters you will use to border your window in the following order: top left corner, top border, top right corner, left border, right border, lower left corner, bottom border, and lower right border. If you don't use this keyword at the file or record level, the system-specified defaults will be used, creating the familiar AS/400 window with the blue dots around it — the same as specifying:

```
WDWBORDER((*COLOR BLU)                                       +
          (*CHAR '...::::.:'))).
```

Interestingly, if you do change the window border and you also use the User Interface Manager (UIM) to display help panels for your application display, UIM's help panels will use the same borders you specify for the display file. (For more information on UIM's help function, see Chapter 47, "UIM Help for Programs.")

The RMVWDW record-level keyword (at D in Figure 43.3) tells the system to remove all the old windows from the display before showing this one. While building this example, I realized I needed to use this keyword because executing an option from the window may result in the CL command prompter being displayed. OS/400 uses a UIM feature that IBM hasn't shared with us to display the command prompter, and the system seems to treat the prompter screen as a full-screen window. Without the RMVWDW instruction, returning to the application window under certain conditions (for example, after pressing F12 (Cancel) when the command prompter is displayed), leaves the command prompter window on the screen instead of redisplaying the underlying PDM display and causes the border attributes for the HEADER format to be lost.

Finally, you can specify USRRSTDSP at the record level (E in Figure 43.3) if your application will restore the previous display after you are done with the window. If you use this keyword, the system won't bother to restore the original display, resulting in faster performance, especially on remote workstations. Because PDM does restore the underlying display, I decided to use the keyword in this example. For more details about DDS windows, refer to the AS/400 *DDS Specifications Reference* (SC41-9620).

One other section of the code for DSPUDOD bears explanation. When workstation management opens a new display file in a program, it defaults to clearing the display the first time you write to the display file. This usually isn't a problem. For example, you will probably want to clear the menu from the screen before you display an order entry display, or else you'll mix the order entry format with the menu format display. In the case of this example, however, the first (and only) write to the display file is the window itself, and I didn't want the system to clear the underlying PDM display. The DUMMY format with the ASSUME keyword (A in Figure 43.3) causes the computer to open and write to the display file without clearing the screen first. I didn't even need to write the DUMMY format to the display; its mere presence in the display file accomplished my goal.

RPG Plus

Program DSPUDOR (Figure 43.4) displays the window that shows your user-defined PDM options and lets you select one of the options to be executed. To run an option, type a 1 before it, then press Enter. If you want the system to show you the CL prompter display for an option, type a 1 before the option, then press F4 (Prompt).

Program DSPUDOR is pretty mundane, but there are a few new features worth mentioning in connection with this code. Two new figurative constants, *ON and *OFF, are shown at A, H, and elsewhere in Figure 43.4. These constants simply return '1' for *ON or '0' for *OFF, lending to the readability of the code.

The lines of code at C, D, F, G, and elsewhere are also examples of readability enhancements for RPG/400. The so-called "structured" opcodes (CASxx, IFxx, DO, DOUxx, and DOWxx) now have parallel ending operation codes (ENDCS, ENDIF, and ENDDO). Using these new end statements is purely optional, but if you do use them, you must use them properly. Specifying ENDIF to close a DO loop, for example, causes a compiler error.

Figure 43.4

RPG Program DSPUDOR

```
 *...+....1....+....2....+....3....+....4....+....5....+....6....+....7
 *****************************************************************
 *
 *     Program - DSPUDOR - Display user-defined options in PDM
 *
 *     To create this object: CRTRPGPGM PGM(DSPUDOR)
 *
 *****************************************************************
 FQAUOOPT IF  E                    DISK
 FDSPUDOD CF  E                    WORKSTN      KINFDS INFDS
 F                                       SFLRRNKSFILE SUBFIL
 E                    EXC     3000  1
 E                    WRK     3000  1
 IQPDMOPT     99
 I              COMMAND                         COMMAN
 IINFDS       DS
 I                                         369 369 KEY
 IWRKEXC      DS                                3000
 I                                           13000 EXC
 IWRKWRK      DS                                3000
 I                                           13000 WRK
 *****************************************************************
 *
 *     MAIN PROGRAM LOGIC
 *
Ⓐ C           *INLR     DOUEQ*ON
 C                     WRITEHEADER
 C                     EXFMTSUBCTL
 **
 C           KEY       CASEQF03       ENDPGM
 C           KEY       CASEQF05       REFRSH
 C           KEY       CASEQF12       ENDPGM
Ⓑ C           KEY       CASEQROLLUP    LODNEX
 C           KEY       CASEQROLLDN    LODPRV
 C                     CAS            PROCES
 C                     ENDCS
 **
Ⓒ C                     ENDDO
 *
 *****************************************************************
 *
 *     SUBROUTINE - BLDCMD - BUILT COMMAND TO BE EXECUTED
 *
 C           BLDCMD    BEGSR
 C                     MOVE *BLANKS   WRKEXC
 C                     MOVE *BLANKS   WRKWRK
 *
 C           KEY       IFEQ F04
 C           '?'       CAT  SFLCOM:0  WRKEXC
 C                     ELSE
 C                     MOVELSFLCOM    WRKEXC
Ⓓ C                     ENDIF
 *
 C           Y         DOUEQ0
```

Figure 43.4 Continued

Figure 43.4

RPG Program DSPUDOR *Continued*

```
*...+....1....+....2....+....3....+....4....+....5....+....6....+....7
C                    Z-ADD1         Y       50
C          '&'       SCAN WRKEXC:Y  Y                 99
**
C          Y         IFGT 0
C                    MOVEAEXC,Y     SUBSTI  2
C          Y         ADD  2         Z       50
C                    MOVEAEXC,Z     WRK
C                    MOVEA*BLANKS   EXC,Y
***
C                    SELEC
C          SUBSTI    WHEQ '&A'
C                    MOVEA@A        EXC,Y
C          SUBSTI    WHEQ '&B'
C                    MOVEA@B        EXC,Y
C          SUBSTI    WHEQ '&C'
C                    MOVEA@C        EXC,Y
C          SUBSTI    WHEQ '&D'
C                    MOVEA@D        EXC,Y
C          SUBSTI    WHEQ '&E'
C                    MOVEA@E        EXC,Y
C          SUBSTI    WHEQ '&F'
C                    MOVEA@F        EXC,Y
C          SUBSTI    WHEQ '&G'
C                    MOVEA@G        EXC,Y
C          SUBSTI    WHEQ '&H'
C                    MOVEA@H        EXC,Y
C          SUBSTI    WHEQ '&J'
C                    MOVEA@J        EXC,Y
C          SUBSTI    WHEQ '&L'
C                    MOVEA@L        EXC,Y
C          SUBSTI    WHEQ '&N'
C                    MOVEA@N        EXC,Y
(E) C          SUBSTI    WHEQ '&O'
C                    MOVEA@O        EXC,Y
C          SUBSTI    WHEQ '&P'
C                    MOVEA@P        EXC,Y
C          SUBSTI    WHEQ '&R'
C                    MOVEA@R        EXC,Y
C          SUBSTI    WHEQ '&S'
C                    MOVEA@S        EXC,Y
C          SUBSTI    WHEQ '&T'
C                    MOVEA@T        EXC,Y
C          SUBSTI    WHEQ '&U'
C                    MOVEA@U        EXC,Y
C          SUBSTI    WHEQ '&V'
C                    MOVEA@V        EXC,Y
C          SUBSTI    WHEQ '&W'
C                    MOVEA@W        EXC,Y
C          SUBSTI    WHEQ '&X'
C                    MOVE QUOTE     EXC,Y
C                    ADD  1         Y
C                    MOVEA@X        EXC,Y
C                    ADD  50        Y
C                    MOVE QUOTE     EXC,Y
```

Figure 43.4 Continued

Figure 43.4

RPG Program DSPUDOR *Continued*

```
 *...+....1....+....2....+....3....+....4....+....5....+....6....+....7
 C                    ENDSL
 ***
 C           WRKEXC    CAT  WRKWRK:Ø  WRKEXC
 C                     MOVE *BLANKS   WRK
Ⓕ C                    ENDIF
 **
Ⓖ C                    ENDDO
 *
 C                     ENDSR
 *****************************************************************
 *
 *     SUBROUTINE - ENDPGM - END OF PROGRAM
 *
 C           ENDPGM    BEGSR
 C                     MOVE *ON       *INLR
 C                     ENDSR
 *****************************************************************
 *
 *     SUBROUTINE - LODNEX - LOAD NEXT DISPLAY PAGE
 *
 C           LODNEX    BEGSR
 *
Ⓗ C          *IN94     IFEQ *OFF                         *IN94-BOTTOM
 C                     MOVE *ON       *IN93              *IN93-SFLINZ
 C                     WRITESUBCTL
 C                     MOVE *OFF      *IN93
 C                     ADD  11        RRN
 C           RRN       SETLLQAUOOPT
 **
 C           1         DO   11        SFLRRN  4Ø
 C           SFLRRN    CHAINSUBFIL                  99
 C                     READ QAUOOPT                   9494
 ***
 C           *IN94     IFEQ *OFF
 C                     MOVE *BLANKS   SFLSEL
 C                     MOVE OPTION    SFLOPT
 C                     MOVE COMMAN    SFLCOM
 C                     MOVELCOMMAN    SFLCMD              ADDED...
Ⓘ C*---                EXSR BLDCMD                        DELETED FOR
 C*---                 MOVELWRKEXC    SFLCMD               PERFORMANCE
 C           SFLOPT    COMP @C                          95  *IN95=DSPATR(ND
 C*                                                               PR)
 C                     ELSE
 C                     MOVE *ON       *IN95
 C                     ENDIF
 ***
 C                     UPDATSUBFIL
 C                     ENDDO
 **
 C                     ENDIF
 *
 C                     ENDSR
 *****************************************************************
 *
```

Figure 43.4 Continued

Figure 43.4

RPG Program DSPUDOR *Continued*

```
*...+....1....+....2....+....3....+....4....+....5....+....6....+....7
*     SUBROUTINE - LODPRV - LOAD PREVIOUS DISPLAY PAGE
*
C           LODPRV    BEGSR
C                     SUB  22        RRN
*
C           RRN       IFLT -10
C                     Z-ADD-10       RRN
C                     ENDIF
*
C                     MOVE *OFF      *IN94                *IN94-BOTTOM
C                     EXSR LODNEX
C                     ENDSR
*****************************************************************
*
*     SUBROUTINE - PROCES - PROCESS SELECTION
*
C           PROCES    BEGSR
*
C           1         DO   11        SFLRRN
C           SFLRRN    CHAINSUBFIL               99
**
C           SFLSEL    IFEQ '1'
C                     LEAVE
C                     ENDIF
**
C                     ENDDO
*
C           SFLSEL    IFEQ '1'
C                     EXSR BLDCMD
C                     CALL 'QCMDEXC'              96   *IN96-ERROR
C                     PARM           WRKEXC
C                     PARM 3000      CMDLEN 155
C     N96             MOVE *ON       *INLR
C                     ENDIF
*
C                     ENDSR
*****************************************************************
*
*     SUBROUTINE - REFRSH - REFRESH DISPLAY
*
C           REFRSH    BEGSR
C                     SUB  11        RRN
C                     MOVE *OFF      *IN94                *IN94-BOTTOM
C                     MOVE *OFF      *IN96                *IN96-ERROR
C                     EXSR LODNEX
C                     ENDSR
*****************************************************************
*
*     SUBROUTINE - *INZSR - FIRST PASS
*
C           *INZSR    BEGSR
C           *ENTRY    PLIST
C                     PARM           @A      10           ATTRIBUTE
C                     PARM           @B      10           LIST TYPE
```

Figure 43.4 Continued

Figure 43.4

RPG Program DSPUDOR *Continued*

```
*...+....1....+....2....+....3....+....4....+....5....+....6....+....7
C                   PARM           @C      2         OPTION
C                   PARM           @D      8         MBR CHG DATE
C                   PARM           @E     10         RUN IN BATCH
C                   PARM           @F     10         FILE NAME
C                   PARM           @G     10         JOBD LIB
C                   PARM           @H     10         JOBD
C                   PARM           @J     21         LIB/JOBD
C                   PARM           @L     10         LIBRARY NAME
C                   PARM           @N     10         ITEM NAME
C                   PARM           @O     10         OBJECT LIB
C                   PARM           @P     10         BATCH COMPILE
C                   PARM           @R     10         REPLACE OBJ
C                   PARM           @S     10         ITEM TYPE
C                   PARM           @T     10         *ITEM TYPE
C                   PARM           @U     10         UDO FILE
C                   PARM           @V     10         UDO LIB
C                   PARM           @W     10         UDO MEMBER
C                   PARM           @X     50         TEXT
C                   BITOF'01234567'F03     1
C                   BITON'2367'    F03
C                   BITOF'01234567'F04     1
C                   BITON'235'     F04
C                   BITOF'01234567'F05     1
C                   BITON'2357'    F05
C                   BITOF'01234567'F12     1
C                   BITON'2345'    F12
C                   BITOF'01234567'ROLLUP  1
C                   BITON'012357'  ROLLUP
C                   BITOF'01234567'ROLLDN  1
C                   BITON'01235'   ROLLDN
C                   BITOF'01234567'ENTER   1
C                   BITON'01237'   ENTER
C                   BITOF'01234567'QUOTE   1
C                   BITON'123457'  QUOTE
C                   Z-ADD-10       RRN     40
C                   EXSR LODNEX
C                   ENDSR
```

Speaking of structured operations, RPG finally has a useful conditional switch statement. RPG/400 has had the CASxx operation code for some time, allowing you to conditionally execute alternative subroutines, based upon matching the contents of Factor 1 and Factor 2. If the factors matched, the subroutine named in the Result field was executed and the program continued with the first statement after the group (B in Figure 43.4). This construction was fine if you wanted to code a subroutine for each case, but often it led to clumsy single-line subroutines (e.g., ENDPGM in Figure 43.4). If you wanted to use a similar construction but leave out the subroutine, you had to code multiple nested IFxx groups, guaranteeing at least one failed compilation and a maintenance nightmare.

Starting with V2R1, you can now code a single SELEC (Select) group using the following construction:

```
SELEC
WHxx
. . . statements
WHxx
. . . statements
OTHER
. . . statements
ENDSL
```

The code following a WHxx (When) statement is executed if the WHxx statement comparing Factor 1 and Factor 2 is true; then the program continues processing with the first statement following the ENDSL (or END) statement. The optional OTHER statement can be specified as a catch-all condition. This new construction is illustrated at D in Figure 43.4.

Epilogue

One more note is in order for the RPG program. The window program defaults to showing you the user-defined option without first substituting the PDM variables in the command; for example, you'll see "CALL &L/&N" instead of "CALL QGPL/PGMA" when you display the window. This was done to speed up the window display. You can display the substituted variables by using the command prompter, but if you want to perform the necessary substitutions before displaying the window, comment out the first line at E in Figure 43.4 and take the comment notation out of the second and third lines in that group so they are executable lines of code.

IBM provides a tool in the QUSRTOOL library that is similar to the DSPUDO program. But, unfortunately for all but a handful of AS/400 installations, IBM's program requires that you have the BASIC compiler installed on your system. For more information about IBM's PDM window, check the information in file QUSRTOOL/QATTINFO, member TPSINFO.

Chapter 44

Subfile Record Retrieval

by Ron Harvey

Code point and execute on your AS/400 to select subfile records or subfile menu options

Selecting data or functions on a PC is usually simple. You view the data or functions on the display and position an action bar or mouse arrow on the record or action you want. Press a key and, *voilà*, your selection is made. This method is called *point and execute* because that's exactly what you do — point to what you want to select, and execute an action.

In contrast, on the AS/400, the conventional method for selecting a subfile record or an option from a subfile menu is to type an X or some other character into a 1-byte, input-capable field at the beginning of the subfile record. This antediluvian technique has worked since the advent of subfiles and will probably be an option until Presentation Manager is available on OS/400.

Few AS/400 programmers are aware, however, that point and execute is easy to code on their machines and often more efficient than the conventional method. With point and execute, the user places the cursor directly on the desired field, which reduces the likelihood of incorrect selections. With this technique, no unnecessary I/O or changed records occur, as often happens with the conventional method when the user presses Field exit or the space bar to move the cursor. Using point and execute requires fewer keystrokes and less head and eye movement. And at least two positions on the screen (the 1-byte, input-capable field and the space immediately following it) are freed, which may reduce or eliminate the need to truncate fields to fit text across the screen.

To take advantage of the point-and-execute record retrieval method, you need to control the cursor location. You also need to define a file information data structure for each display file, the cursor location and subfile relative record number fields within that data structure, the initial cursor position, and the extents of the subfile on the screen. With these steps accomplished, you can use a subroutine to retrieve the subfile record.

Controlling Cursor Placement

There are two commonly used ways to control cursor placement. One is to let OS/400 do it; the operating system places the cursor in position one of the first input-capable field on the display. Another method is to use the PC (position cursor) keyword on the display file Data Description Specifications (DDS), which puts the cursor in position one of the first field containing the keyword.

As an alternative to these methods, a more flexible placement technique is to use the DDS record-level keyword CSRLOC (cursor location) and define row and column fields in the display file. These fields determine where the WRITE or EXFMT operation places the cursor.

Figure 44.1 shows the Screen Design Aid (SDA) Select Output Keywords panel, on which you can specify the field names that will contain the values for row and column (I like SETROW and SETCOL) to control the cursor's position on your screen. Unfortunately, specifying the row and column fields for the CSRLOC keyword does not define these hidden fields to the compiler. To define the fields, use the SDA Work with Fields prompt (F4) — Figure 44.2 shows the Work with Fields panel. Figure 44.3 shows the DDS with the CSRLOC keyword and the row and column fields defined (A), and the specified hidden fields (B).

Figure 44.1

SDA Select Output Keywords Panel

```
                      Select Output Keywords

Record ....: CTL

Type choices, press enter.

                                       Keyword  Y=Yes  Ind

   Blink cursor . . . . . . . . . .    BLINK     _     _ _ _
   Sound the Alarm  . . . . . . . .    ALARM     _     _ _ _
   Do not unlock keyboard . . . . .    LOCK      _     _ _ _
   Write record to joblog . . . . .    LOGOUT    _     _ _ _
   Invite devices for later read  .    INVITE    _     _ _ _
   Allow graphics . . . . . . . . .    ALLOW     _     _ _ _
   Put data before buffer is full .    FRCDTA    _     _ _ _

Hidden fields with
   cursor position for output:           CSRLOC
   Row Number . . . . . . . . .                    SETROW  Name
   Name Column Number . . . . .                    SETCOL  Name


F3=Exit  F12=Previous
```

Figure 44.2

SDA Work with Fields Panel

```
                          Work with Fields

Record . . . :   CTL

Type information, press enter.
 Number of fields to roll . . . . . . . . . . 7


Type options, change values, press Enter.
 1=Select keywords   4=Delete field


Option  Order  Field     Type Use   Length    Row/Col   Ref

          10   SETROW     S    H     3,0
          20   SETCOL     S    H     3,0
          30   ASG100     C          6        001 003
          40   AMOUNT     B          7,2      006 028

                                    More...

Add      ___  ______      H    ____  Hidden


F3=Exit  F6=Sort by row/column  F12=Previous
```

Using CSRLOC to position the cursor gives you more flexibility than conventional methods in at least two ways. First, instead of appearing on the first input-capable field or in position one of the first field with the PC keyword, the cursor appears in the row and column you specify. For example, if the key field on a screen is someone's last name, but the subfile record also contains first and middle names, you might want to have your program put the cursor on the last name rather than the first name. Similarly, you might want to put the cursor somewhere other than the first position of a field to draw the user's attention to the middle of that field, speeding up identification. Only by using the CSRLOC method can you choose where to place the cursor.

Second, when program-defined fields control the cursor position, you can reposition the cursor to any location. For example, say the user selects a line item on an order inquiry screen by cursor position and then presses a function key to call a shipment history program. When control returns to the order inquiry program, you may want the cursor to re-appear in the same position — on the line item selected for inquiry. You can specify this placement simply by having the program move into SETROW and SETCOL the cursor row and column values from the file information data structure when the user presses the function key. When the order inquiry program re-issues the READ or EXFMT

Figure 44.3

Sample DDS for Display File DISPLAY

```
*... ... 1 ... ... 2 ... ... 3 ... ... 4 ... ... 5 ... ... 6 ... ... 7
     ********************************************************************
     *                                                                  *
     *      SAMPLE DDS FOR DISPLAY FILE "DISPLAY"                       *
     *                                                                  *
     *       NOTE ESPECIALLY THE "CSRLOC" KEYWORD                       *
     *       AND THE "SETROW" AND "SETCOL" HIDDEN FIELDS                *
     *                                                                  *
     ********************************************************************
     *
    A                                      DSPSIZ(24 80 *DS3)
    A          R SFL                       SFL
    A            CUSTNO         7  00   6 10EDTCDE(Z)
    A            CUSTNA        25   0   6 28
    A            ORDBAL        11  20   6 58EDTCDE(K $)
    A          R CTL                       SFLCTL(SFL)
    A                                      CF03
    A                                   CF12
    A                                      HELP
    A                                      ROLLUP
    A                                      ROLLDOWN
    A                                      BLINK
(A) A                                   CSRLOC(SETROW SETCOL)
    A  52                                  SFLDSP
    A  51                                  SFLDSPCTL
    A  50                                  SFLCLR
    A                                      SFLSIZ(0025)
    A                                      SFLPAG(0012)
(B) A            SETROW         3  0H
    A            SETCOL         3  0H
    A                                 1  3'Example'
    A                                 1 33'XYZ Corporation'
    A                                 1 57DATE
    A                                      EDTCDE(Y)
    A                                 1 69TIME
    A                                 2 28'Customer Review/Selection'
    A                                 4  9'Customer #'
    A                                 4 28'Custmer Name'
    A                                 4 56'Order Balance'
    A          R S1
    A                                19  2'-----------------------------
    A                                      -----------------------------
    A                                      ------'
    A                                20 12'Place the Cursor on the Customer
    A                                     you wish to select'
    A                                21 26'Press ENTER to select'
    A                                23 16'F3-Exit  F12-Prev    HELP
    A                                      Down'
```

operation, the cursor appears at the row and column specified by the values in SETROW and SETCOL.

Retrieving a Subfile Record

When you know how to control cursor placement with the CSRLOC keyword, you can use this knowledge to retrieve a subfile record on which the cursor is placed. One of the nicest features of the point-and-execute record retrieval method is that the operating system does most of the work for you — if you take a few simple steps.

First, using a continuation specification, define a file information data structure for each display file you want to use this technique for. The sample RPG code in Figure 44.4 defines the display file and names the data structure the operating system uses to store data.

Next, you define the fields CURSOR and SRRN in the file information data structure (Figure 44.5). CURSOR, a binary field located in positions 370 and 371 of the information data structure, contains the row and column where the cursor was positioned at the last EXFMT or READ operation. SRRN, a binary field in positions 378 and 379, contains the number of the first subfile relative record on the current page. (For example, if your subfile has a page size of 12 and the first page is currently displayed, the value of SRRN is 1. As the user presses the Roll up key, the value of SRRN changes to 13, 25, 37, and so on.)

The final step is to define the number of records in the subfile and the initial cursor position. To ensure cursor placement on a valid subfile record, you must identify the beginning and ending extents of the subfile, usually by using a setup subroutine. Figure 44.6 shows a sample block of code that specifies that the first

Figure 44.4

F-Specifications for the Display File

```
Figure 44.4

 *... ... 1 ... ... 2 ... ... 3 ... ... 4 ... ... 5 ... ... 6 ... ... 7

     FDISPLAY CF E                      WORKSTN
     F                                          RRN  KSFILE SFL
     F                                               KINFDS DSPDS
```

Figure 44.5

Defining Fields CURSOR and SRRN

```
 *... ... 1 ... ... 2 ... ... 3 ... ... 4 ... ... 5 ... ... 6 ... ... 7

     IDSPDS      DS
     I                                B 370 3710CURSOR
     I                                B 378 3790SRRN
```

Figure 44.6

Defining Subfile Extents and Cursor Position

```
*... ... 1 ... ... 2 ... ... 3 ... ... 4 ... ... 5 ... ... 6 ... ... 7

     C                    Z-ADD6     FSTLIN  20
     C                    Z-ADD17    LSTLIN  20
     C                    Z-ADD6     SETROW
     C                    Z-ADD32    SETCOL
     C                    Z-ADD12    PAGSIZ  20
```

subfile record appears on line 6 of the display and the last subfile record on line 17. The cursor is initially placed in row 6, column 32. Figure 44.6 also defines a work field that indicates the subfile page size is 12.

I make it a regular practice to identify the extents in all subfile programs. When you define the extents and page size once in the program and use the field names throughout all other calculations, you have only one place (the initialization subroutine) to modify if the size of your subfile changes.

After you define the extents and page size of your subfile, the program can load the subfile with data as usual and issue a READ or EXFMT operation to the control record. In the customer order inquiry program mentioned earlier, you could place the cursor on the line containing the product you want to review and press the function key for shipment history. The only remaining task is to determine on which subfile record the cursor is located, retrieve the information from that subfile record, and pass that information to the shipment history inquiry program. You can do this by executing a RTVSFL subroutine like the one in Figure 44.7.

The subroutine first converts the cursor row and column position (retrieved from the file information data structure) from binary to decimal and puts the values into variables LINE and COL. Then the routine checks whether the cursor is positioned within the subfile. If it is not, the routine displays an error message to the user. Otherwise, the routine subtracts the first subfile line number from the line number on which the cursor is located and adds the difference to the first subfile record number on the current page. The result is the subfile record number of the record the user selected. Finally, the subroutine chains to the correct record.

Some Limitations of Point and Execute

Although point and execute is clean, slick, and accurate, it is not the most efficient method of retrieval when you want to select multiple records before pressing an action key. The best use of point and execute is to select a single record or function from a list. Also, this technique might not be available if you have an old terminal — for my method, you need full-byte cursor capability, in which the cursor location is illuminated rather than underlined, and some old terminals don't have this capability. Although point and execute is not always appropriate, it is a good alternative method to conventional subfile retrieval.

Figure 44.7

Sample RTVSFL Subroutine

```
*... ... 1 ... ... 2 ... ... 3 ... ... 4 ... ... 5 ... ... 6 ... ... 7

     C           RTVSFL     BEGSR
     C                      MOVE *ZEROS    GETRRN  40
      *
      *    Convert cursor position from file INFDS to decimal.
 *
     C           CURSOR     DIV  256       LINE    20
     C                      MVR            COL     20
      *
      *    Determine if cursor is within the subfile extents.
      *
     C           LINE       IFLT FSTLIN
     C           LINE       ORGT LSTLIN
     C                      MOVE 'Y'       ERROR
      *
     C                      ELSE
      *
      *    Determine subfile record number of the chosen record.
      *
     C           LINE       SUB  FSTLIN    DWNPAG   20
     C           DWNPAG     ADD  SRRN      GETRRN
      *
      *    Retrieve the subfile record.
      *
     C           GETRRN     CHAINSFL                      98
      *
      *    Place any highlighting or other subfile operations
      *    here followed by an update subfile operation.
      *
     C                      END
     C                      ENDSR
```

Chapter 45

Side-by-Side Subfiles

by Ron Harvey

You can create the illusion of side-by-side subfiles using the point-and-execute technique

Anyone can place more than one active subfile on a display. The usual method is to design the display so that a control record and corresponding subfile occupy the top half of the screen and a second control record and subfile take up the bottom half. When you use this method, the subfiles appear one above the other, as ORDERS and SHIPMENTS do in Figure 45.1.

Sometimes, however, it might be difficult to compare all the data in subfiles displayed one above the other, or users might want to view a greater number of subfiles than the screen can accommodate (more than two subfiles displayed this way tend to clutter the screen). For example, users might want to review the payments as well as the orders and shipments for a specific customer.

If you place ORDERS, SHIPMENTS, and PAYMENTS next to each other in one subfile (as shown in Figure 45.2), the program can search all three files for the lowest order number and use that order number as the equal argument to set limits and read for equal. In this case, the program fills and displays one order at a time — a tried, true, and completely valid technique.

Loading a subfile with data for more than one order is not difficult — the problem arises when users are viewing a particular order, for example, and they want to roll the ORDERS information but view the same SHIPMENTS currently displayed.

Although such side-by-side subfiles don't yet exist, you can create a single subfile that *looks* and *performs* like multiple subfiles. In Chapter 44, "Subfile Record Retrieval," I introduced a way to select subfile records, using the point-and-execute technique (with my RTVSFL subroutine). You can also use the point-and-execute technique to create the illusion of separate, side-by-side subfiles.

Figure 45.1

Two Subfiles Displayed One Above the Other

```
SFLDEMO                   Order Status Review          9/03/90   18:50:57

  KLUTZ & KLUTZ MOVERS                            Total Orders    $ 45,000.00
  111 BETTER INSURE IT ROAD                       Credit Limit    $100,000.00
  KISS IT GOODBYE       NY 12121                  A/R Balance     $ 32,000.00
-----------------------------------------------------------------------------
                           O  R  D  E  R  S
-----------------------------------------------------------------------------
    Ord #         Date Promised        Part Number            Quantity Ordered
    12345            3/08/90              AA10                           250
    12345            3/08/90              AA25                           500
    12345            4/10/90              AA35                           850
    12345            4/10/90              AA45                           450
------------------------------------------------------------------------------
                        S  H  I  P  M  E  N  T  S
------------------------------------------------------------------------------
    Ord #         Date Shipped         Part Number            Quantity Shipped
    12345            3/08/90              AA10                            50
    12345            3/08/90              AA35                           100
    12345            3/10/90              AA10                            25
    12345            3/10/90              AA35                           125
------------------------------------------------------------------------------
           F3=Exit    Rollup/Rolldown    Other user instructions
```

Figure 45.2

Single Subfile Displaying One Order

```
SFLDEMO                   Order Status Review          9/03/90   18:57:57

  KLUTZ & KLUTZ MOVERS                            Total Orders    $ 45,000.00
  111 BETTER INSURE IT ROAD                       Credit Limit    $100,000.00
  KISS IT GOODBYE       NY 12121                  A/R Balance     $ 32,000.00
-----------------------------------------------------------------------------
|     O R D E R S        |   S H I P M E N T S      |  P A Y M E N T S |
|----------------------------------------------------------------------------
| Ord# Prm Dt Part   Qty | Ord# Shp Dt  Part   Qty  | Ord#   Pd Dt   Amt |
|---------------------------------------------------------------------------|
| 12345 30890 AA10   250 | 12345 30890  AA10    50  | 12345  40890 1,200 |
| 12345 30890 AA25   500 | 12345 30890  AA35   100  | 12345  41290 2,500 |
| 12345 41090 AA35   850 | 12345 31090  AA10    25  |                    |
| 12345 41090 AA45   450 | 12345 31090  AA35   125  |                    |
|                        | 12345 31090  AA45    75  |                    |
|                        | 12345 32290  AA10   125  |                    |
|                        | 12345 32290  AA25   400  |                    |
|                        | 12345 32290  AA35   600  |                    |
|                        | 12345 32290  AA45   375  |                    |
|                        | 12345 32290  AA65   750  |                    |
|                        | 12345 40190  AA65   350  |                    |
-----------------------------------------------------------------------------
                  F3=Exit  Roll Key Instructions, etc.
```

Subfile Sections

If you divide a subfile into three logical sections and display them side by side, you can fill each one with order, shipment, or payment information for a selected customer. The result is three independent, but related, "windows" of information that look like the "subfiles" in Figure 45.3.

If users are interested in payment information only, they can roll the PAYMENTS section and then key some scan criteria, select a particular payment for maintenance, or perform some other payment-related functions. Because, in this example, users have three side-by-side subfile sections that can roll independently, each section is available for viewing separately or in combination with the other two.

I created the display file for the screen in Figure 45.3 the way I always create a display file except that I divided the subfile into three logical sections. Figure 45.4 shows the DDS that produces this subfile illusion. I call the subfile SFL (A in Figure 45.4, page 618) and the control record CTL (B), and set the subfile page equal to the subfile size (C). For the purposes of this demonstration program, I hard-coded the amounts for total orders (D), credit limit (E), and A/R balance (F). The DDS creates a one-page subfile that contains 11 subfile records.

The next step to building a side-by-side subfile illusion is to define, in your RPG program, the file information data structure for the display file (A in Figure 45.5, page 620) with a field that contains the binary equivalent of the cursor location (I call this field CURSOR). Then you write a program initialization subroutine in

Figure 45.3

The Illusion of Side-by-Side Subfiles

```
SFLDEMO                     Order Status Review           9/03/90    19:01:16

  KLUTZ & KLUTZ MOVERS                               Total Orders    $ 45,000.00
  111 BETTER INSURE IT ROAD                          Credit Limit    $100,000.00
  KISS IT GOODBYE        NY 12121                    A/R Balance     $ 32,000.00
--------------------------------------------------------------------------------
|       O R D E R S          |     S H I P M E N T S        |   P A Y M E N T S |
|-------------------------------------------------------------------------------
| Ord# Prm Dt Part    Qty    | Ord# Shp Dt  Part    Qty     | Ord#    Pd Dt   Amt |
|-------------------------------------------------------------------------------|
| 12345 30890 AA10    250    | 12345 30890  AA10     50     | 12345   40890 1,200 |
| 12345 30890 AA25    500    | 12345 30890  AA35    100     | 12345   41290 2,500 |
| 12345 41090 AA35    850    | 12345 31090  AA10     25     |                     |
| 12345 41090 AA45    450    | 12345 31090  AA35    125     | 12498   40890   850 |
|                            | 12345 31090  AA45     75     |                     |
| 12498 31290 AA85    900    | 12345 32290  AA10    125     |                     |
|                            | 12345 32290  AA25    400     |                     |
| 14000 50190 AA12    350    | 12345 32290  AA35    600     |                     |
|                            | 12345 32290  AA45    375     |                     |
| 27123 61590 AA99    750    | 12345 32290  AA65    750     |                     |
| 27123 71590 AA99    810    | 12345 41090  AA65    350     |                     |
--------------------------------------------------------------------------------
                      F3=Exit  Roll Key Instructions, etc.
```

which you declare the subfile extents and page size. If you define the extents and use the field names throughout your program, you have only one place in the program to change if the size or location of the subfile changes.

You must also specify where the SHIPMENT and PAYMENT columns begin, as I have done with the initialization of STRSHP and STRPAY. Five lines of code that define the subfile parameters in Figure 45.5 (K) establish the following facts:

- The first line of subfile data is on display file line 11 (FSTLIN).
- The last line of subfile data is on display file line 21 (LSTLIN).
- The subfile has a page size of 11 records.
- If users place the cursor within the subfile and at a column less than 30, they select ORDERS (the subfile section to the left of SHIPMENTS — STRSHP).
- If users place the cursor within the subfile and at a column beyond 29 (the end of ORDERS) and before 59 (the beginning of PAYMENTS — STRPAY), they select SHIPMENTS.
- If users place the cursor within the subfile and neither of the above two conditions is true, they select PAYMENTS.

As shown in Figure 45.5 (L), the program initialization subroutine performs a DO loop for the same number of times as there are pages in the subfile (PAGSIZ). This DO loop initially writes a complete page of blank records. It is best to perform this DO loop in an initialization subroutine because it needs to be executed only once in the program. (Using an indicator with the SFLINZ keyword performs the same function.)

Loading the Subfile

The program is now ready to load the first 11 subfile records with order information. Three subroutines (LODORD, LODSHP, and LODPAY) load the subfile sections one at a time. Figure 45.5 (G) shows subroutine LODORD, which loads the ORDERS section. The LODORD subroutine uses the customer number to find a match in the ORDERS logical file (ORDL1), moves the database fields to the multiple-occurrence data structure, updates the subfile record with order information, and tracks how many orders have been read from disk.

LODSHP (Figure 45.5 (H)) and LODPAY (Figure 45.5 (I)) are almost identical to LODORD: The only differences in the three subroutines are the database operations, any data manipulation required, and the subroutine called (i.e., ZERORD, ZERSHP, or ZERPAY) to put a blank line between orders or to blank out the unused portion of the screen when end of file is reached.

In Figure 45.5 (J), ZERORD, ZERSHP, and ZERPAY set to zeros or blanks the subfile and multiple-occurrence data structure fields in each subfile section, depending on whether the field is numeric or character. For example, subroutine ZERORD sets to zeros or blanks the subfile fields associated with orders (ORD1, DATE1, PART1, and QTY1). It also sets to zeros or blanks the fields in the order multiple-occurrence data structure, ORDDS.

Displaying the Subfile

Now you have not one but three subfiles (or so it appears). After the program displays the side-by-side subfile illusion, it waits for a user response. Suppose the user places the cursor in the ORDERS section, and presses the Roll up key. Based on the position of the cursor, the program displays the next page of the ORDERS subfile section (Figure 45.5 (C)).

You can give the user a rolling technique that makes the program perform efficiently if you create multiple-occurrence data structures that contain database field names for ORDERS, SHIPMENTS, and PAYMENTS (Figure 45.5 (B)). By storing information in multiple-occurrence data structures, you reduce the number of times the program has to go to the database to retrieve subfile records. Code the program so that each time subroutine LODORD, LODSHP, or LODPAY updates part of the subfile, the program stores the database fields in the next occurrence of the appropriate data structure. When the program loads a new subfile page, it stores the occurrence number of the first subfile record in a subfile hidden field (HO, HS, or HP) and tracks the highest (total) occurrence number (TO, TS, or TP) stored so far (Figure 45.5 (G1)).

When users press the Roll up key, the program increments the occurrence of the first subfile record on the page by the page size. If the result is greater than the highest occurrence stored, the program executes either the LODORD, LODSHP, or LODPAY subroutine (Figure 45.5 (D)), depending on where the user has placed the cursor. If the result is less than the highest occurrence stored, the subfile is loaded from one of the data structures rather than from the database (Figure 45.5 (F)).

Similarly, when users press the Roll down key, the program decrements the occurrence by the subfile page size (Figure 45.5 (E)). The subfile is then reloaded from one of the data structures; however, it always performs data structure OCUR operations rather than database READ operations (Figure 45.5 (F)).

When the program performs either rolling routine, it updates only one set of fields within a subfile. If users place the cursor within the ORDERS subfile section, the SHIPMENTS and PAYMENTS sections remain intact, thus creating the illusion that a separate subfile has been rolled.

Adding Point and Execute

You can use the point-and-execute technique described in Chapter 44, "Subfile Record Retrieval," to further enhance your side-by-side subfile program. For example, say the user chooses order number 14000 and presses the Enter key to request an action (e.g., add or review comments, perform order maintenance, or review additional information that would not fit into the subfile). Using the RTVSFL subroutine, the program can easily determine which order the user selected and perform the requested action, having already retrieved all the data (including hidden fields) that the subfile record contains.

Figure 45.4

DDS for Side-by-Side Subfile Illusion

```
*... ... 1 ... ... 2 ... ... 3 ... ... 4 ... ... 5 ... ... 6 ... ... 7

     A*  90/09/03  18:25:08    HARVEY      REL-R02M00  5728-PW1
     A*
     A*****************************************************************
     A*                                                               *
     A*             DDS FOR DISPLAY FILE SFLEX2D                      *
     A*      "SIDE-BY-SIDE" SUBFILE EXAMPLE/DEMO PROGRAM              *
     A*                                                               *
     A*****************************************************************
     A*
     A                                      DSPSIZ(24 80 *DS3)
     A                                      PRINT
     A                                      CF03
     A                                      ROLLUP
     A                                      ROLLDOWN
     A                                      HOME
     A                                      HELP
(A)  A          R SFL                       SFL
     A*  90/09/03  18:19:53    HARVEY      REL-R02M00  5728-PW1
     A*
     A*  HIDDEN FIELDS USED TO HOLD THE CURRENT DATA STRUCTURE
     A*   OCCURRENCE NUMBER.
     A*
     A            HO             3S 0H
     A            HS             3S 0H
     A            HP             3S 0H
     A                                 11  2'|'
     A                                      DSPATR(HI)
     A*
     A*  ORDER FIELDS
     A*
     A            ORD1      R        O 11  4REFFLD(ORDF/ORORD# DEMO/ORD)
     A                                      EDTCDE(Z)
     A            DATE1     R        O 11 10REFFLD(ORDF/ORPMDT DEMO/ORD)
     A                                      EDTCDE(Z)
     A            PART1     R        O 11 17REFFLD(ORDF/ORPART DEMO/ORD)
     A            QTY1      R        O 11 22REFFLD(ORDF/ORQTY DEMO/ORD)
     A                                      EDTCDE(2)
     A                                 11 29'|'
     A                                      DSPATR(HI)
     A*
     A*  SHIPMENT FIELDS
     A*
     A            ORD2      R        O 11 31REFFLD(SHIPF/SHORD# DEMO/SHIP)
     A                                      EDTCDE(Z)
     A            DATE2     R        O 11 37REFFLD(SHIPF/SHDATE DEMO/SHIP)
     A                                      EDTCDE(Z)
     A            PART2     R        O 11 45REFFLD(SHIPF/SHPART DEMO/SHIP)
     A            QTY2      R        O 11 51REFFLD(SHIPF/SHQTY DEMO/SHIP)
     A                                      EDTCDE(2)
     A                                 11 58'|'
     A                                      DSPATR(HI)
     A*
     A*  PAYMENT FIELDS
```

Figure 45.4 Continued

Figure 45.4

DDS for Side-by-Side Subfile Illusion *Continued*

```
*... ... 1 ... ... 2 ... ... 3 ... ... 4 ... ... 5 ... ... 6 ... ... 7
     A*
     A            ORD3      R        0 11 60REFFLD(PAYF/PYORD# DEMO/PAY)
     A                                      EDTCDE(Z)
     A            DATE3     R        0 11 66REFFLD(PAYF/PYDATE DEMO/PAY)
     A                                      EDTCDE(Z)
     A            AMTPD     R        0 11 73REFFLD(PAYF/PYAMTP DEMO/PAY)
     A                                      EDTCDE(2)
     A                                 11 79'|'
     A                                      DSPATR(HI)
(B)  A          R CTL                       SFLCTL(SFL)
     A*  90/09/03  18:25:08    HARVEY     REL-R02M00  5728-PW1
(C)  A                                      SFLSIZ(0011)
     A                                      SFLPAG(0011)
     A                                      BLINK
     A                                      CSRLOC(SETROW     SETCOL)
     A                                      OVERLAY
     A                                      PUTOVR
     A  51                                  SFLDSP
     A  51                                  SFLDSPCTL
     A  50                                  SFLCLR
     A            SETROW         3S 0H
     A            SETCOL         3S 0H
     A                                  1  3'SFLDEMO'
     A                                  1 29'Order Status Review'
     A                                      DSPATR(HI)
     A                                  1 56DATE
     A                                      EDTCDE(Y)
     A                                  1 67TIME
     A            MMNAME    R        0  3  5REFFLD(CLIENTF/MMNAME DEMO/CLIENT)
     A                                  3 48'Total Orders'
     A                                      DSPATR(HI)
(D)  A                                  3 63'$ 45,000.00'
     A            MMADD1    R        0  4  5REFFLD(CLIENTF/MMADD1 DEMO/CLIENT)
     A                                  4 48'Credit Limit'
     A                                      DSPATR(HI)
(E)  A                                  4 63'$100,000.00'
     A            MMCITY    R        0  5  5REFFLD(CLIENTF/MMCITY DEMO/CLIENT)
     A            MMSTAT    R        0  5 26REFFLD(CLIENTF/MMSTAT DEMO/CLIENT)
     A            ZIP            5A  0  5 29
     A                                  5 48'A/R Balance'
     A                                      DSPATR(HI)
(F)  A                                  5 63'$ 32,000.00'
     A                                  6  2'-----------------------------------
     A                                      -----------------------------------
     A                                      ---------'
     A                                      DSPATR(HI)
     A                                  7  2'|      O R D E R S        |    S-
     A                                       H I P M E N T S      |   P A Y M E-
     A                                       N T S  |'
     A                                      DSPATR(HI)
     A                                  8  2'|---------------------------------
     A                                      -----------------------------------
     A                                      --------|'
     A                                      DSPATR(HI)
```

Figure 45.4 Continued

Figure 45.4 — DDS for Side-by-Side Subfile Illusion *Continued*

```
*... ... 1 ... ... 2 ... ... 3 ... ... 4 ... ... 5 ... ... 6 ... ... 7
     A                                  9  2'| Ord#  Prm Dt Part   Qty  |  Ord -
     A                                       Shp Dt  Part    Qty  |  Ord  Pd Dt-
     A                                           Amt |'
     A                                         DSPATR(HI)
     A                                 10  2'|----------------------------------
     A                                       ----------------------------------
     A                                       --------|'
     A                                         DSPATR(HI)
     A          R S1
     A*  90/09/03  18:19:53    HARVEY      REL-R02M00  5728-PW1
     A                                 22  2'----------------------------------
     A                                       ----------------------------------
     A                                       ---------'
     A                                         DSPATR(HI)
     A N43                             23 22'F3-Exit  Roll Key Instructions etc-
     A                                       ...'
     A                                         DSPATR(HI)
     A  44                             24  3'Invalid cursor position for operat-
     A                                       ion selected - Press ENTER'
     A                                         DSPATR(HI)
     A  45                             24  3'Roll up/down invalid at beginning/-
     A                                       end of data - Press ENTER'
     A  45                                     DSPATR(HI)
     A  46                             24  3'Retrieving Client Comments - Pleas-
     A                                       e wait'
     A                                         DSPATR(HI)
     A  47                             24  3'Retrieving Transaction Comments - -
     A                                       Please Wait'
     A  47                                     DSPATR(HI)
```

Figure 45.5 — RPG for Side-by-Side Subfile Illusion

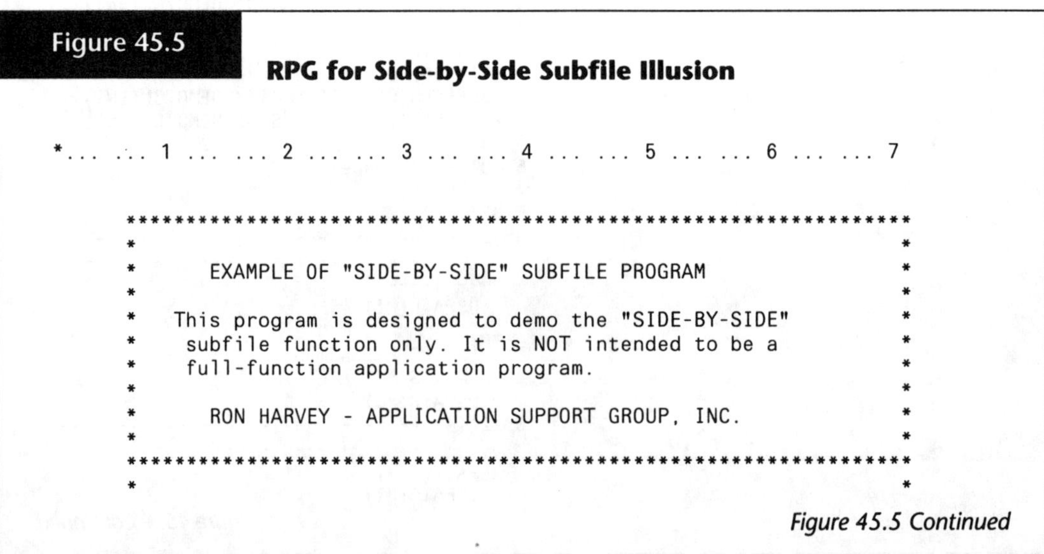

```
*... ... 1 ... ... 2 ... ... 3 ... ... 4 ... ... 5 ... ... 6 ... ... 7

      ***************************************************************
      *                                                             *
      *      EXAMPLE OF "SIDE-BY-SIDE" SUBFILE PROGRAM              *
      *                                                             *
      *   This program is designed to demo the "SIDE-BY-SIDE"       *
      *    subfile function only. It is NOT intended to be a        *
      *    full-function application program.                       *
      *                                                             *
      *      RON HARVEY - APPLICATION SUPPORT GROUP, INC.           *
      *                                                             *
      ***************************************************************
      *                                                             *
```

Figure 45.5 Continued

Figure 45.5

RPG for Side-by-Side Subfile Illusion

```
*... ... 1 ... ... 2 ... ... 3 ... ... 4 ... ... 5 ... ... 6 ... ... 7
     FORDL1   IF  E           K        DISK
     FSHIPL1  IF  E           K        DISK
     FPAYL1   IF  E           K        DISK
     FCLIENTL1IF  E           K        DISK
     FSFLEX2D CF  E                    WORKSTN
     F                                        RRN   KSFILE SFL
     F                                              KINFDS DSPDS
      *
      *
      *  File Information Data Structure
(A)   *
      *    KEY    - "Aid Byte" - Key pressed (HEX)
      *    CURSOR - Cursor Position (Row & Column in Binary)
      *    SRRN   - Subfile Record Number of the 1st subfile record
      *               on the current subfile page.
      *
     IDSPDS       DS
     I                                          369 369 KEY
     I                                        B 370 3710CURSOR
     I                                        B 378 3790SRRN
      *
      *  External DATA STRUCTURE "KEYS" -

     IKEYDS     E DSKEYS *
      *   Multiple Occurrence Data Structures
      *
      *     Used to store the data base fields used in each
      *     subfile record to avoid reading the same
      *     database record more than once as the user presses
      *     the roll keys.
      *
      *   NOTE: 50 OCCURRENCES (Alter for your environment)
      *
      *-------ORDERS DATA STRUCTURE
      *
     IORDDS       DS                          50
     I                                         1   50ORORD#
     I                                         6  110ORPMDT
     I                                        12  15 ORPART
     I                                        16  190ORQTY
      *
      *-------SHIPMENTS DATA STRUCTURE
      *
     ISHPDS       DS                          50
     I                                         1   50SHORD#
     I                                         6  110SHDATE
(B)  I                                        12  15 SHPART
     I                                        16  190SHQTY
      *
      *-------PAYMENTS
      *
     IPAYDS       DS                          50
```

Figure 45.5 Continued

Figure 45.5

RPG for Side-by-Side Subfile Illusion *Continued*

```
*... ... 1 ... ... 2 ... ... 3 ... ... 4 ... ... 5 ... ... 6 ... ... 7
     I                                          1  5ØPYORD#
     I                                          6 11ØPYDATE
     I                                         12 15ØPYAMTP
      *
      *   Hold DATA STRUCTURE for ORDERS/SHIPMENTS.
Ⓑ     *     Used to save database field names during
      *     OCUR operations.
      *
     IHOLD1      DS
     I                                          1  19 H1
      *
      *   Hold DATA STRUCTURE For PAYMENTS
      *
     IHOLD2      DS
     I                                          1  15ØH2
      *
      *   1 Time SETUP Steps
      *
     C                     EXSR SETUP
     C                     EXSR LODORD
     C                     EXSR LODSHP
     C                     EXSR LODPAY
      *
      *   MAIN LINE LOOP
      *
     C           KEY       DOUEQF3
      *
     C                     WRITES1
     C                     EXFMTCTL
      *
     C                     MOVEA'ØØØ'     *IN,43            setoff errors
      *
      *   Check for FUNCTION KEY Requests
      *
     C           KEY       CASEQROLLUP    ROLL
     C           KEY       CASEQROLLDN    ROLL
      *
      *  In a "NORMAL" application program, something similar to
      *  the following CAS statements would probably be found.
      *
      *          KEY       CASEQENTER     INQ               more info
      *          KEY       CASEQHELP      HELP              help
      *          KEY       CASEQF11       MAINT             maintenance
      *          KEY       CASEQF21       ADDCMT            comment maint
      *
     C                     END
     C                     END
      *
     C                     MOVE '1'       *INLR
     C                     RETRN
      *
      ************************************************
```

Figure 45.5 Continued

Figure 45.5

RPG for Side-by-Side Subfile Illusion *Continued*

```
*... ... 1 ... ... 2 ... ... 3 ... ... 4 ... ... 5 ... ... 6 ... ... 7
     *  PROCESS ROLL KEYS                               *
     ***********************************************
     *
    C           ROLL      BEGSR
     *
     *  Convert binary CURSOR position to decimal
     *
    C           CURSOR    DIV  256       ROW
    C                     MVR            COL
     *
     *  Determine if CURSOR placed in a valid position
     *
    C           ROW       IFLT FSTLIN
    C           ROW       ORGT LSTLIN
    C                     MOVEA'110'     *IN,43          cursor error
     *
    C                     ELSE
     *
     *------ Roll key pressed while CURSOR was within the subfile area.
(C)  *------ Determine which transaction type should be rolled.
     *------ Update the subfile reocrd with fields for selected type only.
     *
    C           COL       CASLTSTRSHP    ROLORD          orders
    C           COL       CASLTSTRPAY    ROLSHP          shipments
    C                     CAS            ROLPAY          payments
    C                     END
    C                     END
     *
     *   Set CURSOR to remain where the user placed it.
     *
    C                     Z-ADDROW       SETROW
    C                     Z-ADDCOL       SETCOL
     *
    C                     ENDSR
     *
     *************************************
     *  ROLL ORDERS SUBROUTINE
     *************************************
     *
    C           ROLORD    BEGSR
     *
     *   Retrieve the 1st SUBFILE RECORD on the current page.
     *
    C                     Z-ADD1         RRN
    C           RRN       CHAINSFL                 99
     *
     *   Determine if ROLL UP/DOWN is valid
     *
     *   If ROLLUP requested, see if the next page of orders
(D)  *   has already been placed into the ORDDS data structure.
     *
    C           KEY       IFEQ ROLLUP
```

Figure 45.5 Continued

Figure 45.5

RPG for Side-by-Side Subfile Illusion *Continued*

```
*... ... 1 ... ... 2 ... ... 3 ... ... 4 ... ... 5 ... ... 6 ... ... 7
     *
     *  Take the ORDDS occurrence number from the 1st subfile record
     *  currently displayed (subfile hidden field "HO") and add the
     *  subfile page size to it. The result will be the ORDDS
     *  occurrence of the 1st subfile record to appear on the new
     *  page. If that occurrence is greater than the highest occurrence
     *  already loaded ("TO"), the next page of ORDERS must be
     *  retrieved from the database (call subroutine LODORD). If there
     *  are no more orders for the customer (EOFORD = 'Y'), issue error
     *  message - "ROLL UP INVALID AT END OF FILE."
     *
     *     "O"  - Current occurrence of ORDDS
     *     "TO" - Highest occurrence loaded
     *     "HO" - Current occurrence (subfile hidden field)
     *
     C          HO        ADD  PAGSIZ    O
     *
     C          O         IFGT TO
     *
     C          EOFORD    IFEQ 'Y'
     C                    MOVEA'110'     *IN,43
     *
(D)  *  Note: Until the "Exit Subroutine" operation code is added to
     *        RPG, I consider exiting a subroutine to be the only
     *        valid use of the "GOTO" or "CABXX" operations.
     *
     C                    GOTO ENDORD
     C                    ELSE
     C                    EXSR LODORD
     C                    GOTO ENDORD
     C                    END
     *
     C                    END
     *
     C                    ELSE                              roll down
     *
     *  If ROLLDOWN Requested
     *  See if the beginning of ORDDS has been reached.
     *  If it has, issue "ROLL DOWN INVALID AT BEGINNING OF SUBFILE."
     *
     C          KEY       IFEQ ROLLDN
     C          HO        SUB  PAGSIZ    O
     *
(E)  C          O         IFLT 1
     C                    MOVEA'101'     *IN,43             roll error
     C                    GOTO ENDORD
     C                    END
     C                    END
     C                    END
     *
     *  At this point it has been determined that:
     *
```

Figure 45.5 Continued

Figure 45.5

RPG for Side-by-Side Subfile Illusion *Continued*

```
*... ... 1 ... ... 2 ... ... 3 ... ... 4 ... ... 5 ... ... 6 ... ... 7
     *    The ROLLUP or ROLLDOWN function is valid at this time.
     *    The next page of ORDERS information has been loaded into ORDDS.
     *    The value of field "O" has been set to the ORDDS occurrence
     *      containing the fields for the 1st subfile record to display
     *      on the new page.
     *
    C                      DO   PAGSIZ    X
     *
    C           X          CHAINSFL                  99
    C           O          OCUR ORDDS
     *
     *    Move fields from ORDDS into subfile field names.
     *    Move the current ORDDS occurence into the subfile
     *     hidden field used to hold the current ORDDS occurrence ("HO")
     *
(F) C                      Z-ADDORORD#    ORD1
    C                      Z-ADDORPMDT    DATE1
    C                      Z-ADDORQTY     QTY1
    C                      MOVE ORPART    PART1
    C                      Z-ADDO         HO
    C                      UPDATSFL
    C                      ADD  1         O
    C                      END
     *
    C           ENDORD     ENDSR
     *
     *************************************
     *  ROLL SHIPMENTS SUBROUTINE
     *************************************
     *
    C           ROLSHP     BEGSR
     *
     *    Retrieve the 1st SUBFILE RECORD on the current page.
     *
    C                      Z-ADD1         RRN
    C           RRN        CHAINSFL                  99
     *
     *    Determine if ROLL UP/DOWN is valid.
     *
     *    If ROLLUP requested, see if the next page of SHIPMENTS
     *    has already been placed into the SHPDS data structure.
     *
    C           KEY        IFEQ ROLLUP
     *
     *    Take the SHPDS occurrence number from the 1st subfile record
     *    currently displayed (subfile hidden field "HS") and add the
     *    subfile page size to it. The result will be the SHPDS
     *    occurrence of the 1st subfile record to appear on the new
     *    page. If that occurrence is greater than the highest occurrence
     *    already loaded ("TS"), the next page of SHIPMENTS must be
     *    retrieved from the database (call subroutine LODSHP). If there
     *    are no more shipments for the customer (EOFSHP = 'Y'), issue error
```

Figure 45.5 Continued

Figure 45.5

RPG for Side-by-Side Subfile Illusion *Continued*

```
*... ... 1 ... ... 2 ... ... 3 ... ... 4 ... ... 5 ... ... 6 ... ... 7
     *   message - "ROLL UP INVALID AT END OF FILE."
     *
     *      "S"  - Current occurrence of SHPDS
     *      "TS" - Highest occurrence loaded
     *      "HS" - Current occurrence (subfile hidden field)
     *
    C         HS        ADD  PAGSIZ    S
     *
    C         S         IFGT TS
     *
    C         EOFSHP    IFEQ 'Y'
    C                   MOVEA'110'     *IN,43
     *
     *  Note: Until the "Exit Subroutine" operation code is added to
     *        RPG, I consider exiting a subroutine to be the only
     *        valid use of the "GOTO" or "CABXX" operations.
     *
    C                   GOTO ENDSHP
    C                   ELSE
    C                   EXSR LODSHP
    C                   GOTO ENDSHP
    C                   END
     *
    C                   END
     *
    C                   ELSE                               roll down
     *
     *   If ROLLDOWN requested, see if the beginning of the SHPDS
     *   has been reached. If it has, issue "ROLL DOWN INVALID AT
     *   BEGINNING OF SUBFILE."
     *
    C         KEY       IFEQ ROLLDN
    C         HS        SUB  PAGSIZ    S
     *
    C         S         IFLT 1
    C                   MOVEA'101'     *IN,43              roll error
    C                   GOTO ENDSHP
    C                   END
    C                   END
    C                   END
     *
     *   At this point it has been determined that:
     *
     *   The ROLLUP or ROLLDOWN function is valid at this time.
     *   The next page of SHIPMENT information has been loaded into SHPDS.
     *   The value of field "S" has been set to the SHPDS occurrence
     *     containing the fields for the 1st subfile record to display
     *     on the new page.
     *
    C                   DO   PAGSIZ    X
     *
    C         X         CHAINSFL                 99
```

Figure 45.5 Continued

Figure 45.5

RPG for Side-by-Side Subfile Illusion *Continued*

```
*... ... 1 ... ... 2 ... ... 3 ... ... 4 ... ... 5 ... ... 6 ... ... 7
     C           S         OCUR SHPDS
      *
      *   Move fields from SHPDS into subfile field names
      *   Move the current SHPDS occurence into the subfile
      *    hidden field used to hold the current SHPDS occurrence ("HS")
      *
     C                     Z-ADDSHORD#    ORD2
     C                     Z-ADDSHDATE    DATE2
     C                     Z-ADDSHQTY     QTY2
     C                     MOVE SHPART    PART2
     C                     Z-ADDS         HS
     C                     UPDATSFL
     C                     ADD  1         S
     C                     END
      *
     C           ENDSHP    ENDSR
      *
      *************************************
      *  ROLL PAYMENTS SUBROUTINE
      *************************************
      *
     C           ROLPAY    BEGSR
      *
      *   Retrieve the 1st SUBFILE RECORD on the current page.
      *
     C                     Z-ADD1         RRN
     C           RRN       CHAINSFL                  99
      *
      *   Determine if ROLL UP/DOWN is valid
      *
      *   If ROLLUP requested,
      *   see if the next page of PAYMENTS has already been placed into
      *    the PAYDS data structure.
      *
     C           KEY       IFEQ ROLLUP
      *
      *   Take the PAYDS occurrence number from the 1st subfile record
      *   currently displayed (subfile hidden field "HP") and add the
      *   subfile page size to it. The result will be the PAYDS
      *   occurrence of the 1st subfile record to appear on the new
      *   page. If that occurrence is greater than the highest occurrence
      *   already loaded ("TP"), the next page of PAYMENTS must be
      *   retrieved from the data base (call subroutine LODPAY). If there
      *   are no more payments for the customer (EOFPAY = 'Y'), issue error
      *   message - "ROLL UP INVALID AT END OF FILE."
      *
      *      "P"  - Current occurrence of PAYDS
      *      "TP" - Highest occurrence loaded
      *      "HP" - Current occurrence (subfile hidden field)
      *
     C           HP        ADD  PAGSIZ    P
      *
```

Figure 45.5 Continued

Figure 45.5

RPG for Side-by-Side Subfile Illusion *Continued*

```
*... ... 1 ... ... 2 ... ... 3 ... ... 4 ... ... 5 ... ... 6 ... ... 7
     C           P         IFGT TP
     *
     C           EOFPAY    IFEQ 'Y'
     C                     MOVEA'110'     *IN,43
     *
     *   Note: Until the "Exit Subroutine" operation code is added to
     *         RPG, I consider exiting a subroutine to be the only
     *         valid use of the "GOTO" or "CABXX" operations.
     *
     C                     GOTO ENDPAY
     C                     ELSE
     C                     EXSR LODPAY
     C                     GOTO ENDPAY
     C                     END
     *
     C                     END
     *
     C                     ELSE                               roll down
     *
     *   If ROLLDOWN Requested, see if the beginning of the PAYDS
     *   has been reached. If it has, issue "ROLL DOWN INVALID AT
     *   BEGINNING OF SUBFILE."
     *
     C           KEY       IFEQ ROLLDN
     C           HP        SUB  PAGSIZ    P
     *
     C           P         IFLT 1
     C                     MOVEA'101'     *IN,43              roll error
     C                     GOTO ENDPAY
     C                     END
     C                     END
     C                     END
     *
     *   At this point it has been determined that:
     *
     *   The ROLLUP or ROLLDOWN function is valid at this time.
     *   The next page of PAYMENT information has been loaded into PAYDS.
     *   The value of field "P" has been set to the PAYDS occurrence
     *     containing the fields for the 1st subfile record to display
     *     on the new page.
     *
     C                     DO   PAGSIZ    X
     *
     C           X         CHAINSFL             99
     C           P         OCUR PAYDS
     *
     *   Move fields from PAYDS into subfile field names.
     *   Move the current PAYDS occurence into the subfile
     *    hidden field used to hold the current PAYDS occurrence ("HP").
     *
     C                     Z-ADDPYORD#    ORD3
     C                     Z-ADDPYDATE    DATE3
```

Figure 45.5 Continued

Figure 45.5

RPG for Side-by-Side Subfile Illusion *Continued*

```
*... ... 1 ... ... 2 ... ... 3 ... ... 4 ... ... 5 ... ... 6 ... ... 7
     C                    Z-ADDPYAMTP    AMTPD
     C                    Z-ADDP         HP
     C                    UPDATSFL
     C                    ADD  1         P
     C                    END
      *
     C          ENDPAY    ENDSR
      *
      ********************************************************
      *    LOAD ORDERS SUBROUTINE
      ********************************************************
      *
      * -----------------------------------------------------
      *   This subroutine is only called when the next page  -
      *    of ORDERS has NOT been loaded into the ORDERS     -
      *    data structure.                                   -
      * -----------------------------------------------------
      *
     C          LODORD    BEGSR
      *
      *   1st time through - set lower limits to selected customer.
      *
      *   NOTE: 1st time through need NOT be only once for the program.
      *         A "NORMAL" production program would probably allow
      *         the user to select another CUSTOMER without having
      *         to exit the program.
      *
     C          FSTORD    IFEQ 'Y'
     C          CUST      SETLLORDF
     C                    MOVE 'Ø'       *IN1Ø            eof
     C                    END
      *
      *   Loop to read and load orders to subfile & ORDERS data structure.
      *
 B1  C                    DO   PAGSIZ    X
      *
      *   Increment the highest ORDER occurrence used "TO"
      *    set ORDDS to next occurrence.
      *
     C                    ADD  1         TO
     C          TO        OCUR ORDDS
      *
(G1)  *   Retrieve the next ORDER record for the customer from database
      *    and the next subfile record.
      *
     C          CUST      READEORDF                   1Ø
     C          X         CHAINSFL               99
      *
(G)   *   If end of file, set EOF condition and zero/blank fields.
      *
 B2  C          *IN1Ø     IFEQ '1'
     C                    MOVE 'Y'       EOFORD
```

Figure 45.5 Continued

Figure 45.5

RPG for Side-by-Side Subfile Illusion *Continued*

```
*... ... 1 ... ... 2 ... ... 3 ... ... 4 ... ... 5 ... ... 6 ... ... 7
     C                    EXSR ZERORD
X2   C                    ELSE
      *
      *   NOT end of file
      *   If first time for this customer, force an equal ORDER condition.
      *   The purpose of tracking the order number is to place a blank
      *   subfile record between order numbers.
      *
B3   C          FSTORD    IFEQ 'Y'
     C                    MOVE 'N'       FSTORD
     C                    Z-ADDORORD#    HORD#
E3   C                    END
      *
      *   If order number has changed, place a blank subfile record.
      *   NO blank records on the FIRST subfile line of a page, hold
      *   database fields before executing blanking subroutine.
      *   Load the blank record to both the subroutine and data structure
      *   to preserve the blank subfile record if ROLL BACK
      *   requested without repeating the blanking logic.
      *
      *   ORORD# - Order number from the database file
      *   HORD#  - Hold order # field
      *   ORDDS  - Current occurrence of order data structure
      *   HOLD1  - Single occurrence data structure defined as the same
      *              size as ORDDS.
      *
B3   C          ORORD#    IFNE HORD#                    new order #
     C          X         IFNE 1                        1st record
     C                    MOVE ORDDS     HOLD1
     C                    EXSR ZERORD
     C                    Z-ADDTO        HO
     C                    UPDATSFL
     C                    ADD  1         X
     C                    ADD  1         TO
      *
      *   The blank subfile record has been written, and the current
      *     occurrence has been incremented by 1.
      *   Retrieve the next occurrence and reload the fields from
      *     the HOLD data structure.
      *   Change the order number in process field (HORD#) to current.
      *
     C          TO        OCUR ORDDS
     C                    MOVE HOLD1     ORDDS
     C                    END
      *
     C                    Z-ADDORORD#    HORD#
      *
      * If the blank line has filled the subfile page,
      *  "back up" one database record and exit subroutine.
      *
      * If not, get the next subfile record.
      *
```

Figure 45.5 Continued

Figure 45.5

RPG for Side-by-Side Subfile Illusion *Continued*

```
*... ... 1 ... ... 2 ... ... 3 ... ... 4 ... ... 5 ... ... 6 ... ... 7
     C           X         IFGT PAGSIZ
     C                     READPORDF                     10
     C                     GOTO EXTORD
 Ⓖ   C                     END
     *
     C           X         CHAINSFL              99
  E3 C                     END
     *
     *   Move database fields into subfile fields.
     *
     C                     Z-ADDORORD#    ORD1
     C                     Z-ADDORPMDT    DATE1
     C                     Z-ADDORQTY     QTY1
     C                     MOVE ORPART    PART1
  E2 C                     END
     *
     *   Move current ORDDS occurrence into subfile hidden field
     *    update subfile.
     *
     C                     Z-ADDTO        HO
     C                     UPDATSFL
     *
     C                     END
     *
     C           EXTORD    ENDSR
     *
     *********************************************************
     *    LOAD SHIPMENTS SUBROUTINE
     *********************************************************
     *
     * ------------------------------------------------------
     *   This subroutine is only called when the next page  -
     *    of SHIPMENTS has NOT been loaded into the SHPDS   -
     *    data structure.                                   -
     * ------------------------------------------------------
     *
     C           LODSHP    BEGSR
     *
     *   1st time through - set lower limits to selected customer.
     *
     *   NOTE: 1st time through need NOT be only once for the program.
     *         A "NORMAL" production program would probably allow
     *         the user to select another CUSTOMER without having
     *         to exit the program.
     *
     C           FSTSHP    IFEQ 'Y'
     C           CUST      SETLLSHIPF
     C                     MOVE '0'       *IN11          eof
     C                     END
     *
     *   Loop to read and load shipments to subfile & data structure.
     *
```

Figure 45.5 Continued

Figure 45.5

RPG for Side-by-Side Subfile Illusion *Continued*

```
*... ... 1 ... ... 2 ... ... 3 ... ... 4 ... ... 5 ... ... 6 ... ... 7
 B1  C                     DO   PAGSIZ     X
      *
      *    Increment the highest SHIPMENT occurrence used ("TS");
      *     set SHPDS to next occurrence.
      *
     C                     ADD  1          TS
     C           TS        OCUR SHPDS
      *
(H)   *    Retrieve the next SHIPMENT record for the customer from database
      *     and the next subfile record.
      *
     C           CUST      READESHIPF                    11
     C           X         CHAINSFL                  99
      *
      *    If end of file, set EOF condition and zero/blank fields.
      *
 B2  C           *IN11     IFEQ '1'
     C                     MOVE 'Y'        EOFSHP
     C                     EXSR ZERSHP
 X2  C                     ELSE
      *
      *    NOT end of file:
      *    If first time for this customer, force an equal ORDER condition.
      *    The purpose of tracking the order number is to place a blank
      *    subfile record between order numbers.
      *
 B3  C           FSTSHP    IFEQ 'Y'
     C                     MOVE 'N'        FSTSHP
     C                     Z-ADDSHORD#     HSHP#
 E3  C                     END
      *
      *    If order number has changed, place a blank subfile record.
      *    NO blank records on the FIRST subfile line of a page,
      *    hold database fields before executing blanking subroutine.
      *    Load the blank record to both the subroutine and data structure
      *      to preserve the blank subfile record if ROLL BACK
      *      requested without repeating the blanking logic.
      *
      *    SHORD# - Order number from the database file
      *    HSHP#  - Hold order # field
      *    SHPDS  - Current occurrence of order data structure
      *    HOLD1  - Single occurrence data structure defined as the same
      *               size as SHPDS.
      *
 B3  C           SHORD#    IFNE HSHP#                         new order #
     C           X         IFNE 1                             1st record
     C                     MOVE SHPDS      HOLD1
     C                     EXSR ZERSHP
     C                     Z-ADDTS         HS
     C                     UPDATSFL
     C                     ADD  1          X
     C                     ADD  1          TS
```

Figure 45.5 Continued

Figure 45.5

RPG for Side-by-Side Subfile Illusion *Continued*

```
*... ... 1 ... ... 2 ... ... 3 ... ... 4 ... ... 5 ... ... 6 ... ... 7
      *
      *   The blank subfile record has been written, and the current
      *     occurrence has been incremented by 1.
      *   Retrieve the next occurrence, and reload the fields from
      *     the HOLD data structure.
      *   Change the order number in process field (HSHP#) to current.
      *
     C           TS        OCUR SHPDS
     C                     MOVE HOLD1     SHPDS
     C                     END
      *
(H)  C                     Z-ADDSHORD#    HSHP#
      *
      * If the blank line has filled the subfile page,
      *  "back up" one database record and exit subroutine.
      *
      * If not, get the next subfile record.
      *
     C           X         IFGT PAGSIZ
     C                     READPSHIPF                  11
     C                     GOTO EXTSHP
     C                     END
      *
     C           X         CHAINSFL                99
   E3 C                    END
      *
      *   Move database fields into subfile fields.
      *
     C                     Z-ADDSHORD#    ORD2
     C                     Z-ADDSHDATE    DATE2
     C                     Z-ADDSHQTY     QTY2
     C                     MOVE SHPART    PART2
  E2 C                     END
      *
      *   Move current SHPDS occurrence into subfile hidden field;
      *    update subfile.
      *
     C                     Z-ADDTS        HS
     C                     UPDATSFL
      *
     C                     END
      *
     C           EXTSHP    ENDSR
      *
      ******************************************************
      *    LOAD PAYMENTS SUBROUTINE
      ******************************************************
      *
      * --------------------------------------------------------
      *   This subroutine is only called when the next page   -
      *    of PAYMENTS has NOT been loaded into the PAYDS     -
      *    data structure.                                    -
```

Figure 45.5 Continued

Figure 45.5

RPG for Side-by-Side Subfile Illusion *Continued*

```
*... ... 1 ... ... 2 ... ... 3 ... ... 4 ... ... 5 ... ... 6 ... ... 7
       * ------------------------------------------------------------
       *
      C           LODPAY    BEGSR
       *
       *    1st time through - set lower limits to selected customer.
       *
       *    NOTE: 1st time through need NOT be only once for the program.
       *          A "NORMAL" production program would probably allow
       *          the user to select another CUSTOMER without having
       *          to exit the program.
       *
      C           FSTPAY    IFEQ 'Y'
      C           CUST      SETLLPAYF
      C                     MOVE 'Ø'       *IN12          eof
      C                     END
       *
       *    Loop to read and load payments to subfile & data structure.
       *
(I)B1 C                     DO   PAGSIZ    X
       *
       *    Increment the highest PAYMENT occurrence used ("TP");
       *     set PAYDS to next occurrence.
       *
      C                     ADD  1         TP
      C           TP        OCUR PAYDS
       *
       *    Retrieve the next PAYMENT record for the customer from database
       *     and the next subfile record.
       *
      C           CUST      READEPAYF                         12
      C           X         CHAINSFL                      99
       *
       *    If end of file, set EOF condition and zero/blank fields.
       *
   B2 C           *IN12     IFEQ '1'
      C                     MOVE 'Y'       EOFPAY
      C                     EXSR ZERPAY
   X2 C                     ELSE
       *
       *    NOT end of file:
       *    If first time for this customer, force an equal ORDER condition.
       *    The purpose of tracking the order number is to place a blank
       *    subfile record between order numbers.
       *
   B3 C           FSTPAY    IFEQ 'Y'
      C                     MOVE 'N'       FSTPAY
      C                     Z-ADDPYORD#    HPAY#
   E3 C                     END
       *
       *    If order number has changed, place a blank subfile record.
       *    NO blank records on the FIRST subfile line of a page,
       *    hold database fields before executing blanking subroutine.
```

Figure 45.5 Continued

Figure 45.5

RPG for Side-by-Side Subfile Illusion *Continued*

```
*... ... 1 ... ... 2 ... ... 3 ... ... 4 ... ... 5 ... ... 6 ... ... 7
      *   Load the blank record to both the subroutine and data structure
      *     to preserve the blank subfile record if ROLL BACK
      *     requested without repeating the blanking logic.
      *
      *   PYORD# - Order number from the database file
      *   HPAY#  - Hold order # field
      *   PAYDS  - Current occurrence of order data structure
      *   HOLD2  - Single occurrence data structure defined as the same
      *               size as PAYDS.
      *
 B3  C           PYORD#    IFNE HPAY#                      new order #
     C           X         IFNE 1                          1st record
     C                     MOVE PAYDS     HOLD2
     C                     EXSR ZERPAY
     C                     Z-ADDTP        HP
     C                     UPDATSFL
     C                     ADD  1         X
     C                     ADD  1         TP
      *
      *   The blank subfile record has been written, and the current
(1)   *     occurrence has been incremented by 1.
      *   Retrieve the next occurrence and reload the fields from
      *     the HOLD data structure.
      *   Change the order number in process field (HPAY#) to current.
      *
     C           TP        OCUR PAYDS
     C                     MOVE HOLD2     PAYDS
     C                     END
      *
     C                     Z-ADDPYORD#    HPAY#
      *
      * If the blank line has filled the subfile page,
      *  "back up" one database record and exit subroutine.
      *
      * If not, get the next subfile record.
      *
     C           X         IFGT PAGSIZ
     C                     READPPAYF                  12
     C                     GOTO EXTPAY
     C                     END
      *
     C           X         CHAINSFL                 99
 E3  C                     END
      *
      *   Move database fields into subfile fields
      *
     C                     Z-ADDPYORD#    ORD3
     C                     Z-ADDPYDATE    DATE3
     C                     Z-ADDPYAMTP    AMTPD
 E2  C                     END
      *
      *   Move current PAYDS occurrence into subfile hidden field;
```

Figure 45.5 Continued

Figure 45.5

RPG for Side-by-Side Subfile Illusion *Continued*

```
*... ... 1 ... ... 2 ... ... 3 ... ... 4 ... ... 5 ... ... 6 ... ... 7
     *   update subfile.
     *
    C                    Z-ADDTP        HP
    C                    UPDATSFL
     *
    C                    END
     *
    C          EXTPAY    ENDSR
     *
     *********************************************************
     *   ZERO ORDER FIELDS
     *********************************************************
     *
    C          ZERORD    BEGSR
    C                    MOVE *ZEROS    ORD1
    C                    MOVE *ZEROS    DATE1
    C                    MOVE *ZEROS    QTY1
    C                    MOVE *BLANKS   PART1
    C                    MOVE *ZEROS    ORORD#
    C                    MOVE *ZEROS    ORPMDT
    C                    MOVE *ZEROS    ORQTY
    C                    MOVE *BLANKS   ORPART
    C                    ENDSR
     *
     *********************************************************
     *   ZERO SHIPMENT FIELDS
(J)  *********************************************************
     *
    C          ZERSHP    BEGSR
    C                    MOVE *ZEROS    ORD2
    C                    MOVE *ZEROS    DATE2
    C                    MOVE *ZEROS    QTY2
    C                    MOVE *BLANKS   PART2
    C                    MOVE *ZEROS    SHORD#
    C                    MOVE *ZEROS    SHDATE
    C                    MOVE *ZEROS    SHQTY
    C                    MOVE *BLANKS   SHPART
    C                    ENDSR
     *
     *********************************************************
     *   ZERO PAYMENT FIELDS
     *********************************************************
     *
    C          ZERPAY    BEGSR
    C                    MOVE *ZEROS    ORD3
(J) C                    MOVE *ZEROS    DATE3
    C                    MOVE *ZEROS    AMTPD
    C                    MOVE *ZEROS    PYORD#
    C                    MOVE *ZEROS    PYDATE
    C                    MOVE *ZEROS    PYAMTP
    C                    ENDSR
     *
```

Figure 45.5 Continued

Figure 45.5

RPG for Side-by-Side Subfile Illusion *Continued*

```
*... ... 1 ... ... 2 ... ... 3 ... ... 4 ... ... 5 ... ... 6 ... ... 7
     ********************************************************
     *    INITIALIZATION SUBROUTINE
     ********************************************************
     *
    C           SETUP     BEGSR
     *
     *   Accept cust number selected
     *
    C           *ENTRY    PLIST
    C                     PARM           CUST    50
     *
     *   Call program LODKEY to fill data structure "KEYS."
     *
    C                     CALL 'LODKEY'               99
    C                     PARM           KEYDS
     *
     *   Define misc work fields.
     *
    C           *LIKE     DEFN SETROW    ROW                actual curs row
    C           *LIKE     DEFN SETROW    COL                actual curs col
    C           *LIKE     DEFN SETROW    TO                 # of ord (ordds)
    C           *LIKE     DEFN SETROW    TS                 # of shp (shpds)
    C           *LIKE     DEFN SETROW    TP                 # of pay (payds)
    C           *LIKE     DEFN SETROW    O                  current ocur ord
    C           *LIKE     DEFN SETROW    S                  current ocur shp
    C           *LIKE     DEFN SETROW    P                  current ocur pay
    C           *LIKE     DEFN SETROW    X                  counter
    C           *LIKE     DEFN ORORD#    HORD#              sfl hidden ord#
    C           *LIKE     DEFN ORORD#    HSHP#              sfl hidden ord#
    C           *LIKE     DEFN ORORD#    HPAY#              sfl hidden ord#
    C           *LIKE     DEFN FSTORD    EOFORD             eof orders
    C           *LIKE     DEFN FSTORD    EOFSHP             eof shipments
    C           *LIKE     DEFN FSTORD    EOFPAY             eof payments
    C           *LIKE     DEFN FSTORD    FSTSHP             1st shp for cust
    C           *LIKE     DEFN FSTORD    FSTPAY             1st pay for cust
     *
     *   Define subfile parameters.
     *
(K) C                     Z-ADD11        FSTLIN  20         1st line
    C                     Z-ADD21        LSTLIN  20         last line
    C                     Z-ADD11        PAGSIZ  20         sfl page size
    C                     Z-ADD30        STRSHP  20         start shipments
    C                     Z-ADD59        STRPAY  20         start payments
     *
     *   Set initial cursor position and 1st time fields.
     *
    C                     Z-ADD11        SETROW             initial row
    C                     Z-ADD4         SETCOL             initial col
    C                     MOVE 'Y'       FSTORD  1
    C                     MOVE 'Y'       FSTSHP
    C                     MOVE 'Y'       FSTPAY
     *
```

Figure 45.5 Continued

Figure 45.5

RPG for Side-by-Side Subfile Illusion *Continued*

```
*... ... 1 ... ... 2 ... ... 3 ... ... 4 ... ... 5 ... ... 6 ... ... 7
     *    Get selected customer master record.
     *
    C           CUST      CHAINCLIENTF              03
    C                     MOVELMMZIP     ZIP
     *
     *    Build a blank subfile page.
     *      Set on SFLDSPCTL & SFLDSP indicator.
     *
    C                     DO   PAGSIZ    X
(L) C                     Z-ADDX         RRN     40
    C                     WRITESFL
    C                     END
     *
    C                     MOVE '1'       *IN51
     *
    C                     ENDSR
```

Chapter 46

Virtual Subfiles

by Ron Harvey

Use windows for virtually limitless subfile displays

How many times have you been unable to fit all the information you needed into a subfile? More than twice, I'll wager. How often have you had to truncate fields within a subfile to accommodate the *required* fields, never mind the non-essential ones you would *like* to provide? And how do you work around these common programming situations? Do you set up multiple subfiles to show the additional information? Do you require the user to select one subfile record (using "point and execute" techniques, of course) and then display the supporting data on a separate display format? Do you — heaven forbid — use a folded subfile? Or do you (hint, hint) use a virtual subfile?

I'll bet you're thinking, "Virtual subfiles? I know about virtual memory and virtual devices, and I remember virtual disks, but what the heck is a virtual subfile?" Well, for one thing, virtual subfiles are not some unannounced OS/400 feature. The term "virtual" generally refers to something that is not really there. To create something virtual, you borrow space from something else. Virtual memory, for example, merely borrows space occupied by information that isn't immediately needed. The original information is temporarily replaced and then reacquired when it is needed. We know this as paging, and it is the same principle I use to create virtual subfiles.

Suppose you want to display customer identification (e.g., customer number, name, type, status, salesman, and date of last order) and customer address in a subfile. There are several programming alternatives you could use to meet the objectives of this theoretical application: You could create multiple subfiles, display detail information for a selected customer on a different screen, or use folded subfiles. However, each of these methods has substantial drawbacks.

The main problem with multiple subfiles is knowing when to synchronize them. Figure 46.1 shows a conventional, one-above-the-other dual subfile display. The user may want to roll the Orders section, the Shipments section, or

Figure 46.1

Conventional Dual Subfile Display

```
SFLDEMO                 Order Status Review            1/10/91    19:05:01
    KLUTZ & KLUTZ MOVERS                           Total Orders    $ 45,000.00
    111 BETTER INSURE IT ROAD                      Credit Limit    $100,000.00
    KISS IT GOODBYE       NY 12121                 A/R Balance     $ 32,000.00
----------------------------------------------------------------------------
                              O  R  D  E  R  S
----------------------------------------------------------------------------
      Ord #        Date Promised           Part Number          Quantity Ordered
      12345           3/08/90                 AA10                     250
      12345           3/08/90                 AA25                     500
      12345           4/10/90                 AA35                     850
      12345           4/10/90                 AA45                     450
----------------------------------------------------------------------------
                           S  H  I  P  M  E  N  T  S
----------------------------------------------------------------------------
      Ord #         Date Shipped           Part Number          Quantity Shipped
      12345           3/08/90                 AA10                      50
      12345           3/08/90                 AA35                     100
      12345           3/10/90                 AA10                      25
      12345           3/10/90                 AA35                     125
----------------------------------------------------------------------------
              F3-Exit   Rollup/Rolldown  Other user instructions
```

both. If you create the subfile with subfile size equal to subfile page, your program can react to a roll key in all circumstances and roll one subfile or both subfiles depending on cursor location.

If you create the subfile with subfile size not equal to subfile page and the next page to display has already been created, your program is not even "aware" that the roll key has been pressed. This technique makes for easier coding in your program, but also makes it impossible to roll both subfiles with a single keystroke. To roll both subfiles, the user must press the roll key twice; once with the cursor positioned in each subfile. Workable, but cumbersome.

If you require the user to select a customer, the program displays only one address at a time, either elsewhere on the screen (perhaps replacing the function key section, as in Figure 46.2) or on a separate screen. Either display supplies the requested information, but it may take the user a couple of tries to determine the correct customer record. For example, if Alliance Chemicals has six locations, and the user has not memorized all the customer numbers (a pretty safe bet), there may not be a way to distinguish the different locations in an already crowded subfile.

If you use folded subfiles, the user must press the function key assigned to the SFLDROP keyword, and the system displays any additional lines for each subfile record. (For more information about folded subfiles, see the SFLDROP keyword in the *Data Description Specifications Reference*, SC41-9620.) Although folded subfiles may sound like a neat way to view the needed information, take a look

Figure 46.2

Detail Display in Function Key Area

```
WDEMO010  1/11/91            The Demo Company
          21:25:12           Customer Selection      Customer Number  002
                                                     Customer Name
Customer name sequence
Cust       Customer Name                     TS     Representative            LOD
018     ABC AUTO REPAIR                      NA   JIM MASON                   0489
003     ADMIRALTY APPLIANCE                  NA   JIM MASON                   0589
029     AHEARN & AHEARN                      NA   ED JONES                    0191
016     ALLIANCE CHEMICALS                   NA   RON HARVEY                  0489
017     ALLIANCE CHEMICALS                   NA   JOSEPH PARK                 1290
025     BARNES AND NOBLE BOOKS               NC   RON HARVEY                  0391
010     BOSTON SCHOOL DISTRICT               RC   RON HARVEY                  1289
014     CARLSON DRUGS                        RC   RICHARD DANNER              0191
005     CARTER PEANUT VENDORS                NA   ED JONES                    0589
011     CLARK EQUIPMENT                      RA   JOSEPH PARK                 0291
012     EDWARD LEE PLUMBING                  NA   RICHARD DANNER              1190
002     EXXON DOWN THE STREET                RA   RON HARVEY
------------------------------------------------------------------------------
 ABC AUTO REPAIR
  9927 STATE STREET     DEDHAM, MA   02026
```

at the folded subfile in Figure 46.3. What a horrible thing to do to a poor, unsuspecting user!

Fortunately, virtual subfiles give you a better way to display multiple subfile records simultaneously without the inconveniences of these techniques.

Virtual Subfiles

The information we need for our sample application falls into three groups. The first group contains customer identification information (i.e., customer number and name), the second contains the customer address information (i.e., street, city, and state), and the third contains information about the relationship between the customer and the company (i.e., customer type, status, and salesperson).

Suppose the user doesn't need to view both the customer address *and* the customer/company relationship simultaneously. If you could condition fields in a subfile (as you can on a regular display), you could create a single subfile that displays different data fields and different control record headings according to external conditions (e.g., the press of a function key or the use of a "mode" selection field). Although you can't condition subfile fields, you *can* use a virtual subfile that temporarily borrows an area of the display.

Figure 46.4 shows a subfile partly covered by a window containing customer address information. Using a window this way makes the amount of data a subfile can display virtually limitless. There are many approaches to creating a virtual subfile window; the approach I use in this example performs well and is easy to program.

Figure 46.3

Sample Folded Subfile

```
WDEMO10  1/11/91          The Demo Company
         22:14:08         Customer Selection      Customer Number  025
                                                  Customer Name
Customer name sequence
Cust       Customer Name                   TS   Representative          LOD
018    ABC AUTO REPAIR                     NA  JIM MASON               0489
9927 STATE ST            DEDHAM          MA
003    ADMIRALTY APPLIANCE                 NA  JIM MASON               0589
255 COMMANDANT'S WAY     CHELSEA         MA
029    AHEARN & AHEARN                     NA  ED JONES                0191
85 CONCORD STREET        FRAMINGHAM      MA
016    ALLIANCE CHEMICALS                  NA  RON HARVEY              0489
41 STATE RD ROUTE 6      N. DENVER       MA
017    ALLIANCE CHEMICALS                  NA  JOSEPH PARK             1290
818 HAZARDOUS DUMP       NIMBY           MA
888    ALLIANCE CHEMICALS                  RA  JOE SMITH               0988
20 FIRST STREET          WELLESLEY       MA
-------------------------------------------------------------------------------
 Place Cursor on the CUSTOMER you wish to select and press a key listed below
-------------------------------------------------------------------------------
 Help/Roll    3-Exit       5-Cust# Seq  6-Name Seq   7-Name Scan  10-New Cust
 11-Maint     12-Cust Add  21-ADD Cmnt  22-CHG Cmnt
```

Figure 46.4

Virtual Subfile with Customer Address Window

```
WDEMO10  1/11/91          The Demo Company
         10:16:52         Customer Selection      Customer Number  002
                                                  Customer Name
                                      ........................................
Customer name sequence                :       Customer's Address Display     :
Cust       Customer Name              :......................................:
018    ABC AUTO REPAIR                : 9927 STATE ST           DEDHAM      MA :
003    ADMIRALTY APPLIANCE            : 255 COMMANDANT'S WAY CHELSEA        MA :
029    AHEARN & AHEARN                : 85 CONCORD STREET       FRAMINGHAM  MA :
016    ALLIANCE CHEMICALS             : 41 STATE RD ROUTE 6     N. DENVER   MA :
017    ALLIANCE CHEMICALS             : 818 HAZARDOUS DUMP      NOT HERE    MA :
025    BARNES AND NOBLE BOOKS         : 141 PLEASANT BOX 85     S WEYMOUTH  MA :
010    BOSTON SCHOOL DISTRICT         : 20 MAPLE STREET         BOSTON      MA :
014    CARLSON DRUGS                  : 11 FIRST STREET         DEDHAM      MA :
005    CARTER PEANUT VENDORS          : RT 18 336 BEDFORD ST LAKEVILLE      MA :
011    CLARK EQUIPMENT                : 497 MAIN STREET         SMALLVILLE  KS :
012    EDWARD LEE PLUMBING            : 1147 HANCOCK STREET MILLIS          MA :
002    EXXON DOWN THE STREET          : PARADISE WAY            MAUI ISLAND HI :
------------------------------------  :......................................:
 Place Cursor on the CUSTOMER you wis :        F3-Exit    Rollup/Down        :
------------------------------------  :......................................:
 Help/Roll    3-Exit       5-Cust# Seq  6-Name Seq   7-Name Scan  10-New Cust
 11-Maint     12-Cust Add  21-ADD Cmnt  22-CHG Cmnt
```

I almost always create windows in separate, standalone programs. I try to make each window program as generic as possible so that I can use the same one to service many different applications. This application's window program is a little less generic than a basic window that displays a list of data and asks the user to choose from the list. You can, however, create a fairly generic window program that is still specific enough to meet the requirements of our sample application.

Programming the Application

In most programming situations, the most "expensive" operation is database I/O, so it is good practice to avoid database rereads whenever possible. When the subfile is being loaded with the customer information, your application can take that opportunity to store the address information in an array, a multiple-occurrence data structure, or a subfile hidden field. In the sample application in Figure 46.5, the multiple-occurrence data structure CUSADD has already been loaded with the customer addresses when the database is read to load the subfile.

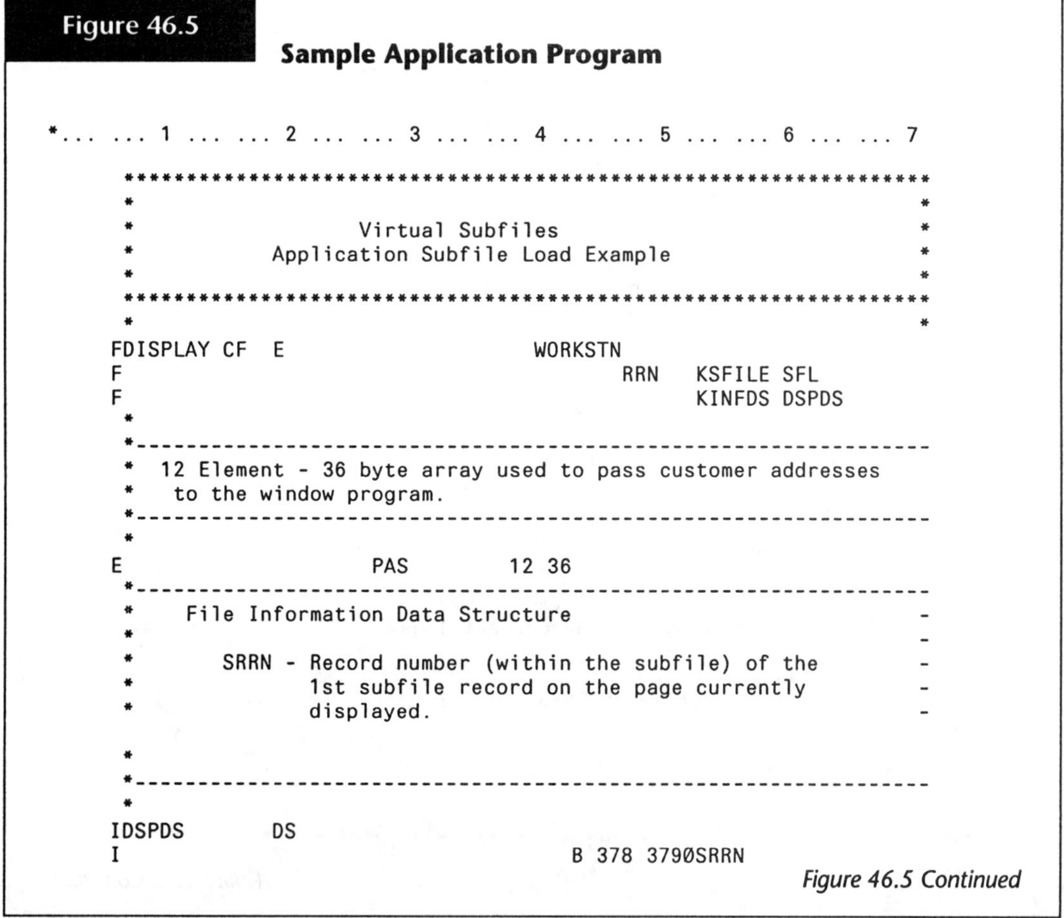

Figure 46.5

Sample Application Program

```
*... ... 1 ... ... 2 ... ... 3 ... ... 4 ... ... 5 ... ... 6 ... ... 7
     *****************************************************************
     *                                                               *
     *                     Virtual Subfiles                          *
     *              Application Subfile Load Example                 *
     *                                                               *
     *****************************************************************
     *                                                               *
    FDISPLAY CF  E                    WORKSTN
    F                                        RRN   KSFILE SFL
    F                                              KINFDS DSPDS
     *
     *----------------------------------------------------------------
     *  12 Element - 36 byte array used to pass customer addresses
     *   to the window program.
     *----------------------------------------------------------------
     *
    E                    PAS        12 36
     *----------------------------------------------------------------
     *    File Information Data Structure                            -
     *                                                               -
     *       SRRN - Record number (within the subfile) of the        -
     *              1st subfile record on the page currently         -
     *              displayed.                                       -
     *
     *----------------------------------------------------------------
     *
    IDSPDS       DS
    I                                      B 378 3790SRRN
```

Figure 46.5 Continued

Figure 46.5

Sample Application Program *Continued*

```
 *----------------------------------------------------------------
 *  Customer Address Data Structure                              -
 *    Set for 50 occurrences - modify for your environment       -
 *----------------------------------------------------------------
 *
ICUSADD      DS                              50
I                                             1  20 STREET
I                                            22  33 CITY
I                                            35  36 STATE
 *
 *----------------------------------------------------------------
 *                                                               -
 *   F12 - Show Customer's Street and City                       -
 *                                                               -
 *----------------------------------------------------------------
 *
C            CUSCTY    BEGSR
 *
 *  If there are NO RECORDS in the subfile - EXIT SUBROUTINE
 *   Until RPG has an Exit Subroutine Op Code, I consider
 *   this to be the only valid use of GOTO/BRANCH.
 *
C            RRN       CABLT2          ENDADR
 *
C                      MOVE ' '        END12   1
 *
 *   Loop to fill ONE PAGE of customer addresses

C            END12     DOUEQ'Y'
C                      Z-ADDSRRN       SFLPAG
C                      Z-ADDSRRN       SFRRN   40
 *
 *   Page size loop
 *
C                      DO   PAGSIZ     Z       20
 *
 *   Use the subfile record number of the 1st subfile
 *   record on the current page to begin the chaining
 *   process.
 *
C            SFRRN     CHAINSFL                    52
 *
 *   If NO subfile record retrieved - move blanks to
 *   the parameter array for the current line
 *
C            *IN52     IFEQ '1'
C                      MOVE *BLANKS    PAS,Z
C                      ELSE
 *
 *   Move the customer's address into the parameter array
 *
C            RRN       OCUR CUSADD
C                      MOVE CUSADD     PAS,Z
```

Figure 46.5 Continued

Figure 46.5

Sample Application Program *Continued*

```
     C                      END
      *
      *   Increment the SFL CHAIN argument
      *
     C                      ADD  1         SFRRN
     C                      END
      *
      *   Call the address WINDOW program
      *
     C                      CALL 'WDEMO20'
     C                      PARM           FUNC    1
     C                      PARM           PAS,1
     C                      PARM           PAS,2
     C                      PARM           PAS,3
     C                      PARM           PAS,4
     C                      PARM           PAS,5
     C                      PARM           PAS,6
     C                      PARM           PAS,7
     C                      PARM           PAS,8
     C                      PARM           PAS,9
     C                      PARM           PAS,10
     C                      PARM           PAS,11
     C                      PARM           PAS,12
      *
      *   If user pressed a roll key, display either the next
      *   or previous page of data, then loop back to display
      *   the customer addresses associated with the new page.
      *
      *
      *   If user pressed ROLL UP
      *   see if the next page has been built
      *   if it has, set the SFLREC to display the 1st
      *   subfile record from that page.
      *
      *   If the last page is currently shown - execute the subroutine
      *   which will load another page of subfile records from the
      *   customer data file.
      *
     C           FUNC      IFEQ 'U'
     C           SRRN      ADD  SFLPAG    CHKRRN  40
     C           CHKRRN    IFLT NXTRRN
     C                     Z-ADDCHKRRN    SFLREC
     C                     ELSE
     C                     EXSR BLDSUB
     C                     Z-ADDRRN       SFLREC
     C                     END
      *
      *   Display the new subfile page
      *
Ⓐ    C                     WRITECTL2
     C                     WRITECTL
     C                     Z-ADDSRRN      SFLREC
     C                     Z-ADDSRRN      SFRRN   40
```

Figure 46.5 Continued

Figure 46.5

Sample Application Program *Continued*

```
     *
     C                     ELSE
     *
     *    If the user pressed ROLL DOWN - Display the
     *    previous page.
     *
     C            FUNC     IFEQ 'D'
     C            SRRN     SUB  SFLPAG    CHKRRN  40
     C            CHKRRN   IFLT 1
     C                     Z-ADD1         SFLREC
     C                     ELSE
     C                     Z-ADDCHKRRN    SFLREC
     C                     END
     *
(A)  C                     WRITECTL2
     C                     WRITECTL
     C                     Z-ADDSRRN      SFLREC
     C                     Z-ADDSRRN      SFRRN   40
     *
     C                     ELSE
     C                     MOVE 'Y'       END12
     C                     END
     C                     END
     *
     C                     END
     C                     Z-ADDRRN       SFLREC
     *
     C            ENDADR   ENDSR
```

The occurrence of each CUSADD record matches the corresponding subfile record number.

In a typical subfile application where I expect a user to roll through a minimal number of screens, I use the multiple-occurrence data structure approach to eliminate redundant database access. If I expect more rolling to occur, I use subfile hidden fields to hold the additional information, because subfile expansion is dynamic, and multiple-occurrence data structures must be preset with a maximum number of occurrences.

When the user views the subfile and presses the function key, the program executes subroutine CUSCTY. (Some fields in CUSCTY are defined elsewhere in the program; see Figure 46.6 for a list of those fields and their definitions.) CUSCTY uses the subfile record number from the file information data structure field SRRN to begin the chaining process to the subfile. When the program retrieves a subfile record, it also retrieves from CUSADD the multiple-occurrence data structure record that contains the address for the customer just retrieved from the subfile record. Because array PAS is the same length as CUSADD, when the application moves the current occurrence of CUSADD to the current element of PAS, the address is stored as a parameter.

Figure 46.6

CUSCTY Fields and Definitions

FUNC — Field used to indicate whether a roll key was pressed in the window program.

NXTRRN — Next subfile record number to add. When you chain or read a subfile record, the field specified for the SFILE keyword on the continuation line (F-spec for workstation file) is set to the subfile record retrieved (RRN in the sample application program). In this program we need to know whether another subfile page is already built. NXTRRN keeps track of the size of the subfile.

PAS — Array used to pass the customer addresses to the window program.

RRN — Subfile record number.

SFLPAG — The subfile page size. (For more information about SFLPAG, see "Subfile Record Retrieval," Chapter 44.)

SFLREC — Field assigned to the SFLRCDNBR keyword in the display file DDS. When a subfile record number is placed into this field, the subfile page that contains the record is displayed at the next WRITE or EXFMT to the subfile control record.

SFRRN — Subfile relative record number work field.

SRRN — Relative record number of the first subfile record on the page currently displayed (defined in the file information data structure).

After loading array PAS, the application calls the window program. The window program display file (WINDOWD, Figure 46.7) uses the keyword USRDSPMGT to accomplish the windowing function. This keyword, which came to the AS/400 from the S/36, has two major limitations:

- It is not available on the S/38.
- Because you can't use response indicators with USRDSPMGT, you can't assign indicators to function keys in the display file.

The application program passes the customer addresses to the window program (Figure 46.8) as 12 individual array elements rather than as one large array parameter. The parameter list loads the window display file, making data structures and moves unnecessary in the window program.

When the user presses the Roll up or Roll down key, the window program fills parameter field FUNC with a "U" or a "D" to indicate the direction of the roll. Subroutine CUSCTY in the application program then uses field SRRN in calculations (A in Figure 46.5) to determine what subfile page to present. The application displays the next subfile page and repeats the parameter array load and window call. If the user hasn't pressed a roll key, the do group ends, and control returns to the EXFMT opcode in the application's mainline routine.

A variation of the virtual subfile technique may work better in your particular situation. Here are several alternatives:

- Place the window formats in the application program. Combining the window with the application reduces the generic value of the window program but increases performance.
- Code the application program to load only one subfile page at a time (subfile size equals subfile page). This increases the complexity of the application program somewhat but again improves performance.
- If you keep the window function separate, you may want to use the DDS keyword SLNO(*VAR) or the new Version 2 keyword WINDOW, which allows placement of both row and column at execution time. These keywords let you give the user some choice in the location of the window. When you use DDS windowing options, you are no longer required to use user-defined data streams to determine window location at execution time.

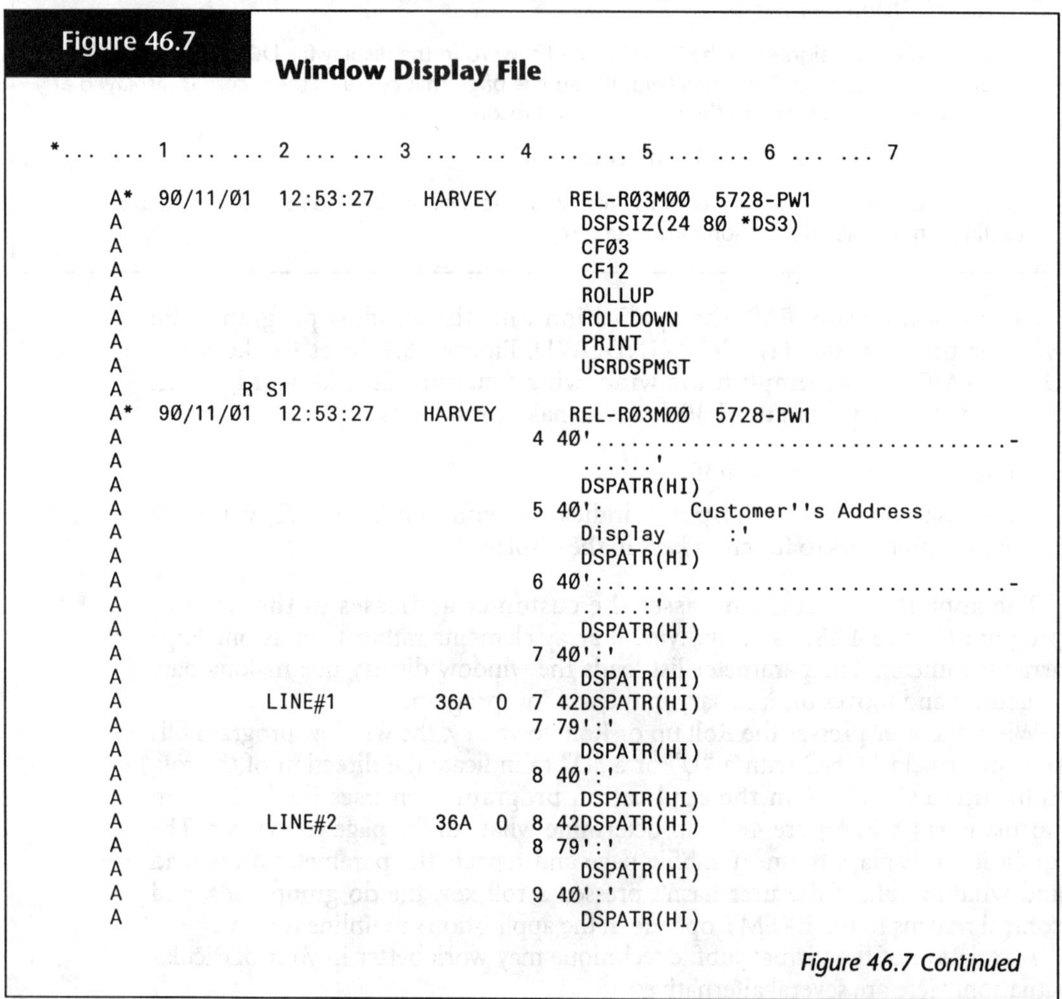

Figure 46.7

Window Display File

```
*... ... 1 ... ... 2 ... ... 3 ... ... 4 ... ... 5 ... ... 6 ... ... 7

     A*  90/11/01  12:53:27    HARVEY      REL-R03M00  5728-PW1
     A                                       DSPSIZ(24 80 *DS3)
     A                                       CF03
     A                                       CF12
     A                                       ROLLUP
     A                                       ROLLDOWN
     A                                       PRINT
     A                                       USRDSPMGT
     A          R S1
     A*  90/11/01  12:53:27    HARVEY      REL-R03M00  5728-PW1
     A                                   4 40'.................................-
     A                                       ......'
     A                                       DSPATR(HI)
     A                                   5 40':         Customer''s Address
     A                                       Display       :'
     A                                       DSPATR(HI)
     A                                   6 40':................................-
     A                                       ......:'
     A                                       DSPATR(HI)
     A                                   7 40':'
     A                                       DSPATR(HI)
     A            LINE#1        36A  O   7 42DSPATR(HI)
     A                                   7 79':'
     A                                       DSPATR(HI)
     A                                   8 40':'
     A                                       DSPATR(HI)
     A            LINE#2        36A  O   8 42DSPATR(HI)
     A                                   8 79':'
     A                                       DSPATR(HI)
     A                                   9 40':'
     A                                       DSPATR(HI)
```

Figure 46.7 Continued

Figure 46.7

Window Display File *Continued*

```
*... ... 1 ... ... 2 ... ... 3 ... ... 4 ... ... 5 ... ... 6 ... ... 7
     A            LINE#3         36A  0  9 42DSPATR(HI)
     A                                   9 79':'
     A                                       DSPATR(HI)
     A                                  10 40':'
     A                                       DSPATR(HI)
     A            LINE#4         36A  0 10 42DSPATR(HI)
     A                                  10 79':'
     A                                       DSPATR(HI)
     A                                  11 40':'
     A                                       DSPATR(HI)
     A            LINE#5         36A  0 11 42DSPATR(HI)
     A                                  11 79':'
     A                                       DSPATR(HI)
     A                                  12 40':'
     A                                       DSPATR(HI)
     A            LINE#6         36A  0 12 42DSPATR(HI)
     A                                  12 79':'
     A                                       DSPATR(HI)
     A                                  13 40':'
     A                                       DSPATR(HI)
     A            LINE#7         36A  0 13 42DSPATR(HI)
     A                                  13 79':'
     A                                       DSPATR(HI)
     A                                  14 40':'
     A                                       DSPATR(HI)
     A            LINE#8         36A  0 14 42DSPATR(HI)
     A                                  14 79':'
     A                                       DSPATR(HI)
     A                                  15 40':'
     A                                       DSPATR(HI)
     A            LINE#9         36A  0 15 42DSPATR(HI)
     A                                  15 79':'
     A                                       DSPATR(HI)
     A                                  16 40':'
     A                                       DSPATR(HI)
     A            LINE#A         36A  0 16 42DSPATR(HI)
     A                                  16 79':'
     A                                       DSPATR(HI)
     A                                  17 40':'
     A                                       DSPATR(HI)
     A            LINE#B         36A  0 17 42DSPATR(HI)
     A                                  17 79':'
     A                                       DSPATR(HI)
     A                                  18 40':'
     A                                       DSPATR(HI)
     A            LINE#C         36A  0 18 42DSPATR(HI)
     A                                  18 79':'
     A                                       DSPATR(HI)
     A                                  19 40':.................................-
     A                                       ......:'
     A                                       DSPATR(HI)
     A                                  20 40':'
```

Figure 46.7 Continued

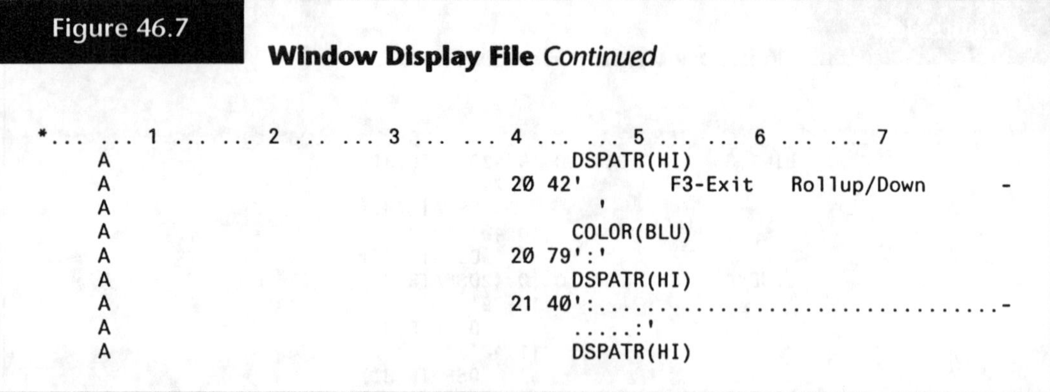

Figure 46.7

Window Display File *Continued*

```
*... ... 1 ... ... 2 ... ... 3 ... ... 4 ... ... 5 ... ... 6 ... ... 7
     A                                          DSPATR(HI)
     A                                     20 42'       F3-Exit    Rollup/Down      -
     A                                               '
     A                                          COLOR(BLU)
     A                                     20 79':'
     A                                          DSPATR(HI)
     A                                     21 40':................................-
     A                                          .....:'
     A                                          DSPATR(HI)
```

Figure 46.8

Customer Address Window Program

```
*... ... 1 ... ... 2 ... ... 3 ... ... 4 ... ... 5 ... ... 6 ... ... 7
      *****************************************************************
      *             Customer Address Window                           *
      *****************************************************************
      *
     FWINDOWD CF  E                    WORKSTN      KINFDS DSPDS
      *
      *  KEYDS - External Data Structure-hold hex values of AID Byte
      *
      *  DSPDS - File Information Data Structure
      *
     IKEYDS      E DSKEYS
     IDSPDS        DS
     I                                        369 369 KEY
     I                                      B 370 3710CURSOR
      *
     C                     EXSR SETUP                      PROG SETUP
     C                     EXFMTS1
      *
     C           KEY       IFEQ ROLLUP
     C                     MOVE 'U'       FUNC
     C                     ELSE
     C           KEY       IFEQ ROLLDN
     C                     MOVE 'D'       FUNC
     C                     ELSE
     C                     MOVE ' '       FUNC
     C                     END
     C                     END
      *
     C                     RETRN
      *********************************
      *    SETUP SUBROUTINE           *
      *********************************
     C           SETUP     BEGSR
```

Figure 46.8 Continued

Figure 46.8

Customer Address Window Program *Continued*

```
*... ... 1 ... ... 2 ... ... 3 ... ... 4 ... ... 5 ... ... 6 ... ... 7
     *
     C           *ENTRY    PLIST
     C                     PARM           FUNC    1
     C                     PARM           LINE#1 36
     C                     PARM           LINE#2 36
     C                     PARM           LINE#3 36
     C                     PARM           LINE#4 36
     C                     PARM           LINE#5 36
     C                     PARM           LINE#6 36
     C                     PARM           LINE#7 36
     C                     PARM           LINE#8 36
     C                     PARM           LINE#9 36
     C                     PARM           LINE#A 36
     C                     PARM           LINE#B 36
     C                     PARM           LINE#C 36
     *
     *   Fill the FUNCTION KEY data structure
     *
     C                     CALL 'LODKEY'                99
     C                     PARM           KEYDS
     C                     ENDSR
```

Note: The LODKEY program called at the end of this program is included in Appendix C, page 735.

Chapter 47

UIM Help for Programs

by Bryan Meyers

Use UIM to add help text to a DDS-defined display file

Chapter 39 explored the new Version 2 access to IBM's User Interface Manager (UIM), which you can use to implement help for user-defined commands and programs. This method of presenting help offers the same windowing, index searching, and hypertext linking functions IBM uses for AS/400 system help. In that chapter, I showed you how to design help screens that pop up to describe a user-defined command (extended help), as well as cursor-sensitive screens to explain individual parameters in that command (contextual help). In this chapter, I'll show you how to use UIM to add help text to a DDS-defined display file.

A Review of Panel Groups

UIM manages AS/400 objects called *panel groups* (analogous to display files), which are created by entering UIM tag statements into a PNLGRP source member. In its simplest form, panel group source uses the following format:

```
.* Comment
:PNLGRP.
:HELP NAME=module-name.
Help Title
:P.
Help text.
:EHELP.
:EPNLGRP.
```

The `:PNLGRP` and `:EPNLGRP` tags identify the source between them as a panel group (just like the PGM and ENDPGM commands identify the CL source between them as a program). One panel group may contain many help modules; the `:HELP` and `:EHELP` tags are the boundaries for each help module within a panel group (similar to RPG's BEGSR and ENDSR tags). These tags identify the source information; other tags, such as the :P (paragraph) tag, format the information in the panel group window. Once you have entered the source statements, you compile the panel group with the new CRTPNLGRP (Create Panel Group) CL command. Finally, when you create your command, you specify two new V2R1 parameters:

```
CRTCMD ... HLPPNLGRP(panel-group-name)                +
       HLPID(help-module-name)
```

Defining Help Areas

In addition to defining help for your own commands, you can use panel groups to display help for any DDS-defined display file. Integrating help panel groups into your application this way standardizes the help function across your entire system.

Many of the same principles we used for command help also apply to display files. But one extra step is required when you define help for display files: You must break your display file into *help areas* in the DDS source. That is, you must include specifications to identify screen locations that correspond to the appropriate help panels. When the user presses the Help key, the system determines the cursor location, decides whether the cursor is in a help area, and, if it is, displays the help associated with that area. If you redesign the display and move a field to another location, you must remember to respecify the appropriate help area. (When you define help for commands, this step is not necessary; the help panels follow the command parameters wherever they may be displayed.) In addition to specific locations, you can also define help that's active for the entire display (extended help).

The examples I'm defining help for are from a command I built called "WRKOBJUSG". The highlighted areas of Figure 47.1 show the additions to the WRKUSGD DDS that are necessary to implement help. The HELP and ALTHELP keywords enable the Help key and the default alternate help key, F1. The HLPTITLE keyword indicates a default title to be displayed on the full-screen help displays you create.

The two lines at A in Figure 47.1 contain the specification for extended help for this record. The HLPPNLGRP specification identifies the appropriate help module and panel group to be displayed when the user asks for help but the cursor is not in a specific help area, and the HLPARA(*RCD) specification defines the extended help area (i.e., the entire record).

The HLPARA statements at B define contextual help areas. For example, the first HLPARA specification defines a rectangle on the display from row 8, column 2 in the upper left corner to row 22, column 5 in the lower right corner. When the user requests help while the cursor is within this rectangle, help module OPTION in panel group WRKUSGHLPD is displayed.

One feature missing in the help support for DDS is the ability to use help keywords at the field level; all help keywords are valid only at the file level or record level. You cannot tie a particular help module to a specific field on the display; you can only tie it to a screen location. It would be a great productivity boost to be able to define the HLPPNLGRP keyword at the field level, then have

Figure 47.1

WRKUSGD DDS with UIM Help

```
*...+....1....+....2....+....3....+....4....+....5....+....6....+....7
     A*****************************************************************
     A*
     A*     WRKUSGD - WORK WITH OBJECT USAGE (DSPF)
     A*
     A*     CRTDSPF FILE(WRKUSGD)
     A*
     A*****************************************************************
     A                                      DSPSIZ(24 80 *DS3)
     A                                      PRINT
     A                                      ALTPAGEUP
     A                                      ALTPAGEDWN
     A                                      HELP ALTHELP
     A                                      CA03(03 'F3=Exit')
     A                                      CA05(05 'F5=Refresh')
     A                                      CF10(10 'F10=Command Entry')
     A                                      CA12(12 'F12=Cancel')
     A                                      CF21(21 'F21=Print list')
     A          R WRKUSG1
     A                                      HLPTITLE('Work with Object Usage In-
     A                                      formation')
(A)  A          H                           HLPPNLGRP(GENERAL WRKUSGHLPD)
     A                                      HLPARA(*RCD)
(B)  A          H                           HLPPNLGRP(OPTION  WRKUSGHLPD)
     A                                      HLPARA(08 002 22 005)
     A          H                           HLPPNLGRP(OBJECT  WRKUSGHLPD)
     A                                      HLPARA(08 006 22 016)
     A          H                           HLPPNLGRP(TYPE    WRKUSGHLPD)
     A                                      HLPARA(08 017 22 025)
     A          H                           HLPPNLGRP(DATE    WRKUSGHLPD)
     A                                      HLPARA(08 026 22 034)
     A          H                           HLPPNLGRP(DAYS    WRKUSGHLPD)
     A                                      HLPARA(08 035 22 040)
     A          H                           HLPPNLGRP(RESET   WRKUSGHLPD)
     A                                      HLPARA(08 041 22 049)
     A          H                           HLPPNLGRP(SIZE    WRKUSGHLPD)
     A                                      HLPARA(08 050 22 058)
     A          H                           HLPPNLGRP(TEXT    WRKUSGHLPD)
     A                                      HLPARA(08 059 22 080)
     A          H                           HLPPNLGRP(FKEYS   WRKUSGHLPD)
     A                                      HLPARA(23 001 23 080)
     A                                  1 24'Work with Object Usage Information'
     A                                      DSPATR(HI)
     A                                  3  2'Library:'
     A            I@LBNM    R        O  3 13REFFLD(QLIDOBJD/ODLBNM QSYS/QADSPOB-
     A                                      J)
     A                                  3 27'Objects:'
     A            I@OBNM    R        O  3 38REFFLD(QLIDOBJD/ODOBNM QSYS/QADSPOB-
     A                                      J)
     A                                  3 52'Type:'
     A            I@OBTP    R        O  3 60REFFLD(QLIDOBJD/ODOBTP QSYS/QADSPOB-
     A                                      J)
     A                                  5  2'Type options, press Enter.'
     A                                      COLOR(BLU)
     A                                  6  4'2=Change'
```

Figure 47.1 Continued

Figure 47.1

WRKUSGD DDS with UIM Help *Continued*

```
*...+....1....+....2....+....3....+....4....+....5....+....6....+....7
     A                                      COLOR(BLU)
     A                                    6 15'4=Delete'
     A                                      COLOR(BLU)
     A                                    6 26'5=Display'
     A                                      COLOR(BLU)
     A                                    6 38'7=Reset usage'
     A                                      COLOR(BLU)
     A                                    6 54'9=Save'
     A                                      COLOR(BLU)
     A                                    6 63'11=Move'
     A                                      COLOR(BLU)
     A                                    8 26'--- Object Used ---'
     A                                      DSPATR(HI)
     A                                    9  2'Opt'
     A                                      DSPATR(HI)
     A                                    9  6'Object'
     A                                      DSPATR(HI)
     A                                    9 17'Type'
     A                                      DSPATR(HI)
     A                                    9 28'Date'
     A                                      DSPATR(HI)
     A                                    9 36'Days'
     A                                      DSPATR(HI)
     A                                    9 43'Reset'
     A                                      DSPATR(HI)
     A                                    9 50'Size(K)'
     A                                      DSPATR(HI)
     A                                    9 59'Text'
     A                                      DSPATR(HI)
     A          R WRKUSGS                   SFL
     A  95                                  SFLNXTCHG
     A            ODOBAT    R        H      REFFLD(QLIDOBJD/ODOBAT QSYS/QADSPOB-
     A                                      J)
     A            S@OPT          2A  B 10  2DSPATR(PC)
     A            ODOBNM    R        O 10  6REFFLD(QLIDOBJD/ODOBNM QSYS/QADSPOB-
     A                                      J)
     A            ODOBTP    R        O 10 17REFFLD(QLIDOBJD/ODOBTP QSYS/QADSPOB-
     A                                      J)
     A            S@UDAT    R   +2   O 10 26REFFLD(QLIDOBJD/ODUDAT QSYS/QADSPOB-
     A                                      J)
     A            ODUCNT    R        O 10 35REFFLD(QLIDOBJD/ODUCNT QSYS/QADSPOB-
     A                                      J)
     A                                      EDTCDE(3)
     A            S@TDAT    R   +2   O 10 41REFFLD(QLIDOBJD/ODTDAT QSYS/QADSPOB-
     A                                      J)
     A            S@OBSZ    R   -3   O 10 50REFFLD(QLIDOBJD/ODOBSZ QSYS/QADSPOB-
     A                                      J)
     A                                      EDTCDE(3)
     A            S@OBTX    R  -29   O 10 59REFFLD(QLIDOBJD/ODOBTX QSYS/QADSPOB-
     A                                      J)
     A          R WRKUSGC                   SFLCTL(WRKUSGS)
     A                                      SFLSIZ(0120)
     A                                      SFLPAG(0012)
     A 92                                   SFLDSP
     A 93                                   SFLDSPCTL
```

Figure 47.1 Continued

Figure 47.1

WRKUSGD DDS with UIM Help *Continued*

```
*...+....1....+....2....+....3....+....4....+....5....+....6....+....7
     A  94                                  SFLCLR
     A  91                                  SFLEND
     A                                      ROLLUP(90)
     A                                      OVERLAY
     A            MAXRRN         4  0H      SFLRCDNBR
     A                                 23  2'F3=Exit'
     A                                      COLOR(BLU)
     A                                 23 12'F5=Refresh'
     A                                      COLOR(BLU)
     A                                 23 25'F12=Cancel'
     A                                      COLOR(BLU)
     A                                 23 38'F10=Command entry'
     A                                      COLOR(BLU)
     A                                 23 58'F21=Print list'
     A                                      COLOR(BLU)
```

the operating system automatically define the help area, regardless of where you move that field on your screen.

There's one other minor restriction: The DDS compiler prevents you from mixing help panel groups with help records or help documents in the same display file. Help records and help documents are the other two officially supported AS/400 methods of providing help to application displays, and they use similar DDS specifications — HLPRCD and HLPDOC instead of HLPPNLGRP keywords. But if you specify HLPRCD or HLPDOC keywords in your DDS, you cannot also specify HLPPNLGRP.

Building the Panel Group

After you define the help areas in the display file and create the file, you finish the job by keying the help text into a PNLGRP source member and creating the panel group. The source in Figure 47.2 uses several UIM markup tags we discussed in Chapter 39, and it introduces a couple of new ones.

The `:NT` and `:ENT` tags (at A) mark the boundaries of a note. Notes are blocks of text, of one or more paragraphs, that UIM formats as indented copy preceded by the label "`Note:`" in boldface. You might use a note in your help text to accent a paragraph, further explain a phrase, or explain a restriction in your program.

You can also embed help information from one help module into another, even if the two modules are not in the same panel group. Help information for each of the function keys is contained in separate help modules, and at B in Figure 47.2, the `:IMHELP NAME` tags tell UIM to also include the help information from each of the modules in a combined help module called FKEYS. You can then refer to the single combined help module in your DDS, instead of to each individual module.

Another use for the `:IMHELP` tag is to let you use the same help information in more than one module of a panel group, without rekeying the text. For

Figure 47.2

UIM Source for WRKUSGD Help

```
*...+....1....+....2....+....3....+....4....+....5....+....6....+....7
**********************************************************************
.*
.*      Panel group - WRKUSGHLPD - Help for WRKOBJUSG command
.*
.*      This PNLGRP contains help for the WRKUSGD display file.
.*
.*      CRTPNLGRP PNLGRP(WRKUSGHLPD)
.*
**********************************************************************
:PNLGRP.
**********************************************************************
:HELP NAME=GENERAL.
Work with Object Usage Information - Help
:P.
This display shows a list of objects in a library, along with object
usage information for each object.  This display results from execution
of the Work with object usage (WRKOBJUSG) command.
:P.
The object name, type attributes, last date used, number of days used,
reset date, object size, and text of each object are shown.  From this
list several object-oriented options can be performed.
:P.
The WRKOBJUSG command was originally described in "Working out with
WRKOBJUSG," :CIT.News 3X/400,:ECIT. February, 1991.
:EHELP.
**********************************************************************
.*
.*      Option - Help Text
.*
:HELP NAME=OPTION.
OPT (Options) - Help
:XH3.OPT (Option)
:P.
Type the option you want.
:PARML.
:PT.2=Change
:PD.
Changes an object.
:PT.4=Delete
:PD.
Deletes an object.
:PT.5=Display
:PD.
Displays an object.
:PT.7=Reset usage
:PD.
Resets usage count to zero, and clears last date used, for an object.
:PT.9=Save
:PD.
Saves an object.
:PT.11=Move
:PD.
Moves an object to another library.
:EPARML.
```

Figure 47.2 Continued

Figure 47.2

UIM Source for WRKUSGD Help *Continued*

```
*...+....1....+....2....+....3....+....4....+....5....+....6....+....7
:EHELP.
**********************************************************************
.*
.*     Option - Help Text
.*
:HELP NAME=OBJECT.
Object - Help
:XH3.Object
:P.
The names of the objects you can use.
:EHELP.
**********************************************************************
.*
.*     Type - Help Text
.*
:HELP NAME=TYPE.
Type - Help
:XH3.Type
:P.
The type of object that is displayed, such as a command (*CMD), a file
(*FILE) or a program (*PGM).
:EHELP.
**********************************************************************
.*
.*     Date - Help Text
.*
:HELP NAME=DATE.
Object Used: Date - Help
:XH3.Object Used: Date
:P.
The date the object was last used.
:NT.
If object usage data is not recorded for this object, "*Not upd" is
displayed in this column.
:ENT.
:EHELP.
**********************************************************************
.*
.*     Days - Help Text
.*
:HELP NAME=DAYS.
Object Used: Days - Help
:XH3.Object Used: Days
:P.
The number of days this object has been used since last being reset.
:EHELP.
**********************************************************************
.*
.*     Reset - Help Text
.*
:HELP NAME=RESET.
Object Used: Reset - Help
:XH3.Object Used: Reset
:P.
The date this object was last reset.
```

(A) marks the line "If object usage data is not recorded for this object, "*Not upd" is"

Figure 47.2 Continued

Figure 47.2

UIM Source for WRKUSGD Help *Continued*

```
*...+....1....+....2....+....3....+....4....+....5....+....6....+....7
:EHELP.
**********************************************************************
.*
.*      Size - Help Text
.*
:HELP NAME=SIZE.
Size - Help
:XH3.Size
:P.
The size of this object, in kilobytes (K).  A kilobyte is 1,024
characters.
:EHELP.
**********************************************************************
.*
.*      Text - Help Text
.*
:HELP NAME=TEXT.
Text - Help
:XH3.Text
:P.
A brief, user-created description of the object.
:EHELP.
**********************************************************************
.*
.*      F-Keys- Help text
.*
:HELP NAME=FKEYS.
Function Keys - Help
:XH3.Function Keys
:IMHELP NAME=FKEY01.
:IMHELP NAME=FKEY03.
:IMHELP NAME=FKEY05.
:IMHELP NAME=FKEY10.
:IMHELP NAME=FKEY12.
:IMHELP NAME=FKEY21.
:EHELP.
**********************************************************************
.*
.*      F1=Help- Help text
.*
:HELP NAME=FKEY01.
:PARML.
:PT.F1=Help
:PD.
Provides additional information about using the display.
:EPARML.
:EHELP.
**********************************************************************
.*
.*      F3=Exit - Help text
.*
:HELP NAME=FKEY03.
:PARML.
:PT.F3=Exit
:PD.
```

(B) — callout beside line ":IMHELP NAME=FKEY03."

Figure 47.2 Continued

Figure 47.2

UIM Source for WRKUSGD Help *Continued*

```
*...+....1....+....2....+....3....+....4....+....5....+....6....+....7
Ends the current task and returns to the display from which the task
was started.
:EPARML.
:EHELP.
**********************************************************************
.*
.*     F5=Refresh - Help text
.*
:HELP NAME=FKEY05.
:PARML.
:PT.F5=Refresh
:PD.
Updates the information displayed.
:EPARML.
:EHELP.
**********************************************************************
.*
.*     F10-Command line - Help text
.*
:HELP NAME=FKEY10.
:PARML.
:PT.F10=Command line
:PD.
Displays a command line that allows you to enter system commands.
:EPARML.
:EHELP.
**********************************************************************
.*
.*     F12=Cancel - Help text
.*
:HELP NAME=FKEY12.
:PARML.
:PT.F12=Cancel
:PD.
Cancels this display and returns to the previous display.
:EPARML.
:EHELP.
**********************************************************************
.*
.*     F21=Print list - Help text
.*
:HELP NAME=FKEY21.
:PARML.
:PT.F21=Print list
:PD.
Prints the list.
:NT.
This function uses AS/400 Query Management.
:ENT.
:EPARML.
:EHELP.
:EPNLGRP.
```

simplicity in this example, the individual function key modules are defined in the same panel group as the combined module — but they could be in another panel group altogether. To pull text from another panel group into the one you're creating, use the following UIM tag just after the :PNLGRP tag, before any :HELP tags:

```
:IMPORT PNLGRP=pnlgrp-name                                    +
        NAME=help-name.
```

This tag makes help modules that are defined in another panel group available to the current panel group. Then you can use the :IMHELP tag to place the text in the current panel group.

A feature similar to RPG's /COPY statement inserts source from another member in the same source file at the time you compile the panel group. To use this feature, key the following directive, beginning in column 1, at the location in your panel group where you want to include the other source member:

```
.IM member-name
```

At first glance, this instruction appears to offer the same function as the :IMPORT tag, but there is a subtle difference. The :IMPORT tag lets you merge text from a compiled panel group into your current panel group at the time you display it. In this respect, it is similar to calling a program from within another program; the text from the two panel groups is combined seamlessly into one window. The .IM directive, on the other hand, includes text from another source member at the time you compile the panel group.

Figure 47.3 shows some examples of the help windows I created in the WRKUSGD display file. Note that the UIM help panels rarely cover the area that the help window is referencing. UIM automatically and dynamically handles window size and position, or you can override the dynamic sizing by specifying an absolute width and depth on the :HELP tag.

Enabling the Help Index

Once you master help panel groups, you'll want to enable the search index function to supplement the help information that you write for each display. With Version 2, you can easily incorporate this feature of the AS/400 help interface into your applications. Here's how it works from the user's perspective: If a user needs more information about a particular topic but doesn't know where to start, he or she can press Help. When the help panel is displayed, the user can press F11 (Search Index), then type a search argument into the display. The search argument may be a simple question, such as "How do I delete a customer?" or it may consist solely of search words, such as "deleting customer." The search index function responds by displaying all the help topics that relate to the search words and predefined synonyms, and the user may select the topic to display or print.

The search index is an easy way to organize the help text for an entire application into an on-line reference guide. You can use panel groups that are already being used to display help windows, and you can create supplementary panel groups that will appear only when users call up the search index.

Figure 47.3

Sample Help Windows

```
                       Work with Object Usage Information

Library:   N3XLIB        Objects:   WRK*          Type:   *ALL

Type options, press Enter.
  2=Change   4=Delete   5=Display   7=Reset usage   9=Save   11=Move

                                  -- Object Used --
Opt Object      Type       Date   ...........................................
___ WRKUSG1     *PGM       07/17/91  :        Object Used: Date - Help        :
___ WRKUSG2     *PGM       07/16/91  :                                        :
___ WRKUSG3     *PGM       07/17/91  :  The date the object was last used.    :
___ WRKUSGD     *FILE      07/16/91  :                                        :
___ WRKOBJUSG   *CMD       07/17/91  :     Note:  If object usage data is not :
___ WRKUSGHLP   *PNLGRP    07/17/91  :     recorded for this object, "*Not    :
___ WRKUSGHLPD  *PNLGRP    07/16/91  :     upd" is displayed in this column.  :
___ WRKUSGQ     *QMQRY               :                                 Bottom :
___ WRKUSGQF    *QMFORM              :  F2=Extended help    F10=Move to top   :
                                     :  F12=Cancel          F24=More keys     :
                                     :                                        :
                                     :........................................:

F3=Exit   F5=Refresh   F12=Cancel   F10=Command entry   F21=Print list
```

```
                       Work with Object Usage Information
  ............................................................................
  :                            Function Keys - Help                            :
  :                                                                            :
  :  F1=Help                                                                   :
  :      Provides additional information about using the display.             :
  :                                                                            :
  :  F3=Exit                                                                   :
  :      Ends the current task and returns to the display from which the task  :
  :      was started.                                                          :
  :                                                                            :
  :  F5=Refresh                                                                :
  :      Updates the information displayed.                                    :
  :                                                                            :
  :  F10=Command line                                                          :
  :      Displays a command line that allows you to enter system commands.     :
  :                                                                            :
  :                                                                   More...  :
  :  F2=Extended help   F3=Exit help    F10=Move to top   F12=Cancel           :
  :  F13=User support   F14=Print help  F20=Enlarge                            :
  :                                                                            :
  :............................................................................:
  F3=Exit   F5=Refresh   F12=Cancel   F10=Command entry   F21=Print list
```

To implement a search index, you specify the root search words that link to a specific help module, using the `:ISCH ROOTS` (Index Search Roots) tag in the panel group source. Root words are keywords that actually appear in the help module. You may also specify synonyms for search words with the `:ISCHSYN ROOT` (Index Search Synonym Root) tag.

Figure 47.4 illustrates the panel group source for a whimsical search function inspired by my six-year-old daughter. She could press F11 at a help window (being somewhat precocious), and type in "Why are there bunnies in the sky?" My trusty AS/400 would then take over answering the hard questions, and I could stick to the easy ones.

Once you finish the admittedly tedious job of specifying roots and synonyms in your panel group source, three more steps are necessary to implement the search index. You build a search index object using the CRTSCHIDX (Create Search Index) CL command, and you link a panel group to the search index using the ADDSCHIDXE (Add Search Index Entry) CL command. Enter these commands at any command line. Finally, you must enable the search function in the DDS source for each display with the DDS file-level keyword HLPSCHIDX (Help Search Index), which also specifies which search index to use for the display.

In addition to accessing a search index from within a help panel, you can start the search function with the STRSCHIDX (Start Search Index) CL command. An application menu option could execute this command to display the user guide/search index directly, without first going through Help or the F11 key.

Figure 47.4

UIM Search Index Source

```
*...+....1....+....2....+....3....+....4....+....5....+....6....+....7

:PNLGRP.
:ISCHSYN ROOT='cloud'.clouds cloudy cloudiness overcast
:ISCHSYN ROOT='cloud'.cirrus cumulus nimbus stratus
:ISCHSYN ROOT='moisture'.precipitation rain water snow hail
:ISCHSYN ROOT='storm'.storms stormy
:ISCHSYN ROOT='rabbit'.rabbits bunny bunnies hare hares
:HELP NAME=clouds.
:ISCH ROOTS='cloud weather moisture storm sky'
ROOTS='shapes formations fluffy rabbit'.
Clouds
:P.
Clouds are weather formations containing moisture.  Occasionally, they appear
to take on the shapes of common objects, such as bunny rabbits.
:P.
Dark clouds usually precede a storm.
:EHELP.
:EPNLGRP.
```

A Little Light Reading

IBM's *Guide to Programming Displays* (SC41-0011), which is also available on the CD-ROM AS/400 SoftCopy Library, describes UIM tag language for help panels. But in case you don't have this (optional) documentation, I've provided a quick reference to the tag language (Figure 47.5). Use the explanations in this figure along with the sample code from this chapter to explore this easy method of providing and maintaining help displays for your applications.

This should be enough to get you started, but we haven't covered a number of optional keywords available for some tags. For example, the hypertext `:LINK` tag, described in Chapter 39 as a means of linking two help modules together, has a number of optional conditional expressions that may change the link operation, depending upon the user class of the person displaying the help, the existence of a specific object on your system, or the user's authority to an object. If you plan to use these features, I advise you to study Appendix A in the *Guide to Programming Displays.*

Nearly every IBM-supplied display you see on the AS/400 is implemented using UIM rather than DDS-defined display files. For example, list panels, which are the hallmark of the many "Work with" commands on the system and which (unlike subfiles) comply with CUA, are UIM panels. While the panel group may never become a complete replacement for DDS, perhaps in the future IBM will see fit to open this function further to mere mortal customers.

Figure 47.5

UIM Quick Reference

Panel Control Tags

Tag	Description
`:HELP NAME=help-module-name.` `:EHELP.`	Indicate the boundaries of a help module.
`:IMHELP NAME=help-module-name.`	Embeds another help module within the module where this tag occurs. The other help module must be in the same panel group, or must be :IMPORTed from another panel group.
`:IMPORT PNLGRP=pnlgrp-name +` `NAME=imported-name.`	Imports help modules from another panel group into the current panel group. Must occur just after the :PNLGRP tag.
`:ISCH ROOTS='root-word-list' +` `.index-entry-text`	Identifies the help module to be used when an index search matches a word in the root word list. Must occur just after the appropriate :HELP tag.
`:ISCHSYN ROOT=root-word.synonyms`	Builds a table of synonyms for a root word during an index search.

Figure 47.5 Continued

Figure 47.5

UIM Quick Reference *Continued*

Panel Control Tags

Tag	Description
:LINK PERFORM='DSPHELP help-module'. :ELINK.	Identify a reference phrase to be linked (via hypertext) to another help module.
:PNLGRP. :EPNLGRP.	Indicate panel group boundaries. One set is allowed; they must be the first and last tags in the source.

Panel Markup Tags

Tag	Description
:CIT. :ECIT.	Identify the title of a publication (to be underlined).
:DL. :DT.definition-term :DD.definition-description :EDL.	Used to format a definition list. List must be bounded by :DL and :EDL tags. One or more sets of :DT and :DD tags may occur within the list.
:FIG. :EFIG.	Identify a figure, diagram or other illustration. All formatting is turned off.
:H1.heading-text :H2.heading-text :H3.heading text :H4.heading-text	Identify main topics and subtopics of help information. :H1 centered, underlined, bold :H2 left-justified, underlined, bold :H3 left-justified, bold :H4 left-justified, underlined
:HPØ.text:EHPØ. :HP1.text:EHP1. :HP2.text:EHP2. :HP3.text:EHP3. :HP4.text:EHP4. :HP5.text:EHP5. :HP6.text:EHP6. :HP7.text:EHP7. :HP8.text:EHP8. :HP9.text:EHP9.	Identify the boundaries of a phrase to be highlighted when displayed: :HP0 = normal :HP1 = underlined :HP2 = bold :HP3 = underlined, bold :HP4 = normal :HP5 = reverse image :HP6 = underlined, reverse image :HP7 = bold, reverse image :HP8 = nondisplay :HP9 = reverse image
:LINES. :ELINES.	Identify unformatted lines of text.
:LP.	Identifies a comment or explanation within a list.
:NT. :ENT.	Identify the boundaries of a note, indented with "Note:" preceding the text.
:OL. :LI.list-item-text :EOL.	Identify an ordered list. Ordered lists are formatted with identifiers (1, a, etc.) to the left. One or more :LI tags may occur within the list.
:P.	Starts a paragraph — a block of text separated from other text by a blank line.

Figure 47.5 Continued

Figure 47.5

UIM Quick Reference *Continued*

Panel Markup Tags

Tag	Description

`:PARML.`
`:PT.parameter-term`
`:PD.parameter-description`
`:EPARML.`
	Format a list of parameter terms and descriptions, identifed by the :PT and :PD tags.

`:PC.`	Continues a paragraph when it has been interrupted by another tag.

`:PK.keyword:EPK.`
`:PK DEF.keyword:EPK.`
`:PV.variable:EPV.`
	Indicate programming keywords and variables. :PK DEF indicates a default keyword.

`:SL.`
`:LI.list-item-text`
`:ESL.`
	Format a simple list, with no identifiers or bullets. One or more :LI tags may occur within the list.

`:UL.`
`:LI.list-item-text`
`:EUL.`
	Format an unordered list, with bullets or dashes to the left. One or more :LI tags may occurs within the list.

`:XH1.heading-text`
`:XH2.heading-text`
`:XH3.heading-text`
`:XH4.heading-text`
	Identify heading text for extended help.
	:XH1 = centered, underlined, bold
	:XH2 = left-justified, underlined, bold
	:XH3 = left-justified, bold
	:XH4 = left-justified, underlined

`:XMP.` `:EXMP.`	Identify the boundaries of unformatted example text.

Miscellaneous UIM Tags

Tag	Description
`.*`	Comment identifier. Must start in column 1 of source.
`.IM member-name`	Embeds source from another member at compile time.

`&.`
`&COLON.`
`&CONT.`
`&PERIOD.`
`&SLR.`
	Handle punctuation marks that may conflict with UIM notation. & becomes an ampersand (&). &COLON becomes a colon (:). &CONT concatenates the next line to the current line for unformatted text. &PERIOD becomes a period (.). &SLR becomes a right slash (/).

`&MSG.(message-id, message-file, +` `library)`	Extracts the appropriate message at panel group compile time. You may use this feature as part of National Language Support implementation.
`'dd'x`	Used to enter hexadecimal data. You can include one or more pairs of hex digits within the single quotation marks.

Chapter 48

Group Jobs

by Paul Conte

Add flexibility to existing applications and simplify future program development with a "master menu" for group jobs

In this chapter, I furnish a group job example (which I call the "master menu" approach) that uses one group job as a "dispatcher" for transfers among up to 15 other group jobs in which application menus or application functions execute.

Figure 48.1 shows the general structure of the master menu approach. The first group job ("MSTMNU" in Figure 48.1) is established by using the CHGGRPA GRPJOB(MSTMNU) command and invoking the master menu program. The MSTMNU group job has two roles: First, it is the only group job that starts a new group job or transfers control to a suspended group job to make it active; second, if a predefined selection of the next group job is not made via a "hot key," the MSTMNU group job displays a menu that lets the user select the next group job. In the master menu approach, other group jobs execute either application menu programs (e.g., in Figure 48.1 group job LONMNUl executes CL menu program LONMNUCTL) or application function programs such as displaying database records (e.g., in Figure 48.1 group job UPDLONAPP executes the CL "shell" program UPDLONCTL and the HLL program UPDLONAPP).

Once in the group job environment, a user can transfer among the application menus and functions by pressing the Attention key to return to the MSTMNU group job and view a menu of group jobs. As an alternative, for those menus and functions that have "hot key" support (i.e., the capability to switch between applications with a single function key), the user can press a function key to preselect the next group job and thus bypass the display of the group job menu. When a master menu option is selected for the first time, a new group job starts,

Figure 48.1

Group Job "Master Menu" Processing

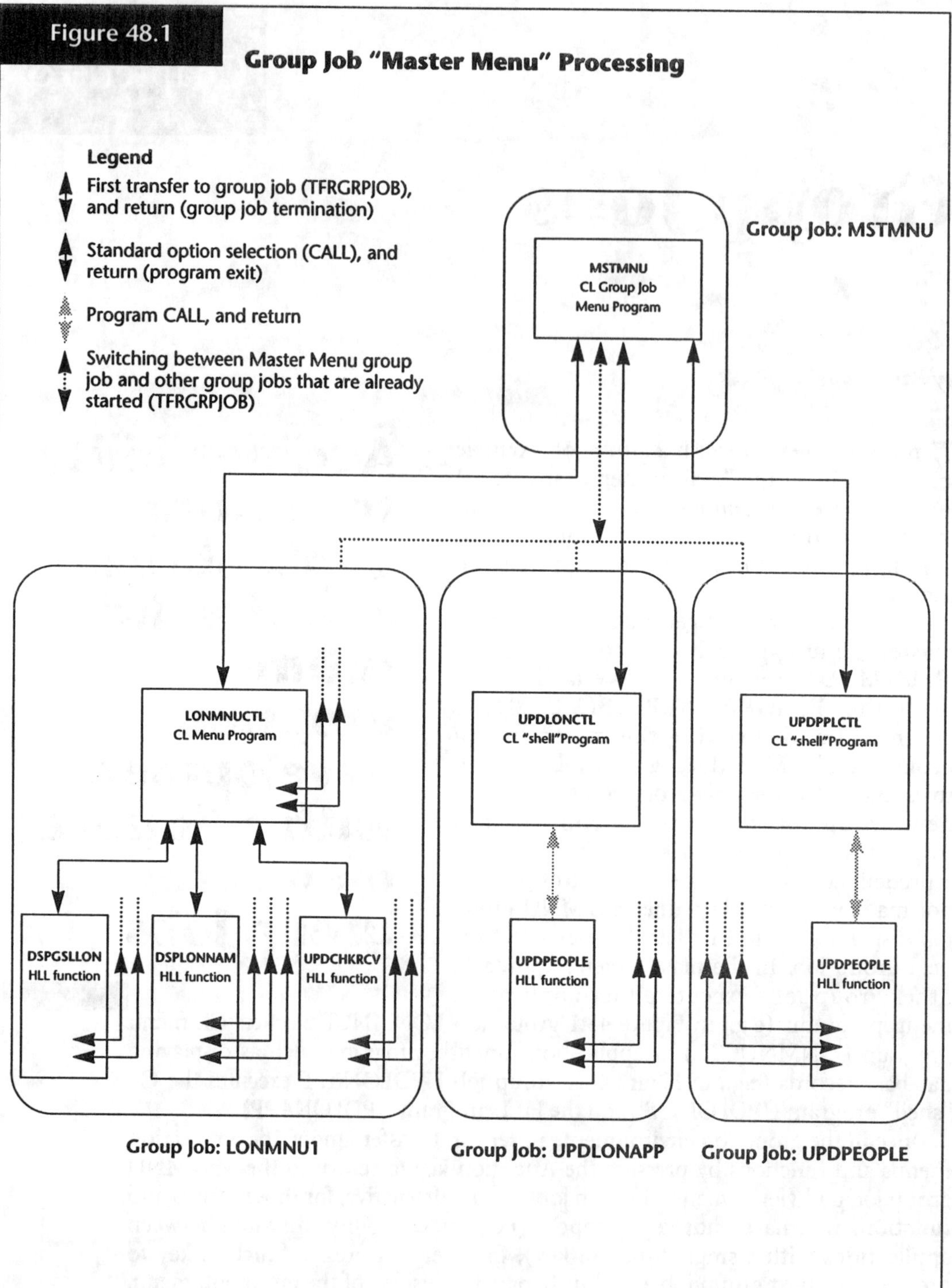

Legend
First transfer to group job (TFRGRPJOB), and return (group job termination)
Standard option selection (CALL), and return (program exit)
Program CALL, and return
Switching between Master Menu group job and other group jobs that are already started (TFRGRPJOB)
Group Job: MSTMNU
MSTMNU
CL Group Job
Menu Program
LONMNUCTL
CL Menu Program
UPDLONCTL
CL "shell" Program
UPDPPLCTL
CL "shell" Program
DSPGSLLON
HLL function
DSPLONNAM
HLL function
UPDCHKRCV
HLL function
UPDPEOPLE
HLL function
UPDPEOPLE
HLL function
Group Job: LONMNU1
Group Job: UPDLONAPP
Group Job: UPDPEOPLE

and the group job's initial program executes. When the user finishes with an application menu or function that is a group job's initial program, the menu or function can be exited. At that point, the completed group job terminates and the MSTMNU group job once again displays a menu of group jobs.

Within an application menu (e.g., within LONMNUCTL in Figure 48.1), lower-level menus or functions (e.g., HLL functions DSPGSLLON, DSPLONNAM, and UPDCHKRCV in Figure 48.1) can be selected as they would be in a standard interactive job. Attention-key and hot-key transfers can occur to and from points in these lower levels; however, all transfers must be to and from points in other group jobs, not within the same group job. That is, a user can use the Attention key to transfer back to the MSTMNU group job from the DSPGSLLON function, or a user can press a hot key to switch from the UPDPEOPLE function to the lower level UPDCHKRCV function of the LONMNUCTL menu. However, to select a new option within the same group job's application menu, a lower-level function — for example, the DSPLONNAM function — must be exited and a new option — for example, the DSPGSLLON function — selected from the menu.

Group Jobs From the User's Perspective

Now that I've described the general structure of the master menu approach, let's look at how the programs presented later in the chapter work for a user. Figure 48.2 shows the Master Menu that appears when the user first enters the group job environment. Five alternate group jobs are available: loan processing menu (1), loan processing menu (2), display/update loan applications, display/update loan transactions, and display/update people), and the user also can sign off (option 90).

Note that both the first and second options select the loan processing menu, but they start the menu in separate group jobs. This approach allows the user two

Figure 48.2

The Master Menu (No Option Selected)

```
                              MASTER MENU

Select one of the following:                              CF Key
  1.   Loan Processing menu (1)                             20
  2.   Loan Processing menu (2)                             21
  3.   Display/Update loan applications                     22
  4.   Display/Update loan transactions                     23
  5.   Display/Update people                                24
  90.  Signoff

Option: __

F3=Exit                      F6=Messages                        HELP
```

open-ended options in addition to the specific functions available in the other three master menu group job options. That is, a loan menu option to display daily check receipts can be in use in one group job while the loan menu option to display defaulted loans is in use in another group job. Use of multiple group jobs to access the same menu helps keep the Master Menu itself simple yet provides extensive selection to the user, without forcing the user to back out of a lower-level function to enter a different lower-level function from the same menu. The only cost is an increase in the menu "depth" of some of the group jobs — a performance, not a functional, consideration; because once the user reaches the desired function, the menu depth is of no concern.

In Figure 48.2, note also that when a user first enters the group job environment, the Master Menu lets the user exit the group job environment by pressing F3. The Master Menu also supports F6 to display workstation messages and the Help key to invoke a locally written help facility.

The final thing to note about the Master Menu in Figure 48.2 is that it lets the user assign keys F20 through F24 as hot keys for preselecting transfers. The hot keys take the default assignment shown in Figure 48.2; however, the user can reassign them as he or she prefers. Granted, when only five group jobs are available, hot-key designations are of limited value. However, if the master menu includes more than five group jobs, users find it valuable to be able to assign hot key designations to the options they use most frequently.

From the Master Menu in Figure 48.2, the user can select a group job by entering an option or by pressing a command function key. For example, to select the "Display/ Update loan applications" function, a user can enter a 3 on the "Option:" line or press F22. Then anywhere the selected group job (e.g., the UPDLONAPP application) reads a display file (i.e., requests input from the user), the user can press the Attention key to return to the Master Menu. From the Master Menu, the user can select another group job.

Figure 48.3 shows the Master Menu after three group jobs have been started. A literal — "(active)" — is displayed beside each group job that has been started. (The term "active" is more meaningful to a user than the more precise group job status of "suspended.") On the bottom line of the display appears the name of the previously active group job (in this case, UPDLONAPP) if it did not terminate. The user can press F2 to resume this group job. Because both application menu group jobs and application function group jobs exist, option 90 for signing off is no longer displayed. A sign-off ends not just one group job, but all other group jobs within the group without allowing each group job an orderly completion. Thus, if any group job besides the Master Menu group job has been started, it is unwise to let a user sign off from the Master Menu. In addition, F3 is not available to exit the Master Menu until all other group jobs are terminated. From the Master Menu in Figure 48.3, the user can select one of the "active" group jobs to resume, or the user can start a new group job.

Figures 48.4, 48.5, and 48.6 show examples of screens displayed by the group jobs selected with Master Menu options 1, 3, and 5. From any of these displays, the user can press the Attention key to display the Master Menu and select another group job. Because support for hot keys has been included in the programs for the

Figure 48.3

The Master Menu (Three Options Selected)

```
                              MASTER MENU

  Select one of the following:                               CF Key
    1.    Loan Processing menu (1)                  (active)    20
    2.    Loan Processing menu (2)                              21
    3.    Display/Update loan applications          (active)    22
    4.    Display/Update loan transactions                      23
    5.    Display/Update people                     (active)    24


  Option:.__


  F2=Prior job: UPDLONAPP   F6=Messages
 HELP
```

Figure 48.4

An Application Menu Using Option 1 of the Master Menu

```
                              LOAN   MENU

  Select one of the following:
     1.  Display GSL loans/applications
     2.  Display loans received by name
     3.  Check receipting
     4.  Query reports
     5.  GSL - Correct loan information
     6.  GSL - Enter endorsed applications
     7.  GSL - Enter other transactions
     8.  GSL - Move Applic. to Loan Master
     9.  SCR - Update SCR file
    10.  CLC - Display Defaults by Name
    11.  CLC - Display Defaults by SSN
    12.  PLS - Display PLUS Loans
    13.  PLS - Update PLUS Loans
    14.  LON - Update Refund Checks
    98.  Training menu

  Option: __

  F3=Exit    F6=Messages               F2x=Alternate Group Job   HELP
```

three "active" group jobs, the user also can press F20 to switch immediately from the display in either Figure 48.5 or 48.6 to the display in Figure 48.4; or the user can press F22 to switch immediately to the display in Figure 48.5; or the user can press F24 to switch immediately to the display in Figure 48.6. If the user presses either

Figure 48.5

A HLL Application Using Option 3 of the Master Menu

```
3/23/86 11:51:58            LOAN APPLICATION DETAIL 1                +++

SSN:               501-22-8440
Name:              ORR                           , MONICA       E
Seq:               0                 Loan number:        325735
EDD agency:        741               Birthdate:         53/10/13
US citizen:        Y                 Elg. Alien:        _
Org. enr. sts.:    FT                Nbr. cosign.:       0
Loan period:       85/12/01          Through:           87/01/01
Academic Year:      3                Acd. Cpl. Date:    89/06/01
Org. College:      688923            Dep. Status:       D
AGI:                    $23,500.00   Educ. cost:              $5,700.00
w10  aid amt.:             $900.00   Family Ctrb.:            $1,200.00
Clg. Ctf. Date:    85/07/03          Org. lender:       12892
Itr. rate (%):       7.00            Itr. subsidy:      Y
   Dsb. Date       Dsb. Amount       Fee   Amount
(1)  86/01/01             $1,000.00          $20.00
(2)  86/06/01             $1,000.00          $20.00
(3)   0/00/00                 $0.00           $0.00
(4)   0/00/00                 $0.00           $0.00
Org. principal:           $2,000.00  Endorsed: 85/09/01

CF3=Exit                     CF12=Cancel    CF2x=Alt. group job   HELP
```

Figure 48.6

A HLL Subfile Display Using Option 5 of the Master Menu

```
3/23/86 11:49:41                  PEOPLE

Access ID: SSN

SSN          Last name             First        MI Seq Grt Lon Dft
501-22-8440  ORR                   MONICA       E       Y   Y
501-28-2148  GROSCHE               DARLENE      D
501-30-5507  FOSS                  VELMA        _       Y
501-34-1225  DECOTEAU              DORIS        M           Y   Y
501-36-2822  HALE                  BETTY        A       Y
501-44-2174  BROOKS                MARY         J
501-44-4740  FORVILLY              LORRAINE     H       Y
501-46-3094  HOLT                  LAURAJO      _       Y   Y
501-46-7122  BARON                 AMANDUS      L       Y   Y
501-48-0616  MORRISON              KAY          M       Y
501-48-2775  SCHLECHT              CATHAY       L       Y
501-50-7935  ANDERSON              LINDA        E       Y                +

1-Detail  3-Print                        9-Delete
F3=Exit  F5=Refresh  F8=Display  F9=Add  F2x=Alt. group job  HELP
```

F21 or F23 from any of these three displays, a new group job for option 2 or option 4 of the Master Menu is started, and the appropriate program's first display is presented. The ability to switch rapidly between an individual's detail display of a loan application (e.g., Monica Orr in Figure 48.5) to a subfile display that shows what other financial aid that individual has with the agency (Figure 48.6) is an example of using related functions "simultaneously" with group jobs.

Eight Steps to Implement Group Jobs

Now that you've seen how the Master Menu approach works on the "outside," let's look at the eight steps involved in implementing the approach. One step necessitates adding the CHGGRPA command to the program that calls the program to display the Master Menu (Figure 48.7). Another step involves the creation of the display file for the Master Menu (Figure 48.8). You also need to develop the master menu program (Figure 48.9). And you must add group job-related commands to application menu programs and CL "shell" programs available from the Master Menu (Figure 48.10). If you want hot key support in high-level language (HLL) programs that implement application functions (e.g., the UPDPEOPLE function in Figure 48.1), you must add the appropriate code to the programs (Figure 48.11). In addition, you need to create an external TRFGRPJOB subroutine for use by HLL programs (Figure 48.12). You also must develop an Attention key handling program (Figure 48.13). And if you want to protect your group jobs from the improper use of the SIGNOFF command, you must create an alternate SIGNOFF command (Figure 48.14). I'll consider each step separately.

Using the CHGGRPA Command

To use the master menu program (in this case, program MSTMNU) as a group job "dispatcher," it first must be a group job itself. Thus, in the program that calls program MSTMNU, you must execute the CHGGRPA command shown in

Figure 48.7 **User Profile's Initial Program to Establish Group Job Environment**

```
/*  Establish that this is a group job with name MSTMNU.              */

CHGGRPA    GRPJOB(mstmnu)


/*  Initialize the group data area.                                   */
/*  Bytes 1 and 2 hold function key identifier for a predefined      */
/*  application to which transfer is made.  This user will start     */
/*  with function key identifier "20", selecting the loans menu.     */

CHGDTAARA  DTAARA(*gda (1 2)) VALUE('20')


/*  Transfer to the Master Menu.  The parameter is set to "Y" so     */
/*  that the master menu can be exited with CF3.                      */

CALL       PGM(prdmnu/mstmnu)  PARM('Y')
```

Figure 48.8

MSTMNU Display File

```
* MSTMNU Display file

* Use CRTDSPF RSTDSP(*yes) when creating this display file

                                      PRINT(PRINTKEY)

  91                                  CA03(03 'CA3  - Exit'   )
  92 93                               CA02(02 'CA2  - PRVGRPJOB')
                                      CA06(06 'CA6  - DSPMSG')
  93                                  CA20(20 'CA20 - Hot key')
Ⓐ 93                                  CA21(21 'CA21 - Hot key')
  93                                  CA22(22 'CA22 - Hot key')
  93                                  CA23(23 'CA23 - Hot key')
  93                                  CA24(24 'CA24 - Hot key')
                                      HELP(25 'Help - HELP')

                                      INDTXT(46 'OVERLAY/PUTOVR')
                                      INDTXT(60 'Display messages')
                                      INDTXT(61 'Job  1 active')
                                      INDTXT(62 'Job  2 active')
                                      INDTXT(63 'Job  3 active')
                                      INDTXT(64 'Job  4 active')
                                      INDTXT(65 'Job  5 active')
                                      INDTXT(90 'Invalid option    +
                                                 error message')
                                      INDTXT(91 'Enable CA1')
                                      INDTXT(92 'Enable CA2')
                                      INDTXT(93 'Group job')
                                      INDTXT(97 'Invalid hot key used')
                                      INDTXT(98 'Invalid CF key    +
                                                 assigned as hot key')
                                      INDTXT(99 'Enable Signoff')

          R MENU                      BLINK
  46                                  OVERLAY
  46                                  PUTOVR

                                  1 32'MASTER MENU'     DSPATR(HI)
                                  2  2'Select one of the following:       '
  93                              2 59'CF Key'          DSPATR(UL)

                                  3  4'1.'              DSPATR(HI)
                                  3  9'Loan Processing menu (1)'
                                  3 50'(active)'
 N61                                  DSPATR(ND)
  46                                  OVRATR
            CF_OP1        2A  B   3 61VALUES(' ' '20' '21' '22' '23' '24')
 N93                                  DSPATR(ND PR)
  46                                  OVRDTA
  98                                  ERRMSG('Invalid or duplicate CF key-
                                      (s) assigned as ''hot'' keys.')
                                  4  4'2.'              DSPATR(HI)
                                  4  9'Loan Processing menu (2)'
                                  4 50'(active)'
 N62                                  DSPATR(ND)
```

Figure 48.8 Continued

Figure 48.8

MSTMNU Display File *Continued*

```
     46                                          OVRATR
               CF_OP2      R           B  4 61REFFLD(CF_OP1)
    N93                                          DSPATR(ND PR)
     46                                          OVRDTA
     98                                          ERRMSG(' ')

                                          5  4'3.'              DSPATR(HI)
                                          5  9'Display/Update loan applications'
                                          5 50'(active)'
    N63                                          DSPATR(ND)
     46                                          OVRATR
               CF_OP3      R           B  5 61REFFLD(CF_OP1)
    N93                                          DSPATR(ND PR)
     46                                          OVRDTA
     98                                          ERRMSG(' ')

                                          6  4'4.'              DSPATR(HI)
                                          6  9'Display/Update loan transactions'
                                          6 50'(active)'
    N64                                          DSPATR(ND)
     46                                          OVRATR
               CF_OP4      R           B  6 61REFFLD(CF_OP1)
    N93                                          DSPATR(ND PR)
     46                                          OVRDTA
     98                                          ERRMSG(' ')

                                          7  4'5.'              DSPATR(HI)
                                          7  9'Display/Update people'
                                          7 50'(active)'
    N65                                          DSPATR(ND)
     46                                          OVRATR
               CF_OP5      R           B  7 61REFFLD(CF_OP1)
    N93                                          DSPATR(ND PR)
     46                                          OVRDTA
     98                                          ERRMSG(' ')

                                         11  4'90.'             DSPATR(HI)
    N99                                          DSPATR(ND)
     46                                          OVRATR
                                         11  9'Signoff'
    N99                                          DSPATR(ND)
     46                                          OVRATR

                                         20  2'Option:'
               MNUOPT           2Y 0B 20 11EDTCDE(Z)
                                                 DSPATR(PC)
                                                 VALUES( 1  2  3  4  5 90)
                                                 CHECK(AB)
     46                                          OVRDTA
    *                                            Invalid option message.
     90                                          ERRMSGID(SDA2007 QSDAMSG)
    *                                            Invalid hot key message.
```

Figure 48.8 Continued

Figure 48.8

MSTMNU Display File *Continued*

```
     97                                ERRMSG('Unassigned CF key cannot be-
                                        used as ''hot'' key.')

            CFKPMT         21A  O 23  1
     46                                OVRDTA
            PRVJOBOUT      10A  O 23 15
     46                                OVRDTA
                                  23 27'F6=Messages'
                                  23 69'HELP'
 *                                    Message subfile is used for errors.
Ⓑ        R MNUMSGSFL                   SFL
                                       SFLMSGRCD(24)
            MSGOUTKEY                  SFLMSGKEY
            PGMMSGQ                    SFLPGMQ
          R MNUMSGCTL                  SFLCTL(MNUMSGSFL)
                                       LOCK
                                       OVERLAY
                                       SFLSIZ(5)
                                       SFLPAG(1)
     60                                SFLEND
     60                                SFLDSP
     60                                SFLDSPCTL
     60                                SFLINZ
            PGMMSGQ                    SFLPGMQ
```

Figure 48.7. The CHGGRPA command changes the standard job the user signs on to into a group job. You can use a CHGDTAARA (Change Data Area) command as it is used in Figure 48.7 to set up a function key identifier (in this example, "20") in the group data area to preselect the first group job to start; in this partial program, when program MSTMNU is called, it actually bypasses the display of the Master Menu in Figure 48.2 and immediately transfers to the preselected group job (the Loan Menu in Figure 48.4). The CALL that follows the CHGDTAARA command invokes program MSTMNU with the parameter that controls use of F3 set to "Y," so the user can exit the group job menu. In many cases, you may want to specify "N" for the MSTMNU parameter, so the user remains in program MSTMNU.

Create the Master Menu Display File

The Master Menu display file Data Description Specifications (DDS) (Figure 48.8) conditionally enable the command function keys (A) that can be used as hot keys in the group job environment. The display file DDS also includes the OVERLAY, PUTOVR (Put with Explicit Override), OVRATR (Override Attributes), and OVRDTA (Override Data) keywords to avoid resending constant fields (such as the labels for the menu options) when the display is written. The use of data and attribute overrides is not necessary for group jobs; however, it results in flicker-free display of menus and shorter response time over communications lines because less data is transmitted. Display file MSTMNU should be created with RSTDSP(*YES) specified in the CRTDSPF (Create Display File) command, so the display will be restored after another group job transfers back to the MSTMNU group job.

Also note that group jobs affect the operation of the display file WAITRCD (Wait for Record) parameter, which limits the number of seconds a program waits for a read to an invited device. The WAITRCD parameter sometimes is used to prevent an interactive job from holding record locks too long or to sign off an inactive workstation automatically. In a group job environment, a suspended group job may exceed the wait limit while another group job is in use because the WAITRCD time limit is compared to the total elapsed time (i.e., the time the group job is active as well as the time it is suspended). However, the suspended group job is not notified of the display file time-out until the group job is again active. Thus, where group jobs are concerned, the use of the WAITRCD parameter is an ineffective means of controlling record locks. In addition, a program that tests for a display file time-out to sign off inactive workstations must incorporate some means of determining whether the period of inactivity occurred while the group job was active.

Display file MSTMNU includes a message subfile (B) with subfile record format MNUMSGSFL and subfile control record MNUMSGCTL. This subfile is used to display the MSTMNU program message queue's messages in a single operation.

Develop the Master Menu Program

The master menu program, MSTMNU, is shown in Figure 48.9 (page 684). After initializing variables, program MSTMNU begins a loop that processes an option selected from the Master Menu. The RTVGRPA command (A) retrieves the list of group jobs that currently exist in the group and the group job count. The group job count will be zero if program MSTMNU is executing in a standard (nongroup) job environment; if that is the case, the menu functions like a normal application menu. The group job count will be 1 if only the MSTMNU group job exists in the group. If MSTMNU is the only group job, the sign-off option (option 90) is enabled (C).

Once the group job attributes are retrieved, a function key identifier is retrieved from bytes 1 and 2 of the group data area (B). This function key identifier is used to preselect the menu option that currently has the same function key identifier value associated with it as a hot key. Although this example only demonstrates use of the function key identifier with the "real" keys F20 through F24, the function key identifier can be expanded to allow values other than "20" through "24," including alphabetic codes, and can be used with application display file fields to allow preselection from a large number of menu options. For example, if the function key identifier were expanded to three characters and application programs included a three-character NXTGRP (Next Group) field on the display, many more than five preselected options would be available.

After the function key identifier is retrieved, indicators 91 and 92 are set to control the prompt text that displays on the last line, and then the group job list is scanned to set on the indicators that control the "(active)" literal that appears beside group jobs that currently exist in the group (D).

Next the program tests (E) for a valid predefined menu selection (using a hot key). If a function key identifier was put in the group data area by the previous group job and if the identifier is currently associated with one of the Master Menu options, the menu display is skipped, and the preselected option is taken. Because the user can change the assignment of function keys, if no match is found for the function-key identifier at this point, it is not treated as an error; instead, the menu is displayed as if no hot key were pressed. This technique makes it unnecessary for the application programs to keep track of the function keys currently valid as hot keys.

If no function-key identifier is found in the group data area, program MSTMNU displays the menu. At that point, the user can change the assignment of the hot keys or select an option. If the user changes a hot-key assignment, that assignment is checked to be sure that no function key is associated with more than one menu option (F).

The last major step in each loop iteration is a CASE statement that handles the option selected when a hot key is pressed or when a Master Menu option is entered. The selected option puts its unique group job name in the field for the last group job transferred to by program MSTMNU (G). Then, if program MSTMNU is executing in a group job environment, a TFRGRPJOB command is executed (H) to start or resume the group job for the selected option. In a standard (nongroup) job, a CALL is executed (I). In a group job environment, control returns to the statement after the TFRGRPJOB command (J) when the MSTMNU group job is resumed either because the previous group job terminated or because the previous group job executed a TFRGRPJOB GRPJOB(*PRV) command. When control returns, the CASE statement completes, and the loop is repeated (K).

Add Group Job-Related Commands

Figure 48.10 (page 696) shows the code that must be added to each initial group job program for each application menu available from the Master Menu. In this case, the initial group job program displays the application menu shown in Figure 48.4. The code segment in Figure 48.10 uses the RTVGRPA command to get the group job count (A). The CPF1311 message must be monitored because no GRPJOB parameter is included in the RTVGRPA command. If there is a GRPJOB parameter in the RTVGRPA command and if the job is not a group job, no escape message is sent and "*NONE" is placed in the variable specified for GRPJOB. Without the GRPJOB parameter, if the program is not executing in a group job environment, an escape message occurs.

If the application menu program is executing in a group job environment, the SETATNPGM command (B) sets up program ATNPGM as the one invoked when the user presses the Attention key. Program ATNPGM remains in effect as this group job's attention key handling program until the initial group job program exits. (For nonmenu application functions — e.g., UPDLONAPP in Figure 48.1 — a similar SETATNPGM command should be executed at the beginning of the CL "shell" program — e.g., UPDLONCTL in Figure 48.1.)

The code segment for the application menu program in Figure 48.10 includes code to support hot keys. The CAxx keyword for keys F20 through F24 must be specified in each application menu's display file DDS. If the user presses one of these command function keys, a corresponding function key identifier is put in bytes 1 and 2 of the group data area (C), and the previous group job (i.e., MSTMNU) is resumed (D).

When the user exits the application menu by pressing F3, the program executes a RETURN command (E). In a group job environment, this terminates the group job and resumes the previous group job (MSTMNU).

Add Hot-Key Support to HLL Programs

The previous section explained how to add hot-key support to application menu programs accessed through the Master Menu. Hot-key support also can be added to HLL programs that implement application functions. To add hot-key support, you must add the command function keys to the application display file and test for the user pressing one of these command function keys when your program reads the display file. This test is accomplished most easily if you read the display file in a single place in each program (using an RPG subroutine, a COBOL section, or a PL/I procedure). Having a single point for display file reads is a technique also useful for processing other common display functions, such as online help, available from all application system displays. The COBOL code segment in Figure 48.11 (page 699) demonstrates how to add hot-key support to existing help-key and other command function-key support. A common section that reads the display (A) is performed repeatedly until no "subordinate" action, such as Help or group job transfer, has been requested by the user. (The concept of a "subordinate" action is applicable to RPG, COBOL, and PL/I; it is simply an action that can be performed without affecting the status of the current program. Such functions as displaying Help text, displaying workstation messages, printing a currently displayed record, and transferring to another group job do not affect the current program's status. The current program's display file must be created with RSTDSP(*YES), so when the subordinate action is completed and the current program regains control, the display file can be reread without having to be rewritten.)

After every read, a test is made (B) to see if the user pressed a hot key. If a hot key was pressed, a subroutine is called (C) to transfer control back to the MSTMNU group job. The TFRGRPJOB subroutine is passed a two-character function-key identifier to be put in the group data area. (The LAST-FUNCTION-KEY variable has the system-provided function-key identifier put in it automatically by the COBOL runtime system; RPG programs can set this argument by testing indicators KA through KY or by using the hexadecimal value in byte 369 of the File Information Data Structure (INFDS); PL/I programs can test variables IN01 through IN24 or use the hexadecimal value in byte 147 of the argument of the PLIIOFDB built-in subroutine.) Keep in mind that you don't need this additional HLL code to use the Attention key; the additional HLL code is required only to add hot-key support.

Create External Subroutine

Figure 48.12 (page 700) shows the TFRGRPJOB subroutine to be called by HLL programs, such as the program partially shown in Figure 48.1, when a hot key is pressed. The subroutine simply puts the function-key identifier in bytes 1 and 2 of the group data area (A) and transfers control to the previous group job, which will be the MSTMNU group job. When the application group job is once again selected, control resumes after the TFRGRPJOB statement in the TFRGRPJOB subroutine. The TFRGRPJOB subroutine then exits and execution resumes in the HLL program with the display file read loop. If a hot key is pressed when the HLL program is in use in a standard job, the TFRGRPJOB program sends an informational message and returns immediately to the application program. Thus, HLL application programs are not required to determine whether a group job environment exists.

Develop an Attention Key Handling Program

The CHGGRPA and TFRGRPJOB commands provide the ability to start and transfer among group jobs. But with only these commands, you would have to implement explicit TFRGRPJOB commands at every point in your application where the user might want to switch between group jobs. However, the SETATNPGM command mentioned earlier simplifies handling user transfers between group jobs by letting you specify a program to function as an externally called subprogram whenever your application program is waiting for input from a display file and the user presses the Attention key.

Figure 48.13 (page 702) shows the Attention key handling program (ATNPGM) set up by the SETATNPGM command in Figure 48.10. This Attention key handling program is simply a TFRGRPJOB command to transfer back to the MSTMNU group job. Attention key handling programs should be kept simple, and the use of a separate group job for the Master Menu makes ATNPGM about as simple a program as possible. The Attention key support must be added only to the program that is the group job's initial program (either a CL menu program or a CL "shell" program); the Attention key is then available at all points where the application programs execute display file reads.

An Alternate SIGNOFF Command

The code presented in Figures 48.8 through 48.13 demonstrates all the necessary components of a flexible group job approach. However, one final program can make your use of group jobs more effective. Figure 48.14 (page 703) shows a command processing program (CPP) to be used with a locally created SIGNOFF command. The locally created SIGNOFF command should be placed in an alternate system library (ALTQSYS), which is placed before the IBM-supplied system library QSYS in the system part of the library list. (Refer back to Chapter 7, "Library Standards," for additional information about using an alternate system library such as ALTQSYS.) This causes the local version of the SIGNOFF CPP to execute when a SIGNOFF command is entered or when option 90 is entered from an IBM-supplied menu.

The program shown in Figure 48.14 checks to make certain the user is not trying to sign off while application functions are still in progress. In a group job environment, the user can sign off if either a single group job (implicitly the MSTMNU) or two group jobs (one of which must be the MSTMNU; the other is assumed to be an application menu) exist. Otherwise, the user must exit (thus terminating) some of the remaining group jobs. In addition, a sign-off from the System Request Menu is allowed only if the user is the security officer or a special user profile used by the application system administrator, or if a confirmation is provided in reply to a message. It is important to allow sign-off from the System Request Menu under some circumstances because this is one way of obtaining useful job log information when there are problems with an interactive job. One word of caution, though — be certain any alternative SIGNOFF CPP is "bullet-proof" by using MONMSG commands to trap unexpected errors. You will find an unreliable SIGNOFF command a very irksome "enhancement."

Design Considerations

I designed the master menu approach to keep to a minimum the interconnection between separate group jobs, which enables them to be combined into different groups on alternate master menus. The implementation of menus in this example allows a menu to be a group job's initial program in one case and a subordinate menu in other cases. In addition, this approach allows application menu and function programs to be used in either a standard or group job environment. Granted, this approach incurs a slight performance penalty because it requires that all transfers occur through the master menu (thus requiring execution of two TFRGRPJOB commands — one to the master menu and one to the selected group job — instead of one), but the result is a structure that is simple to understand, easily retrofitted to existing CL and HLL applications, and one from which alternate, differently structured master menus can be built without requiring changes to the individual applications included on a master menu.

The support for hot keys is designed to allow the gradual incorporation of hot keys into old applications; to be included in the master menu, old applications need only have commands added to set up the Attention key handling program. No change is required to use existing application programs in a group job if they are invoked through a menu that has the SETATNPGM command added to it.

As you implement your own group job approach, you may want to mix a different combination of techniques; nevertheless, all the commands you need have been demonstrated in this example. So once you set up your own "master menu" program, add the SETATNPGM command to existing application menus, and replace the SIGNOFF CPP, you are ready to take advantage of the flexibility of group jobs. As a next step, you can add "hot key" support to existing and new application programs. With minimal coding, you then will be able to sit back and enjoy the appreciation of your users — who will have greatly expanded flexibility, your programmers — who will be able to write simpler more modular programs, and maybe even your controller — who may see your AS/400 performance improved.

Figure 48.9

MSTMNU Program

```
/*  MSTMNU                                                           */

/*  Abstract: Menu to control group jobs.  Can be invoked by         */
/*  user pressing Attention key or by any group job executing a      */
/*  TFRGRPJOB GRPJOB(*PRV) to return to it.                          */

/*  This menu program can be used either in a standard interactive   */
/*  job, or in a group job.  To use in a group job, execute a        */
/*  CHGGRPA GRPJOB(mstmnu) command prior to calling this program.    */

/*  The menu will be displayed if a valid function key identifier    */
/*  has not been put in bytes 1 and 2 of the group data area.        */
/*  Otherwise, the valid function key identifier is used to          */
/*  transfer to a predefined group job.                              */

PGM                                                                   +
PARM(                                                                 +
     &alw_cf3            /* IN     Allow CA3 as exit and RETURN.     */+
                         /*        (Y/N)                             */+
    )

/*-----------------------------------------------------------------*/


DCL &alw_cf3    *CHAR  1                    /* Allow CA3 for RETURN     */
DCL &bgnidx     *DEC   7                    /* String index             */
DCL &cde_ok     *CHAR  1 VALUE('1')         /* HLL return code - OK     */
DCL &cde_esc    *CHAR  1 VALUE('E')         /* HLL return code - Escape */
DCL &cf_20      *CHAR  2 VALUE('20')        /* Mnemonic - soft CF key   */
DCL &cf_21      *CHAR  2 VALUE('21')        /* Mnemonic - soft CF key   */
DCL &cf_22      *CHAR  2 VALUE('22')        /* Mnemonic - soft CF key   */
DCL &cf_23      *CHAR  2 VALUE('23')        /* Mnemonic - soft CF key   */
DCL &cf_24      *CHAR  2 VALUE('24')        /* Mnemonic - soft CF key   */
DCL &cf_key_id  *CHAR  2                    /* CF identifier in *GDA    */
DCL &errcnt     *DEC   1 VALUE( 0 )         /* Error count              */
DCL &false      *LGL   1 VALUE('0')         /* Mnemonic                 */
DCL &fmt        *CHAR 10                    /* DSPF format              */
DCL &grpjob     *CHAR 10                    /* Current group job name   */
DCL &grpidx     *DEC   3                    /* Group job list index     */
DCL &grpjobcnt  *DEC   3                    /* Group job count, decimal */
DCL &grpjobl    *CHAR  1056                 /* Group job list           */
DCL &grplib_1   *CHAR 10 VALUE('PRDMNU')       /* Opt  1 pgm library    */
DCL &grplib_2   *CHAR 10 VALUE('PRDMNU')       /* Opt  2 pgm library    */
DCL &grplib_3   *CHAR 10 VALUE('*LIBL' )       /* Opt  3 pgm library    */
DCL &grplib_4   *CHAR 10 VALUE('*LIBL' )       /* Opt  4 pgm library    */
DCL &grplib_5   *CHAR 10 VALUE('*LIBL' )       /* Opt  5 pgm library    */
DCL &grpnam_1   *CHAR 10 VALUE('LONMNU1')      /* Opt  1 group job name*/
DCL &grpnam_2   *CHAR 10 VALUE('LONMNU2')      /* Opt  2 group job name*/
DCL &grpnam_3   *CHAR 10 VALUE('UPDLONAPP') /* Opt  3 group job name*/
DCL &grpnam_4   *CHAR 10 VALUE('UPDLONTRN') /* Opt  4 group job name*/
DCL &grpnam_5   *CHAR 10 VALUE('UPDPEOPLE') /* Opt  5 group job name*/
DCL &grpnam_tmp *CHAR 10                       /* Group job name (temp)*/
DCL &grppgm_1   *CHAR 10 VALUE('LONMNUCTL') /* Opt  1 inl group pgm */
DCL &grppgm_2   *CHAR 10 VALUE('LONMNUCTL') /* Opt  2 inl group pgm */
DCL &grppgm_3   *CHAR 10 VALUE('UPDLONCTL') /* Opt  3 inl group pgm */
```

Figure 48.9 Continued

Figure 48.9

MSTMNU Program *Continued*

```
DCL &grppgm_4    *CHAR 10 VALUE('UPDTRNCTL') /* Opt  4 inl group pgm */
DCL &grppgm_5    *CHAR 10 VALUE('UPDPPLCTL') /* Opt  5 inl group pgm */
DCL &helptitle   *CHAR 50                    /* Help display title   */+
                          VALUE('                 GROUP JOB MENU')
DCL &op_sgnoff   *DEC   2 VALUE(90)       /* Mnemonic - Signoff option */
DCL &pgmname     *CHAR 10 VALUE('MSTMNU')/* This program's name       */
DCL &pgmlib      *CHAR 10 VALUE('PRDMNU')/* This program's library    */
DCL &rtncde      *CHAR  1                /* HLL return code           */
DCL &true        *LGL   1 VALUE('1')     /* Mnemonic                  */

DCLF prdmnu/mstmnu                       /* The menu display file     */
/*    -- Indicators --------------          -- Variables ------------*/
/*    03 - Exit menu                        cf_op1     *CHAR  2       */
/*    02 - Previous group job               cf_op2     *CHAR  2       */
/*    20, 21, 22, 23, 24 - Hot keys         cf_op3     *CHAR  2       */
/*    25 - Display Help                     cf_op4     *CHAR  2       */
/*    46 - OVERLAY/PUTOVR/OVRATR/OVRDTA     cf_op5     *CHAR  2       */
/*    60 - Display program message queue                              */
/*    61, 62, 63, 64, 65                    &mnuopt    *DEC   2       */
/*         Display "active" literal         &cfkpmt    *CHAR 21       */
/*    90 - Invalid menu option              &prvjobout *CHAR 10       */
/*    91 - Enable CA1                                                 */
/*    92 - Enable CA2                                                 */
/*    93 - Job is group job                                           */
/*    97 - Invalid hot key (CA20-24) used                             */
/*    98 - Invalid CF key assignment                                  */
/*    99 - Enable signoff                                             */

/*  - - - - - - - - - - - - - - - - - - - - - - - - - - - - - - - - */

MONMSG (cpf9999) EXEC(GOTO failed) /* Unmonitored messages           */

/* (Note that some command-specific MONMSG's have been removed from */
/*  this program to condense it for publication.)                   */


/*-------------------------- BEGIN ---------------------------*/
/*============================================================*/
/*                                                              */
/*                          Initialization                      */
/* . . . . . . . . . . . . . . . . . . . . . . . . . . . . . .  */


/* Allocate this program so it can't be deleted while in use.     */

ALCOBJ     OBJ((&pgmlib/&pgmname *pgm  *shrrd ))
MONMSG    (cpf9999) EXEC(GOTO badalcobj)

/* Turn on the program msgq display indicator. The pgm msgq is     */
/* displayed each loop through after a valid option is processed.  */
/* This gets diagnostic and info messages as well as escape msgs.  */

CHGVAR     &in60  &true
```

Figure 48.9 Continued

Figure 48.9

MSTMNU Program *Continued*

```
/* Set that there is currently NOT a wrong option selected.              */

CHGVAR     &in90  &false


/* Set that there is currently NOT an unassigned hot key entered.        */

CHGVAR     &in97  &false


/* Initialize so that the soft CF keys are in the same order as the  */
/* menu options.                                                      */
/* (If more than 5 options are on the menu, blank out the rest.)     */

CHGVAR     &cf_op1 &cf_20
CHGVAR     &cf_op2 &cf_21
CHGVAR     &cf_op3 &cf_22
CHGVAR     &cf_op4 &cf_23
CHGVAR     &cf_op5 &cf_24


/*  . . . . . . . . . . . . . . . . . . . . . . . . . . . . . . . .  */
/*  . . . . . . . .    BEGIN Menu Loop   . . . . . . . . . . . . . .  */

/*  Begin dispatching loop that ends when user signs off or enters  */
/*  CA3.                                                              */

MAIN_LOOP:


/*  Initialize variables that will control the group job selected.  */

CHGVAR     &cf_key_id  ' '
CHGVAR     &mnuopt     0

/*  Get the info on currently active group jobs (if any).           */

CHGVAR     &grpjobcnt  0

(A) RTVGRPA    GRPJOB(&grpjob) GRPJOBL(&grpjobl) GRPJOBCNT(&grpjobcnt)
MONMSG     (cpf1311)      /* Not a group job -- fall through      */+
           EXEC(DO)       /* Note that CPF1311 is never sent if the*/
           ENDDO          /* GRPJOB parameter is used.             */


/*  If the count is > 0, then enable group job related fields (in93)*/

CHGVAR     &in93  (&grpjobcnt >  0)


/*  If this is a group job, get any function key identifier put in  */
/*  bytes 1 and 2 of the group data area by the most recently active*/
/*  group job or by the user profile's initial program.  Then blank */
/*  out these two bytes in the group data area.                     */
```

Figure 48.9 Continued

Figure 48.9

MSTMNU Program *Continued*

```
Ⓑ IF        (&grpjobcnt >= 1)                                      +
              DO
              RTVDTAARA  DTAARA(*gda (1 2))  RTNVAR(&cf_key_id)

              CHGDTAARA  DTAARA(*gda (1 2))  VALUE('  ')
              ENDDO

  /*  If there is only 1 group job, enable option '90' (Signoff) on   */
  /*  menu. Otherwise, the user cannot signoff until all active group */
  /*  jobs are exited. IN99 on allows the display of Signoff option.  */

Ⓒ CHGVAR     &in99  (&grpjobcnt <= 1)


  /*  If there is only 1 group job, and CA3 is allowed, then enable   */
  /*  CA3 on the menu. Otherwise, don't allow the user to exit.       */
  /*  IN91 on enables CA3.                                            */
  CHGVAR     &in91 ((&grpjobcnt <= 1) & (&alw_cf3 = 'Y'))
  /*  If the count is two or more, and the last group job still exists*/
  /*  as the most recently active group job, enable the CA2 key for   */
  /*  transferring back to it.                                        */
  /*  If CA2 is not enabled, blank out the previous group job.        */

  CHGVAR      &in92   (&grpjobcnt >  1)

  IF        ( &in92)  (CHGVAR  &in92  (&prvjobout = %SST(&grpjobl 67 10))

  IF        (*&in92)  (CHGVAR  &prvjobout ' ')


  /*  Now that indicators 91, 92, and 93 are set, put the appropriate */
  /*  prompt text in line 23.  This technique is used rather than     */
  /*  conditioned literal fields so that PUTOVR can be used.          */

  IF        ( &in91 *and  &in93) (CHGVAR &cfkpmt 'F3=Exit')
  ELSE IF   ( &in91 *and *&in93) (CHGVAR &cfkpmt 'F3=Exit'      )
  ELSE IF   (*&in91 *and  &in92) (CHGVAR &cfkpmt 'F2=Prior job:')
  ELSE                           (CHGVAR &cfkpmt ' '                 )


Ⓓ /* Set the indicators that control display of the "(active)" literal*/
  /* beside each menu option.                                         */

  /* Turn off the "(active)" literal for all options on the display.  */
  /* Then, turn on if found in group job list.  Indicators 61 - 65    */
  /* control the non-display attribute.                               */

  CHGVAR     &in61  &false
  CHGVAR     &in62  &false
  CHGVAR     &in63  &false
  CHGVAR     &in64  &false
  CHGVAR     &in65  &false

  CHGVAR     &grpidx  1        /* Skip the first entry in the group   */
```

Figure 48.9 Continued

Figure 48.9

MSTMNU Program *Continued*

```
                    /* list, it is the MSTMNU.          */

BGN_SETACT:

IF        (&grpidx >= &grpjobcnt)  (GOTO end_setact)

CHGVAR     &grpidx  (&grpidx + 1)

CHGVAR     &bgnidx  (((&grpidx - 1) * 66) + 1)

CHGVAR     &grpnam_tmp (%SST(&grpjobl &bgnidx 10))

CHGVAR     &in61       ((&grpnam_tmp = &grpnam_1) *or (&in61))
CHGVAR     &in62       ((&grpnam_tmp = &grpnam_2) *or (&in62))
CHGVAR     &in63       ((&grpnam_tmp = &grpnam_3) *or (&in63))
CHGVAR     &in64       ((&grpnam_tmp = &grpnam_4) *or (&in64))
CHGVAR     &in65       ((&grpnam_tmp = &grpnam_5) *or (&in65))

GOTO       bgn_setact

(E) END_SETACT:

/*  See if a valid predefined selection has been made.              */

IF      (((&cf_key_id *= '  '   )     )                              +
                    *and                                              +
         ((&cf_key_id  = &cf_op1) *or                                 +
          (&cf_key_id  = &cf_op2) *or                                 +
          (&cf_key_id  = &cf_op3) *or                                 +
          (&cf_key_id  = &cf_op4) *or                                 +
          (&cf_key_id  = &cf_op5)     ))                              +
          DO

          /* Turn on the wrong option message, any valid option    */
          /* will turn it back off.                                */

          CHGVAR &in90  &true

          /* Skip displaying and receiving the menu, a predefined  */
          /* transfer will be used.                                */

          GOTO   CHKOPT
          ENDDO

/* Display menu and get option.                                    */


/*        Send the display file.                                   */

/*        This sends the whole display, which is mostly constants, */
/*        the first time. From then on, OVERLAY/PUTOVR/OVRDTA is in*/
/*        effect and the send overlays the attributes and data or  */
/*        the ERRMSGID for wrong option. Note that most wrong      */
/*        options should be caught by the VALUES keyword in the DDS*/
/*        for the display file.                                    */
```

Figure 48.9 Continued

Figure 48.9

MSTMNU Program *Continued*

```
SEND:

/* Reset the option field to Ø, if it was previously valid. Then     */
/* with EDTCDE(Z), it will appear blank. If it was an invalid        */
/* option (IN9Ø is on), just leave as it is.                         */

IF         (* &in9Ø)    (CHGVAR    &mnuopt  Ø)


/* Send the display file.  Note that if a critical error occurs, the*/
/* IBM-supplied (not the local) SIGNOFF is executed.                 */

SNDF        DEV(*file)  RCDFMT(menu)
MONMSG     (cpf4101)    EXEC(GOTO baddspf )          /* File not found */
MONMSG     (cpf4131)    EXEC(GOTO badfmt  )          /* Lvl Chk on Fmt */
MONMSG     (cpf4168)    EXEC(QSYS/SIGNOFF *list)     /* Bad device file*/
MONMSG     (cpf5143)    EXEC(QSYS/SIGNOFF *list)     /* Bad device file*/
/* From this point on, just send the attributes and data, not       */
/* constant information. (&in46 turns on OVERLAY/PUTOVR/OVRDTA).    */

CHGVAR     &in46       &true


/* Display the message file withe program message queue messages.  */
/* Messages may be sent by this program to its own program message */
/* queue or by a called program.  Messages are removed before a    */
/* new option is called or if the user enters blank in the option  */
/* field.                                                           */

CHGVAR     &pgmmsgq    &pgmname

SNDF        RCDFMT(MNUMSGCTL)
MONMSG     (cpf4101)    EXEC(GOTO baddspf )          /* File not found */
MONMSG     (cpf4131)    EXEC(GOTO badfmt  )          /* Lvl Chk on Fmt */
MONMSG     (cpf4168)    EXEC(QSYS/SIGNOFF *list)     /* Bad device file*/
MONMSG     (cpf5143)    EXEC(QSYS/SIGNOFF *list)     /* Bad device file*/


/*          The label RECEIVE:   is used to avoid the resending of   */
/*          display file. It can be used when the display file       */
/*          is "suspended" by a call to DSPHELP or the DSPMSG cmd.   */
/*          The display file must be created with RSTDSP(*YES).      */

RECEIVE:


/*          Receive input.                                           */

RCVF        DEV(*file)  RCDFMT(menu)
MONMSG     (cpf4101)    EXEC(GOTO baddspf )          /* File not found */
MONMSG     (cpf4131)    EXEC(GOTO badfmt  )          /* Lvl Chk on Fmt */
MONMSG     (cpf4168)    EXEC(QSYS/SIGNOFF *list)     /* Bad device file*/
MONMSG     (cpf5143)    EXEC(QSYS/SIGNOFF *list)     /* Bad device file*/
```

Figure 48.9 Continued

Figure 48.9

MSTMNU Program *Continued*

```
/* If CA3, return to caller.  For group jobs, change back to a      */
/* standard job before returning.                                   */

IF          &in03                                                    +
            DO
            IF      (&grpjobcnt = 1)                                 +
                    DO
                    CHGGRPA GRPJOB(*none)
                    ENDDO
            GOTO    deallocate
            ENDDO

/* If CA2, return to the previous group job.  When transfer comes   */
/* back to this point, loop to process another transfer.            */

IF         (&in02 *and (&grpjobcnt > 1))                             +
            DO
            RMVMSG    CLEAR(*all)
            TFRGRPJOB GRPJOB(*prv)
            GOTO main_loop
            ENDDO


/* If CA6, display workstation messages, then get input again.      */

IF          &in06                                                    +
            DO
            DSPMSG
            GOTO    receive
            ENDDO


/* Help key - display help, then get input again.                   */
/* (DSPHELP is a locally written program.)                          */

/* Note that the member name is the same as the menu (program).     */

IF          &in25                                                    +
            DO
            CALL    dsphelp  PARM('HLPSRC' 'PRDDOC' &pgmname         +
                                  &helptitle  &rtncde)
            GOTO    receive
            ENDDO


/*  See if a valid hot key has been entered.  If it has, treat it   */
/*  just like a predefined selection.  Note that other input fields */
/*  are ignored, because these are Command Attention keys.          */
/*  Start with no invalid hot key error, set if an unassigned one   */
/*  is entered.                                                     */

CHGVAR      &in97  &false

IF       ((&in20) *and (&grpjobcnt >= 1)) (CHGVAR &cf_key_id  &cf_20)
```

Figure 48.9 Continued

Figure 48.9

MSTMNU Program *Continued*

```
ELSE IF  ((&in21) *and (&grpjobcnt >= 1)) (CHGVAR &cf_key_id  &cf_21)
ELSE IF  ((&in22) *and (&grpjobcnt >= 1)) (CHGVAR &cf_key_id  &cf_22)
ELSE IF  ((&in23) *and (&grpjobcnt >= 1)) (CHGVAR &cf_key_id  &cf_23)
ELSE IF  ((&in24) *and (&grpjobcnt >= 1)) (CHGVAR &cf_key_id  &cf_24)
ELSE                                       (CHGVAR &cf_key_id  ' '  )
IF       ( &cf_key_id  = ' '   )    /* Skip hot key checking       */

ELSE IF  ((&cf_key_id  = &cf_op1) *or                              +
          (&cf_key_id  = &cf_op2) *or                              +
          (&cf_key_id  = &cf_op3) *or                              +
          (&cf_key_id  = &cf_op4) *or                              +
          (&cf_key_id  = &cf_op5)    )                             +
          DO

          /* Turn on the wrong option message, any valid option    */
          /* will turn it back off.                                */

          CHGVAR &in90  &true

          /* Skip displaying and receiving the menu. Predefined    */
          /* transfer will be used.                                */

          GOTO   CHKOPT
          ENDDO

ELSE      DO
          /* An unassigned hot key was used.  Turn on an error     */
          /* message and resend the display. (&in97 controls msg.) */

          CHGVAR &in97  &true
          GOTO   send
          ENDDO


/* At this point, no Command Attention key has been entered, so     */
/* process any input fields.                                        */

(F) /* Check the CF key assignments to hot keys. (&in98 controls msg.)  */

CHGVAR      &in98 ((( &cf_op1 *= ' '            ) *and              +
                   ((&cf_op1  = &cf_op2) *or                        +
                    (&cf_op1  = &cf_op3) *or                        +
                    (&cf_op1  = &cf_op4) *or                        +
                    (&cf_op1  = &cf_op5)     )      )               +
                            *or                                     +
                  (( &cf_op2 *= ' '            ) *and               +
                   ((&cf_op2  = &cf_op3) *or                        +
                    (&cf_op2  = &cf_op4) *or                        +
                    (&cf_op2  = &cf_op5)     )      )               +
                            *or                                     +
                  (( &cf_op3 *= ' '            ) *and               +
                   ((&cf_op3  = &cf_op4) *or                        +
                    (&cf_op3  = &cf_op5)     )      )               +
                            *or                                     +
```

Figure 48.9 Continued

Figure 48.9

MSTMNU Program *Continued*

```
                 (( &cf_op4 *= ' '            ) *and              +
                  ((&cf_op4  = &cf_op5)       )    )              +
              )

IF          &in98  (GOTO send)

/* Turn on the wrong option message, any valid option will turn it  */
/* back off.                                                        */

CHGVAR      &in90  &true

/* Find the option and handle it. ALL options below should monitor  */
/* for escape messages that may be sent; and whether an error occurs*/
/* or not, after the option is processed, execute a GOTO OPTEND.    */


/*  0   A value of 0 may occur when they blank out the field.       */
/*      Treat as a valid option, then just clear the messages.      */

IF          (&mnuopt =  0)                                        +
             DO
             CHGVAR  &in90    &false
             RMVMSG  CLEAR(*all)
             GOTO    optend
             ENDDO


/*  The CHKOPT label begins the checking of non-zero display options*/
/*  or predefined selections.                                       */


CHKOPT:


/*  CASE statement using either predefined function key or menu     */
/*  option selected by user.                                        */

IF        (((&cf_key_id = &cf_op1) *and (&cf_key_id *= ' '))      +
                    *or                                           +
           ((&mnuopt    = 1)                               ))     +
             DO
             CHGVAR       &in90      &false       /* Valid option. */
             RMVMSG       CLEAR(*all)             /* Clear pgm msgq*/
             CHGVAR       &prvjobout &grpnam_1

             IF     (&grpjobcnt > 0)                              +
                    DO
                    TFRGRPJOB  GRPJOB(&grpnam_1)                  +
                               INLGRPPGM(&grplib_1/&grppgm_1)
                    MONMSG    (cpf0000) /* Any messages, incl. CPF9999*/
                    ENDDO
             ELSE   DO
                    CALL        PGM(&grplib_1/&grppgm_1)
                    MONMSG    (cpf0000) /* Any messages, incl. CPF9999*/
                    ENDDO
```

Figure 48.9 Continued

Figure 48.9

MSTMNU Program *Continued*

```
          GOTO    optend
          ENDDO
IF      (((&cf_key_id = &cf_op2) *and (&cf_key_id *= ' '))              +
                    *or                                                  +
         ((&mnuopt    = 2)                                  ))           +
          DO
          CHGVAR       &in90      &false           /* Valid option. */
          RMVMSG       CLEAR(*all)                 /* Clear pgm msgq*/
          CHGVAR       &prvjobout &grpnam_2

          IF     (&grpjobcnt > 0)                                        +
                 DO
                 TFRGRPJOB  GRPJOB(&grpnam_2)                            +
                            INLGRPPGM(&grplib_2/&grppgm_2)
                 MONMSG    (cpf0000) /* Any messages, incl. CPF9999*/
                 ENDDO
          ELSE   DO
                 CALL       PGM(&grplib_2/&grppgm_2)
                 MONMSG    (cpf0000) /* Any messages, incl. CPF9999*/
                 ENDDO

          GOTO    optend
          ENDDO
IF      (((&cf_key_id = &cf_op3) *and (&cf_key_id *= ' '))              +
                    *or                                                  +
         ((&mnuopt    = 3)                                  ))           +
          DO
          CHGVAR       &in90      &false           /* Valid option. */
          RMVMSG       CLEAR(*all)                 /* Clear pgm msgq*/
          CHGVAR       &prvjobout &grpnam_3

          IF     (&grpjobcnt > 0)                                        +
                 DO
                 TFRGRPJOB  GRPJOB(&grpnam_3)                            +
                            INLGRPPGM(&grplib_3/&grppgm_3)
                 MONMSG    (cpf0000) /* Any messages, incl. CPF9999*/
                 ENDDO
          ELSE   DO
                 CALL       PGM(&grplib_3/&grppgm_3)
                 MONMSG    (cpf0000) /* Any messages, incl. CPF9999*/
                 ENDDO

          GOTO    optend
          ENDDO
IF      (((&cf_key_id = &cf_op4) *and (&cf_key_id *= ' '))              +
                    *or                                                  +
         ((&mnuopt    = 4)                                  ))           +
          DO
          CHGVAR       &in90      &false           /* Valid option. */
          RMVMSG       CLEAR(*all)                 /* Clear pgm msgq*/
          CHGVAR       &prvjobout &grpnam_4

Ⓖ         IF     (&grpjobcnt > 0)                                        +
```

Figure 48.9 Continued

Figure 48.9

MSTMNU Program *Continued*

```
                 DO
Ⓗ                TFRGRPJOB  GRPJOB(&grpnam_4)                          +
                            INLGRPPGM(&grplib_4/&grppgm_4)
                 MONMSG     (cpf0000) /* Any messages, incl. CPF9999*/
                 ENDDO
         ELSE    DO
                 CALL       PGM(&grplib_4/&grppgm_4)
Ⓘ                MONMSG     (cpf0000) /* Any messages, incl. CPF9999*/
                 ENDDO

Ⓙ        GOTO     optend
         ENDDO

 IF       (((&cf_key_id = &cf_op5) *and (&cf_key_id *= ' '))          +
                  *or                                                  +
           ((&mnuopt    = 5)                               ))          +
         DO
         CHGVAR       &in90      &false          /* Valid option. */
         RMVMSG       CLEAR(*all)                /* Clear pgm msgq*/
         CHGVAR       &prvjobout &grpnam_5

         IF     (&grpjobcnt > 0)                                       +
                 DO
                 TFRGRPJOB  GRPJOB(&grpnam_5)                          +
                            INLGRPPGM(&grplib_5/&grppgm_5)
                 MONMSG     (cpf0000) /* Any messages, incl. CPF9999*/
                 ENDDO
         ELSE    DO
                 CALL       PGM(&grplib_5/&grppgm_5)
                 MONMSG     (cpf0000) /* Any messages, incl. CPF9999*/
                 ENDDO


         GOTO     optend
         ENDDO

 IF       ((&grpjobcnt <= 1          )    *and                         +
           (&mnuopt      = &op_sgnoff))                                +
         DO
         ALTQSYS/SIGNOFF    /* Local version of SIGNOFF              */
         GOTO    optend     /* In case signoff prevented             */
         ENDDO

/* The end of the options - send messages and check results.        */

OPTEND:

/* If there was an invalid option, redisplay with error message.    */

IF        (&in90)     (GOTO send)


/*  When control is transfered back to this group job, loop to       */
/*  select another group job to make active.                         */
```

Figure 48.9 Continued

Figure 48.9

MSTMNU Program *Continued*

```
(K) GOTO       main_loop

 MNULOOPEND:
 /* . . . . . . . . .   END   Menu Loop   . . . . . . . . . . . . . . . */
 /* . . . . . . . . . . . . . . . . . . . . . . . . . . . . . . . . . . */



 /*-------------------------------------------------------------------*/
 /*----------------------SPECIAL ROUTINES ---------------------------*/

 /*----------------------- DEALLOCATE    --------------------------*/

 DEALLOCATE:  /*  Deallocate the program.                             */


 DLCOBJ      OBJ((&pgmlib/&pgmname *pgm  *shrrd ))
 MONMSG     (cpf9999)                                                   +
                 EXEC(DO)
                 SNDPGMMSG MSGID(cpf9898) MSGF(qcpfmsg)                 +
                           MSGDTA('Failed DLCOBJ in ' 33 &pgmname)      +
                           MSGTYPE(*escape)
                 GOTO      exit
                 ENDDO

 GOTO          exit

 /*----------------------- ERROR   RTNS --------------------------*/
 /* (Several error handling routines have been removed from this    */
 /*  program to condense it for publication, one sample is included.)*/


 BADALCOBJ:   /*  Bad allocate of the program.                        */

 SNDPGMMSG  MSGID(usr1606) MSGF(usrmsgf)                                +
            MSGDTA(&pgmname)                                            +
            MSGTYPE(*escape)

 GOTO        exit

 /*-------------------------------------------------------------------*/
 /*----------------------- ERROR   EXIT --------------------------*/


 FAILED:          /* The subroutine has failed because of some error   */
                  /* that was not handled explicitly. Any special      */
                  /* handling that is desired can be done here. The    */
                  /* test on error count is essential to prevent       */
                  /* looping because of the global MONMSG.             */

 IF           (&errcnt > 0)        (GOTO exit)
 CHGVAR        &errcnt             (&errcnt + 1)
```

Figure 48.9 Continued

Figure 48.9

MSTMNU Program *Continued*

```
/*  Deallocate the program.                                          */

DLCOBJ     OBJ((&pgmlib/&pgmname *pgm  *shrrd ))
MONMSG    (cpf0000)                                                  +
              EXEC(DO)
              SNDPGMMSG MSGID(cpf9898) MSGF(qcpfmsg)                 +
                        MSGDTA('Failed DLCOBJ in ' 33 &pgmname)      +
                        MSGTYPE(*escape)
              ENDDO


/*  Send escape message                                              */


SNDPGMMSG  MSGID(cpf9898) MSGF(qsys/qcpfmsg) MSGTYPE(*escape)        +
           MSGDTA('The menu CL program ' 33 &pgmname 33 'failed.')
MONMSG    (cpf0000)

/*-------------------------------------------------------------------*/
/*----------------------- PROGRAM EXIT ------------------------------*/


EXIT:

RETURN
ENDPGM
```

Figure 48.10

Initial Group Job Program That Is an Application Menu

```
   .
   .
   .
DCL  &atnkey_pgm   *CHAR  10    VALUE('ATNPGM')
DCL  &atnkey_lib   *CHAR  10    VALUE('PRDCLP' )
DCL  &false        *LGL    1    VALUE('0')    /* Mnemonic            */
DCL  &grpjobcnt    *DEC    3                  /* Group job count     */
DCL  &cf_key_id    *CHAR   2                  /* CF key code         */
DCL  &true         *LGL    1    VALUE('1')    /* Mnemonic            */

DCLF prdmnu/lonmnuctl
   .
   .
   .
/* Allocate this program so it can't be deleted while in use.        */

ALCOBJ     OBJ((&pgmlib/&pgmname *pgm  *shrrd ))


/*  See if this is a group job.                                      */
```

Figure 48.10 Continued

Figure 48.10 **Initial Group Job Program That Is an Application Menu** *Continued*

```
   CHGVAR     &grpjobcnt  0

Ⓐ  RTVGRPA    GRPJOBCNT(&grpjobcnt)
   MONMSG     (cpf1311)      /* Not a group job -- fall through       */

   /*  If a group job, establish the program that will be invoked by   */
   /*  Attention key.  Also set on IN93 to enable CF2x for transfers.  */

   IF        (&grpjobcnt >  0)                                         +
              DO
Ⓑ             SETATNPGM  PGM(&atnkey_lib/&atnkey_pgm)  SET(*on)
              ENDDO

   CHGVAR     &in93   (&grpjobcnt >  0)
      .
      .
      .
   /* Loop sending and receiving the menu display and processing the   */
   /* selected option on each loop.  The following segments show how   */
   /* function keys are handled when entered on the menu.              */

   MAIN_LOOP:
      .
      .
      .
   RCVF        DEV(*file)  RCDFMT(menu)
      .
      .
      .
   /* If CF3, or CF2 and not group job, then exit.                     */

   IF        ((&in03) *or (&in02 *and (&grpjobcnt < 1)))               +
               GOTO deallocate


   /* If CF2 and more than 1 group job, return to the previous group   */
   /* (this should be the master menu).                                */

   IF        (&in02 *and (&grpjobcnt > 1))                             +
               DO
               TFRGRPJOB GRPJOB(*prv)
               GOTO       optend
               ENDDO
      .
      .
      .
   /*  If predefined function key entered, put the corresponding       */
   /*  identifier in the group data area and then transfer to the      */
   /*  master menu.  Upon return, loop to display the loan menu again. */

Ⓒ  IF        ((&in20) *and (&grpjobcnt >  0)) (CHGVAR &cf_key_id  '20')
   ELSE IF   ((&in21) *and (&grpjobcnt >  0)) (CHGVAR &cf_key_id  '21')
   ELSE IF   ((&in22) *and (&grpjobcnt >  0)) (CHGVAR &cf_key_id  '22')
```

Figure 48.10 Continued

Figure 48.10 **Initial Group Job Program That Is an Application Menu** *Continued*

```
ELSE IF  ((&in23) *and (&grpjobcnt >  Ø)) (CHGVAR &cf_key_id  '23')
ELSE IF  ((&in24) *and (&grpjobcnt >  Ø)) (CHGVAR &cf_key_id  '24')
ELSE                                       (CHGVAR &cf_key_id  '  ')


IF       ((&cf_key_id *= '  ')  *and                                      +
          (&grpjobcnt >  Ø   ))                                           +
           DO
           CHGDTAARA  DTAARA(*gda (1 2))  VALUE(&cf_key_id)
(D)        TFRGRPJOB  GRPJOB(*prv)
           GOTO       optend
           ENDDO
    .
    .
    .
/* Find the option and handle it as with standard job menus, then      */
/* loop to display the menu and process another option.                */
    .
    .
    .
/* The following label is the target if the menu is to be exited.      */

DEALLOCATE:  /*  Deallocate the program.                                */

DLCOBJ      OBJ((&pgmlib/&pgmname *pgm  *shrrd ))

GOTO         exit
    .
    .
    .
/* If this is the initial group job program, then when the return     */
/* is executed, this group job will be terminated and the most         */
/* recently active group job (the master menu) will be resumed.        */

EXIT:
(E) RETURN
ENDPGM
```

Figure 48.11 **COBOL Application Program That Supports "Hot Keys"**

```
  .
  .
  .
      *----------------------------------------------------------------
      *    Get the next display after processing subordinate actions
      *    like Help, CF6-Display Messages, and group job "hot keys".
      *    Subordinate actions are handled within the loop below
      *    by a subroutine call.  The display must have RSTDSP(*YES) so
      *    upon return, it can just be re-read.

           SET SUBORDINATE-ACTION TO TRUE.

(A)        PERFORM  GET-DISPLAY-INPUT
             UNTIL  NO-SUBORDINATE-ACTION.
  .
  .
  .
      *----------------------------------------------------------------

       GET-DISPLAY-INPUT SECTION.

           SET      NO-SUBORDINATE-ACTION TO TRUE.

           PERFORM READ-LONAPPDSP.

           IF       LAST-FUNCTION-KEY = CF03-KEY

                    SET      EXIT-PGM           TO TRUE

           ELSE IF LAST-FUNCTION-KEY = CF06-KEY

                    SET      SUBORDINATE-ACTION TO TRUE
                    PERFORM CALL-DSPWRKMSG

           ELSE IF LAST-FUNCTION-KEY = CF15-KEY

                    SET      SUBORDINATE-ACTION TO TRUE
                    PERFORM CALL-PRTCURRCD

(B)        ELSE IF LAST-FUNCTION-KEY = CF20-KEY OR
                    LAST-FUNCTION-KEY = CF21-KEY OR
                    LAST-FUNCTION-KEY = CF22-KEY OR
                    LAST-FUNCTION-KEY = CF23-KEY OR
                    LAST-FUNCTION-KEY = CF24-KEY

                    SET      SUBORDINATE-ACTION   TO TRUE
                    PERFORM CALL-TFRGRPJOB
           ELSE IF LAST-FUNCTION-KEY = HELP-KEY

                    SET      SUBORDINATE-ACTION TO TRUE
                    PERFORM CALL-DSPHELP

           ELSE     NEXT SENTENCE
```

Figure 48.11 Continued

Figure 48.11 **COBOL Application Program That Supports "Hot Keys"** *Continued*

```
    .
    .
    .
      *-----------------------------------------------------------

       CALL-TFRGRPJOB SECTION.

      *    Transfer to preselected group job.

           CALL   "TFRGRPJOB" USING LAST-FUNCTION-KEY.
```

©

Figure 48.12 **Group Job Transfer Program Called by High-Level Languages**

```
/*  TFRGRPJOB                                                     */

/*  Abstract: Preselect a group job to transfer to.               */

/*  The calling program must pass in a 2 character code representing*/
/*  the function key that was entered.  Generally, this is '01'     */
/*  through '24' representing a "real" function key.  However, other*/
/*  codes can be used (by convention defined between the master menu*/
/*  and the applications accessed via the menu).  This program      */
/*  tests to see if this is a group job, and if it is puts the code */
/*  in bytes 1 and 2 of the group data area and then transfers      */
/*  control to the previous group job which should be the master    */
/*  menu.  The master menu then transfers to the preselected job or */
/*  displays the master menu.                                       */

/*  If this program is called and the job is not a group job, an    */
/*  info message is sent and the program returns to the caller.     */

PGM                                                                  +
PARM(                                                                +
    &cf_key_id         /* IN     The function key id to preselect  */+
                       /*        the next group job.               */+
   )

/*--------------------------------------------------------------*/


DCL &cf_key_id   *CHAR  2                /* CF identifier parameter   */
DCL &errcnt      *DEC   1 VALUE(0)       /* Error count               */
DCL &grpjob      *CHAR 10                /* Group job (current)       */
DCL &grpjobcnt   *DEC   3                /* Group job count           */
DCL &grpcnt_chr  *CHAR  3                /* Group job count (charactr)*/
DCL &pgmname     *CHAR 10 VALUE('TFRGRPJOB') /* Program name          */
DCL &pgmlib      *CHAR 10 VALUE('PRDCLP')    /* Program library       */


/*  - - - - - - - - - - - - - - - - - - - - - - - - - - - - - - - - */
```

Figure 48.12 Continued

Figure 48.12 Group Job Transfer Program Called by High-Level Languages *Continued*

```
MONMSG (cpf9999) EXEC(GOTO failed) /* Unmonitored messages         */


/*-------------------------- BEGIN ----------------------------*/
/*-------------------------------------------------------------*/

/*  Find out how many group jobs (if any)                      */

CHGVAR     &grpjobcnt  0

RTVGRPA    GRPJOB(&grpjob) GRPJOBCNT(&grpjobcnt)
MONMSG     (cpf1311)      /* Not a group job -- fall through   */

/*  If not at least 2 group jobs, send message and return.     */
/*  (There should be at least the master menu and the current  */
/*   application group job active.)                            */

IF        (&grpjobcnt < 2)  (GOTO  not_grpjob)

/*  Put the function key identifier in the group data area.    */

(A) CHGDTAARA  DTAARA(*gda (1 2))  VALUE(&cf_key_id)


/*  Transfer back to the group job that activated the current  */
/*  group job.  This is normally the controlling menu.         */
/*  If the transfer fails, just fall through and resume the    */
/*  current group job.                                         */

(B) TFRGRPJOB  GRPJOB(*prv)
MONMSG     MSGID(cpf9999)


/*  When this group job is reactivated, it will be at this point.  */
/*  Just exit and resume the application program at the point where */
/*  the function key was entered, (ie. this program was called.)   */

GOTO       exit
/*-------------------------------------------------------------*/
/*----------------------- ERROR   RTNS -------------------------*/

NOT_GRPJOB:  /*  Either this was not a group job, or it was the only*/
             /*  group job.  Send info message.                  */

/* Put the "0" or "1" into character field for sending the message.  */

CHGVAR    &grpcnt_chr  &grpjobcnt
MONMSG    (cpf9999)     EXEC(CHGVAR &grpcnt_chr  '***')


SNDPGMMSG  MSGID(usr1212) MSGF(usrmsgf) MSGTYPE(*info)          +
           MSGDTA(&grpcnt_chr)
MONMSG    (cpf9999)
```

Figure 48.12 Continued

Figure 48.12 **Group Job Transfer Program Called by High-Level Languages** *Continued*

```
GOTO        exit


FAILED:           /* The subroutine has failed because of some error     */
                  /* that was not handled explicitly.                    */

IF          (&errcnt > 0) THEN(GOTO exit)
CHGVAR       &errcnt           (&errcnt + 1)


/*  Send diagnostic message (to avoid blowing up HLL program).          */

SNDPGMMSG  MSGID(cpf9898) MSGF(qsys/qcpfmsg) MSGTYPE(*diag)              +
           MSGDTA('The CL program' 33 &pgmname 33 'failed.')
MONMSG     (cpf9999)

/*==================================================================*/
/*======================== PROGRAM EXIT ===========================*/

EXIT:

RETURN
ENDPGM
```

Figure 48.13 **Attention Key Handling Program**

```
/*  ATNPGM                                                          */

/*  Abstract: Program that is invoked by attention key.  It         */
/*            transfers back to the group job that invoked the      */
/*            current group job (which should be the master menu).  */

PGM

/*  - - - - - - - - - - - - - - - - - - - - - - - - - - - - - - - - */

/*  Transfer back to the group job that activated the current       */
/*  group job.  This is normally the controlling menu.              */
/*  If the transfer fails, just fall through and resume the         */
/*  current group job.                                              */

TFRGRPJOB  GRPJOB(*prv)
MONMSG     MSGID(cpf0000)


/*  When this group job is reactivated, it will be at this point.   */
/*  Just exit and resume the application program at the point where */
/*  the attention key was entered, or this program was called.      */

RETURN
ENDPGM
```

Figure 48.14

ALternate SIGNOFF Command Processing Program

```
/*  SIGNOFF (Alternate CPP)                                            */

/*  Abstract: An alternate SIGNOFF CPP to replace the IBM-supplied     */
/*            one.  It first checks to determine that no application*/
/*            function is in progress in a group job.  If there is   */
/*            none, a normal IBM-supplied SIGNOFF is executed.  If    */
/*            there is potentially an application in progress, the   */
/*            signoff is prevented.  A SIGNOFF from the System        */
/*            Request Menu is also checked.  If the user is the       */
/*            Application System Administrator or Security Officer   */
/*            the signoff is allowed.  If a different user,           */
/*            confirmation is required before the signoff is done.   */

PGM                                                                     +
PARM(                                                                   +
     &log                /* IN     *LIST/*NOLIST                      */+
     &drop               /* IN     *DEVD/*YES/*NO                     */+
    )


DCL &alwsgnoff   *LGL   1                 /* Allow signoff             */
DCL &cfmsgnoff   *LGL   1                 /* Confirmed signoff         */
DCL &confirm     *CHAR 10 VALUE('CONFIRM')   /* Confirm special val   */
DCL &drop        *CHAR  5                 /* Drop current device parm  */
DCL &errcnt      *DEC   1 VALUE( 0 )      /* Error count               */
DCL &false       *LGL   1 VALUE('0')      /* Mnemonic                  */
DCL &grpjob      *CHAR  10                /* Group job (current)       */
DCL &grpjobcnt   *DEC   3                 /* Group job count           */
DCL &grpjobl     *CHAR  1056              /* Group job list            */
DCL &appadm      *CHAR 10 VALUE('APPADM')/* Applic Sys. Admin. Usrprf*/
DCL &jobuser     *CHAR  10                /* Job's User                */
DCL &list_arg    *CHAR  7                 /* List job log argument     */
DCL &log         *CHAR  7                 /* List job log parm         */
DCL &msgid       *CHAR  7                 /* MSGID command parm        */
DCL &msgrpy      *CHAR 10                 /* User msg reply            */
DCL &mstmnu      *CHAR 10 VALUE('MSTMNU')/* Master menu group job     */
DCL &none        *CHAR  5 VALUE('*NONE')/* Mnemonic                   */
DCL &pgmname     *CHAR 10 VALUE('SIGNOFF')/* Program name              */
DCL &pgmlib      *CHAR 10 VALUE('ALTQSYS')/* Program library           */
DCL &secofr      *CHAR 10 VALUE('QSECOFR')   /* Secur. Ofcr.   Usrprf*/
DCL &sysrqs      *LGL   1                 /* SysRqs is in use          */
DCL &true        *LGL   1 VALUE('1')      /* Mnemonic                  */
DCL &yes         *CHAR  4 VALUE('*YES') /* Mnemonic                   */
/*  - - - - - - - - - - - - - - - - - - - - - - - - - - - - - - - - - */

/*  Initialize the list argument to the value passed in.               */

CHGVAR      &list_arg  &log

/*  Initialize that Signoff is allowed, change to false if not.       */

CHGVAR      &alwsgnoff &true
/*  Find out how many group jobs (if any)                              */

RTVGRPA     GRPJOB(&grpjob) GRPJOBL(&grpjobl) GRPJOBCNT(&grpjobcnt)
```

Figure 48.14 Continued

Figure 48.14 **ALternate SIGNOFF Command Processing Program** *Continued*

```
MONMSG      (cpf9999)       /* Unexpected error, allow signoff      */+
                            /* But force *LIST                      */+
            EXEC(DO)
            CHGVAR   &list_arg  &yes
            ENDDO


/*  If not group job, or only group job, or 2 group jobs               */
/*  and second is MSTMNU -- it's OK to signoff.                        */
/*  (Note that if MSTMNU is second group job, it means that they are*/
/*   currently in the only active application group job, and have     */
/*   the ability to signoff.  That means they are either at a menu,  */
/*   or in System Request (which is checked later.))                   */

IF       (( &grpjobcnt           <= 1            )                     +
                                 *or                                   +
          ((&grpjobcnt           = 2        ) *and                     +
           (%SST(&grpjobl 67 10) = &mstmnu)      )       /* Do nothing */

ELSE        CHGVAR      &alwsgnoff &false


/*  If allowed to do signoff so far, check to see if System Request */
/*  (If signoff not allowed because of group jobs, no attention is   */
/*   paid to whether or not System Request is in use.  It is treated*/
/*   as if NOT in use.)                                                 */
/*  Send a blank status message to the System Request message queue,*/
/*  then test for there being no current invocation of the System    */
/*  Request program, QMNSYSRQ (which means it is not in use).         */

CHGVAR      &sysrqs &false

IF         (&alwsgnoff)                                                +
            DO
            CHGVAR     &sysrqs &true

            SNDPGMMSG MSGID(cpi9801)             MSGF(qcpfmsg)         +
                      TOPGMQ(*same qmnsysrq)  MSGTYPE(*status)
            MONMSG    (cpf2469)  /* Command failed, look for diagnostc*/+
                                 /* CPF2479 - Program not active.     */+
                      EXEC(DO)
                      CHGVAR   &msgid ' '
                      RCVMSG   MSGTYPE(*diag)    RMV(*no) MSGID(&msgid)
                      MONMSG (cpf0000) /* CPF2479 not present         */+
                              EXEC(DO)
                              CHGVAR  &sysrqs &false
                              ENDDO
                      IF      (&msgid = 'CPF2479')                     +
                              DO
                              CHGVAR  &sysrqs &false
                              ENDDO
                      ENDDO
            MONMSG    (cpf0000)  /* Other unexpected error, treat as  */+
                                 /* if SysRqs in use.                 */
            ENDDO
```

Figure 48.14 Continued

Figure 48.14 ALternate SIGNOFF Command Processing Program *Continued*

```
/*  If System Request, get confirmation of signoff.                  */
/*  (If not Sys Rqs, treat as if confirmation was given.)             */
/*  (If Application System Administrator or Security Officer, always*/
/*   allow.)                                                          */

CHGVAR     &cfmsgnoff &true

IF        (&sysrqs)                                                   +
           DO
           CHGVAR   &cfmsgnoff &false
           CHGVAR   &jobuser  ' '

           RTVJOBA  USER(&jobuser)
           ENDDO

IF      (((&sysrqs) *and (&jobuser = &appadm   ))   *or              +
         ((&sysrqs) *and (&jobuser = &secofr   )))                   +
           DO
           CHGVAR   &cfmsgnoff &true
           ENDDO

ELSE IF   (&sysrqs)                                                   +
           DO
           CHGVAR    &msgrpy ' '

           SNDUSRMSG MSG('Signoff from System Request requires ' 33   +
                         'confirmation. Press Enter to ignore.')      +
                     MSGRPY(&msgrpy)
           MONMSG  (cpf0000)   /* Error sending user message, treat */+
                               /* as no confirmation                */+
                    EXEC(DO)
                    ENDDO

           IF       (&msgrpy = &confirm)                              +
                    DO
                    CHGVAR   &cfmsgnoff &true
                    ENDDO
           ENDDO


/*  Reset whether signoff is allowed from system request             */

CHGVAR     &alwsgnoff  (&alwsgnoff *and &cfmsgnoff)

/*  If allowed, do signoff.                                          */
/*  QSYS/SIGNOFF is the original IBM-supplied SIGNOFF.               */

IF        (&alwsgnoff)                                                +
           DO
           QSYS/SIGNOFF    LOG(&list_arg) DROP(&drop)
           MONMSG  (cpd0000 cpf0000) /* Error on command, try with  */+
                                     /* no arguments.               */+
                    EXEC(DO)
```

Figure 48.14 Continued

Figure 48.14 **ALternate SIGNOFF Command Processing Program** *Continued*

```
                    QSYS/SIGNOFF
                    MONMSG (cpd0000 cpf0000)  /* Return              */
                    GOTO   exit
                    ENDDO
           ENDDO

/*  If not allowed, and not System Request, send Group Job msg.     */

ELSE IF    (*&sysrqs)                                                 +
           DO
           SNDPGMMSG  MSG('Signoff not allowed, group jobs active.')  +
                      MSGTYPE(*diag)
                      MONMSG (cpf9999)
           ENDDO


EXIT:
RETURN
ENDPGM
```

Appendix A

QUSRTOOL

by Wayne Madden

As an experienced programmer, you have to find — or write — the right routine for the right job. Consequently, you probably collect programs and commands to help you with new jobs, much as an experienced craftsman designs and acquires specialized tools not often found on the average do-it-yourselfer's workbench. Having useful, specialized tools readily available can save you time and effort. Many user groups circulate libraries of tools that group members have written. *NEWS 3X/400* publishes a wide range of programming tools, and NEWSLINK subscribers have access to nearly all of them.

In addition to the tools you develop or acquire, you have a built-in "programmer's toolbox" on the AS/400: QUSRTOOL. QUSRTOOL contains source code for a variety of commands and command processing programs that can help you develop applications and manage your system.

QUSRTOOL comes to you courtesy of IBMer Jim Sloan, now retired, who developed most of the tools in the library. Sloan wrote the tools over the seven or so years he has been presenting his popular COMMON session on CL tips and techniques. Each of the 13 sessions he has presented has provided a new set of tips and techniques and has resulted in a remarkable collection of unofficial but very useful tools that can enhance your toolbox.

According to Sloan, the tools originally had a threefold purpose: to provide practical, working examples; to educate; and to tickle the imagination. He says, however, that a fourth purpose soon emerged: to provide examples that would inspire "smart people" to do something better.

Sloan's fourth purpose suggests that QUSRTOOL is simply a seed. The library contains only the source code for these tools. But you can access, copy, and modify this source code and then create the working objects yourself. The documentation IBM provides guides you, and you can learn as you go.

To get an idea of how easily you can access and create these tools, let's open up the QUSRTOOL library — your AS/400 programming toolbox — and look at the tools inside.

What's in Library QUSRTOOL?

Execute command WRKLIB LIB(QUSRTOOL) or use the Program Development Manager (PDM) to work with the contents of library QUSRTOOL. You will find one source file, QATTINFO, and several save files. Each save file contains a source physical file with the same name. These source files must be "unpackaged" before the tools can be used. All of the V2.R2 source code files are listed in Figure A.1. QUSRTOOL has source files for routines coded in every language that the AS/400 supports, including RPG, PL/I, and Pascal. You need the appropriate compiler to create these tools. QPGMR owns these files, and QSYS owns the QUSRTOOL library.

As you begin to work with these tools, the most important source code file is QATTINFO. This file contains text members that provide detailed overviews of each tool and its function. For instance, member AAAMAP in file QATTINFO holds the official IBM overview of the library and the tools provided. This documentation member contains a complete list of the tools and vital information about the creation and use of the tools.

You access member AAAMAP or any of the documentation members by using the DSPPFM (Display Physical File Member) command or by using Source Entry Utility (SEU). From a command line, key in DSPPFM QUSRTOOL/QATTINFO AAAMAP and press the Enter key. The text of documentation member AAAMAP appears on your screen.

IBM has organized QUSRTOOL into 16 sets of tools that perform various functions:

- *Access Path Protection Tool* manages a journaling environment for the access paths of files with a given number of records.

Figure A.1

Source Files in Library QUSRTOOL, V2.R2

File Name	Description
QATTBAS	Contains Source for BASIC programs
QATTCBL	Contains Source for COBOL programs
QATTCL	Contains Source for CL Programs
QATTCMD	Contains Source for Command Definitions
QATTDDS	Contains Source for Files and Menus
QATTINFO	Contains Documentation of the Various Tools
QATTPAS	Contains Source for Pascal Programs
QATTPL1	Contains Source for PL/I Programs
QATTQM	Contains Source for Query Definitions
QATTREX	Contains Source for REXX Programs
QATTRPG	Contains Source for RPG Programs
QATTSYSC	Contains Source for C Programs
QATTUIM	Contains Source for UIM Panels

- *Converting Office Documents to SEU Text Files* allows office users to use the familiar text manipulation provided by SEU.
- *Data Structure/Include for APIs* provides HLL data structures to assist in the access of system APIs.
- *Display Overflowed Object(s) Tool* displays all objects that have overflowed from a user ASP into the system ASP.
- *Example Communications Configurations* provide a menu-driven interface for creation and maintenance of communications objects.
- *Graphics Tools* provide commands that support the conversion of pictures and images into image graphics compatible with the AS/400 Graphical Data Display Manager (GDDM). These tools also let you display, print, or plot these image graphics files.
- *Group Jobs Made Easy* provides commands that simplify the use of group jobs.
- *Make Utility* checks and maintains the dependencies between the various components of an application.
- *Programming and Management Tips* provide a large collection of usable functions, commands, files, and programs for application development and systems management.
- *Publication Examples* is a listing of IBM manuals that use examples from QUSRTOOL.
- *SQL Trace* creates a report of SQL requests and performance information based on the TRCJOB outfile.
- *Storage Space Management Tools* provide support facilities to automate procedures that manage auxiliary storage. These tools support the cleanup of old history logs, problem log entries, and previously saved journal receivers.
- *Teleos Network Manager Utility* collects Call Detail Records and Alarms from a T-R attached Teleos device.
- *Save/Restore Spool File Tool* saves and retrieves selected spooled files into a designated library.
- *Trace 36E Tool* identifies CPU-intensive jobs in S/36E programs and procedures.
- *Package/Unpackage of QUSRTOOL Files* converts the supplied QUSRTOOL save files into physical files to allow the tools to be created.

Figure A.2 lists the 16 sets of tools. Each set has a two-character identifier, a documentation member in source file QATTINFO that summarizes the tools in that set, and an install member that contains source code for an installation program in source code file QUSRTOOL/QATTCL. In addition, each set of tools is contained in a save file of a source physical file. Each tool consists of one or more

Figure A.2

Description of Sets of Tools

Tool	ID	Documentation Member	Install Member
Access Path Protection Tool	JA	TJAINFO	TJAINST
Converting Office Documents	OF	TOFINFO	TOFINST
Data Structures for APIs	OP	TOPINFO	n/a
Display Overflowed Objects Tool	SM	TSMINFO	TSMINST
Example Communications Configurations	DC	TDCINFO	TDCINST
Graphics Tools	GR	TGRINFO	TGRINST
Group Jobs Made Easy	GJ	TGJINFO	TGJINST
MAKE Utility	MK	TMKINFO	TMKINST
Package/Unpackage of QUSRTOOL	TT	TTTINFO	TTTINST
Programming/Management Tips	AA	TAASUMMARY	n/a
Publication Examples	**	TPSPUBS	n/a
Save/Restore Spooled Files	SR	TSRINFO	TSRINST
SQL Trace	SQ	TSQINFO	TSQINST
Storage Space Management Tools	SP	TSPINFO	TSPINST
Teleos Network Manager Utility	NM	TNMINFO	TNMINST
Trace 36E Tool	TS	TTSINFO	TTSCRT

*The documentation member CRTTAATOOL in the source file QUSRTOOL/QATTINFO provides instructions on how to install the TAA tool functions.

members within the source files in QUSRTOOL. These members contain the source code for the actual commands, files, and programs that provide the functions for each tool. You can copy the sample tools and modify them for your own use.

Once you choose a set of tools from the list, you can ready it for use by reading the documentation member and then creating and executing the installation program. For example, if you want to use the Storage Space Management Tools, read the documentation in member TSPINFO in source file QUSRTOOL/QATTINFO, and then create and execute the installation program from member TSPINST in source file QUSRTOOL/QATTCL. Likewise, for each of the other tools you can elect to install the entire set at one time. The only exception is the Programming and Management Tips set of tools. Due to the many commands, files, and programs that make up this set of tools, you probably want to create only those tools you intend to implement.

Using the Programming and Management Tips Tools

Let's take a close look at the Programming Tips and Techniques tools and work through an example of implementing one of the tools in this set. To familiarize yourself with the various tools in the set, examine member TAASUMMARY in source file QUSRTOOL/QATTINFO. This text member provides both a one-line summary by category and a brief summary of each tool alphabetically. (Member TAAUPDAT in source file QUSRTOOL/QATTINFO documents all new release additions and updates to the Programming Tips and Techniques tools.) Within member TAASUMMARY, you will find the following set of tools:

CRTTAATOOL	Create TAA Tool
CPYTAATOOL	Copy TAA Tool
DLTTAATOOL	Delete TAA Tool
DSPTAACMD	Display TAA Commands
DSPTAATOOL	Display and/or Print TAA Tool
SCNTAATOOL	Scan TAA Tools
TAASUMMARY	TAA Tool Summary

This list shows source members that you can use to display information about, create, and manage the Programming Tips and Techniques tools.

Using the CRTTAATOOL Command

The CRTTAATOOL command provides a means of creating one or all of the tools in the Programming Tips and Techniques set. To use this command, you must first create it and the programs associated with it. The documentation in member CRTTAATOOL in source file QATTINFO describes the steps necessary to create and use this command. Briefly, the steps are:

- Create library TAATOOL (if it does not already exist):

```
CRTLIB LIB(TAATOOL)                                                  +
   TEXT('TAA Tools Library')
```

- Then create CL program TAATOLAC in library TAATOOL:

```
CRTCLPGM                                                             +
   PGM(TAATOOL/TAATOLAC)                                             +
   SRCFILE(QUSRTOOL/QATTCL)
```

- Finally, call CL program TAATOLAC:

```
CALL PGM(TAATOOL/TAATOLAC)
```

Because TAATOLAC is a long-running procedure, you should submit a call to TAATOLAC as a batch job. The spooled files the procedure creates are placed in output queue TAATOOL/TAAOUTQ, which the procedure automatically creates if it does not already exist.

At this point, you have in library TAATOOL the CRTTAATOOL command and the programs CRTTAATOOL uses. The CRTTAATOOL command parameter CMDLIB defaults to TAATOOL, which means that CRTTAATOOL will place the tools it creates in library TAATOOL. If you decide to place the tools in a different library, you can specify a library each time you execute CRTTAATOOL, or you can change the default for parameter CMDLIB by executing the command

```
CHGCMDDFT                                    +
   OBJ(TAATOOL/CRTTAATOOL)                   +
   NEWDFT('CMDLIB(lib_name)')
```

Then move the CRTTAATOOL command into the library you selected. (The TAATOOL library will not change when you load a new release of OS/400; thus, you can safely leave your tools in that library. Remember, however, that any new release of the operating system deletes all source code in library QUSRTOOL.)

Add the library containing the CRTTAATOOL command to your library list. Then type CRTTAATOOL, and press F4 to prompt for the parameters. The parameters you will see are:

TOOL	The tool you want to create. Enter *ALL to create all the tools. To specify *ALL, you must have security officer authority because some tools require such authority to function.
SRCLIB	The source library name. The default is QUSRTOOL.
CRTFILLIB	Some tools create and use database files. This is the library where those files will be created. This library cannot be TAATOOL.
CMDLIB	This is the library in which the tool command objects will be placed. The default is TAATOOL.
RESTART	If you are creating all the tools, you can specify a restart value. This value must be the name of a tool. For example, if you requested that all the tools be created, but then a failure occurred, you could correct the problem and then specify the name of the tool to restart within the create *ALL process.
AFTER	This parameter is used in conjunction with the RESTART parameter. It allows you to specify the command after which you will begin creating the remaining tools.
RMVOBS	Removes observability from the *PGM objects that are created.
ALWRTVSRC	Does not store the source code when the tool is created. Not storing the source will save about 15 percent of the disk space required for the tool but you will not be able to modify the tool if you use this parameter.

Now that you are familiar with the tools and the CRTTAATOOL command, let's create one of the tools.

The CHGLIBOWN Command

The tool we will create is CHGLIBOWN (Change Owner of a Library and Its Objects). This command helps clean up ownership of objects on a system. For instance, if you decide to combine all your programmers into the QPGMR group profile, you can use the CHGLIBOWN command to change the ownership of all objects in your development libraries so they are owned by the QPGMR profile.

First, let's examine the documentation member CHGLIBOWN in source file QATTINFO (Figure A.3). The command documentation has four sections: Command Description, Command Parameters, Implementation, and Objects Used by the Tool. Each tool documentation member has the same sections, making the documentation easy to read and understand. Note, however, that the documentation for command CHGLIBOWN does not include one important fact (as you would quickly find out if you attempted to create CHGLIBOWN without creating all of the other tools in the set). TAALIBBC, the CL program that serves as the command processing program (CPP) for this command, uses

Figure A.3 **Member CHGLIBOWN in Source File QUSRTOOL/QATTINFO**

```
CHGLIBOWN  CHANGE OWNER OF A LIBRARY AND IT'S OBJECTS  TAALIBB
---------  -----------------------------------------  -------

The  CHGLIBOWN  command changes the owner of a library and it's objects
to  another  owner. If an object in the library is already owned by the
new  owner,  no change occurs. An option exists to remove any authority
of the old owner to the object.

The typical use of the command is:

       CHGLIBOWN   LIB(ABC) NEWOWN(JONES)

Command parameters
------------------

  LIB           The library containing the objects to be changed.

  NEWOWN        The new owner name.

  OLDOWN        The old owner  name.  The  default  is  *ANY meaning to
                change any object  found.  If a name is specified, only
                those objects owned by the named owner will be changed.

  RVKOLDOWN     Revoke old owner's authority. This is a *YES/*NO value
                that defaults to *YES meaning to revoke the old owner
                from any authorization to the object.

The library object as well as the objects in the library are checked.

To  execute  the  command,  the user invoking the command must meet the
authorities required by the CHGOBJOWN command. In general these are:

    - Read on the library

    - Delete on the old user profile
```

Figure A.3 Continued

Figure A.3 **Member CHGLIBOWN in Source File QUSRTOOL/QATTINFO** *Continued*

```
     - Add on the new user profile

     - Object existence to the object

The Security Officer may execute the command for any library and owner.

Implementation
--------------

If the tool does not already exist, create it as:

      CRTTAATOOL    TOOL(CHGLIBOWN)
**NEWPAGE
Objects used by the tool
------------------------

   -------- TAATOOL library ---------        ---- QUSRTOOL library ----

   Object          Type        Attribute      Src member       Src file
   ------          -----       ---------      ----------       -----------

   CHGLIBOWN       *CMD                       TAALIBB          QATTCMD
   TAALIBBC        *PGM           CLP         TAALIBBC         QATTCL
```

the EDTVAR command, which is another command in library QUSRTOOL. Thus, you must also create the EDTVAR tool for CHGLIBOWN to execute.

To create the CHGLIBOWN tool, enter the following command:

```
CRTTAATOOL TOOL(CHGLIBOWN)
```

The spooled files this command generates are placed in output queue TAATOOL/TAAOUTQ, but are deleted if creation of the tool is successful.

Figure A.4 lists command source member TAALIBB in source file QUSRTOOL/QATTCMD. Figure A.5 shows the source member for the CPP TAALIBBC in source file QUSRTOOL/QATTCL. Before creating the CHGLIBOWN tool, you may decide to copy the source members into a user-defined library. You can then modify the tool without worrying about losing the source code when you load the next release.

The documentation for CHGLIBOWN specifies that the user invoking the command must have certain authorities to the libraries to be changed and to the objects in those libraries. In general, the security officer would invoke this type of ownership change. If you have the proper authority, type CHGLIBOWN on a command line and press F4 to prompt the command. You will be prompted to enter values for the parameters LIB (library), NEWOWN (new owner name), OLDOWN (old owner name), and RVKOLDOWN (revoke old owner authority). Parameter OLDOWN lets you enter a specific owner name or the value *ANY. If you enter a specific owner name, like QDFTOWN, only the

Figure A.4

Member TAALIBB in Source File QUSRTOOL/QATTCMD

```
/* TAALIBB - Change library owner - CHGLIBOWN cmd                    */
/*PARMS PGM(TAALIBBC) PRDLIB(TAATOOL)                                */
/*                                                                   */
/*  The CHGLIBOWN command finds whatever objects are owned by the    */
/*    old owner parameter and changes them to the new owner. A       */
/*    special value of *ANY may be used in the old owner parameter   */
/*    if sufficient authorization exists. An option exists to        */
/*    revoke the old owner from being authorized to the object.      */
/*                                                                   */
/* The CPP is TAALIBBC                                               */
/*                                                                   */
             CMD        PROMPT('Change Library Owner')
             PARM       KWD(LIB) TYPE(*NAME) LEN(10) MIN(1) +
                          PROMPT('Library')
             PARM       KWD(NEWOWN) TYPE(*NAME) LEN(10) MIN(1) +
                          PROMPT('New owner name')
             PARM       KWD(OLDOWN) TYPE(*NAME) LEN(10) DFT(*ANY) +
                          SPCVAL(*ANY) +
                          PROMPT('Old owner name')
             PARM       KWD(CUROLDOWN) TYPE(*CHAR) LEN(7) RSTD(*YES) +
                          VALUES('*REVOKE' '*SAME') DFT(*REVOKE) +
                          PROMPT('Current owner authority')
```

objects QDFTOWN owns will be changed. For the parameter NEWOWN, enter the new owner's user profile. The parameter RVKOLDOWN lets you enter *YES if you want to revoke the previous owner's authority to these objects. If you enter *NO, the old owner retains authority to the objects.

CHGLIBOWN is just an example of the type of tool in library QUSRTOOL. Figure A.6 is a complete list of the Programming Tips and Techniques tools available in V2.R2. You can find this list in member AAAMAP in file QUSRTOOL/QATTINFO, and you can find the documentation for each tool in the list in the member of the same name in file QATTINFO.

Whether you are an entry-level AS/400 programmer or a senior programmer, QUSRTOOL contains tools you can access, learn from, and implement to help you develop applications and manage systems. Examine the list of tools closely. You have the resources to write some amazing programs: You can print a journal analysis; check database dependencies; compare two source members and print the changes; print your local device configurations in the form of a workable chart; print security violations from the QHST log; send a break message to everyone currently active on the system; or send a nice message to users who encounter a locked record (instead of the nasty CPF message, which they always answer incorrectly, generating a multipage system dump).

With QUSRTOOL, you might find the right size programming wrench or the bigger hammer routine you need to get the job done. So start today. Print member AAAMAP in source file QUSRTOOL/QATTINFO and take advantage of your AS/400 programming toolbox.

Figure A.5 **Member TAALIBBC in Source File QUSRTOOL/QATTCL**

```
/* TAALIBBC - CPP for CHGLIBOWN - Change library owner */
             PGM        PARM(&LIB &NEWOWN &OLDOWN &CUROWNAUT)
             DCLF       QSYS/QADSPOBJ
             DCL        &LIB *CHAR LEN(10)
             DCL        &NEWOWN *CHAR LEN(10)
             DCL        &OLDOWN *CHAR LEN(10)
             DCL        &CUROWNAUT *CHAR LEN(7)
             DCL        &ALLOBJ *DEC LEN(5 0)
             DCL        &ALLOBJA *CHAR LEN(22)
             DCL        &CHGOBJ *DEC LEN(5 0)
             DCL        &CHGOBJA *CHAR LEN(22)
             DCL        &NOTOLDOWN *DEC LEN(5 0)
             DCL        &NOTOLDOWNA *CHAR LEN(22)
             DCL        &SAMEOWN *DEC LEN(5 0)
             DCL        &SAMEOWNA *CHAR LEN(22)
             DCL        &NOAUTH *LGL
             DCL        &ALLOC *DEC LEN(5 0)
             DCL        &ALLOCA *CHAR LEN(22)
             DCL        &ERRORSW *LGL                     /* Std err */
             DCL        &MSGID *CHAR LEN(7)               /* Std err */
             DCL        &MSGDTA *CHAR LEN(100)            /* Std err */
             DCL        &MSGF *CHAR LEN(10)               /* Std err */
             DCL        &MSGFLIB *CHAR LEN(10)            /* Std err */
             MONMSG     MSGID(CPF0000) EXEC(GOTO STDERR1) /* Std err */
             CHKOBJ     QSYS/&LIB OBJTYPE(*LIB)
             DSPOBJD    OBJ(QSYS/&LIB) OBJTYPE(*LIB) DETAIL(*FULL) +
                          OUTPUT(*OUTFILE) OUTFILE(QTEMP/DSPOBJP1)
             DSPOBJD    OBJ(&LIB/*ALL) OBJTYPE(*ALL) DETAIL(*FULL) +
                          OUTPUT(*OUTFILE) OUTFILE(QTEMP/DSPOBJP)
             CPYF       FROMFILE(QTEMP/DSPOBJP1) +
                          TOFILE(QTEMP/DSPOBJP) MBROPT(*ADD) /* Add +
                          lib obj from QSYS */
             DLTF       QTEMP/DSPOBJP1 /* Delete temp file */
             OVRDBF     QADSPOBJ TOFILE(QTEMP/DSPOBJP)
 LOOP:       RCVF       /* Read DSPOJBD output records */
             MONMSG     MSGID(CPF0864) EXEC(GOTO ENDLOOP)
             CHGVAR     &ALLOBJ (&ALLOBJ + 1) /* Count all */
             IF         (&ODOBOW *EQ &NEWOWN) DO /* Same owner */
             CHGVAR     &SAMEOWN (&SAMEOWN + 1)
             GOTO       LOOP
             ENDDO      /* Same owner */
             IF         (&OLDOWN *EQ '*ANY') GOTO ALC
             IF         (&OLDOWN *NE &ODOBOW) DO /* Not owned by old */
             CHGVAR     &NOTOLDOWN (&NOTOLDOWN + 1)
             GOTO       LOOP
             ENDDO      /* Not owned by old */
 ALC:        ALCOBJ     OBJ((&ODLBNM/&ODOBNM &ODOBTP *EXCL)) WAIT(0)
                        /* Some obj types cannot be allocated */
             MONMSG     MSGID(CPF0001) EXEC(GOTO CHG)
             MONMSG     MSGID(CPF1002) EXEC(GOTO ALCERR)
                        /* Only DB files with mbrs can be allocated */
             MONMSG     MSGID(CPF1085) EXEC(GOTO CHG)
             DLCOBJ     OBJ((&ODLBNM/&ODOBNM &ODOBTP *EXCL))
```

Figure A.5 Continued

Figure A.5 **Member TAALIBBC in Source File QUSRTOOL/QATTCL** *Continued*

```
CHG:       CHGOBJOWN  OBJ(&ODLBNM/&ODOBNM) OBJTYPE(&ODOBTP) +
                        NEWOWN(&NEWOWN) /* Change owner */
           MONMSG     MSGID(CPF2230) EXEC(DO) /* Lack auth to chg */
           CHGVAR     &NOAUTH '1'
           GOTO       LOOP
           ENDDO      /* Lack authority to change */
           IF         (&CUROWNAUT *EQ '*REVOKE') DO /* Revoke */
           RVKOBJAUT  OBJ(&ODLBNM/&ODOBNM) OBJTYPE(&ODOBTP) +
                        USER(&ODOBOW) AUT(*ALL) /* Revoke old own */
           MONMSG     MSGID(CPF0000) /* Ignore not authorized */
                      /* The previous MONMSG was added to allow */
                      /*   the command to operate on Rel 1.4    */
                      /*   where the CUROWNAUT parameter was    */
                      /*   added to CHGLIBOWN and the default   */
                      /*   is *REVOKE                           */
           ENDDO      /* Revoke */
           CHGVAR     &CHGOBJ (&CHGOBJ + 1) /* Count changes */
           GOTO       LOOP /* Read again */
ALCERR:    SNDPGMMSG  MSGID(CPF9898) MSGF(QCPFMSG) MSGTYPE(*DIAG) +
                        MSGDTA('Object ' *CAT &ODOBNM *TCAT +
                        ' in ' *CAT &ODLBNM *TCAT ' type ' *CAT +
                        &ODOBTP *TCAT ' cannot be allocated +
                        to change owner')
           CHGVAR     &ALLOC (&ALLOC + 1)
           GOTO       LOOP
ENDLOOP:   EDTVAR     CHROUT(&ALLOBJA) NUMINP(&ALLOBJ)
           EDTVAR     CHROUT(&CHGOBJA) NUMINP(&CHGOBJ)
           EDTVAR     CHROUT(&NOTOLDOWNA) NUMINP(&NOTOLDOWN)
           EDTVAR     CHROUT(&SAMEOWNA) NUMINP(&SAMEOWN)
           EDTVAR     CHROUT(&ALLOCA) NUMINP(&ALLOC)
           DLTF       QTEMP/DSPOBJP /* Delete temp file */
           IF         &NOAUTH SNDPGMMSG MSGID(CPF9898) +
                          MSGF(QCPFMSG) MSGTYPE(*ESCAPE) +
                          MSGDTA('Authority to change was lacking +
                            on one or more objects. See the job log')
           SNDPGMMSG  MSG('Lib ' *CAT &LIB *TCAT +
                        '   Objs rd-' *CAT &ALLOBJA +
                        *TCAT '   Objs chgd-' *CAT +
                        &CHGOBJA *TCAT '   Objs not owned by +
                        old owner-' *CAT &NOTOLDOWNA *TCAT +
                        '      Objs already owned by new owner-' +
                        *CAT &SAMEOWNA *TCAT +
                        '   Objs cannot be allocated-' *CAT +
                        &ALLOCA) MSGTYPE(*COMP)
           RETURN     /* Normal end of program */
STDERR1:              /* Standard error handling routine */
           IF         &ERRORSW SNDPGMMSG MSGID(CPF9999) +
                        MSGF(QCPFMSG) MSGTYPE(*ESCAPE) /* Func chk */
           CHGVAR     &ERRORSW '1' /* Set to fail ir error occurs */
STDERR2:   RCVMSG     MSGTYPE(*DIAG) MSGDTA(&MSGDTA) MSGID(&MSGID) +
                        MSGF(&MSGF) MSGFLIB(&MSGFLIB)
           IF         (&MSGID *EQ '       ') GOTO STDERR3
           SNDPGMMSG  MSGID(&MSGID) MSGF(&MSGFLIB/&MSGF) +
```

Figure A.5 Continued

Figure A.5 **Member TAALIBBC in Source File QUSRTOOL/QATTCL** *Continued*

```
                          MSGDTA(&MSGDTA) MSGTYPE(*DIAG)
            GOTO        STDERR2 /* Loop back for addl diagnostics */
STDERR3:    RCVMSG      MSGTYPE(*EXCP) MSGDTA(&MSGDTA) MSGID(&MSGID) +
                          MSGF(&MSGF) MSGFLIB(&MSGFLIB)
            SNDPGMMSG   MSGID(&MSGID) MSGF(&MSGFLIB/&MSGF) +
                          MSGDTA(&MSGDTA) MSGTYPE(*ESCAPE)
            ENDPGM
```

Figure A.6 **Programming Tips and Techniques Available in V2.R2 of QUSRTOOL**

Function	Description
ACCSECLIB	ACCESS SECURE LIBRARY
ADDDAT	ADD DATE COMMAND
ADDDTAARA	ADD TO A DATAAREA
ADDSRCMBR	ADD A SOURCE MEMBER WITH SOURCE TYPE
ADDTIM	ADD A TIME IN NUMBER OF SECONDS
ALCDBF	ALLOCATE DATA BASE FILE
APYUSRCHG	APPLY USER CHANGE
ATNPGM	SIMPLE ATTENTION KEY HANDLING PROGRAM
BINSEARCH	BINARY SEARCH TECHNIQUE
BKP	BREAKPOINT TOOL
BLDCALL	BUILD CALL FOR SBMJOB COMMAND
BLDPRTLIN	BUILD PRINT LINE CVTDAT CONVERT DATE CL PROGRAM
BRKMSGQN	BREAK MESSAGE QUEUE N TIMES
CAPJOBA	CAPTURE AND RETURN JOB ATTRIBUTES
CHGGRPPRF	CHANGE GROUP PROFILE
CHGLIBOWN	CHANGE OWNER OF A LIBRARY AND IT'S OBJECTS
CHGMSGD2	CHANGE MESSAGE DESCRIPTION # 2
CHGSRCTYP	CHANGE SOURCE TYPE
CHGUSRPWD	CHANGE USER PASSWORD
CHKACTPGM	CHECK ACTIVE PROGRAM
CHKAPOST	CHECK APOSTROPHES
CHKASPOBJ	CHECK ASP OBJECT
CHKCFGCHG	CHECK CONFIGURATION CHANGES
CHKDAT	CHECK DATE COMMAND
CHKDBD	CHECK DATA BASE DEPENDENCIES
CHKDBF	CHECK DATA BASE FILE
CHKGENERC	CHECK GENERIC VARIABLE
CHKJOBDUSR	CHECK JOBD USER PARAMETER
CHKLEAP	CHECK LEAP YEAR
CHKLIBOWN	CHECK LIBRARY OWNER
CHKLMTCPB	CHECK LIMITED CAPABILITY *USER TYPES
CHKNAM	CHECK NAME
CHKOBJDMG	CHECK OBJECT DAMAGE
CHKSAV	CHECK SAVE STRATEGY COMMAND
CHKSAVRST	CHECK SAVE/RESTORE JOB LOG FOR PROBLEMS
CHKSAVTAP	CHECK SAVE TAPE

Figure A.6 Continued

Figure A.6 **Programming Tips and Techniques Available in V2.R2 of QUSRTOOL** *Continued*

Function	Description
CHKSRCTYP	CHECK FOR VALID SOURCE TYPES IN A SOURCE FILE
CHKSYSCND	CHECK SYSTEM CONDITION
CHKS38CMD	CHECK CL SOURCE FOR USE OF S/38 COMMANDS
CHKUSRAUT	CHECK USER AUTHORITY WITHOUT PROGRAM ADOPT
CHKWEEK	CHECK DAY OF WEEK FOR EXECUTION
CHK400CMD	CHECK CL SOURCE FOR USE OF AS/400 COMMANDS
CLCDATDIF	CALCULATE DATE DIFFERENCES
CLCTIMDIF	CALCULATE TIME DIFFERENCE
CLRLFM	CLEAR LOGICAL FILE MEMBER
CMDLINE	PROVIDE COMMAND LINE SUPPORT
CMPDAT	COMPARE DATE
CMPDBF	COMPARE DATA BASE FILE
CMPSRC	COMPARE SOURCE MEMBER COMMAND
CMPSRC2	COMPARE SOURCE MEMBERS #2
CNFDLTOBJ	CONFIRM DELETE OBJECT
CNFRMVM	CONFIRM REMOVE MEMBER
CPYCHGMBR	COPY CHANGED MEMBERS
CPYDSTTAP	COPY IBM DISTRIBUTION TAPE
CPYFRMOUTQ	COPY FROM OUTPUT QUEUE
CPYFRMSAVF	COPY FROM SAVE FILE
CPYGENSRC	COPY GENERIC SOURCE
CPYJOBLOG	COPY JOB LOG COMMAND
CPYMNYSRCF	COPY MANY SOURCE FILE MEMBERS
CPYSPLTXT	COPY SPOOLED FILE TO TEXT MEMBER
CPYTAATOOL	COPY TAA TOOL SOURCE
CPYUSRPRF	COPY USER PROFILE
CRTPRTPGM	CREATE PRINT PROGRAM
CRTTAATOOL	CREATE TOOLS IN TAATOOL LIBRARY
CRTUSRSPC	CREATE USER SPACE
CVTALLJOBQ	CONVERT ALL JOB QUEUES TO A DATA BASE FILE
CVTALLOUTQ	CONVERT ALL OUTPUT QUEUES TO A DATA BASE FILE
CVTBINDEC	CONVERT BINARY VALUE TO DECIMAL
CVTBIN4DEC	CONVERT A BINARY 4 VALUE TO DECIMAL
CVTCFGSTS	CONVERT WRKCFGSTS TO A DATA BASE FILE
CVTDAT	CONVERT DATE COMMAND
CVTDAYN	CONVERT DAY N TO A NEW DATE
CVTDDSSRC	CONVERT DDS SOURCE COMMAND
CVTDSKSTS	CONVERT DISK STATUS
CVTDSPDTA	CONVERT DISPLAY DATA
CVTFRMHEX	CONVERT FROM HEX
CVTHEX	CONVERT A FIELD'S CONTENTS TO A HEX STRING
CVTJOBQ	CONVERT WRKJOBQ TO A DATA BASE FILE
CVTJRNA	CONVERT JOURNAL ATTRIBUTES COMMAND
CVTJRNRCVA	CONVERT JOURNAL RECEIVER ATTRIBUTES
CVTMSGF	CONVERT MESSAGE FILE
CVTOBJLCK	CONVERT WRKOBJLCK TO A DATA BASE FILE
CVTOUTQ	CONVERT WRKOUTQ TO A DATA BASE FILE
CVTPGMA	CONVERT PROGRAM ATTRIBUTES
CVTQHST	CONVERT QHST FILE TO NORMAL DATA BASE FILE
CVTSAVFD	CONVERT SAVE FILE DESCRIPTION
CVTSYSSTS	CONVERT WRKSYSSTS OUTPUT TO A DATA BASE FILE

Figure A.6 Continued

Figure A.6 **Programming Tips and Techniques Available in V2.R2 of QUSRTOOL** *Continued*

Function	Description
CVTTAPSAVD	CONVERT TAPE SAVE DESCRIPTION
CVTVOLSTAT	CONVERT VOLUME STATISTICS TO A DATA BASE FILE
CVTWRKACT	CONVERT WRKACTJOB OUTPUT TO A DATA BASE FILE
CVTWRKSBS	CONVERT WRKSBS OUTPUT TO DATA BASE FILE
CVTWRKSPLF	CONVERT WRKSPLF OUTPUT TO A DATA BASE FILE
CVTWRKUSR	CONVERT WRKUSRJOB TO A DATA BASE FILE
DLTDEPLGL	DELETE DEPENDENT LOGICALS
DLTOBJ	DELETE OBJECT
DLTOLDSPLF	DELETE OLD SPOOLED FILES
DLTQHST	DELETE QHST
DLTTAATOOL	DELETE TAA TOOL
DLYCMD	DELAY COMMAND
DSPADP	DISPLAY ADOPT TOOL
DSPAUDLOG	DISPLAY AUDIT LOG
DSPCLPDO	DISPLAY CL DO GROUP
DSPDB	DISPLAY DATA BASE RECORD
DSPDBF	DISPLAY DATA BASE FILE
DSPDTAQ	DISPLAY DATA QUEUE COMMAND
DSPFDTAQ	DISPLAY FILE DATA QUEUE EXAMPLE
DSPMBRD	DISPLAY MEMBER DESCRIPTION COMMAND
DSPMSGDTA	DISPLAY MESSAGE DATA
DSPMSGTXT	DISPLAY MESSAGE TEXT
DSPPRTSPC	DISPLAY PRINT SPACING
DSPPWD	DISPLAY PASSWORD
DSPRPGIGN	DISPLAY RPG IGNDECERR OPTION
DSPSECRVW	DISPLAY SECURITY REVIEW
DSPTAACMD	DISPLAY OR PRINT TAA COMMAND DESCRIPTIONS
DSPTAATOOL	DISPLAY OR PRINT TAA TOOL DESCRIPTIONS
DSPUSRSPC	DISPLAY USER SPACE
DUPFILFMT	DUPLICATE FILE FORMAT WITHOUT A KEY
DUPMSGD	DUPLICATE MESSAGE DESCRIPTION
DUPSAVTAP	DUPLICATING A SAVE/RESTORE TAPE
DUPSPLF	DUPLICATE SPOOLED FILE
DUPSRC	DUPLICATE SOURCE MEMBER
DUPTAPIN	DUPLICATE A TAPE USING A SINGLE TAPE DEVICE
EDTDTAARA	EDIT DATA AREA COMMAND
EDTJOBD	EDIT JOB DESCRIPTION COMMAND
EDTNETA	EDIT NETWORK ATTRIBUTES COMMAND
EDTOBJAUT2	EDIT OBJECT AUTHORITY 2
EDTUSRPRF	EDIT USER PROFILE
EDTVAR	EDIT VARIABLE COMMAND
ENAUSRPRF	ENABLE USER PROFILE
ENDDUPJOB	END DUPLICATE JOBS COMMAND
EXCCMD	EXECUTE COMMAND
EXPVOLID	EXPAND VOLUME ID
EXTCMD	EXTRACT COMMAND
EXTLST	EXTRACT AN ELEMENT FROM A LIST
FILEFDBCK	FILE FEEDBACK DEFINITION
FIND	FIND OBJECT
FREE	FREE A PROGRAM FROM CL
GENRANNBR	GENERATE RANDOM NUMBER COMMAND DESCRIPTION

Figure A.6 Continued

Figure A.6 Programming Tips and Techniques Available in V2.R2 of QUSRTOOL *Continued*

Function	Description
JOBSCH	JOB SCHEDULING FUNCTION DESCRIPTION
LOCKMSG	PRODUCING A MESSAGE ON A LOCKED RECORD
LOGCL	LOG CL STATEMENTS
MOVCHRDEC	MOVE CHARACTER TO DECIMAL COMMAND
MOVLIBOBJ	MOVE LIBRARY OBJECTS
MOVM	MOVE MEMBER COMMAND
MOVMNYOBJ	MOVE MANY OBJECTS
MOVSPLF	MOVE SPOOLED FILE FROM ONE OUTQ TO ANOTHER
MOVTODEC	MOVE TO DECIMAL
MSGCTL	MESSAGE CONTROL
MTNJRN	MAINTAIN JOURNAL
OR	OR TWO VARIABLES TOGETHER
PMTOPR	PROMPT OPERATOR COMMAND
PRINT	PRINT COMMAND
PRTASPLIB	PRINTS THE LIBRARIES IN ONE OR ALL ASPS
PRTASPUSE	PRINT ASP USE
PRTBIGCHR	PRINT BIG CHARACTER
PRTCHGIBM	PRINT CHANGED IBM OBJECTS
PRTCHGMSGD	PRINT CHANGED MESSAGE DESCRIPTIONS
PRTCMDUSE	PRINT COMMAND USEAGE
PRTDBFANL	PRINT DATA BASE FILE ANALYSIS
PRTDBFEXP	PRINT DATA BASE FILE EXCEPTIONS
PRTDEVCFG	PRINT DEVICE CONFIGURATION TO A SOURCE FILE
PRTGENSRC	PRINT GENERIC SOURCE
PRTHDWSUM	PRINT HARDWARE SUMMARY
PRTJOBACG	PRINT JOB ACCOUNTING
PRTJRNANL	PRINT JOURNAL ANALYSIS
PRTJRNSUM	PRINT JOURNAL SUMMARY
PRTLIBANL	PRINT LIBRARY ANALYSIS
PRTLIBDTL	PRINT LIBRARY DETAIL
PRTLIBSAV	PRINT LIBRARY SAVE INFORMATION
PRTLSTCHG	PRINT LAST CHANGE DATE INFORMATION
PRTLSTUSE	PRINT LAST USE INFORMATION
PRTMNYSRCF	PRINT MANY SOURCE FILE MEMBERS COMMAND
PRTQHSTANL	PRINT QHST ANALYSIS
PRTPGMA	PRINT PROGRAM ATTRIBUTES
PRTSAVSTS	PRINT SAVE STATUS
PRTSECVIL	PRINT SECURITY VIOLATIONS FROM QHST
PRTSRCF	PRINT SOURCE FILE MEMBER COMMAND
PRTSRCSUM	PRINT SOURCE SUMMARY
PRTSYSANL	PRINT SYSTEM ANALYSIS
PRTSYSSUM	PRINTS SYSTEM SUMMARY
PRTUSECNT	PRINT USE COUNT
QRYF	FRONT END TO OPNQRYF
RBLDBF	REBUILD DATA BASE
RMVOLDMSG	REMOVES OLD MESSAGES FROM WORKSTATION MESSAGE QUEUES
RPGVALCHK	RPG VALIDITY CHECKING DEMONSTRATION
RPGSTSDS	RPG STATUS DATA STRUCTURE DEFINITION
RPLCMD	REPLACE COMMAND
RPLDSPF	REPLACE DISPLAY FILE
RPLPGM	REPLACE PROGRAM

Figure A.6 Continued

Figure A.6 Programming Tips and Techniques Available in V2.R2 of QUSRTOOL *Continued*

Function	Description
RPLPRTF	REPLACE PRINTER FILE
RSTALLCHG	RESTORE ALL CHANGES
RSTALLLIB	RESTORE ALL LIBRARIES
RSTANYLIB	RESTORE ANY LIBRARY
RSTFIL	RESTORE FILE COMMAND
RTVCLSA	RETRIEVE CLASS ATTRIBUTES COMMAND
RTVCMDA	RETRIEVE COMMAND ATTRIBUTES
RTVDAT	RETRIEVE DATE IN VARIOUS FORMATS
RTVDSPFA	RETRIEVE DISPLAY FILE ATTRIBUTES
RTVGENMBR	RETRIEVE GENERIC MEMBER
RTVJOBD	RETRIEVE JOB DESCRIPTION PARAMETERS
RTVJOBSTS	RETRIEVE JOB STATUS
RTVLFA	RETRIEVE LOGICAL FILE ATTRIBUTES
RTVLSTCHG	RETRIEVE LAST SOURCE CHANGE DATE
RTVNBRACT	RETRIEVE NUMBER OF ACTIVE USERS PER SUBSYSTEM
RTVOUTQA	RETRIEVE OUTPUT QUEUE ATTRIBUTES
RTVPFA	RETRIEVE PHYSICAL FILE ATTRIBUTES
RTVPGMA	RETRIEVE PROGRAM ATTRIBUTES
RTVPRTFA	RETRIEVE PRINT FILE ATTRIBUTES
RTVSPCAUT	RETRIEVE SPECIAL AUTHORITIES
RTVSPLA	RETRIEVE SPOOL ATTRIBUTES WITHIN A PRINTER FILE
RTVSPLFA	RETRIEVE SPOOLED FILE ATTRIBUTES
RTVTIMSTM	RETRIEVE TIME STAMP COMMAND
RTVUSRSPCE	RETRIEVE USER SPACE ENTRY
RTVUSRSPCI	RETRIEVE USER SPACE INITIALIZATION
RTVWSDA	RETRIEVE WORK STATION ATTRIBUTE
SAVALLCHG	SAVE ALL CHANGES TO TAPE
SAVICHDTA	SAVE INTERCHANGE DATA
SAVWHLACT	SAVE WHILE ACTIVE
SBMPARMS	EXTRACT PARMS FROM SOURCE AND ADD TO CRT CMDS
SBMPDMOVR	SUBMIT PDM OVERRIDES
SCNALLSRC	SCAN ALL SOURCE FILES
SCNSRC	SCAN SOURCE FILE COMMAND
SCNTAATOOL	SCAN TAA TOOLS COMMAND
SCNVAR	SCAN A VARIABLE
SCNVARRGT	SCAN A VARIABLE FROM THE RIGHT
SCRAMBLE	SCRAMBLE BYTES WITHIN A FIELD
SETJOBLOG	FORCE JOB LOG TO BE SPOOLED
SHOUT	SHOUT A MESSAGE
SNDBRKACT	SEND BREAK MESSAGE TO ACTIVE WORK STATIONS
SNDDTAQ	SEND DATA QUEUE
SNDNETOUTQ	SEND NETWORK OUTPUT QUEUE
SORTDB	SORT A DATA BASE FILE (FRONT END TO FMTDTA)
SORTTXT	SORT TEXT
SPLCTL	SPOOL CONTROL
SRCARC	SOURCE ARCHIVE
SRCCTL	SOURCE CONTROL
STACK	STACK OF DATA IN CL PROGRAMS
STRKEY	START AT A KEY VALUE
STSMSG	SENDING WORK STATION MESSAGES AS STATUS MESSAGE
SUMJRNENT	SUMMARIZE JOURNAL ENTRIES

Figure A.6 Continued

Figure A.6 **Programming Tips and Techniques Available in V2.R2 of QUSRTOOL** *Continued*

Function	Description
SYSRQSCMD	ACCESS COMMAND ENTRY FROM THE SYSTEM REQUEST DISPLAY
VALDBF	VALIDATE DATA BASE FILE
WHO	WHO IS ABUSING THE SYSTEM
WRTSRC	WRITE SOURCE STATEMENTS TO A SOURCE MEMBER

Note: These commands are provided as part of an example tool. As such, the commands may be changed or deleted in a future releases or there may be a system-provided command which uses the same name. It is therefore recommended that you qualify the use of these commands with the name of the user library where they exist.

QUSRTOOL Summary

Using any new tool requires caution, and getting the hang of QUSRTOOL may take a little more effort than snapping a 9/16-inch socket onto a ratchet handle. A few warnings will keep you from skinning your knuckles when you get the tools out and go to work.

Warning #1: The tools come with an explicit disclaimer: "What you see is what you get." There is no guarantee that the tools will work, nor can you call Level 1 support to report program bugs. It is up to you to review the code and make changes to meet your own programming standards.

Warning #2: You should also use the QUSRTOOL documentation warily. AAAMAP and other documentation members contain some errors, such as incomplete lists of tools or descriptions that do not match the tools. And there may be no internal documentation within the commands and programs. You should examine each tool closely and verify the documentation before use.

Warning #3: Library QUSRTOOL contains only the source code for programming tools, and each new release of OS/400 replaces this library. New releases may add new sample tools and modify or delete existing tools. To prevent a new release from destroying your existing tools, do not create the tools in library QUSRTOOL. Instead, create the actual objects in a user-defined library.

Don't let these warnings discourage you. As a good programming mechanic, you can still use these tools easily, even if you do have to clean them up first.

Appendix B

APIs

by Ken Kelley

For as long as IBM has been producing computers, system programmers have been developing tools that augment the capabilities of the operating system. 3X/400 toolsmiths have produced useful software packages that work with (and sometimes replace) operating system modules. Many of these third-party tools have gained wide acceptance in the marketplace.

Despite this progress, system programming for the midrange has become increasingly difficult as IBM first restricted materials about the operating system and then ceased publishing technical specifications for the internals of the S/38 and the AS/400 altogether. AS/400 system programmers have had to work almost entirely in the dark, without tools or information for constructing their software.

Object Domains and Program States

Starting with Release 3.0, IBM introduced to system programmers two important new concepts. One is the introduction of object domains, of which there are only two — *SYSTEM and *USER. Every object belongs to one or the other. Virtually all IBM-supplied objects and those created during operation belong to the system domain. User-written programs and data files are an exception; they belong to the user domain.

The second new concept is that all programs must operate in one of two states — again, either system or user. Every program created under OS/400 executes in the user state. Only IBM-supplied programs operate in the system state.

A new security option — level 40 — brings these concepts together and enforces domain integrity. Under level 40, user state programs cannot cross the domain boundary, so system domain objects are strictly off limits to user-written programs. Consequently, programmers cannot create programs that directly address or manipulate OS/400 objects. (For more information about AS/400 security, see Chapter 5, "OS/400 Security Exposures.")

Gateways to the System Domain

Under level 40, user programs may not call system programs, access system data areas, or reference OS/400 objects. This presents two choices to OS/400 system programmers. They can waive level 40 operation and continue creating software that works (as before) under security levels 10, 20, and 30. Or they can use the new IBM programs that serve as gateways to the system domain.

These new programs, collectively known as Application Programming Interfaces (APIs), are special because they belong to the user domain but operate in the system state. As a result, they can be referenced by user-written programs, yet they can access system domain objects. user domain programs can request information and services from the API programs, which manipulate the requested system objects in an IBM-controlled fashion.

API Attributes

The available APIs are documented in the *System Programmer's Interface Reference* manual, document number SC41-8223-01, program number 5738-SS1. There are seven categories of APIs, but all have three characteristics in common.

First, APIs provide performance or function unachievable through a high-level language (HLL). APIs are faster than output-file-oriented CL commands and, in some cases, offer access to otherwise unavailable operating system objects and information.

Second, APIs are available through the external call capabilities of all HLLs. Parameter lists serve as the vehicle for API I/O, eliminating the overhead associated with a CL interface (e.g., the RTVJOBA (Retrieve Job Attributes) command).

APIs support only character and binary data types. None of the information returned by the APIs contains any pointer or bitwise data (i.e., data in which each bit represents a different flag or state of information). Conversion from bitwise or coded format to external character form occurs within the API, so the HLL program never views the details of system format. In addition, APIs return information in fixed-length data structures rather than the variable-length form in which information is usually stored.

While at first blush it may seem advantageous to be able to access APIs via HLLs such as RPG and COBOL, some of the tradeoffs associated with this compatibility can have a serious impact on API performance. The conversion of data from variable-length to fixed-length formats and the inability to use pointers results not only in a more voluminous representation of data and more data movement, but less efficient movement of that information. Thus, while providing performance advantages over HLLs, APIs are not as fast as they could be if they were not burdened with HLL-compatibility baggage.

The third characteristic of APIs is that they remain compatible with OS/400 through future releases of the operating system. As APIs are enhanced, future information will either be added to data currently returned by the API or will be placed into a new API data format. Therefore, compatibility with future OS/400 releases is guaranteed for programs that use the APIs as long as you properly use offset and length information returned by the APIs and do not hard-code positional and length information for returned data elements.

Retrieving System Object Information

Most of the APIs are designed to retrieve system object information the way equivalent CL commands do. Information passes between the user program and the API via API data formats and OS/400 user space (*USRSPC) objects. Most APIs return fixed-length information (e.g., object description, member description, spool attributes) to the requesting program through a data structure, and many can return varying levels of information. A format parameter passed by the requesting program tells the API which data set to return, and the API fills the return data structure accordingly.

Several APIs return lists (e.g., of objects, fields, and spool files) into a user space object. For the sake of consistency, every API that lists information does so through a common data structure. The data structure consists of a fixed-length header, followed by a variable number of fixed-length entries. The header and list data can "float" in the user space because they are located by using offsets also returned in the user space object.

Accessing the information in the user space is easiest with pointer-capable languages (i.e., C/400, System C/400, MI, Pascal, PL/I), but RPG and COBOL users can invoke an API to retrieve data from the user space based on the starting position and length of the data.

API Types

The APIs are stored in library QSYS and fall into several categories. Figure B.1 shows the categories, the APIs in each, and their function. Let's take a quick look at a few of the most interesting categories.

One group, the user object APIs, lets you create and manipulate the new user space (*USRSPC), user queue (*USRQ), and user index (*USRIDX) objects. Each of these is created as a permanent object in a specified library and belongs to the user domain. User-written programs can access and modify these objects directly, unlike their OS/400 counterparts (data areas, data queues, and logical files), which belong to the system domain and can be addressed or modified only with CL commands. Once you create one of these new user objects, however, you must use either the DLTUSRSPC (Delete User Space), DLTUSRQ (Delete User Queue), or DLTUSRIDX (Delete User Index) CL command to delete it.

Although you can manipulate queue and index entries only by using MI instructions (or System C/400 equivalents), three user object APIs let programs work with user spaces. A user space is similar to a data area in that it is an unstructured space for holding program-described data. HLL programs retrieve and modify user space contents via the retrieve and change user space APIs (QUSRTVUS and QUSCHGUS, respectively). Pointer-capable languages can access the space directly if a pointer is made available, which you can do using the retrieve pointer API (QUSPTRUS).

Currently, there is no provision for explicitly updating object usage information (e.g., when the object was last modified or used) for user objects, although the retrieve/change APIs implicitly update usage information for user spaces. Neither have any APIs been provided to support locking — therefore, concurrency between jobs that must refer to the same user space is a problem.

IBM has made the OS/400 MI assembler accessible to anyone who has operational authority to QPRCRTPG, the create program API. QPRCRTPG accepts creation parameters and an Intermediate Representation of a Program (IRP) string, which can be presented through a user space or a sufficiently large program variable. The IRP string is compiled to become a new user state program in the user domain. (IRP syntax is documented in the *System Programmer's Interface Reference* manual (SC41-8223).)

Only the change pool attributes API (QUSCHGPA) lets you change system object information. It is equivalent to the WRKSYSSTS (Work with System Status) display that lets you modify storage pool sizes and activity levels. Although you must use QUSCHGPA with the Materialize Resource Management Data (MATRMD) MI instruction, this API lets user-written programs modify machine performance characteristics.

Only the Beginning

An old proverb states that a journey of a thousand miles begins with a single step. APIs represent a movement in the right direction by starting to grant passage to OS/400. Although the APIs do not provide access to many operating system functions, and the performance of applications that rely on APIs is still in question, IBM has firmly embarked on a path that lets independent developers create stable, useful software for accessing some of the capabilities of the operating system.

Figure B.1

APIs by Category

User-Defined Communications Support

Disable Link (QOLDLINK)
Enable Link (QOLELINK)
Query Line Description (QOLQLIND)
Receive Data (QOLRECV)
Send Data (QOLSEND)
Set Filter (QOLSETF)
Set Timer (QOLTIMER)

Data Stream Translation APIs

End Data Stream Translation Session (QD0ENDTS)
Start Data Stream Translation Session (QD0STRTS)
Start Data Stream Translation Session (QD0STRTS) API
Translate Data Stream (QD0TRNDS) API

Database File APIs

List Database File Members (QUSLMBR) API
List Database Relations (QDBLDBR) API

Figure B.1 Continued

Figure B.1

APIs by Category *Continued*

Database File APIs

List Fields (QUSLFLD) API
List Record Formats (QUSLRCD) API
Query (QQQQRY) API
Retrieve File Description (QDBRTVFD) API
Retrieve Member Description (QUSRMBRD) API

Commitment Control APIs

Add Commitment Resource (QTNADDCR) API
Remove Commitment Resource (QTNRMVCR) API
Retrieve Commitment Information (QTNRCMTI) API

Edit Function APIs

Convert Edit Code (QECCVTEC) API
Convert Edit Word (QECCVTEW) API
Edit (QECEDT) API

Hierarchical File System APIs

Change Directory Entry Attributes (QHFCHGAT) API
Change File Pointer (QHFCHGFP) API
Close Directory (QHFCLODR) API
Close Stream File (QHFCLOSF) API
Control File System (QHFCTLFS) API
Copy Stream File (QHFCPYSF) API
Create Directory (QHFCRTDR) API
Delete Directory (QHFDLTDR) API
Delete Stream File (QHFDLTSF) API
Force Buffered Data (QHFFRCSF) API
Get Stream File Size (QHFGETSZ) API
List Registered File Systems (QHFLSTFS) API
Lock and Unlock Range in Stream File (QHFLULSF) API
Move Stream File (QHFMOVSF) API
Open Directory (QHFOPNDR) API
Open Stream File (QHFOPNSF) API
Read Directory Entries (QHFRDDR) API
Read from Stream File (QHFRDSF) API
Rename Directory (QHFRNMDR) API
Rename Stream File (QHFRNMSF) API
Retrieve Directory Entry Attributes (QHFRTVAT) API
Set Stream File Size (QHFSETSZ) API
Write to Stream File (QHFWRTSF) API

Using New File Systems with the HFS

Register File System (QHFRGFS) API

Figure B.1 Continued

Figure B.1

APIs by Category *Continued*

Using New File Systems with the HFS

Deregister File System (QHFDRGFS) API
Exit Program for Change Directory Entry Attributes (QHFCHGAT) API
Exit Program for Change File Pointer (QHFCHGFP) API
Exit Program for Close Directory (QHFCLODR) API
Exit Program for Close Stream File (QHFCLOSF) API
Exit Program for Control File System (QHFCTLFS) API
Exit Program for Copy Stream File (QHFCPYSF) API
Exit Program for Create Directory (QHFCRTDR) API
Exit Program for Delete Directory (QHFDLTDR) API
Exit Program for Delete Stream File (QHFDLTSF) API
Exit Program for Force Buffered Data (QHFFRCSF) API
Exit Program for Get Stream File Size (QHFGETSZ) API
Exit Program for Lock and Unlock Range in Stream File (QHFLULSF)
Exit Program for Move Stream File (QHFMOVSF) API
Exit Program for Open Directory (QHFOPNDR) API
Exit Program for Open Stream File (QHFOPNSF) API
Exit Program for Read Directory Entries (QHFRDDR) API
Exit Program for Read from Stream File (QHFRDSF) API
Exit Program for Rename Directory (QHFRNMDR) API
Exit Program for Rename Stream File (QHFRNMSF) API
Exit Program for Retrieve Directory Entry Attributes (QHFRTVAT)
Exit Program for Set Stream File Size (QHFSETSZ) API
Exit Program for Write to Stream File (QHFWRTSF) API

Application Development Manager/400 APIs

Get Space Status (QLYGETS) API
Read Build Information (QLYRDBI) API
Set Space Status (QLYSETS) API
Write Build Information (QLYWRTBI) API

COBOL/400 APIs

Change COBOL Main Program (QLRCHGCM) API
Retrieve COBOL Error Handler (QLRRTVCE) API
Set COBOL Error Handler (QLRSETCE) API

Message Handling APIs

Move Program Messages (QMHMOVPM) API
Receive Nonprogram Message (QMHRCVM) API
Receive Program Message (QMHRCVPM) API
Remove Nonprogram Messages (QMHRMVM) API
Remove Program Messages (QMHRMVPM) API
Resend Escape Message (QMHRSNEM) API
Retrieve Message (QMHRTVM) API
Retrieve Request Message (QMHRTVRQ) API

Figure B.1 Continued

Figure B.1

APIs by Category *Continued*

Message Handling APIs

Send Break Message (QMHSNDBM) API
Send Nonprogram Message (QMHSNDM) API
Send Program Message (QMHSNDPM) API
Send Reply Message (QMHSNDRM) API

Network Management APIs

Change Mode Name (QNMCHGMN) API
Deregister Application (QNMDRGAP) API
End Application (QNMENDAP) API
Filter Problem (QSXFTRPB) API
Generate Alert (QALGENA) API
Receive Data (QNMRCVDT) API
Receive Operation Completion (QNMRCVOC) API
Register Application (QNMREGAP) API
Retrieve Alert (QALRTVA) API
Retrieve Mode Name (QNMRTVMN) API
Send Alert (QALSNDA) API
Send Error (QNMSNDER) API
Send Reply (QNMSNDRP) API
Send Request (QNMSNDRQ) API
Start Application (QNMSTRAP) API
Work with Problem (QPDWRKPB) API

OfficeVision/400 APIs

Change Office Program (QOGCHGOE) API
Control Office Services (QOCCTLOF) API
Display Directory Panels (QOKDSPDP) API
Retrieve Office Programs (QOGRTVOE) API

Operational Assistant APIs

Attention-Key-Handling (group jobs) (QEZMAIN) API
Attention-Key-Handling (nongroup jobs) (QEZAST) API
Save Information (QEZSAVIN) API
Send Message (QEZSNDMG) API
Work with Jobs (QEZBCHJB) API
Work with Messages (QEZMSG) API
Work with Printer Output (QEZOUTPT) API

Program and CL Command APIs

Create Program (QPRCRTPG) API
Retrieve Command Information (QCDRCMDI) API
Retrieve Program Information (QCLRPGMI) API

Figure B.1 Continued

Figure B.1

APIs by Category *Continued*

Security APIs

Change User Password (QSYCHGPW) API
Check User Authority to an Object (QSYCUSRA) API
Check User Special Authorities (QSYCUSRS) API
Convert Authority Values to MI Value (QSYCVTA) API
Get Profile Handle (QSYGETPH) API
List Authorized Users (QSYLAUTU) API
List Objects Secured by Authorization List (QSYLATLO) API
List Objects That Adopt Owner Authority (QSYLOBJP) API
List Objects User Is Authorized To or Owns (QSYLOBJA) API
List Users Authorized to Object (QSYLUSRA) API
Release Profile Handle (QSYRLSPH) API
Retrieve Information about User (QSYRUSRI) API
Retrieve User Authority to Object (QSYRUSRA) API
Set Profile (QWTSETP) API

Spooled File APIs

Close Spooled File (QSPCLOSP) API
Create Spooled File (QSPCRTSP) API
Get Spooled File Data (QSPGETSP) API
List Spooled Files (QUSLSPL) API
Open Spooled File (QSPOPNSP) API
Put Spooled File Data (QSPPUTSP) API
Retrieve Output Queue Information (QSPROUTQ) API
Retrieve Spooled File Attributes (QUSRSPLA) API

User Interface APIs

Display Command Line Window (QUSCMDLN) API
Display Help (QUHDSPH) API

User Interface Manager APIs

Add List Entry (QUIADDLE) API
Add List Multiple Entries (QUIADDLM) API
Add Pop-Up Window (QUIADDPW) API
Add Print Application (QUIADDPA) API
Close Application (QUICLOA) API
Delete List (QUIDLTL) API
Display Panel (QUIDSPP) API
Get Dialog Variable (QUIGETV) API
Get List Entry (QUIGETLE) API
Get List Multiple Entries (QUIGETLM) API
Open Display Application (QUIOPNDA) API
Open Print Application (QUIOPNPA) API
Print Panel (QUIPRTP) API
Put Dialog Variable (QUIPUTV) API

Figure B.1 Continued

Figure B.1

APIs by Category *Continued*

User Interface Manager APIs

Remove List Entry (QUIRMVLE) API
Remove Pop-Up Window (QUIRMVPW) API
Remove Print Application (QUIRMVPA) API
Retrieve List Attributes (QUIRTVLA) API
Set List Attributes (QUISETLA) API
Set Screen Image (QUISETSC) API
Update List Entry (QUIUPDLE) API

User Space APIs

Change User Space (QUSCHGUS) API
Create User Space (QUSCRTUS) API
Delete User Space (QUSDLTUS) API
Retrieve Pointer to User Space (QUSPTRUS) API
Retrieve User Space (QUSRTVUS) API

User Index APIs

Create User Index (QUSCRTUI) API
Delete User Index (QUSDLTUI) API

User Queue APIs

Create User Queue (QUSCRTUQ) API
Delete User Queue (QUSDLTUQ) API

Object APIs

Change Object Description (QLICOBJD) API
Convert Type (QLICVTTP) API
List Objects (QUSLOBJ) API
Retrieve Object Description (QUSROBJD) API

Virtual Terminal APIs

Close Virtual Terminal Path (QTVCLOVT) API
Open Virtual Terminal Path (QTVOPNVT) API
Read from Virtual Terminal (QTVRDVT) API
Send Request for OS/400 Function (QTVSNDRQ) API
Write to Virtual Terminal (QTVWRTVT) API

Work Management APIs

Change Pool Attributes (QUSCHGPA) API
Dump Flight Recorder (QWTDMPFR) API
Dump Lock Flight Recorder (QWTDMPLF) API
List Active Subsystems (QWCLASBS) API
List Job (QUSLJOB) API

Figure B.1 Continued

Figure B.1

APIs by Category *Continued*

Work Management APIs

List Job Schedule Entries (QWCLSCDE) API
List Subsystem Job Queues (QWDLSJBQ) API
Retrieve Job Description Information (QWDRJOBD) API
Retrieve Job Information (QUSRJOBI) API
Retrieve Job Queue Information (QSPRJOBQ) API
Retrieve Subsystem Information (QWDRSBSD) API
Set Lock Flight Recorder (QWTSETLF) API

Work Station Support APIs

Query Keyboard Buffering (QWSQRYWS) API
Set Keyboard Buffering (QWSSETWS) API

Miscellaneous APIs

Convert Date and Time Format (QWCCVTDT) API
Convert Graphic Character Strings (CDRCVRT) API
Get CCSID for Normalization (CDRGCCN) API
Get Encoding Scheme (CDRGESP) API
Get Related Default CCSID (CDRGRDC) API
Get Short Form CCSID (CDRSCSP) API
Remove All Bookmarks from a Course (QEARMVBM) API
Retrieve Main Storage (QVTRMSTG) API

Appendix C

The LODKEY Program to Identify Keys

by Ron Harvey

If you write interactive programs, you have probably experienced the frustrations of the many inconvenient techniques for identifying the key the user has pressed. Take indicators, for example. Using the function key indicators KA through KY with the *IN array works, but you must document the indicators (unless you enjoy counting on your fingers to find out what key *INKQ, for example, represents). Other problems arise with identifying the Enter, Roll up, Roll down, Help, and Print keys. You must assign indicators to each key except Enter, which you must handle with the VLDCMDKEY keyword or the "none of the above" technique ("if it's not any of these, it must be Enter"). You end up with three sets of indicators (KA through KY, your display file indicators, and the VLDCMDKEY indicator).

Hex conversions are another frustration. The attention identification (AID) byte (i.e., the 1-byte hex character found in the file information data structure for display files) provides a convenient way to identify the key pressed. (For more information on the AID byte, see *RPG/400 Reference* (SC09-1349) and *Data Management Guide* (SC41-9658) for the AS/400.) But there are drawbacks. You may need some sort of hex conversion. For example, you may use a table to translate the hex characters into a more usable form for comparisons (e.g., "F4"). And, whatever technique you use with hex conversions and the AID byte, you must document your code to avoid maintenance headaches.

Let me suggest a better solution, one that works well on both the S/38 and the AS/400. Simply test the AID byte against a list of hex values that identify the key pressed. This method eliminates indicator assignment in the display file, allows direct access to all keys (including Enter), requires no hex conversion, and is almost self-documenting. The solution has three pieces: an externally defined data structure to hold the list of hex values, an RPG program to do the hex comparison (you create the data structure and the RPG program only once for setup), and a small modification to each application program that identifies pressed keys.

For the first step, create an externally defined data structure (i.e., a physical file definition without data) called KEYS. Figure C.1 shows the DDS for the data structure. Create KEYS as you would any other physical file by using the CRTPF

Figure C.1

DDS for KEYS Data Structure

```
*... ... 1 ... ... 2 ... ... 3 ... ... 4 ... ... 5 ... ... 6 ... ... 7
     *****************************************************************
     *                                                               *
     * KEYS -- EXTERNAL DATA STRUCTURE FOR KEY PRESSED FIELD NAMES   *
     *                                                               *
     *****************************************************************
     A          R KEYSF
     A            ENTER          1         COLHDG('ENTER KEY')
     A            ROLLUP         1         COLHDG('ROLL UP KEY')
     A            ROLLDN         1         COLHDG('ROLL DOWN')
     A            HELP           1         COLHDG('HELP KEY')
     A            PRINT          1         COLHDG('PRINT KEY')
     A            BSPACE         1         COLHDG('BACK SPACE')
     A            CLEAR          1         COLHDG('CLEAR KEY')
     A            F1             1         COLHDG('F1 KEY')
     A            F2             1         COLHDG('F2 KEY')
     A            F3             1         COLHDG('F3 KEY')
     A            F4             1         COLHDG('F4 KEY')
     A            F5             1         COLHDG('F5 KEY')
     A            F6             1         COLHDG('F6 KEY')
     A            F7             1         COLHDG('F7 KEY')
     A            F8             1         COLHDG('F8 KEY')
     A            F9             1         COLHDG('F9 KEY')
     A            F10            1         COLHDG('F10 KEY')
     A            F11            1         COLHDG('F11 KEY')
     A            F12            1         COLHDG('F12 KEY')
     A            F13            1         COLHDG('F13 KEY')
     A            F14            1         COLHDG('F14 KEY')
     A            F15            1         COLHDG('F15 KEY')
     A            F16            1         COLHDG('F16 KEY')
     A            F17            1         COLHDG('F17 KEY')
     A            F18            1         COLHDG('F18 KEY')
     A            F19            1         COLHDG('F19 KEY')
     A            F20            1         COLHDG('F20 KEY')
     A            F21            1         COLHDG('F21 KEY')
     A            F22            1         COLHDG('F22 KEY')
     A            F23            1         COLHDG('F23 KEY')
     A            F24            1         COLHDG('F24 KEY')
```

(Create Physical File) command. KEYS never contains data; it only defines the data structure's fields. Put KEYS into a library accessible to all programs that will use this technique (I use a user-defined library in the system library list).

You can select field names that correspond to the name for each key that you use in your programs. If you migrated from a S/38 and still have routing data coded in some of your display files, you may want to change the field names in KEYS to match the routing data names (e.g., RA, UP, DN) so that you will have fewer changes to make in the RPG C-specifications when you re-create the display files on the AS/400.

Your next step is to create RPG program LODKEY. Figure C.2 shows the source code. LODKEY loads each field of data structure KEYS with the hex value that the AID byte will contain when a given key is pressed. LODKEY merely identifies function keys (i.e., F1 through F24, Backspace and Clear (included simply because the AID byte supports them), Enter, Roll up, Roll down, Help, and Print) — it does not define allowable keys within your display files. You must still define the allowable keys, but you don't need to assign resulting indicators to them. As with KEYS, put LODKEY into a library accessible to all programs that will use this technique.

Your final step is to add the code that calls LODKEY to your application programs. Figure C.3 shows a shell RPG program that calls LODKEY. You need to insert three lines of code: the I-specification that defines data structure KEYS (A in

Figure C.2

Source Code for Program LODKEY

```
*... ... 1 ... ... 2 ... ... 3 ... ... 4 ... ... 5 ... ... 6 ... ... 7
     ****************************************************************
     *                                                              *
     *    LOAD KEY PRESSED DATA STRUCTURE WITH "AID" BYTE VALUES    *
     *                                                              *
     ****************************************************************
     IKEYDS      E DSKEYS
     *
     C           *ENTRY    PLIST
     C                     PARM           KEYDS
     *    NOTE:  KEYDS IS AN OUTPUT PARAMETER.                      *
     *
     C                     BITOF'01234567'ENTER
     C                     BITOF'01234567'ROLLUP
     C                     BITOF'01234567'ROLLDN
     C                     BITOF'01234567'HELP
     C                     BITOF'01234567'PRINT
     C                     BITOF'01234567'BSPACE
     C                     BITOF'01234567'CLEAR
     C                     BITOF'01234567'F1
     C                     BITOF'01234567'F2
     C                     BITOF'01234567'F3
     C                     BITOF'01234567'F4
     C                     BITOF'01234567'F5
     C                     BITOF'01234567'F6
     C                     BITOF'01234567'F7
     C                     BITOF'01234567'F8
     C                     BITOF'01234567'F9
     C                     BITOF'01234567'F10
     C                     BITOF'01234567'F11
     C                     BITOF'01234567'F12
     C                     BITOF'01234567'F13
     C                     BITOF'01234567'F14
     C                     BITOF'01234567'F15
     C                     BITOF'01234567'F16
     C                     BITOF'01234567'F17
     C                     BITOF'01234567'F18
     C                     BITOF'01234567'F19
     C                     BITOF'01234567'F20
     C                     BITOF'01234567'F21
     C                     BITOF'01234567'F22
```

Figure C.2 Continued

Figure C.2

Source Code for Program LODKEY *Continued*

```
*... ... 1 ... ... 2 ... ... 3 ... ... 4 ... ... 5 ... ... 6 ... ... 7
     C                         BITOF'Ø1234567'F23
     C                         BITOF'Ø1234567'F24
      *
     C                         BITON'Ø1237'   ENTER          X'F1
     C                         BITON'Ø12357'  ROLLUP         X'F5
     C                         BITON'Ø1235'   ROLLDN         X'F4
     C                         BITON'Ø12367'  HELP           X'F3
     C                         BITON'Ø12356'  PRINT          X'F6
     C                         BITON'Ø1234'   BSPACE         X'F8
     C                         BITON'Ø23457'  CLEAR          X'BD
     C                         BITON'237'     F1             X'31
     C                         BITON'236'     F2             X'32
     C                         BITON'2367'    F3             X'33
     C                         BITON'235'     F4             X'34
     C                         BITON'2357'    F5             X'35
     C                         BITON'2356'    F6             X'36
     C                         BITON'23567'   F7             X'37
     C                         BITON'234'     F8             X'38
     C                         BITON'2347'    F9             X'39
     C                         BITON'2346'    F1Ø            X'3A
     C                         BITON'23467'   F11            X'3B
     C                         BITON'2345'    F12            X'3C
     C                         BITON'Ø237'    F13            X'B1
     C                         BITON'Ø236'    F14            X'B2
     C                         BITON'Ø2367'   F15            X'B3
     C                         BITON'Ø235'    F16            X'B4
     C                         BITON'Ø2357'   F17            X'B5
     C                         BITON'Ø2356'   F18            X'B6
     C                         BITON'Ø23567'  F19            X'B7
     C                         BITON'Ø234'    F2Ø            X'B8
     C                         BITON'Ø2347'   F21            X'B9
     C                         BITON'Ø2346'   F22            X'BA
     C                         BITON'Ø23467'  F23            X'BB
     C                         BITON'Ø2345'   F24            X'BC
      *
     C                         RETRN
```

Figure C.3) and the CALL and PARM statements for LODKEY (B). The LODKEY call is outside the display execution loop and needs to be done only once — preferably from an initialization subroutine. (Even though the file information data structure statement is required, I do not count it as additional code because most of my display file programs already use information from this data structure.)

Rather than using literals in factor 2, the CASEQ section of the program in Figure C.3 uses field names from data structure KEYS. This technique eliminates the need for hex conversion because LODKEY simply compares hex characters instead of converting them into some other form before comparison.

LODKEY is easy to implement and offers many benefits. Inserting the lines of code needed to call LODKEY from an application is a snap. And, as you can see from the CASEQ section in Figure C.3, this technique is self-documenting, which simplifies maintenance. LODKEY also provides shop standardization: Programs

Figure C.3

Shell RPG Program to Call LODKEY

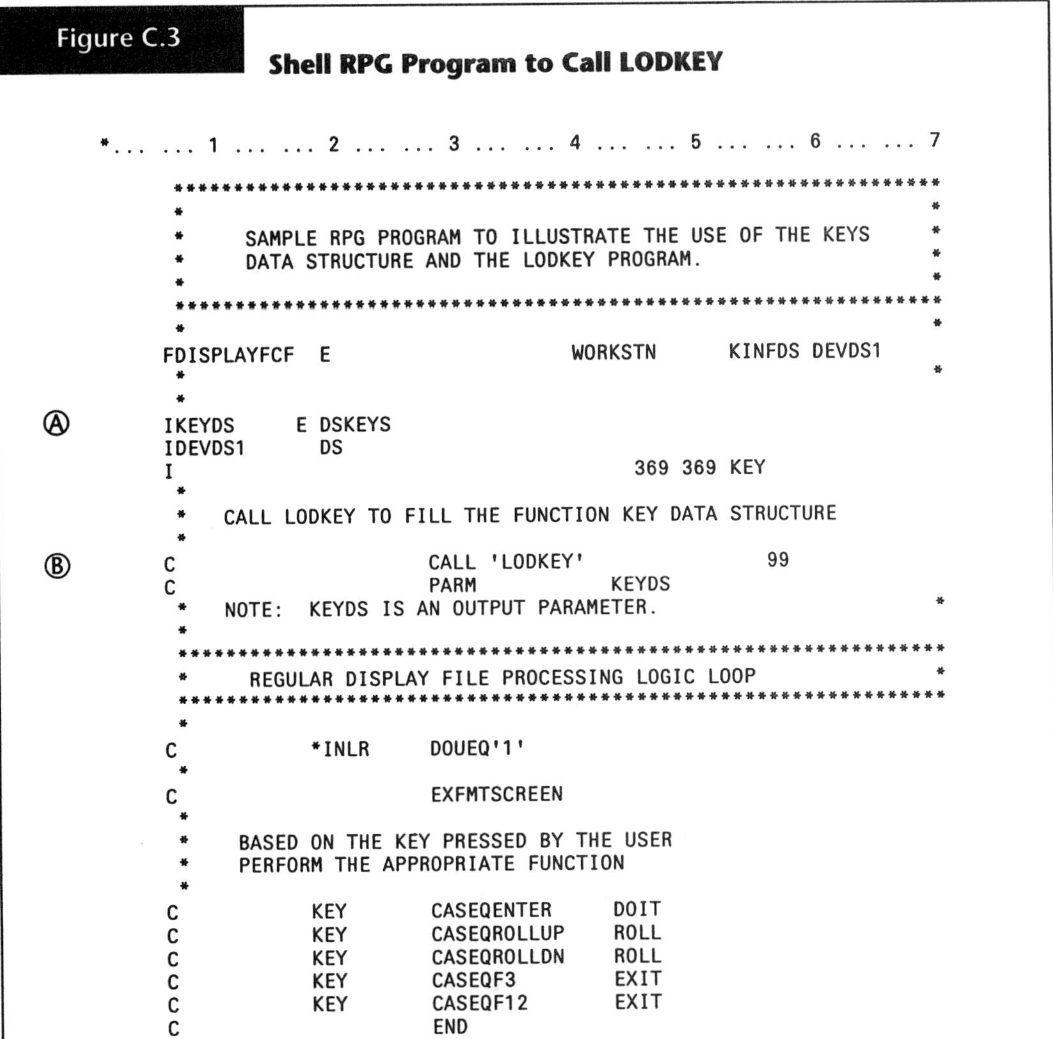

```
    *... ... 1 ... ... 2 ... ... 3 ... ... 4 ... ... 5 ... ... 6 ... ... 7

      *************************************************************
      *                                                           *
      *     SAMPLE RPG PROGRAM TO ILLUSTRATE THE USE OF THE KEYS  *
      *     DATA STRUCTURE AND THE LODKEY PROGRAM.                *
      *                                                           *
      *************************************************************
      *                                                           *
     FDISPLAYFCF  E                    WORKSTN      KINFDS DEVDS1
      *                                                           *
      *
Ⓐ    IKEYDS     E DSKEYS
     IDEVDS1      DS
     I                                        369 369 KEY
      *
      *   CALL LODKEY TO FILL THE FUNCTION KEY DATA STRUCTURE
      *
Ⓑ    C                     CALL 'LODKEY'               99
     C                     PARM           KEYDS
      *   NOTE:  KEYDS IS AN OUTPUT PARAMETER.                    *
      *
      *************************************************************
      *     REGULAR DISPLAY FILE PROCESSING LOGIC LOOP            *
      *************************************************************
      *
     C           *INLR     DOUEQ'1'
      *
     C                     EXFMTSCREEN
      *
      *    BASED ON THE KEY PRESSED BY THE USER
      *    PERFORM THE APPROPRIATE FUNCTION
      *
     C           KEY       CASEQENTER     DOIT
     C           KEY       CASEQROLLUP    ROLL
     C           KEY       CASEQROLLDN    ROLL
     C           KEY       CASEQF3        EXIT
     C           KEY       CASEQF12       EXIT
     C                     END
```

can use the standard name for keys, instead of programmer-selected indicators. Because LODKEY uses an externally described data structure to contain the hex values, you need to call LODKEY only once for the duration of the application, instead of calling it every time the user presses a key. And LODKEY has a low overhead because it passes a pointer only and doesn't open any files. LODKEY is about as simple and efficient as an external program call can get.

Although some key-identification techniques (i.e., internal tables) offer a slight edge in performance, LODKEY's significant maintenance advantages and ease of use more than make up for its being slightly slower. Try this technique on for size. If nothing else, it eliminates yet another instance of required indicator usage.

The author thanks Jennifer Hamilton of the IBM Toronto Laboratory for her assistance and suggestions during the development of this technique.

Appendix D

The Complete CVTOUTQ Command

by Wayne Madden

Figure D.1

Command Definition (CVTOUTQ)

```
/*-----------------------------------------------------------------*/
/*  Convert Output Queue Entries to Outfile                        */
/*  Written by:  Wayne Madden                                      */
/*               February 28, 1992                                 */
/*-----------------------------------------------------------------*/

             CMD        PROMPT('Convert Output Queue Entries')

             PARM       KWD( OUTQ )                 +
                        TYPE( QUAL1 )               +
                        MIN(1)                      +
                        PROMPT('Output Queue:')

             PARM       KWD( OUTFILE )              +
                        TYPE( QUAL2 )               +
                        MIN(1)                      +
                        PROMPT('Outfile name:')

 QUAL1:      QUAL       TYPE(*NAME) LEN(10)
             QUAL       TYPE(*NAME) LEN(10) DFT(*LIBL)               +
                          SPCVAL((*LIBL)) EXPR(*YES) PROMPT('Library +
                          name:')

 QUAL2:      QUAL       TYPE(*NAME) LEN(10)
             QUAL       TYPE(*NAME) LEN(10) DFT(QTEMP)               +
                          EXPR(*YES) PROMPT('Library name:')
```

Figure D.2

DDS (QACVTOR)

```
     *
     A          R QACVTOR                         TEXT('Convert Output Queue FORMAT')
      *
     A            FILE          10A               COLHDG('Spool file name')
     A            SPLNBR         4A               COLHDG('Spool file number')
     A            JOB           10A               COLHDG('Job name')
     A            USER          10A               COLHDG('User profile name')
     A            JOBNBR         6A               COLHDG('Job number')
     A            PAGES          5A               COLHDG('Number of pages')
     A            STATUS         4A               COLHDG('File status')
     A            COPIES         3A               COLHDG('Number of copies')
     A            FRMTYP        10A               COLHDG('Form type')
     A            SPLDTE         8A               COLHDG('Spool file date')
     A            SPLTIM         8A               COLHDG('Spool file time')
```

Figure D.3

CPP Program (CVTOUTCL)

```
/*-------------------------------------------------------------------*/
/*   Program name :  CVTOUTQCL                                        */
/*   Program type :  CPP  -  for command CVTOUTQ                      */
/*   Author name..:  Wayne Madden                                     */
/*   Date created :  March 1, 1992                                    */
/*                                                                    */
/*   Purpose......:  Convert output queue list of entries to an       */
/*                   externally described database file.             */
/*                                                                    */
/*   Program Summary                                                  */
/*   -------------------------------------------------------------    */
/*   1. Verify existence of selected outq named in &i_ql_outq         */
/*   2. Create work files.                                            */
/*   3. WRKOUTQ of outpur queue to OUTPUT(*PRINT)                     */
/*   4. Copy the spool file of above step to flat file DSPOUTQ        */
/*   5. Use HLL program CVTOUTQR to convert spool file entry records  */
/*         found in DSPOUTQ to the externally described outfile       */
/*         named in &i_ql_outf.                                       */
/*                                                                    */
/*                                                                    */
/*   Revision Summary                                                 */
/*   -------------------------------------------------------------    */
/*   Wayne Madden    03/01/92    Modify escape message handling to    */
/*                               ensure cleanup operations performed. */
/*                                                                    */
/*-------------------------------------------------------------------*/

   PGM  PARM( &i_ql_outq  /* IN Output queue name (qualified)     */ +
              &i_ql_outf  /* IN Outfile name (qualified)          */ +
            )
```

Figure D.3 Continued

Figure D.3

CPP Program (CVTOUTCL) *Continued*

```
/* Incoming Parameters from command CVTOUTQ                              */

  DCL  &i_ql_outq   *CHAR   20
  DCL  &i_ql_outf   *CHAR   20

/* Work variables for incoming parameters                                */

  DCL  &outq        *CHAR   10
  DCL  &outqlib     *CHAR   10
  DCL  &outfile     *CHAR   10
  DCL  &outflib     *CHAR   10

/* Work variables for message handling                                   */

  DCL  &msgdta      *CHAR  256
  DCL  &msgf        *CHAR   10
  DCL  &msgflib     *CHAR   10
  DCL  &msgid       *CHAR    7
  DCL  &rtntype     *CHAR    2

/* General work variables                                                */
  DCL  &fl1exist    *LGL     1  VALUE('0')
  DCL  &fl2exist    *LGL     1  VALUE('0')
  DCL  &io_rtncode  *CHAR    1  VALUE('0')
  DCL  &msg_flag    *LGL     1  VALUE('0')

/* Work variables for defining mnemonics                                 */

  DCL  &@blanks     *CHAR    1  VALUE(' ')
  DCL  &@diag       *CHAR    2  VALUE('02')
  DCL  &@escape     *CHAR    2  VALUE('15')
  DCL  &@false      *LGL     1  VALUE('0')
  DCL  &@rtn_norec  *CHAR    1  VALUE('1')
  DCL  &@rtn_ok     *CHAR    1  VALUE('0')
  DCL  &@true       *LGL     1  VALUE('1')

/* Program-level monitor message                                         */

  MONMSG CPF9999 EXEC(GOTO GLOBAL_ERR)

/* Create actual work variables from qualified name parameters           */

  CHGVAR  &outq     (%SST(&i_ql_outq 1 10))
  CHGVAR  &outqlib  (%SST(&i_ql_outq 11 10))

  CHGVAR  &outfile  (%SST(&i_ql_outf 1 10))
  CHGVAR  &outflib  (%SST(&i_ql_outf 11 10))

/*=====================================================================*/
/* Validation and setup                                                  */
/*=====================================================================*/
```

Figure D.3 Continued

Figure D.3

CPP Program (CVTOUTCL) *Continued*

```
/* Check for the Outq Object.                                          */

   CHKOBJ OBJ(&outqlib/&outq) OBJTYPE(*OUTQ)
   MONMSG CPF9801 EXEC(DO)
     SNDPGMMSG MSGID(CPF9898)                                          +
               MSGF(QSYS/QCPFMSG)                                      +
               MSGDTA('Output queue' |>                                +
                      &outqlib       |<                                +
                      '/'            ||                                +
                      &outq          |>                                +
                      'not found')                                     +
               TOPGMQ(*SAME)                                           +
               MSGTYPE(*DIAG)
     CHGVAR &msg_flag &@true
     GOTO CLEAN_UP
   ENDDO

/* Set up work file in QTEMP.                                          */

   CHGVAR &fl1exist &@true
   CHKOBJ OBJ(QTEMP/DSPOUTQ) OBJTYPE(*FILE)
   MONMSG CPF9801 EXEC(DO)
     CHGVAR &fl1exist &@false
   ENDDO
   IF (&fl1exist) DO
     CLRPFM QTEMP/DSPOUTQ
   ENDDO
   ELSE DO
     CRTPF FILE(QTEMP/DSPOUTQ) RCDLEN(132)
     CHGVAR &fl1exist &@true
   ENDDO
   OVRDBF  FILE(DSPOUTQ) TOFILE(QTEMP/DSPOUTQ)

/* Create outfile named in &outfile and &outflib variables             */

   CHGVAR &fl2exist &@true
   CHKOBJ OBJ(&outflib/&outfile) OBJTYPE(*FILE)
   MONMSG CPF9801 EXEC(DO)
     CHGVAR &fl2exist &@false
   ENDDO
   IF (&fl2exist) DO
     CLRPFM &outflib/&outfile
   ENDDO
   ELSE DO
     CRTDUPOBJ OBJ(QACVTOTQ)                                           +
               FROMLIB(KWMLIB)                                         +
               OBJTYPE(*FILE)                                          +
               TOLIB(&outflib)                                         +
               NEWOBJ(&outfile)
     CHGVAR &fl2exist &@true
   ENDDO
   OVRDBF FILE(QACVTOTQ) TOFILE(&outflib/&outfile)

/*  Override spool file to HOLD(*YES). QPRTSPLQ is spoool file         */
/*    created by WRKOUTQ OUTPUT(*PRINT).                               */
```

Figure D.3 Continued

Figure D.3

CPP Program (CVTOUTCL) *Continued*

```
    OVRPRTF FILE(QPRTSPLQ) SCHEDULE(*IMMED) HOLD(*YES)
    WRKOUTQ &outqlib/&outq OUTPUT(*PRINT)

 /*  Copy the spool file to disk file DSPOUTQ.                                */
 /*  Override the declared disk file to the one in QTEMP.                     */

    CPYSPLF FILE(QPRTSPLQ) TOFILE(QTEMP/DSPOUTQ) SPLNBR(*LAST)
    DLTSPLF FILE(QPRTSPLQ) SPLNBR(*LAST)
    MONMSG (CPF3303 CPF3344) /* file not found or no longer on system */


 /*------------------------------------------------------------------------*/
 /* Call HLL program CVTOUTQR to perform data conversion                   */
 /*      &io_rtncode values:   '0' = successful operation                  */
 /*                            '1' = no spool file entries found           */
 /*------------------------------------------------------------------------*/

    CALL CVTOUTQR PARM( &io_rtncode  /* IN/OUT return code          */ +
                      )

    MONMSG CPF0006 EXEC(DO)
      SNDPGMMSG MSGID(CPF9898)                                         +
                MSGF(QSYS/QCPFMSG)                                     +
                MSGDTA('Call to program CVTOUTQR ended in error')      +
                TOPGMQ(*SAME)                                          +
                MSGTYPE(*DIAG)
      CHGVAR &msg_flag &@true
      GOTO CLEAN_UP
    ENDDO

    IF (&io_rtncode = &@rtn_norec) DO
      SNDPGMMSG MSGID(CPF9898)                                         +
                MSGF(QSYS/QCPFMSG)                                     +
                MSGDTA('No entries found in output queue' |>           +
                       &outqlib                           |<           +
                       '/'                                ||           +
                       &outq)                                          +
                TOPGMQ(*SAME)                                          +
                MSGTYPE(*DIAG)
      CHGVAR &msg_flag &@true
      GOTO CLEAN_UP
    ENDDO

    IF (&io_rtncode = &@rtn_ok) DO
      SNDPGMMSG MSGID(CPF9898)                                         +
                MSGF(QSYS/QCPFMSG)                                     +
                MSGDTA('Output queue'        |>                        +
                       &outqlib              |<                        +
                       '/'                   ||                        +
                       &outq                 |>                        +
                       'entries converted')                            +
                MSGTYPE(*COMP)
    ENDDO
```

Figure D.3 Continued

Figure D.3

CPP Program (CVTOUTCL) *Continued*

```
  GOTO CLEAN_UP

/*-----------------------------------------------------------------*/
/* Program level MONMSG detected, flag for messages.               */
/*-----------------------------------------------------------------*/
GLOBAL_ERR:
  IF (&msg_flag) DO  /* To protect from error looping */
    SNDPGMMSG MSGID(CPF9898)                                      +
              MSGF(QSYS/QCPFMSG)                                  +
              MSGDTA('Error in message handling process ' ||      +
                'detected during a program failure.'    |>        +
                'See joblog for details')                         +
              MSGTYPE(*ESCAPE)
    MONMSG CPF0000 EXEC(RETURN)
  ENDDO
  CHGVAR &msg_flag &@true

/*-----------------------------------------------------------------*/
/* Perform any program cleanup operations.                         */
/*-----------------------------------------------------------------*/

CLEAN_UP:
  IF (&f11exist) DLTF QTEMP/DSPOUTQ

/*-----------------------------------------------------------------*/
/* Error handling - resend messages to calling program             */
/*    IF &msg_flag, then error messages are in queue to be sent.   */
/*-----------------------------------------------------------------*/

RSND_BGN:
  IF (&msg_flag) DO

    RSND_RPT:
      RCVMSG RMV(*YES)                                            +
             MSGDTA(&msgdta)                                      +
             MSGID(&msgid)                                        +
             RTNTYPE(&rtntype)                                    +
             MSGF(&msgf)                                          +
             MSGFLIB(&msgflib)
      MONMSG CPF0000 EXEC(GOTO RSND_END)
      IF (&msgid = &@blanks) GOTO RSND_END /* no more messages */
      IF (&rtntype = &@diag *OR &rtntype = &@escape) DO
        SNDPGMMSG MSGID(&msgid)                                   +
                  MSGF(&msgflib/&msgf)                            +
                  MSGDTA(&msgdta)                                 +
                  MSGTYPE(*DIAG)
        MONMSG CPF0000 EXEC(GOTO RSND_END)
      ENDDO
      GOTO RSND_RPT

    RSND_END:
      SNDPGMMSG MSGID(CPF9898)                                    +
                MSGF(QSYS/QCPFMSG)                                +
                MSGDTA('Operation ended in error. ' ||            +
                  'See previously listed messages')               +
```

Figure D.3 Continued

Figure D.3

CPP Program (CVTOUTCL) *Continued*

```
               MSGTYPE(*ESCAPE)
     MONMSG CPF0000 EXEC(GOTO FINISH)

   ENDDO

/*-----------------------------------------------------------------*/
/* End of program                                                  */
/*-----------------------------------------------------------------*/

FINISH:
   RETURN
   ENDPGM
```

Figure D.4

RPG Program (CVTOUTQR)

```
*-----------------------------------------------------------------*
*    IBM AS/400    2/28/92    K WAYNE MADDEN                        *
*                                                                  *
*    Convert Outputq Queue Entries to Outfile                      *
*                                                                  *
*    PROGRAM FUNCTION:  This program converts output               *
*      queue entries to a work file.                               *
*                                                                  *
*    FILES: DSPOUTQ - SEQUENTIAL FILE                              *
*                     ACCESS BY RELATIVE RECORD NUMBER             *
*                     PROGRAM DESCRIBED                            *
*                     RECORD LENGTH - 132                          *
*                                                                  *
*    FIELD DESCRIPTIONS OF "DSPOUTQ"                               *
*                                                                  *
*    FROM   TO   DESCRIPTION              LENGTH  TYPE             *
*                                                                  *
*       2   11   SPOOL FILE NAME            10      A              *
*      13   22   USER ID                    10      A              *
*      35   38   SPOOL STATUS                4      A              *
*      42   46   NUMBER OF PAGES             5      A              *
*      50   52   NUMBER OF COPIES            3      A              *
*      55   64   FORM TYPE                  10      A              *
*      73   76   SPOOL NUMBER                4      A              *
*      82   91   JOB NAME                   10      A              *
*      93   98   JOB NUMBER                  6      A              *
*     100  107   DATE (MM/DD/YY)             8      A              *
*     109  116   TIME (HH:MM:SS)             8      A              *
*                                                                  *
*    *IN99 ................    READ THE WORK FILE (DSPOUTQ)        *
*                                                                  *
*-----------------------------------------------------------------*
*
FDSPOUTQ IF  F     132              DISK
```

Figure D.4 Continued

Figure D.4

RPG Program (CVTOUTQR) *Continued*

```
FQACVTOTQO   E                     DISK                A
 *
E                   NO          4  1                 SPOOL NUMBER
 *
IDSPOUTQ NS  01
I                                           1 132 DATA
 *
I            DS
I                                           1 132 DATA
I                                           2  11 QSPFIL
I                                          13  22 QSPUSR
I                                          35  38 QSPSTS
I                                          42  46 QSPPAG
I                                          50  52 QSPCPY
I                                          55  64 QSPFMT
I                                          66  75 QUEIN
I                                          73  76 QSPNBR
I                                          82  91 QSPJOB
I                                          82  91 LIBIN
I                                          93  98 QSPJNB
I                                         100 107 QDATE
I                                         109 116 QTIME
 *
 *-----------------------------------------*
 *   Write out file.                       *
 *                                         *
 *   The first record always contains the  *
 *   name of the QUEUE and LIBRARY that is *
 *   selected.                             *
 *                                         *
 *   From the other entries, only those    *
 *   identified as spool file entries are  *
 *   selected (QSPJNB) Job number will be  *
 *   a numeric value, therefore TESTN.     *
 *-----------------------------------------*
 *
C           *ENTRY    PLIST
C                     PARM O#RTN     I#RTN   1
 *
C                     MOVE 'Ø'       O#RTN   1
C                     Z-ADDØ         COUNT   5Ø
 *
C                     READ DSPOUTQ                 98 Read Work File
C           *IN98     IFEQ *ON                        No records
C                     MOVE '1'       O#RTN
C                     GOTO FMEND
C                     ELSE
C                     MOVE 'Ø'       O#RTN
C                     ENDIF
 *
 * First read has QUEUE & LIBRARY name (HEADER RECORD)
C                     MOVE QUEIN     OUTQ   1Ø        Outq
C                     MOVE LIBIN     OUTQLB 1Ø        Outq Library
 *
 * Read again after first record
```

Figure D.4 Continued

Figure D.4

RPG Program (CVTOUTQR) *Continued*

```
C                     READ DSPOUTQ                   99 DSPOUTQ    In
 *
 * Read Loop
C           *IN99     DOWEQ*OFF
C                     TESTN          QSPJNB      02
C           *IN02     IFEQ *ON
C           QSPFIL    ANDNE'QPRTSPLQ'
C                     MOVE QSPFIL    FILE              In QACVTOTQ
C                     EXSR @FXSN
C                     MOVE QSPNBR    SPLNBR            "  "  "
C                     MOVE QSPJOB    JOB               "  "  "
C                     MOVE QSPUSR    USER              "  "  "
C                     MOVE QSPJNB    JOBNBR            "  "  "
C                     MOVE QSPPAG    PAGES             "  "  "
C                     MOVE QSPSTS    STATUS            "  "  "
C                     MOVE QSPCPY    COPIES            "  "  "
C                     MOVE QSPFMT    FRMTYP            "  "  "
C                     MOVE QDATE     SPLDTE            "  "  "
C                     MOVE QTIME     SPLTIM            "  "  "
 * Write out record
C                     WRITEQACVTOR
C                     ADD  1         COUNT
C                     ENDIF
 *
C                     READ DSPOUTQ                   99 DSPOUTQ    In
C                     END
 *
C           COUNT     IFEQ 0                           No records
C                     MOVE '1'       O#RTN
C                     ENDIF
 *
C           FMEND     TAG                              FMEND        Tag
C                     MOVE *ON       *INLR
C                     RETRN
 *
 *-----------------------------------------------------------*
 * Subroutine for padding spool number with '0's on the left. *
 *-----------------------------------------------------------*
 *
C           @FXSN     BEGSR
 * Make sure the spool number is padded with '0's on the left.
C                     MOVEAQSPNBR    NO
C                     DO   4         X       20
C           NO,X      IFEQ *BLANK
C                     MOVE '0'       NO,X
C                     END
C                     END
C                     MOVEANO        QSPNBR
 *
C                     ENDSR
```

Index

D

E

F

G

H

I

M

N

O

P

S

T

U

V

W

X

Also Published by *NEWS 3X/400*

C FOR RPG PROGRAMMERS

By Jennifer Hamilton, a **NEWS 3X/400** *author*

Written from the perspective of an RPG programmer, this book includes side-by-side coding examples written in both C and RPG to aid comprehension and understanding, clear identification of unique C constructs, and a comparison of RPG op-codes to equivalent C concepts. Includes many tips and examples covering the use of C/400. 292 pages, 23 chapters.

COMMON-SENSE C

Advice and warnings for C and C++ programmers

By Paul Conte, a **NEWS 3X/400** *technical editor*

C programming language has its risks; this book shows how C programmers get themselves into trouble, includes tips to help you avoid C's pitfalls, and suggests how to manage C and C++ application development. 100 pages, 9 chapters.

CONTROL LANGUAGE PROGRAMMING FOR THE AS/400

By Bryan Meyers and Dan Riehl, **NEWS 3X/400** *technical editors*

This comprehensive CL programming textbook offers students up-to-the-minute knowledge of the skills they will need in today's MIS environment. Progresses methodically from CL basics to more complex processes and concepts, guiding readers toward a professional grasp of CL programming techniques and style. 512 pages, 25 chapters.

DESKTOP GUIDE TO CL PROGRAMMING

By Bryan Meyers, a **NEWS 3X/400** *technical editor*

This first book of the *NEWS 3X/400 Technical Reference Series* is packed with easy-to-find notes, short explanations, practical tips, answers to most of your everyday questions about CL, and CL code segments you can use in your own CL programming. Complete "short reference" lists every command and explains the most-often-used ones, along with names of the files they use and the MONMSG messages to use with them. On-line Windows Help diskette available. 205 pages, 36 chapters.

DESKTOP GUIDE TO AS/400 PROGRAMMERS' TOOLS

By Dan Riehl, a **NEWS 3X/400** *technical editor*

This second book of the *NEWS 3X/400 Technical Reference Series* gives you the "how-to" behind all the tools included in *Application Development ToolSet/400* (ADTS/400), IBM's Licensed Program Product for Version 3 of OS/400; includes Source Entry Utility (SEU), Programming Development Manager (PDM), Screen Design Aid (SDA), Report Layout Utility (RLU), File Compare/Merge Utility (FCMU) — *new in V3R1*, and Interactive Source Debugger — *new in V3R1*. Highlights topics and functions specific to Version 3 of OS/400. On-line Windows Help diskette available. 266 pages, 30 chapters.

DESKTOP GUIDE TO THE S/36

By Mel Beckman, Gary Kratzer, and Roger Pence, **NEWS 3X/400** *technical editors*

This definitive S/36 survival manual includes practical techniques to supercharge your S/36, including ready-to-use information for maximum system performance tuning, effective application development, and smart Disk Data Management. Includes a review of two popular Unix-based S/36 work-alike migration alternatives. Diskette contains ready-to-run utilities to help you save machine time and implement power programming techniques such as External Program Calls. 387 pages, 21 chapters.

IMPLEMENTING AS/400 SECURITY, SECOND EDITION

A practical guide to implementing, evaluating, and auditing your AS/400 security strategy

By Wayne Madden, a **NEWS 3X/400** *technical editor*

Concise and practical, this second edition brings together in one place the fundamental AS/400 security tools and experience-based recommendations that you need and also includes specifics on the latest security enhancements available in OS/400 Version 3 Release 1. Completely updated from the first edition, this is the only source for the latest information about how to protect your system against attack from its increasing exposure to hackers. 389 pages, 16 chapters.

AN INTRODUCTION TO COMMUNICATIONS FOR THE AS/400

By Ruggero Adinolfi; Technical editor, John Enck, a **NEWS 3X/400** *technical editor*

This guide to basic communications concepts and how they operate on the IBM AS/400 outlines the rich mix of communications capabilities designed into the AS/400 and relates them to the concepts that underlie the various network environments. 183 pages, 13 chapters.

JIM SLOAN'S CL TIPS & TECHNIQUES

By Jim Sloan, developer of QUSRTOOL's TAA Tools

Written for those who understand CL, this book draws from Jim Sloan's knowledge and experience as a developer for the S/38 and the AS/400, and his creation of QUSRTOOL's TAA tools, to give you tips that can help you write better CL programs and become more productive. Includes more than 200 field-tested techniques, plus exercises to help you understand and apply many of the techniques presented. 564 pages, 30 chapters.

MASTERING THE AS/400

A practical, hands-on guide

By Jerry Fottral

This introductory textbook to AS/400 concepts and facilities has a utilitarian approach that stresses student participation. A natural prerequisite to programming and database management courses, it emphasizes mastery of system/user interface, member-object-library relationship, utilization of CL commands, and basic database and program development utilities. Also includes labs focusing on essential topics such as printer spooling; library lists; creating and maintaining physical files; using logical files; using CL and DDS; working in the PDM environment; and using SEU, DFU, Query, and SDA. 484 pages, 12 chapters.

OBJECT-ORIENTED PROGRAMMING FOR AS/400 PROGRAMMERS

By Jennifer Hamilton, a **NEWS 3X/400** *author*

Explains basic OOP concepts such as classes and inheritance in simple, easy-to-understand terminology. The OS/400 object-oriented architecture serves as the basis for the discussion throughout, and concepts presented are reinforced through an introduction to the C++ object-oriented programming language, using examples based on the OS/400 object model. 114 pages, 14 chapters.

POWER TOOLS FOR THE AS/400, VOLUMES I AND II

Edited by Frederick L. Dick and Dan Riehl

NEWS 3X/400's Power Tools for the AS/400 is a two-volume reference series for people who work with the AS/400. *Volume I* (originally titled *AS/400 Power Tools*) is a collection of the best tools, tips, and techniques published in *NEWS/34-38* (pre-August 1988) and *NEWS 3X/400* (August 1988 through October 1991) that are applicable to the AS/400. *Volume II* extends this original collection by including material that appeared through 1994. Each book includes a diskette that provides load-and-go code for easy-to-use solutions to many everyday problems. *Volume I*: 709 pages, 24 chapters; *Volume II*: 702 pages, 14 chapters.

PROGRAMMING IN RPG IV

By Judy Yaeger, Ph.D., a **NEWS 3X/400** *technical editor*

This textbook provides a strong foundation in the essentials of business programming, featuring the newest version of the RPG language: RPG IV. Focuses on real-world problems and down-to-earth solutions using the latest techniques and features of RPG. Provides everything you need to know to write a well-designed RPG IV program. Each chapter includes informative, easy-to-read explanations and examples as well as a section of thought-provoking questions, exercises, and programming assignments. Four appendices and a handy, comprehensive glossary support the topics presented throughout the book. An instructor's kit is available. 450 pages, 13 chapters.

PROGRAMMING IN RPG/400, SECOND EDITION

by Judy Yaeger, Ph.D., a **NEWS 3X/400** *technical editor*

This second edition refines and extends the comprehensive instructional material contained in the original textbook and features a new section that introduces externally described printer files, a new chapter that highlights the fundamentals of RPG IV, and a new appendix that correlates the key concepts from each chapter with their RPG IV counterparts. Includes everything you need to learn how to write a well-designed RPG program, from the most basic to the more complex, and each chapter includes a section of questions, exercises, and programming assignments that reinforce the knowledge you have gained from the chapter and strengthen the groundwork for succeeding chapters. An instructor's kit is available. 450 pages, 14 chapters.

THE QUINTESSENTIAL GUIDE TO PC SUPPORT

By John Enck, Robert E. Anderson, Michael Otey, and Michael Ryan

This comprehensive book about IBM's AS/400 PC Support connectivity product defines the architecture of PC Support and its role in midrange networks, describes PC Support's installation and configuration procedures, and shows you how you can configure and use PC Support to solve real-life problems. 345 pages, 11 chapters.

RPG IV JUMP START

Moving ahead with the new RPG

By Bryan Meyers, a **NEWS 3X/400** *technical editor*

Introducing the "new" RPG, in which the columnar syntax has been challenged (all the specifications have changed, some vestigial specifications from an earlier era have been eliminated, and new specifications and data types have been added), this book shows you RPG IV from the perspective of a programmer who already knows the old RPG. Points out the differences between the two and demonstrates how to take advantage of the new syntax and function. 193 pages, 12 chapters.